THE REPUBLIC IN PRINT

TRISH LOUGHRAN

THE REPUBLIC IN PRINT

Print Culture in the Age of U.S. Nation Building, 1770–1870

COLUMBIA UNIVERSITY PRESS . *New York*

Columbia University Press
Publishers Since 1893
New York   Chichester, West Sussex

Copyright © 2007 Trish Loughran
All rights Reserved

Library of Congress Cataloging-in-Publication Data

Loughran, Trish, 1968–
The republic in print : print culture in the age of U.S. nation building, 1770–1870 /
Trish Loughran.
p.   cm.
ISBN 978-0-231-13908-3 (cloth : acid-free paper) — ISBN 978-0-231-13909-0 (pbk. : acid-free paper) —
ISBN 978-0-231-51123-0 (e-book)
Includes bibliographical references.
1. Publishers and publishing—United States—History—18th century.   2. Publishers and
publishing—United States—History—19th century.   3. Press and politics—United States—
History—18th century.   4. Press and politics—United States—History—19th century.
5. Press—United States—History—18th century.   6. Press—United States—History—
19th century.   7. Book industries and trade—United States—History—18th century.
8. Book industries and trade—United States—History—19th century.   9. Books and
reading—United States—History—18th century.   10. Books and reading—United
States—History—19th century.
Z473.L826   2007   2007001348
070.50973/09033 22

Columbia University Press books are printed on permanent and durable acid-free paper
Printed in the United States of America
c 10 9 8 7 6 5 4 3 2
p 10 9 8 7 6 5 4 3 2 1
References to Internet Web Sites (URLs) were accurate at the time of writing.
Neither the author nor Columbia University Press is responsible for Web sites that may have
expired or changed since the book was prepared
Portions of chapter 2 appear in slightly different form in *American Literature* 78,
no. 1 (2006):1–28.
Portions of chapter 4 appear in slightly different form in George Boudreau
and William Pencak, eds., *Explorations in Early American Culture* 5
(University Park, PA: Pennsylvania Historical Association, 2001).

For KT Langton

I am contending for the rights of the *living*, and against their being willed away, and controlled and contracted for, by the manuscript assumed authority of the dead. ... Those who have quitted the world, and those who have not yet arrived in it, are as remote from each other, as the utmost stretch of moral imagination can conceive. What possible obligation, then, can exist between them; what rule or principle can be laid down, that of two nonentities, the one out of existence, and the other not in, and who never can meet in this world, that the one should control the other to the end of time?

—Thomas Paine, *The Rights of Man*, 1791–92

CONTENTS

PART TWO
THE NATION IN FRAGMENTS:
FEDERAL REPRESENTATION AND ITS DISCONTENTS,
1787–1789

PART THREE
THE OVEREXTENDED REPUBLIC:
SLAVERY, ABOLITION, AND NATIONAL SPACE,
1790–1870

ILLUSTRATIONS

ACKNOWLEDGMENTS

I am grateful to the many teachers and colleagues who helped me create this book, which began as a dissertation at the University of Chicago under the generous direction of Christopher Looby, with Bill Brown, Janice Knight, and Kenneth Warren serving as readers. I owe these four my moorings in this project, and I thank them for their example and encouragement. For helping me transform the dissertation into a book, I owe many more recent thanks to my colleagues at the University of Illinois. Nina Baym was an especially formative influence while Leon Chai was a tireless champion of the more Napoleonic side of my imagination. Stephanie Foote, Robert Markley, Carol Neely, Robert Dale Parker, and Joseph Valente all generously supported me, intellectually and professionally, through many revisions. Nor could I have succeeded without the friendship and collegiality of Vernon Burton, Nancy Castro, Shefali Chandra, Jed Esty, Lauren Goodlad, Debbie Hawhee, Suvir Kaul, Susan Koshy, Ania Loomba, Janet Lyon, William Maxwell, Cris Mayo, Bruce Michelson, Cary Nelson, Lori Newcomb, Leslie Reagan, Julia Saville, Simona Sawhney, Julia Walker, and Zohreh Sullivan. Several exceptionally gifted Illinois graduate students helped me with portions of my research: Sarah Dennis did important bibliographic research; Andrew Moss did detailed archival reconnaissance; and Sara Luttfring and Spencer Snow helped proofread. I thank them for their labor.

Beyond my home institutions, I have benefited from the indispensable institutional support of libraries, museums, presses, and universities, along with the people who work in them. I am grateful for fellowship support from the American Bibliographic Society, the CBS Bicentennial Narrators Fund, the David Library of the American Revolution, the Huntington Library, the Library Company of Philadelphia, the McNeil Center for Early American Studies, the Mellon Foundation, the University of Chicago, and the Research Board at the University of Illinois. I thank the reference staffs at each of the libraries named, as well as those at the American Philosophical Society, the Newberry, the Rosenbach, the Ohio Historical Society, the Vermont Historical Society, and the rare book rooms at the University of Chicago, the University of Pennsylvania, and the University of Illinois. For sundry acts of encouragement and kindness, I thank Richard Dunn, David Fowler, Phillip Lapsansky, Robert McNeil, Robert Ritchie, and Jerome Singerman. For valuable feedback on specific ideas and chapters, I thank James Green, Robert Gross, David Hall, Ronald Hoffman, John Kaminski, David Shields, Julia Stern, Frederika Teute, Alfred Young, and Michael Zuckerman. At Columbia University Press, Kabir Dandona and Anne Routon graciously walked me through the details of submission and production, while Anita O'Brien, my copy editor, and Leslie Bialler, my production editor, worked patiently through a long and sometimes twisting manuscript. Peter Dimock, my editor, was remarkably generous and patient. This book would never have been published in its current form without him, nor without the savvy readers' reports filed on my behalf while the book was under submission, including insightful readings by the gracious Cindy Weinstein, Jay Fliegelman, and several anonymous readers, all of whom challenged the book in ways that made it stronger.

Finally, like many academics, I am lucky enough to say that some of my best readers have also been my best friends. For that privilege, I thank Lisa Brawley (whose work on fugitive slavery much inspired my own thinking here), Ronald Christ, Seth Cotlar, Caroline Eastman, Elaine Freedgood, Cathy Jurca, Margaret Keller, and Laura Rigal. I also appreciate those few people who did not read for me but were nevertheless deeply important in my life in the years while I was writing, especially Dorothy Grice, Barbara Nordhaus, and the Langtons: Bob, KT, Katie, and Connor. At the end of this long list of friends, family, and colleagues stands my girlfriend Siobhan Somerville—a Jeter among women and an intellectual rock. Everything I make and think is made better because of her intelligence and her generosity: thank you.

Thomas Paine once said, "I know but one kind of life I am fit for, and that is a thinking one and, of course, a writing one." My friend KT Connors Langton modeled that maxim for me and helped me make it my own. For that, I dedicate this book to her, in memory of a creative life: February 1, 1950–November 9, 2005.

FIGURE I.1 *Inauguration of President Lincoln at U.S. Capitol, March 4, 1861.* Library of Congress, Prints and Photographs Division, LC-USZ62-48564.

INTRODUCTION
A VIEW FROM THE CAPITOL
The Unfinished Work of U.S. Nation Building

A Klee painting named "Angelus Novus" shows an angel looking as though he is about to move away from something he is fixedly contemplating. His eyes are staring, his mouth is open, his wings are spread. This is how one pictures the angel of history. His face is turned toward the past. Where we perceive a chain of events, he sees one single catastrophe which keeps piling wreckage and hurls it in front of his feet. The angel would like to stay, awaken the dead, and make whole what has been smashed. But a storm is blowing in from Paradise; it has got caught in his wings with such a violence that the angel can no longer close them. This storm irresistibly propels him into the future to which his back is turned, while the pile of debris before him grows skyward. This storm is what we call progress.
—Walter Benjamin, "Theses on the Philosophy of History," 1940

To make a claim on behalf of the fragment is also, not surprisingly, to produce a discourse that is itself fragmentary. It is redundant to make apologies for this.
—Partha Chatterjee, *The Nation and Its Fragments*, 1993

The Library of Congress holds a rare photograph that portrays the in-auspicious inauguration of Abraham Lincoln on March 4, 1861 (see facing page). Recording the moment just before Lincoln took the oath of office on the steps of the half-built Capitol, this photograph captures the profoundly unfinished nature of the republic, even eighty-five years after it declared itself an autonomous nation-state. The image tells a story that I elaborate on in every chapter of this book: it suggests not only that the foundational project of American nation building was not yet complete in 1861, but that the work left to be done really was, quite literally, an issue of *building*. Lincoln's nation was not, in other words, merely a matter of an incoherent or not-yet-worked-out ideology (though, with the shameful legacy of slavery yet unresolved, it was also that); it was like-wise an essentially *material* business—a matter of unmortared bricks and not-yet-raised roofs. The drama of the photograph is in the way that it captures, beneath the half-built dome of the national Capitol, the half-taken oath of a president whose second term we know, in retrospect, will never be completed. So it is with nations. However immemorially they might appear to loom from a deep and distant past, nations are in fact always incomplete, cross-generational, noninevitable, and *ongoing* enterprises.

Like this photograph, *The Republic in Print* describes the unfinished work of U.S. nation building as it proliferated both as an ideology and as a set of material practices in the years between the Revolution and the Civil War. This double focus has allowed me to explicitly address the question of print culture and its role in nation formation as well as to consider a series of larger questions about the relationship between the two most epochal of nation-making and nation-breaking American moments: how a country nearing a century of history could rend so completely around the figure of one man; how slavery, the larger issue in the War between the States, could persevere for so long in one part of the country while being rejected in another; and why we still think—and should think—of the founding compacts of 1776 and 1789 as successful, even though they begat such a flawed constitution, such a divided people, and such a horrible civil war.

This book gathers answers to these questions from the numberless fragments and piece-fictions from which the United States literally produced itself in the years between 1770 and 1870—the photographs, engravings, novels, newspapers, magazines, tracts, pamphlets, plays, laws, maps, and debates of early American print culture. I focus on print culture because it provides an explicitly materialist base from which to examine questions of representation *and* because print continues to dominate our national narratives about early national founding. Americans have historically had a mundane faith in the infallibility of their own written origins. When asked where America began, many will answer *"in print."* From the dissemination of *Common Sense* to the printed reproduction of the Declaration of Independence to the newspaper debates over the Constitution, the founding has long been understood as a text-based process, with the citizens of the early republic cast as readers and writers who organize themselves collectively through the institutions of a thriving print culture. But the republic in print is not just a popular narrative. It has an illustrious history in the field of early American studies and has, in fact, been widely reenacted in recent years by arguments that link the rise of nationalism to the emergence of print capitalism, a thesis made iconic by Benedict Anderson with the 1983 publication of *Imagined Communities*. Numerous scholarly accounts of early American culture follow Anderson in presuming a coherent and connected print culture as the crucial apparatus that successfully knits together dispersed North American communities from the colonial period forward. Print serves, in such analyses, as the central and centralizing agent in the processes of American nation formation. *The Republic in Print* takes a different view. It challenges this account as ahistorical, a postindustrial fantasy of preindustrial print's efficacy as a cross-regional agent and of federalism itself as an inevitable outcome. I argue instead that there was no "nationalized" print public sphere in the years just before and just after the Revolution, but rather a proliferating variety of local and regional reading publics scattered across a vast and diverse geographical space. While classic eighteenth-century texts like *Common Sense* or *The Federalist* may serve today as powerful emblems of early national consensus, their actual history as material objects tells another story—one in which fragmented pieces of text circulated haphazardly and unevenly in a world still largely dominated by the limits of locale.

In this way, the book builds two primary strands of argument. The first focuses on the issue of print culture per se and its allegedly determinant role in the processes of nation formation; under this heading I address the question of when and how a "national" print culture might be said to emerge and consider the problems inherent in the abstracted model of the print public sphere that currently underwrites our understanding of early American print culture. The second strand of argument traces the nation-state itself as a material and historical form that emerges across time from its own theorized origins (in constitutional federalism) into an actual infrastructure embedded in real institutions: a nation. In defining the nation (and the nation-state) in the most materialist way possible, I follow the work of theorists and historians like Richard Brown, Rogers Brubaker, John Brueilly, Anthony Giddens, Richard John, Michael Mann, John Torpey, and Eugen Weber. As Torpey writes, "the nation state is more than a 'structure of ideas.'" It is also "a more or less coherent network of *institutions*." This book asks how this "coherent network of institutions" was theorized from a position of absence (in 1776 and 1787) that nevertheless called forth the material world we live in today.[1]

I begin, then, by dismantling the text-based model of U.S. nationbuilding on which the field of early American studies depends—a tale in which both nation and citizen are mutually and inevitably constituted through the institutions of early industrial print culture. I undo this argument with a paradox, suggesting that it was not the connectedness of early American print cultures or the commonness of common texts that enabled U.S. founding, but instead the very localness of early print cultures that made founding possible in the first place. I then turn from these eighteenth-century fantasies to their nineteenth-century consequences, exploring the ways that an increasingly connected American book market, once it finally did emerge, spectacularly failed to use its new technologies to manufacture consensus, particularly in regard to slavery. By 1850, I argue, the United States was an actual and an uncomfortable *E pluribus unum*, a nation whose differences could no longer be contained in constitutional language because language itself could no longer be contained in loosely and locally organized print economies.

This larger thesis is developed through seven chapters. Chapter 1 lays out the book's central thesis, describing the methodology, scholarly stakes, and historical arc of the book as a whole. Here, I introduce my readers to what I call the "virtual nation" and describe several of its citizens: itinerant printers, painters, authors, booksellers, politicians, and pamphleteers who all see America unfolding in front of them but who each in his own way fails to reach it. Infusing recent "print theory" with a materialist dose of "print culture," this chapter suggests why we might more usefully think of print culture as the factory that produced the nation-fragments called regions and sections rather than as the great unionizer and unifier it is so often remembered as. The rest of the book follows a tripartite structure, organized conceptually (rather than just chronologically) around three specific issues: the history of the early national book, the theoretical and material problems behind emerging structures of federalist representation, and the historical contest between abolition and slavery, which played out between 1790 and 1850 both in the abstract space of "the nation" at large and within the material confines of antebellum print culture.

Part 1 poses the early national period as a materialist tableau against which the figure of the early national book is theorized as both object and ideology. Chapter 2 offers a material history of the fabled circulation of Thomas Paine's 1776 pamphlet *Common Sense*, arguing that Paine's pamphlet was more limited in its circulation than scholars have supposed and exploring the uses that the myth of its exorbitant circulation numbers have served, both at the moment of the Revolution and in national histories ever since. Chapter 3 likewise describes the scene of constitutional ratification as first and foremost a material process, using *The Federalist Papers* and other articles of the ratification debate to foreground the crucial role that distance and disinformation played in the limited but continually expanding public sphere engineered by federalist partisans throughout the crucial months of 1787 and 1788. In describing this public sphere as a material realm in which actual objects circulated (and failed to circulate), I explicitly revisit Michael Warner's influential "republican print ideology" thesis (put forth in his 1990 *Republic of Letters*). I conclude that print paradigms that organize themselves around singular ideologies ultimately collude with the historically noninevitable fantasy of an organized and homogenous federalist state, a "phantom" that antifederalists unsuccessfully tried to describe to populations their writings simply could not reach. The more fruitful object of our cultural study, I suggest, is not so much any singular ideology (whether it be republicanism, federalism, or printedness itself), but the varied terrain over which these monolithic models eventually sought to spread themselves.

Part 2 explores the spatial, historical, and rhetorical architecture of what I call "virtual nationalism"—understood here as 1787's bold commitment to far-flung, and highly centralized, modes of representation (as opposed to 1776's investment in populism, democracy, embodied governance, and polycentric confederation). The federalists of 1787 ultimately succeeded in erecting what their opponents called a governmental "superstructure" (dubbed the "extended republic"), but they were able to do so, in large part, because the various domains that constituted that extended space were not yet a unified field of exchange. Both chapters in this part focus on how the federal state (then as now) relies on populations dispersed across both space and time in order to assure its ongoing hegemony over subjects who never actually consent to its construction. Chapter 4 makes this argument primarily through Royall Tyler's 1787 stage play *The Contrast*, re-locating it within the now largely forgotten era of the post-Revolutionary Confederation. Although the play is usually read as a nationalist artifact ("the first American stage comedy"), I reposition it here within the regionalized identity politics of the 1780s, arguing that the contrast of the title is not an external (British versus American) one but an internal (American) one rooted in the intensely localist (or state-based) political imaginaries of the Confederation period. Chapter 5 uses connected readings of *The Federalist Papers* and William Hill Brown's 1789 seduction novel, *The Power of Sympathy*, to argue that spatial dislocation was essential not just to the ratification of the Constitution but also to the federalists' understanding of the long-term viability of the nation as a perpetual construct. Like *The Contrast*, Brown's *Power of Sympathy* evokes a shifting series of highly differentiated local terrains. Unlike *The Contrast*, however, Brown explores two complicating features of such disarticulated spaces: the problem of unlike scales (a crucial feature in the theory of federalism) and the problem of historical lineage, or national reproduction, across time. In this way, *The Power of Sympathy*, celebrated as the "first American novel," poses a sharp rebuke to the "first American comedy": while Tyler lingers on the possibilities of the federalist imaginary for members of a mobile and metro-identified elite (like himself), Brown explores the local wreckage that those at the new nation's peripheries feared that federalism, at its worst, might leave in its wake.

Part 3 moves into the antebellum period to consider some of the ways that the nation-in-progress ultimately found itself tangled up in the painful consequences of its own historical emergence. Chapter 6, for example, describes the material content of the long shift from gradual abolition (starting in the 1790s) to the immediatist program of the 1830s. Here I compare the always interrelated spatial and publishing imaginaries of gradual abolition and immediate abolition, considering the role that print culture played in each. I focus in particular on the American Anti-Slavery Society of 1833–40, which exploited an increasingly centralized print network in order to foment public debate about something proslavery secessionists began to call "practical amalgamation"—a phrase that refers, in this period of dramatic market expansion, to the feared rupture of both regional and racial boundaries. Chapter 7 uses the backdrop of the 1850s to reread Stowe's *Uncle Tom's Cabin*, Solomon Northup's *Twelve Years a Slave*, and William Wells Brown's *Clotel*. Here, I develop several arguments about the production of federalist scale begun in previous chapters. Using the Fugitive Slave Law of 1850 as a materialist warrant, I describe how relations between the (now) materially immanent nation and the local citizen had finally caught up to the framing fictions of 1776 and 1789, as the once-distinct tiers of federalism began to buckle under the force of emerging industrial networks. The result, I suggest, is less federalism (in the sense of two balanced scales of national life existing in harmonious equipoise) than nationalism: that sense of hyper-self-saturated space in which regional differences are increasingly felt to be lost.

Over the course of these chapters, I draw on a wide range of methodological and theoretical positions. I am indebted to the classic *histoire du livre* method of Roger Chartier, Robert Darnton, and (in American studies), Cathy Davidson, David Hall, Meredith McGill, and Ronald Zboray; to the thick cultural histories of Stanley Elkins and Eric McKitrick, Eric

Foner, Alexander Saxton, Charles Sellers, and Sean Wilentz; as well as to the class-based investigations of nineteenth-century print culture of Michael Denning, Eric Lott, and Shelley Streeby—and of course to many others. Though these scholars are diverse, I share with each of them a materialist method that is integrated into the wider conceptual content of the book. Within early American studies per se, I am indebted to scholars like Jay Fliegelman, Christopher Looby, Laura Rigal, Joseph Roach, Nancy Ruttenberg, David Waldstreicher, Michael Warner, and many others—creative readers of early American culture who all curate their own museumized archive against which to write innovative revisions of the early republic. Following the heterogeneous methodology these scholars have modeled for me, this book examines a range of texts, genres, and objects (from pamphlets, plays, novels, newspapers, and reform tracts to engravings, paintings, diaries, statues, and other material artifacts) in order to confront American culture on the ground of its own making.

Alongside this expanded archive, *The Republic in Print* constructs a spacious genealogy of the U.S. nation as a developing cultural form, mounting a connected analysis of two often sharply periodized moments in American literary history: on one hand, the Enlightenment republic of letters that was foundational to the political contracts of 1776 and 1789, and, on the other, the era of high literary nationalism associated with figures like Emerson, Douglass, Hawthorne, Melville, Stowe, and Whitman. While U.S. literary studies continues to rely on sharply periodized conceptions of the early national versus the antebellum periods, this book binds these two moments together into one interconnected story about the slowly emerging apparatus of one truly nationalized culture industry. In this, I take my methodological cue from those literary scholars who have unfolded a similar story (especially Jay Grossman in his work on the Constitution and the American Renaissance) and from the many gifted historians who have colored my thinking, teaching me the nuances of what Ian Baucom calls "temporal accumulation" and what Walter Benjamin tropes as the ongoing scene of modernity's wreck-in-progress: history itself.

Even so, this book is not meant to be an exhaustive history but is instead a partial and a hybrid endeavor, joining history, literature, and cultural theory in equal parts to produce a wide-ranging cultural history of the early American nation-state. This history is posed argumentatively as a dialectic between the moment of union (in 1776 and 1787) and that of disunion (in 1861–65) and is narrated not through the language of continuous national chronology, but in and through the cultural fragments produced by people on the ground at several staggered historical intervals: 1776, 1787, 1835, 1853, and so on. In covering a century rather than a few decades, I have been necessarily selective, omitting many important problems and events. To the degree that I have addressed several important questions (from party politics to religion), I have done so, not by relying calendrically on common narratives of antebellum transition (by rehearsing a shift, for instance, from Federal Party federalism into Jeffersonian Republicanism or by describing in detail the War of 1812), but by thinking instead about these and other problems from *inside* the materials the book excavates and the long story it wants to tell about print culture. In this way, the larger argument joins the early national and antebellum periods in a tight narrative that exposes the balance and tensions between them even as individual chapters give sustained attention to local moments, texts, and places. The book thus plumbs the phenomenological details of historically lived experience even as it insists on the familiar horizontal rhetoric of Revolution, Constitution, Secession, Civil War, and Reconstruction that is America's national narrative.

Tracing the ways the nation unevenly progressed into a more unified form over the course of many decades (as opposed to insisting on its spectacular and instantaneous invention in 1776 or 1787) should do much to displace the text-based fantasies to which the United States as a nation continues to subscribe, both in the academy and in popular culture. As a scholar, however, I look not merely to overturn but to turn over and really look at the hegemonic narratives that frame my field: from the privileging of print that we see in the foundational work of Benedict Anderson to the abstractions of the public sphere model to the antimaterialist ideality that often still pervades American historiography of the Revolutionary period. I have worked hard to challenge these central theses without agonistically reifying them, and to do so by speaking simultaneously to a dense field of interlocutors that includes scholars in many different fields. It is my hope that my ideas will challenge the dichotomized paradigms that continue to dominate discussions of early American culture—dichotomies not just of the eighteenth versus the nineteenth century but of oral versus print culture, the abstract versus the embodied, the grand versus the particular, and the literary versus the historical. This book doesn't choose between the two sides of such binaries: instead, it says yes to each of them, acknowledging that in the mixed up world of early industrial expansion, both are always in play.

While this book begins, then, as a critique of existing accounts of early national print culture, it sometimes slips the straightjacket of that thesis altogether in order to discuss instead the complicated ways that the world itself was being reorganized by early industrial transformations that were simultaneously material and discursive—problems both of materialist history and of cultural representation. In this way, *The Republic in Print* enters the critical field mapped out by existing accounts even as it aims to produce on its own terms a vivid new account of the imperfect emergence of the postcolonial American nation-state and its vexed relations to a host of its own embodied and disembodied competitors—the family, the tavern, the regiment, the church, the village, the marketplace, the local state, the region, and even the ever more cosmopolitan (if also imagined) world of transatlantic exchange—that were all emerging as possible modes of identification and affiliation throughout the last half of the eighteenth century. American nationalism is, in this account, hopelessly mediated and yet hopefully virtual—right up until it actually disintegrates into cross-regional rivalry and civil war.

THE PROGRESS OF THE CENTURY.

THE LIGHTNING STEAM PRESS.   THE ELECTRIC TELEGRAPH.   THE LOCOMOTIVE.   THE STEAMBOAT.

FIGURE 1.1   *The Progress of the Century: The Lightning Steam Press, the Electric Telegraph, the Locomotive, [and] the Steamboat.* New York: Currier & Ives, 1876. Library of Congress, Prints and Photographs Division, LC-USZ62-102264.

1. U.S. PRINT CULTURE
THE FACTORY OF FRAGMENTS

> Every thing is local.
> —J. Hector St. John de Crèvecoeur, *Letters from an American Farmer*, 1782

1. LOOKING BACKWARD: THE PRINT CULTURE THESIS

1876 was a year of epochal, periodizing fictions in the United States, marking for Americans the first national centennial, an astounding one hundred years of independence. In a commemorative print (fig. 1.1) titled "The Progress of the Century," Currier and Ives celebrate this manmade event, evoking the grandeur of the unified state through the icons of the communications and transportation revolutions. The print tells its story in several distinct scenes of national improvement, arranged in raggedly clockwise manner. The result is a montage of American ingenuity that evolves from a barely noticeable gesture toward preindustrial production (a man working with his hands at the left margin of the frame) to ever more modern innovations as the viewer makes the visual rounds of the print's circular composition. The story starts at nine o'clock with a residual artisanal figure lifting hammer and hand in an old-fashioned act of autonomous bookmaking. A few notches upward, at about ten o'clock, his handiwork has already been displaced by the cylindrical steam press that revolutionized printing in the 1830s, marking the definitive end of artisanal control of the book trade in the United States and the start of a more capitalized industry relying, as we see here, not on one hand but on a division of labor among many hands. Several notches past these three emergent Bartlebys, at about two o'clock, the print's expansionist plot thickens with a battery of internal improvements, including canals, tunnels, steamboats, railroads, and a suggestive set of telegraph wires that leads us to the composition's focal point: an isolated white-collar worker, looking quite tailored and Taylorized, who sits alone encoding a telegraph message into the Morse clicker while a pithy unionist epigram ticks off below him. As the historian Richard Brown has noted, the telegraph message serves as the picture's motto, "join[ing] Daniel Webster's 1830 unionist epigram" ("LIBERTY AND UNION NOW AND FOREVER ONE AND INSEPARABLE") "with the universal message of Luke in the Bible" ("GLORY TO GOD IN THE HIGHEST, ON EARTH PEACE, GOOD WILL TOWARD MEN") to suggest "that progress in communications promotes national union, piety, and peace."[1]

The connection between national progress and technological innovation is a familiar one. But there are problems with the fictional unit of time this image labors to create. Despite the print's epic title, the chief innovations depicted here do not represent the gradual evolution of American ingenuity but are instead specific technologies whose historical innovation dates to a narrower window in American history: the mid-1820s to the mid-1840s. The cylindrical steam press, for example, came into wide use only after 1825 and did not significantly impact American printing until 1833, with the rise of the penny press and the institution of large book factories like Harper and Brothers in New York; the steamboat likewise emerged in the 1820s, permanently altering the social and economic geography of the Northeast and West with the completion of the Erie Canal in 1825; railroads dominated expansion everywhere—but only after 1830; and the telegraph finally arrived in the 1840s to conquer utterly, as antebellum Americans liked to say, the national divides of time and space. By presenting these innovations within the unified space of the centennial picture frame, "The Progress of the Century" seems to suggest they were spread out over the course of one hundred years, in the process conflating the largely preindustrial moment of founding with its increasingly industrialized afterlife. Why are the technological innovations of two decades celebrated as the engines of an entire century? Like much nationalist rhetoric, this image represses the relative modernity of 1830s industrialism in a way that makes both the nation and its technologies of expansion seem to "loom" without rupture "out of an immemorial past."[2] This narrative in turn enacts an indispensable amnesia, insisting that these years were doing the work of unification in a way that conveniently covers over the skeleton in the national closet—that casket marked, in survey courses, "sectionalism" and "secession."

This book tells a different story about the production of both printed texts and the American nation—a story that begins to take shape only when we note the specific origins of the technologies celebrated here. When we remember the emergence and proliferation of such technologies as historically specific events, we begin the work of contesting an official and retrospective narrative that casts technology as progress, nationally written. The dramatic industrial transformations of the 1830s, '40s, and '50s—so oddly telescoped in master narratives of American economic and literary history—provide ample opportunities to think about and theorize the ongoing processes of cultural integration (celebrated by historians as a "market revolution" and by literary scholars as an "American Renaissance"). But the timing of these transformations ought to point us in another direction as well: in short, toward the simultaneous experiences of *dis*integration and national fragmentation that mark these same years, in all their technological wonder.

Print culture lies at the center of this account because print is, without rival, American nationalism's preferred techno-mythology. In local historical societies, rare book rooms, history classrooms, literature surveys, and PBS documentaries, print culture dominates America's national narrative of how it began. But just as Currier and Ives telescope the industrial transformations of the 1830s to tell a story of triumphant union, so these text-based accounts of U.S. founding conveniently forget that there was no "national" print culture before the industrial revolution slowly centralized literary production in the 1830s, '40s, and '50s. Recognizing the material conditions under which a national print culture can and cannot function requires that we revisit and revise existing accounts of the relationship between print culture and nation formation. This book asks two questions in this regard: first, how do we account for nation formation in the material absence of a national print culture? And second, how do we account for the profound cultural fragmentation that accompanied the eventual emergence of national print networks between 1820 and 1860?

I argue that it was not the presence of a national print culture but the absence of one that ensured U.S. founding in 1776 and 1789. But even though no national print network existed at the moment of the American Revolution, that period still bequeathed to its heirs a profound belief in the possibilities of a more perfect, more material union—a union made increasingly "real" through the spread of post roads, canals, railroad tracks, and national periodicals that hailed an ever more reachable American public to recognize itself as a community in print. Cross-regional communication is, in fact, the fiction on which the founding based itself, and the antebellum period would serve as both the fulfillment of that founding fantasy and its undoing. Like some long-forgotten Rip Van Winkle, the United States finally wakes up after fifty years to find itself deeply entangled in the embrace of two contradictory developments—its own unionist rhetoric and an expanding regime of internal improvements that are meant to promote union and commerce but that actually only erode the one through the expansion of the other. After 1830, these newly awakened Americans must grapple with a national culture that is only just beginning to be made institutionally immanent as the many incompatible parts of the union are brought into increasingly uncomfortable alignment—an alignment visibly registered in and through the institutions of antebellum print culture.

Though one of the most identifiable agents of a wished-for and integrated national public, the printing industry not only was *not* celebrated in the 1830s for its role in the work of national consolidation but instead called forth scenes of deep division and dissent. It is no coincidence that the decade in which the technologies of steam and rail came into widespread use was also a decade that saw an astounding rise in mob violence against printers across the United States as well as the earliest threats of Southern secession and the ultimate entrenchment of stubborn sectional blocks. These developments were reinforced by the rise of the mass party system, which was in turn circularly reinforced by the rise of a mass media system—a system of interlinked antebellum newspapers that had an increasing capacity to share information both with each other and with distant subscribers in a reliable and timely fashion.[3] Against the optimism of Currier and Ives—and I might add, much of our own retrospective optimism about the power of print to link dispersed citizens—I argue that this newly predictable set of connections did not create an ever-widening sense of imagined community so much as it disturbingly displaced one that was already rigidly in place. Indeed, the world of 1830s and '40s print culture (and especially its ubiquitous periodical constituents—the newspaper, the magazine, the city directory, the trade annual, the gift book, and the almanac) called forth for antebellum Americans a new and destabilizing episode in the long history of what Benedict Anderson has called, in a more positive context, national "simultaneity." For antebellum Americans, this sense of shared time and space was not a solution to the geographic displacement of one part of the population from the next; it was instead a new and frightening problem for those previously distinct and culturally autonomous populations. By focusing on the production of print networks and the circulation of actual objects within those networks, this book tracks the way that the textually imagined connections of 1776 and 1787 were eventually reified and then tested (after the nationalist fact) by more sustained, highly integrated systems of cross-regional contact. I take it for granted that such contact is largely produced by commerce but is ultimately figured, ideologically, by culture. What happens when the official national narrative of continental union, so entrenched in the nation's local celebrations of itself, comes face to face with the material mechanisms that would seem to make it possible—canals, trains, telegraphs, and a thriving mass print culture? In the case of the early United States, the rhetoric that powered this proliferating infrastructure was an ever more literally understood "Union," but the actual consequence was secession and civil war.

2. The Imagined Community and the Actual Archive

One of the most compelling accounts of nationalism in the past thirty years has been Benedict Anderson's *Imagined Communities*, and much of its well-deserved lure resides in its first word: *imagined*. Against the antinationalist pessimism that preceded him, Anderson eloquently described the role that desire, affect, creativity, and wishfulness play in the epochal world-building work of nations, states, and empires.[4] But *Imagined Communities* also famously links the longevity and appeal of the nation as a form to the rise of capitalist networks more generally, describing nationalism as an affect that rides on the back of material objects. Anderson gives print pride of place among the many objects that circulate through these networks, arguing that the "territorial stretch" inhabited by New World populations "could be imagined as nations" only with "the arrival of print-capitalism" and that the sphere of circulation in which printed artifacts moved explains the territorial boundaries of particular nations

(61). In this argument, print capitalism both registers a new comparative consciousness among different geographical populations *and* circulates the affect that attaches to such consciousness.

I would like to retheorize the relation of the "imagined" to the "material" in this argument by revisiting these interconnected claims, especially the question of whether networks of (print) exchange produce a circulatory and circulating field of affect. To this end, consider the case of a forgotten Enlightenment functionary named Hugh Finlay. Finlay was a British postal employee who, in 1772, was appointed by the Crown to inspect the King's Post Road in North America.[5] Traveling overland from his most recent post in Quebec, Finlay spent ten painstaking months between September 1773 and June 1774 surveying every postal office between Falmouth and Georgia, methodically recording everything he could find out about each road, bridge, horse, ferry, postal deputy, and rider on his route. Because the post road was the only inland material infrastructure that linked one colony to the next in the eighteenth century, Finlay's journal represents one of our few comprehensive records of the material conditions attending the circulation not just of letters but of newspapers, pamphlets, novels, and every other imaginable printed (or tradable) object—things that could have moved from colony to colony only over sea by boat or over land by post road. The *Journal* thus offers nothing less than a material account of textual circulation on the eve of the American Revolution and in doing so allows us to test, on North American ground, some of Anderson's central arguments about the ways that networks of exchange help to produce nations.

Finlay does, in fact, display a notable enthusiasm for translocal community, suggesting that dispersed collectivities were indeed being fantasized as connected entities via institutions like the post road. To this end, Finlay uses the *Journal* to propose (to himself) a series of postal improvements that might make greater use of the post road's circulatory potential, advocating the wide distribution of "postal horns" to announce the arrival of new mail; the establishment of proper postal spaces (as opposed to the more customary use of private houses or public taverns); the introduction of new accounting methods; and sundry other "regulations" and "forms" (52). The *Journal* itself is a product of Finlay's investment in such regulation: "written in a small, exceedingly neat, and perfectly legible hand" and later "bound in official vellum," the journal never leaves Finlay's possession (v). He carries it with him at all times because he hopes one day to use his notes to compute uniform distances for every rider in the king's service. He expects to gather that document, in turn, into that most Enlightenment of orderly spaces—a printed book, a postal directory that will describe the movement of the mail in the most detailed, transparent, and organized way possible (90). Always empire's creature, Finlay even suggests (to himself) that the service advertise his improvements in coffee houses throughout the empire in order to drum up more revenue for the king, from Wales to Savannah.

But Finlay's *Journal* is a text divided between imagined communities and real ones. Finlay thinks of himself as one "whose business is to further the interest of the General Post Office, and facilitate correspondence by every possible means" (24). But seamless correspondence between colonial fragments was not only impossible in the early 1770s; it was in many ways undesirable to local populations who were deeply invested in a local autonomy they defined not only against England (or Canadian postal inspectors) but against each other as well. Finlay's fantasies are thus not only highly bureaucratic; they prove unrealistic as well. Finlay may have earnestly believed in the post road as a highly functional network of exchange, but his administrative enthusiasm rarely met with success. The *Journal* thus unfolds as an unintentional picaresque, with Finlay recording his every movement in the hopes of producing a master administrative text for empire and for king—even as that goal, like Finlay himself, is comically resisted in every colonial nook it enters. Indeed, much of the *Journal*'s comic appeal derives from the fact that Finlay never sees what every reader must: the utter impracticability of his desire to organize and control the provincial mails against the combined forces of custom, weather, and technological impediment. The chaotic forces of disorganization appear on almost every page of the *Journal*. Not only are the roads bad and the postal riders cunningly resistant to regulation, but there are no inns for Finlay when he needs rest and often no horses to transport him when he needs to move. Some customers are too "indigent" to pay for their mail, while their neighborly postmasters are too kind not to deliver it (16). In some places, mail is routinely delayed while printers set its content in type for local news gazettes (31). Some riders are known to ride drunk (55); others carry letters "privately," burdening their horses with extra packages the king is never compensated for. As one deputy tells Finlay, "there's two post offices in New Port, the King's and Mumfords, and … the revenue of the last is the greatest" (32).

This last problem might suggest that the problems Finlay faces are proto-Revolutionary ones (with incipient Americans—like Mumford—resisting the king's entitlement). But even in loyalist colonies, Finlay's elaborate plans are pragmatically foiled by any number of local problems—from bad roads to lost papers. He often arrives to find offices whose accounts have gone unsettled for decades—if ever settled at all: in one, the postmaster has died, leaving no records behind (63); in another, the postmaster "says he cannot settle ... because his children and negroes in his absence from home got into his office and destroy'd his Papers" (58); a third postmaster absconds to the West Indies, taking the king's profits with him (89, 92); while a fourth has moved to another colony and taken up a new profession (89, 92). Those who have kept records, on the other hand, have struggled for decades with severe paper shortages, keeping their accounts on "scrap[s]" of which nobody can now make sense (83).

The post office is, in short, a mess, and Finlay's figure for this cacophony is the postal rider's "portmanteau." The box or bag in which official mail was, by law, to be locked, the portmanteau is one thing in theory but quite another in practice:

> The Portmanteaus seldom come locked: the consequence is that the riders stuff them with bundles of shoes, stockings, canisters, money or any thing they can get to carry, which tears the Portmanteaus, and rubs the letters to pieces. [One rider's] Portmanteau was not lock'd; it was stuff'd with bundles of different kinds, and crammed with news papers: the letters for the different stages were not put up in bags, the rider had saddle bags quite full besides, so that his horse (a poor looking beast) was loaded too much to make the necessary speed. (41–43)

Here and elsewhere, the portmanteau tropes in miniature the confusion of Finlay's long and unexpectedly arduous journey even as it offers the *Journal*'s most compressed figure for postal circulation, with all its attendant losses, delays, deferrals, and confusions. In the end, the portmanteau figures the combined force of custom and contingency that made the post road so resistant to Finlay's administrative interventions. Finlay, of course, is a believer in the locked and well-ordered portmanteau, but even he must learn firsthand the inevitability of postal contingency: in one humorous episode, he arrives in a rainstorm at "a poor hut without windows called a Tavern" to find that "the rain had soak'd thro' my portmanteau" (54), damaging his letters of introduction. The damaged, overstuffed, or unlocked portmanteau resonates with similar figures that proliferate up and down the route and everywhere throughout the *Journal*. We find one such counterpart, for instance, in several tavern tables Finlay describes, where mail is (against regulation) carelessly thrown for public retrieval, especially in towns where postal deputies have been lost to death, resignation, or emigration, leaving the mail to autodisseminate—in other words, to deliver itself. But disorder is never the exception in Finlay's world. It is, to his chagrin, the eighteenth-century rule.

Finlay's *Journal* thus documents in painstaking detail the restrictive material contexts in which early American textual circulation took place. As an early U.S. travel narrative, it suggests a world of profound noncorrespondence and nonsimultaneity, a world in which mail is marked not by speedy delivery but by deferrals of every imaginable kind. Indeed, the *Journal* itself is rather like one of Finlay's portmanteaus—a motley compendium of information delivered to us from the past (after a brief delay), overstuffed with the unexpected and the unlikely. Within the *Journal*, the progress of Finlay's trip is repeatedly delayed as he waits for mail from his superiors that (ironically) never comes. In New York, for instance, he defers his trip indefinitely as the entire city waits for the October packet to arrive from England. When it finally does arrive, "there came no Instructions for a Surveyor" (49). In this way, Finlay's will-to-organize is continually frustrated both by the empire at large and by the local institutions that would seem to subtend it (including packets, ferries, horses, portmanteaus, postal employees, and, most recurrently, the post road itself), none of which can live up to the bureaucratic fantasies he piles upon them. The *Journal* thus unwittingly reveals the very thing that *Imagined Communities* does not address: the historically specific ways that both artifacts and affect circulated under the still emerging relations of early industrial North American (nation) production.

Finlay's *Journal* is neither a novel nor a newspaper, the two forms that *Imagined Communities* specifically links to the origins of nationalist consciousness and especially to that crucial sense of simultaneity-across-space that allows reading subjects to imagine themselves as part of a larger, translocal community. Anderson famously suggests that "these forms provided the technical means for 're-presenting' the *kind* of imagined community that is the nation." The novel, for instance, in following a cast of characters who do not necessarily know each other but who nevertheless coexist within the same narrative, works as "a device for the presentation of simultaneity," making it "a complex gloss upon the word 'meanwhile'" (25). Likewise, the newspaper is organized around "calendrical coincidence," giving it a "novelistic format" (33) in which the characters are other communities. The columns that separate their narratives serve as the technical means of expressing a fundamental relation of modernity: the idea of temporal coincidence across space. The newspaper is thus, like the novel, another "gloss on the word 'meanwhile.'"

What then of Finlay's journal as a *form*? Like all journals, it rejects the word "meanwhile," disavowing it for something more like the word "now" (and in Finlay's case, "here"). Nevertheless, because it is no less invested in calendrically recording the topography—the literal spatial sprawl—of the emerging nation, the *Journal* poses an uncanny countertext to Anderson's discussion of novels and newspapers. Finlay details his travels, for example, in exacting diary entries that map emerging national space through the use of geographic and calendrical bylines (October 2 at Falmouth, November 13 at New Haven, December 14 at Charles Town, and so on). But while the dates and locations at the top of each entry look like newspaper bylines, the *Journal* repudiates the sense of simultaneity that Anderson describes. The eighteenth-century newspaper collects a proliferating archive of remote information and reproduces it in a singular location that makes the events it records appear simultaneous (because collected in one space and consumed by the reader at one time). Finlay's journal, on the other hand, describes a body that rarely stopped moving. His bylines consistently record a single consciousness moving slowly across the tightly linked coordinates of time and space, describing the precise somatic conditions of early American travel, which include (for Finlay) not just illiterate tour guides and resistant locals but extremes of heat and cold, rain and snow, leaky canoes, boggy swamps, fallen trees, serpentine rivers, dead creeks, "wild beasts," bad bridges, frozen ground, "fatiguing" mountains, a smallpox outbreak, late ferries, a sore back, rivers filled with rocks and shallows, darkness, and a series of lame horses ("starv'd, weak, lean, small brutes" that are quickly "knocked up" by travel [53–54]). As the trip continues and entries accumulate, the *Journal* becomes an extension for Finlay's specific body, collecting information while continually on the move rather than collecting it within the (temporarily) fixed site of the newspaper office or a newspaper. The *Journal* thus records not only what the newspaper does not express but the very thing that the newspaper, in a sense, is designed to repress—the vast distances between bylines, which Finlay mathematically expresses in his compulsive computation of the exact distances (or exact travel times) between each entry.

But if the newspaper denies, in its casual columnar form, the scattered-ness of the spaces from which it collects its information, it nevertheless bears, like Finlay's *Journal*, the telltale traces of that scatteredness. Every colonial newspaper records the gaps between metropole and colony (and between colony and colony) in its bylines. In the eighteenth-century pro-vincial newspaper, such bylines serve as eloquent registers of the banal displacements that empire's sprawl had long produced for readers living at its edge. For instance, the January 3, 1776, issue of the *Pennsylvania Ga-zette* amply records the temporally disjunct and random fashion in which information was received and relayed through the makeshift network of Revolutionary print culture. Reports from Watertown, Massachusetts, are dated December 14—a nineteen-day lag in "national" intelligence; information from Cambridge is dated December 31; from Providence, December 16; from New York, December 28; from Montreal, Decem-ber 4; from St. George, Grenada, November 4; and from outlying Bucks and Chester counties, December 26. The January 10 issue would likewise carry news from London, dated October 28.[6] The newspaper thus power-fully registers not just an imagined sense of simultaneity-across-space, but its more materialist corollary: a sense of scatteredness, or dispersion-across-space.

In the age of jets, cell phones, and e-mail, we rarely think about the gaps between bylines (indeed, online newspaper stories are no longer dated by month or day but by minute and second). These gaps were, however, very much on the mind of American revolutionaries in 1776. Indeed, it was the very sense of simultaneity that Anderson has suggested makes nations feel complete, the very sense of cohesion and brother-hood with their British kin, that was perpetually taxed by the strains of geographic space and by imperial policies that exacerbated such strains. American colonists experienced this taxation as both an imperial (fiscal) policy and the unwanted affective content of their structural relationship within the empire as a whole, and it eventually produced—in print—an elaborate provincial discourse devoted to cataloguing and theorizing the dangers of dislocation and "foreign" (or spatially removed) administra-tion—as, for instance, the Declaration of Independence would later do in seeking to reject "distant" rule in favor of "home" rule. Print culture thus did not, in the American case, simply reinforce a sense of simultaneity. On the contrary, it actually worked in many cases to register the failures of such simultaneity and the consequent lack, in Jefferson's word, of "consanguinity" across the sweep of British empire.

Anderson, of course, precisely targets the nation (rather than the empire) as the unit of simultaneity. It would be a mistake, however, to think that the scale of the nation was more conducive to a sense of shared, or simultaneous, experience than empire had been. To be sure, imperial sprawl—and what the colonists dubbed its "virtual" administration of far-off spaces—was a primary target of Revolutionary critique, and one promise of independence was undoubtedly the much sought-after sense of self-identicality that had long been denied colonial populations living at the edge of a large, disintegrated empire. By this, I mean not just the self-identicality of cherished Enlightenment truisms (such as "all men are created equal"), but of geographical self-sameness—the ability finally to be at home, as it were, in America. But though we frequently forget it, the Revolution did not produce this kind of integration on a national scale—nor was it meant to. The later fetishization of July 4 notwithstanding, 1776 produced not a nation but a confederation—a compact among former colonial units (each one dubbed a "state")—and it was these smaller units that were meant to make good on the promise of self-identicality and local self-governance. More than one new American was puzzled, after 1776, about what it might mean to feel "nationly" (as one Massachusetts woman asked in her diary).[7] The nation, such as it was, was simply less legible—more literally speaking, less *available*—as a mode of affective affiliation than were the state, the county, and the village.

Given Finlay's position as a colonial functionary, one might expect him to bond with the other colonial characters he meets up with in his travels. Indeed, Finlay very much resembles the foundational nationalist figure that Anderson focuses on in his argument about "Creole Pioneers." Anderson describes these incipient, or "first-wave," nationals as traveling bureaucrats engaged in a series of journeys that are "vertically barred" and laterally "cramped," colonial administrators who prove degraded and suspect to their metropolitan brethren but are finally legible to their cofunctionaries as a new kind of imperial companion—in short, a fellow national (57). Though Anderson's argument primarily targets Spanish administrators (the "viceroyalty") that have no British counterpart in North America (and likewise emphasizes "the fatality of trans-Atlantic birth" over and against permanent emigrations), the Glasgow-born Fin-

lay nevertheless resembles this sort of eighteenth-century traveling sales-
man—one of countless "pilgrim" "functionaries" sent by his king not,
as in old days, on a religious pilgrimage but on an "administrative pilgrimage," a "looping climb" that Finlay hoped would lead to ever more
prestigious positions.

As scholars have sometimes noted, however, problems emerge when
trying to fit a real body into Anderson's framework.[8] Most persistently,
the issue of geographical diversity (along with a complex range of local
political affiliations) arises to complicate the simple binary of metropole
and colony, center and periphery. Finlay was an imperial functionary in
1775, but he was stationed in Canada, not the thirteen colonies, and he
was sent to inspect a postal system that had long been under the control
of an absentee Pennsylvania printer (Benjamin Franklin). As the *Journal*
makes clear, the administrative unit that would later come to be called
the "thirteen colonies" had a different set of political squabbles with
Britain—and a different culture of local autonomy—than Canada had.
Finlay was never recognized as a fellow traveler in the communities he
visited, nor did he recognize their inhabitants as potential fellow Americans—even though there was, in 1775, an ongoing attempt to organize
resistance across the entire arc of British empire (from Quebec to Maine,
Philadelphia, Savannah, Cuba, and Barbados). Instead of antimetropoli-
tan solidarity, Finlay's travels reveal a complex rivalry between his own
Canadianness, the king's Britishness, and the postal route's incipient (but
deeply fragmented) Americanness.

One might argue that these tensions merely reflect the future nationalisms that would eventually emerge in this area of the globe. But even this
tripartite model minimizes the ways that more local geography works in
Finlay's *Journal* to fracture collective (incipiently nationalist) affect. Not
even the post road, for instance, can be lumped under a single structure
of feeling (such as "Americanness"). The *Journal* itself is starkly divided
between the "North" road and the "South" (each with very different material conditions and quality of life). It records, moreover, far more local
divides from town to town and colony to colony. In New England, for instance, improvements cannot be made to the road because Massachusetts
and New Hampshire refuse to pay for changes that they believe might
benefit rival colonies' economies more than their own. Even within the
smallest towns, rival factions attend the answering of Finlay's every question, and more than one deputy asks not to be named as the source of
information, even as he gladly offers it. In the deferential world of the

eighteenth-century American colonies, these factions are primarily organized around status (an elusive category that had not yet, in 1775, congealed into "class"). Indeed, Finlay himself identifies not with the riders
who travel the roads but with the more incipiently bourgeois deputies
who administer them (one, he says approvingly, "seems to be a Post Master in his heart" [34]). His is not a horizontal kinship, one Briton (or
North American) to another, but a vertical one—one postal employee
to the next as they inhabit the great chain of imperial administration—a
mode of organizing social relations that not only marks Finlay's relations
with colonial populations but finally saturates all social relations described in the *Journal*, even those between townsmen.

Though Finlay hoped to use his diary as a report to the Crown, he
was reassigned to a new post before he finished his postal tour, and the
Journal's entries break off partway through. The *Journal* was thus abandoned, a forgotten manuscript that disappeared from the historical record until it was serendipitously rediscovered in 1866 in the bankruptcy
auction of a failed Swedenborgian missionary. Purchased by a member of
the Brooklyn Mercantile Library who sensed "that it must possess some
intrinsic value," it was published in an edition of 150 copies, few of which
sold or survived (v). The *Journal's* checkered composition, production,
and reception history poses an ironic postscript to Finlay's own understanding of it as an indispensable administrative master text. Though he
never stops trying, Finlay the post manager simply cannot beat back the
peculiar force of the local—whether it comes in the shape of provincial
custom or colonial cunning, a muddy road or a lame horse, a damaged
portmanteau or a dead postal inspector. Though he never sees it himself, the *Journal* registers on nearly every page a profound disjunction between Finlay's own utopian-imperial project to collect and control the
mails and the many delays, miscarriages, missing instructions, and unanswered letters that otherwise litter his narrative.

Composed hundreds of years later, Anderson's formulations about
imagined communities rely on a similar fantasy about the ability of print
to erase local differences and to install, in their place, a formal homogeneity, whether in fact or in feeling. Anderson's arguments finally work
best when we sever his ungrounded account of early national circulation
from his more ingenious reading of novels and newspapers as registers
of a specific worldview, objects that reflect a new model of history within
which any number of forms and allegiances might take root. Isolated artifacts and genres may appear in retrospect to have been produced and re-

ceived in a uniform way across the disparate spaces of empire and region, but the actual archive tells a different story about what kinds of communities were being imagined in 1774—or 1776—and how and why.

3. Carey's *Museum* and Franklin's Wheelbarrow

Finlay believed in the post office's ability to organize, connect, and make productive the disparate spaces and populations of North America. The first generation of post-Revolutionary Americans inherited that belief from the British Empire, parlaying it into a number of popular republican discourses about the diffusion of knowledge and into nationalist calls for internal improvements that were expected to pave the way for more regular interregional communication and trade.[9] In the inaugural essay for Mathew Carey's *American Museum* (first published in 1787), Benjamin Rush is every inch a Finlay, displaying an administrative optimism much like the *Journal*'s in calling for any number of ambitious internal innovations that directly engage the fantasy of both centralization and mass diffusion, including a federal university and extended postal service, "for the purpose of diffusing knowledge as well as extending the living principle of government to every part of the united states—every state—city—county—village—and township in the union." Carey's *Museum* was itself an attempt to create just these sorts of national connections through a widely distributed print forum, and his editorial aspirations were no less utopian and forward-looking than either Rush's or Finlay's. In his preface to the first number, Carey modestly envisioned his new print venture as a "repository" for "perishable" print productions collected from across the American continent, pieces of writing that "after a confined period of usefulness and circulation" would otherwise be condemned to "oblivion." Just three years into the venture, however, the theme of drawing together the "genius" of the continent into a single space was already being reversed, elaborated, and extended into a commercial fantasy of mass distribution throughout the continent. Reflecting on the *Museum*'s success in 1790, Carey boasts that the magazine's "patronage has so far increased as to far exceed the most sanguine expectations of the original proprietor. It now circulates in almost every corner of this extensive continent." These remarks are signed, corporately, by the newly formed partnership of "Carey, Stewart, and Company—July 20, 1790."[10]

Carey's corporate signature marks his rising entrepreneurial status from local printer to nationally prominent publisher—an ambition that emerged hand-in-hand with the rise of the federal state itself, the reorganization of which, under the Constitution, had been codified just one year earlier. But Carey's optimism in this preface belies the material state of publishing in the late 1780s. Corporate publishing ventures of this sort were not common in 1787, and Carey himself had serious doubts about the probability of their success.[11] Just a year before he began work on the *Museum*, he had pulled out of a similar corporate partnership for the short-lived *Columbian Magazine* because, as he later wrote, common business sense dictated "the utter improbability of such a work producing any profit, worth the attention of five persons."[12] Despite Carey's enthusiastic declarations in its various prefaces and advertisements, the *Museum* posed a similar problem, and it was, in fact, never profitable—not even in 1790, when Carey boasted most loudly of its success. Looking back on the other side of the nineteenth century, from a vantage point of far greater success than he could have imagined in 1790, Carey remembers a profound failure: "During the whole six years, I was in a state of intense penury. My pecuniary embarrassments were so great, and so constant, that I am now astonished, how I was able to muster perseverance and fortitude to struggle through them.... When I married at 31, my whole property consisted in cart-loads of odd volumes, and odd numbers, of the American Museum, which, when I finally abandoned the work, proved almost valueless" (22–24).

What accounts for the discrepancy between the promise of the first number and the failures of later ones? According to Carey, his "embarrassment" arose in large part from his own irrational ambition toward ever more expansive markets that were not within practical reach. "I printed," he complains, "quite too many copies, in the vain hope of ultimately procuring a large increase of subscribers," but "more than half of my subscribers lived in remote situations, 2, 3, 4 and 500 miles from me; and their remittances were so extremely irregular that I was obliged to hire collectors to dun them, at a heavy expense, which averaged at least 30 per cent of the slender modicum, I was entitled to receive!" In the end, Carey's ambition was not realizable: "I was much attached to the work, and had great reluctance to abandon it, unproductive and vexatious as was the management of it; but at length I sang its requiem, as I have said, at the close of the year 1792" (23).

Writing as an older man to a new generation of Jacksonian entrepreneurs, Carey positions his *Autobiography* as one part self-advertisement, one part nostalgia. Nevertheless, his well-documented struggles with *The American Museum* suggest a discrepancy between how booksellers talked in early America and how they did business. This often unnarrated gap between the world of things and the world of words used to describe those things should prove instructive to critics of this period who continue to use local linguistic declarations as unfettered evidence of more general material situations. In 1787, printers, publishers, and even consumers may have begun to imagine and discuss the potential of an emergent federal market that could connect "every corner of this extensive continent," but a functional national market zone, or unified field of exchange, had still not materialized across the landmass of eastern North America. Indeed, when Carey began his *Museum*, there were few roads, no rails, and, in fact, very little money in the United States.

This is not to say that the early republic was a series of localities as disjunct in 1787 and 1789 as they had been in 1774 when Finlay first rode his lean, starved beast through the American South. The tumults of the Revolution were in many ways deeply geographic ones, initiating high rates of mobility and exchange among various North American populations. The 1770s saw the emergence of a protonationalist network of contacts (overseen by the Continental Congress and local committees of correspondence), the mobilization of various populations across several regional fronts, and increasingly predictable postal and commercial contacts, particularly in the Northeast. These are the very shifts in material life that made diffusionist fantasies so appealing in the first place to a scattered, often isolated, but also increasingly mobile series of local reading publics looking for ways to imagine unity across a vast space—with little in the way of material infrastructure to bolster such imaginings. As I argue in chapter 2, Paine's *Common Sense* served as the epochal cornerstone in the emergent discourse of republican diffusion, and the memory of Paine's popular 1776 pamphlet posed an inspirational example to a post-Revolutionary generation of entrepreneurs and literate elites who wanted to believe that a national market for books *already* existed, if only it could be tapped. It is no coincidence that one of the first essays Carey chose to extract in the *Museum* was, in fact, Paine's *Common Sense*, for the *Museum* perpetually confused its own project of editorial collection with a Painite program of mass diffusion.

The American Museum's vexed business history calls into question our own backwards sense of what the earliest American "mass" markets must have looked like, especially in regard to the domestic circulation of printed goods. In the end, Carey had the ability to imagine a national periodical but not the means to produce and distribute one profitably. If Carey learned one thing from this episode, it was that the surest path to commercial stability in the early republic was to concentrate first on a small area and to give up, at least for a time, large-scale publishing projects in favor of smaller jobbing contracts in and around Philadelphia.[13] "When I relinquished the ill-fated Museum," he later wrote,

> I commenced bookselling and printing on a small scale. My store, or rather my shop, was of very moderate dimensions; but small as it was, I had not full-bound books enough to fill the shelves—a considerable portion of them were occupied by spelling books. I procured a credit at the Bank, which enabled me to extend my business; and by care, indefatigable industry, the most rigid punctuality, and frugality, I gradually advanced in the world. (25)

Carey's rise in the world thus coincided, paradoxically, with his decision to give up the *Museum's* investment in national diffusion; only when he settled down to serve the needs of a more local community of readers did Carey rise, like Benjamin Franklin before him, to the status of representative printer and man of letters.[14]

Carey's route to national success was, however, decidedly un-Franklinian. Compare Carey's "cartload" of magazines to Franklin's more famous wheelbarrow episode in the *Autobiography*. Carey, of course, uses his cart to move to smaller quarters after the *Museum* nearly bankrupts him: his "whole property" at the age of thirty-one "consisted in cart-loads of odd volumes, and odd numbers, of the American Museum," which by 1792 were "valueless." Franklin's wheelbarrow, on the other hand, is the very opposite of Carey's. As Franklin writes:

> In order to secure my Credit and Character as a Tradesman, I took care not only to be in *Reality* Industrious & frugal, but to avoid all *Appearances* of the Contrary. I drest plainly; I was seen at no Places of idle Diversion; I never went out a-fishing or Shooting; a Book, indeed, sometimes debauch'd me from my Work; but that was seldom, snug, & gave no Scandal: and to show that I was not above my Business, I

sometimes brought home the Paper I purchas'd at the Stores, thro' the Streets on a Wheelbarrow. Thus being esteem'd an industrious thriving young Man, and paying duly for what I bought, the Merchants who imported Stationary solicited my Custom, others propos'd supplying me with Books, & I went on swimmingly.[15]

While Carey's cart is a sign for failure, Franklin's wheelbarrow is a mark of success. In the end, however, Franklin's wheelbarrow is not really a sign of anything in particular but just, cannily, a sign—one that Franklin elastically uses to create and promote an appearance, among his neighbors and customers, of integrity, frugality, industry, and success. When set beside Carey's account of carting around the "valueless" "odd volumes" of his failed print venture, Franklin's story suggests that his various constructions of and about print literacy should not be treated, as they so often are, as transparent descriptions of eighteenth-century life: in particular, his persona as printer-turned-statesman needs to be more carefully considered as a performance that may not finally have been based in fact but that instead served Franklin's needs by exploiting what his audience expects or wants to be true. Critics, in other words, who use Franklin's *Autobiography* as the centerpiece for arguments about print's general and diffuse centrality at the moment of national founding ought to keep in mind that Franklin's wheelbarrow is above all a *floating* (or to use Franklin's favorite metaphor for slippery signification, a "swimming") sign—as much a performance for us, his readers, as the historical wheelbarrow it signifies was a performance put on by Franklin for his neighbors. Carey's pathetic cart, in other words—and all it connotes about the material limits of the book trade in the early republic—is at least as valid a figure for describing and understanding the state of national communication and community (and the status of representative texts and text-makers) as is Franklin's wheelbarrow.

Long after the Revolution, the United States would continue, as a series of independently operating local or state-based economies, to be oriented more toward exporting raw materials to and importing manufactured goods from marketplaces abroad than toward making real its own interior myths of domestic connection. While a nationalist discourse raged all through the Revolution (in the "Continental" Congress and the "Continental" Army), the mass circulation of American manufactured goods through diffuse American markets would not be a reality until Britain's later successful blockade of U.S. maritime trade finally forced the U.S.

government to begin funding internal improvements that, before 1816, were often discussed, debated, proposed, and fantasized but almost never funded or built. In the earliest days of the republic, not even raw staples were being exchanged on any massive scale among the most distant parts of the union, and in the absence of roads and canals to carry goods into the western interior, up to the Canadian border, and throughout most of the South, luxury items like Carey's *Museum* (as well as numerous locally produced engravings, newspapers, novels, plays, and pamphlets) had an even more limited potential for domestic circulation. In the end, American staples were far more likely to circulate in a predictable way thousands of miles *east* of Philadelphia (across the Atlantic in England's urban centers and then beyond with other foreign trading partners) than to circulate just hundreds of miles west or south of Philadelphia—in those areas of the continental United States that were the most isolated and the most dependent on land transportation.

Carey's story demonstrates in particularly materialist fashion how Franklin's wheelbarrow colludes with other Franklinian fictions—most notably, the fiction of union itself. Just as Franklin pretends to be working with his wheelbarrow, he would, as an aged (and sometimes ignored) delegate to the Federal Convention of 1787, strenuously argue that the delegates must perform unanimity as they tendered their creation to their constituents—especially in those flummoxed delegations most marked by interior dissent. Like the federalists who followed him, Franklin sensed the need to promote a fiction of federal consensus in the face of those innumerable local particulars that threatened to stall the union before it ever got going. This strategy was translated into print and engraved on every copy of the Constitution that was forwarded to the state legislatures, each one corporately signed not by individuals (who may or may not have concurred with its contents), but by state delegations (in which majority votes carried the day). The convention thus used a printed fiction to create a veneer of official consensus that was, because of the difficulties of acquiring accurate intelligence from Philadelphia, difficult to critique or verify. As we shall see, it is precisely this way of handling, or holding, dissent that is actually representative of this period (rather than particular texts themselves). Indeed, Franklin's embrace of evasion and dissemblance, of willful pretense and pretending, actually prefigures the cultural work of federalism as it proliferated from a topic of debate within various local communities into an immensely successful discourse for negotiating the relations of self-centered parts to the centerless whole of the union at large.

4. From Print Theory to Print Culture

Carey's story tells us what social and economic historians have long known: that print was a small part of a small early national world. Even in 1800, most Americans lived beyond the reach of any printed matter that was not produced by their own local printer or privately sent to them through personal connections. As William Charvat and Cathy Davidson note, both printers and the reading public lay scattered in these years in local communities that were hard to connect via print because publishing activity tended to be local and decentralized. A writer like Royall Tyler lived in New Hampshire and so published in New Hampshire—with the consequence that readers in Boston (the nearest city, over one hundred miles south) who might have wanted a book like Tyler's *Algerine Captive* could not get their hands on it.[16] Likewise Hugh Henry Brackenridge, writing in Pittsburgh, was unsure if readers in Philadelphia, roughly three hundred miles east, were even conscious of his "performance": "What? Ho!" he writes in the third volume of *Modern Chivalry* (which was published at Pittsburgh), "are ye all asleep in the hold down there at Philadelphia?" Brackenridge threatens to take "revenge" on his absentee readers "by dropping my pen altogether," but he finally resolved the problem of maintaining a Philadelphia audience in a more conventional way: by publishing his next installment there.[17]

Though aspiring printers and authors like Carey, Tyler, and Brackenridge might have wished otherwise, print played a smaller role in daily life than we might imagine. According to Richard Brown, "word-of-mouth transmission together with signed, handwritten messages furnished the primary means of spreading information, with print—newspapers and broadsides—playing only a secondary role." News of an important "national" event like Washington's death in 1799 traveled through the republic at a relatively quick pace, but not because there were sophisticated or reliable print networks to do the job. In fact, "hours or even days before the first locally printed newspaper accounts appeared," most people had already heard the news through commercial or political networks, passed mouth to mouth and by private letter.[18] Newspapers and topical broadsides were not quick enough—printing as an industry was not yet capitalized enough—to consistently and reliably spread important information nationally. The rhetorical grandeur of early nationalist fantasy aside, texts of this period leave a compelling record of the ways in which the potential unity of a still emerging American book market was routinely disrupted by material circumstances that were local in origin and localizing in effect—including, among others, geographic isolation, competing political affiliations, regional identification and diversity, and temporal lags in the production and dissemination of texts themselves. The routine ruptures that mark the real-life locales in which early national books and their readers traveled suggest that these books played two different roles in early national culture: on one hand, they served as symbols of unity; on the other, they were actual objects with limited circulations. In the first guise, they have historically figured a coherent site of national origin, calling forth a unified audience to act the role of national public. In the second, this same "public" emerges as a series of locally bound and locally defined communities—"publics" in the most plural, and fragmented, sense of the word.

Print was of course important, but it was indispensable only to a small part of the population. As Brown tells us, "printed matter was generally an imported luxury available, with certain exceptions such as the Bible and devotional books, only to the wealthy few."[19] Print was central to men like Franklin, Jefferson, and Adams—and to every member of those privileged elites that controlled the formal creation of the new state apparatus in 1776 and beyond. But even as provincial print cultures multiplied and proliferated in the years before and after the Revolution, they did so first in urban centers, taking as their initial audiences a growing urban middle class whose literacy and hunger for printed commodities has been well documented.[20] Arguments that foreground the importance of print, making it a monolithic and representative cultural practice across differentiated locales and populations, also necessarily foreground these highly literate classes—(men) who either were wealthy enough to amass private libraries or inhabited an early urban cash economy that allowed them to buy and read print products regularly or to join circulating libraries. Studies that focus on these groups—and almost every account of early American print culture in literary studies does—do not explain what nation and national consciousness meant to the Kentucky frontiersman who pushed the national border west, to the Florida speculator who sat out the Revolution in the swamps of the St. Johns River, or to the rural minuteman who lost his life fighting redcoats in the remote reaches of Vermont or Maine. These margins sit not just at the edge of the printed page but quite often somewhere outside of it. It is, in other words, only when we begin to think about what print meant outside of the coastal urban loop that dominates this country's official history that we will finally be able to scrutinize in new ways the more limited meaning of printed texts from inside the urban loop, breaking up the fiction of their nation-making embrace from within.[21]

In the end, any one theory of print threatens to reduce the plural possibilities of multiple cultures to one false meaning. Yet too few literary accounts of print culture in the early national period emphasize its provincial and plural nature, nor have we thought enough about how American nationality was inflected (and imploded) following the centralization of industrial production and the subsequent transformation of the continental interior into a vast market for northeastern goods in the 1830s, '40s and '50s.[22] Prior to these transformations (integrated by Charles Sellers and others under the banner of "market revolution"), many authors and printers dreamed of a mass book market, but none could locate or serve such an audience across any significant amount of geographic space. Geography continually trumped the entrepreneurial will-to-national-being of a host of early U.S. cultural producers—at least until the mantra of internal improvements finally trumped geography by helping to produce an internal national market. The emergence of such a market collapsed the republic's original time-space barriers through the creation of new and faster travel routes via steam, canal, and rail (a process greatly aided, in the 1840s, by the invention of the telegraph). These developments, well under way by the 1830s, allowed for greater rates of domestic tourism (a new mobility of persons) and for more massive exports of local productions of every kind, including newspapers, from one region to the next (a new mobility of things). One of the claims of this book is that a mutually informed, or *national*, discourse did not emerge via print until different areas of the country were in just this sort of sustained contact. Cass Sunstein has suggested that the founding of the republic rested on a series of "incompletely theorized agreements," and I will argue that it was precisely their incompleteness that was initially fortuitous and finally disastrous.[23] But this incompleteness rested less on an emerging or inexact ideology than on an insufficiently developed interior infrastructure (or material framework), the absence of which led to a constitutional compact based largely on ignorance and miscommunication, producing in turn a union untested by the pressures of actual contact or sustained exchange.[24] Traditional American historiography usually marks the end of the so-called early national period with that series of economic and social transformations called the domestic market revolution. But as we shall see, this transformation, because it called forth a novel degree of cross-regional contact, actually coincides with a new kind of nationalizing moment altogether.

5. VERNACULAR CULTURE, NATIONAL NARRATIVE

There were many Hugh Finlays and Mathew Careys in this period: pamphleteers like Thomas Paine, politicians like Alexander Hamilton, and playwrights like Royall Tyler populate the pages that follow, traveling or writing about spaces far away from the ones where they started or the ones they know best. Christopher Colles, an early national surveyor, walks the roads of early America making extensive roadmaps that no one needs to buy. John Trumbull, portraitist of the fading Revolution, moves from site to site, seeking to recover the lost facts and faces of founding for inclusion in his massive painting, *The Declaration of Independence.* Benjamin Lundy, an itinerant abolitionist printer, travels up and down the eastern seaboard as well as west (and south) in his attempt to spread the gospel of abolition to the most diffuse audience possible, taking his newspaper on the road with him and inventing a new genre: "the itinerant periodical." Amos Dresser, eventually one of many traveling agents for the American Anti-Slavery Society, is publicly whipped by (other) white men for traveling through Nashville with a valise full of antislavery pamphlets while Theodore Weld, an AASS manager, sits at home with his family clipping advertisements from southern newspapers at his kitchen table in Fort Lee, New Jersey. Behind them all, the figure of the mobile, sometimes "fugitive," slave—of Dred Scott and William Wells Brown— casts in stark relief the stakes of such travel: the disintegrative potential of bodies moving too quickly through space, making disparate populations finally feel somatically connected not just to their racial others but also to their regional others—North and South, East and West.

These are the citizens of the virtual nation—a term I use to describe the extended but nonintegrated republic in the years between the Revolution and the Civil War. The federal state that superintended this vast, unintegrated (and hence "virtual") nation operated in these years at several removes from the local worlds of village and town even as it struggled to make good on the Revolutionary promise of embodied democracy. As many critics have noted, the "We" in "We the People" is a rhetorical device meant to get around the embarrassing fact that the "people" were and had to be absent in order for the business of nationality to proceed— even though the Constitution paradoxically authorizes itself via the ideal of popular sovereignty.[25] But the problem of representative dislocations was already an old one in 1787. The Revolution itself produced a torrent of pamphlets theorizing just how close to the "real" representation could get, and from the 1760s forward, the phrases "actual representation" and "virtual representation" were used to designate the level of representative dislocation that was considered tolerable to American colonials in their engagements with the British Empire: "actual representation" described a representative drawn from North America (usually tied to constituents through the use of "express," or written, instructions), while "virtual representation" indicated a British-born (and nonelected) representative who was said to represent the interests of the Americas merely because he represented the interest of the empire at large. Used in the narrow context of a pamphlet war with England, actual representation made sense, but extrapolated as an ideal of emerging American political economy, its promise necessarily went unfulfilled: as the federalists of 1787 knew, representations can never be actual, and a country as big as the United States requires some form of representation if the federal government is to function as an effective state apparatus.[26] The United States was thus built from the start on the insurmountable fact of dislocation—that of the representative from the constituents he represents, of one group of citizens in one area from another group in the next, and of local knowledge from region to region. The surprising thing about the regional conflict of the nineteenth century is not that different parts of the country had so little in common with one another, but that they seem to have so fully forgotten that local differences and dislocations were the founding prerequisite of the representative government they (commonly) cherished.

Ontologically, of course, there are no gradations of "realness" or "imaginedness" from one moment of national life to the next: nations are always, at the end of the day, ideas—theoretical figments of the various local lives they are said to encompass. While I am interested, then, in the "fiction" of federalism, I am not suggesting that there was no "real" nation in 1776 or in 1787 while there was one, finally, in 1830, 1850, or 1870. Nor do I want to claim that the dissent of 1850 was somehow more "real" than the staged consensus of 1776 and 1787. But the federal state *was* initially imagined and discussed before a shared national culture had materially taken hold, and these untested and necessarily incoherent imaginings would eventually have profound consequences in the face of ongoing integration. Early national culture is something that *is*, but it derives most of its significance, like all things virtual, from what it is *not*—from extended contacts that have not yet been made and from things that are not knowable or within the realm of local experience but that are nevertheless talked about as if they were. Indeed, the thing that makes it possible for the thirteen sovereignties of the early United States to emerge, rhetorically, as one seemingly univocal, unified thing in the 1770s and 1780s is the dispersion of its parts, their generative dislocation out of actual face-to-face ties into the elusive realm of the (early) national.

If material conditions matter, however, they clearly matter after the rhetorical fact. Rhetorical projections of nationalist sympathy among different regions preceded sustained material connections by many decades. In the period between the War for Independence and the domestic trading and building boom that followed the War of 1812, the United States was connected less by roads or rivers than by the confused language let loose during the Revolution—the affective rhetoric of "consanguinity" first mobilized in opposition to England and then recirculated unevenly through a series of ever-shifting local economies. As Christopher Looby has said, "nations are not born, but made"—and made, he tells us, "in language."[27] It is the largely rhetorical nature of early nationalist sentiment—the fact that connections are fantasized and cemented in language long before they are tested by travel—that creates the special historical problem of dissent, secession, and civil war when material connections eventually do emerge. It is not enough, then, to write a material history of print culture, foregrounding the history of internal improvements or elaborating the history of emerging publishing houses. We need to set alongside this materialist framework of nation and nation building a history of the locally bound rhetorics, or cultural vernaculars, of the early national period and of those counterrhetorics eventually raised in regionalized protest in the second quarter of the nineteenth century. For this reason, this book narrates two different and yet mutually productive processes: on one hand, the rise of nationalism and its rhetorical display in any number of cultural forms and, on the other, the process of nation building, understood in the most material (road building, canal digging, steamboat inventing, railroad running) forms possible.

Revolutionary rhetoric called forth these material improvements, but they in turn threatened the coherence of the national discourse that had produced them. An increasingly integrated antebellum print culture raised into view the impracticality of Revolutionary discourse—from the promise of equality to the immensely popular language of "self-evident truths" and "inalienable" rights. The Declaration's claims to "self-evidence" and "inalienablity" were sufficiently unifying fictions in a nation so locally constituted as to be unsure of the goings-on in all its relative parts. But this appeal to self-evidence grew increasingly untenable as those parts came slowly into a more knowing alignment with one another and as the distinctive Revolutionary inheritances of each were finally revealed to have been geographically relative all along. In response to the proliferation of self-*non*-identical knowledge, powerful reform movements emerged in the antebellum period devoted both to mass memberships across space *and* to making transparent the faulty nationalist and semicontractual claims of the Declaration and the Constitution. As I argue in chapter 6, abolition posed the most radical and successful of these rebukes to the logic of federalism, and it did so from the inside out, using national institutions (including the post office and an increasingly centralized publishing industry) against the very union these institutions were thought to be producing.[28] In sending traveling lecturers, book agents, and New York-produced periodicals through the southern and western territories, the American Anti-Slavery Society proves what Anderson's theory of imagined communities chooses to overlook: the fact that although English as a "print language" had long displaced the vernacular languages of town and region on the "type"-faced pages of books and newspapers, it had not done so in a way that ensured the erasure of vernacular material cultures—the local worlds of town, state, and region. Abolition thus took advantage of something that federalism had long repressed—the peculiarly disintegrative power of local knowledge.

The ongoing integration of the local into the national found its exemplary spokesperson in Harriet Beecher Stowe. *Uncle Tom's Cabin* invited its reader to travel America in print and to use those travels as sites of imagined resistance to the inevitability of a proslavery union, infiltrating those national spaces too far off for readers to visit themselves. What else is Simon Legree's backwater plantation if not a vestige of an older economy so local that no national newspaper can penetrate it? Legree's desolate plantation is many long miles off the river. Located deep in the southern interior, it takes several days on a small river and then a long wagon ride on a barely traveled road to get there. Stowe titles the chapter that describes this trip "Dark Places," and even the foliage is described in foreign and exotic terms. But the irony—and the painful problem— for Stowe's readers is that there seemingly was no place by 1850 that was not penetrable by or accessible via print—and as the new Fugitive Slave Law was about to demonstrate, by national law. That's what made Stowe's book such a huge success: by 1852, the print market had expanded far beyond the local routes that had put a cap on the dissemination of *The Federalist* in the 1780s.[29] What a book like *The Federalist* was and never was—on one hand, a highly iconic figure for national consensus and yet, on the other, never a really nationally disseminated text—Stowe's novel mirrored in what it too both was and was not—on one hand, a highly *divisive* discourse; on the other, a widely reprinted and mass-disseminated text.

Stowe tapped the regional nerve of an increasingly nationalized North. While radical abolitionists had been working to produce this outcome for decades, it was only after 1850 that mainstream Northerners began to fear what had once been unthinkable—that slavery itself would finally come knocking on northern doors. As Henry Carey declared in 1853, "slavery now travels North, whereas only twenty years ago freedom was traveling South."[30] The idea that slavery had become a cultural import, dissolving boundaries and differences between states and regions, underwrites Thoreau's "Slavery in Massachusetts," in which he identifies the capture and return of fugitive slaves from Massachusetts with the (re)legalization of slavery there. Lincoln, too, in a famous (and much reprinted) 1854 speech on the Kansas-Nebraska Act identified what he saw as an inevitable trend toward legalizing slavery in the North; indeed, after 1854, Lincoln repeatedly argued that the Supreme Court would eventually rule it unconstitutional to bar a southern slaveholder from moving his human property to, say, Illinois—which is indeed what the Court decided in *Dred Scott* in 1857. Because of these fears of regional encroachment, antislavery was no longer a fringe cause by the mid-1850s but an increasingly common sentiment in the liberal North, which, as Eric Foner has shown, was invested not so much in the abolition of southern slavery as in the maintenance of its own free-wage, free-labor regional identity.[31]

The Currier and Ives print with which I began carefully avoids the sectional issues I have raised here as corollaries to the rise of certain kinds of technology. That lithograph is set nowhere in particular, and it resists the spatial and temporal fragmentation of national disunity blandly— which is to say, as an act of repression, masterfully and seamlessly. It is little wonder that Americans in 1876 would have wanted to mark off a unit of time and call it a day—or its grander equivalent, a century. The year 1876 marked the official end of Reconstruction throughout most of the South and the formal withdrawal of those mildly punitive postwar northern institutions that the South considered carpet-bagging imperialism. In 1776, the colonies declared their independence from England; by 1877, the South would once again be independent of an imposing North. Thus 1876 is a moment when the country seeks closure and reconciliation, a new way of thinking about the relation of the parts of the union to the whole and a new way of remembering how these new relations were brokered—or, perhaps more precisely, a new way of *forgetting* how they had been brokered. In 1876, the United States finally closed the chapter of sectional conflict that had ignited in the 1830s and that Webster and Clay so famously failed to avert by means of "peaceful" compromise or national "good will." Thus if Currier and Ives make one sort of overt claim about the efficacy of material connections and national union, the opposite claim lurks just under the surface: with the advent of a materially united United States, statements like Webster's became part of a necessary (but not necessarily true) rhetorical campaign for union that attempted to create a veneer of national consensus, continental progress, and national union in the midst of the most severe sectional dissent the United States has ever known.

PART ONE

THE BOOK'S TWO BODIES
Print Culture and National Founding, 1776–1789

FIGURE 2.1 Political cartoon of Thomas Paine. London: 1792. Library of Congress, Prints and Photographs Division, LC-USZCN4-5.

2. DISSEMINATING *COMMON SENSE*
THOMAS PAINE AND THE SCENE OF REVOLUTIONARY PRINT CULTURE

What a poor, ignorant, malicious, short-sighted, crapulous mass is Tom Paine's "Common Sense." . . . And yet history is to ascribe the American Revolution to Thomas Paine.
—John Adams writing to Thomas Jefferson, 1819

This book—COMMON SENSE—calling the American people to arms, and to set up a free government, may be called the book of Genesis, for this was the beginning. From this book sprang the Declaration of Independence, that not only laid the foundation of liberty in our own country, but the good of mankind throughout the world.
—S. Bryant, preface to *Common Sense*, 1856

1. TOM PAINE'S BODY

The most interesting thing about Tom Paine's body is that it's missing. Unlike other Revolutionary noteworthies, Paine became, as he grew older, less rather than more popular in the United States, and from the 1780s on, his role in the American Revolution was increasingly obscured by popular accounts of his personal behavior and beliefs. By the time he died in 1809, his atheism and alcoholism were so notorious that he was denied conventional burial in consecrated ground and was buried quietly instead on his farm in New Rochelle, New York, in a marked but untended grave. Ten years later, William Cobbett, the conservative-turned-radical who had once attacked Paine under the pen-name Peter Porcupine, decided to exhume Paine's body and bring it to England, where he planned a more suitable resting place for a man he took to be one of the great Enlightenment *philosophes*. While Cobbett was planning his monument, however, something embarrassing happened: Paine's body went astray. Cobbett died and the bones he carried with him to England were lost, and so all we have left of the organic Tom Paine is the place where he should be buried, marked by a stone that signifies nothing but a memory.

This missing body is a fitting image for Paine's career as an American man of letters in that ghostly arena we commonly call the public sphere, a phrase that by now resonates not only with Jürgen Habermas's specific arguments about eighteenth-century European salons and newspapers but also with our more specific understanding of how print culture works in the early American republic. The disembodied author, anonymously circulating through the virtual networks of print culture, has become a major figure in recent discussions of republican print culture. Indeed, it has become almost a truism in early American literary studies to speak of the ways that printed texts, by virtue of their printedness, are able to "abstract" or disembody their authors in culturally useful ways, separating them from their particular personalities and local realities in ways that make their arguments and actions seem disinterested and public—or, in eighteenth-century terms, republican and virtuous.[1]

But nothing is ever *always* abstract, especially a book. This is especially true, as we shall see, of Paine's most famous American pamphlet, *Common Sense*. Though Paine's title mines the fantasy of abstracted generality, his life as an aspiring author in Revolutionary Philadelphia registers at every turn the gross counterclaims of locality and materiality. Yet it is precisely the "local" and the "material" that have been missing in our common understanding of both Paine and his pamphlet. While *Common Sense* is frequently cited as "the first American bestseller," it remains one of the most mystified objects in the museum of American history. No printed text has garnered so much responsibility for inciting American nationalism as *Common Sense*, yet its history as a material text has been largely ignored by historians, literary critics, and political scientists alike.[2] This chapter attempts to fill that gap, first by reading the Painite legend of universal diffusion from within a material account of *Common Sense*'s actual production and dissemination over the landmass of the early United States and then by asking what such a book history can tell us about Paine, his pamphlet, the Revolution, and the scene of American founding itself.

These subsequent questions are necessary because book history, as a method, proves not quite enough, in the end, to explain the pamphlet's power. *Common Sense*'s legend has its roots in many locations, not just geographically but ideologically and narratively as well. Paine himself first began the long historical rumor of *Common Sense*'s monumental success. He promoted the pamphlet throughout his life as "the greatest sale that any performance ever had since the use of letters."[3] But his authorial fantasy about the protracted reach of *Common Sense* was also firmly rooted in a more widely held belief in republican diffusion (or "universal" circulation), an immensely popular social discourse that allowed Paine to believe that his book could and did reach every household in America. In imagining a monumental circulation for *Common Sense*, Paine called forth a radically democratic model of nation building that transcended his own self-interests as an author—believing that every citizen might participate, by reading his pamphlet, in the formation of the coming state.

Yet *Common Sense* was never as evenly produced or as spontaneously consumed as this rumor would have it. Paine's pamphlet was, materially speaking, an unprecedented and immensely popular call to American nationalism. But even in its own time, *Common Sense* was less useful as a fixed text, a revolutionary handbook circulating through predictably connected networks of internal commerce, than as a symbolic repository, a (material) signifier that was used locally within various early American communities to imagine what the coming Revolution might be. An object of curiosity, speculation, and gossip, Paine's text certainly contributed (as both object and discourse) to the wartime consensus, but that consensus was more limited than the myth of *Common Sense*'s meteoric cross-continental dissemination would suggest. Indeed, as I argue here, the legend of *Common Sense* as "the best of bestsellers" has made it easier for later generations to ignore not just the mixed (Tory) underside of the Revolution but the provisional and noninevitable character of the supposedly continental alliance it produced.[4] Despite Paine's ardent belief in it, the alliance of 1776 was never held together by sophisticated community structures (like a strongly linked print network and the roads, boats, stages, canals, rails, and steamboats that would make such a thing possible). It was composed instead of a series of disconnected locales, pieced together in quite distinctive (and at times conflicting) ways in the many local worlds that constituted it. In the post-Revolutionary era, this patchwork of shifting locales was inscribed (with some additions and deletions) into a lasting union by the Constitution of 1787, and texts like the Constitution—and *Common Sense*—are now read retroactively as the signs of universal consent. But the Revolution, as well as the people and the nation it subsequently produced, was never a uni-vocal phenomenon, any more than Paine's pamphlet could have been universally diffused. The production of Paine's "national" pamphlet was, in fact, a highly fragmented affair, varying significantly from town to town and colony to colony. The local scenes of production that dominate eighteenth-century book culture thus offer a welcome antidote to the more totalizing accounts of nation formation that often accompany tales of *Common Sense*'s success.

This last point begins to get at why *Common Sense* has proven such an enormously attractive legend in American history. In its own time, the myth of a best-selling *Common Sense* helped the colonists appear coher-ent to themselves in the face of imperial disintegration. In ours, it con-tinues to secure a coherent and legitimate scene of U.S. founding years after the fact. Paine may have made ingenious use of emergent nationalist sentiment in *Common Sense*, but nationalism has in turn made ample use of *Common Sense* in the years ever since. Taking up the full implications of this insight, this chapter unfolds the story of *Common Sense* in several different ways. I begin by surveying popular historiographic accounts of *Common Sense*'s role in the Revolution and countering them with a material history of the pamphlet's production, dissemination, and recep-tion. This material history is then transposed in two ways: first, through a theoretical account of the mythic pamphlet's ideological (nationalist) functions, and second, through a close reading of Paine's arguments in *Common Sense*, which actually deploys numerous tropes of "continental" hyperbole quite similar to the ones that underwrite our stories about the pamphlet's cross-continental transmission. Finally, I end the chapter by tracing this penchant for hyperbole to Paine's troubled authorial career in Revolutionary Philadelphia, suggesting some of the ongoing scholarly stakes (in both literary studies and social history) of remembering *Com-mon Sense* as a populist Revolutionary textbook while effacing the real-life movements of its author, who was simultaneously a member of the abstracted literary world we call the republic of letters and the painfully material world of the lower sorts.

Considered as an episode in material history, the idea of hundreds of thousands of printed pamphlets circulating uniformly and instan-taneously across the disjointed fringe of the eighteenth-century British Empire may appear more than a little unlikely. Nevertheless, the Painite myth of mass diffusion is a powerful Enlightenment metanarrative that we continue to consume in early American studies, one in which the practices of book making and nation building continue to be imagined as inseparable practices. To the degree that we continue to uphold this master narrative, we remain objects of the Enlightenment rather than critics of it. In providing a material history of one its foundational texts, then, this chapter also offers what Michel-Rolph Trouillot would call "an alterative history" of the American Enlightenment—and of the revolution and the nation it produced.[5] Joining material history, cultural theory, close reading, critical biography, and social history, this chapter seeks to reconstruct the specific North American scene in which Paine and his book moved as a vast tableau against which a new, human-powered account of the Revolution can take its place alongside the currently mystified narrative of a spontaneously self-disseminating *Common Sense*. This new human-powered account is meant to serve, in turn, as a materialist extension to recent discussions of republicanism's investment in abstraction and to print's presumed utility in procuring such abstraction through acts of textual disembodiment. Paine's body may be missing today, but in its own time it was always painfully present at the scene of every social exchange—repeatedly described by observers as "unshaven," "unwashed," "reeling," and yet authorially and politically desiring.[6] When Paine's body is returned to the scene of American founding (along with the numerous others that might be said to have produced his text—from the printers, teamsters, and congressional delegates of 1776 to a host of U.S. historians ever since), the Revolution itself comes newly into view—not so much as an occasion in which democratically mobilized populations erected new political and cultural forms on top of older, more elite forms, but as a place where the necessary persistence of such older forms has simply required special myths to disguise them. And these myths, more often than not, happen to come in the shape of a book.

2. THE CULT OF *COMMON SENSE*

Before Paine adopted it, "Common Sense" was three things in the English-speaking world: first, an idiomatic expression denoting the common understandings of common (nondreaming, nonlunatic) people; second, a pseudonym that writers sometimes used to sign essay series in London and, in one notable instance, in Boston in the 1770s; and third, a phrase associated with a school of Scottish philosophy that set itself the formidable task of unraveling the anti-empiricist binds of George Berkeley and David Hume. In the early months of 1776, "Common Sense" continued, for those who cared, to operate in these three ways, but it also gained three new uses along the eastern seaboard of North America and in its refracted recirculation back through the heart of British empire. First, Paine took it up from January onward as a signature in many of his American policy polemics, continuing to use it throughout the war. Second, it became both widely known (as a title) and widely owned (as an actual text) by Revolutionary Americans and their imperial interlocutors, especially in England. And third, as a consequence of Paine's notoriety, it became a repopularized phrase within the American vernacular that then recirculated, as vernaculars will, in intractably untraceable ways, changing forever the language we speak in ways we can never fully know.[7]

Common Sense would eventually become both more and less than the sum of these foundational parts. What began as a forty-six-page pamphlet expanded in time into a discourse, a phenomenon of national imagining after the fact and a key component in the metanarratives now associated with "the Whig interpretation of history."[8] It would not be hard to find a hundred instances of this narrative in American historiography, but we can start with just one unexceptional example: Henry Cabot Lodge's 1898 *Story of the Revolution*. Here, as in many popular histories of the Revolution, the historian explicitly connects the production of nationalist affect to the mythic impact of *Common Sense*. As Lodge tells it:

> his pamphlet went far and wide with magical rapidity. It appeared in every form, and was reprinted and sold in every colony and town of the Atlantic seaboard. Presently it crossed the ocean, was translated into French, and touched with unshrinking hands certain chords in the Old World long silent but now beginning to quiver into life. In the colonies alone it is said that one hundred and twenty thousand copies were sold in three months. This means that almost every American able to read, had read "Common Sense."[9]

In this, as in other late-nineteenth-century histories of the Revolution, *Common Sense* has already become a phenomenon of national storytelling, a tale in which Paine is at once both present and absent, his text central but his name effaced. Indeed, the passage cedes enormous agency to the pamphlet itself. *Common Sense* (the thing) takes charge syntactically here, a grammatical as well as an historical agent. The pamphlet "went," for example, apparently of its own accord, "far and wide." People don't seem responsible for carrying the book from place to place or for choosing how and when it would be presented to readers; it simply "appeared" in multiple forms, "cross[ing] the ocean" and "touch[ing]" all of Europe with "hands" as suspiciously invisible as the one Adam Smith was to theorize in *The Wealth of Nations* the same year Paine wrote *Common Sense*. In foregrounding what he calls the "magical" agency of the book and telling its story through an array of passive verbs, Lodge de-emphasizes human agents and historical actors. Who did the considerable work of reprinting *Common Sense* when, as Lodge tells us, "it was reprinted"? Who did the translating when it "was translated"? Who was it that "said" that "one hundred and twenty thousand copies were sold in three months"? And who was responsible for selling them when they "*were* sold"? On the material mechanisms that underwrote the "magical rapidity" of *Common Sense*'s success, Lodge is silent, and so is American historiography more generally.

But this story of the Revolution does more than just reiterate a common myth about *Common Sense*. It actually reifies, through the trope of *Common Sense*'s ubiquitous dissemination, our mythic national conception of the Revolution and of founding itself as a text-driven phenomenon. Not only is a printed text given magical agency in such a way that it elides the social forces that would seem to make it possible—including printers, booksellers, cart haulers, and ferrymen (not to mention the frozen ports, icy rivers, muddy roads, barter relations, and illiteracy that marked the world such people lived in). But the very "magic" of the book's widespread dissemination produces, by passage's end, the new, nationally affiliated subject ("Americans"), who emerge simultaneously here as readers of Paine's pamphlet and as political entities, as if the pamphlet itself could hail its Revolutionary audience into being at the very moment of contact. In this way, *Common Sense* essentially performs the act of popular founding, turning North American colonials into American nationals by treating them as one massive, interconnected reading community.

Taken apart verb by verb, Lodge's account looks unlikely. Nevertheless, this story of the Revolution cannot simply be dismissed. Indeed, the problem with writing a revisionist account of *Common Sense* is that the myth has its basis in fact. Lodge is right: *Common Sense was* an exception, what one bibliographer calls "something of a freak."[10] At a time when political pamphlets had restricted geographical circulations, *Common Sense* was reprinted an unusual number of times and had a tremendous influence in (parts of) the colonies and Europe. A pamphlet like Jefferson's *Summary View of the Rights of British America* had two modest printings in North America (one at Williamsburg and one at Philadelphia). But *Common Sense* went through twenty-five American editions—almost twice as many as any other pamphlet of its time.[11] Its closest runner-up would (according to Thomas Adams) be a printed 1774 speech by Jonathan Shipley (now largely forgotten), with twelve American editions; a distant third would be John Dickinson's *Letters from a Farmer in Pennsylvania*, with seven. Indeed, *Common Sense* was reprinted so often (and so quickly) that its publication history more nearly resembles that of a London imprint than anything produced in America before the nineteenth century.[12]

The other reason Lodge's account cannot be dismissed is because it recurs so often in other histories of the Revolution. Even in the numbers it cites, Lodge's story echoes down through the decades. Lodge was neither the first nor the last to cite such numbers. Indeed, circulation figures are cited so often and so consistently that the figures themselves have become a persistent part of the Painite legend. The most repeated estimates range from 100,000 to "120,000 in three months" to 150,000, but they have at times inflated all the way up to 500,000 (a number first cited by Moncure Conway in his 1892 biography of Paine and later adopted by Philip Foner in the authoritative *Complete Writings*).[13] In citing these numbers, many nineteenth- and early twentieth-century historians noted (as Lodge did not) the apparent disjunction between a still-developing print culture and the pamphlet's grand success, but for most this apparent contradiction merely proved the pamphlet's importance. John Fiske, writing in 1891, references no source when he notes that "it was difficult for the printers, with the clumsy presses of that day, to bring out copies of 'Common Sense' fast enough to meet the demand for it. More than a hundred thousand copies were speedily sold."[14]

The large circulation numbers cited by postbellum historians were retained throughout the twentieth century, but with a twist: claims to their unlikelihood gradually disappeared while attempts to link *Common Sense* to the phenomenon of the modern bestseller began to multiply. Thus, in 1926, W. E. Woodward kept the tale intact but extended it with a new *topos*—an analogy to modern sales figures. Calling *Common Sense* "the phenomenal 'best seller' of its time," Woodward enlarged on an already large claim: "In three months one hundred thousand copies were sold. This is equivalent to a sale of five million to-day."[15] In 1950, Lynn Montross likewise valorized the pamphlet as a mathematical wonder, noting that "before the end of the year, 120,000 copies had come off the presses, establishing a record for a best seller which has never been equaled in the history of American publishing. In order to reach the same proportion of the total population in the middle of the twentieth century, it would be necessary for a book to achieve a circulation of six million copies during its first year."[16] Nor are such numbers merely the work of outdated or unsubtle scholars. Some of our most powerful and radical contemporary historians continue to articulate the value of *Common Sense* through sales figures. A recent edition of Blackwell's *Companion to the American Revolution* cites "enormous" circulation figures on three different occasions in essays written by three different scholars (two putting the number at 100,000; the other, at 150,000).[17] Nor is this sentiment any longer entirely Whiggish at base. As strong a critic of America's bourgeois Revolution as Howard Zinn calls the pamphlet "perhaps the most important publication in the history of the United States" because it "sold hundreds of thousands of copies," making it "the best of best sellers."[18]

Such numerical insistence would be encouraging if the numbers cited did not derive from that most unreliable of narrators: the author himself.[19] In the most unstable moments of the early Revolution, as General Washington lost battles and his armies scrambled for supplies, Paine began to speculate freely about the number of copies his pamphlet had sold. His earliest estimate comes in the dubious context of a newspaper debate with the anti–*Common Sense* editorialist Cato, a forum that would have inspired even a lesser polemicist than Paine to hyperbole. Writing under the pen name "Forester" on April 8, 1776—a few days *less* than three months after the pamphlet's initial publication—Paine responded to Cato's attack by staking his pamphlet's virtue on its circulation: "I am certain that I am within compass when I say one hundred and twenty thousand" copies of the pamphlet have been sold (2:67). Three years later, in 1779, writing an autobiographical account of himself for Henry Laurens, he raised the overall number, speculating that "the number of copies printed and sold in America was not short of 150,000," making it "the greatest sale that any performance ever had since the use of letters"

(2:1163). Modifying these numbers one last time in the 1790s, Paine finally claimed in *The Rights of Man* that "the demand ran to not less than one hundred thousand copies" (1:406).

None of these estimates was based, however, on actual knowledge. Though Paine claimed that he "gave the copy-right to every state in the Union" (2:406), implying a working knowledge of when and where the pamphlet was published, we know that he had little to do with the dissemination of *Common Sense* across the eastern seaboard (other than a handful of copies he carried with him to New York early in 1776), and at no time was he in contact with the printers across the colonies who set the pamphlet in type. Indeed, he jumbles the facts when he says he "gave the copy-right" to the states. In fact, he gave over copyright not to the dispersed states but to that far more centralized entity, the Continental Congress (gathered in one place, where he too happened to be), a sentimental act that was not all that meaningful in 1776, given that there was no (colonial) copyright law in effect at the time. Ultimately, Paine could only have known of the success of his pamphlet the same way everyone else did—through the considerable word-of-mouth notoriety it generated in the circles in which he himself was physically moving.[20]

Paine promoted the book, however, despite the limitations any particular perspective might have produced—including his own. Posing the pamphlet's dissemination as a vivid material extension of the continental union he was agitating for *inside* the pamphlet, he did what he could to confuse the book's alliance-building arguments with the scattered facts of everyday life. Paine may well have been the first author both to address every inhabitant of the colonies rhetorically and to believe (or to behave as if) he had actually succeeded. We, of course, should know better, though it remains tempting to say otherwise. Robert Middlekauff, for example, merely reinscribes the Painite myth of *Common Sense*'s ubiquitous distribution when he claims that "since the controversy involved the 'continent,' *Common Sense* was reprinted in all the major American cities and the minor ones as well."[21] What is more likely is that because "the controversy involved the 'continent,'" many colonists wanted to believe that its distribution was—or could be—continental as well. If dispersed North Americans could, as Paine had challenged his readers, imaginatively "transport" themselves "to Boston," then how hard could it be to get a few boxes of pamphlets there too (1:22)?

In the middle of January, it was hard to get anything from Philadelphia to British-occupied Boston, and there was certainly no precedent for the mass movement of large numbers of something as ephemeral as a pamphlet.[22] Books in general were not yet being moved easily from colony to colony, and even the most established and ambitious colonial booksellers had long accepted two facts of American life that Paine, as a writer, could (and in this case had good political reasons to) dismiss: first, the colonies' economic dependence on the British book trade, and second, the dispersion of colonial populations—would-be book buyers—across the mythic continent hailed by *Common Sense.* So splintered and embryonic was the American book trade at the moment of independence that one scholar insists there was not one but "thirteen separate book cultures in the colonies" at this time.[23] Pamphlets like Paine's, if they circulated at all outside the area that produced them, were usually distributed not in mass numbers but in single copies carried piecemeal here and there along the coastal post route and reprinted wherever they came to rest. As James Gilreath notes, "the American book distribution system on the eve of the Revolution consisted of informal networks of friends, temporary laborers, independent agents, peddlars, [and] bookstore owners whose income came only partially from books."[24] In this localized economy, it was not political treatises—however timely—but almanacs that were the perfect bestsellers, "because their astronomical calculations pertained to the locale in which they would be used."[25]

Common Sense's circulation numbers, often posed in the language of accounting, carry with them the objective force of the mathematical, but like accounting itself, they stand instead as relics of the cultures of production that made them. *Common Sense*'s success was produced in multiple locales, not just across differentiated space but across time as well, spanning generations of nation-building discourses. One source for the account we now have is Paine, but another is the emerging industry of historiography itself. Many first-generation historians of the Revolution (including David Ramsey, Jonathan Boucher, and Mercy Otis Warren) favored speculative theses about the origins of resistance and consensus, and none of them mentions *Common Sense* as a decisive factor in the decision to separate.[26] Second- and third-generation historians (like Lodge), however, increasingly relied, as Arthur Schaffer has argued, on a newly accruing archive of official state papers, where the citation of contemporary political actors was becoming a new standard for how history should be written.[27] After 1820, the construction of such an archive became a primary concern of American historians: in 1822, Hezekiah Niles published the first extensive archival record of the Revolution with his

Principles and Acts of the Revolution; in 1829–30, Jared Sparks edited *The Diplomatic Correspondence of the American Revolution;* in 1837 the first edition of the *American Archives* project appeared; and in 1836, Jonathan Elliot began to publish his collection of constitutional papers, *The Debates in the Several State Conventions,* the authenticity of which continues to be debated. By 1830, then, numerous multivolume documentary projects were under way (even though many American archives had, ironically, to be repossessed from British keepers). From that time forward, textual sources (and textual origins) became the preferred mode in the retroactive production of early American history, even though the archive being produced and drawn on was naturally a partial one, favoring (as Gordon Wood has argued) not the reality of the Revolution but the rhetoric of its victors.[28] These "elite archives" (especially the papers of the Continental Congress) are, as we shall see, one genealogical source for the cult of *Common Sense.*[29]

3. CONTINENTAL DRIFT

On January 13, 1776, Christopher Marshall, a prominent Philadelphia Whig, noted in his diary: "Went to Bell's; bought a pamphlet called *Common Sense.*"[30] Marshall does not tell us how he heard of the pamphlet— whether through an ad in that day's newspaper or through his everyday connections to other like-minded patriots. But in that single, sparse diary entry, we have a rarity: a historical record of the local transmission of a pamphlet that within weeks would begin the process of becoming the notorious and celebrated object that has burned bright enough in popular history to obscure its own origins. On January 13, however, *Common Sense* was just a new pamphlet printed by Philadelphia's Robert Bell. A well-known local republican and Scottish immigrant, Bell routinely published pamphlets on Anglo-American relations, a commercially lucrative topic in Philadelphia, which had been the site of the First Continental Congress in 1774 and was hosting the Second Congress when Paine's pamphlet hit the bookstalls in January 1776. Marshall's diary reminds us of something that Paine's later rhetoric (both within and about *Common Sense*) might make us forget: that the story of *Common Sense* is also the story of the local book trade that first produced it. And so, as in most national narratives, the first in a series of local subtexts waits in the wings to be narrated.

Its oft-cited circulation numbers aside, we know with certainty the number of imprints in only a small number of *Common Sense*'s early Philadelphia editions. Several anecdotal accounts indicate that Bell's initial printing of 1,000 copies sold out in a week, and that he immediately put out a second edition at least as large as the first.[31] Paine, angry with Bell for not consulting him before going to press a second time, immediately engaged another printing house—William and Thomas Bradford—to bring out an authorized and extended edition. Entrepreneurially alert, the Bradfords quickly jobbed out the presswork to two local printers who each put out 3,000 copies within several weeks.[32] But before the Bradfords could produce their version, the original printer, Bell, had profited enormously: Benjamin Franklin alone bought 100 copies from Bell, while Robert Aitken ordered two dozen for his bookstore on January 10, two dozen more on January 15, another dozen on January 17, and two dozen more on January 22.[33] Bell's success did not stop the Bradfords, however, from selling a large number too when their new extended edition came out, and several other Bradford editions soon followed. In all, sixteen Philadelphia editions came out—nine from Bell, six from the Bradfords, and one German edition from Steiner and Cist. Within these certainties, however, several questions remain. How many copies were produced in each edition? Were later editions smaller, as local markets approached saturation? And in the case of the competing Bell and Bradford editions (which differed significantly), did some readers buy both, viewing each as a distinct commodity?[34]

These sixteen early editions make one thing clear: *Common Sense* was vividly in view in and around 1776 Philadelphia. But it was not just the pamphlet's genius, or the self-evidence of its truths, that produced that visibility. Paine's antimonarchical tirade fortuitously arrived in bookstalls, coffeehouses, and taverns on the same day that a long-awaited anticolonial speech by King George III also arrived from London. This coincidence lent the pamphlet's arguments a surreal sense of timeliness at a time when few printed artifacts could boast such newslike quality. But *Common Sense* was also sensational in a much more mundane way, due to the loud commercial dispute that erupted between Paine and his initial printer. This squabble was in many ways as crucial to the book's early celebrity as were its arguments for independence. Not only did this dispute ensure, quite apart from the issue of demand, that twice the number of copies would be printed in Philadelphia (one set by Bell and the other by the Bradfords), but it also made the book a glaring local scandal whose fifteen minutes of fame lasted several months as Bell (at his own expense) and Bradford (at Paine's expense) inserted dueling full-page ads in opposite columns of the *Pennsylvania Evening Post*, each making claims not for or against independence but for and against the characters of the locally identifiable disputants. Paine used the Bradfords' advertisements to criticize Bell for proceeding to a second edition "without orders" from him. Bell responded with several extensive and vitriolic attacks on Paine's character and on the Bradfords' craftsmanship, defending his own rights as a master craftsman and dubbing Paine with a motley array of half-comical, half-hateful monikers—calling him a "weak man," a "Feeble author," "a rascally PUPPY," an "illnatured cur," a "wretched reptile," a "self-conceited Englishman," and "a villainous THIEF."[35] Thus over the course of its first few months, *Common Sense* was at times the topic of a full four of the *Pennsylvania Evening Post's* eight columns (or two of the paper's four pages), but only half of this coverage involved actual political debate.

Because of the special conditions attending *Common Sense*'s early appearance, massive print runs are most likely to have occurred at the site of origin. Philadelphia was Anglo-America's largest city, the seat of American Enlightenment, and the largest book-producer in the British colonies, with a population estimated at more than twice that of Boston.[36] James Warren's much-cited testimony about *Common Sense*—about the "Pamphlet which has made so much noise to the Southward"—initially reads like evidence of the pamphlet's cross-regional, seamlessly unifying impact, from New England to Georgia.[37] Writing, however, from Plymouth, Massachusetts, Warren was actually referring to the "noise" the pamphlet had made in Philadelphia. This stir, though local in origin, was hardly inconsequential to the book's later legend, for the myth of *Common Sense*'s "general" success throughout the colonies was directly enabled by its timely and distinctive appearance in the first local print culture that produced it. No other American city had Philadelphia's production, marketing, or distribution capacity on the eve of the Revolution, nor could any other city approach the level of demand for the pamphlet that political Philadelphia, site of the ongoing Continental Congress, must have had. Philadelphia, with its high concentration of printers, its literate urban audience, and its strategic location in terms of trade and transport, was specially poised to create a big book.[38] But even Philadelphia had its limits. Because of the decentralized nature of early American printing, the city's printers never had more than fragmentary access to the rest of the continent, access made more limited by the wintertime conditions that accompanied the early months of the pamphlet's reception. Because there was no preexisting commercial network through which to circulate the pamphlet, no single printer could capitalize on *Common Sense*'s enormous success. Even Robert Bell, who through his aggressive marketing campaign probably sold more copies than any other printer in the colonies, was not prepared to supply massive demand outside Philadelphia, where other printers, following the familiar, dispersed pattern of the colonial book trade, printed their own copies for local distribution.[39]

This is where the cult of *Common Sense* can and should be called to account. *Common Sense* was immensely popular, but it is not true that it "was reprinted and sold in every colony and town." In fact, the pamphlet with the reputation for having been everywhere at once was eventually reprinted in just thirteen towns in only six of the thirteen colonies. It did not appear at all (in 1776) in Canada, Vermont, Maine, Florida, or the western hinterlands—territories that in some cases lacked the same provincial status of the North American colonies but that nevertheless engaged in imperial debates and often in Revolutionary battles.[40] Because Philadelphia was closely linked to New York via an express mail corridor, *Common Sense*'s early distribution was probably quickest and most complete on this axis and in those counties directly surrounding Philadelphia. Its initial distribution, however, along more far-flung parts of the post route was only as reliable as the eighteenth-century mails—which were, in fact, not reliable at all.[41] *Common Sense*'s early reprint history suggests that it had its greatest impact in the northern colonies, particularly in parts of New England that had already been radicalized by military engagement or in those, like Philadelphia, that had a willing and already highly politicized audience. Thus while it was eventually reprinted as a pamphlet in Pennsylvania, New York, Connecticut, Massachusetts, and Rhode Island, it was reprinted only once south of Philadelphia (in Charleston). And with the exception of Lancaster, Pennsylvania, every city in which it was reprinted lay directly on the King's Post Road, making its dissemination from printer to printer not magical (as Lodge suggests) but fairly mechanical and predictable.

This is not to say that *Common Sense* was never read where it was not reprinted, nor even that it *could* have been reprinted in all of the places where it was not. *Common Sense* was not strictly bound to its local reprint sites. Many copies circulated individually across regions, and in many locations no reprint was possible because there was no printer available to produce it.[42] The question is not whether the pamphlet was or was not present at such sites, but, rather, how many copies might have been there, where did they come from, and how did they arrive? How evenly, in short, was *Common Sense* produced, distributed, and consumed? The pamphlet's reprint sites cannot tell us everything about its plural travels, but they do tell us it was not produced homogenously through every part of the early republic. Nor was it consumed simultaneously and ubiqui-tously. We can reconstruct the pamphlet's staggered reception by look-ing at extant newspaper advertisements from distant reprint sites, which register temporal lags in the pamphlet's reproduction across space—lags that tell us that the twenty-five American reprintings of *Common Sense* came out more slowly than Paine's boast of early April would suggest. Numerous ads describe the pamphlet as "in the press" or on sale as of early February in New York and late February (or early to mid-March) in lower New England (including parts of Connecticut and Rhode Island). The pamphlet was not advertised for sale, however, until mid- to late April in most northern New England towns. The earliest Boston adver-tisement, dated March 4, announces that there are "a few of those cel-ebrated Pamphlets entitled COMMON SENSE . . . to be Sold (if applied for soon)"—language that indicates imports rather than a local reprint.[43] Edes & Gill, the only Boston printers of *Common Sense*, did not advertise their edition until April 8 (announcing "Tomorrow will be published" *Common Sense*).[44] We see a similar timeline in Andover, where Samuel Phillips published a single edition of Paine's pamphlet. The first mention of this pamphlet comes on April 19 (twelve days *after* Paine's celebrated estimate), when the *Essex Journal, & New-Hampshire Packet* ran an ad-vertisement stating the book was "Now in the press." On April 26, a new ad promised the book would be "published . . . in a fortnight." And on May 10, the *Packet* finally declared that "This day is published" *Common Sense*.[45] Though random copies were no doubt circulating in from other areas, these advertisements indicate a predictable lag in dissemination across the sprawling arc of the eastern seaboard. At the very least, they tell us that the pamphlet had probably not reached all its reprint sites when Paine offered his most cited estimate ("120,000 copies in three months"), thus calling that number into question (2:67).

In the end, however, no circulation number can ever be verified, for while we know *where* the pamphlet was reprinted, we do not know the *size* of each print run or the inevitable variations in local demand from site to site. In New York and perhaps parts of New England, editions could theoretically have been almost as large (even though they were never nearly as numerous) as in Philadelphia. But even in the densely literate enclaves of rural New England and the well-settled towns of the middle colonies, the book business was in a state of constant disruption from 1775 forward. In a scene made familiar by battle and British occupation, printers from Albany to Boston to Newport buried their presses and waited out the war, leaving settled print cultures deprived of their usual production sites.[46] Even towns and cities that maintained their presses during the war contended with labor and supply crises. Large parts of New England, greatly affected by British troops and blockades, suffered colony-wide shortages of paper through the early months of 1776.[47] In Hartford, Connecticut, Ebenezer Watson wanted to bring out an early edition of *Common Sense* but printed a public apology to his customers in mid-February, claiming that the "difficulty of . . . obtaining suitable paper to print it as a pamphlet" would force him to serialize it in his newspaper instead.[48] Solomon Southwick of Newport, Rhode Island, likewise struggled to put out a timely edition, battling a shortage of workers and supplies throughout the early months of 1776, as he had before the war. When he finally advertised his first edition of *Common Sense*, it was a partial reprinting of just sixteen slim pages (undoubtedly a small run), followed later by another partial edition (of thirty-one pages), which continued where the first one left off.[49] Given the pervasiveness of such material pressures even in what were then (relatively) large-scale local print economies, it seems all the more unlikely that smaller towns like Lancaster or resource-poor Charleston would have put out massive, Philadelphia-sized editions.

Even Boston, historically an important publishing site and a center of radical political activity, must be brought into local perspective because so many Bostonians (and their outlying neighbors) had fled the city with the advent of fighting at Lexington and Concord. Boston's hard times in 1775 forced Isaiah Thomas to move his presses out of town (in the middle of the night) to outlying Worcester, where he continued to publish his *Massachusetts Spy*. The publishers of the *Boston Gazette* likewise shifted to Watertown, Massachusetts, for the entirety of 1776, a wise move given that the publication schedule of every other Boston paper was disrupted through the rest of the year, with one paper issuing printed apologies through the early months of 1776 for its disrupted service to subscribers in outlying areas. One Salem printer's resources were so strained that he printed a note inside his edition of *Common Sense* apologizing for the imprint's poor quality, which he attributed to "the present Scarcity of all kinds of Paper."[50] The known travails of Boston-area printers suggest the chaotic scene of Revolutionary New England, which saw troubled production and disrupted dissemination—problems that suggest that Boston lacked the resources and labor (not to mention the stable reading public) that might have produced the spectacularly large runs seen in Philadelphia.[51]

Richard Gimbel, the great twentieth-century bibliographer of *Common Sense*, argues that Paine's early quarrel with his "noisy" Philadelphia printer boosted *Common Sense*'s local circulation and consequently made Paine's book "the most discussed and widely circulated pamphlet in America."[52] In making such a claim, however, Gimbel embraces an ideologically loaded generalization, suggesting that the known history of a distinctive and essentially urban part of early U.S. culture can stand in for the unknown histories of other parts, almost in the way that republican forms of representation allow one man to stand in for many others through an elective process. But a city is not a senator (it cannot, like a person, move from place to place); nor does this generalization account for the significant geographic and political diversity of early U.S. cities (more properly called towns)—a diversity that posed a real-world problem to Paine's ardent belief in the power of "transport." If there remains, then, an occluded narrative in the history of this pamphlet, it would be the story of how and why it got out of Philadelphia in the first place, and how it then spread through the scattered print cultures that ultimately did reproduce and consume it. How do we account for what surely was, for an American imprint, an astonishingly high degree of continental drift?

History has retained and fetishized an answer to this question in any number of unlikely metaphors, citing the pamphlet as a protoliberal meteor that spread through the colonies "like wildfire," an "electric" "landflood," "a torrent," or, in military parlance, "a shot heard round the world" that "exploded like a bombshell."[53] Such metaphors speak colorfully to the book's popularity, but they also suggest models of transmission that carry with them narrative implications about the origins and spread of revolutionary sentiment. Metaphors that emphasize instantaneous transmission (and its corollary, simultaneous reception) implicitly figure an original unity across a diverse space even as they elevate the pamphlet to textbook status as the people's choice: the first American bestseller, freely consumed by a desiring population. Yet this laissez-faire model of continental transmission is inconsistent not just with the state of the early U.S. economy and the structure of early American print culture, but also with what little we know about the pamphlet's actual production and consumption within the local economies in which it did, in fact, circulate. Indeed, the pattern of *Common Sense*'s known transmissions out of Philadelphia suggests that its early success as a reprint was not the work of natural (meteoric or "wildfire"-like) forces nor the disinterested hand of an already free market so much as the work of a small handful of men living in Philadelphia—a calculated and partial act of promotion in which the logic of partiality has simply been repressed. Propaganda in the most traditional sense of the word, *Common Sense* was knowingly dispersed early on to whatever population would use it, a tool deployed within the networks of deferential custom that, despite the coming reorganization of American life, continued to frame many different versions of social relations in late-eighteenth-century America—from political culture to book selling to the scene of revolution itself.[54]

Paine's status as a newly arrived British immigrant served in this regard a crucial function: it made him the perfect transitional object through which a number of radical Whigs might express their own, still unstated preferences for separation in a way that both tested and shaped public opinion. Indeed, the pamphlet has much of its traceable source in a handful of men who had themselves already decided that separation was the answer to the Anglo-American problem, but who were unwilling to attach their names to that position in any public way because they were, in effect, what Paine was not: insiders who were dependent on their local communities—both the home communities they had come to Philadelphia to represent and the new Philadelphia community that was their Congress (and which made them twice-dependent). Several of these men were congressional delegates, but others were local characters with no congressional affiliation, or continental standing, at all. These men—beginning with Benjamin Rush and Benjamin Franklin but eventually extending to a larger group (including Samuel Adams, James Wilson, and David Rittenhouse)—encouraged Paine to write the pamphlet in the first place, arranged to have Robert Bell print it, helped retitle it "Common Sense" when Paine preferred "Plain Truth," and judiciously spread it through their home constituencies.[55]

Common Sense's known pattern of reprintings closely corresponds to this understanding of its original dissemination. Having first been solicited by powerful Philadelphia locals, the pamphlet saw its greatest success in Philadelphia. It then spread to numerous other locales, but it clearly did not do so either in the random way that books usually circulated in eighteenth-century Anglo-America or in the unanimous and spontaneously enthusiastic way that many later accounts would suggest. As Pauline Maier notes, "the pamphlet's usefulness was recognized by Congressmen, who sent copies to their home constituencies."[56] Most of the book's dispersed production sites (from Boston to New York to Andover) are registered at early dates in the correspondence of congressional delegates, many of whom either carried the pamphlet home in their cross-continental travels or sent it through the public post or via privately paid couriers. New Hampshire's Josiah Bartlett, for example, promised as early as January 13 to send a copy to an ally in Portsmouth, "which you will please lend round to the people."[57]

Because it was patronized by these protonational but locally identified representatives, the uneven spread of *Common Sense* across the continent ultimately mirrored the sectional factions that had formed in the Congress itself—especially the line between radical (often northeastern) Whigs who already privately favored separation from Britain and more moderate to conservative delegates who wished to see the dispute amicably settled in a way that might restore the old order. In primarily loyalist colonies like New Jersey, Maryland, and Delaware, the pamphlet was never independently reprinted, and while patriot readers in these colonies certainly received copies through their everyday trade relations with Philadelphia, a spontaneous and overwhelming public demand is not reflected either in local advertisements or in reprinted newspaper excerpts. It is hardly a coincidence, then, that the line between pro– and anti–*Common Sense* colonies was drawn most starkly in the same terms in which it was daily articulated on the congressional floor—a sharp line that divided New Englanders (who had suffered the most at British hands) from southerners (who retained a disproportionate number of trade and cultural relations with the metropolis even after the onset of armed conflict). As its delegates undoubtedly knew, the North was ready to receive and retransmit the message of *Common Sense* in a way that the southern colonies were not. Thus when congressional delegates from Connecticut, Rhode Island, Massachusetts, and New Hampshire sent small numbers of copies back to their hometowns, they did not need to pressure anybody to have the pamphlet reprinted. Instead, the book followed an obvious path from post rider to private recipient, making the expected interim stop in the hands of the local printer (who was usually also the local postmaster), who either commandeered a copy for himself, copied all or parts of it longhand, or set it in type before sending it on to its rightful owner. Only in Rhode Island, which had chronic paper shortages throughout the war, did the Philadelphia delegate write follow-up letters, detailing suggestions for the pamphlet's production there.[58]

In the South, the pamphlet's dissemination was spottier. As in New England, southern print cultures were routinely disrupted throughout the war, as presses were seized and newspaper production was suspended. But southern print cultures were never nearly as productive as northern ones were, either before or after the war.[59] In Virginia, historians describe a swing toward independence in the months leading up to July 1776, but there is little hard evidence to show how *Common Sense* might have been disseminated there—either by whom or for whom. Paine's own newspaper note "To the Public" announcing his appended edition trumpeted the news that "several hundreds are already bespoke, one thousand for Virginia," and while it seems likely that many copies got there, we do not know how, or when, or who read them.[60] Most extant evidence involves not detailed descriptions of *transmission* but partial accounts of *reception,* an archive of evidence that requires special consideration, since it often relays not on-the-spot information but second-hand reports, stories, and gossip that circulated through distant cities that were themselves saturated with their own local tales about *Common Sense* (and independence). John Adams, for instance, learned from a traveling John Penn that "Common sense and Independence . . . was the Cry, throughout Virginia," while Washington, from his post as commander in chief of the Continental Army, likewise reported (to a correspondent in Massachusetts) that "by private letters which I have lately received from Virginia, I find that Common Sense is working a powerful change there in the minds of many men."[61]

Hearsay testimonials like these are among the most common textual traces to be found about *Common Sense* in any colony, but they pose a special problem in one that reprinted only a few newspaper extracts of the essay and never advertised it as a pamphlet. The problem of *Common*

Sense's impact in Virginia is further complicated by competing anecdotal evidence that suggests the pamphlet was not always widely available there. Jefferson, for example (for many years a Paine ally), tended to minimize the pamphlet's early impact:

> at the annual election in April 1776, a convention for the year was chosen. Independence, and the establishment of a new form of government, were not even yet the objects of the people at large. One extract from the pamphlet called Common Sense had appeared in the Virginia papers in February, and copies of the pamphlet itself had got in a few hands. But the idea had not been opened to the mass of the people in April, much less can it be said that they had made up their minds in its favor.[62]

Jefferson's account poses many of the same problems as the testimonials cited above. His sense of the pamphlet's limited availability is corroborated, however, by the sparse number of surviving records of southern transmissions and reprints and by the fact that Virginia elites, as Woody Holton has suggested, were resistant to the pamphlet.[63] Some letters suggest that the pamphlet was originally disseminated tentatively in the Tidewater states, cited more as a "Curiosity" than an item of propaganda to be reproduced.[64] In February, for instance, Thomas Nelson sent two dozen copies to Jefferson at Monticello, but neither man ever mentioned them again.[65] In February, one "worn" copy was accidentally mailed to Richard Henry Lee in Williamsburg and wound up instead in the hands of the planter John Page. This misdirected copy was then apparently used by the printer of the *Virginia Gazette*, who copied "extracts" out of the pamphlet and then published them in his paper.[66] Passing up the opportunity to print his own edition, the printer likely knew the climate in which such arguments would be received — or the lack of readers willing to openly buy such an object. The only further mention of Paine's text came, in the months to come, not (as in New England) in the form of advertisements, but in several essays by the anti–*Common Sense* editorialist Cato, the Tory critic who first prompted Paine to coin the number "one hundred and twenty thousand."[67]

South of Virginia, the pamphlet evoked more clearly negative responses. When congressional delegate Christopher Gadsden returned home to South Carolina in February for his colony's provincial congress, he brought several copies with him. When Gadsden tried to read pieces of Paine's argument on the floor during debate, he was immediately denounced: "Henry Laurens thought the idea 'indecent'; John Rutledge found it treasonable; and Rawlins Lowndes was shocked. The arguments in Paine's work were 'too strong to be gainsay'd,' wrote Josiah Smith, yet the pamphlet was called '*Nonsense.*' A committee buried Gadsden's proposal."[68] While some copies eventually spread to other readers in South Carolina and, finally, to Savannah, Georgia, no southern printer reprinted the pamphlet except David Bruce of Charleston. This limited circulation no doubt troubled radical southern Whigs who had seen the pamphlet's effects in Philadelphia and heard of its success (through congressional colleagues) in the Northeast. John Penn of North Carolina, perhaps realizing that the underresourced and conservative North Carolina press would not put out its own edition, arranged to have a "Waggonload" sent to Edenton for the Committees for Correspondence to distribute to their members. But "the roads being very bad" between Philadelphia and North Carolina, Penn and his fellow delegate Joseph Hewes had to arrange to "put five horses on the Waggon" and in the end could only "hope they [would] be delivered safe."[69] No further mention is made in either man's correspondence of that late-winter wagon or its paper pamphlets, but it is clear that conditions throughout the South—including conservatism, lack of resources, notoriously difficult travel conditions, a widespread investment in social hierarchies, and a dispersed and in some cases illiterate population—all converged to dampen the impact of Paine's monumentalizing arguments there.

Because its known dissemination mimics factions already present in Congress, *Common Sense*'s success in different colonies might make that body seem like a functional reflection—to use a commonplace Enlightenment metaphor—of the will of its many rural constituencies. But this line of influence has perhaps been read too frequently in inverted order—a possibility that, in turn, raises questions about the limits and legitimacy of the Congress at a moment when many local populations favored an aggressively anti-imperial model of actual representation, with their delegates expected to mirror their constituents and follow their express instructions. But Congress was not, of course, the pamphlet's only, or even its "official," distributor.[70] *Common Sense*'s six-month spread was ultimately powered by many people, in many places, in different ways—with individual Philadelphians influencing Paine, northern delegates influencing their constituencies, and radicalized northern constituencies in turn influencing others as word of the pamphlet's popularity spread.[71] No theory more unified than this is ever likely to fully explain *Common Sense*'s popularity. The number of reprint sites and the variety of interests involved are too numerous to be collected within one master narrative without oversimplifying the scattered series of contingent events let loose by its real-world reception. The important thing to remember is that *Common Sense* had a staggered geographic reception, making its arrival across the continent not a spontaneous and instantaneous event but a slow, uneven, fragmented, and dispersed *series* of events that played out across a vast, protonational field of exchange that was, in early 1776, still very much in the process of uniting itself economically, politically, materially, and discursively.

The rest of *Common Sense*'s history as a material text is a mystery. Nobody will ever know how many copies were printed or sold, how many were purchased and how many given away, for whom most copies were printed, by whom they were read, or how many readers came into contact with any single copy. In citing large circulation numbers, historians have relied on Paine's own account of the pamphlet's success and, of course, the large number of times Continental delegates mention *Common Sense* in letters home (even though such mentions do not indicate anything except the pamphlet's high visibility in Philadelphia). If one looks beyond the letters of invested congressional delegates, archival evidence for *Common Sense*'s cross-continental transmission becomes more difficult to locate.[72] The printers' records that might reconstruct a definitive account of its production and distribution either were not kept at all or are now lost. In the face of such archival gaps, all we can do is guess. But even if we guessed that every American edition was printed in a bestselling, Philadelphia-like batch of 3,000 (and this is not possible, since we already know that not even every Philadelphia edition was this large), its circulation would not have exceeded 75,000. A more likely estimate would probably be lower and still would not account for repeat buyers in Philadelphia or the copies that did not reach any reader at all.[73] And while the book certainly had a phenomenal circulation in the Northeast, this circulation still does not meet the vastness and variety of the early American population writ large. There were three million people living in Anglo-America in 1776 (2.4 million of them white and free), with many scattered on farms. Even if we concede the largest of large circulations, is it really likely that "every American able to read, had read 'Common Sense'"?[74] And what about the ones who couldn't read?

For two hundred years, the legend of *Common Sense* has repressed the potentially disruptive dissonances of time, geography, split political affiliation, and (most recurrently) class. Through its tricornered emphasis on unanimity, spontaneity, and ubiquity, the myth of *Common Sense* as "the first American bestseller" relocates the desire for independence away from congressional elites and onto the people at large (nationally conceived as a populist monolith). In doing so, it works to make the story of founding look national—homogenously uniform from site to site—rather than what it more often was: local—a broken, heterogeneous, chaotic scene from locale to locale. Many scholars have sought to resolve the problem of whom the book affected (and in what order) by locating two simultaneous audiences for it. Philip Foner, for example, suggests that "the common people" quoted Paine's most "contempt[uous]" passages while "more cautious and conservative Americans quoted other sections," a model that posits a singular field of reception temporally and geographically while dividing that united field into two classes. In this way, Foner avoids locating the desire for independence on either side of the status divide.[75] But even if we waived class and regional variation and determined that a large majority of (mostly white) men in urban settings and a smaller majority of such men in rural settings read and debated the pamphlet's contents, we would still be omitting slaves, women, non-English and non-German speakers (including many Native Americans), German speakers who lived beyond the reach of the one German edition, children and adolescents, territorially peripheral populations from Maine to Florida, and (especially in rural areas that lacked sufficiently enlightened coffeehouses, taverns, or general stores) illiterates of every sort. Though contemporary social history has labored to reintegrate such figures into the scene of Revolution, the myth of *Common Sense* silently reenacts their casual erasure, suggesting that a part—in this case, a group of readers (many of them white, male, urban or suburban, and literate)—can stand in for the whole protonational American population.

This is the challenge posed by *Common Sense*. On one hand, Paine's pamphlet must be recognized as a novel print phenomenon—a pamphlet that sold far more copies than similar artifacts of its day. On the other hand, our sense of its success can and should be qualified by a better material understanding of how it was produced and where it circulated. We cannot say (because we cannot prove) that *Common Sense* did or did not sell a specific number of copies, but we can question how much purchase the notion of a runaway "bestseller" can hold in eighteenth-century (protocapitalist but preindustrial) terms.[76] The bestseller as a cultural form is finally anachronistic to the particular moment of U.S. economic development in which *Common Sense* was produced, the material conditions of which could not really have sustained the legendarily spontaneous and simultaneous dissemination we have so long assigned to *Common Sense*. If it could have, it would be reasonable to assume that more such bestsellers would have followed. But as numerous scholars note when they describe *Uncle Tom's Cabin* as *Common Sense's* second coming (a second civic blockbuster), more such bestsellers did not follow—for almost a hundred years.

4. In America, the Book Is King

"Not any fiction can pass for history."[77] Why then the myth of *Common Sense*? It is clear that print was in fact crucial to American founding, even if particular printed texts were not themselves as seamlessly consumed as the myth of *Common Sense* suggests. Indeed, one possibility that scholars of the early republic have yet to explore is that books may have been important to founding not despite but *because* they were local and so importantly limited in both production and circulation. *Common Sense's* history as a material text illustrates this point nicely, for Paine's pamphlet was one of many founding documents whose goal was to repress the dispersed conditions of its own production—a text whose primary political and rhetorical task was to fantasize, through the figure of its own widely heralded circulation, an original unity that could be translated across a proliferating set of locales before the war was even won or the union agreed to. As I will suggest here, the localness of its reception across a diverse array of disconnected sites is exactly what enabled it to achieve this.

T. H. Breen has recently theorized questions of production and consumption within colonial economies by describing 1776 as part of an Atlantic world "consumer revolution," suggesting that American nationalism was first embraced not merely in the local worlds of tavern and town meeting but within a globally conceived marketplace that colonists had been avidly participating in for many years.[78] In this argument, Breen reminds us that it is never enough to think locally about events in the eighteenth century. We must think globally (and, in this case, nationally) as well—for different spatial scales are always *potentially* in play in this period, even if they were not always easily integrated through commerce (including commerce in print). To recognize the local production of *Common Sense* should not, in other words, reduce us to insisting that the world of 1776 was *only* local. Indeed, as Breen amply demonstrates, the Revolution was imaginatively powered by social relations that were both local and global at once, with the earliest successful compacts between states consisting of local nonimportation agreements through which radicalized colonists boycotted British goods and hence oppressive mercantile policies that were playing themselves out on a transnational scale.

But the local is an illuminating subtext to almost any Atlantic world argument, and the aftermath of these nonimportation agreements is a case in point. In renouncing imperial consumption, defiant American communities placed their faith in provincial production.[79] In official boycotts, political debate, and popular discourse, a new investment in the local was being theorized throughout the 1760s and 1770s as a solution to British tyranny. Within this context, domestically produced (or "homespun") material objects became a legible sign of self-identity for colonial populations as surely as local (North American-born) representatives were thought to be more "self-identical" in representing American interests than were British-appointed representatives. Provincially produced hats and belt buckles, locally produced books and ideas, and the human resources of local legislatures and provincial congresses— all these were invoked as antidotes to the infringements of an increasingly present yet foreign-seeming British administration that made its presence known through any number of imported practices, including taxes, legislative edicts, and standing armies, but extending as well to metropolitan-produced cultural products (like pamphlets and speeches) that failed to get the colonial scene right.

Paine's pamphlet directly intersected this sense of conflicting, or nonintegrated, spatial scales within the empire at large. I have already described one example of this: the fact that *Common Sense* appeared in print on the same day that a speech by King George III arrived from England. For lifelong Philadelphians, this coincidence was sensational—a spectacular moment of hypersimultaneity for readers who spent most of their time waiting for news from England rather than actually receiving it. "Had the spirit of prophecy directed the birth of this production," Paine later wrote, "it could not have brought it forth at a more seasonable juncture. . . . The bloody-mindedness of the one, shows the necessity of pursuing the doctrine of the other" (1:40). In receiving both texts on the same day, Philadelphia readers experienced a novel integration of two disarticulated spatial scales. The empire at large (represented by news from far-away London) was for a moment temporally integrated with everyday life in Philadelphia, much the way that *Common Sense*'s later dissemination would be thought to integrate disparate regions (North and South) and distinct spatial scales (local and national). Distance was, of course, central to this effect (since Paine could not have written the pamphlet anywhere *but* at a distance from the Crown). But no matter: in *seeming* to appear in concert with the king's speech, *Common Sense* allowed its first Philadelphia readers to feel less like the abject periphery of imperial administration (waiting months on end for British news and packets) and more like the new centered kind of self that a locally administered republic might be, debating issues on the scene in person, as they came up, rather than having news of important debates and edicts circulated back second- and third-hand through the virtual networks of empire.[80]

But this early experience of simultaneity was also a local one, available primarily to those readers who were on the scene as the two texts entered the field of public debate and became momentarily linked not just in the abstract sense of discursively connecting but in the real-time sense of being passed hand to hand and mouth to mouth as simultaneous objects of conversation and exchange. For most British subjects living within the larger context of an administratively decentered, dispersed, and relatively disintegrated empire, colonial-metropolitan relations were more often marked by the opposite experience—by the lags, delays, deferrals, and misunderstandings that were the material and perceptual content of colonial subjectivity.[81] This sense of dislocation was at the center of Revolutionary debate over whether to continue on as a colony or pursue a new destiny as a nation. Indeed, the colonies eventually developed an elaborate critique of their marginal geographic position within the empire at large, in part by theorizing the dangers of dislocation and "foreign" (or spatially removed) British rule. Paine participates in this critique in *Common Sense*, not only by plaintively marking the gaps between England and America (as the Declaration of Independence would later do), but by recoding and reversing them in order to make metropolitan Britons seem less British than their colonial counterparts. In one such inversion, Paine elaborates on the topos of British foreignness by suggesting that the monarchy's seemingly "honorable origin" is merely a phantasmatic function of its "antiquity," a displacement that will not, Paine insists, "bear looking into." Dubbing George III a "royal brute" and a "ruffian," Paine traces the king's "bastard" claim to the Norman (and thus biologically illegitimate) invasion of William the Conqueror (1:13–16). Such inversions in the logic of British authenticity (with the rightful sovereign revealed as a French invader) in turn drive an ongoing reversal of geographic legitimacy and centrality throughout the text, so that by essay's end North American colonists, however resistant to England's authority or remote in birth from London's center, are shown to be more British than their metropolitan counterparts—up to and including the royal ruffian.

This chain of reasoning makes clear something that many colonial petitions, including the Declaration of Independence, emphatically deny: the fact that if the colonists were, as they often claimed, injured by their peripheral geographical status within the circuits of empire, they were also made imaginatively privileged by it. As Paine well knew, the gap between center and periphery came in many ways to be decisively productive for colonial populations, many of whom used their relative distance from London to safely imagine a new world order in the form of a reorganized and reprioritized body politic. But being able to imagine (or even make) a new world does not make that new world legitimate or coherent. Indeed, as many Tories would later argue, the North American colonies were no more geographically integrated than the flawed British Empire had been. In the face of this contradiction, Paine struggles to make the coming revolution appeal to common sense, calling for a new era, with new rites:

> But where, say some, is the King of America? I'll tell you, friend, he reigns above, and doth not make havoc of mankind like the royal brute of Great Britain. Yet that we may not appear to be defective even in earthly honors, let a day be solemnly set apart for proclaiming the charter; let it be brought forth placed on the divine law, the Word of God; let a crown be placed thereon, by which the world may know, that so far as we approve of monarchy, that in America the law is king.

For as in absolute governments the king is law, so in free countries the law ought to be King; and there ought to be no other. But lest any ill use should afterwards arise, let the crown at the conclusion of the ceremony be demolished, and scattered among the people whose right it is. (1:29)

In the Western world, one way the binds of illogic have been repeatedly mended is through the invocation of a presumably always rational law. So it is in *Common Sense*, which at this crucial moment interposes a law that does not need to be consented to because it is already intact—"in America," Paine insists, "the law is king"—and it is made so here not through mechanisms like prior elections or public debates but through the magnificent force of an already-assuming present tense. Lest this rhetorical solution appear "defective," however, Paine also offers a second, more material one, literalizing the scene of revolution as an embodied rite that is perfectly commensurate with the dispersion of modern populations. Both at the moment of the Revolution and long after its official end, the challenge posed by national dispersion would be the most recurrent problem in American political economy, forcing Paine and those who followed him to try to secure the scene of founding as a legitimate one, despite its own displaced production (first in space and later in time) from the populations who are said to have called for it and those who continue to sustain it. If "the people" could not, in other words, be literally present at the scene of founding (as they are when Paine or Locke describes the origins of human government), then the founding itself needs to become real and come to them. The story of *Common Sense* indicates that this was achieved, for a time, in the form of a book.

Paine himself imagines the Revolution made legitimate in this moment not in the theoretical language of liberalism or classical republicanism (because it is just or virtuous to do so) but in the form of a spectacle centered on material objects (a holy book, a charter, and a crown), the last of which can, after a rite that collapses all three, be broken into pieces and dispersed "among the people," much as a printed text is reproduced and disseminated to consensus-constituting majorities in many of our text-based myths of founding. Michael Warner has used this passage to indicate how the Constitution later established its legitimacy through the condition of its printedness, which, he argues, allowed it "to emanate from no one in particular, and thus from the people"(108). But as my discussion of *Common Sense*'s local circulation might suggest, I am less concerned here with the discursive uses of print (including its patently fabricated claim to nonparticularity) than with the interplay between discursive claims to abstraction and the challenge perpetually posed to them through the embodiment of the real—including material texts, living actors, and geographical space. In American culture, this interplay—like the foundational gap between imperial center and colonial periphery—has been surprisingly productive. Indeed, to the degree that printed texts solve key problems in modern political economy, it is not just because they emanate from no place, or no person, in particular, but because they have the peculiar ability to be both particular and nonparticular at once. Both a thing capable of being held in one reader's hands and something that could potentially be everywhere else at the same time, Paine's pamphlet was both an object under local control and a sign for the democratic work being done elsewhere, an assertion of egalitarian diffusion, circulation, and exchange among enlightened citizens of the (American) world.

This is an essentially postcolonial fantasy, in which a democratic totem is invoked to disperse authority across geographical space rather than allowing it to remain condensed, metropolitan-fashion, in a capital—or a king. In suggesting that such work must be done in order to make U.S. founding legitimate (and in later offering up *Common Sense* to do it), Paine sought to reorganize the colonial periphery into the kind of densely privileged center that a nation is. While any well-circulated object could theoretically reorganize space in this way (and today, many different ones do), Paine's pamphlet was, in 1776, a peculiarly effective one. As one of few *speaking* objects available to early American publics, the freestanding political pamphlet, or manifesto, bears an explicitly stated politics in a way that newspapers and magazines (as miscellanies containing multiple points of view) do not. Indeed, Paine himself insisted that the essay be produced as a freestanding pamphlet rather than having it reprinted as part-essays in newspapers, objecting to the latter plan because of "the impossibility in getting them generally inserted."[82] In doing so, he mobilized both ends of the dialectic, articulating a fantasy of fixed reality as well as one of dispersed generality. On one hand, he believed he had maintained authorial control over the material text by (seeming to) control all the potential sites of the book's production. On the other, he cultivated a far more imaginary relation to the potential vastness of its implied but unverifiable dissemination.

   The fantasy of a "generally inserted" *Common Sense* thus worked from
the outset to naturalize the not-yet-realized nation and to nationalize
Paine's chosen sign for it: the freestanding printed political pamphlet.
Common Sense openly figures the territorial frontier of the nation's imagined community as an imagined market zone in which a freely circulating commodity (explicitly conceived of as a bestseller) has been repeatedly invoked as the key instrument in securing nationalist affect. But the
question of whether the book secured that affect by reflecting something
that was already there or by installing something that was not has never
been made clear in subsequent accounts. The material rite of circulation
is simply assumed in Paine's fantasy to ensure the abstract rights of the
people who receive its goods. In this way, *Common Sense* enables that
most democratic of fictions: the idea that all the people were (or could
be) equally present at the scene of their subjection—all interested and
invested readers in a common culture of consent.

   Where, then, did the spirit of 1776 originate? The relation between
national base (figured in democratic rhetoric as "the people") and intellectual superstructure (figured in Painite fantasy as the Revolutionary or
foundational text) is doomed to call forth chicken-and-egg arguments
about lines of transmission and influence that are essentially untraceable.
But the question of whether "the people" of early 1776 were a signified or
a signifying constituency (an already existent mindset merely reflected in
Paine's pamphlet or a mindset actually created and called forth by it) is a
crucial one, if only because Paine's text continues to be seen as the pen-
ultimate and determining textual event in the long argument with England, culminating less than six months later in the very thing Paine had
argued for—official separation, itself expressed textually within a written
(and then printed) Declaration that would become popularly reinscribed
as the official act of founding (even though the Declaration technically
founded a Confederation that no longer exists).[83] It was in turn this Declaration that produced, juridically, a state of war between sovereign nations, in which citizens' local bodies (a kind of irreducible material base)
were mobilized en masse in the service of a war they may, or may not,
have consented to.

   Although Paine was himself an ardent believer in the most democratic
forms of representation possible, he too was taken in by the figure a book
makes. He romantically promoted the success of *Common Sense* as a
democratic rite for the rest of his life—as would later Whig historians.

But the Revolution was never, as this story suggests, an act authorized by a "unanimous people assembled in the self-presence of its speech," and this is why the myth of *Common Sense* will probably never go away.[84] While the surviving correspondence of congressional delegates offers the best evidence for how the pamphlet was initially disseminated throughout the Northeast, that partial story is not likely to take hold, for it does not do nearly as much cultural work for founding as the myth of the bestseller. The word "bestseller" projects an already-present nationalist affect onto the majority of citizen-readers, even though the known history of *Common Sense*'s early transmissions out of Philadelphia suggests the possibility that this affect initially existed in a relatively small group only to be secondarily circulated back through the body politic (in different places and in different ways) in and by the actual pamphlet. If this is true, then Whig history is not just inaccurate in its account of the magical diffusion of a disembodied *Common Sense*. This story of the Revolution actually uncritically extends the original narrative silently put in place by the necessarily partial group who produced it in the first place—the first Americans to join the practices of book making and nation building into a unified story of founding that critics of both political and book culture have yet to dismantle.[85]

The myth of the well-diffused book was not just useful, then, two centuries ago but remains crucial to the ways we recall and sustain a belief in the legitimate origins of democratic consent—even today. Most notably, *Common Sense* continues to authorize the potentially nongrounded juridical act of independence itself within a popular narrative that demonstrates its sovereign *national* origins in the "minds of the people," who, according to Lodge, agreed to the premises behind independence even though they remained inarticulate—or "dumb"—until Paine spoke their thoughts for them.[86] By helping later generations dissociate the scene of Revolution from its fragmented origins, the myth of *Common Sense* does for latter-day America exactly what its arguments claim to be dismantling for the eighteenth-century monarchy: it lends legitimacy to murky origins. Indeed, as one of the inaugural acts of the political American Enlightenment, the legend of *Common Sense* works much the way that Horkheimer and Adorno have suggested that the Enlightenment worked more generally—as an emphatic reenchantment of ancient institutions for modern purposes.[87]

Common Sense is thus to democracy what the crown (or the king) is

to monarchy. Reflecting on the peculiar way that the crown manages to
be both material and symbolic at once, the British legal historian F. W.
Maitland wryly notes:

> There is one term against which I wish to warn you, and that term is
> "the crown." You will certainly read that the crown does this and the
> crown does that [but] as a matter of fact we know that the crown does
> nothing but lie in the Tower of London to be gazed at by sight-seers.
> No, the crown is a convenient cover for ignorance: it saves us from
> asking difficult questions.[88]

Printed texts like *Common Sense* (and the Declaration of Independence,
the Constitution, and *The Federalist*) all form a piece of America's peculiar crown, democratic metonymies that will undoubtedly continue to
draw "sight-seers" at museums and in popular histories. The difference,
however, is that printed texts have historically done more for America
than "lie in the Tower of London" (or the Library of Congress). Indeed,
the printed text does cultural work that neither the crown (fixed by its
singularity) nor the king (fixed by his mortality) could ever do. While
it does not *actually* solve the problem of popular participation and consent, the printed text mines a fantasy of generality over and through
one of fixity, and it achieves this balance in a way that no (single) sovereign could hope to, seeming to organize and integrate vast spaces in
very material ways. A book can do this because every book has, like the
king before it, two bodies—one that is present in the form of a reliably
fixed, real, and always self-identical material text, and the other that is
promised by its endlessly reproducible, presumably identical (but always
only imagined) counterparts, which are to be diffused evenly among "the
people whose right it is." The book dispenses with the thorny issue of
biological succession by remaining self-identical not just across territorial space but through generations of time as well. In this way, the myth
of the bestseller continues to speak to and for modern citizens in a way
that solves many problems for them—including the ongoing problems
of consensual founding and popular participation, both of which can be
endlessly inferred but never proven or disproven through the existence
of a printed text. In figuring the Revolution as a populist spectacle not
unlike the one Paine himself imagines in *Common Sense*, we have secured
in perpetuity our own will-to-founding, which must always be an (im-

possible) will-to-have-been-founded in order to serve the purposes of legitimation.

5. UNION FROM THE OUTSIDE IN

Robert Ferguson has recently noted that retrospective discussions of *Common Sense* have never sufficiently accounted for its arguments and its legend as related acts of hyperbole, nor (I would add) have Paine's literal claims to continental transmission been adequately recognized for what they are: a crucial departure from the rhetoric Paine found when he arrived on the colonial scene.[89] Ferguson's goal is to bring together an account of the pamphlet's material "impact" with its rhetorical "brilliance." I will likewise argue here that the pamphlet's material impact and its discursive contribution form two ends of a nationalist dialectic, neither of which can be ignored: a reading of Paine's rhetoric is an indispensable corollary to a material history of his text. Regardless of how many copies it sold, *Common Sense* became the icon it did for good reasons: it registers spectacularly—both in the plural sceneries of its production and in its arguments for a newly abstracted yet still locally grounded American identity—the paradox between diffuse imaginings and local realities that underlies nationalism itself.

When *Common Sense* came out in early 1776, the title page of many Philadelphia editions announced only that it was "Written By an Englishman," a claim many eighteenth-century readers chose not to believe, preferring to speculate that the "Englishman" was a straw man, a ruse to protect an American author from imperial wrath. In our own day, that element of disbelief has been sustained as yet another part of the Paine myth. Scholars have often wondered, for instance, how an unknown British staymaker just off the boat from England could step from one continent so completely into another and within fourteen months become the spokesman for the American patriot movement. How could the little book that started the Revolution have been written by an outsider?[90]

The truth is that *Common Sense*, in its radical and original articulation of the North American continent as a distinct and newly imaginable geographical subject, could only have been written by an outsider uninitiated and unassimilated to the fierce local attachments of late-eighteenth-century provincial politics. When Paine arrived in Philadelphia in November 1774, he was not a Virginian or a New Yorker, a Bostonian or even a Pennsylvanian—distinctions that, with the rejection of metropolitan identifications, grew increasingly important from the mid-eighteenth century forward. While the Revolution would eventually create new conditions of mobility for at least some of the colonial population, most late-eighteenth-century Americans still lived entire lifetimes in one place and still felt dependent on and loyal to the local economies where they were born or had settled. But Paine never had this problem to sort through: as a native Englishman, he was routinely exposed to a metropolitan discourse that cast the colonies as a discrete object in the curio cabinet of empire—a discursive practice that, paradoxically, made him the perfect spokesman for a new American union.

But Paine's status as outsider was not just central to what we now take to be the peculiar insight, or genius, of his work. It also made him strategically mobile in the kinds of arguments he was willing to make. As Paine later wrote in *The Crisis*, "I happened to come to America a few months before the breaking out of hostilities. I found the disposition of the people such, that they might have been led by a thread or governed by a reed. Their suspicion was quick and penetrating, but their attachment to Britain was obstinate, and it was at that time a kind of treason to speak against it" (1:143). The Philadelphia Whigs who instrumentalized Paine knew the threat that union posed to the local identifications that powered anti-imperial provincial politics and so underwrote their own authority within their home communities. Benjamin Rush first met the newly arrived immigrant at Robert Aitken's Philadelphia bookstore at a time when he was himself thinking of writing a pamphlet advocating separation from England. Having heard Paine declaim on the issue of independence, Rush decided that Paine would make a better author precisely because, unlike Rush himself, Paine had no local standing:

> I had before this interview put some thoughts upon paper upon this subject, and was preparing an address to the inhabitants of the colonies upon it. But I had hesitated as to the time, and I shuddered at the prospect of the consequence of its not being well received. I mentioned the subject to Mr. Paine, and asked him what he thought of writing a pamphlet upon it. I suggested to him that he had nothing to fear from the popular odium to which such a publication might expose him, for he could live anywhere, but that my profession and connections, which tied me to Philadelphia, where a great majority of the citizens

and some of my friends were hostile to a separation of our country
from Great Britain, forbad me to come forward as a pioneer in that
important controversy.[91]

Rush's anxiety demonstrates two things about early American print culture. First, regardless of how well Benjamin Franklin might have made
himself disappear into the theoretical abstractions of the printed text,
most authors still expected their writing to be received into a known
(and knowing) community, and they understood that they would have to
live with the face-to-face consequences of the words they put on paper.
Second, like many eighteenth-century Americans, Rush felt "tied" to the
specific place in which he lived both through a series of economic depen-
dencies (the time and capital he had invested setting up a medical practice in Philadelphia) *and* through loyalty to the feelings of the community itself, which Rush interpreted in late 1775 as predominantly "hostile
to a separation." Thus while Rush can imagine rhetorically addressing
a diffuse protonational group—"the inhabitants of the colonies"—he
is more decisively wary of the pamphlet's potential reception among the
more local readers he understood would be its primary audience.[92]

Rush's Philadelphia neighbors were "hostile" to independence for a
number of reasons. Provincial politicking had long put at odds those diverse populations that were now being asked to unite. Exploiting these
highly visible regional rivalries early in the war, the Maryland loyalist
Jonathan Boucher tried to dissuade Philadelphians from entering a permanent intercolonial alliance by calling New Englanders "Goths and
Vandals" and warning that cross-regional ties could not last: "'Tis a monstrous and an unnatural coalition; and we should as soon expect to see
the greatest contrarieties in Nature to meet in harmony, and the wolf and
the lamb to feed together, as Virginians to form a cordial union with the
saints of New England."[93] As Boucher knew, colonists in different regions
had real differences that stood in the way of potential alliances, not least
the perpetual territorial disputes that pit landholders in one colony against
those in another. "The Province of New York," Carter Braxton noted in
1776, "is not without her Fears and apprehensions from the Temper of
her Neighbors, their great swarms and small Territory. Even Virginia is
not free from Claims on Pennsylvania nor Maryland from those on Virginia. Some of the Delegates from our Colony carry their Ideas of right to
Lands so far to the eastward that the middle Colonies dread their being
swallowed up between the Claims of them and those from the East."[94]

Paine was not the first to try to imagine union in the face of provincial jealousies. Franklin first posed his Albany Plan in 1754, and intercolonial political gatherings from the 1760s onward often simulated the flowery rhetoric of potential union. Yet they tended to do so in artificial and official contexts that coercively called for the imaginative negation of local identities. Franklin's *Join or Die* cartoon is just the most famous of these coercive calls "to associate" into a functional political union. In 1765, Christopher Gadsden invoked the bleak logic of a negatively generated union when he declared, during the Stamp Act crisis, that "there ought to be no New England man, no New Yorker, &c., known on the Continent, but all of us Americans."[95] Nine years later, in 1774, Patrick Henry (ironically a future antifederalist and fierce defender of Virginia's supreme sovereignty) famously echoed the same thought at the first Continental Congress: "The distinctions between Virginians, Pennsylvanians, New Yorkers, and New Englanders are no more. I am not a Virginian, but an American. . . . All distinctions are thrown down; all America is thrown into one mass."[96] Following this logic, Virginia and Pennsylvania signed an historic agreement in 1775 (negotiated in part by Franklin) intended to set aside a longstanding boundary dispute. The following "Proclamation" was then printed in Pennsylvania and Virginia newspapers: "Friends and Countrymen. . . . All animosities which have heretofore subsisted among you, as inhabitants of distinct colonies, may now give place to generous and concurring efforts for the preservation of everything that can make our common country dear to us."[97] In agreements like this, elite groups of merchants and planters attempted to repair provincial breaches by offering official statements of peace among neighboring colonies. But as a call to union, this declarative proclamation is forced and, like most declarations of its kind, ludicrously inadequate: one cannot order, via an imperative proclamation, the kind of affective sentiment that might make people "generous" and "dear" to one another. Indeed, such declarations were themselves largely official expressions, feebly masking the conspicuous problem of competition within the congressional bodies that produced them. As Richard Merritt notes, "when representatives of the individual colonies met at intercolonial congresses, they behaved more as ambassadors of sovereign nations than as compatriots, and seemed more interested in preserving than in breaking down existing barriers."[98]

In treating each other this way, the colonies were fulfilling a common Enlightenment theory about the relation between geography and politics.

It was a commonplace in the eighteenth century that a land mass as large as the future United States had to be subjected to the disciplinary control of a territorially bound metropolis: the colonies were considered too unwieldy, too widely spaced one from the other, to function as a cooperative, independent, republican unit. And if independent nations may be said to inhere in national institutions—roads, churches, trade relations—then there was little of the national to bind the colonies together, even as late as the 1770s. Merritt, discussing the lack of "amalgamated community structures" prior to the Revolution, notes that throughout the colonial era, "contacts with the mother country were often easier to maintain, and perhaps more fruitful, than those with neighboring colonies" (1). Even in 1781, after Yorktown had secured the inevitability of official autonomy, an English clergyman named Josiah Tucker predicted a dire future for the colonies for precisely this reason. Noting the "Difference of Governments, Habitudes, and Manners" that marked the thirteen colonies, Tucker concluded that

> the *Americans* will have no *Center of Union* among them, and no *Common Interest* to pursue, when the Power and Government of *England* are finally removed. Moreover, when the Intersections and Divisions of their Country by great Bays of the Sea, and by vast Rivers, Lakes, and Ridges of Mountains;—and above all, when those immense inland Regions, beyond the Back Settlements, which are still unexplored, are taken into the Account, they form the highest Probability that the *Americans* never can be united . . . under any Species of Government whatever. Their Fate seems to be—A DISUNITED PEOPLE, till the End of Time.[99]

"Till the End of Time"—no. But for much of the Revolution and the early national period, Tucker was right. While London was the indisputable hub of the British Empire, early national America had no "Center of Union," no centralized location from whose seat industry and government could rule the republic as a whole. The American capital would move four times in the first three decades of independence and be inauspiciously likened, for its trouble, to a hot-air balloon gone astray in the North American sky. The problem of geographical "Divisions" would last longer: not only did the technology not yet exist to forge links across "great Bays," "vast Rivers, Lakes, and Ridges of Mountains," but also the content and shape of American territory would for many decades keep changing, with populations shifting west at a greater rate than any centralized network (either of transportation or communication) could keep pace with until well into the nineteenth century.

In the face of such geographic skepticism, Paine needed to produce a new way of thinking about the extended colonies that would neutralize the deeply appealing but divisive rhetoric of local attachment while offering a convincing model of the continent as an autonomous (and non-imperially integrated) unit rather than a series of disintegrating colonial fragments. As his circulation estimates for *Common Sense* suggest, one answer to this problem was to imagine a monolithic reading audience, a seamless circuit of unruptured dissemination for his own abstracted point of view. But even before *Common Sense* emerged as a legend in book lore, Paine had already begun the project of theorizing what he called "continental minds," and he did so in a strikingly effective nonofficial voice (1:20). Writing in 1775 in the *Pennsylvania Journal*, he reversed the common order of previous proclamations (in which intercolonial congresses had released statements of unity to "the people" in the imperative voice of command), speaking instead as a private man addressing the congressional body, urging them to act "not PROVINCIALLY but CONTINENTALLY." As he declared in a later letter: "I despise the narrow idea of acting PROVINCIALLY and reprobate the little unworthy principle, conveyed in the following words, '*In Behalf of this colony*,' and the more so because by a late resolve, all Colony distinctions are to be laid aside. 'TIS THE AMERICAN CAUSE, THE AMERICAN CONGRESS, THE AMERICAN ARMY."[100] This call to tighten the continental belt (as he would later characterize it) would become the driving argument of *Common Sense* as well, which repeatedly deploys the newly visible divisions of the "provincial" versus the "continental," the "local" versus the "universal." In fact, the words "continent" and "continental" appear sixty-four times in *Common Sense*'s fifty (or so) pages, as Paine prods his reader to "get over local or longstanding prejudices" and to "generously enlarge his views" (1:7, 17). America was, as Paine liked to say, "a vast scene," and in *Common Sense* he encourages his readers to look at the whole, rather than identifying with just one part (1:496). In fact, he naturalizes this unwieldy idea of the continent through the repeated use of organic metaphors (the continent as growing tree, the continent as aging man), reframing the seemingly unnatural idea of a noncolonial America by turning it into a monolithic entity already independent from Britain in day-to-day life if not in decisive political act.

In calling for independence, Paine was well aware of the arguments about geographical dispersion that would seem to make his plan risky and novel. Indeed, one of the pamphlet's greatest contributions to the rhetorical debates of 1776 is its rethinking of existing arguments about the politics of size in the implausibly extended republic that people were beginning to imagine for North America, and in this sense, the pamphlet was not a reflection of the popular mind at all, for it hardly reflected common wisdom. "It hath lately been asserted in Parliament," Paine writes, "that the colonies have no relation to each other but through the parent country, i.e., that Pennsylvania and the Jerseys, and so on for the rest, are sister colonies by the way of England" (1:19). Warning his readers not to buy into the oppressive binary of imperial versus local attachment, he concludes that "the king and his worthless adherents are got at their old game of dividing the continent" (1:44). In fact, Paine turns on its head the widely accepted commonplace about the dangerously decentered and dispersed variety of the American colonies by suggesting that it is not the colonies but the empire that is too dispersed: "Even the distance at which the Almighty hath placed England and America is a strong and natural proof that the authority of the one over the other, was never the design of heaven" (1:21).

Paine reenacts this reversal on almost every page of *Common Sense*, countering the feared scene of postcolonial disintegration with one of monumental U.S. integrity: "The sun never shone on a cause of greater worth. 'Tis not the affair of a city, a county, a province, or a kingdom; but of a continent—of at least one eighth part of the habitable globe" (1:17). America's huge land mass and the expansive possibilities of its "continental seed-time" are explicitly offered as positive alternatives to British narrowness, particularly the physical narrowness of England, which Paine delights in lampooning for its miniature size ("there is something absurd," he notes, "in supposing a Continent to be perpetually governed by an island" [1:24]). He inverts the spatial logic of empire-to-colony so successfully that England itself, rather than her satellite colonies, begins to look like an insular and isolated province:

> In this extensive quarter of the globe, we forget the narrow limits of three hundred and sixty miles (the extent of England) and carry our friendship on a larger scale. . . . It is pleasant to observe by what regular gradations we surmount the force of local prejudices, as we enlarge our acquaintance with the world. A man born in any town in England

divided into parishes, will naturally . . . distinguish [his fellow parish-
ioner] by the name of *neighbor*; if he meet him but a few miles from
home, he drops the narrow idea of a street, and salutes him by the name
of *townsman*; if he travel out of the county and meet him in any other,
he forgets the minor divisions of street and town, and calls him *coun-
tryman, i.e., countyman*; but if in their foreign excursions they should
associate in France, or any other part of *Europe*, their local remembrance would be enlarged into that of *Englishman*. And by a just parity
of reasoning, all Europeans meeting in America, or any other quarter
of the globe, are *countrymen*; for England, Holland, Germany, or Sweden, when compared with the whole, stand in the same places on the
larger scale, which the divisions of street, town, and county do on the
smaller ones; distinctions too limited for continental minds. (1:19–20)

Here the island-bound Englishman stands as the most reductive unit of
empire. Trapped within "the narrow limits of three hundred and sixty
miles," he strongly feels the "force" of English "prejudices" grafted onto
the land in the form of parishes, streets, towns, and counties. It is only
midway though the passage that the Englishman gets, as it were, his passport out of provinciality through one of Paine's most favored tropes:
travel. Like Paine himself, who had only a few months before emigrated
from one country to another, this Englishman is able to traverse, through
a circuit of movement that takes him across the globe, the boundaries of
both England and its narrow "distinctions," thus "enlarg[ing]" all "local
remembrance" and attaining the status of the "continental mind."

But while *Common Sense* repeatedly calls for an "enlarged" identity,
it never attempts to deny local attachment or provincial variety. On the
contrary, Paine imagines the colonies' heterogeneity as a generative scene
of ethnic Babel, where people from "England, Holland, Germany, or
Sweden" as well as those from Boston, New York, and Charleston can
all, through individual acts of real or imagined mobility, share the same
collective space. Allowing both localist and universalist identifications to
function simultaneously, *Common Sense* overrides the priority of either
imperial or local attachment by cultivating a new universalizing localism—a model of American nationality that is both local and cosmopolitan at once (and hence not necessarily national at all).

Such notions of translocal identity, though useful at the moment
of separation, would ultimately have limited appeal and utility in the
border-patrolling politics of the 1780s and 1790s. In 1776, however, the

possibility of a world revolution played out in innumerable local sites throughout the Atlantic world was very much within reach of Paine's mobile imagination, and scenes of such translocal imagining permeate *Common Sense*, though they are often evoked, paradoxically, in the most intimate and local register imaginable. Describing the regionally specific scene of a blockaded Boston, for instance, Paine famously declares that "our affections [are] wounded through a thousand pores" (1:30). Imagining the political violence of separation as having already occurred at the microlevel of pores, this sentence tropes the nation as a collection of local sites, punningly evoking, with the word "pore," the American ports at the center of colonial trade disputes while at the same time figuring resistant Americans as a damaged and plural yet organic and unified body politic. The sentence thus evokes the spectacle of the slain and "wounded" bodies at Lexington and Concord even as it calls to mind the scene in the port of Boston that brought on the British military's blockade of that city—the defiant dumping of British tea into Boston Harbor. And this is a canny mechanism for calling forth a sense of translocal attachment, because if the colonies had united in any one way in the decade prior to the Revolution, it was in their shared decision to assent to a groundbreaking cross-continental nonimportation agreement—a unanimous shutting down of ports at the local level of city and state.

But translocality was, like separation, just another argument that had to be made to *seem* commonsensical. Because so many colonists had no reason to care about the Boston blockade, Paine had to work hard to connect this colonial scene with every other one in a way that did not recur to the prior common bond of the metropolis as a unifying prism. After the fashion of Adam Smith, whose theory of moral sentiments theorized the production of sympathy among disparate subjects, *Common Sense* finds itself in the business of theorizing feelings and triangulating them through spectatorial third parties. Paine would masterfully resolve this problem—we might call it the dilemma of locality—through the mechanism of his book, omitting the familiar imperial third party and replacing it with a provincial one made newly visible and reachable to Paine's imagined audience (the "you" who was the owner and reader of Paine's pamphlet and whose sympathetic identification could be called forth in the act of reading it):

> It is the good fortune of many to live distant from the scene of present
> sorrow; the evil is not sufficiently brought to their doors to make them

feel the precariousness with which all American property is possessed.
But let our imaginations transport us a few moments to Boston. . . .
The inhabitants of that unfortunate city who but a few months ago
were in ease and affluence, have now no other alternative than to stay
and starve, or turn out to beg. . . . But if you say, you can still pass
the violations over, then I ask, hath your house been burnt? Hath your
property been destroyed before your face? Are your wife and children
destitute of a bed to lie on, or bread to live on? Have you lost a parent
or a child by their hands, and yourself the ruined and wretched survi-
vor? If you have not, then are you not a judge of those who have. . . .
This is not inflaming or exaggerating matters, but trying them by those
feelings and affections which nature justifies. (1:22)

Presuming a consensus between two separate points of origin (and so
eluding potential dissent), this passage transforms the "I" who is the
speaker into part of an "us" (in alliance with his readers), even as it tries
to enfold a "them" (of potential Tories) into that same group of patriots.
Like the narrow-minded Englishman who learned to think continentally
by traveling the globe, colonial provincials are invited to use the text in
front of them to "let [their] imaginations transport [them] a moment
to Boston." Paine then asks his imagined audience to see these Bostonians as mirrors of their own families, capitalizing on the sentimental
rhetoric of family ties previously monopolized by loyalists, who deployed
the trope of mother-country to infant-colony to make the imperial status
quo seem natural. Paine's passage resists this commonplace, recircuit-
ing American affections in a way that undermines imperial metaphors
of kinship without collapsing them into the language of primitive local
attachment: filial affections once held toward England are now simply
transported "to Boston."[101]

   This was a good solution—rhetorically. It is only in the real world,
after all, that transportation proves limited as a model for political attachment and social affection. It was (and still is) difficult for people to
move from place to place without simply reattaching themselves to their
new destination (as congressional delegates eventually did by reorienting
themselves away from their constituents and toward their Philadelphia
colleagues). But Paine's version of "transport"-ation fortuitously relies,
in the end, on something other than literal mobility, something more like
interior enlightenment—the sort of "transport" that turns on a powerful

leap of the mind. Even so, *Common Sense* almost always insists that such inner epiphanies turn on an appeal to the local, or the embodied. Thus at the end of *Common Sense*, Paine insists on reimagining the relation of colonist to colonist through the thrillingly implausible image of a cross-continental handshake:

> Instead of gazing at each other with suspicions or doubtful curiosity, let each of us hold out to his neighbor the hearty hand of friendship, and unite in drawing a line. . . . Let the names of Whig and Tory be extinct; and let none other be heard among us, than those of *a good citizen; and open and resolute friend; and a virtuous supporter of the* RIGHTS OF MANKIND, *and of the* FREE AND INDEPENDENT STATES OF AMERICA. (1:46)

Rather than evoking a call to a more traditional negative nationalism ("We are not Virginians or Bostonians but Americans"), Paine projects a positive nationalism based on the local ideal of face-to-face relations—the nation as village, the citizen as "neighbor" and "friend." His new American subject is so successfully conceived that the potentially incoherent, or self-splitting, act of "unit[ing] in drawing a line" (i.e., separating), comes to seem productive rather than destructive. And as that line is drawn, Paine subtly substitutes an altogether different kind of defining division—that of Whigs and Tories—to displace more provincial identifications (the appeal of which nevertheless ironically underwrites the scene as a whole). By pamphlet's end, the continental mind has been so "enlarged" that the only meaningful distinction between colonists is whether or not they support the pamphlet's call to independence—whether, in short, they possess the same natural common sense as their intercolonial "neighbors."

The tropes of embodiment that *Common Sense* deploys (from travel to wounds to handshakes) would eventually prove a troubled route to the end-ideal of abstracted citizenship. But Paine's willingness to mobilize his "Countrymen" through a language that was both abstract and embodied, local and translocal, was, in 1776, a distinctive achievement. In making this appeal, Paine capitalized on the slippage then emerging in the concept of the word "country" (as one would emerge, in years to come, in the word "state"). In 1776 and for some time after, the word "country" would signify both the continental alliance and more local attachments, both the nascent United States as country and whatever local county citizens came from — their "home" country. Daniel Roberdeau, a Pennsylvania delegate to the Second Continental Congress, invokes both senses when he writes to the president of Pennsylvania on January 26, 1778, to apologize for the fact that Pennsylvania farm produce cannot reach the Continental Army: "I could weep," he writes (with Paine-like emotion), "over my suffering Country [the united colonies, figured by the Continental Army], cramped at this season for vigorous exertion, by want of provisions, with which our Country [Pennsylvania] abounds."[102]

In his best moments, Paine saw and exploited the generative "line" *and* linkage between these two different kinds of "Country" in a way that his contemporaries did not and in ways that never cut one side of the dialectic off from the other. For all his talk of tightening the continental belt, he insisted on thinking about America as an almost unimaginable, or infinite, number of heterogeneous local cultures ("a thousand pores," a thousand porous ports). More than once during the war, Paine would argue that the dispersion of rural Anglo-American culture could be turned to the Revolution's advantage — but only if common attachments could be forged while buffers still existed between colonies (while the possibility of cross-regional transport, in other words, remained imaginary). "It might be difficult, if not impossible," he argues in *Common Sense*, "to form the continent into one government half a century hence. The vast variety of interests, occasioned by an increase of trade and population, would create confusion. Colony would be against colony" (1:36). Thus where other eighteenth-century writers saw doom in dispersion, Paine saw a way to float local differences in the isolated variety of the massively conceived whole. He never doubted that if the colonies decided to fight, Britain would lose the war: "Like a game of drafts, we can move out of *one* square to let you come in, in order that we may afterwards take two or three for one. . . . In all the wars which you have formerly been concerned in you had only armies to contend with; in this case you have both an army and a country to combat" (1:67). Here, Paine's single use of the word "country" is as semantically diffuse as Roberdeau's two uses of it. On one hand, "country" signifies the nascent nation, an abstracted people. On the other hand, because of Paine's analogy of it to the spaces on a checkerboard, it also signifies the land itself as a number of dispersed locales, or specific topographical terrains, within which that monolithically imagined people might materially take form and resist.

It has been a cultural commonplace to regard the Revolution as a moment of union and the post-Revolutionary 1780s as a moment of local partisanship and disunion, to which the Constitution of 1787 was an innovative antidote. But localism was a problem not just before and after but all *through* the Revolution—something Paine, arriving from London without any local affiliations whatsoever, could oppose with exceptional clarity but could not in the end change, except by participating rather flamboyantly in a compelling counterdiscourse. His peculiar innovations of that discourse have been overshadowed by the myth of *Common Sense*'s commercial success, but Paine's powerful imagining of North America as an already unified whole makes him something he clearly wanted to be—the first theorist of *E pluribus unum*, a federalist in the making whose sense of the new forms that social relations were taking was cannier than even Franklin's, who in 1775 helped to draft an early version of the now defunct Articles of Confederation after the fashion of his own long-outmoded Albany Plan. While it is true that the first fitful uses of "continental" (or protofederal) discourse emerged several years before Paine arrived (and were in fact splashed everywhere in 1776—from the "Continental Congress" to the "Continental Army"), such uses were more descriptive than prescriptive. In these cases, the "continental" modifier was used to describe concentrations of people literally gathered together from dispersed sites to form discrete collective bodies. But Paine does not imagine parts standing in for wholes (as imperial metonymies had long done and as later constitutional metonymies would continue to do) so much as he makes transcendent claims upon the whole multi-self-differentiating field itself, shifting beyond the literal act of bodily collection to the imagined world of mass collectivity that was the future.

6. The Would-Be Author and the Real Bookseller

To the degree that Paine was able to balance the abstractions of mass collectivity with the materiality of being an embodied revolutionary, he did so through novel acts of authorship. For this reason, I want to end this chapter by describing Paine's entrance into American literary culture and using it to revisit Habermas's well-known (and much critiqued) model of the public sphere.[103] Habermas, of course, valorizes eighteenth-century

newspapers, pamphlets, coffeehouses, salons, circulating libraries, and
debating clubs as potentially utopian sites in which men joined an abstracted, universalizing field of debate based on their "common humanity," sites where "the laws of the market were suspended as were laws of
the state" so that all could equally participate in a rational critique of the
state. *Common Sense* would appear to be an exemplary artifact of such
Enlightenment debate. Its very title embraces two of the eighteenth century's more attractive cultural fictions about its own public institutions,
with "common" suggesting universality and "sense" suggesting rationality. Indeed, when read under the mythic sign of the bestseller, *Common
Sense* offers itself as a promising location not just for applying but for
expanding and relegitimating Habermas's notoriously limited (white,
male, urban, propertied) formulation, a privileged site where the public
sphere's theoretical universality finally meets the practical application of
universal diffusion—a truly utopian moment of transparent communication that produces, in Gordon Wood's words, "the most egalitarian nation in the history of the world."[104]

But despite *Common Sense*'s storied role in the history of eighteenth-
century American print culture, Paine's local experiences as an author
in Enlightenment Philadelphia provide a powerful antiexemplum to this
Americanized fantasy of a populist public sphere. My purpose here will
be to demonstrate how nonuniversalizing the phenomenon of *Common
Sense* actually was, not merely as a matter of reception across its multiple mixed audiences but for Paine, its lower-class author. Paine heartily
believed both in the fiction of universality *and* in simple acts of authorship and readership as the sites at which such fantasies might be secured
as a reality. Paine's embrace of textual abstraction occurred, in fact, at
two distinct scales. At the level of the national, he believed that the many
everyday worlds across the American "continent" could be abstracted
into a national community through acts of reading; at a more personal
level, he believed he could escape the humiliating markers and limits of
his own social history and merge himself, as an author, with the Revolutionary phenomenon we call "Common Sense." Such fantasies, however,
only proved impoverishing for Paine in the end, providing the grounds
for the last chapter of his effacement from the scene of American founding. Try as he might to play the part of the disinterested republican, Paine
never managed to diffuse his particular self into the body politic via the
abstractions of the printed text. On the contrary, his experience of print's
abstractions was a decidedly frustrated one. Though he constantly articu-

lated fantasies about print culture's capacity to generalize and popularize, he routinely came up against the material limitations of such fantasies. As an author, Paine never achieved the status of representative republican that his patron Franklin patched together, nor could he transcend the limits of the particular moment and scene in which he found himself. His struggles to locate a model of authorship that bridged a democratic politics with the actually existing social hierarchies of Revolutionary Philadelphia reveal a ground upon which the fictions of the public sphere prove not just inaccessible but also devastatingly damaging to those who cannot profit from them.

Common Sense is a case in point. While Whigs upheld Paine's argument as the people's rational choice ("common sense"), Tories vilified it from the start as nonsense, an example not of rational debate but its degradation into the more common kind of cultural consumption that marks the historiographic limit of Habermas's model. Tories thus read the word "common" not positively (as universality) but negatively (as vulgarity). Yet, as we shall see, even good Whigs who embraced *Common Sense* tended to treat Paine himself more circumspectly than his text, denying him full credentials in the republic of letters by particularizing him in any number of ways—marking out his poverty, his bodily habits, his authorial ambitions, and his social politics. His pamphlet may have been instrumentalized by revolutionaries in good standing from John Adams to George Washington, but Paine himself was often rejected as a gatecrasher at the (republican) scene of American founding.

After the Revolution, John Adams recalled that Paine "was extremely earnest to convince me that, Common Sense was his first born: declared again and again that he had never written a Line nor a Word that had been printed before Common Sense."[105] "In England," Paine insisted, "I never was the author of a syllable in print" (2:1229). "It was the cause of America that made me an author" (1:235). But Paine's authorial aspirations both precede and transcend 1776. Though Paine lauded *Common Sense* as his inaugural act of authorship, he had actually embarked on pamphleteering in London in 1772 with *The Case of the Officers of Excise*. This pamphlet was expressly written for British tax collectors (Paine among them) in order to plead their case to the House of Commons. Though never widely circulated (and not released to the general public until 1793), the *Excise* pamphlet is an instructive starting point for a discussion of Paine's conception of authorship, for it has its origins in England's own unevenly developing public sphere, where Paine's experiences in many respects resembled his patron Franklin's. As a tax collector and customs officer living in Lewes, England, Paine worked for the Crown (as Franklin did, in his position as postmaster), but he spent much of his free time participating in local debating clubs, where he composed numerous songs, poems, and speeches for a group of young men that resembles Franklin's famous Philadelphia Junto. In producing the *Excise* pamphlet, Paine moved (literally) between this smaller world in Lewes and the larger world of London, where he adopted a new identity as Parliamentary petitioner and pamphleteer.[106]

But while the *Excise* pamphlet had its origins (like *Common Sense*) in the eighteenth-century world of coffeehouses, debating clubs, and print shops, it offers an ironic contrast to Paine's American writings. For one thing, the *Excise* pamphlet was explicitly self-interested (seeking a pay raise) in a way that Paine's American writings are not. For another, its dissemination and reception did not remotely resemble that of his later, more successful writings. While *Common Sense* was disseminated along the North American post road without Paine's overt involvement, he actually hand-carried the *Excise* pamphlet throughout London, where he spent six months personally distributing copies to members of Parliament, who chose not to engage its arguments either in print or on the floor of the debate. In its financial self-interestedness, contracted circulation, failed project of persuasion, and ignominious end (Paine was dismissed from his post because of it, for dereliction of duty), *The Case of the Officers of Excise* is an anti–*Common Sense*. It is little wonder, then, that Paine sought to reinvent himself authorially when he arrived in Philadelphia. Not only was his first act of authorship a failure, but it did not organize itself (politically) in the way that Paine's later writings would. Paine did not, for this very reason, recognize it as an authentic act of either "authorship" or "publication"—a fact that tells us much, finally, about what these words meant to him.[107] Four years later, Paine would appeal to and for the American people against the oppressive structures of a distant state. But the *Excise* pamphlet of 1772 was written, conversely, by a state employee and directed both to other such employees and to the state itself. We do not yet see, in other words, the generative splitting in Paine's thinking and writing of the state from itself in the fictional figure of "the author," who, within the impartial arena of the public sphere, is able to stand as a disinterested medium between a people and their government. Thus while the *Excise* pamphlet is essentially a labor document (pointing out "the voice of general want" and the "misery" of its subjects' economic lives), it never successfully moved a wider populace, which, as many scholars have noted, had little interest in the complaints of tax collectors (2:4–11).

But even though the *Excise* pamphlet differs sharply from Paine's American writings, we can already see in it many of the political, social, and literary ambitions that later produced his self-mythologies about *Common Sense*. For one thing, it had a large print run for a "nonpublication" (totaling 4,000 copies), with Paine expecting to distribute 3,000 of these to other excise officers and "the remaining 1,000 reserved for presents" (2:1129). On arriving in London, furthermore, to dispense these presents, Paine used the opportunity to circulate through the center of political and social power, attending lectures on mathematics and astronomy and trying to connect not just with members of Parliament (as he later would with members of the Continental Congress) but with Enlightenment luminaries like Franklin, Oliver Goldsmith, and (unsuccessfully) Sir Isaac Newton. Its eventual failure aside, Paine was pleased enough with the pamphlet to present a copy to Goldsmith (a potential patron), noting that "I have received so many letters of thanks and approbation for the performance, that were I not rather singularly modest, I should insensibly become a little vain" (2:1129).

After 1776, Paine did become, of course, "a little vain." For one thing, he believed *Common Sense*'s success was "beyond anything since the invention of printing" (1:406). For another, he frequently took credit for nearly every aspect of that success, crafting an elaborate cult of genius around his authorship that denied the involvement of other thinkers and that seized narrative control of many apparently contingent aspects of its dissemination:

> I determined with myself to write the pamphlet. . . . As I knew the time of the Parliament meeting, and had no doubt what sort of King's speech it would produce, my contrivance was to have the pamphlet come out just at the time the speech might arrive in America, and so fortunate was I in this cast of policy that both of them made their appearance in this city on the same day. (2:1162)

In an era when colonial populations waited months on end for British packets to arrive in local ports, Paine suggests that he intentionally planned *Common Sense*'s publication to coincide with the arrival of the king's speech. In this narrative, nobody consults with the author (no Rush, no Franklin, no Rittenhouse). Instead, he independently "determine[s]" to write *Common Sense* and then arranges its sensational appearance alongside a packet and a speech whose arrival could not have been predicted with any certainty. In variations on this theme, Paine would eventually claim extraordinary intentionality regarding many other aspects of the pamphlet's success. As already noted, he often cited his gift of "copy-right to every state in the Union" as the moving cause behind the pamphlet's continental dissemination (even though local printers would undoubtedly have printed it, as Bell did, whether he had given his blessing or not), and he likewise took responsibility for the pamphlet's wide reading base by describing to friends how he had fixed the price of the pamphlet at "one shilling each" (2:1162).

As this last example suggests, money is a recurring theme in Paine's remarks about *Common Sense*. In deeding his "first born" to his adopted country, Paine believed he had deprived himself of a personal fortune. While no profits ever actually accrued (either to him or to the entities he philanthropically deeded them to), he maintained an imaginary relation to their potentiality, much like the imaginary relation he cultivated to the pure potentiality of the pamphlet's circulation numbers. As he later declared, "the single pamphlet 'Common Sense,' would at that time of day have produced a tolerable fortune, had I only taken the same profits from the publication that all writers had ever done," for "the sale was the most rapid and extensive of any thing that was ever published in this country, or perhaps any other" (2:182–83). Rather than reading the lack of profits as an effect of the colonial economic conditions attending his authorship (conditions in which there was no such thing as copyright, and few profits for any author), Paine believed he had *chosen* to make no money from it: "In order to accommodate that pamphlet to every man's purchase and to do honor to the cause, I gave up the profits I was justly entitled to, which in this city only would at the usual price of books [have] produced me £1,000 at that time [of] day, besides what I might have made by extending it to other States" (2:1163). Such remarks indicate that even years after the war, Paine was still counting his Revolutionary chickens, not just imagining a wide dissemination for the pamphlet across space but theorizing reverse capital flows as well, whereby royalties would return to him through the same routes by which the book had circulated away from him.

In statements like these, Paine was crafting a complicated understanding of his own authorship—one part of it classical republican (and self-effacing) and the other liberal (and self-aggrandizing). Though it is rarely mentioned in discussions of *Common Sense*, Paine's "noisy" marketing feud with Robert Bell forms an important episode in his emerging conception of this newly empowered yet virtuous kind of literary production. Here, in a public contest between "the Would-Be Author and the Real Bookseller" (as the printer Bell characterized it), we can see traces of Paine's previous failures *and* the increasingly self-congratulatory mythos he would later use to promote *Common Sense*.[108] In fact, Paine's first mistake with Bell was in trying to puff his own authorial accomplishments and to seize control of them. On January 25, 1776, he denounced Bell (in print), announcing that "the great demand" for *Common Sense* "hath induced the publisher of the first edition to print a new edition unknown to the author," even though "the author" had "expressly directed him not to proceed therein without orders."[109] Although Paine declared that "this is all the notice that will ever be taken" of Bell, he continued the argument in print for several more weeks, promising his readers more and better material ("written by the Author of COMMON SENSE") if they waited for his new "authorized" edition.[110] In this way, Paine sought to establish a direct connection to his reading base and at the same time began the lifelong project of claiming a central role for his Revolutionary literary production.

But the historical record of this conflict strongly suggests that Paine misread not just his potential place in the coming Revolution, but the local (and literary) site from which he was to participate in it. Bell, of course, made no such mistake. He promptly labeled Paine a "self-conceited Englishman" while representing himself as a simple "brother bookseller" who had been taken advantage of, the artisanal "godfather" of *Common Sense*, who had, in the public interest, "only charged one penny each" for an astonishing amount of work (described in loving detail as "the stitching [of] one thousand pamphlets, containing eleven thousand different half sheets to be folded, gathered, pressed, and collated, which goeth through the artists hands five different times before the pamphlet can be ready for the public"). Bell's material labor as a "real bookseller" ("by whose knowledge in business the pamphlet was made respectable") was repeatedly held up in this debate against the more abstract contributions of Paine, the "ostensible author," "whose self-imagined importance hath swelled him into contemptible consequentiality" and who, in his excessive authorial pride, seemed to "insinuate there is no WRITERS in America but the would-be author of Common Sense." Against the cult of genius that Paine was already cultivating about himself, Bell proffered a more traditional republican model of group authorship, targeting the presumed originality of the pamphlet by calling Paine "the ostensible," "the would-be," and "the Foster-Father Author." In such moments, Bell relentlessly highlighted the debt that Paine owed to local Philadelphians (who had initially served as a go-between for Paine, thus securing Bell's agreement to print the pamphlet in the first place). Indeed, Bell finally reduces Paine's role to that of an "Amanuensis to a group of authors," casting him as an imposter whose individual literary reputation was "usurped" and "BORROWED." In this way, Bell exposed Paine's attempts both to gain control of and to profit from his authorship not financially but socially, skewering Paine for having "condescendeth again to puff his pamphlet" and being so taken with his own "imaginary triumph" that he only looked, in the end, "ridiculous."[111]

Paine was undoubtedly more available for such attacks because of his unusual social status in Philadelphia, both as an immigrant outsider and as a member of an ambiguous, but lower, social tier. John Adams conflates both these positions when he describes Paine's language as "suitable for an Emigrant from New Gate."[112] But Paine's feud with Bell also suggests how unstable Philadelphia's tiered social relations were in 1776. On one hand, Paine appears to have made the error of not treating Bell like the "brother" craftsman that he was, giving him "an order" and then publicly criticizing Bell when he felt himself ignored. On the other hand, Bell's enraged response suggests that it was not equal standing that he sought from Paine, but the everyday social deference due to a productive member of society (Bell, the master craftsman and "real bookseller") from a relatively obscure and nonproductive one (Paine, "the would-be author"). To put it simply, Paine treated the publication of Common Sense like a market transaction, while Bell viewed it from within a more traditional social model structured by deferential codes that Paine clearly violated. In this sense, Paine was acting out, as a local author, the same seizure of power that he was advocating politically in the pamphlet, a slippage that Bell recognized and reacted against. In trying to control the production of his pamphlet, Paine had (in Bell's telling words) "declared his desirable independence from the trammels of catch-penny authorcraft."[113] Bell's response to this impudent declaration tells us that however much he might have believed in the project of American (political) independence, he resisted the arrival of a potentially revolutionary social logic when it threatened his master status in his own local world.

In the weeks that followed, Paine responded to Bell's attacks by invoking a model of authorship that might serve as both an engine for his own social rise and a screen against accusations of licentiousness—one that looks very much like the model that Michael Warner describes as republican print ideology. Finding himself at the center of "an unpleasant situation," Paine tried to recoup a sense of public honor by emphasizing his anonymity and disinterested financial relation to the outcome of his work. Addressing an open letter "To the Public," he defended himself in absentia first by citing his public go-betweens ("two gentlemen . . . whose names are left at the bar of the London Coffee-house" and who might "authenticate" his account of the dispute) and then by announcing in the same sentence his desire to use all profits from *Common Sense* "for the purpose of purchasing mittens for the troops" in Canada. Try as he might, however, to rehearse a textbook rendition of republican virtue, he could not resist ending this set of remarks by threatening to see Bell "sued" should he fail to "perform" the author's wishes and "settle" the profits of *Common Sense* immediately.[114]

But Paine's missteps at this late date did not really matter. At no point in this long, public argument did Bell ever let Paine disappear into the abstracting logic of his pamphlet's pseudonym. His advertisements for *Common Sense* throughout January and February repeatedly linked Paine's "disinterested generosity" to base authorial ambitions that were, in turn, continually collapsed into degraded corporeal desires: "You say you wanted to remain unknown," Bell wryly notes, "but, in practice, [you] yourself [are] telling it in every beer-house."[115] While Paine tried to use the Habermasian coffeehouse as a neutral site at which the dispute might be justly resolved, Bell linked him back at every turn to degraded spaces like the local tavern—always, for Paine (who drank too much), the site of unenlightened embodiment rather than abstracted rationality.[116] In this way, Bell effectively labeled Paine an antirepublican pretender, aspiring to a brand of honor, disinterestedness, and anonymity that his own licentious desires—for fame, profit, and control—had already made impossible. Indeed, Bell tied Paine back to his body in a far more literal way, by adding to the title page of every one of his editions (after the first) the vengeful line "Written By an Englishman" (which also ran in Bell's advertisements and was, of course, reprinted up and down the eastern seaboard in every reprint set from Bell's expanded edition).

Readers farther afield would eventually misread this byline as a register of its author's unlikely genius. But in 1776 Philadelphia, those four words outed Paine as the author of *Common Sense* even as they sought to alienate him from a local (Pennsylvanian) identity.

From our perspective, it might seem that Bell, rather than Paine, acted most problematically in this dispute. Bell's attacks on Paine were blisteringly rude, while Paine's responses often seem anemic, confused, and perhaps even (in afterthought) well intended, if still ineffectual. But in the end, Bell's campaign against Paine only reinforced his own status as a Philadelphia insider—and Paine's as an outsider.[117] Francis Hopkinson was among the first, but hardly the last, to take the local printer's side in the dispute, following Bell's lead by poking fun at the hilarious presumption of a very ungentlemanly and nonanonymous character that he, and many other Philadelphia gentlemen, already knew was named "Tom":

> Tom mounted on his sordid load,
> And bawling, d—n ye, clear the road;
> His shovel grasp'd firm in his hands,
> Which far and near the street commands,
> No hardy mortal dares approach,
> Whether on horseback, foot, or coach;
> None in his wits the risque would choose,
> Who either wears a coat or nose.
> So——in pomp, on Billingsgate,
> His arms display'd in burlesque state;
> Scurrility and impudence,
> Bombast and Bedlam eloquence,
> Defiance bids——to COMMON SENSE.[118]

Billingsgate was an urban fish-market in a poor section of London and a synonym, by 1776, for the coarse language of the lower sorts. Paine's proverbial use of such a language continues to stand today as a celebrated sign of his text's integrative cross-class project, the coalition-building discourse that helped to make America classless (because appealing to and speaking for the widest possible base), from the very beginning. But Paine's vulgar language is not cited here as a unifying accomplishment but as a spectacle of foreignness and even (to borrow a word from Paine's description of King George) as brutishness—something so alienating that it allows Hopkinson to respond in decidedly diversifying, snobbish, and nonunifying poetic turn.

By citing Billingsgate, Hopkinson rightfully locates in Paine's impoverished British past (as corsetmaker, storekeeper, sailor, tax collector, and, of course, failed Parliamentary pamphleteer) the likely origins of the tirade imagined here. Indeed, as an account of Paine's will to authorial agency in the local Philadelphia book trade, this tirade smacks of pretensions to metropolitan, rather than provincial, modes of cultural production, for the centralized organization of London print culture was far more likely to produce profits for its authors (and crucial forms of celebrity and agency) than were less capitalized, more dispersed, and more deferentially organized colonial book cultures. Yet Hopkinson, careful not to alienate an emerging force in Philadelphia politics, does not align Paine with the urban mechanic class to which he did in fact (as a corsetmaker) originally belong. Instead, Hopkinson presents Paine as an indeterminate composite of the lower sorts, part farmer come to town on market day, part day laborer—a mad minuteman brandishing not a musket (or a pen) but a shovel of foul-smelling shit, a compost of "Scurrility and impudence/ Bombast and Bedlam eloquence." Just one of several local satires that defamed Paine in the most specific and "common" terms possible, Hopkinson's poem is a telling analogue to hagiographic accounts of *Common Sense* as a bodiless voice that spoke the people's generalized will to and for them. Seen from atop this "sordid load," *Common Sense* comes into view not as an occasion in which the differences within early America were either set aside or integrated into seamless consensus, but as a place where the disintegrative power of such difference has, in fact, simply been in special need of suppression.[119]

The myth of text-based founding has done the work of such suppression for generations of remembering Americans, integrating a vast and primarily rural mass of eighteenth-century North Americans into the largely northern and often urban scenes of print culture and political nation formation. The irony, as we shall see, is that Paine himself enthusiastically embraced the discourses that were the most responsible, in the end, for his own erasure from the scene of founding. As a theorist of what he called "a new system, *that of representation*," Paine was acutely aware of the fragmented social scene on his newly imagined continent, but he naively thought that as an author he could (in Habermasian fashion) transcend and integrate such differences in his writings—and indeed, in his very person. In describing "the various classes and merits of men in society" to his friend and patron Henry Laurens, Paine listed as necessary constituents in any new scheme of federal representation the following three "classes": first, "farmers and cultivators," "citizens of the first necessity, because every thing comes originally from the earth"; second, "various orders of manufacturers and mechanics," who "contribute to the accommodation rather than to the first necessities of life"; and third, "merchants and shopkeepers," "convenient but not important" because "they produce nothing themselves . . . but employ their time in exchanging one thing for another and living by the profits" (2:1142–43). Intuiting, however, an obvious occlusion, Paine then adds: "Perhaps you will say that in this classification of citizens I have marked no place for myself; that I am neither farmer, mechanic, merchant, nor shopkeeper. I believe, however, I am of the first class. I am *a farmer of thoughts*, and all the crops I raise I give away. I please myself with making you a present of the thoughts in this letter" (2:1143). In a way that recalls but reverses Hopkinson's sense of social distinctions, Paine uses the heterogeneity of the social sorts listed here as an opportunity to conflate the activities of rural farmers with his own urban practice of authorship, insisting on the usefulness of representation as a form of production rather than (like the work of merchants) a scene of mere exchange.

In letters like this, Paine does something he did not do with Robert Bell: he capitalizes on the norms of an older model of cultivated civility, "making . . . a present of the thoughts in this letter" (very like the one he offered Goldsmith when he presented him with the *Excise* pamphlet and then signed his name, via an unexamined cultural commonplace, with the deferential words your "Humble servant") (2:1129). Courtly gestures like these appeal to a more traditional model of cultural production than Paine had initially embraced in his contest with Bell. They reveal Paine's ongoing investment in (some) social hierarchies, enacting a thorough reinscription of deference that allows the emergent language of the yeomen republic and the radical potential of pure democracy to rest uncritically within the residual model of patronage—the same model through which local elites would, in future years, attempt to construct a national organization of linkages among themselves (via the backwards-looking Articles of Confederation) while still retaining maximum control over the local worlds they had overseen for several generations.

Yet Paine never found buyers for this mixed story in the Philadelphia circles in which he moved. Much as he yearned for it, that world never allowed him the luxury of being the nation's representative (every)man of letters. One anecdote recalled years after the Revolution epitomizes the paradox of Paine's painfully embodied, decidedly unrepresentative position:

> Clothier-General Mease, of Philadelphia, had invited a number of gentlemen of the army to dine with him in the city, among whom were . . . several members of the Legislature. . . . All the gentlemen heartily approved of Paine's political essays, for they were to a man good Whigs, but his general bearing inspired a feeling of repugnance. . . . As you may readily suppose, the excellent wine of General Mease exhilarated the company. When returning to their lodgings Colonel Atlee observed Paine coming towards them down Market Street. "There comes 'Common Sense,'" says Atlee to the company. "D—n him," says Slough, "I'll 'Common Sense' him." As he approached the party they took the wall. Slough tripped him and threw him into the gutter. . . . You may think this act cruel and unnecessary, yet these men were some of the most eminent in the State, who staked their all on the issue of the war.[120]

Paine's abjection here at the hands of "the most eminent [men] in the State" suggests once again the corporeal limits of Enlightenment universality, which disastrously erupts here into what Michael Warner might call "the humiliating positivity of the particular."[121] While Paine's "political essays" are "heartily approved" by his Revolutionary fellows, "his general bearing" repels them, perhaps because "the good Whigs" in question have themselves momentarily been caught being bodies ("exhilarated" by "excellent wine"). But this story is no exception. In the aftermath of *Common Sense*, Paine became just such an object of derision to many Philadelphia gentlemen, who as good Whigs undoubtedly followed the attacks on his character that appeared in the local press, playing out in a public sphere that was less united in critique of a distant state than viciously partisan, divided against itself on all sorts of local issues (many of them—like price controls—breaking down along the axis of class). There, in barbs aimed straight at his most republican aspirations, Paine was knowingly dubbed "Mr. Anonymous," "Mr. Nonsense," and just plain ridiculous "Common Sense."[122] Because he had tried (and failed) to transcend the local limits of the trade that produced his pamphlet (in the sense of trying unsuccessfully to control its printing and profits, of which there finally were none), "Common Sense" the author was perpetually respecified in the months that followed as "Tom Paine," the degraded immigrant "whose general bearing inspired a feeling of repugnance"—"a shadow of an author" (in Bell's words) whose pretensions to republican honor had only proven that he was incapable "of making proper distinctions."[123]

Paine himself habitually resisted the idea that he could (as an author) be reduced to his particular person. But the phrase "Common Sense" proved in the end to be an unstable double entendre, one that neatly encapsulates the untenable material basis of the disembodied (or representative) authorship he aspired to. On one hand, "Common Sense" was meant to figure national consensus and assent—the setting aside of provincial politics for a higher, continental, anti-British union based on colonist-to-colonist consanguinity. But "Common Sense" was also a much more specific signifier as well: Paine used the phrase repeatedly both as a pseudonym in his published writings *and* as a signature in private letters. Yet as much as Paine enjoyed this "title" (tied as it was to a book rather than to feudal privilege), it was a Revolutionary oxymoron waiting to disappoint him. While he originally used the pseudonym to deflect attention away from his authorship (the preface to the second edition of *Common Sense* claims that "Who the author of this production is, is wholly unnecessary to the public" [1:4]), "Common Sense" became in the end less an expression for a peculiarly American state of mind than a nickname for Paine himself, who for the rest of his life was frequently referred to, in both private letters and public conversations, as "the celebrated author of 'Common Sense'" and, more often, simply as "Common Sense" itself. One old woman, recounting how she had met Paine at a "village fete" when she was a young woman, recalled that, knowing him only "as 'Common Sense,'" she simply "supposed that was his name."[124] The words "Common Sense" thus ironically became the narrowest, most local of signifiers, with Paine himself as their only referent.

Paine's troubled history as an author does more, however, than simply describe the failure of the public sphere as a liberatory model for one individual. It also challenges the larger idea that the institutions of the public sphere (including print culture) helped to produce a functionally disembodied and disinterested revolutionary collectivity, or national "public." If anything, the American Revolution calls forth a special problem in the history of such idealized publics. For Habermas, the public

sphere is that category of society that is separate from the state, functioning in an extralegal supervisory fashion. Revolutionary culture, however,
allowed for a foundational slippage of such categories, since those who
criticized the old, outgoing (British) state were also forming themselves
simultaneously into the vanguard of the new (American) state. However
acute Habermas's descriptions of a supervisory public sphere may be as a
description of eighteenth-century European culture, they entail a public
that maintains subjection to (and thus differentiation from) the state it
critiques. This fantasy of a pure public sphere, a world divided cleanly
between two social functions, if it can be said to describe any world at
all, cannot describe the in-between state in which organs of scrutiny, via
acts of revolution, seize power for themselves and shift from watchers
to actors in the dramas of nation formation. In the face of the intense
investments of elite colonial publics in the formation of a freestanding
American state, the notion of a distinct and nonstate-identified public
sphere wishfully calls forth and invests itself in a form of virtuous abstraction that did not actually exist in colonial political culture, except
as a kind of disclaimer whereby self-interested political actors (like Rush
and Franklin) defended themselves from accusations of corruption (and
treason) by claiming a patently fabricated form of disinterestedness. As a
model that thrills to the Enlightenment's own metanarratives about the
relationship between power and print, the public sphere merely provides
theoretical cover for the Revolutionary generation's own need to abstract
the Revolution into a unanimous, nonparticular, and populist event,
long after the fact of founding had secured its rewards for a far more
limited group.

7. THE ONCE AND FUTURE PAINE

As the French Revolution bred hysteria in the 1790s, Paine became an
object of intense European scrutiny, maligned in both the British press
and popular satirical prints. But even as early as 1783, his participation
in the Anglo-American conflict earned him the dubious honor of a partially spurious portrait, one which might stand, at the end of this chapter,
as new kind of revolutionary icon—a symbol for the same set of material disconnections and dilemmas that originally enabled the myth of
Common Sense. As British and Americans citizens awaited the Treaty of

FIGURE 2.2 James Watson. *Thomas Paine*. London: 1783. The National Portrait Gallery, Smithsonian Institution.

Paris, a London printmaker named James Watson produced a mezzotint portrait of Paine (figure 2.2.) that recirculated back through the colonial market by way of Philadelphia. Targeting patriot consumers, the print arrived in Philadelphia in early 1783, where its importer advertised it in a local newspaper along with other merchandise from the same ship.[125] Even though the print tries to resolve questions about its authenticity before they arise (describing itself as authoritatively taken "from an original portrait in the possession of Henry Laurens, Esq."), it badly mistakes its subject, misidentifying Thomas Paine as "Edward Payne Esq."[126] Since Paine would, by the early 1780s, have been fairly well known to urban Philadelphians, we can assume that the printmaker's gaffe would have been obvious to local buyers of the portrait, who were likely to have been urban devotees of Paine's Revolutionary writings (explicitly referenced in the portrait, as "Edward Payne" holds a text titled "In the Cause of Liberty and My Country[:] The Crisis [and] Common Sense"). In the end, the print's displaced production in London limits its ability to meet the expectations of its provincial audience. The printmaker's ignorance of his subject thus performs once again the telltale breakdown in imperial signification that had powered colonial resistance in the first place, making the print yet another example of corrupt imperial representation—the inability of metropolitan cultural forms to maintain commonsensical correspondences to distant provincial referents.

Yet as I have already pointed out, the same problem of displaced and partial representation that powered colonial rejection of British rule also paradoxically enabled the founding of the new American state. In describing this dilemma, I have tried to reconstruct the prenational American world, focusing on those moments when the ideal of commonsensical correspondence might be said to break down, or when it starts to do work that extends beyond the commonsensical—as when the figure of a single book comes to stand in as the indispensable agent of nation building. We have inherited in *Common Sense* a book persistently remembered as both an artifact and an abstraction rather than just a book like other books, a narrative that disarticulates the scene of production from the object of its making and in doing so privileges the federal outcome of founding over and against that process's far more splintered origins. This insistence on national outcomes has not only elevated Paine's pamphlet to the status of secular scripture and overemphasized the unilateral importance of print culture in the emerging material order of the early American republic; it has also distorted our understanding of the man who produced it and the people he was said to produce it for.

No one paid a greater price for the fantasy of "Common Sense" than Paine did. His pamphlet may be remembered in schoolbooks and museum culture as ubiquitous and foundational, but the myth of its magical agency has obscured other potential stories about Paine's role in the Revolution, and even in his own day, his contributions went largely unacknowledged and uncompensated. Paine's post–*Common Sense* career as an American man of state poses an ironic and revelatory addendum to the utopian vision of a perfectly disseminated *Common Sense*. The years just after the pamphlet's publication were marked by many public failures for the aspiring statesman. Having called the continent to metaphoric attention, Paine momentarily allowed himself to be pulled, in the later 1770s, into the vortex of provincial politics. Eric Foner writes that "the very success of the pamphlet plunged Paine into an intense involvement in the tangled and divisive politics of Philadelphia and Pennsylvania"—including disagreements about city price controls and the state constitution. In the midst of these local debates, Paine made the mistake that would permanently undo him with his early patrons in the Congress. Enraged with the deception of Silas Deane, who in 1778 used his position as an ambassador to France to profit unfairly from the Philadelphia price controls that Paine and his local allies opposed, Paine in turn used his position as secretary to the Committee on Foreign Affairs to leak confidential state correspondence implicating Deane in unethical practices. Having sacrificed national security for the good of a local (city-based) cause, the author of *Common Sense* found himself stripped of his congressional appointment and "denounced in the press as a 'stranger without either connections or apparent property in this country.'"[127]

But even if Paine had managed to avoid the minutiae of provincial politicking, it is unlikely he would have found a niche in the new government that was forming after Yorktown. As a "stranger" without "connections" or "property," Paine remained to many members of Congress an immigrant and an Englishman, never successfully assuming an American identity in post-Revolutionary culture. Nor was there much use for the continental rhetoric of *Common Sense* (or his similarly titled later manifesto, *Public Good*) in the state- and city-based debates of the 1780s. Like many Revolutionary worthies, Paine spent most of the mid-1780s soliciting support from each of the new states in recognition of his contributions to the cause, but he got little response. Pennsylvania offered him a small sum to live on, and New York, after much debate, donated a seized loyalist farm. Most of the states simply ignored his requests for support, but in Virginia the Assembly hotly debated the question of a Paine pension and finally rejected it (in spite of strong support from Washington and Jefferson) on the grounds that Paine's federal position on western lands was a threat to Virginia's local sovereignty. The very insistence upon continental priorities that had made Paine famous also, in the end, helped make him poor, obscure, and suspect in the new American nation-state, made up, as it was, of a series of sovereign microstates whose autonomy had been secured, in part, by cultural work like his. No other state voted him a pension, and in 1787, as the states finally brokered a lasting union with the new Constitution, Paine returned to Europe, where he spent the rest of the eighteenth century in France theorizing another revolution, for which he remains to this day more fondly remembered in the Old World he spent his life rejecting than in the new one he helped to create.[128]

This is not to say, however, that Paine was physically absent (or outcast) on every occasion and in every social setting for the rest of his time in Philadelphia. On the contrary, the paradox of Paine's position in these years was that he was simultaneously celebrated as the author of *Common Sense and* made socially marginal because of it. Peter Thompson has described a 1782 garden party at the home of the Chevalier de la Luzerne (then minister from France), the guest list of which included, among others, "the most eminent men" of the (new) state: George Washington, Benjamin Rush, John Dickinson, Robert Morris—and "the celebrated author of *Common Sense*," Thomas Paine. Rush later described "the assembly" as "truly republican. The company was mixed, it is true, but the mixture formed the harmony of the evening":

> Here were to be seen men conversing with each other, who appeared in all the different stages of the American War. . . . Here were to be seen statesmen and warriors from opposite ends of the continent, talking of the history of the war in their respective States. . . . Here were to be seen men who had opposed each other in the councils and parties of their country, forgetting all former resentments and exchanging civilities with one each other. . . . An Indian chief in his savage habits, and the count Rochambeau in his expensive and splendid military

uniform, talked with each other, as if they had been the subjects of the same governments, generals in the same army.[129]

Thompson uses this anecdote to illustrate how the institutions of the public sphere were becoming less heterogeneous and open at the end of the eighteenth century. His larger project is to show how public commercial spaces (which had once been "mixed" settings catering to clientele from across the social spectrum) increasingly catered to more homogenous clienteles (certain coffeehouses, for example, tending to appeal more to elites and certain taverns more to commoners). Rush's use of the word "mixed" initially seems to signal an older, more heterogeneous kind of space, but as Thompson makes clear, the private garden party (like the public garden) was very much a site of homogenous respectability (quite the opposite of a barroom). A certain kind of person, in other words, is invited to this party while certain others are left looking on (literally) through the windows, where "a crowd" gathers while "the gentlemen" on the inside fret over the possibility of a riot. The company at this party is thus "mixed" in a different (and new) way—not because it sets forth a potentially democratic (or universalizing) space in which men of all ranks can participate, but precisely because it does not. Elite men with sharp differences (Tory and patriot, northerner and southerner) are thrown together and chat amiably because their "good breeding" allows them to do so. This kind of "mixture" is, as Rush notes, very "republican," precisely because difference is present yet (in protofederalist fashion) also contained and effaced in the very act of assembly, which convivially diminishes the frictions of space, region, and party loyalty, and so balances potential chaos into "harmony."

But what of "Common Sense"? As his feud with Robert Bell suggests, Paine could not keep the two ends of this emerging institutional dialectic separate, with his coffeehouse authorship always blending embarrassingly into alehouse boasts. His behavior at the French minister's party was representative of this ambivalent position. Unlike even the "Indian chief" (who harmoniously balances Rochambeau, right down to his party dress), Paine is, according to Rush, "a solitary character" who does not "mix" well with the evening's "mixed company." While old enemies politely "reclined together against the same pillar," "conversing," "the celebrated author of 'Common Sense' retired frequently from the company to analyze his thoughts and to enjoy the repast of his own original ideas." In such moments, Paine sits awkwardly at the line of a reorganized social ladder, both inside and outside at once. While Rush's description of Paine is polite (and politic), it also serves as a gentle send-up, calling out Paine's singularity as a cluster of intellectual pretensions that finally reduce Paine and his thoughts to a "company" of one. If this is so, it is because Paine never completely identified with either side of the emerging divide that Thompson describes but instead straddled both worlds, one foot firmly on the respectable ground of republican citizenship and the other stuck in a disreputable stall at Billingsgate.

The diary of a conservative early-nineteenth-century Federalist named Grant Thorburn records one last telling anecdote about Paine's paradoxical place in post-Revolutionary America—the world he returned to, hopefully, after his storied brush with the French Terror. Arriving in Baltimore in the spring of 1802 at the invitation of President Jefferson, Paine "found letters . . . urging him onto Washington," where "a splendid dinner was got up at the White House":

> Burr, Barlow, and all of the sect of Freethinkers were present, a feast of Reason, and a flow of souls was anticipated. But O, tell it not . . . Paine entered *late,* His feet shad with a preparation of Coal-dust—and Ashes, his shirt unwashed, his beard—unshaven, and reeling like a Drunken-man, Consternation flashed from face to face, He was voted a Bore, and no Company for a Gentleman; one by one the Company went out, Leaving Paine on his Chair fast asleep; next morning a Letter was sent him by a messenger, desireing him to set out for New york, forthwith the messenger was instructed to keep him in Tow,—till they arrived at thir Point of destination.[130]

In the "feast of Reason" we call the American Enlightenment, Thomas Paine never got his just desserts. Even among other American "radicals" of the sort Thorburn can't stand—"King Thomas" (Jefferson), Burr, Barlow, and "the sect of Freethinkers"—Paine stands out as unassimilable, once again received and rejected in the most bodily terms possible: "unwashed," "unshaven," "reeling like a Drunken-man," "asleep," and finally abandoned by an elite group of freethinking "gentlemen" whose solidarity with one another is reinforced by their unanimous rejection of Paine, a common and unkempt "Bore." But that is not all. Upon arriving afterwards, "in Tow," in New York City, Paine is promptly refused residence in each of the city's "two or three respectable Hotels" while "'No Admittance for Paine' was written on the door-post and Lintals of every Reputable Boarding-house in the City." According to Thorburn, "the dirty News" of Paine's "*Intemperance* and its *Consequences*" had circulated first among "the servants" and then to "the Proprietor" of the City Hotel and then on to every other establishment in the city. "In this dilema," Paine was finally taken in by one "Wm Carver, A Journeyman-Blacksmith and a Native of the Same town in England where Paine was Born." Carver's act of solidarity is especially ironic, based as it is on a nostalgic identification with Paine's local birthplace in England rather than a more nation-based identification with the author of *Common Sense* or a class-based embrace of the author of *The Rights of Man*. Such kindness proved, furthermore, to be the exception rather than the new American rule, as Paine continued in his final years to be rejected, as he is here, not just by "gentlemen" in the White House but quite often by boarding-house "servants" as well.

It is in this last regard that James Watson's print of a smiling "Edward Payne" is especially articulate, for Watson mistakes Paine in two ways, one of which is still often in play in our renderings of a revolutionized early republic. Erroneously presenting Paine not only as an "Edward" but as a gentlemanly "Esquire," the portrait badly mistakes who Paine was in the social world in which both he and the print circulated. In using the word "Esquire," the print confers, if not the official rank of older English tradition (in which an esquire was a landed gentleman), then at least an honorary rank that would have greatly appealed to Paine, who through much of his life sought out the privileges of status from those who already had it, including, while in England, Goldsmith and Franklin and, in his early years in America, the likes of the affluent southern planter Laurens (more accurately labeled by the printmaker an "Esquire" as well). As this chapter suggests, however, such status eluded Paine, not only through his early, itinerant life in England (as corsetmaker, shopkeeper, and tax collector), but also in his most successful and highly visible years as one of the key cultural producers of Euro-American Enlightenment.

Paine told Robert Morris in 1782 that he thought of himself as one of "the founders of a new Independent World" (2:1207). But "Common Sense" (the man) will never be remembered either as an American or as a founding father, even though his pamphlet will always remain central to each new story of the Revolution. To the extent that Paine is present in mainstream narratives of U.S. nation formation, he is present as the understood but often effaced author of *Common Sense* rather than, as is often the case in labor histories, the radical author of *The Rights of Man* or *The Age of Reason*.[131] E. P. Thompson in *The Making of the English Working Class* directly ties Paine's European cultural work in the 1790s to the radical labor organizations that would proliferate throughout western Europe in the early nineteenth century. It would be appealing to claim a similarly radicalizing role for Paine's work in the American Revolution and for the Revolution itself as a scene of utopic liberation by and for every kind of social sort across every imaginable U.S. terrain. But we would do so with difficulty. The making of discernible working class populations was decades removed from the mixed modes of preindustrial production that made the Revolution possible and that are in fact epitomized in the localized drift from town to town, world to world, of *Common Sense* (the thing). This projection, furthermore, of a more foundational (yet still radical) American Paine must always find some way to manage the troubling problem of his mixed politics—including the Hamiltonian economic policies he persistently favored to the end of his life, which led him to support, among other things, a national bank over and against the claims of impoverished local debtors. When organized working-class radicalism finally did emerge in the United States, it was not a function of a radicalized Enlightenment but an industrially motivated phenomenon that emerged well after the Revolution. And when it did gain ground, it was with more limited momentum than it found in Europe, doing so not because of Paine's direct involvement in its Americanized version but in the wake of his conspicuous post-Revolutionary absence. By claiming Paine as the founding father of a radical yet abstract American crowd, we merely appropriate him in much the same way that populist histories have appropriated his book. And to do so is to invest the Revolution after the fact with leveling goals in which its key engineers were never really invested. As Grant Thorburn knew, the author of *Common Sense* was "no Company for a Gentleman," and the American Revolution was in many respects more of a gentleman's club than a scene of social "upheaval" (or Paris Commune).[132]

This is not to say that there were no socially progressive moments in the Revolution or that everyday people did not participate in the Revolution and drive it forward as a material event. They did: in tavern debates, battles, boycotts, crowd actions, and any number of other ways. But the participation of lower social tiers was less organized and its impact less ongoing on the national level than that of elites, and its forms did not revolve merely or primarily around books, letters, and manuscripts, as it so often did for highly mobile founding elites. The American Revolution was in this sense very much a "mixed" social event, one part gentleman's club and one part riot, but Paine's role as an author, instead of seamlessly joining these two, finally made him unable to inhabit either side of this growing split—rather like his experience at the French minister's garden party, where he sat poised between a host of stuffy republican luminaries and a crowd of riotous lookers-on. Had Paine identified more readily upward, he might have become, like Franklin, the token self-made man circulating within the upper tiers of American political life; had he identified only downward, he would probably have been drawn more quickly into local (class-based) disputes and would not have gone continental in *Common Sense*. But authorship was never an either/or proposition for Paine, who stood instead on the wishful middle ground of the Gramscian "would-be" (or wannabe), a hybrid class position that was both self-effacing and self-aggrandizing, abstracted and embodied, disinterested and yet desiring. Paine stood at the ambivalent juncture of each of these things, thinking he could close the gap, through acts of authorship, between the populist and the elite and so usher in a new era in human history. In the end, however, his pamphlet became merely another chapter in the long social process of class coverture, a bourgeois fiction just powerful enough to hide the hyphen in a would-be populist revolution.

This unwillingness to choose sides would recur later in life when Paine refused to settle definitively on a local (national) identity, seeking instead a place in a translocal, and transnational, republic of letters. This cosmopolitan refusal to be fixed in space eventually led to accusations that Paine was a literary mercenary—a pen for hire who would write anything for any cause. The plaintive caption of one such satire—"Who Wants Me?"—is an apt epitaph for the would-be author whose aspirations to founding fatherhood were never ultimately fulfilled. In the end, the particularities of Paine's subject position, set against the pretensions to universal eloquence so evident in his writing, help explain both his book's notoriety and his own effacement. Though Paine remained more committed than most to the cosmopolitan networks that empire had produced and that he seemed to believe that nationalist revolutions would (more locally and hence more justly) sustain, his tendency to prioritize the whole over the part, the universal over the particular, was his undoing in history. Identifying finally as a citizen of the world rather than a citizen of someplace more particular, Paine's person failed, in short, to circulate the way a book—or a theory of a book—was thought to circulate: he was never able to maintain the perfectly reciprocal relation between embodiment and universal diffusion that the myth of the bestseller allows. In the end, his expansive cultural commitments did more than simply fail to make him the opposite of provincial; they actually made him illegible within every local community he tried to inhabit—a would-be founder who is conspicuously absent in early national history, like so many of the other non-esquires for whom his own investment in Enlightenment abstraction would not allow him to stand in particular.

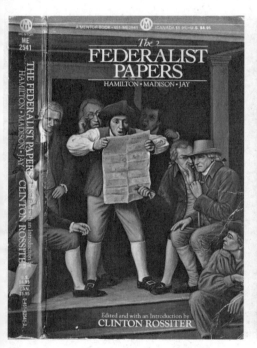

FIGURE 3.1A (LEFT)   *The Federalist Papers.* New York: New American Library, 1961. Book cover. Courtesy of the Penguin Group.
FIGURE 3.1B (RIGHT)   Richard Caton Woodville. *War News from Mexico.* 1848. Oil painting. Private collection.

3. THE REPUBLIC IN PRINT
RATIFICATION AS MATERIAL TEXT, 1787–1788

The new Constitution! The new Constitution! is the general cry this way. Much paper is spoiled on the subject, and many essays are written which perhaps are not read by either side.
—Henry Knox to John Sullivan, 1788

1. THE PURLOINED NEWSPAPER AND THE TEXT-BASED NATION

In 1961, the New American Library published a cheap paperback edition of *The Federalist Papers*, which remained unchanged, inside and out, for roughly forty years, until its cover was redesigned with an American flag. The image on the older cover (shown in figure 3.1a) nevertheless remains familiar, for this is the "classic" edition used for several decades to teach undergraduates, law students, graduate students, and, appropriately, the American people at large (that now undifferentiated mass of modern North American consumers) about the Constitution's history and meaning. Even more familiar than this particular edition of *The Federalist*, however, is the kind of image portrayed. Taking the scene of constitutional ratification as its topic, the image conjures several eighteenth-century men avidly discussing the contents of a newspaper. The scene thus makes several interconnected claims, suggesting a bustling eighteenth-century public sphere peopled by private citizens rather than professional politicians and casting the scene of the founding as one of participatory and even democratic (if gendered) debate, a debate that is, in turn, grounded in the circulation of a printed text. Placed on the front of a widely selling mass-market paperback, this image sold for decades something that the American public has been consuming for centuries: a cultural truism linking modern citizenship to a printed text. Few images could be more legible within the larger grammar of modern nationalisms in which this book has so routinely circulated.

The master trope organizing this image is an old one, but so is the image itself. Though the book cover does not cite its source, it craftily impersonates a historically specific image not of the eighteenth but of the nineteenth century: Richard Caton Woodville's well-known local color painting *War News from Mexico* (1848) (shown in figure 3.1b). Woodville's canvas is one in a long series of representational attempts of the late 1840s and 1850s that seek to sustain the troubled illusion of union by absorbing, rather than foregrounding, local difference. In Woodville's federalist iconography, for example, a group of men gathers to read "War News from Mexico" on the porch of "The American Hotel," whose trademark is the same nationalist symbol that appears today on the one-dollar bill: the American bald eagle, carrying in its beak a banner that reads *E pluribus unum*. The neoclassical design of the porch—a pediment atop four simple pillars—recalls the pyramidal shape of federalism imagined by the founders in 1787. Under this federalized roof, the scene of reading is remarkably and appropriately nonspecific—strikingly so, given that the debate at its center focuses not just on a specific geographic territory (Polk's Mexican conquest), but also on the specific geographic argument that would prove permanently sectionalizing for the young United States, dividing the union in a long contest over the extension of slavery into the American Southwest and finally culminating thirteen years later in civil war. Given this context, Woodville's rendering of the scene seems willfully opaque. The most we can know is that this is a small town: it does not have a separate post office but one that shares space in a hotel; the sign for the post office as well as several advertisements tacked to the wall behind the men are handwritten (or painted) rather than printed, perhaps suggesting that the town lacks a working press and imports its printed goods from elsewhere. From there, however, Woodville's geographic signifiers are mixed, gesturing to no place, no state, and no section in particular. The black workman sitting at the foot of the porch suggests a racially hierarchized slave economy, but the plaid pants, flowing cravats, silk hats, and patent leather shoes of the reading men suggest a northern industrial economy. Since the scene could plausibly be imagined as either a northern or a southern one, the painting implies that under the federal roof, North, South, and the expanding West are or can be one.

To Woodville's conflation of regions, the *Federalist* paperback adds a new wrinkle: a conflation of time-frames, repackaging Woodville's dated antebellum scene as an early national one meant to depict the ratification debates of 1787–88. This purloined image, and the amnesia it enacts, is connected to the story of U.S. origins that the book's insides (as well as its outside) will tell. For one thing, it suggests that American reading practices are not fundamentally different from one historical moment to the next, that from 1787 to 1848 little more changed than hats and socks. Evoking national life as a scene populated by interchangeable mannequins, the image sutures not just two but several historical moments into one: the figure at the center of the scene, wearing a pair of old-fashioned knee britches and a tricornered hat, plays the part of the mobile messenger—a folk reference to Paul Revere and his midnight ride around the perimeters of Concord. The Revolution is thus conflated with the scene of 1780s Constitutional debate, in a picture that cribs its source material from a painting of the 1840s—all to sell a book to audiences in the late twentieth century. In this way, the book establishes, from the outside in, the illusive sense of perpetuity on which nations and constitutions are founded. The practice of making, buying, and displaying industrial goods—from coats, cravats, and patent leather shoes to newspapers and of course mass market paperbacks—"looms" in this image "out of an immemorial past," without discernible beginning or end.[1]

At the center of this ahistorical claim lies an unaltered newspaper. Readers of Woodville's painting have noted the way that the newspaper visually organizes the scene, its shape echoed in numerous other rectangles placed throughout the painting, determining the shape both of the porch on which these debaters sit and the larger staged set (the framed painting) in which they act out the drama of literate citizenship.[2] While the book cover makes a number of crucial editorial interventions in order to make the scene look more homogenous to its twentieth-century readers (in particular, the racial lightening of the black figure in the foreground and the erasure of both the child in the foreground and the woman at the right margin), the newspaper is left utterly intact—right down to the shape and number of printed columns and even a graphic image in one column that all come directly from Woodville's painting. It is the newspaper, then, more than any other object, that seamlessly links each moment evoked here, from 1776 and 1787 to 1848 to today.

In collapsing two newspapers into one, this image fabricates an implausible claim to print-sameness. But as similar as they look here, these two newspapers would necessarily have been quite different objects in the worlds in which they circulated. A 1780s newspaper organized the world around it, from labor to audience, in different ways than an 1840s newspaper eventually would, in large part because the material world around that 1780s newspaper had not yet been reorganized by the machines, canals, turnpikes, trains, and telegraphs that would make both the war with Mexico and timely news of that war possible just sixty years later. Woodville's newspaper was a product of advanced and still advancing technology. It was quite possibly made on high-speed cylinders with massproduced inks, and on paper that itself may have been made in a factory on a high-speed machine; it may have cost as little as a penny, and because it was so inexpensive, its manufacturer probably had to make many thousands like it to turn a profit, and he probably had to give over a significant amount of space on each page to advertisements. Finally, because a large number of copies were printed, some of them were probably carried on a steamboat or train from the factory or shop that manufactured them—maybe the same steamboats and trains that carried flowing cravats and silk top hats to eager cross-regional consumers in the same painting. This is of course all conjectural (printing in the late 1840s remained in many places quite localized), but even so, it is possible and even probable that the newspaper depicted in Woodville's painting was mass produced and reached something approaching what antebellum writers had come to call the "multitude"—that truly massed reading public that is both serviced and produced by the antebellum culture industry. More important, it is almost certain that the news in this newspaper was, thanks to the telegraph, fairly reliable, uniform, and recent.[3]

But in 1787 (when *The Federalist Papers* were first serialized), newspapers were made and used in entirely different ways. Each page of a newspaper was produced manually on a hand press by an individual printer's apprentices in an artisanally organized shop. The division of labor and heavy capital investment that would help make cheap newspapers possible just sixty years later was perhaps unevenly emerging in the printing trade at this point, but the printing technology of the 1780s was literally medieval, in that the wooden hand press being used was the same machine that had been used since Gutenberg. As for paper, the printer might have purchased rag-based paper stock from one of the numerous paper mills that were popping up along the coast, but more than likely even this degree of division of labor had not yet occurred, and the printer himself probably played a part in collecting rags in his local community to be recycled into paper. The actual shape of the newspaper in Woodville's painting—that familiar half broadsheet that we see today—was determined and made uniform by the machine that made it, but this was not necessarily true in the eighteenth century, and anyone who has spent time in an archive thumbing through eighteenth-century newspapers knows that they came in different shapes and sizes—usually smaller than Woodville's broadsheet, and with only woodcuts for graphics.[4]

The content of each newspaper would also have been different. The *Federalist* paperback suggests a local community reading news about the progress of ratification or perhaps eagerly checking out the latest installment of Publius's serialized essays. But news in 1787 was not the same thing as news in 1848. Historians have long known that eighteenth-century American newspapers were only inconsistently able to link U.S. communities together via domestic news networks. As Allan Pred has demonstrated, these early American newspapers devoted most of their space (even after the Revolution) to international rather than domestic news. Before 1776, most domestic news had been received, circularly, through networks that reached not from colony to colony but back through the metropole, with Boston papers, for example, reprinting Virginia news that had been circuitously received from London papers. But even as late as 1794, Pred suggests that "only a few issues of one major Philadelphia paper had more column space allocated to American news than to European news." Foreign news was simply easier to get on the North American coast than was news from more disparate and scattered American communities. According to Pred, domestic news did not gain much cultural currency until the War of 1812 cut off foreign trade and thus prompted "American communications . . . to develop into a well-integrated system."[5]

The late 1780s are of course a special case, and the ratification crisis is even more special. It is safe to assume that the Federal Convention had given every state a reason to care, at least momentarily, about what every other state was doing and thinking.[6] There was, however, an inarguably uneven quality to the circulation of such information. In order for news of any kind—from gossip to newspapers—to migrate from one state or city to another, one of several specific types of embodied transmission had to occur. An actual person had to bring news orally or send it in handwritten or printed form; essays like *The Federalist* had to be carried either by postal riders or by private citizens carrying items for friends or for hire. Newspapers like the one depicted on the cover of *The Federalist* tended to be locally produced and locally consumed. Those that did circulate translocally were transmitted along the post road by riders who carried either entire papers or partial clippings from printer to printer, post office to post office. In times of crisis, like that of ratification, private citizens who could afford to send entire newspapers did in fact do so, but they were not always sending them to printers in their home constituencies so much as to political contacts or close friends. Federal officeholders were lucky in this respect: their postage was franked—paid from the public coffers—and it was common for members of Congress to send complete copies of newspapers back to their home constituencies, a practice that, as we shall see, has ramifications for how *The Federalist* was disseminated. Before 1792, however (when Congress passed a bill that allowed whole newspapers to be sent through the post as cheaply as letters), the high cost of sending entire newspapers was prohibitive for nearly everyone except such officials. As Pred notes, printers often relied on each other to share knowledge via the partial and partializing practice of clipping (an early version of the exchange system), passing printed items along piecemeal and then reprinting (some of) them in an endless process of inclusion and exclusion that made the circulation of information not only nonuniversal but highly uneven and unpredictable.[7]

This chapter asks what we can learn by looking at *The Federalist* in print and, in turn, by reconsidering federalism itself as it circulated through the various print cultures of the early extended republic. While the federalist invention of the extended republic has been written about at length, I engage the problem of an emerging federalist space in two novel ways. First, I want to suggest how discussions *about* the extended republic traveled materially *across* extended spaces. Such discussions, though national in scope, were necessarily local in origin and often stayed that way as they circulated through any number of texts or were passed, viva voce, from person to person, in conversation and gossip. Second, I will use this wide array of texts and their real-world travels to recall the scattered scene of ratification (or what we might call ratification-in-space), treating that scene less as a political process than as a material one, crucially bound by the limits of the time and places in which it was produced. Though too rarely thought of in this way, ratification is the complicated mise-en-scène of U.S. founding: a plurality of historical sites filled with readers, printers, authors, newspapers, pamphlets, and political partisans, all of which only intermittently and imperfectly overlapped with one another. It is this material scene (rather than the discourse of antifederalism) that offers the real countertext to the monolithic singularity of early national union.

I begin by focusing on *The Federalist*, that now iconic defense of the Constitution coauthored (under the pen name "Publius") by John Jay, Alexander Hamilton, and James Madison in the months leading up to the New York Ratifying Convention. Like Paine before him, Publius offers himself as an exemplary spokesman for the early national print public sphere, and like Paine, he uses his position in print to posit both a viable union and a mass audience, one that is often presumed, over the course of *The Federalist*'s eighty-five papers, to be already integrated and already whole. As with *Common Sense*, however, the history of *The Federalist*'s production and dissemination necessarily denies its own central premise: union. Indeed, *The Federalist*'s piecemeal dissemination within the everyday circuits of eighteenth-century print culture reveals a vast gap between the print public sphere we routinely invoke in critical discourse and the actual territorial spaces in which textual production, dissemination, and reception materially unfolded. It is only by considering the field of ratification in its entirety (as a series of semiconnected debates circulating across a large, unintegrated field of exchange) that a new reading of *The Federalist* can emerge to stand alongside the older, more iconic one we have inherited from its makers. While I use *The Federalist*, then, as one point of departure, my real object is to describe the vast archive of ratification writ large. This materialist context is not merely a tableau for an old story—a backdrop for the unfolding of an inevitable historical outcome—but serves instead as the contingent but indispensable condition for constitutional consolidation.

I use the word "indispensable" because the facts of this setting—its materiality—were never merely incidental; indeed, the limited material structures (or infrastructure) within which printed debate about ratification circulated ultimately enabled consensus by producing inevitable (and largely agentless) loopholes—gaps in communication from site to site and state to state that finally proved crucial to ratification's success. Not only will I argue here that the process of ratification unfolded unevenly across large spaces that were only imperfectly connected via print; I will argue that consensus and consolidation could have succeeded *only* under such scattered conditions. Federalism succeeds, in other words, not in spite of early American localism but *because* of it—a fact illustrated by the process of ratification itself as it proliferated (in print and in speech) across that wide variety of imperfectly connected, highly pluralized political cultures we call "states."

This is not how the story of ratification is usually remembered. We usually think of the federal Constitution (and the print culture that diffused it across the nation) as a magical antidote, a "miracle" made at Philadelphia that saved the Revolutionary experiment from a bonfire of local prejudices, creating a unified nation out of a chaotic variety of self-interested parts. In this narrative, ratification as a process finally produced a definitive national totality, saving the parts of the union from political "dismemberment" (or worse) and doing so unanimously, after an extended period of *national* public debate made possible, in large part, by a print public sphere that is imagined as coextensive with the nation-space in question (yet somehow separate from the state it wants—or does not want—to form). Such a figment—a coherent, connected, self-intelligible, and autonomous public sphere—was, no doubt, a necessary phantom of the ratification process (legitimating its outcome both in 1787 and for future generations). As I argue here, however, the federalists' attempts to construct such a monolithic public succeeded only because one did not yet exist to resist such a representation. Ratification's own labyrinthine archive makes it clear that the emerging federal state was imagined and discussed in the face of profound material disconnections amongst the different parts of the union, gaps in time and space that eighteenth-century print culture did not, because it could not, overcome. There never was, in other words, a truly national discussion of what a ratified Constitution would mean for everyone involved—even if today we routinely imagine *The Federalist* to stand in for such a discussion. On the contrary, it is precisely the incomplete and fractured underside of early American communication that made possible the fiction of bounded, seamless collectivity that has come to be called the federal state.

2. The Problem with Publius: Republican Print Ideology and the Case of *The Federalist*

It would be hard to overstate the adulation that *The Federalist* has received in American culture in the centuries since ratification. Thomas Jefferson, urging the University of Virginia to adopt the essays as required reading in 1825, hailed it as an American classic, "an authority to which appeal is habitually made by all, and rarely declined or denied by any."[8] Clinton Rossiter, writing an introduction to *The Federalist* a century and a half later, spoke for many latter-day federalists when he essentially agreed: "It would not be stretching the truth more than a few inches to say that *The Federalist* stands third only to the Declaration of Independence and the Constitution itself among all the sacred writings of American political history. It has a quality of legitimacy, of authority and authenticity, that gives it the high status of a public document."[9] What was true in 1822 and 1961 is still true today: *The Federalist*'s hermeneutic credentials are unquestioned in the United States, extending even to the most learned and powerful circles. *The Federalist* has been cited repeatedly, for example, in Supreme Court briefings and rulings, by plaintiffs, defendants, and even the justices themselves, who frequently consult Publius to defend the logic of their arguments and decisions. Publius's opinions on constitutional matters are, like print itself, a formidable cultural authority by now.[10]

This triple conflation—which links the cultural authority of the Constitution, *The Federalist*, and print culture more generally—is not entirely rhetorical, nor is it entirely my own. Instead, it references an influential and important set of arguments made by Michael Warner in his account of "republican print ideology," understood as the widespread early national investment in print and printedness, which Warner rightly reads as an ideological solution to the ongoing problems of localism and licentious self-interest that were so troubling to the founding generation. In *Letters of the Republic*, Warner argues that it was the printedness of the Constitution that allowed American consensus to be achieved in perpetuity. As Warner notes, revolutionary ideology insisted that the legality of state institutions must derive not from embodied persons but from "the people" en masse, abstractly conceived. "For this reason it was of utmost importance that the legal-political order be constituted not just by a written text"—since written texts are supposedly associated with particular authors—"but by a printed one. . . . The Constitution's printedness allows it to emanate from no one in particular, and thus from the people" (106, 108). As a vivid figure for this procedure, Warner cites the same passage from Thomas Paine that I discussed in chapter 2—the moment when Paine fantasizes a postmonarchical rite whereby the "crown of law" might be shattered and fantastically diffused among the people in what Warner suggests will be printed form.

Warner makes two distinct points about print's usefulness here, both

of which depend on its perceived generality. The first involves its ability
to be diffused—scattered to the four corners of the kingdom like Paine's
shattered crown—and the second involves its potential transcendence,
its ability to kick free from association with particular persons—like bad
kings, would-be tyrants, or (in the language of federalist anxiety) licentious characters—and to become instead the generalized property of the
people as a whole. Having focused in this way on print's generalized and
generalizable potential, it takes only a short leap to identify the authority (in print) of the Constitution with the authority (in print) of Publius;
thus, the same print ideology that legitimates the Constitution's constitu-
tionality can "also be seen animating the ratification debates, especially
in the aggressive print campaign of the 'Publius' who stands forth in the
Federalist papers" (109). Indeed, "the new paradigm [of impersonality in
print] . . . finds its exemplary 'spokesman' . . . [in] 'Publius' . . . [whose]
very identity . . . dramatizes the conditions of authority in representational polity, for Publius—like the People, in 'We the People'—is emphatically a pen name, a composite voice made articulable only in his
written pseudonymity. Throughout the ratification debate he was lauded
and attacked only as 'Publius' because he was not known by any other
name." Citing Publius's diffusion "in a barrage of print"—he appeared
"in four newspapers in New York and another in Virginia, with occa-
sional appearances elsewhere to boot"—Warner concludes that "Publius
speaks in the utmost generality of print, denying in his very existence the
mediation of particular persons" (113).

Warner never claims to do more in this argument than describe a historically specific ideology of the late eighteenth century. Nevertheless, his
much-cited arguments have produced a far more hegemonic narrative
about the workings of early American print culture. This is partly because
Letters of the Republic tends to explore and explicate the inner logic of the
ideology it unpacks, describing republican print ideology from the inside
out and rarely attending to the ruptures and contradictions effected by its
production and deployment in material space or to its numerous rivals
within that space. This focus on the ideological insides of one particular discourse poses several problems for our reading of ratification across
space. First: a problem of medium. Warner's model grants an overwhelming centrality to printedness over and against other forms of affiliation
that were still very much competitors to print and its ideologies at this
moment—forms like handwritten letters, oratory, privately circulated
manuscripts, public debate, and private conversations. As critics like Jay

Fliegelman, Christopher Grasso, Sandra Gustafson, Christopher Looby, David Shields, and others have shown, print culture did not dominate these other forms but was embedded within them.[11] The meanings of printedness were thus continually recircuited through a complex system of representational production that Warner's print-centered model obscures. Second: a problem of materiality. Warner suggests that print enables an almost total denial of "the mediation of particular persons." But, as my account of the 1780s newspaper suggests, printing in the 1780s was still very often a matter of personal relations. Early national books, newspapers, and magazines were not yet being made in factories by faceless workers toiling in separate rooms but in small, artisanally organized shops that were themselves part of a wider culture still organized around deferential values and personal relationships (as opposed to the mass, and cash, transactions that would organize American literary culture just fifty years later). Like other forms of preindustrial production, print often leads back to actual bodies in the eighteenth century—whether those bodies belong to the master printers who run shops, the journeymen and apprentices who work in them, or the authors who are often known to the printers who print their writings and in many cases to the audiences who read them (even when those writings are signed with pseudonyms). Finally: a problem of reception. The very phrase "republican print ideology" evokes the discourse that surrounds print culture as if it were a singular and transcendent force doing uniform cultural work for different early national populations. This assumes either the utility of an urban metonymy (since print shops were primarily urban) or a uniformity of reception across an already coherent and coherently linked North American setting. But print did not have the same meanings on the Kentucky frontier or in the Georgia backcountry that it had in the densely literate and more economically integrated villages of Massachusetts, nor could it mean the same thing for the Philadelphia merchant and the Pittsburgh farmer. Although *Letters of the Republic* begins with geography (citing the different cultures of the New England, middle, and southern colonies), it is less interested finally in the local deployment of republican print ideology than in the paradigm itself, the basic structure of an ideology that is understood to operate nationally, constitutionally—in short, foundationally.

It is true that, when imagined abstractly (or in its most ideally fungible—or exploitable—form), print did indeed promise early American authors and readers a compelling solution to certain intractable problems in emerging American political economy—including, as Warner points out, the pressing need to legitimate the U.S. Constitution as the work of the people (as opposed to the platform of an interested elite). But no ideology, however hegemonic, functions seamlessly when circulated back through the microspaces of everyday life. Indeed, "circulation" is the first term we might put forward to complicate this paradigm. While eighteenth-century Anglo-American print culture was caught up in a process of infinite expansion (infinite, that is, in that it continues to this day), the development of that ever-expanding network of readers, writers, and publishers was slow and uneven. This unevenness is amply indexed throughout the early national archive, which is strewn with the wreckage of imperfect or aborted communications—lost (and crossed) letters, suspended newspapers, failed magazines, and books that went unbought and unread. Such failures were produced by a complex interaction between material forces and ideological ones, but the interaction itself produced new and unexpected outcomes—with none more consequential, to the future of the nation, than those that occurred at the moment of ratification.

The national debates surrounding the Constitution were marked from the start by lags in communication and failures of dissemination that threatened to divide the public from itself at the very moment the federalists were trying to imagine themselves (and "the people") as a unified and connected whole. While pamphlets like *The Federalist* may have aspired to conditions of disinterested generality, they did so within the restrictive material contexts of early American print culture—a phrase meant to denote the many specific material publishing practices that form the larger subject of this book. These practices include but are not reducible to the actual writing of pages by authors; the physical production of types, ink, and paper; the manual presswork performed by journeymen and apprentices; the always exhausting and incomplete work of manually disseminating printed objects by hand, foot, boat, cart, and horse; and of course the reception of such objects by savvy audiences who may or may not have actually believed everything inside of them (or even read them at all). These are the workings not of print or printedness per se, but of print *culture* as it slowly developed its own concrete practices on the ground, filtering the ideological from inside the domain of the material—and back again.

The Federalist itself makes these points clear, but only if we view it as a material object produced (manually, by discernible human agents) within a particular space and time. One of the great of ironies of *The*

Federalist is that it has its origins in the contracted world of state politics. Organized by Alexander Hamilton in 1787, the series originally took shape within a circle of local political rivalries among a small group of men who knew each other intimately. This local origin is permanently inscribed in its newspaper form, which initially paired the headline "The Federalist" with an opening line addressed "To the People of the State of New-York." This pairing was meant to suggest that a local citizen can and should be "federal" or "federalist" as well. But the early newspaper printings also remind us of something that latter-day Publiophiles often forget: that these essays were primarily written to sway voters in New York State. While Publius dubs himself "The Federalist" and then projects throughout his papers the fantasy of a federal public, the essay series was mounted against a specific number of antifederalist writings written and published locally in Manhattan by someone Hamilton personally knew and disliked—the antifederalist New York governor, George Clinton. Indeed, Hamilton so disliked and distrusted Clinton that when he first returned to New York City from the Federal Convention, he wrote under the pen name Caesar a series of papers that specifically attacked Clinton. Those papers, however, were so badly received—not only were they attacked for what they said, but Hamilton was singled out as the obvious author hiding behind a tyrannical pseudonym—that Hamilton abandoned the series. The next time he appeared in print, he had become Publius.[12]

But if Hamilton invented the figure of Publius in the context of a local feud, he also saw national potential for him. He and John Jay went out of their way to look for partners for the writing venture who were in New York City representing other regions—men like William Duer, who was from upstate New York; Rufus King, from Massachusetts; and of course Madison, from Virginia. Even Hamilton (a New Yorker), was well connected in other states, maintaining regular correspondences with powerful men throughout the union. If Hamilton hoped to see *The Federalist* spread to other states, he had several factors in his favor. For one thing, no newspapers circulated more consistently throughout the other states than New York City's: the port of New York was considered the most reliable source of the most coveted kind of news—foreign events. In addition, New York was the seat of government in 1787 and 1788, with prominent delegates from all over the country on hand in New York to read the local newspapers in which the early *Federalist* was daily appearing. These men could easily have sent Publius home in the mails (as members of Congress, their postage was free), or they could have carried numbers back with them and had them reprinted in their home constituencies when they returned to attend local ratifying conventions, as many of them did.

As Elaine Crane has instructed us, however, Publius saw little press time in the provinces.[13] Though most printers likely saw some part of the series in the recirculated New York newspapers that were sporadically exchanged up and down the postal route, few spontaneously picked up the series for their own newspapers. Later in life, Madison suggested that the essays autocirculated through other regions: "It being found that they were republished in other States and were making a diffusive impression in favor of the Constitution, [their] limited character [i.e., the appeal to New York] was laid aside."[14] But Madison's telltale use of the passive voice marks a conspicuous, because actual, absence; the agent of this republication is syntactically repressed because there was no agent. There did not need to be one, because *The Federalist* was not widely republished. To the degree that the essays did circulate outside New York, that circulation can be traced to the usual suspects: the authors themselves. Correspondence from both Hamilton and Madison amply illustrates their attempts to disseminate the series across regions to an elite core of federalist supporters who were urged to have the essays republished or to share them with other federalists as a debating manual in preparation for various state ratifying conventions. Hamilton personally sent copies of the earliest newspaper installments to Benjamin Rush in Philadelphia and George Washington in Virginia, urging both to use their influence to get the essays reprinted in local papers. Madison likewise circulated the papers to friends in Philadelphia and Virginia, urging their dissemination.[15] Their efforts, however, met with only modest success. Few numbers of *The Federalist* appeared in print elsewhere, and Hamilton's fantasy of a cross-regional cult of Publius petered out beyond the outskirts of New York State.

New York City, however, was a different story. While neither Hamilton nor Madison could engineer a wide-scale geographical diffusion for the essays, Hamilton used his local influence to saturate Manhattan with Publius appearances between October 1787 and August 1788. In a curious innovation that looks a little bit like *Common Sense* in reverse (in that it explicitly targeted a contracted rather than a protracted audience), Hamilton blanketed Manhattan with Publius's eighty-five essays by arranging to have the same essays published repeatedly and simultaneously in different New York City papers. The first number of *The Federalist*, for instance, appeared not just in one New York paper but in three, and all eighty-five essays appeared in more than one New York newspaper—sometimes in as many as four, sometimes in as few as two, but never in just one. Publius's ubiquity—and his incredible prolixity—was so obnoxious to some New Yorkers that on January 1, 1788, twenty-seven subscribers wrote to the printer of the *New-York Journal* begging him to discontinue the series, arguing that Publius's prominence in every major city paper amounted to "a new mode of abridging the liberty of the press."[16] The printer, Thomas Greenleaf, complied soon after by dropping the series from his pages, but Hamilton countered by arranging for another paper, the *New-York Packet*, to pick up the series. The newspaper publication of *The Federalist* was thus, at the outset, an intensely local spectacle, targeting the southern tip of the tiny island of Manhattan. Publius's essays appeared 322 times in print between October 1787 and August 1788, but 279 of these were in New York State, and an amazing 238 comprise merely the Manhattan printings. Outside of New York State, Publius made a total of only forty-three appearances in twelve newspapers in only five other states. If this sounds like a lot, we should remember that there were (according to Crane) eighty-nine newspapers in the United States in these years—only twelve of which outside of New York State picked up any of Publius's columns, with most printing only a few numbers. Not only were Publius's reprintings sparse, they were not particularly well spread out either, with only seven numbers reprinted south of Philadelphia, and all of these appearing in Virginia, where coauthor James Madison, a Virginian, sent many copies.[17]

The conditions of *The Federalist*'s original newspaper publication eloquently refute Warner's construction of Publius as the spokesman of republican print ideology. That model reinscribes the fantasy of a coherent and successfully generalized Publius (he appears, Warner tells us, in "a barrage" of print). In doing so, it does the work of proleptically *pre-remembering* the unified state that eventually emerged while at the same time retroactively forgetting the scattered political and print cultures that allowed that state to emerge. It thus works to reify the fiction of an already federal union that Publius and other federalists were peddling in 1787, allowing us latter-day nationals to misread the rhetorical for the already empirical that it would one day be.

The same conditions that made the extended republic seem so implausible to antifederalists in 1787 also make anything approaching a uniform national public equally improbable. Though it sounds (retrospectively) plausible, it does not really make sense to say that eighteenth-century subjects were constitutionally interpellated in 1787 by reading pamphlets like *The Federalist* and that this is how we became a nation—through the mechanism of national debate that print made possible. Too many people did not read or did not have access to the same texts or, in some regions, to very many texts at all, and far too many people mistrusted printed accounts. We might argue instead that Publius at least does the work of constructing the public he does reach, that he speaks to (and probably already for) a quite specific constituency, and in doing so he at least hails those (elite) readers as national subjects. But this story in itself would not account for the awesome and geographically dispersed power of nationalist sentiment as it developed in the federal and postfederal period. More problematically, it gives Publius far too much credit, even within the contracted circles of his own target audience. But there is perhaps a third, more antifederalist alternative. What if there were too many Publiuses to count—and not all of them met or even knew about each other? Conceived of in this way, ratification emerges as a material field of immense but uneven exchange, in which multiple authors reached multiple publics, each one necessarily narrower than the whole of the union and many overlapping with one another, but none cohering in the more predictable ways that would characterize mass-market exchange in decades to come. This would, however, mean admitting that ratification was never materially commensurate with the nation it managed to call forth, but was instead a contingent, disconnected, and above all partial process.

This is in fact what ratification looked like. It was, as Michael Allen Gillespie and Michael Lienesch have argued, "a complex and convoluted process," and its complexities extend not just to the ideological tangle of ideas that continue to preoccupy us, but to the material circulation of those ideas.[18] Debate for and against the Constitution was decentralized and unorganized; while some attempts were made to coordinate campaigns in different states, debate was never carried out on a national level—in the sense that every part of the union did not have access to arguments being made in every other part of the union. The fantastic device that makes *The Federalist* so memorable is that it projects the fiction of a far wider public, one that does not yet exist in fact but that Publius can posit in language because it is the province of representation (both political and linguistic) to project parts as if they were wholes. *The Fed-*

eralist and its audience have thus, through a combined trick of language and history, come to seem representative. But in fact these papers speak for only one of the innumerable local publics that made up the early national world. This is the genius and the ingenuity of federalism—the fact that the federalists were able to overcome and even exploit the absence of federal infrastructure in order to create something that, in future years, would forever *look* federal. But this is not a fiction we should be repeating in our accounts of early national printing and reading practices. In fact, it is precisely the gap between the local practices of print production and dissemination (on one hand) and the language of federal inevitability (on the other) that we need to keep in view when we try to get at just what constituted the fantasy of the early federal public sphere.

3. PUBLIUS THE OBSCURE: READING *THE FEDERALIST*

Its heterogeneous authorship and original reception history aside, most people will insist that *The Federalist* makes sense, and they will insist on this whether they have read the eighty-five essays or not. Publius's reputation for rationality, for clear, composed, well-reasoned, and candid debate, often precedes many readers' actual experience of reading his sentences. But if we revere *The Federalist*, we revere it for a reason: because it tells us to. Hamilton built a fantasy of structural rationality into the very making of *The Federalist*. It was methodically mapped out for its readers in its early numbers: twenty-five essays were promised, each expected to cover a predictable set of issues and all to be published in a predictable sequence. One newspaper promised an orderly publication schedule early on: "In order that the whole subject of these Papers may be as soon as possible laid before the Public, it is proposed to publish them four times a week, on Tuesday in the *New-York Packet*, on Wednesday and on Thursday in the *Daily Advertiser*."[19] The argumentative arrangement of the finished product, furthermore, self-consciously mirrors the structure of the Constitution itself (frequently admired for its geometrical precision). Promising to give his readers "a survey" of the Constitution's "interior structure" (165), Publius follows that document whenever possible (rather than engaging with this or that local antifederalist attack and allowing the timeliness of such debates to control the rhythm and order of his text). In this way, Publius projects a systemic and highly organized treatise; indeed, his early plan of composition suggests from the start that he is not writing merely a string of essays but a whole book—a unified object, undivided from itself by the simple fact of circulation or piece-meal publication.

But for all its investment in systemic "structure," "just reasoning," and "rational alternative[s]" (150–51), *The Federalist* was not an orderly affair. The promised plan of publication was repeatedly altered as the essays were being composed. The twenty-five short essays initially promised by Hamilton ballooned, through the winter and spring of 1788, into eighty-five long, digressive, and repetitious papers. Publius's prolixity appeared irrational to his readers and unprofitable to his printers. Having imagined a timely political pamphlet after the fashion of *Common Sense* or *The Federal Farmer*, multiple printers in New York City vied for the favor of printing a bound collection of *The Federalist* articles by doing special jobs for Hamilton throughout the year.[20] But printer Archibald McLean, who eventually won the honor, found himself stuck instead with an impossibly unprofitable albatross. In an early advertisement for the proposed collection, the printer noted that he could not estimate the total number of pages the volume would comprise, for "the Author has not yet done publishing" and "does not seem . . . nigh a close."[21] The book eventually dried up McLean's profits when the anticipated text ran over into two volumes. Even Hamilton, in the preface to the first edition, apologizes for the book's excesses, pointing out "violations of method and repetitions of ideas which cannot but displease a critical reader."[22]

But the "critical reader" who reads all eighty-five papers finds more than just repetition to test his pleasure: he finds essays that are out of order, arguments that extend awkwardly and telegraphically across many different papers, and others that divide and self-divide (also across papers), making argumentative threads hard to follow, even when gathered in book form. But these lapses are not, as one might imagine, merely markers of bad writing. Instead, *The Federalist*'s labrynthine and repetitious argumentation gestures to the scene of its hurried production. As Hamilton noted in his 1788 preface, "the particular circumstances under which these papers have been written, have rendered it impractical to avoid" such problems. Madison later recalled that the "deficiency" and "repetition" of *The Federalist* was an effect of the "shortness of time allowed" and the "great haste" "with which many of the papers were penned." Here and elsewhere Madison stressed not ideological matters but the contingent scene of *The Federalist*'s production schedule, citing the need "to get thro the subject whilst the Constitution was before the public, and to comply with the arrangement by which the printer was to keep his newspaper open for four numbers every week. . . . It frequently happened that whilst the printer was putting into type the parts of a number, the following parts were under the pen, & to be furnished in time for the press."[23] The composition of the essays was disorganized enough that Madison could not finally keep track of them, even while they were appearing (piecemeal) in print: one correspondent, requesting missing numbers, was told he would have to wait for the collected edition, since only the printer knew where all the pieces were.[24]

Rushed as its original publication schedule was, *The Federalist* labors as a literary text to repress all evidence of disorganization. Publius does this by invoking schedules and structures, even if they are later broken. At other times (when evidence is absent), he makes claims to self-evidence, as in *Federalist* No. 1, when he insists that "the subject speaks its own importance," or in No. 31, when he presses his tired reader to submit to a higher "order" of reason:

> In disquisitions of every kind, there are certain primary truths or first principles upon which all subsequent reasonings must depend. These contain an internal evidence, which antecedent to all reflection or combination commands the assent of the mind. Where it produces not this effect, it must proceed either from some defect or disorder in the organs of perception, or from the influence of some strong interest, or passion, or prejudice. (193–94)

This passage, like *The Federalist* as a whole, is concerned with "command[ing] the assent" of its readers. It suggests that those who fail to see the "primary truths or first principles" of the new system are either deficient (their confusion arising from "some defect or disorder in the organs of perception") or self-interested (creatures of "passion, or prejudice"). Either way, the resisting reader requires a virtuous caretaker (such as the Constitution—or a federalist elite) to organize or control him. Federalism emerges, in these instances, as a relentless imposition of coherent boundaries that the reader is coerced not to question: cool candor is opposed to licentious self-interest, reason to "defect or disorder," federalism to antifederalism, and union to permanent dismemberment. In this way, Publius slowly constructs a field of pure contradiction that is agonistic and yet perfectly coherent—even, in a strange way, unified.

And those who cannot keep up with this elevated and highly rational view are simply left behind to the chaos and limited horizons of the local.

Many antifederalists, of course, saw through this claustrophobic "structure," attempting to lay out a full and varied critique of the Constitution. The fuller and more various their critique, however, the more vulnerable they became to the singularity of the federalist attack. Indeed, one way that *The Federalist* achieves its own veneer of rationality is by constructing criticisms to the Constitution (and hence to itself) as incoherent and irrational. Publius repeatedly tropes the antifederalist "survey" of the Constitution's flaws as disorganized and scattered in large part because it is not united in a singular book-to-be (a book, that is, like *The Federalist*) (231). Thus Publius complains that "there is a striking incoherence in the objections which have appeared" in newspapers, authored as they are by many different antifederalists (182).[25] In one of his most extended attacks, he goes so far as to ventriloquize "the publications which have swarmed against the Convention," lampooning their variety (263). In one particularly obnoxious move, he proclaims, "Let them speak for themselves"—and then proceeds to speak for them, listing this or that objection as just so many random pet peeves:

> From this quarter, we are alarmed with the amazing expense from the number of persons who are to administer the new Government. From another quarter, and sometimes from the same quarter, on another occasion, the cry is that the Congress will be but the shadow of a representation, and that the Government would be far less objectionable, if the number and the expense were doubled. A patriot in a State that does not import or export, discerns insuperable objections against the power of direct taxation. The patriotic adversary in a State of great exports and imports, is not less dissatisfied that the whole burden of taxes may be thrown on consumption. This Politician discovers in the constitution a direct and irresistible tendency to monarchy. That is equally sure, it will end in aristocracy. Another is puzzled to say which of these shapes it will ultimately assume, but sees clearly it must be one or other of them. Whilst a fourth is not wanting who with no less confidence affirms that the constitution is so far from having a bias towards either of these dangers, that the weight on that side will not be sufficient to keep it upright and firm against its opposite propensities. . . . Let each one come forward with his particular explanation and scarce any two are exactly agreed upon the subject. (244–45)

This list goes on at far greater length; indeed, its length is part of its performative power. Defending this maneuver, Publius explains that he has
"exhibited" this "sample of opinions" to his readers so that they might
take part in his more integrated view of the current crisis (246). The result, however, is a devastating revelation of the mess that is antifederalism. Rather than adopting a more systemic view (like federalism) that
would unify all contradictions within a larger field of debate, the antifederalists make the mistake of disagreeing *with each other*—indeed, sometimes with themselves. The result is a form of chaos that, *The Federalist*
suggests, is not only destructive but also politically, culturally, and perceptually unnecessary.[26]

   As Melancton Smith later drily noted, "any argument may be placed
in a ridiculous light, by taking only detached parts."[27] But *The Federalist* does more than parody the discombobulated minutiae of conflicting
grounds of dissent. Against the argumentative fragments of circulating
newspaper and pamphlet debates, Publius cultivates a countervailing
sense of the general, the complete, and the systemic, elevating the whole
(or the federal) to a newly privileged status that can only properly take
effect within the new federal sphere of representation. In some papers,
Publius challenges the antifederalists to adopt this elevated kind of view,
asking them "to prove, not merely, that particular provisions in [the
Constitution] are not the best . . . but that the plan upon the whole is
bad and pernicious" (444–45). But no such iconic antifederalist master-
text ever emerged to take its place alongside *The Federalist*, nor should
this surprise us: as Sheldon Wolin suggests, the proliferation of diverse
antifederalist arguments was, in a sense, inevitable. Not only were the antifederalists geographically scattered, but they were forced to "generalize
about difference," "trying to make a theory about exceptions, local idio-
syncrasies, regional differences."[28]

   Against the disintegrating and disintegrative critique of antifederalism,
Publius posits the "comprehensive" view of the Federal Convention and
its plan, modeling, in his own performance, the singularity and integrity
he claims the antifederalists lack. The language of parts and partialness
is disdained through all eighty-five numbers, for as Publius argues, "the
peace of the whole ought not to be left at the disposal of a part" (509).
Publius's attempts to appear singular in the face of antifederalist dissent
are connected to the book's larger rhetorical project. At the same time
that *The Federalist* works to appear ideologically coherent across its different papers (and in spite of its different authors), it seeks to assure its

scattered readers of the geographical coherence of ratification's ultimate object: the union. *The Federalist* conjures unity in many guises, routinely casting divided or diverse things as already unified. The Federal Convention is said to represent a "unanimity almost . . . unprecedented" (238); "the people" are hailed as a monoglot audience (9); different "classes" are evoked as one unit (216); and the states themselves are often literally lumped together (as in No. 37, where they are "incircle[d]" by foreign nations) (158). Indeed, Publius poses geographic union—a nation that is whole from the start—as the privileged countertext to the fragmenting forces of post-Revolutionary localism and the self-interestedness of antifederalist partisanship:

> It has often given me pleasure to observe, that Independent America was not composed of detached and distant territories, but that one connected, fertile, wide spreading country was the portion of our western sons of liberty. Providence has in a particular manner blessed it with a variety of soils and productions, and watered it with innumerable streams, for the delight and accommodation of its inhabitants. A succession of navigable waters forms a kind of chain round its borders, as if to bind it together; while the most noble rivers in the world, running at convenient distances, present them with highways for the easy communication of friendly aids, and the mutual transportation and exchange of their various commodities. (9)

Publius sees here the providential design of *E pluribus unum* written into the landscape, with "innumerable" "variety" contained by "a chain" of rivers that "bind" the republic's distinctive locales together. In the absence of actual highways, rivers stand in as "easy" and "convenient" venues for the exchange of commodities that commercial nationalists like Hamilton hoped would make the union perpetually binding and, of course, profitable.

But the image of the chain is a troubling one, even in a text as repressed as *The Federalist*. Fifty years after ratification, Garrisonian abolitionists would be trying to break the binding chain of federalism by using rivers and newly built steamboats to disseminate accurate information about the chains of chattel slavery, a practice that continued to proliferate westward in the years after ratification. The word slavery is, of course, never mentioned in the Constitution, which prefers to discuss "persons" rather than "slaves."[29] Similarly, whenever Publius speaks authoritatively in *The Federalist* as a "federal" voice that can transcend self-interest and take in all viewpoints, he too must find ways to cover, in language, the differences between the diverse parts he wants to assimilate within the new frame of federalism.

Given the contested nature of the Federal Convention's willingness to create a union with slaveholders,[30] it is perhaps appropriate that the famous seamlessness of Publius's narrative voice should be broken most dramatically when he is discussing the three-fifths compromise—the deal that brought the three southernmost states into the union by ensuring that southern representation in the federal legislature would be inflated by counting slaves as "three-fifths of a person." Discussing this compromise in *Federalist* No. 54, Madison (the presumed author) breaks with the convention of the federalized voice and introduces instead a discrete second voice—"one of our Southern brethren":

> We subscribe to the doctrine, might one of our Southern brethren observe, that representation relates more immediately to persons, and taxation more immediately to property, and we join in the application of this distinction to the case of our slaves. But we must deny the fact that slaves are considered merely as property, and in no respect whatever as persons. The true state of the case is, that they partake of both these qualities; being considered by our laws, in some respects, as persons, and in other respects as property. . . . The Fœderal Constitution therefore, decides with great propriety on the case of our slaves, when it views them in the mixt character of persons and of property. This is in fact their true character. (367–68)

This passage eloquently captures the uneasy rupture between the republic's diverse cultures and spaces. The breakdown is ironic, for it is Madison (the southerner) who finds himself disavowing (by pretending to ventriloquize) his own identity here, partitioning the southern point of view in a supremely alienating moment of staged regional dialogue. Thus contained, Madison's fictional southerner defends the three-fifths clause to Publius, who presumably does not like it. The insertion of this (literally) distanced point of view momentarily troubles the unitary fiction that underwrites *The Federalist*. Set against the monolithic singularity of Publius's larger narrative voice, the dialogue reveals that parts of the new nation's insides are actually outside—or, at any rate, need to be thought of that way. But this makes sense only if we keep in mind that *The Federalist* essays were primarily intended for an entirely different set of insiders—readers in New York City and New York State.

More than any other number, *Federalist* No. 54 foreshadows the cracked fiction of federalism as it would later emerge in the far different union of the 1830s, '40s, and '50s—a union damaged, as I argue in the latter portion of this book, by increasing dialogue across regions. Indeed, we see the "mixt" (and mixed-up) "character" not just of slavery's logic in this passage but of federalism itself. Though the South lays a larger proportional claim to Publius's supposedly federal attention here (forming at least one-third of the original thirteen states), it is the smaller part (the one-thirteenth part of the union that is New York State) that ultimately marks the median point of view in this passage. The imagined readership (or public) to which Publius is speaking in such moments is far more local than the name of this essay series suggests. While this might be good politics in 1787, it is also bad math (valuing a minor fragment over a mass, or a thirteenth over a third), and it finally catches up to the federalists in 1861. It was, after all, the mathematically unjust disequivalence of Lincoln's Northern and Southern electoral votes (he received not one from the South but won the office anyway) that provoked South Carolina to secede. *Federalist* No. 54 thus demonstrates both the union's and the *Papers'* potential for self-dissolution while at the same time suggesting some of the rhetorical strategies that were adopted to contain that potential. Like Carwin in Charles Brockden Brown's *Wieland*, Publius chooses to ventriloquize that which he cannot otherwise assimilate. More remarkably, the passage unwittingly suggests that the unassimilable other of federalism extends far beyond antifederalism. In moments like this, it is not ideological dissent that must be repressed in order for ratification to proceed; it is the geographic and cultural diversity already marked as Southernness.

Just as Publius tries to broker geographic discontinuities, latter-day readers of *The Federalist* have sought to minimize the discontinuousness of *The Federalist's* original newspaper form. *The Federalist* stands forth today as the premier artifact of constitutional consolidation precisely because it is a collection whose readers have forgotten the original scene of its scattered production and reception—the dispersed places that the original text had to negotiate ideologically (as an argument) and materially (as an object). Indeed, the presumption of coherence and collectedness (over and against the scattered and confused contingency of the

moment of making) is by now deeply ingrained not just in our ideological inheritance of ratification but in its many historiographic depictions
as well. This is true even in the most basic form in which the debate of
1787–88 continues to be transmitted to us and in the most basic ways it
continues to be consumed. For instance, alongside their iconic 1961 edition of *The Federalist Papers*, the New American Library sells a companion volume of antifederalist material. While the *Federalist* volume is offered as a unified object—a "book" or a "treatise" with one narrator and
one point of view—the antifederalist volume is an "anthology"—a collection of excerpts that project a variety of chaotic and often contradictory
positions from across a vast subsection of the antifederalist coalition.[31]

This pairing of unity and cacophony, coherence and contradiction, exactly replicates the terms that *The Federalist* constructed for the debate of
1787–88 and as such represents one of many retrospective reifications (in
print) of known outcomes. Even today, the monolithic singularity of the
collected *Federalist* continues to obscure the manyness of the original "Papers"—published, as they were, in this or that newspaper, in this or that
state, raggedly, over time. In the place of context, there now stands only
text. If this is so, it is because the collectedness of the collected *Federalist*
makes a more useful nationalist artifact than does the memory of the numerous semiconnected print cultures within which the serial papers were
initially, and plurally, disseminated. This is true as well for ratification
more generally, which was plurally and brokenly first performed, from
site to site, in jagged disunison. Debate both for and against the Constitution occurred, after all, in an utterly scattered—or unfederal—way. But
this fact is erased whenever we allow the cool collectedness of Publius's
bound volume of essays or the seeming inevitability of the Constitution
itself to stand in for what was actually the cacophonous truth of 1787.

Publius's creators, no doubt, intended it that way. Despite its rare
moments of dialogue, *The Federalist* suggests that the voice of federalism can be spoken only through a theatrically nonsplit persona, a mask
that screens an unassimilable difference of opinion as if it could be rendered intelligible in one person. The genuine split behind that voice is,
of course, permanently inscribed in the known political differences that
eventually emerged between its two primary authors, Hamilton and
Madison—a West Indian emigrant and a North American Creole; a
commercial nationalist and an agrarian republican; an urbane Manhat-
tanite and a southern squire; a merchant's clerk and a planter's son. Yet
the monolithic persona of the pseudonym presumes and projects union

and unity, and it does so as a way of cutting off opponents, making them seem like untrustworthy innovators. By calling himself "The Federalist," in other words, Publius made his opponents seem like they were actually antifederal, but in fact the antifederalists were not against union; they were simply against the Constitution—which in 1787 was hardly the inevitable statement of U.S. nationalism that it seems today. Far from being inevitable, the Constitution was odd, and it was not the antifederalists who were innovating a new national order by resisting the Constitution, but the federalists who were innovating an entirely new and unheard of contraption called the extended republic, which many antifederalists simply dared to think of as impracticable. When we choose to see the early national landscape from the antifederalist perspective—as innumerable locations of resistance to a false narrative of collected coherence—Publius emerges as one of the early republic's most spectacularly unreliable narrators, foisting a tale of cool candor that many audiences in 1787 considered "dry trash," but that audiences several centuries later have found woefully unsuspect.[32]

Publius thus presents his readers with a formidable irony. On one hand, we have a fictional narrator who speaks for "the founders" so persuasively that *The Federalist* continues to shape public policy at the highest and most official levels of the state. On the other hand, Publius is demonstrably a partisan whose arguments are redundant and at times inconsistent, a tool of political expedience who was quietly disowned in succeeding years by both Hamilton and Madison as each went his separate way in the two-party system that eventually displaced the federalist consensus.[33] Washington famously brushed off these criticisms and claimed a special admiration for Publius, telling Hamilton (prophetically) that "when the transient circumstances and fugitive performances which attended this *crisis* shall have disappeared, that work will merit the notice of posterity."[34] But most eighteenth-century readers were more ambivalent about the essays. The antifederalist Samuel Bryan (writing as Centinel) called *The Federalist* a "hobgoblin," "sprung from the deranged brain of *Publius*," and poked fun at its "myriads of unmeaning sentences," its "torrent of misplaced words," and its "long-winded disquisitions," bemoaning the reader's "fatigue" and the paper it "wasted."[35] Other readers agreed, and enough numbers of the 1788 edition remained unsold to allow John Tieboult to bring out a second edition in 1799 merely by pasting new boards on the unsold remainders. William Maclay no doubt spoke a more common sentiment than Washington's when he called *The Federalist* "a lost book" with no audience to purchase it. Maclay felt sure he could get a copy for free, for "it is not worth" "buying it."[36] Even Madison had his reservations. When Jefferson flatteringly suggested in 1825 that the newly founded University of Virginia should teach the twin texts of founding side by side—his Declaration and *The Federalist*—Madison demurred, remarking that while an "authentic exposition" of the Constitution, *The Federalist* was also overly "detailed" and deeply flawed. Though authorities had "accepted it," "yet it did not foresee all the misconstructions which have occurred; nor prevent some that it did foresee. . . . It may . . . be admissible," he concluded, with the faintest imaginable praise, "as a school book," but he did not recommend it.[37]

Americans today are much more likely to agree with Washington than with Bryan, Maclay, or Madison—in large part because the collected *Federalist* now stands in for the messy scene of ratification, describing the scene of debate from an urbane, detached, and unified point of view and thus making it seem inevitable and correct. No doubt the nation as a form needs the fiction of *The Federalist* in order to remain legitimate and intelligible to itself, just as the book once needed the fiction of an already coherent nation in order to persuade audiences to ratify the Constitution. As I will argue next, however, it was not just the *semblance* of coherence that allowed ratification to slip through in the face of massive dissent from state to state; it was the semblance of coherence deployed across a chaotic and disconnected space. To see how this was achieved, we need to look beyond the singularity of any one text to the larger material tableau of ratification writ large. Leaving the specific history of *The Federalist* behind, we must theorize instead the entire field of exchange in which such texts were circulating.

4. Somebody Versus No One: The Problem with Republican Anonymity

Writing is that neutral, composite, oblique space where our subject slips away, the negative where all identity is lost, starting with the very identity of the body writing. No doubt it has always been that way.

—Roland Barthes, "Death of the Author," 1967

Much recent work on early American print culture depends on a post-structuralist understanding of print (or the condition of printedness) as a pure structure of representation—a series of signs in which signifiers and signifieds are doubly sundered from one another. All printed objects are, as texts, inevitably unmoored from the world to which they refer. As material objects, however, they also have the uncanny ability to escape connection with the conditions of their production once they enter the realm of circulation: as a cluster of self-contained signs produced *as an object* in one place and then consumed in another, they have the potential to leave behind their local origins, obscuring the authors who penned them and the printers who made them into that thing called a book, a newspaper, or a pamphlet. Indeed, the very reproducibility of a printed text (its potential for plurality) ensures that there will be many more sites of reception than sites of production. Perhaps this is one reason why printed texts are the ultimate Enlightenment fetish: icons without origins or, at any rate, icons whose origins are more than likely to be mystified in the process of their reception.

This is the theoretical model upon which Michael Warner's republican print ideology thesis depends, especially his now familiar reading of the eighteenth-century trope of the pseudonym, or authorial anonymity, as the signal gesture of republican abstraction and disembodiment. The name "Publius" is, for example, "emphatically a pen name" for Warner and thus works "like the People, in 'We the People'" to erase the local origins and interests of its authors (113). "No doubt it has always been that way," says Roland Barthes.[38] Warner ingeniously extends this ahistorical insight by converting it into a plausible account of an explicitly historical ideology—early national republicanism. But *The Federalist* proves such a useful example of virtuous abstraction for reasons that extend beyond the use of a pseudonym. For one thing, the supposedly "national" circulation of *The Federalist* ensures its dislocation from the men who produced it (and so obscures the "motives" that, Publius insists, "must remain in the depository of my own breast") (6). For another, the manyness of those men (Madison, Hamilton, and Jay) ensures that the collected *Federalist* can never be traced back to one body.

The problem of authorial attribution is, of course, hardly new in *Federalist* scholarship. But Warner's model raises two new questions beyond the hackneyed one of who-wrote-which-paper. First, does pseudonymous authorship—even when it includes more than one author—effectively amount to a sense that there is *no* author? And second, do printed objects, when unsigned, really appear to "emanate from no one"? I have already argued that printed texts, no matter how widely disseminated, are never entirely sunderable from their origins. This position, however, requires some nuance, for an array of signed and unsigned pamphlets, newspapers, and broadsides did in fact travel up and down the American post route during ratification, shedding their associations with their original producers and resurfacing as part of some other place's product (as in the common practice of reprinting, whereby essays were clipped and reprinted in local newspapers whose audiences may or may not have known the context of the essay's original publication). Though they were never finally detachable from the labor of *somebody's* body (be it the postmaster, the bookseller, the printer, or a politician), the origins of such texts were often mystified and confused in the course of circulation. The answer to the first question, then, lies less in assuming a limited circulation for any given text than in thinking about how historical readers read. Because most objects were reprinted and consumed in local newspapers, location—or the act of locating—was likely to be a routine reading habit in the early republic. This readerly habit of locating texts within a specific context suggests that there is no such thing as "nowhere" (although there is such a thing as somewhere else). While a great deal of information circulated translocally, its production and circulation in material form—as a book, a newspaper, or a pamphlet—was still often a local matter. For this reason, the somewhere else from which texts arrive can never quite be nowhere, and a great many unknown writers, far from being no one, are almost always understood to be someone.

This is another way of saying that anonymity takes on a special meaning within the larger set of cultural commonplaces about rootedness and circulation that mark early national print culture.[39] While the potential anonymity of print could be used, as Warner notes, to promote a fiction of impartiality, this strategy was in no sense hegemonic. As useful as anonymity was in furthering the process of ratification, there are many instances when print's detachment from a known or knowable source was considered troubling or untrustworthy. The federalists, for instance, pressured printers in many states to reveal the names of antifederalist authors, playing on the widespread fear that pseudonymous authors were hiding their self-interest behind pen-and-paper masks. In such moments, print was openly recognized for the screen that it was, and anonymous essayists were deemed *less* trustworthy because they chose to be more shielded from public scrutiny. While the federalists were more influential in muting debate in this way, the desire to see behind the curtain of the pseudonym—to assign printed debate to known persons—was evident on both sides. The antifederalist Samuel Bryan coyly cloaked his adversaries ("the well-born few") in thinly veiled pseudonyms that would have been easily recognizable to his Philadelphia readers. His Centinel essays pointedly refer to "James, the Caledonian" (for James Wilson) and "Robert, the cofferer" (for Robert Morris).[40] In other moments, authors used the more standard eighteenth-century technique of leaving letters out of names, which shielded newspapers from libel charges even as it dared its readers to fill in the blanks, making them knowing participants in the process of critique rather than just passive consumers of it. Centinel, for instance, doubly deflates the disinterested pretensions of republican anonymity when he asks of Philadelphia's most prominent federalist: "Are Mr. W———n, and many of his coadutors in the late C———n, the disinterested patriots they would have us believe?"[41] In both cases, Centinel's primary targets were well known, and their attempts to appear above ambition are openly questioned.

Given Bryan's attempts to personalize debate by using thinly veiled pseudonyms for his major adversaries, it is ironic that he himself wrote under the pseudonym of "Centinel," refusing to reveal his name, even when pressured to do so by his federalist opponents. This refusal was embedded in a larger debate about anonymity and pseudonymity that began in Massachusetts and then circulated back through several major northern cities.[42] It began in Boston on October 10, 1787, when a printer named Benjamin Russell announced that his paper, the *Massachusetts Centinel*, would no longer print any antifederalist essays unless "the writers leave with him their names, to be made publick if desired."[43] Boston federalists widely praised this policy and pressured other printers to adopt it, questioning the virtue of "any production, where the author chooses to remain concealed."[44] Local antifederalists, recognizing that Russell was acting under the direction of wealthy federalist subscribers, responded with an elaborate defense of anonymity, equating pseudonymous debate with freedom of the press while at the same time suggesting that to be known as an antifederalist was simply not feasible in Boston's intensely pro-Constitution climate. The *American Herald*, for instance, noted that "the name of the man who but lisps a sentiment in objection to it, is to be handed to the printer, by the printer to the publick, and by the publick he is to be led to execution."[45] Others, noting "the rage" of local mechanics, declared it "unsafe to be known to oppose it."[46] As Boston newspapers circulated to the middle colonies, the debate was picked up in both New York and Philadelphia—far more readily and fully, in fact, than were the essays of Publius.[47] In Philadelphia, a letter signed (ironically) by an anonymous "Pennsylvania Mechanic" took the federalist side of the argument, casting resisters as part of an "anti-federal junto."[48] Antifederalists in Philadelphia responded here as they had in Boston: to sign one's name, wrote one, "is as much as to say, Give me a stick, and I will break your head."[49]

Though apparently paradoxical, Bryan's refusal to be named as the author of the Centinel essays was actually consistent with his own pointed identification of his most local nemeses. Within the larger context of the anonymity debate, Bryan's refusal reveals the stakes of knowing and not knowing—or more precisely, of being known and not being known. As Bryan undoubtedly knew, anonymity was not always received as a sure signature of disinterest, nor was it always an attempt to screen partiality (or hide licentiousness). It was, instead, a complex response to a public sphere that was for many of its participants a highly local affair, one in which writers often knew their readers (and knew that their readers knew them), leading them to fear personal reprisal—especially in those intensely pro-Constitution, mercantilist urban settings where newspapers were printed and circulated most densely.[50] In Massachusetts, for instance, one anonymous essayist asked that his name be withheld in order to evade "the treatment which has been so liberally bestowed on mr. Gerry, governour Randolph, governour Clinton, and other most respectable characters, who appear to have objected to the plan of confederation." The glare of scrutiny was enough, in this case, to arrest the author's contributions to the debate: a note from the printer in a later issue protected the author's anonymity but "assures" the paper's readers that this antifederalist author "will not trouble them or himself with any more observations on the subject."[51] This fear of losing local standing is the same one that led Benjamin Rush to seek out a newly arrived immigrant to compose the pamphlet that finally became *Common Sense*. In the case of ratification, antifederalists had equally good reasons to disavow their identities. Not only did their reputations and businesses stand to suffer, but their physical safety was imperiled as well: in the tradition of Revolutionary mob violence, tarnished reputations sat on a continuum with broken heads.

Local knowledge proves, of course, to be a central problem for Warner's model as well, for he does not attend to the possibility that a great number of people already knew who was writing what. Instead, he assumes the utmost utility of the pseudonym, especially in the case of Publius, who, he argues, "was lauded and attacked" "throughout the ratification debate" "only as 'Publius' because he was not known by any other name" (113). But this is not quite true. Both Hamilton and Madison had a stake in letting some people know that they had authored *The Federalist*. Both authors informed Washington of their involvement in the project, while Madison let Jefferson in on the secret via cipher. But not everyone needed to be told first hand. Melancton Smith and George Clinton both wrote letters from the floor of the New York Ratifying Convention in which they obliquely but knowingly linked Hamilton—"the little Great man"—with his alter ego, Publius.[52] Hamilton's authorship is also alluded to in more public venues, as in a spurious letter printed in the Philadelphia *Independent Freeman*, in which "Mr. R—h" (i.e., Benjamin Rush) discusses the issue (as well as other federalist intrigues) with "Mr. H—n."[53] Here and elsewhere, we have abundant evidence—both printed and in manuscript—that Publius's identity was, by 1788, an open secret to many readers who cared to know it.[54]

Such examples show that the relationship among print, pseudonymity, anonymity, and publicity was a complicated and unstable one in 1787. To be an author *or* a reader in the early republic was not just to be made an abstract subject of republican discourse, but, as Paul Downes has said, to "negotiate a relationship" to the "disembodying" grammars that structure such discourses.[55] Indeed, general readers did not need to know the precise details of a pseudonymous persona's identity in order to discern the *kind* of person who might be lurking beneath such a persona. In one particularly humorous piece of Philadelphia filler, Publius is never overtly linked to a specific author, but he is satirically called back into the flesh that his pseudonym would seem to disavow:

> Anecdote of PUBLIUS, who pants for a fat office under the new system of government. A Country relation of Publius's calling to see him in New-York, at the time his 18th number appeared; the author enquired of him, what the people up in his part of the country said of the Federalist; the other, not suspecting he was the author of it, answered, that he had read it, but heard little said about it, as the attention of the people was so much occupied on the subject of the New Constitution, they had no time or inclination to read any essay on Foreign Affairs.[56]

This squib skewers *The Federalist*'s pretensions to candor and disinterestedness by supplying a self to the selfless Publius. This self has a body (a walking cluster of corporeal desires who "pants" for something "fat") but also a human history—a family. That family feeds back into the body it produced: not only does it provide a set of biological "relations" for Publius to chat with, but it constructs a back story for his otherwise il-legible ambition as he attempts to distinguish himself from his "Country relation" by asking about the reception of his essays upstate. The punch line here—the fact that folks at home have "no time or inclination to read any essay on Foreign Affairs"—targets *The Federalist Papers'* most oft-remarked flaws—that they are boring and off-topic. But it also sug-gests that Publius's readers (even unlearned "Country" readers) know the difference between the various things that Publius attempts to conflate. This extends not just to the foreign and the domestic in particular, but to the inside and the outside more generally—as Gordon Wood might say, the outwardly worthy versus the inwardly licentious.[57]

The idea of Publius—that most rational, disinterested character in all of early American culture—having such a self (one fraught by desire, ambition, and failure) is comical, but it speaks to more serious questions circulating on the eve of ratification. The problem of authorial identi-fication is linked to a larger cultural crisis in these years surrounding questions of self-identity and self-evidence, a crisis in which an extended number of disconnected populations sought, through representations of various sorts, to abstract themselves into two generalized (though always overlapping) forms: a state and a public sphere. But just as Montesquieu had warned that a large republic would distort the political representa-tion upon which republics depend, so the extended republic proved an open field for the distortion of nonlocal representations of every kind. As Elbridge Gerry argued on the floor of the convention, reliable informa-tion—printed and otherwise—was increasingly difficult to find in the 1780s, a problem that strained the feasibility of the Revolution's demo-cratic experiment across an extended space even as small as a *state*. "The people do not want virtue," Gerry argued, "but are the dupes of pre-tended patriots. In Massts. it has been fully confirmed by experience that they are daily misled into the most baneful measures and opinions by the false reports circulated by designing men, and which no one on the spot can refute."[58]

The ability of local populations to identify certain authors even when screened by a pseudonym must thus be posed against the unstable circu-lation of information *across* space. Men "on the spot" were also men in

the know, but information that circulated into local areas from the outside was a more complex problem. Even Madison's opinion was not as
transparent to his home constituency as one would expect. In December
1787, Lawrence Taliaferro, a local Virginia voter from Madison's district,
wrote to him at New York, declaring, "I dare say you will be grately [sur-
prised]: to hear that it is report'd that you Are Opos'd to the Sistum, & I
was told the other day that you were Actually writing a Pece against it."
Citing the confusion of the local people, the writer confides that it is "our
ernest desier that you will be hear a Week or two before the Elextion by
which Menes I make n[o] doubt but the Citicens of this state wi[ll] be
prevented from being led into an Err[or]."[59] As this letter suggests, the
line between accurate news and corrupt rumor was often hard to distinguish during the ratification crisis. And the circulation of unreliable
information in turn created an anxiety that was often allayed only when
a trusted and knowable source could answer "on the spot" the kinds of
questions that printed accounts simply could not.

For this very reason, much of the work of suasion done during the
ratification crisis was not done in print at all but orally, "on the spot,"
in ratifying conventions, town meetings, and taverns, just as the original debate had been orally (if secretly) argued on the floor of the Federal
Convention. Authority was often invested in persons, in a way that could
be undermined by the abstractions and dislocations of print. Throughout
the fall of 1787, Madison had been sending copies of *The Federalist* to important members of his home constituency in Orange County as well as
to individual elite readers in Richmond. In these transmissions, Madison
often suggests (and sometimes openly admits) his authorship, and numerous letters circulating among the Virginia elite show that Madison's
authorship was known, as in many cases was Hamilton's. As Joseph Jones
noted in a 1787 letter posted at Richmond, "Publius is variously ascribed
to M—d—n, H-lt-n, J-y."[60] Madison's sentiments on the constitutional
question—circulated under the stamp of Publius but known by many
of the Virginia elite to belong to Madison—thus preceded his return to
Virginia in March 1788, when he traveled home from New York to participate in the election of delegates to Virginia's ratifying convention. Yet
Madison's account of what he found when he arrived there in person is
telling. First, he complains of "the badness of the roads & some other
delays that retarded the completion of my journey"—marking the difficulties attending the circulation not just of information but of people.

He then goes on to record a startling sight—Publius, not in print but in person, ascending the podium:

> I had the satisfaction to find all my friends well on my arrival; and the chagrin to find the County filled with the most absurd and groundless prejudices against the fœderal Constitution. I was therefore obliged at the election which succeeded the day of my arrival to mount for the first time in my life, the rostrum before a large body of people, and to launch into a harangue of some length in the open air and on a very windy day. What the effect might be I cannot say, but either from that experiment or the exertion of the fœderalists or perhaps both, the misconceptions of the Government were so far corrected that two fœderalists one of them myself were elected by a majority of nearly 4 to one. It is very probable that a very different event would have taken place . . . if the efforts of my friends had not been seconded by my presence.[61]

Madison divides the public here into two categories—his "friends" and "the County" at large. The passage suggests that the former (members, we can assume, of the Virginia elite) already know his position while the "large body of people" are filled with "groundless prejudices" and "misconceptions" about the Constitution—even though we know that many of them were reading Virginia's newspapers on the topic, including newspapers that reprinted fugitive numbers of *The Federalist*. But misinformation was the rule rather than the exception in Madison's world: as Taliaferro fretted, "it is report'd that you Are Opos'd to the Sistum, & I was told the other day that you were Actually writing a Pece against it." In such cases, it was not print but bodily "presence" and personal knowledge that were the ultimate check on confusion.

But even members of the most well-informed elites sometimes got confused and conflicting information during the ratification debates, and newspapers were often the agents of such confusion. Earlier the previous year Washington had confided in a letter to Madison that he was "anxious" to know if there was any "ground" to a Baltimore newspaper's (false) report that Jay had "become a bitter enemy" of the Constitution. Madison was able to refute the rumor through personal information, calling it an "arrant forgery," but he was forced to direct Washington circuitously to yet another print source: Jay's response in a local Pennsylvania paper, which Washington did not have easy access to (as indeed Madison did not, choosing to cite it rather than send it). Madison complained that "tricks of this sort are not uncommon with the Enemies of the New Constitution," who "mutilated" and "adulterated" information in order to achieve their ends.[62] But such "tricks" were, in fact, practiced on both sides of the debate. Printedness may have been a solution for some (especially for those, like Hamilton, who were disliked and mistrusted by the local audience from whom their pseudonyms sometimes helped to shield them), but the printed condition of news and the unstable ways it circulated also created problems when information or ideas were detached from known persons. Misunderstandings and anxieties like Taliaferro's and Washington's make clear what Warner's model obscures: the fact that print was not just a solution to a crisis of representation but was often perceived as part of a crisis in representation.[63]

This is why the republican print ideology paradigm is such a profoundly postfederal one. Such a model, severed from the wider material contexts that challenge and limit it, reinscribes the story of how ratification's eventual victors obscured their own self-interest, embodiedness, and agency when such strategies were necessary or useful. In addition to effacing the many moments when those same victors *did* use their bodies or their names to get what they wanted—as Madison did when he ascended the pedestal and stumped for the Constitution—Warner neglects to describe the many critics who recognized and denounced this way of using print to promote fictions of generality. Patrick Henry, for instance, wasted no time in exposing the Constitution's central fiction, proclaiming, from the floor of the Virginia Ratifying Convention: "I have the highest veneration for those gentlemen [who participated in the Federal Convention]; but, sir, give me leave to demand, What right did they have to say, We, the people? . . . Who authorized them to speak the language of, We, the people, instead of We, the states?"[64]

This query makes clear that the producers of the Constitution were never entirely invisible from their intended audience. Indeed, when celebrity was useful, the federalists made ample use of it, trumpeting the involvement of well-known statesmen (such as Washington and Franklin) who were recognizable to audiences at either the national or state level. Many antifederalists pointedly responded to this tactic by scorning "the splendor of names."[65] But "names" were a large part of the Constitution's success. Far from emanating from "the people," the Constitution was usually submitted to the legislatures with an elaborate array of carefully worded framing material that meticulously tracked the document's circuit from convention to congress to state legislature and then on to the wider public. This extended apparatus makes it clear that the convention's work was never seriously thought to have come from "no one in particular" (Warner 108). Indeed, the first words many readers saw were not "We the People" but "Dear Gentlemen"—followed by a letter from George Washington, president of the Federal Convention, and another from Charles Thomson, secretary of Congress. When the Constitution was submitted to the states by Congress, there was likewise a framing (and signed) letter that prefaced it. And when it finally circulated to the general public (in locally produced newspapers, almanacs, and broadsides), another framing text was often printed alongside these original documents: a letter from members of the state legislature, signed by prominent state politicians in large, bold-faced, capital letters. This strategy was by no means uniform; the Constitution was printed in many formats, many times over. But this only proves the larger point: that there were many different cultures of print operating in different ways in different locations in these years, and nothing about them was monolithic. "What right did they have to say, We, the people?" asked Patrick Henry, and many eighteenth-century readers clearly knew to whom "we" and to whom "they" referred.

5. The Secrets of the Convention

When the Federal Convention met in Philadelphia in the summer of 1787, one of its first official acts involved an agreement to control the dissemination of information about what the convention delegates were about to do inside the Philadelphia State House. The official journal for Monday, May 28, lists a series of "Rules to be observed as the standing Orders of the Convention."[66] Along with a number of standard parliamentary procedures, the members voted to restrict public access to their debates. "A motion was made by Mr. Butler, one of the Deputies of South Carolina, that the House provide . . . against licentious publication of their proceedings." Butler's suggestion was adapted and adopted in the following form in the Journal for May 29:

> Rules,
>
> . . . . . .
>
> That no copy be taken of any entry on the journal during the sitting of the House without the leave of the House.

That members only be permitted to inspect the journal.

That nothing spoken in the House be printed, or otherwise published, or communicated without leave.[67]

Madison later claimed that this rule was adopted so that members would
feel free to change their votes without appearing fickle in the local press.
But in fact, the secrets of the convention were kept secret long after every
vote was cast. Indeed, the convention closed three months later with the
same compact of secrecy with which it began. Franklin, of course, put
forth the now famous suggestion that the states, rather than individual
delegates, should sign the Constitution, thus promoting the fiction of unanimity, but he also introduced a further dissemblance when he suggested,
on the final day of the convention, that individual delegates should withhold information about convention debates from their constituents: "If
every one of us in returning to our Constituents were to report the objections he has had to it, and endeavor to gain partizans in support of them,
we might prevent its being generally received, and thereby lose all the
salutary effects & great advantages resulting . . . from our real or apparent
unanimity."[68] Once members agreed not to talk about what had happened
in the convention, the only informational loophole left to contain was the
written record. Citing concerns similar to Franklin's, "Mr. KING suggested that the Journals of the Convention should be either destroyed, or
deposited in the custody of the President [i.e., Washington]. He thought
if suffered to be made public, a bad use would be made of them by those
who would wish to prevent the adoption of the Constitution."[69] James Wilson seconded this motion but argued that it would be best not to destroy
the journals because, somewhat ironically, he felt they might be needed
as contradictory proofs should "false suggestions . . . be propagated."[70]

The convention's commitment to secrecy did not necessarily make its
members seem more virtuous, but it did effect a fantastic distortion of information across both time and space. Historically, the decision worked
to rupture the documentary record beyond verifiable recognition—a fact
that bears ironic consequences for judges who believe they can recover
original intent through the medium of a documentary record even more
corrupt and unstable than most.[71] The record we have today is hopelessly
partial. While the secretary of the convention did hand over his official
journal to Washington, he did not do so before destroying "all loose
scraps of paper."[72] The journal that remains comprises undated roll calls
on votes with no names and often no state identifications attached. Indi-

vidual members, sworn to secrecy, kept their piecemeal notes private for decades, and it was not until Congress ordered the official journal printed in 1818 that Robert Yates, the only convention member other than Madison to keep careful notes, finally released the first of these. Titling his text the *Secret Proceedings and Debates of the Convention* (1821), however, Yates significantly altered his records to promote his party's agenda.[73]

But the decision to suppress information had more immediate effects within the context of ratification itself, for even as the convention called for a new form of national consolidation, its commitment to secrecy doomed the debate about that consolidation to a much more local scale. Although the convention was a quintessentially translocal gathering, drawing its delegates from each state in the Confederation (except Rhode Island, which refused to participate), ratification was an insular affair from state to state. No two states officially acted in concert throughout the ratification process, and even if they had wanted to, such timely coordination would have been difficult.[74] The only exceptional attempt for concerted conversation was between Edmund Randolph of Virginia and George Clinton of New York—both antifederalist governors in strong antifederal states who hoped to turn their alliance into a powerful negative that would sway the states around them. Their attempts to coordinate their information were thwarted, however, by the difficulties of communicating quickly and privately across such a large space, and their plan disintegrated as letters from both men were misdirected, delayed, and in some cases lost before they could have an impact on key votes.[75] The success of the convention's secret compact—and its fragmenting effect on the Constitution's scattered opposition—enraged antifederalists across the nation, who began to refer to the proceedings at Philadelphia as "the Immaculate Convention," sardonically deflating the federalists' providential rhetoric while at the same time drawing a conspiratorial inference about the decidedly man-made outcome produced by the convention's secret resolves.[76]

Historians have long noted that the Constitution's scheme of representation judiciously solved the problem of size, brokering an agreement between large and small states while at the same time extending the field of representation to an unprecedented (federal) scale.[77] But the secrets of the convention indicate that the federalists did not solve the problem of size so much as they strategically exploited it. In a world where information was sure to circulate unevenly, the antifederalists worried, quite explicitly and vocally, about the gap that the extended republic might create between representatives and constituents, facts and fictions. But while the antifederalists droned on about the distortions in representation that an expanded political and social sphere would entail, the federalists recognized the more important fact—that if a verbal agreement could be brokered among the disjunct parts of the whole, then size would not necessarily have consequences. Yet even as the federalists ignored the question of distance and difference as a potential *theoretical* problem for the future administration of the early U.S. megastate, they were able, throughout the process of ratification, to turn the *facts* of size to their own rhetorical advantage. As fixed a character as Washington—the national figurehead for the kind of transparent republican candor cultivated by Publius—understood the uses of dissemblance in a world where, as he knew, rumours were often more numerous than facts—and almost as impossible to verify. As Washington wrote to Madison concerning the Continental Congress's decision to transmit the Constitution to the states without a recommendation either for or against its adoption: "feeble as it is . . . this apparent unanimity will have its effect. Not everyone has opportunities to peep behind the curtain; and as the multitude are often deceived by externals, the appearance of unanimity in that body on this occasion will be of great importance."[78] The appearance of unanimity (like the appearance of virtue or disinterestedness) was not likely to "dupe" everyone who encountered it. As it circulated away from its source, however, it created a useful amount of confusion—"a curtain," as Washington says, that made motives less legible to those unable to "peep" "behind" it.

In keeping with this strategy of dissemblance, federalists in key states began a campaign of misinformation, planting false articles in the press. A spurious letter from Daniel Shays was reprinted ten times up and down the eastern seaboard, suggesting that Shays was at the head of "the Antifederal Junto."[79] In Philadelphia, a spurious essay under the antifederalist pen name Centinel appeared and spread pell-mell, over the course of four months, into sixteen different papers in nine states.[80] Several months later, false essays were circulated under the name of Luther Martin, who tried to counteract the federalists' misinformation campaign by publishing a series of essays of his own, although by the time his responses made it into the press (under the title "The Genuine Information"), they probably did not appear any more authentic than the spurious letters to some of his readers.[81]

Antifederalists used some of the same strategies of dissemblance. Rumors were circulated that key federalists—from Madison to Jay to Washington himself—had defected from the Constitution's camp, and some of these false accounts made their way into print, causing considerable confusion and further corroding the authority of printed debate.[82] As the pro-Constitution Phocion, writing in Rhode Island, suggested: "Groundless reports, designed misrepresentations, and absolute falsehoods have been used to raise *innumerable visionary spectres without substance* to affright the people."[83] But by and large, the antifederalist campaign against ratification returned insistently to attempts to verify the truthfulness or untruthfulness of suspect rumors, for in verifying the existence of false reports, the antifederalists were trying to prove a larger point about the instability of representation across a wide geographical field, an argument that buttressed their larger claim that the sphere of political representation was unmanageably large under the new system. The high rate of misinformation circulating on the eve of ratification was, for antifederalists, an inevitable index of how vulnerable the extended federal sphere would be to corrupt representations of every kind. As Robert Yates and John Lansing argued, "the extensive territory of the United States, the dispersed situation of its inhabitants, and the insuperable difficulty of controuling or counteracting the views of a set of men [in a state of] . . . remoteness from their constituents" were problems that could never be resolved under the proposed system.[84]

For the federalists, however, corrupt information worked successfully on two fronts. In its original release, perceived as true, a false report or spurious essay did whatever damage the original dissemblance had intended. But later, when—or if—a truer version of accounts came out, it did something else as well: it demonstrated, in a particularly vivid form, the people's gullible incapacity to make discerning and judicious decisions for themselves. False reports from any camp—federalist or antifederalist—circularly reinforced the perceived need for fixed federal characters—like General Washington, or Publius—to do the work of discernment within the new frame of extended representation. When antifederalists like Elbridge Gerry voiced fears about the inability to get information "on the spot," federalists like James Wilson were able to capitalize on them, calling in turn for spotless men who could transcend local views and adopt a federal point of view. Indeed, the spottiness of men who were or were not on the scene of information was a primary topic of conversation as debate proliferated, in print and speech, up and down the disintegrated eastern seaboard, with no one piece of information and no one person able to be everywhere at once.

There are of course many moments in the archive when key federal-ists are caught at their own game, for even the finest federalist was no more fixed in character than the next man, and if anything the sheer geo-graphical expanse of the federalists' extended republic was, as the anti-federalists suggested, a new and much more serious threat to the fixities of everyday life than the licentious characters of individual men operat-ing in more local spheres of influence. As spotless a republican character as Washington found himself the target of damaging misrepresentations that included misquotes, spurious letters, fictitious portraits, and blatant forgeries. Early in his military career, Washington became wary of the dangers of early industrial publicity, carefully guarding the circulation of his private correspondence and shrinking from overtly public statements on potentially divisive issues. "I feel an unwillingness," he wrote in 1780, "to give any opinion (even in a confidential way) lest my sentiments (be-ing known) should have unfavorable interpretations ascribed to them by illiberal Minds."[85] But while Washington tried to set strict rules about the circulation and republication of his private papers, his attempts to control the dissemination of his words and image were destined to fail in a world that both craved information about him and increasingly had the technology to deliver it. The decentralized print culture that would assure ratification also eventually served to proliferate rumors about Washing-ton and his administration throughout the 1790s, rumors that were not always as becoming—or as easily corrected—as the sensitive new presi-dent might have wished. For this reason, Washington frequently com-plained that he could not control the circulatory field through which his private papers traveled. When one personal letter—devoted to the tame topic of "dogs, Wolves, Sheep, [and] experiments in Farming"—found its way into the press in the form of butchered extracts, a livid Washington felt himself "hurt by the publication."[86] But such interceptions were as in-evitable in the 1780s and '90s as what we now call privacy was impossible. As the first president soon learned, his private opinions could "become known to all the world" merely "by passing through the Post offices."[87]

Much to his distaste, Washington would continue to be an object of both transparent and spurious display in the 1790s, as the federalist con-sensus split and gave rise to the partisan two-party system that in turn produced an explosion of networked but still decentralized political print-ers across the union. But Washington was not the only one to have his opinions circulated back to him in potentially damaging form. Publius's famous commitment to candor made the key architect of *The Federal-*

ist—Hamilton himself—particularly vulnerable to the public scandal of "inconsistency," long before Jeffersonian Republicanism emerged to dog his every move. On June 28, 1788, for example, Hamilton made a lengthy speech on the floor of the New York Ratifying Convention in Poughkeepsie, taking as his topic the differences between the states and the ways those differences would be honored and cultivated under the new Constitution. Having staked himself publicly to a position that ran counter to the arguments he had made on the floor of the Federal Convention in Philadelphia (where he had openly favored both a reconstructed monarchy and the abolition of state distinctions), something embarrassing happened: Hamilton got caught in an intentional misrepresentation of his own views, called to account by fellow New Yorker John Lansing, a delegate to the Federal Convention who had resisted the federal plan all along. As the *Daily Advertiser* reported:

> Mr. Lansing . . . let fall some expressions which tended to shew an inconsistency in Col. Hamilton's conduct. He asserted that in the Federal Convention that gentleman had agreed strongly that the State governments ought to be subverted or reduced to mere corporations. He compared these sentiments to those he had avowed in the present Convention, viz. That the State governments were necessary for the preservation of liberty.[88]

This "altercation" (as note taker Francis Childs called it) took up several days of the ratifying convention's time as Hamilton defended himself against the accusations of Lansing and Robert Yates (another former colleague from Philadelphia). This rhetorical tussle would, ironically, later be excised from the official debate transcript (even though it was, tellingly, the only material about Hamilton that reached the Poughkeepsie newspapers).[89] But it was hardly tangential stuff. The issue of "inconsistency" went to the heart of the structural intervention the Constitution was seeking to make. As I argue in chapter 5, federalism was, in its original iteration, a model for making productive political, economic, and social use of the early republic's incommensurability—the literal fact of its geographical dispersion, in the form of both a scattered population and an extended and infinitely expandable number of spaces that could stand as one thing (a union) even as such populations and spaces maintained the differential self-identity of their own particular locations. At the Poughkeepsie Convention, we see a rare moment in which the strategic potential of this incommensurability was foiled by the presence, "on the spot," of a small number of mobile, highly informed men (Lansing, Yates, and Hamilton) who had all been at the Federal Convention together but who did not agree on its outcome. Whereas most convention members in other state ratifying conventions felt bound by the convention's compact of secrecy, Lansing and Yates rejected it—a decision that damaged Hamilton's credibility once their information was introduced within the singular and decidedly *un*dispersed space of the ratifying convention.

Hamilton's response to this assault on his integrity—his self-identity as a trusted public figure—is telling. He extricated himself from Lansing and Yates's charges, eloquently and memorably, by giving a lengthy speech about the cultural unity of the United States, perorating on the theme of national homogeneity:

> It has been asserted, that the interests, habits, and manners of the Thirteen States are different; and hence it is inferred, that no general free government can suit them. This diversity of habits, &c. has been a favorite theme with those who are disposed for a division of our empire; and like many other popular objections, seems to be founded on fallacy. I acknowledge, that the local interests of the states are in some degree various; and that there is some difference in their habits and manners. But this I will presume to affirm; that, from New-Hampshire to Georgia, the people of America are as uniform in their interests and manners, as those of any established in Europe. This diversity, to the eye of a speculist, may afford some marks of characteristic discrimination, but . . . [t]hough the difference of interests may create some difficulty and apparent partiality, in the first operations of government, yet the same spirit of accommodation, which produced the plan under discussion, would be exercised in lessening the weight of unequal burthens. Add to this that, under the regular and gentle influence of general laws, these varying interests will be constantly assimilating, till they embrace each other, and assume the same complexion.[90]

In mobilizing the language of assimilated "complexion," Hamilton appears to rehearse a familiar racial solution to the impending social conflict—a futuristic version of ethnic nationalism, whereby racial homogeneity is achieved later, rather than in the past. But the language of "complexion" shows us something else as well: it demonstrates in a particularly vivid form that the central problem in the 1780s and '90s was not the polarized racism that would permeate and frame antebellum culture, but the profound differences between white men, who, as Lansing knew—and as Hamilton and Madison were just beginning to learn—could have very different political "complexions."[91] There is no doubt, however, that those differences and their brokerage in practical political arrangements (including compromises on ongoing slave importation and the three-fifths clause for taxation and representation) were constitutive precursors to the systematic racism that would follow in the antebellum years as a coalition of free/white/wage labor arrayed itself powerfully against the rights and needs of unfree/black/slave labor. These were, after all, the very compromises that allowed federalism to emerge in the first place as a compact between individuals, rather than between states. Federalism's ability to extend its reach to individuals, each with a unique racial and/or sexual biology attached, may well be the most modern of its innovations. As I will argue in the chapters that follow, this reallocation of federal identity from the state to the individual not only makes Hamilton's sentimental appeal here affecting, even across centuries; it sets the stage for the embodied conflicts of the still unimaginable antebellum years.

6. Conspiracy Theories, or Antifederalism Cracked

As ratification proceeded and the federalists prevailed in state after state despite many large antifederalist majorities, an entirely new antifederalist critique emerged. While the early ratification debate was taken up with trying to show the strengths and the flaws in the Constitution, some antifederalists turned their attention away from the Constitution later in the process and began instead to theorize the flawed process of ratification itself and the ways the federalists had manipulated it. Thus alongside the antifederalists' original, more fragmented attack on the Constitution (so memorably ventriloquized by Publius in *The Federalist*), there emerged a totalizing account of federalism as a systemic strategy that foreshadowed, for many of its critics, the potentially totalitarian state they feared was coming. Such exposés sought, in the words of the antifederalist Benjamin Workman, "to unhinge every part" of a vast federalist "conspiracy."[92]

In mounting this critique, most antifederalists were careful to adopt the same language of reason that had served the likes of Publius so well.

Thus Samuel Bryan (writing as Centinel) assured his readers that "the term *conspirators* was not, as has been alleged, rashly or inconsiderately adopted; it is the language of dispassionate and deliberate reason."[93] He then proceeded across a number of papers to lay out a relentlessly detailed account of the federalists' "systematic deception,"[94] describing improper parliamentary procedures, rushed votes, and the wide use of spurious essays meant to damage the reputations of all who opposed the Constitution. The whole of Centinel XII dwells on these deceptive and coercive techniques, arguing that the federalists had used their wide-ranging power to create an "empire of delusion."[95] The empire imagined is not, however, run autocratically by an emperor but, like the quintessential legislative gathering of this period (the Congress), by "committee":

> as the task will be arduous, and requires various abilities and talents, the business ought to be distributed, and different parts assigned to the members of the committee, as they may be respectively qualified: some by ingenious sophisms to explain away and counteract those essays of patriotism that have struck such general conviction; some to manufacture extracts of letters and notes from correspondents, to give the complexion of strength to their cause, by representing the unanimity of all corners of America in favor of the new constitution; and others to write reams of letters to their tools in every direction, furnishing them with the materials of propagating error and deception; in short, that this committee ought to make the press groan and the whole country reverberate with their productions.[96]

Centinel describes a highly organized body of men working in concert to achieve a predetermined end. The "distributed" division of labor he describes makes federalism sound less like an ideology than an assembly line, with various workers "assigned" "different parts" "as they may be respectively qualified." The metaphor of divided labor suggests that ratification is an organized process for manufacturing consent through the simultaneous production of unanimity and repression of dissent. This production of fictive unity is, in turn, tightly linked to the literary "productions" that the federalists have produced and artfully "distributed" to gullible audiences.

Centinel's ongoing critique of "the well-born few" was picked up and elaborated by Bryan's Philadelphia neighbor Benjamin Workman. Writing as Philadelphiensis, Workman mocked the Federal Convention as a group of "High Mightinesses" "*locked up in the Statehouse,* guarded by Captain M'Clain's Old Battle-Axe battalion."[97] In one of the most scathing jeremiads to come out of the ratification crisis, Workman warns his readers that a coalition of the wealthy is organizing itself, against the people's interest, into the vanguard of the new state. The federalists make use, when necessary, of the residue of the Revolution, but that residue reveals itself, in Workman's mind, not in the form of a populist ideology (however corrupt or self-serving) but in the leftover apparatus of an aging Continental Army ("Captain M'Clain's Old Battle-Axe battalion")—a coercive structure of authority only in the most pathetic sense (making it eminently resistible). More to the point, Workman identifies a number of highly organized "schemes and collusions" among the "friends of the new constitution" that he believes are meant "to dupe the people in to its adoption."[98] For him, as for Centinel, the political position called federalism is an exercise in "delusion"—a "deception," a "monster," a "*Colossus of Despotism.*"[99]

Workman's accusations are as vivid and inflammatory as Centinel's, but his appeal is less obviously rational. Instead of laying out a careful case against the federalists by detailing verifiable examples of locally known deception, Workman's essays meet rumor with rumor, accusation with accusation. One number, for example, generates rhetorical energy through a series of tried and true epithets, plumbing widespread animosity against groups that had been linked historically (if incorrectly) to secrecy and conspiracy. Workman argues, for example, that "the convention was composed of a variety of characters; ambitious men, Jesuites, tories, lawyers, &c. formed the majority, whose similitude to each other, consisted only in their determination to lord it over their fellow citizens; like the rays that converging from every direction meet in a point, their sentiments and deliberations concentered in tyranny alone."[100] In true Enlightenment fashion, paranoia meets Pythagoras in Workman's essays, with conspiracy suggesting itself as a geometrical axiom in which power naturally aligns with power to the detriment of the people at large: "ambitious men, Jesuites, tories, lawyers"—all combine to "lord" it over their fellow nationals.

The language of lordship does double work for Workman, bearing both an aristocratic and an evangelical referent. If Bryan's Centinel essays targeted the urban elite among which he circulated in everyday life, Workman's are pitched to a more populist audience. Thus while Centinel's essays seek to identify their author with a series of secularist (and at

times legalistic) debates about civil liberties, Workman's are saturated instead with the evangelical fire and brimstone of the coming Second Great
Awakening. The reader of these essays is hailed throughout as a "careless
and insecure sinner" while Workman, in his persona as Philadelphiensis,
takes on the role of a preacher hectoring his fallen audience. Philadelphiensis V, for example, sermonically perorates on the word and plan of
a higher authority, confidently predicting that the federalists will fail because God wants them to:

> Providence has ordered, that they should begin to carry their arbi-
> trary schemes too soon into execution, that, their boundless ambition
> should precipitate their destruction, and that the glory of God should
> be made perfect in the salvation of the poor. Blessed be his name, "He
> hath shewed strength with his arm; he hath scattered the proud in the
> imagination of their hearts. He hath put down the mighty from their
> seat, and exalted them of low degree. He hath filled the hungry with
> good things, and the rich he hath sent empty away." As a villain, who,
> secreted to rob and murder in the silent hour of night, issues forth
> from his lurking place before the people have retired to sleep, and thus
> frustrates his infernal design by impatience; so in like manner the lust
> of dominion has urged these despots on to the adoption of measures
> that will inevitably, and, I hope, immediately unhinge every part of
> their conspiracy.[101]

Workman's belief that Providence would imminently "unhinge every part
of their conspiracy" was out of place in a debate that repeatedly sought to
align itself with Enlightenment ideals of science and reason. His account
treads a line Gordon Wood has identified between two kinds of conspiratorial thinking: one in which Providence has a design for all things and
one in which a purpose can be traced back to the elaborate motives of
other men.[102] For Workman, God's design trumps the federalist design,
but design is nevertheless the trope that structures both accounts: "like
the rays that converging from every direction meet in a point, their sentiments and deliberations concenter."

Regardless of their differences, however, neither Workman nor Bryan
fits the stereotype of the typical antifederalist. Both in our time and in
theirs, the antifederalists have been understood as "men of little faith";
constrained by local concerns, they are remembered as men who were
unwilling or unable to lift their gaze to the elevated view required by fed-

eralism. It is clear, however, that both Workman and Bryan did in fact see the larger picture projected by the Constitution and that both developed visionary accounts of the larger field of debate called ratification. Ed White has detailed the validity of what he identifies as Centinel's four major claims: disingenuousness on the part of the convention, an overly rushed debate, the suppression of alternative points of view, and the despotic nature of the overall proposed system.[103] As White demonstrates, the first three of these are by any standard reasonable accounts of how debate proceeded on both sides of the issue: "it is fair to say that there *were* actions by political elites—Federalists and anti-Federalists—that warrant the proximate designation of conspiracy" (14). This means that when Centinel bemoans the rush with which Pennsylvanians were called to ratify the Constitution, or when he details at length those numerous moments when the freedom of the press was impinged upon, he is not fabricating these events, imagining them, or even exaggerating: a number of coercive techniques *were* mobilized on the way to ratification in Pennsylvania. In the tradition of the Revolutionary mob, delegates were physically coerced and argumentatively silenced; printers were pressured; and debate was suppressed.

As accurate, however, as many of their claims about federalist deception may have been, neither Bryan nor Workman was able to persuade his target audience that the Constitution portended the end of all civil liberties. Perhaps because of the care with which Bryan constructs his key arguments, the Centinel essays have fared better than Workman's in latter-day discussions of ratification debate. But the relative success or failure of these two writers in their own day was not merely (as perhaps it is today) a question of rhetorical appeal. Workman's millennial rhetoric never found its place in Philadelphia's more enlightened ratification debate—but neither did Bryan's more carefully reasoned conspiracy theories. In the end, Centinel and Philadelphiensis both display the "paranoid style" so memorably described by Richard Hofstadter. But while Hofstadter is careful to note that his conspiracy theorists are not really "certifiable lunatics," the federalists were not so generous. Instead, both Bryan and Workman became targets of federalist satires that sought to move them as far off the platform of reason as possible. Francis Hopkinson, for instance, composed a well-known parody of antifederalism titled "The New Roof," in which he portrayed both men in the most marginal eighteenth-century terms possible, with Centinel lampooned as a shrewish old woman named Margery and Workman as a "certifiable lunatic"—

a delusional critic of the Constitution whose hallucinations are spurred on by the more ideologically driven motives of Margery (i.e., Centinel/Bryan). As the venerable "architects" of the "New Roof" of federalism gather to debate their creation, "the windows and doors were crowded with attendants." As the people prepare to witness the debate, a "lunatic" filled with "the most terrible apprehensions from the new roof" is let loose among the crowd

> where he roared and bawled to the annoyance of all by-standers. This circumstance would not be mentioned, but for the opportunity of exhibiting the stile and manner in which a deranged and irritated mind will express itself—one of his rhapsodies shall conclude this narrative.—
>
> "The new Roof! The new Roof! Oh! The new Roof!—Shall demagogues, despising every sense of order and decency, frame a new roof? . . . you are careless and insecure sinners . . . ah! The days of Nero! ah! The days of Caligula! ah! The British tyrant and his infernal junto—glorious revolution—awful crisis—self-important nabobs—diabolical plots and secret machinations—ah, the architects! the architects!—they have seized the government, secured power, brow beat with insolence and assume majesty—oh the architects! they will treat you as conquered slaves . . . –oh that the glory of the Lord may be made perfect—that he would shew strength with his arm, and scatter the proud . . . I will cry day and night—behold is not this my number five?—attend to my words . . . –behold—behold the lurking places, the despots, the infernal designs—lust of dominion and conspiracies . . .
> . . . Do I exaggerate?—no truly . . . they are despots, sycophants, Jesuits, tories, lawyers—curse on the villains! We beseech thee to hear us—Lord have mercy on us—Oh!—Ah!—Ah!—Oh!"—[104]

Hopkinson's strategy here is reminiscent of Publius's ventriloquism, for many of the words placed in this lunatic's mouth are in fact Workman's, set to the tune of a new and comical character. (Phrases like "insecure sinners" and "Jesuits, tories, lawyers" are just a few of the more memorable hallmarks of Workman's prose.) But "The New Roof" does more than just target Workman. It simultaneously lampoons the rhetorical underpinnings of antifederalism writ large as Hopkinson patches together a series of terms that repeated themselves throughout many different anti-Constitution writings. "The New Roof" thus serves as a sort of reverse primer in the lexicon of antifederalism, citing "demagogues," "woe," "tyrants," "junto[s]," the "glorious revolution," an "awful crisis," "conquered slaves," "despots," "designs," "dominion," and "conspiracy." This is the base vocabulary of rhetorical resistance to the Constitution in 1787–88. But while Hopkinson accurately emulates the diction of the antifederalist position, he withholds the attending syntax and grammar that might help a reader make sense of it, instead placing a string of meaningless (because decontextualized) words into the mouth of one of Philadelphia's most flamboyant, impassioned, and evangelical writers. Placing the language of design within an overly apocalyptic, illogical, hyperexclamatory, deeply paratactic (and thus disjointed) syntax, Hopkinson portrays Philadelphiensis—and the antifederalist critique for which he synecdochically stands—not as one who unhinges plots, but as one who is himself unhinged.

But as Hopkinson undoubtedly knew, the antifederalist catalogue of federalist deception was based not on fantasy but in fact. Centinel's and Philadelphiensis's critiques were not irrational at base; they were, if anything, *too* rational, assuming a coherence and connectedness among the federalist coalition that was never actually there. Centinel repeatedly identified the "manoevres" he was cataloguing as part of a vast, well-concerted plan, but as Hofstadter notes of conspiracy theories more generally, this theory "leaves no room for mistakes, failures, or ambiguities." Like many conspiracy theorists, Centinel starts with "defensible assumptions and with a careful accumulation of facts" and proceeds "to marshal these facts toward an overwhelming 'proof.'" This proof is highly organized and coherent, but unfortunately "the paranoid mentality is far more coherent than the real world." Thus while the facts are usually correct in such theories, the generalizations drawn from them are frequently flawed.[105]

These conspiracy theories would not be of much interest to us today, except for one crucial fact: they reveal a fundamental misunderstanding within antifederalist thinking about how the extended republic is *supposed* to work and so suggest one important reason why the federalists succeeded where their opponents failed. A central claim of Centinel's essays was that information was being suppressed not just locally but nationally. What Centinel fails to see, however, is that no information circulated across the thirteen states in any systematic or reliable way, and for this reason debate could not have been systematically controlled by any one group—either federalist or antifederalist. Neither Centinel nor Philadelphiensis recognizes this fact—an insight that is, of course, crucial to Madison's *Federalist* No. 10. Centinel is thus convincing when detailing the local antics of the Pennsylvania Ratifying Convention, but he is far more vulnerable to error when he thinks about how deceptions circulate across space, from site to site. He notes, for instance, that "but two southern papers have come to hand" and that "they contain no information."[106] From this (and similar) evidence, he surmises a full-blown federalist plot—fully backed by the Continental Post Office—to suppress all information from the South. But no such well-orchestrated scheme for the suppression of mail ever existed—because it did not need to. In fact, federalists around the nation were every bit as beleaguered by ratification's informational vacuum as the antifederalists were. Private federalist correspondence demonstrates the pains that federalists in different states took to gather what information they could: Hamilton, understanding the value of up-to-date information, offered to pay express riders personally to bring him news of southern developments; Madison likewise tried to collect as much up-to-date information and as many newspapers as his correspondents could provide.[107] But the replies they received vividly display the precariousness of the federalist information network: Washington, for instance, writing to Madison from Mount Vernon in December 1787, offers up information of "Conventions from the Northward and the Eastward" (as well as other information from the North that turns out to be incorrect). His knowledge of the South, however, is sparse: "what the three Southern States have done, or in what light the new Constitution is viewed by them, I have not been able to learn."[108] In the end, Centinel's thesis is, as Hofstadter says of conspiracy theories more generally, "far more coherent than the real world." The flaw in such analyses is not in their content (or the particular evidence) that they mobilize, but in the structure of their syntax—the failure, we might say, to see the deep architecture of the evidence that they mobilize. And in this sense, Bryan and Workman turn out to have been very bad readers of the New Roof—no matter how intuitive their critiques may be.

Publius himself, that icon of structure and overwhelming logic, points out the overrationality of antifederalist conspiracy theories in an odd turn of argument that momentarily reveals his own investment in the fiction of unity *as a fiction*:

> In reading many of the publications against the Constitution, a man
> is apt to imagine that he is perusing some ill written tale or romance,

which instead of natural and agreeable images exhibits to the mind
nothing but frightful and distorted shapes—Gorgons Hydras and
Chimeras dire—discoloring and disfiguring whatever it represents
and transforming every thing it touches into a monster. (185–86)

These fears of an emerging federal monster are, Publius insists elsewhere,
drawn from "the regions of fiction" (452):

> That the people and the States should for a sufficient period of time
> elect an uninterrupted succession of men ready to betray both; that the
> traitors should throughout this period, uniformly and systematically
> pursue some fixed plan for the extension of the military establishment;
> that the governments and the people of the States should silently and
> patiently behold the gathering storm, and continue to supply the ma-
> terials, until it should be prepared to burst on their own heads, must
> appear to every one more like the incoherent dreams of a delirious
> jealousy, or the misjudged exaggerations of a counterfeit zeal, than like
> the sober apprehensions of genuine patriotism. (320–21)

Publius insists that the coming state will be both benevolent and harm-
less, not least because the Constitution offers a plan of power so perfectly
balanced and checked that no common form of corruption will be able
to undo it. The organization of the new government will, he insists, be
no match for the disorganization of everyday life. Indeed, the Constitution counts on such disorganization, relying upon various forms of dispersion and disaggregation to make the machine go more reliably, more
predictably. Publius notes, for example, that in order to meet the scale of
corruption predicted by the antifederalists, there would need to be not
just one conspiracy but "a continued conspiracy for a series of time,"
carefully linking members of each branch of government across the time
span of several elections (169). He concludes that the success of such a
plot would be unlikely, given the "confederal" scheme of state cooperation: "the Legislatures," Publius argues, "will have better means of information. They can discover the danger [of federal tyranny] at a distance. . . . They can readily communicate with each other in the different
states, and unite their common forces for the protection of their common liberty" (180).

Publius thus offers up, as a counter to claims of conspiracy, his own
version of an alert and active public sphere. Rather than imagining the

states as victims of the national government's coming tyranny, *The Fed-eralist* posits the federal state as a sitting duck in the middle of a reverse panopticon—a fledgling object subject to the surveillance of its state-parts and man-parts rather than something that can exert control and scrutiny over those parts from above or beyond. Later chapters will take up this figure and explore its implications for early national governance at greater length. But for now we can simply be suspicious of this construc-tion of an effectively supervisory and *national* public sphere—especially when offered up by the likes of Publius in the midst of the confusing, rushed, fractured, and plural set of public debates we now monumental-ize under the banner of "ratification." Suffice it to say, the public sphere is not really an adequate model with which to understand the materialist structures that founding *had* to repress in order to go forward, but nei-ther was conspiracy the right way to theorize why antifederalism failed. On the contrary, antifederalism like Centinel's cracked under the pres-sure of its own countervailing fantasy of a tightly networked nation—a phantasm that would not emerge for many years to come.

PART TWO

THE NATION IN FRAGMENTS
Federal Representation
and Its Discontents, 1787–1789

FIGURE 4.1   John Trumbull. *The Declaration of Independence, July 4, 1776.* 1818. Oil painting located in the Rotunda of the U.S. Capitol. Courtesy of the Architect of the Capitol.

4. VIRTUAL NATION
STATE-BASED IDENTITY AND FEDERALIST FANTASY

The government of the Union depends almost entirely upon legal fictions. The Union is an ideal nation which exists, so to speak, only in men's minds and whose extent and limits can only be discerned by the understanding.

—Alexis de Tocqueville, *Democracy in America*, 1835

It takes time for something false to become self-evident.
—Pierre Bourdieu, *Acts of Resistance*, 1998

1. CONTINENTAL CONSEQUENCES

Common Sense never really made sense. In the midst of learned and precise legal debates on both sides of the Atlantic about the rights of citizens and the limits of sovereignty, Paine mixed the vocabulary of political rights with a language of feelings culled from a wide array of unexpected and discontinuous forums—from parliamentary oratory to philosophy to oral tavern debate. Responding to Paine's novel mixture of forms and the famously tenuous reasoning that attended it, loyalists routinely attacked Paine's writings not as common sense but as nonsense. Charles Inglis, whose *True Interest of America* for the most part critiqued Paine's arguments in the drier language of earlier pamphlet debates, considered Paine a "brain-sick enthusiast," "a crack-brained zealot" who could not think straight.[1] Even Whigs who liked the effect of the pamphlet found much of it spurious. As John Adams wrote to his wife, "You ask, what is thought of Common sense. . . . This Writer seems to have very inadequate Ideas of what is proper and necessary to be done, in order to form Constitutions for single Colonies, as well as a great Model of Union for the whole."[2] In remarks like these, Paine's contemporaries mark the gap between *Common Sense*'s rhetorical projections and their imaginable empirical outcome, wondering aloud how the troubled history of Revolution might be translated into something sustainable and real. In Adams's view, Paine's rhetoric had succeeded in importantly destructive ways: it convinced people to separate from England, to abandon longstanding social ties, to take up arms in rebellion. But *Common Sense*—and the Revolution more generally—was less successful in imagining how that rupture might be recontained in a new political order.

The pamphlet's most striking inconsistency involved Paine's projection of the mammoth North American "continent" as an imaginable geographical subject (and reachable audience) even as he repeatedly critiqued England's ability to maintain colonial rule by virtue of the empire's unwieldy size, its sheer distance from the colonies. This was a routine problem in patriot logic throughout the 1770s. On one hand, patriots saw the size of the British Empire as a divine sign that the colonies should and would be independent states: "even the distance at which the Almighty hath placed England and America," Paine claimed, was "a strong and natural proof that the authority of the one over the other, was never the design of heaven" (1:21). Paine repeatedly lampooned the red tape that had flummoxed colonial administration for so many years, proclaiming imperial dispersion absurd: "To be always running three or four thousand miles with a tale or a petition, waiting four or five months for an answer, which, when obtained, requires five or six more to explain it in, will in a few years be looked upon as folly and childishness" (1:24). And yet for every moment in which *Common Sense* critiques the British Empire's unmanageable size, there are two or three in which Paine *celebrates* the equally vast proportions of the potentially independent colonies—an emerging geopolitical unit that Paine, long before the doctrine of Manifest Destiny, repeatedly termed "continental." Boasting that the new United States would account for "one eighth part of the habitable globe," Paine never seemed concerned about the unwieldy consequences that his continental fantasy implied for the future administration of the new United States (1:17).[3]

It is the unanswered geographical paradox at the center of Paine's pamphlet that is referenced by the word "virtual" in the title of this chapter. I use this word to emphasize how dislocated from everyday life the Painite (and later the federalist) fantasy of an extended republic was. But the word "virtual" also has another, more precise meaning in the context of early American political economy, and this involves the longstanding pre-Revolutionary debate about the efficacy of "actual" versus "virtual" representation that I described briefly in my introduction. Every American schoolchild knows the Revolutionary mantra, "No taxation without representation." Throughout the 1760s and 1770s, colonial pamphleteers persistently embroidered this aphoristic slogan in precise and arcane pamphlet debates, theorizing just how close to home colonial citizens could expect their political representation to get. In this context the terms actual and virtual representation were coined to designate removes of representation that were or were not acceptable to distant imperial subjects. The colonists favored actual representation by representatives of their own choosing, drawn from the colonial population. The British countered by insisting that colonists did not need to be "actually" represented in Parliament by their own representatives because they were "virtually" represented by metropolitan representatives who had the needs of the empire—and thus the interests of the colonists—at heart. Proponents of virtual representation believed actual representation to be geographically implausible because it would require distant representatives to travel back and forth between continents or to relocate to London—in the process detaching them from the local interests they were meant to represent. British theorists concluded that imperfect representation of far-flung populations was a de facto condition of expansion—a necessary fact for any population living on the fringe of the British world.[4]

We know, of course, who won the long Anglo-American argument about virtual versus actual representation: the new United States of America, proclaimed "free and independent" by a Declaration of the Continental Congress on July 4, 1776. A number of Jefferson's listed grievances against the Crown exactly engage the rhetoric of this long, complex debate about the unsatisfactory dislocations of imperial representation. Viewed outside the context of this debate, the Declaration's complaints about the "fatiguing" administration of British government at "places unusual, uncomfortable, and distant" read almost like a childish rant, a rage at the king's mere absence from his subjects as well as at the bureaucratic inconveniences of those subjects' necessary dislocation from the imperial capital.[5] But geographic dislocation was very much at the center of intellectual Revolutionary debate. The colonies had long played periphery to Britain's imperial center, and the Revolution might be said to have been fought, at least in part, because Americans fantasized that they could themselves become a meaningful republican center.[6] Independence thus held out the promise that Americans might become, as it were, (geographically) self-identical with themselves, and the languages of independence that eventually articulated this longing repeatedly elevated self-evidence, inalienability, and actuality to the status of national ideals.

But if the Declaration critiques imperial dispersion, it also represses the process of *continental* dispersion that underwrote the new Congress's ability to issue such a monumentalizing text of consensus in the first place. Indeed, one might argue that the Declaration of Independence is such a cherished artifact in popular culture precisely because it restores us rhetorically to the promise of actuality, with little discrepancy between signs (or signings) and the things signified.[7] The text of the Declaration may mediate between colonial assemblies and their chosen representatives or between those chosen representatives and the Crown, but at least there is no mediation, seemingly, in the language itself. Indeed, the Declaration maintains its special popular status precisely because it seems so self-identical in its activity of declaring: as a diplomatic instrument of rupture, it performed its job the same way marriage vows do—in the very utterance. The authority of that utterance is, furthermore, perpetually reproducible, regardless of the way the physical document is manufactured or who (or how many people) may be reading it. No matter how far the handwritten or printed or memorized Declaration might migrate in time or space from its source in 1776 Philadelphia, its various readers are always made invested speakers through the simple device of the first-person plural crossed with the present tense—a combination that cannily turns the Declaration, even today, into a script for performing American consensus. In reading the text of the Declaration, even the most random of readers inhabits, in the space of his or her reading, the voice of this document's authority and so becomes the self-legitimizing source of its directives. In the end, it is the very present-tenseness of this declaration—and of declarations in general as a category of utterance— that compensates for the arcane circuitry of dislocation and representation that had made independence possible in the first place. In this sense, it is something quite other than printedness or writtenness—something closer to the performance of the present tense (or of presence)—that makes this document so peculiarly effective and affecting, even hundreds of years later.[8]

John Trumbull tried to capture the self-identical actuality of the Declaration in the late 1780s when he began painting *The Declaration of Independence, July 4, 1776* (see figure 4.1). As a representation of representatives, the painting records, somewhat anxiously, a number of displacements, even as it seeks to ratify and elevate the political scene it depicts. For one thing, with the transit of what appears here as an insignificant piece of paper, political authority is about to migrate from the British Crown and Parliament to the "people" of the colonies, and it does so through their chosen representatives in the Continental Congress and via the document of the Declaration itself as both the instrument and outcome of colonial self-rule. Both medium and narrative authority are likewise in flux here, because the *written* textuality of the Declaration is being displaced by the painting, and the mantle of authorship is migrating from the painted to the painter. More important, however, is the historical displacement embedded in the painting's composition history: Trumbull was painting a picture about the Revolution, but he began the painting in the very different world of 1787, and he would not finish it until the late 1810s. And therein lies the rupture that interests me most—the displacement of authority from the Declaration of 1776 to the Constitution of 1787, from a revolutionary moment that stressed participatory populism to an era of semiperpetual reconstitution that emphasized restricted representation. The painting figures a moment in 1776, but it was painted and then viewed in a world with very different representational values, needs, and imperatives.

Trumbull's response to the problem of maintaining the self-identicality of the moment of declaring independence (after the fact and in a different medium) was to commit himself absolutely—on the personal advice of Jefferson—to an ethos of verisimilitude—or actuality. As he later wrote in an "Advertisement" for the future engraving:

To preserve the resemblance of the men who were the authors of this memorable act, was an essential object of this painting. . . . Mr. Adams and Mr. Jefferson were consulted, and . . . they particularly recommended, that wherever it was possible, the artist should obtain his portrait from the living person. . . . [I] spared neither labor nor expense in obtaining . . . portraits from the living men. . . . The dresses were faithfully copied from the costume of the time. . . . The room is copied from that in which Congress held their sessions at the time. . . . In fact nothing has been neglected by the artist, that was in his power, to render this a faithful memorial of the great event.[9]

Such precise aspirations were not easily fulfilled in the late 1780s, not least because the populations that had been physically gathered by revolutionary necessity (like the Continental Congress) had, by 1787, long since dispersed back to their local states, towns, villages, plantations, and homes. Yet even when obstacles emerged, Jefferson and Adams stubbornly maintained that "absolute authenticity should be attempted, as far as it could be obtained," and that Trumbull "should by no means admit any ideal representation" (as opposed to an authentic or actual one), "lest, it being known that some such [invented portraits] were to be found in the painting, a doubt of the truth of others should be excited in the minds of posterity" (417). Trumbull's aspiration to create an utterly legitimate representation (of the moment of continental representation being made politically legitimate) engendered, for him, a literally continental set of consequences. To fulfill the fantasy of "absolute authenticity," Trumbull scrupulously wrote to each of the signers' families, and for four years he personally traveled with multiple canvasses across the Atlantic Ocean and up and down the eastern seaboard. Indeed, Trumbull's account of his travels reads like a who's who — or a who's where — of the extended republic: "Mr. Adams was painted in London; Mr. Jefferson in Paris; Mr. Hancock and Samuel Adams in Boston; Mr. Edward Rutledge in Charleston, South Carolina; Mr. Wythe at Williamsburgh, in Virginia; Mr. Bartlett at Exeter, in New Hampshire, &c. &c." (417). By 1791, Trumbull wrote to Jefferson that "the picture will contain Portraits of at least Forty Seven Members:— for the faithful resemblance of Thirty Six I am personally responsible, as they were done by myself from the life." Finishing the picture took over thirty more years, however, during which Trumbull conferred with relatives and surviving signers on the quality of the likenesses he was producing. An overly sanguine advertisement described work on the picture as "considerably advanced" in 1790, but in fact the portrait gathering alone took decades.[10] The first sketches were taken in 1786; the final portraits were inserted (in two different versions) in 1817 and 1819; and the large and (appropriately) life-sized version of the painting finally found a home in 1826, when it was placed in the Rotunda of the Capitol with three other massive historical canvasses, where it can still be viewed today.

Trumbull's labors provide us with a cultural parable, one in a series of available windows onto the problems Americans were experiencing as they tried to sort out the ways that geographic distance and local diversity were inflecting standards of representation that had been raised at the particularly utopian, and still self-identical, moment of independence. It can hardly be a coincidence that a painting that aspires to smooth over a problem in political representation—the transfer of power from one set of representatives to another (also merely representative, or partial) set of representatives—also shows so much anxiety about its own status as a representation displaced from the physical reality of its subjects' literal physiognomies. Trumbull's arduous attempts to reconstruct the moment of founding in every detail instruct us about the necessary dislocations that accompany representations of any kind—political, visual, and verbal. But the story of Trumbull's extensive travels also opens a window onto the literal, day-to-day consequences of Paine's monumentalizing arguments in *Common Sense* and of the Revolutionary ideal of actual representation. In formulating their arguments against the imperfections of imperial representation, the Revolutionary generation portrayed in Trumbull's painting repressed the ways that they themselves were authorized by the same dislocated processes that Parliament had been trying to legitimate throughout the 1760s and 1770s when they insisted on the appropriateness of "virtual" political representation to stand in for colonial interests. And when Trumbull took up the task of painting a key moment in this process, he too repressed the necessarily dislocated origins of his project—and paid the price for that repression in miles traveled and years lost. "To be always running three or four thousand miles with a tale or a petition"—Paine's critique of British administration—hardly seems so different from what Trumbull found himself doing with a canvas.

Trumbull's struggles to reproduce the memory of independence from the unfolding fringe of the extended republic call into question the received relation between Revolution and Constitution on which so many stories about American nationalism depend. The Revolution and Constitution are popularly remembered as inextricably linked events—a continuous and inevitable phenomenon, without intervention.[11] The old Philadelphia Statehouse is today a figure for just this kind of historical confusion in that the National Park Service calls the building "Independence Hall" while the tour of its central rooms focuses not on independence but on the closed sessions of the Federal Convention that were held there over a decade after independence was declared. But there were in fact few physical links between the Continental Congress of 1776 and the Federal Convention of 1787 besides the building that was the shared site where two separate self-mythologizing documents were signed. Indeed, the history of Trumbull's *Declaration of Independence* implies that the movement from the act of 1776 to the act painted in 1787 was not one of progression, fulfillment, or even rupture, so much as it was simply an effect of historical displacement—dislocations from the remembered moment both in space and time that simply could not be recovered, no matter the miles traveled or the details attended to in order to recover the authentic, or actual, facts of founding.

The problem of the (literal) dislocation of one part of the union from the next and of one era of national life from another—both palpable in the story of Trumbull's extended cross-country travels—emerged in the 1780s as part of a larger crisis in representation.[12] If the Revolution mobilized local support through a series of unevenly disseminated discourses, objects, and persons—including pamphlets, newspapers, and soldiers— then the federal moment was concerned with stabilizing and enforcing the federalizing fictions of a coherent American identity that had begun to proliferate across the North American seaboard between 1776 and 1787. This chapter narrates the shift from revolution to constitution and explores the problems this process engendered—both in historical time, as the Revolution faded in memory, and in physical space, as provincial state-units were replaced by an emerging federal imaginary that forced its citizens to accept dislocations in political representation that were often just as far-flung (or virtual) as the ones they had once railed against under British rule. The Revolution's utopian commitment to actual representation and equal rights notwithstanding, it took less than a decade for members of the Federal Convention of 1787 to concede the inherent contradictions of oxymoronic ideals like "actual representation," "self-evident truths," and "inalienable" rights in an extended republic where representations, truths, and individuals were almost always necessarily many miles away from the local origins that supposedly legitimated them. As most members of the Federal Convention knew, the sheer size of the extended republic made the Revolutionary rhetoric of inalienability and actuality impossible to fulfill, and the new republic, if it was to become truly federal, had to leave behind both the Revolution and its rhetoric.

Yet this shift brought its own problems. England had once acted as a foil, allowing colonial policies to emerge as significantly localist and populist by comparison to the metropole. But the reorganization of North America from periphery to center, from colony to consolidated nation-state, threatened to disperse and make marginal the entrenched localism of residual colonial institutions just as the entrenched strength of those residual institutions in turn threatened the "weak" apparatus of union under the Articles of Confederation—the Continental Congress. In order to analyze the ongoing shift from revolution to constitution—from utopian resistance to the limits of imperfect representation to an open acceptance of representative dislocations—I now turn to Royall Tyler's *The Contrast*, a play written and performed in New York just a few weeks before the Federal Convention was scheduled to meet at Philadelphia to consider ways to reinvigorate the unsteady American alliance. Many texts produced by Americans in the 1780s unevenly and overlappingly acknowledge the literal shortcomings of the Declaration's democratic optimism; Tyler goes further, however, and in federal fashion thematizes a new virtual nationalism, a willingness to float America on a playful performance of national affiliation rather than on anything more literal, local, or—in Revolutionary parlance—actual. Tyler's foray into the playhouse thus proposes a deeply rhetorical, decidedly non-Trumbull-like set of strategies for performing the work of nation-making both in the most restricted home spaces and in front of the world.

2. The First American Contrasts

Social history long ago began to wedge open the fist of Whig history by excavating stories other than those of triumphal elites, and this same emphasis on marginal social actors—from women to slaves to the lower sorts—has profoundly altered the face of early American literary studies. Yet that fist holds us tighter than we think, because of the one category of early American identity that we continue to undertheorize: the local category of place, which was already amassing itself, in the 1780s, into more abstracted state- and region-based identities. These local identities vexed the new and shaky nationalism of 1776 and 1787, just as they would later threaten the more entrenched union of 1861. But they also offer an indispensable corrective to the nationalist fantasies that (still) dominate twenty-first-century literary studies, which continues to presume the coherence of white, representative men and their texts against which to posit its "other" narratives. To the degree that we have not yet recovered the foundational contrasts between Americans of different regions, I argue here, we continue to live in a Whiggish account of history, anachronistically assuming constitution as the unproblematic telos of revolution.

Consider the case of Royall Tyler's *The Contrast*, a play whose origins in the uncertain world of 1780s regionalism has been largely erased by the postconstitutional myth of the United States's federal inevitability. While the play languished out of print for decades as a footnote in American literary history (usually cited as the first American stage comedy), recent years have seen a renewed interest in using it to excavate eighteenth-century notions of identity, particularly questions of gender and class. Yet this renewed interest has, paradoxically, not so much excited as deflected prolonged and various intellectual discussion. Indeed, if there has been a sustained problem in the critical history of *The Contrast*, it is that nobody ever disagrees about what it is about. Even today, the play is frequently treated, as it has been for centuries, not as a complicated act of dated (historical) representation but as an archival source, a transparent window onto the eighteenth-century world of hoop skirts and shoe buckles or—to take our newer ideas—onto an equally transparent social world of coquettes and rakes, masters and servants. This tendency toward superficial consensus is one of the play's most curious legacies, but it is also intimately connected to a historical problem internal to the play itself: the pressing need to appropriate a broad form of social consensus within the crisis of the 1780s. This, then, is the feature of the play I want to focus on—both its initial absorption of dissent (in an era of dissent) and its later deflection of multiple readings into a repetitive critical consensus (in its afterlife as an American classic). Such a reading assumes from the outset that the play's bland dichotomies have always been its central cultural contribution (two centuries ago as two centuries later) yet also insists that the play needs a way to be read that will draw it out of its own self-imposed obscurity, blasting open its carefully self-constructed but strangely nongenerative contrasts.

But let me be clear about the kinds of consensus the play has engendered. There have been two key movements in the critical history of *The Contrast*. The first reflected a high literary nationalism, with critics exploring how the play, as a nationalist artifact, stood in the literary field next to other nationalist artifacts. This line of inquiry included discussions of the play's genre, its status as the first American comedy, its imitation of Richard Sheridan's *The School for Scandal* (its long-assumed British counterpart), and arguments about whether Tyler had created a truly American play or an Anglophile knock-off.[13] The second set of readings is more recent, and its opening salvo was fired in 1986 when Richard Pressman and Cathy Davidson began the long process of recovering Tyler from the scrap heap of old literary histories. In that year, Pressman reminded readers that Tyler and his play could be interesting for reasons other than their "firstness," especially because of Tyler's involvement in (and the play's references to) a central historical event of the late 1780s: Shays's Rebellion, an armed conflict in western Massachusetts between cash-poor farmers (and other debtors) and the wealthy, eastern seaboard mercantile elite that tended to run the Massachusetts state government. Davidson, meanwhile, also discussed Shays's but began to pose alongside that problem a similar set of questions about the play's construction of gender. Thus, while *The Contrast* was reductively viewed for many years as a nationalist contrast between British vice and American virtue, it finally began to be more densely elaborated through a series of readings that cast its primary contrasts in more historicist terms as contrasts of class and gender.[14]

This kind of reading revolutionized the way critics approached *The Contrast*. Yet radical as it is, this emphasis on class and gender never essentially disrupts the larger equilibrium upon which these newer contrasts depend. Both generations of critics accept a priori, that is, that there is, in 1787, a coherent national culture that generates stable contrasts. While the earlier nationalist reading assumes that this happens externally, vis-à-vis other nations (Britain versus the United States), the later readings assume that it happens internally, among homogenous subsets of individuals that are nationally recognizable as either upper or lower class (in Pressman's case) or as virtuously feminine or iconically "Manly" (in Davidson's). This later set of readings makes an important intervention into the play's long history of critical consensus, and I will be discussing its insights more as I continue. But for now, I would simply point out that as innovative as it is, this newer reading still presumes a coherent whole from which to theorize difference—a dysfunctional whole, but a whole and already ideologically coherent nation nonetheless from which to evolve a reading of the play's perpetually dull and repetitive contrasts. And in this sense these readings are not "post-"nationalist at all.

Yet the very category of the national, when it comes to discursive goods, should be suspect to us by now, for the national is as constructed and rhetorical a category of identity as class and gender are. Throughout the early national period, there were a number of models for "national" discourse that attempted to short-circuit the perceptual problem of thinking the nation monolithically, in all its innumerable variety, but two of the more salient ones particularly interest me here. One is the myth of the mass-disseminated, ubiquitous text (like *Common Sense*); another is the "representative" geographically determined text, whose American-ness is an effect of its production either on North American land or by a North American author. Both of these models fantasize a fundamen-tally coherent, traceable, and incorruptible source for the monolithic and monumentalizing federal sign. I have, for the time being, talked enough about the first of these, although in relation to Tyler it is worth noting that it is some combination of both that has elevated *The Contrast* to its lengthy tenure as a classic piece of nationalist American literature. As for the second category, Cathy Davidson has pointed out many of the falla-cies that underwrite the geographic valorization of early national texts in her account of the long critical reception of William Hill Brown's *The Power of Sympathy* as the "first" "American" novel. As Davidson ar-gues, both the "firstness" and the "Americanness" of classically received American firsts can be deconstructed by historical research that proves them otherwise. Davidson amply demonstrates that in the mixed up, ex-panding, but still fairly localized world of late-eighteenth-century literary production, there is almost always some obscure precedent to a received "first" or some sort of compromised geopolitical identification to a per-ceived nationalist identity that muddies the waters of our retrospective classifications.[15]

What then of *The Contrast*—which is still taught today as the "first" "American" comedy? Like Brown's novel, the composition of Tyler's play coincided with local conflicts that would later be overwritten by federal reorganization, and in both cases that federal reorganization happened to coincide with the text's *printed* publication. Perhaps it is no surprise, then, that Tyler's play, like Brown's novel, was in large part produced in the museum of American literary history as the "first" "American" stage comedy by virtue of the savvy promotions of another first-class mar-keter—in this case, Thomas Wignell, the celebrated eighteenth-century provincial actor to whom Tyler gave over power of copyright. Looking at the printed edition, it is no wonder that readers have for centuries comfortably presumed its status as a foundational American literary ar-tifact. Wignell aggressively tied his production of the printed book into the rhetoric of federal union that was, in 1790, emerging all around him in postratification Philadelphia. The book is framed for its reader as nationalist entertainment with a title page that is an eloquent text in and of itself (see figure 4.2). It posits its nationalist authenticity on three criteria: first, its prominent declaration that the play was "WRITTEN BY A CITIZEN OF THE UNITED STATES"; second, its declaration that the play has achieved (like *Common Sense* before it) some level of geographic diffuseness, having been "Performed with Applause at the Theatres in NEW-YORK, PHILADELPHIA, and MARYLAND"; and finally, its declaration that as nationalist entertainment, it has been properly sanctified by the federal government "*under an Assignment of the Copy-Right.*" The last declaration is made more significant by the fact that Wignell apparently withheld publication of the book so that he might obtain one of the earliest copyrights under the Federal Copyright Law of 1790. In fact, *The Contrast's* application for copyright was the second application recorded at the federal copyright office, and the first in all of Pennsylvania.[16] And if these three things do not satisfactorily stamp the object before us as an American manufacture, Wignell goes on to include an epigram from Virgil, which he then imitates with an Americanized heroic couplet welcoming the arts to "our shores." Amid such monumentalizing credentials, it is no surprise that the local intersection of the printed play's actual production—"MARKET STREET; BETWEEN SECOND AND FRONT STREETS"—is shrunk into the smallest typeset on the page while the name of its actual, embodied author is elided altogether.

The rest of Wignell's editorial apparatus repeats and elaborates the same nationalist assertions so evident on the title page. Following the title page, for instance, Wignell includes three documents that all promote the national framing of the text. The first is a letter dedicating the play (as "the first essay of *American* genius in the dramatic art") to "the President and Members of the Dramatic Association." Reinscribing the class conflict pointed out by Pressman and others, Wignell (the actor) signs this dedicatory page from "THEIR MOST OBLIGED AND MOST GRATEFUL SERVANT, THOMAS WIGNELL, 1 January, 1790"—a date that, as the first day of the first year of a new decade, once again reinforces a sense of this object's newness, its firstness. Following the dedicatory letter to the Dramatic Association, Wignell next offers a copy of his subscription list, which includes as its first name the most federal of Americans—George Washington (whose inauguration had just been cel-

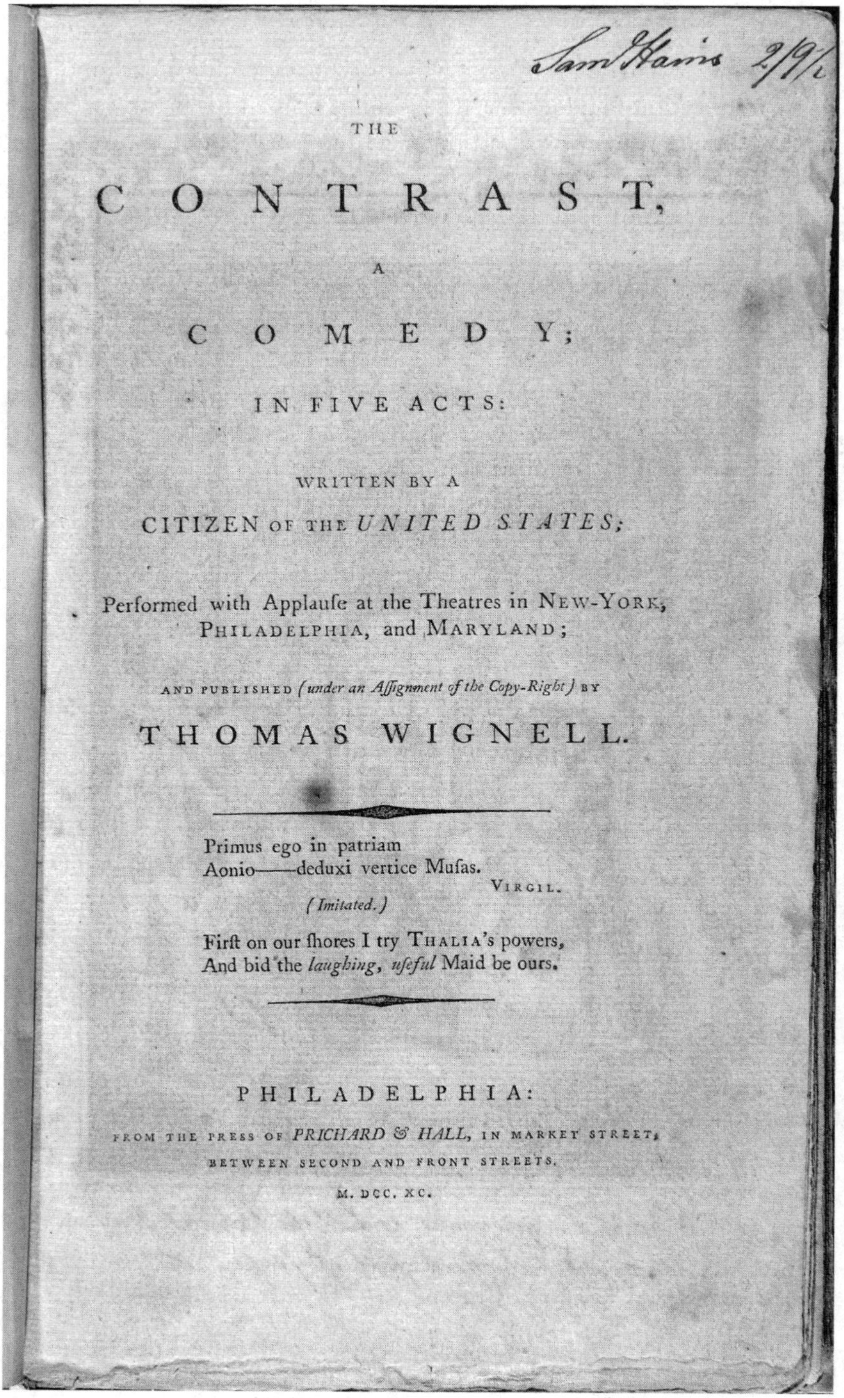

THE

CONTRAST,

A

COMEDY;

IN FIVE ACTS:

WRITTEN BY A

CITIZEN OF THE *UNITED STATES;*

Performed with Applause at the Theatres in NEW-YORK,
PHILADELPHIA, and MARYLAND;

AND PUBLISHED *(under an Assignment of the Copy-Right)* BY

THOMAS WIGNELL.

Primus ego in patriam
Aonio——deduxi vertice Musas.

VIRGIL.

(Imitated.)

First on our shores I try THALIA's powers,
And bid the *laughing, useful* Maid be ours.

PHILADELPHIA:

FROM THE PRESS OF *PRICHARD & HALL,* IN MARKET STREET,
BETWEEN SECOND AND FRONT STREETS.

M. DCC. XC.

FIGURE 4.2 Royall Tyler. *The Contrast.* Philadelphia: Prichard & Hall, 1790. Title page. The Historical Society of Pennsylvania (HSP).

ebrated with great pomp across the United States)—followed by a sundry list of other subscribers that includes residents from locales as diverse as Philadelphia, New York, Boston, Baltimore, Poughkeepsie, Madeira, and Jamaica. Finally, Wignell also includes an introductory "Advertisement" that, like the title page and the subscription list, once again trumpets the play as "the first essay of American genius," "which has been bestowed on numerous audiences in the Theatres of *Philadelphia, New-York,* and *Maryland.*"

All these ways of framing a text—the title page, the assignment of federal copyright, the dedication, the subscription list, and the advertisement (with its testimonial to the play's other, traveling incarnation)—routinely serve in eighteenth-century print culture as discursive indices of how products were being pitched to what their producers hoped would be geographically diverse audiences. Nor is it any surprise that Wignell proffers his play to the widest possible audience. Yet none of these claims for the play's broad appeal proves that the play actually had broad appeal, and in this sense, Wignell's presentation of the play is a little like the well-worn story of Benjamin Franklin wheeling his wheelbarrow about town in a public pantomime of actual labor—yet another print-centered performance that has perhaps been taken a little too literally by succeeding generations of readers. In the end, Wignell's attempts to make the play relevant to the ongoing articulation of *E pluribus unum* in federal Philadelphia all invite critical questioning. The fact that Wignell held out long enough to get a federal copyright, for instance, tells us something about how he envisioned the book, but the firstness of this gesture also indicates the provisional (because new) nature not just of copyright but of the federal government's regulation of such matters.[17] The play's diffuse subscription list, furthermore, does not prove the limitless agency of the printed book at hand so much as it follows the mobile but still finite movements of one man—Wignell himself, who as a player in a traveling theatrical company made very specific trade contacts in the cities he performed in—Baltimore, Annapolis, Williamsburg, New York, and Philadelphia—which together comprise the bulk of the place-names found on the list. Even the printed subscription list evokes a fantasy of broad textual diffusion *and* serves as a record of the ways in which actual dissemination was imperfect and fragmented. To anchor the fantasy of the (imagined) unified nation-state (over and against the disruptions and displacements of lived space), Wignell places Washington's name at the head of the list as a figurehead subscriber. As the new president, Washington was the perfect screen on which to project the semblance of federal patronage and coverage. But even this is more a matter of Wignell's hopes than an endorsement, for Washington does not appear to have actually subscribed. On the contrary, Wignell placed Washington at the head of the subscription list because he intended to send the new president an (unsolicited) copy, a favor that allowed Wignell to use Washington's name on the list.[18] The claim for geographic diffuseness, meanwhile—based on the fact that the play had been "Performed with APPLAUSE at the theatres in NEW-YORK, PHILADELPHIA, and MARYLAND"—does more to indicate the play's relative restriction, given the fact that it was played neither in the lower Chesapeake nor in the deep South, not to mention to the north, in New England, or to the west. Indeed, the play's performance history demonstrates that relatively few audiences saw it performed. While George Seilhamer notes that the premiere of the play was "the chief event of the season in New York," the play's performance schedule prior to the print edition was thin: it had only five performances in New York (spanning from its opening on April 16 to mid-May 1787, plus one more in June 1789), followed by two in Baltimore (in 1787 and 1788), and one in Philadelphia (in December 1787).[19] The range of performances is even less impressive when one realizes that some of these were not full-dress, full-cast performances. The lone Philadelphia production, for instance, was merely a solo reading held by Wignell at the City Tavern as he was passing through Philadelphia on his travels between the only two cities (in all of North America) that had legal playhouses (New York and Baltimore).[20] In fact, the Philadelphia reading seems to have been little more than a promotional tie-in for the impending print edition: tickets to the performance cost a steep seven shillings and six pence each, which entitled the customer to a place on the subscription list and "a copy of the comedy when printed."[21]

The limited impact of the play in Philadelphia accounts for Wignell's dedication to the Dramatic Association. While this might look like a grateful acknowledgment to a powerful national elite that supports the fledgling arts, the Dramatic Association was in fact a small group of Philadelphia merchants then lobbying to reopen the city's theaters in the face of staunch Quaker and lingering populist resistance.[22] It is little wonder that Wignell would have wanted to reach out to these men. Not only was Philadelphia midway between the only two cities in which his company could legally perform, but when he did do readings in Philadelphia, he had to evade the letter of the local law by bribing local officials and disguising his wares as "Lectures" or "Dialogues" rather than "readings" or "plays." One advertisement for a performance of Shakespeare's *Richard III*, for instance, billed itself as "a serious Historical Lecture in five parts—on the Fate of Tyranny." Thus, what looks like a reference to an austere early national dramatic institution actually refers to a local debate that Wignell sought to involve himself in to the betterment of his own touring company.[23]

Given Wignell's aggressive framing of the play in print, is it any wonder that *The Contrast* has long been read as an already postconstitutional, already national text rather than the rare Articles-era artifact that it is? With this problem in view, we might begin to ask a different set of questions. What happens to the shape of the early national canon if we entertain another reading, not just of the play but of the nation that the play is said to be presenting? What if *The Contrast* is not so much the "American" artifact it has been retroactively produced as (in print) but an intensely regional one? I use the word "region" here in the most flexible sense possible (for it is, in fact, an historically plastic term that never stops changing in these years). For my purposes, it includes any abstracted territorial identity that rises above the merely local but falls short of being national, including the familiar Western contrasts of competing geographical locale vis-à-vis relative industrial development (urban vs. rural) but even more so the less grand contrasts between particular place-based identifications—in the case of this play, the Massachusetts-ness of upstanding Massachusetts yeomen vs. the New York-ness of dissolute New York spendthrifts. These place-based (and often, as we shall see, state-based) identities are the most meaningful political and social affiliations in late-eighteenth-century North America, and *The Contrast* explores them in depth by pitting one kind of regionalized character against another in scene after scene. This is not to say that the play does not express a powerful nationalist *wish*; on the contrary, it is because that wish is so artfully constructed that we take it, somewhat like the provincial Jonathan takes the play, for the real thing. Nevertheless, *The Contrast*'s primary concern is not nationalism per se, but the problem of how, within the emerging language of nationalist unity, to make sense of profound regional differences. And in this sense, the play's primary reality is not one of consensus at all but of discord—momentous differences that threaten to render the emergent union unworkable before it ever gets going.

The question of *what happens* in *The Contrast* has been strangely elusive in critical accounts of the play. It is usually described as a work of "a newly awakened nationalism," "aimed at a British target, turning the conventions of the Restoration drama against itself by juxtaposing the homespun honesty of American characters against the calculating hypocrisy and theatricality of their British counterparts."[24] But as valid as this reading might be as an abstracted account of the play's internationalized codes—its meaning, in other words, within a shared transatlantic republic of letters—it does not describe the particular political affiliations of the play's actual characters. Few critics remark on the extraordinary fact that there simply are no "British counterparts" to be found here—that there are no British or European characters in *The Contrast* at all.[25] The play depicts a small circle of New Yorkers whose world is altered by the arrival into their community of two Massachusetts visitors: the upright (and uptight) Colonel Manly and his gullible manservant Jonathan, who quickly become involved in local scenes and scandals because of their readymade relation to Manly's sister Charlotte, who has been living in the city for some time before her brother's arrival. In one such subplot, the New Englanders foil the nefarious seduction schemes of a corrupt local rogue named Billy Dimple; in another, Manly slowly becomes enamored with Dimple's fiancée (and his sister's social rival), Maria Van Rough, heiress to a Dutch New York fortune that Dimple has his eye on, even as he woos several other women with the help of *his* manservant, Jessamy. The plot that ensues plays the virtuous pairing of Manly and Jonathan off that of the corrupt Dimple and Jessamy, following the star-crossed paths of several cross-regional love triangles (Dimple, Manly, and Maria; Charlotte, Maria, and Dimple; Dimple, Charlotte, and Letitia; and Jonathan, Jessamy, and Jenny) even as it arrives, finally, at one single bi-state marriage.

Where, then, are the British? The foppish Billy Dimple has long stood in for the British pole in this international binary while Manly is read as the iconic and foundational American republican. Yet Dimple and Manly are not, in the end, two international types but two regional types—a stereotypical New Yorker and a stereotypical Yankee. If anything, the play's crises are engendered by Americans who simply travel too much—and not just those who travel to Europe. One set of problems is generated by the fact that Dimple leaves New York and sees too much of London, but a host of other—and much more central—problems is instigated by the fact that Jonathan and Manly (and Charlotte) are all "strangers" to the particular mores of New York City. What canonical accounts of the play fail to point out, then, is that every character in this play is American, and the dramatic crises they experience are without exception crises of dislocation brought on by journeys *across* putatively linked ("American") regions. This fact suggests that the contrast of the title is not about America and Britain at all but about local varieties of 1780s Americans, who identify themselves first as members of towns, states, and (when traveling) regions and only secondarily as the proud nationals we postconstitutionalists have retroactively asked them to be.[26]

Jonathan's rendition of his own "town song," "Yankee Doodle," is an apt figure for our retrospective confusions of postconstitutional outcomes with preconstitutional realities. As Jonathan sings: "Marblehead's a rocky place, / And Cape-Cod is sandy; / Charlestown is burnt down, / Boston is the dandy" (46). This is not a verse of the song many of us learn today: it is, after all, provincial to a fault. While history has revised the song into a generically and generalized patriotic artifact, its local origins are still evident here. Its speaker, a regimental foot soldier with a precise (Boston) identification, antagonistically taunts not the British but other "Americans," and not just any other Americans but other Massachusetts citizens on the basis of their inferior origins at places like "Marblehead" (too rocky), "Cape-Cod" (too sandy), and "Charlestown" (burnt to the ground in the Battle of Bunker Hill). As this verse shows, "Yankee Doodle" is not yet (in 1787) the relic of patriotic consensus that later versions would render it. It is instead a song that epitomizes perfectly the local identifications that underwrote everything "continental" in the 1770s and 1780s—including General Washington's fractious Continental Army (whose various regiments sang the song, each with local biases) and the Continental Congress, which was still in session in 1787, when Tyler came to New York and wrote this play. Jonathan's "town-song" thus reminds us—as Jonathan himself repeatedly does—that locale, and localness, is still an important signifier of identity and identification, not just at the moment of the Revolution but in the tumultuous years after as well.[27]

The play begins with a "Prologue" that elusively engages the subject of locale, and it is worth quoting at length:

PROLOGUE
Written by a young gentleman of New-York; spoken by Mr. Wignell.

EXULT each patriot heart!—this night is shewn
A piece, which we may fairly call our own;
Where the proud titles of "My Lord! Your Grace!"

To humble *Mr.* and plain *Sir* give place.
Our Author pictures not from foreign climes
The fashions, or the follies of the times;
But has confin'd the subject of his work
To the gay scenes—the circles of New-York.
On native themes his Muse displays her pow'rs;
If ours the faults, the virtues too are ours.
Why should our thoughts to distant countries roam,
When each refinement may be found at home?
· ·

But modern youths, with imitative sense,
Deem taste in dress the proof of excellence;
And spurn the meanness of your homespun arts,
Since homespun habits would obscure their parts;
Whilst all, which aims at splendour and parade,
Must come from Europe, *and be ready made.*
Strange! we should thus our native worth disclaim,
And check the progress of our rising fame.
Yet *one,* whilst imitation bears the sway,
Aspires to nobler heights, and points the way,
Be rous'd, my friends! his bold example view;
Let your own Bards be proud to copy *you!*
Should rigid critics reprobate our play,
At least the patriotic heart will say,
"Glorious our fall, since in a noble cause.
The bold *attempt alone* demands applause."
Still may the wisdom of the Comic Muse
Exalt your merits, or your faults accuse.
But think not, 'tis her aim to be severe;—
We all are mortals, and as mortals err.
If candour pleases, we are truly blest;
Vice trembles, when compelled to stand confess'd.
Let not light Censure on your faults, offend,
Which aims not to expose them, but amend.
Thus does our Author to your candour trust;
Conscious, the *free* are generous, as just.[28]

This looks at first glance like a familiar outtake from the eighteenth-
century canon. Mobilizing a well-worn discourse about the "refinement"

found in "distant countries" versus the "native worth" of "homespun arts," it tells a familiar story about early American cultural production and its struggles to distinguish itself from the "ready made" culture of Europe. "Vice" is reduced to the impulse to imitate; "candour" is elevated to the status of virtue. When read against the ensuing pairing of the "homespun" Manly and the Europeanized Dimple, these lines seem, once again, to announce the play's aggressive nationalist intentions.[29]

But the prologue also gestures toward the play's embedded, and unexcavated, regional conflicts, and readings that ignore this fact are doomed to sing a tune that sounds more like a latter-day "Yankee Doodle" than the one Jonathan sings in the play. Note, for example, how the prologue begins here—not in the spoken lines but in the set directions that precede it. While the play was billed, both on its title page and in New York advertisements, as having been "Written By A Citizen of the United States," the prologue is distinctively labeled as having been written "By a young gentleman of New-York"—a meaningful and in this case intriguing late 1780s political classification. Today we are used to paying taxes to both our local state and the federal government; there is no political incoherence, in modern American citizenship, in calling oneself a citizen of both New York and the United States at large. But this understanding of a political affiliation deriving from dual sources of equally legitimate, coexisting authority is a legal fiction that was not invented until 1787 when the members of the Federal Convention inserted a new representational standard into the architecture of American citizenship—the plan of proportional representation that created the House of Representatives as a counterpart to the more traditional scheme of state-based representation in the Senate, thus extending federal citizenship not just to states but to individuals.[30] Before the Constitution was ratified in 1789 and this new scheme of representation went into effect, the states (rather than the nation) exercised absolute sovereignty over individuals. After ratification, however, the individual state was no longer the irreducible unit of political representation within the union at large: the individual citizen thereafter played that part and in the process gained a new legal relationship to the distant federal state.[31] While state loyalties remained intact, the Constitution's representational compromise subtly reorganized political life in ways I will discuss at greater length in future chapters. For Madison, this new kind of representation was the central problem of the summer-long debate about how to restructure the Confederation, and indeed, its consequences were profound, for it ensured the long-term feasibility of an extended and infinitely extendable republic, a vast geo-political screen for seemingly unlimited projections of federal fantasy.[32] The idea was radical enough that several (including two of New York's three) delegates left the Federal Convention because they knew they were not authorized to debate a plan that would undermine the very unit of political power—the individual state—that had sent them to Philadelphia in the first place.

We are used to this arrangement now. Most twenty-first-century Americans would probably characterize it as one of the "blessings" of the founding so much so that it is nearly invisible to them as a choice in the structure of their government. But this is a decidedly postconstitutional perception. In the 1780s, fresh from the Revolution, citizens throughout the physical territory that called itself the United States considered themselves first and foremost subjects of their state's primary sovereignty, while the states were in turn members in the larger Confederation.[33] This way of organizing political identities made sense in the eighteenth century: for one thing, it followed the truism that sovereignty must come from a single and uncontested source; for another, it created small, imaginable units of political affiliation rather than the unimaginable community of an entire continent, which (as Charles Inglis pointed out in 1776) was not considered feasible for "the dilatory administration of democracy."[34] State loyalty was so ingrained in the delegates to the Federal Convention that the Committee of Style changed the words in the Constitution's preamble to "We the People of the United States" only at the last possible moment—September 10, just before the final draft was released to the public. For months before that, the working drafts over which the delegates argued began with the more obvious choice of words: "We the People of the States of New-Hampshire, Massachusetts," and so on.[35]

The state-based political identifications of the 1780s create problems for the pervasively nationalist bias that has dominated our reading of *The Contrast*, because in order for the nationalist reading of the play to be intelligible, New York must already be, in 1787, a representative American locale, a specific place that can serviceably function as a metonym for the more generalized American "we" that nationalist readings presume over and against a generalized Britain. But despite the presence of the new federal government (which made New York its capital from 1785 to 1790), New York was not such a generalizable locale in 1787. For one thing, New York had been the most Tory city during the Revolution, occupied by the British from 1776 to 1783, and after the war it remained a haven for many affluent (reassimilated) Tories. New York was not just the *least* American of cities; it was the most visibly British or Anglophile of American cities and, along with other urban centers, a geographical icon not for representative American virtue but for luxury and vice—a set of cultural codes that Tyler knowingly tweaks with (among others) his ruthless caricature of the overly Anglicized, foppish Billy Dimple.

But there is a more immediately explosive set of contemporary issues at work when Tyler codes his New York characters as avaricious and acquisitive importers, Anglophile travelers, reckless speculators, Chesterfieldian rakes, luxury consumers, and outrageous coquettes. All these stereotypes are traceable to the city's cultural role as the North's primary importer of foreign goods, itself a function of its fortuitous geographic location. The boom in New York maritime trade that followed the Treaty of Paris helped raise the local economy from the ashes of the revolutionary fires that had razed many of its buildings, but it did little to make New York seem comfortably representative or "federal" to its sister states. When Tyler arrived in the city in 1787, New York was vying with Philadelphia for the reputation of being the most decadent city in North America. New York's status as a geographical icon known up and down the eastern seaboard for its luxury and vice coincided with the move of the Continental Congress into the city in 1785. As the temporary capital of the union, New York was visited at length by representatives from all over America, many of whom took the opportunity to describe the world they saw in the letters they sent home. Common accounts of life in the city describe a world of "Balls, Concerts, routs, hops, [and] Fandangoes," not to mention rampant inflation brought on by the overimportation and overpricing of British goods.[36]

Still, it was hardly just the number of New York's imports or the ostentation of its self-display that affected its cross-regional persona as a significant (or signifying) locale. It was *how* New York chose to regulate its maritime trade that created divisive debate among neighboring states. Because of the way the Confederation conceived of state sovereignties, New York was able to exploit the geographic advantage of its conveniently located seaport (and, because of its recent Tory past, its strong cultural ties to England) as a way to gouge—and irritate—other states within the regional market it inhabited. New Jersey, poised between Philadelphia and New York City, would seem to have been in a position to profit from this proximity, but because neither city was within its own borders, New Jersey instead found itself like "a cask tapped at both ends," paying extravagantly punitive tariffs for the ironic "fatality" not of "trans-Atlantic birth" (to use Benedict Anderson's phrase) but of New Jersey residence.[37] Indeed, New York's tax practices were more brutal than most: its trade regulations designated other states in the Confederation under the same legal alien status that governed their relations with foreign nations.[38]

Far from standing forth, then, as an acceptable regional representative for Confederate America, New York had made itself infamous as an anti-nationalist city in an antinationalist state. This generalized perception of New York as self-interested was further exacerbated when, in the late 1780s, New York State stubbornly refused to pass the bill known as the Continental Impost.[39] The Impost would have diminished the state's ability to tax other states unfairly while at the same time giving the Continental Congress broader powers under the confederation to collect taxes and thus support itself as a federal entity. For many federalists, the crisis that led to the Federal Convention was brought on by New York's unwillingness to pass the Impost, which led many other states' leaders to conclude that some advantageously located states—like New York—had too much control over such interstate issues while the Continental Congress had too little. Had New York acted with less self-interest and more continental character, the Federal Convention might not have been called when it was. Indeed, New York was frequently cited at the Federal Convention by delegates from other states, who were vocally wary of the Empire State's legendary ability to implode consensus with its self-interested economic policies.[40]

Given the centrality of abstracted state affiliation to 1780s political organization, the prologue's announcement that it was "*Written by a young gentleman of New-York*" becomes perhaps a more meaningful rhetorical gesture than we might at first think. This is not to say that the prologue speaks only in a New York voice (though tellingly, it does not appear as part of Wignell's more nationally conceived print version in 1790). On the contrary, the prologue imagines multiple—and incoherent—audiences, straddling the ambiguities of overdetermined geopolitical identifications to create a sharp regional specificity while at the same time working (like the play that follows) to erase whatever regional discords might potentially torpedo the success of the production at hand. By positing itself as the production of a New Yorker, the prologue subtly identifies its own sensibility with that of its first, actual audience and in doing so works to defuse whatever offenses might be generated by the play—which was widely known in New York circles to be the work of a visiting New England, Major Tyler, who was in New York on a diplomatic mission, sent by the governor of Massachusetts as a state envoy to discuss and negotiate an interstate conflict of interest with the governor of New York.

A prologue is the perfect rhetorical juncture at which to perform such delicate work. For one thing, prologues almost always mark an ambiguous disjunction between the voice or sensibility that produced the play and the one who speaks the prologue, and that disjunction is further reinforced here by the fact that the prologue speaker is labeled as a New Yorker while the play's author is identified as "A Citizen of the United States." As a theatrical convention, prologues are *meant* to stand apart from the text they are attached to; they are spoken first but are understood to have been written last, with the speaker speaking in reflective afterthought, having already seen the play that the audience is about to experience. Wignell had good reason to want to mark a difference between the prologue and the play. We of course, as heirs to a national history that has largely erased the specificities of 1780s political affiliation, hardly notice the differences between the prologue's and the play's sensibility. But *The Contrast's* prologue is self-consciously constructing an ambiguous "we" that sometimes expands to include a protonationalist identification but that more often than not focuses, rhetorically, on the specific audience for which the play was first performed. The prologue needs, in other words, to be excavated as an instructional aside *by* a New Yorker *for* a specifically New York audience. In quipping that "if ours the faults, the virtues too are ours," the prologue's speaker is generically elevating "our" "American" "virtues," but he is also specifically emphasizing the more local New York "faults" that Tyler lampoons so mercilessly throughout the play. The prologue functions in this sense as an elaborate and ambivalent apology to its very first New York audience, acknowledging the potential insult in Tyler's scathing (outsider's) portrayal of Billy Dimple, a New York antihero and the character most marked by the flaws that the prologue tries to smooth over as the mere foibles of "youth."

Once we recover the specificity of New York both as the story's setting and as the target audience for the prologue, it becomes easier to see *The Contrast* as the regionally charged play that it is rather than the nationalist one it has been reconstructed as after the fact. Tyler skewers New York as only an outsider can, casting it as a city of greed, luxury, and licentious self-interest. Tyler's city is, in fact, very much the New York of his own recent touristic experience—the same city that, as a stranger, he was only just beginning to know in the weeks before the play opened. Though few readers have remarked on it, the play is saturated with self-conscious references to the city's most famous local features. Thus, Tyler has several hometown characters offer to show the out-of-towners "the sights" (including famous places like "the Battery," "the Mall," and "Holy Ground"), day trips that give the play all the feel of a cramped and circumscribed travel narrative—an early tourist's guide, if you will, to life in the Big Apple.[41]

But the devices used in delineating setting are nothing compared to those devoted to character. From start to finish Tyler cultivates a recognizable array of New York stereotypes—particularly in the figure of the avaricious Dutch merchant Van Rough; the foppish, Anglophile spendthrift Dimple; the coquettes Charlotte and Letitia; and the overly educated Maria. While the New England pairing of Manly and Jonathan is also lampooned, they are far less troubling (morally) than the play's many New York characters. Manly and Jonathan are far more acceptable, in the end, as potential model citizens than either member of the contrasting New York duo—Dimple and Jessamy. Indeed, while female New York characters like Letitia, Charlotte, Maria, and Jenny (the servant girl) provide oases of identification for both the viewer and, one imagines, Tyler himself (especially in the case of Charlotte), the male New Yorkers are intensely marked as moral failures: the merchant Van Rough is greedy and dottering; Dimple is a debauched and highly unlikable rake (unlike the slightly more attractive rogues found in *The Coquette* or *Charlotte Temple*); while Jessamy is the ape of his master's foolish tastes. As a factory of character, New York looks very bad indeed.

These regionalized caricatures should not surprise us, for Tyler himself was invested in an abstracted political identity at the time he wrote the play. As an officer of the state of Massachusetts, his political commitments on this visit were clearly state-based Massachusetts interests, and yet as a negotiator (someone who was sent from one state to another to broker a resolution to an interstate crisis), his particular identification was also something more than just state-based—even if short of being federal. It is not insignificant, in any case, that these contemptible New York caricatures sprang from the head of a Massachusetts man—indeed, a newly arrived Massachusetts diplomat who in the weeks before this performance was in the process of being received at dinner parties and private balls into the same polite New York society for whom this play was primarily performed at the John Street Theater, and which it nevertheless also targets as the objects of its out-of-town satire. Later in life, Tyler would repeatedly satirize specific regional populations in his major works, and this would prove to be a persistently divisive and problematic feature of his rhetoric. Indeed, later this same year, in May 1787, Tyler wrote a second play for the New York stage, complete with similar regional stereotypes of New Yorkers (but, crucially, no such stereotypes of New Englanders), but this second play was widely criticized on just these grounds. As William Grayson wrote to James Madison:

> We have lately had a new farce wrote by Poet Tyler, called May day. It has plott & incident and is as good as several of the English farces; It has however not succeeded well, owing I believe to the Author's making his principal character a scold; Some of the New York ladies were alarmed for fear strangers should look upon Mrs. Surdus as the model of the gentlewomen of this place.[42]

As a federal delegate from Georgia writing to Madison in Virginia, Grayson could afford to record this moment of regional rejection without personal investment or further analysis. But it is just this kind of regional antagonism that Wignell's prologue is meant to defuse by speaking to New Yorkers in a voice of their own. And if Wignell was trying to frame the play with a set of reading instructions primarily tailored to the play's satiric targets—New Yorkers—then he seems to have succeeded: *The Contrast* managed to pass in the end as an acceptable satire of regional manners. It may have succeeded where later Tyler productions did not because, in addition to its New York targets, it also pokes fun at Massachusetts men, or it may have benefited from the careful jockeying and presentation of Wignell, who in the prologue and elsewhere labored to frame the play as inoffensive, playful, and nationally invested in nonregionally specific aspirations (rather than state-based identifications).[43] In the end, one of the few published criticisms of the play turned out to be, ironically, that it was not regional enough: as the *New-York Daily Advertiser* argued, the play was well done, but "Wignell had not quite the right pronunciation for Jonathan."[44] Tyler's bumpkin Yankee—the template for future stage Yankees—was simply not Yankee enough for its very first New York audience.

In the end, *The Contrast*'s prologue exposes the problem with presuming an always already postconstitutional "we"—a "we" that signifies a homogenized, generalized American audience rather than the more specific, geographically determined audience that sat in the theater for specific performances. The postconstitutional "we" does not merely limit our reading of the literal "we" used in the play's prologue. It also dramatically hampers our ability to see Tyler's play for what it is: an historically unique attempt to think about the grounds of post-Revolutionary community among various geographic parts of the union—particularly in regard to those pervasive and yet now largely invisible place-based identifications that marked everything American in the fractious 1780s. In 1787 when Tyler wrote his play, such territorial differences had yet to be suspended in federal consensus, and they were already congealing into the constructed abstractions of stringent state identification that would make the imagining of the federal constitution—and its ratification— such a remarkable endeavor in the months and years that followed *The Contrast*'s premiere. In brokering a lasting union across these competing sites of identity, federalism did the impossible—raising what John Murrin has called "a roof without walls," a federal framework in a world of localities that (like the mutually suspicious Dimple and Manly) "did not like each other very much."[45]

What is self-evident to us now—the inevitableness of *E pluribus unum*—was a splinter of desperate fragments in 1787. Indeed, even within certain states, competing identifications emerged to threaten what little consensus and cohesion existed at the *state* level. In Massachusetts, for instance, Shays's Rebellion was seen as a "western," "rural," and "farm" problem, and most of the state militia raised to put it down was drawn from the mercantile, monied, eastern seaboard communities. Thus the discourse of class difference that drove Shays's Rebellion also emerged simultaneously as an internal geographic division of the state's actual physical territory that threatened not the federal government but government of any kind—in this case, Massachusetts state government. I am not suggesting, then, that class and gender were not constitutive fragments in the confusing world of 1780s social affiliation—because they were. But these categories were not nearly as coherent in 1787 North America as many readings of *The Contrast* assume. If Charlotte's behavior in New York and her brother's prudish expectations for her can be taken seriously, New York City had an entirely different normative baseline for gendered behavior than did the Manlys' Massachusetts hometown. Likewise we need to take into account the incoherence of early class formation, especially as a category being unevenly formulated across a territorial space that was still defining itself in these years as a monolithic entity—rather than simply accepting the monumentalizing fiction of sameness that class-based readings of the play sometimes suggest.

The play participates, of course, in generating these confusions. *The Contrast* is a quintessentially transitional cultural object, with one foot mimetically planted in the world as Tyler knew it and the other moving nimbly toward some other, imagined future. We can see this in Tyler's complex construction of the problem of class, which is still very much a matter of region in the play yet is experimentally offered up as a potential site for translocal identity in the entertaining friendship that emerges between Manly's (Massachusetts) servant Jonathan and Dimple's (New York) servant Jessamy. In one telling scene, the Yankee Jonathan comically resists reductive class identification with his New York counterpart by declaring that he is not, like Jessamy, "a servant" but "a waiter." Like Jonathan's many other cultural malapropisms, the audience is meant to laugh at this seemingly meager but insistent moment of self-definition, and it is almost certain that the very first New York audience would have found this joke very funny indeed. But what investment does Tyler have in making such a joke? One of the unionizing fictions the play is peddling is that of an already recognizable, cross-regional economic system whereby Massachusetts Shaysites like Jonathan already resemble the servant class of New York or, indeed, the working poor throughout the increasingly racialized poor, white South. This is not so different, it turns out, from the logic that would later drive the formation of the Federal Convention, which took local evidence of class rebellion in Massachusetts and connected it to an array of other social disorders in other states in order to legitimate its radical reorganization of the existing Confederation. As Jack Greene argues, "'by juxtaposing and synthesizing different and previously unconnected kinds of violence and disorder and by treating them all as symptoms of an underlying constitutional problem' that could be solved only by augmenting the authority of the union, [the federalists] . . . 'created a new reality' that, in Washington's words, finally persuaded the 'greater part of the Union . . . of the necessity of foederal measures.'"[46]

This solution is all the more remarkable because of the very real differences the play makes visible between Jonathan and Jessamy. Indeed, if these two lower class characters are similar in a structural sense (within the play's fictional dichotomies, Jonathan is to Manly as Jessamy is to Dimple), then they are also significantly different in terms of the *content* of their intensely regionalized characters. Jonathan, for instance, will very likely return to Massachusetts and become a modest landowner—owner of a small piece of rocky land but a landowner nonetheless whose class inferiority, though distinct, would continue to be structured for several decades more in the pastoral version of deferential lower rank that had marked British social hierarchies for centuries. But Jessamy's class predicament more closely resembles the modern, industrially motivated definition of class that we are used to seeing in classical Marxist analysis, whereby workers are exploited for their surplus value in such a way that they manage to accumulate little property or skill over the course of their working lives. Jessamy is not likely to own anything if he remains a New York servant—except perhaps his master's castoff clothes. Class, then, is not at all unimportant in this play. But its centrality involves the way the play manages to find ways to use very different kinds of lower-class people from entirely different regional economies to create an incipiently federalist consensus among very different kinds of upper-class people— especially those kinds of New Yorkers and Massachusetts men who were most likely to attend federal, and ratifying, conventions the summer after Tyler's play premiered: the first sons of the families named Manly and Van Rough.

3. FEDERAL FRICTIONS:
THE PART-PIECES OF NATIONAL IDENTITY

When *The Contrast* was finally printed, it included a single engraved plate (figure 4.3) that perfectly epitomizes not the fractious state-based realities of 1780s life so evident in the play's regional caricatures but another, wished-for outcome. It expresses a fantasy about how best to suppress the cacophonous problems of state loyalty that Tyler, the Massachusetts envoy, had recently combated and in the process finds a solution that strongly resembles the constitutional outcome that was eventually ratified and elevated into a coherent system for managing cross-regional conflict. The plate illustrates, appropriately, the "scene last"—the comedic finale in which conflict is resolved and future unions assured. The engraving may or may not have been based on an eyewitness account of the performance, but it is the only surviving archival evidence that sug-

FIGURE 4.3 Royall Tyler. *The Contrast.* Philadelphia: Prichard & Hall, 1790. Frontispiece. The Historical Society of Pennsylvania (HSP).

gests what Tyler's play may have looked like on the stage. To this end, the illustrator chose his moment well: the scene portrayed is the only one in which all of the principals are together in the same space, and so we are treated to an illuminating tableau that includes Colonel Manly and his weepy future wife Maria on one side and the good merchant/bad merchant New York duo of Van Rough and Billy Dimple on the other, with the Yankee Jonathan in the middle. Beneath the plate, the illustration is captioned with one of Jonathan's final lines in the play: "Do you want to kill the Colonel? I feel chock full of fight."

It is appropriate that Jonathan should be centrally located here: by all accounts, he was the most popular character in the play and his part was played by Wignell, the most celebrated character actor in the early United States. There is little doubt that Wignell would have placed Jonathan at center stage as often as possible, and as the copyright holder he may even have engaged the engraver to memorialize his character here. It is no surprise, then, that like the other editorial materials that frame the printed play, this plate continues the federal framing of Tyler's uneven imaginings. Many readers have noticed that Jonathan disappears from the play midway through, but the engraving reminds us that while the script of the play may fail to include him verbally in the final scenes (he has virtually no lines and for this reason is largely erased from the printed text), Jonathan is in fact very much present at, and central to, the climax and resolution of the play's regional conflicts as a whole. While Cathy Davidson laments that the problem of class is merely absorbed into the central plot, the engraving suggests the continued centrality of all sorts of differences right up through the ultimate resolution, or absorption, of its portrayed social crisis into union. The particularities of Jonathan's emergent class position are amply inscribed here—in his words, his childish and overly passionate expression, his rather dirty appearance, his backwoods bare-knuckles pose, and even in his thick, dark natural hair, which stands out strikingly against the powdered wigs of the three other men portrayed here. In this scene, a Yankee boy—by his own description a "true blue" son of Bunker Hill (and a modest New England freeholder to boot)—is centrally refigured through the mechanism of the play's resolved plot into a menial servant reduced to defending his social superior with his fists (28).

This silent reworking of Jonathan's pre-Revolutionary identity into a new perpetually inferior post-Revolutionary identity is hinted at earlier in the play. On being introduced to Billy Dimple's servant Jessamy for the first time, Jonathan naively exclaims: "You a waiter! by the living jingo, you look so topping, I took you for one of the agents to Congress!" (27). In yet another of the play's endless jokes on Jonathan, the fellow who looks (to him) like a senator is really a menial servant—not a federal representative except insofar as he represents the emergent, post-Revolutionary class divisions that farmers like Jonathan—or Jefferson, his southern counterpart—found so frightening about northern urban life and so potentially threatening to the heritage of the "true blue" "sons of liberty" who had helped fight the Revolution only to become disenfranchised Jessamys under the new federal system (28). As a (future) Massachusetts freeholder, Jonathan is invested in denying that the same kinds of class divisions that were emerging among free white men in urban areas had any potential for exportation into his home locale. Nevertheless, his claim that he is not a "servant" but a "waiter" aside, the nascent formulation of a divisive identity politics is already present in his own internalized racist logic: within the leveling New England language of liberty (what Jessamy calls "a true Yankee distinction, egad, without a difference"), Jonathan already cannot assert his equality to the colonel he serves without also asserting his superiority to someone else: "Do you take me for a neger?" (26). As outrageous as that question is meant to sound coming from a white man, Jonathan is in fact racialized—indeed, that is one of the ways that he is classed—in the printed play's engraving, which shows the farm boy's heightened color in distinct contrast to the cool, federalist pallor of the social superiors who thus accent his childish pose. As Jonathan's gradual transformation from "true blue son of liberty" to "waiter" to "servant" to borderline "neger" suggests, class is not subordinate to the regional issues this play raises. Rather, the difference-based discourses of federalism are deeply imbricated in the fiction of white elite male consensus the play is trying to achieve.

In the end, *The Contrast* is both intensely regionalized and profoundly unionizing. Indeed, it is precisely its unionizing telos that has made it so hard to relocate as part of the 1780s regionalized landscape. While the play is riddled with the undercurrents of territorial dissent, Tyler's ulterior motives can hardly be called divisive. *The Contrast*, more so than many other texts of this era, clearly seeks an amicable suspension to divisive regional debate. However poorly behaved Tyler's New Yorkers are, he casts them in the most socially lethargic, or conservative, of forms—a drawing room comedy that demonstrates its urbanity by observing its own inconsequentiality with self-ironic aplomb. And as distasteful as the central New Yorkers are, they are not unmatched, in their ridiculousness, by their Massachusetts counterparts—a fact that will continue to give headaches to readers who feel they need to locate the play's notoriously unstable center of moral gravity.

It is worth noting, finally, that Tyler (like Paine before him) manages to float this fiction of an already constructed whole (complete with already properly subjected subjects) without doing what the state-based loyalists of 1787–88 (now called antifederalists) seemed to fear most: at the same time that he partakes of an emergent federal discourse to broker a bi-state (New York/Massachusetts) union, he does little to undermine the geographic coherence of particular kinds of class conflict. Indeed, if anything, he fudges the (literal) grounds of regional consensus in a way that would very likely have been unrecognizable to his New York audience.[47] Jonathan may be very different from Manly when considered individually, but if you put Manly and Jonathan next to Jessamy and Dimple as a set of pairings, you see just how much the play reinforces the Massachusettsness of Massachusetts men (even very different ones) and the New Yorkness of New York men—even as it ends, simultaneously, with a Massachusetts–New York wedding. And while the play ends in cross-regional union, with the Yankee yeoman marrying the Dutch New Yorker's daughter, there is little overt threat to the regional identifications that otherwise saturate the play. One assumes that Manly will take his New York bride back to New England and buy even more Massachusetts land with Van Rough's New York money. Thus at the same time that it creates affective links between upper classes over and against lower classes, the play continues to underwrite an (equally fictitious) account of regional—or in this case, state-based—sovereignty and consensus, and one way it does this is by promising sameness and homogeneity at a national level but hierarchically organized difference at the local level. Indeed, it is the play's protofederalist evocation of every little locality as a mirror for the next—with each small community repeating the same recognizable "contrasts" of class and gender—that floats the fantasy of national homogeneity here.[48]

Gender does special work in this regard—as it must do in a play that structures itself as a seduction plot and resolves its fictional dilemmas through the mechanism of marriage. Tyler uses gendered political identities to broker the fiction of multiple distinct communities that nevertheless have the potential to be peacefully unified. While all the men portrayed in *The Contrast* are regionally inflected, none of the women are regionally identifiable by virtue of their speech or their behavior. Indeed, the women in this play have no political affiliation whatsoever: they appear entirely disconnected from the distinctions of region, race, and class—emergent categories that underwrite the identities of all of the play's male characters. The play never raises questions, for instance, about why a Massachusetts daughter like Charlotte is living in New York (with her Manly uncle) in the first place, or why she and Manly do not seem to share the same features of New England cultural identity that Manly obviously shares with Jonathan. Tyler's women are a little like New York goods: exportable commodities, regionally transcendent, and presumably assimilable to other geographic areas. Thus the unproblematic cross-regional marriage of a young New York girl to "Mr. Indigo, the rich Carolinian" is mentioned early on in order to bolster the play's national imaginings (6). Indeed, Maria (to take another example) is so porous in her subjective identifications that she can identify not just across regional lines (accepting a Massachusetts stranger as a suitor over and against both her New York fiancé and her New York father) but across racial lines as well, as when she sings a rueful ballad in the voice of the already exterminated Native American, Alknomook. The fact that the play's women are not regionally (and thus politically) inflected has profound implications for how Tyler imagines union might eventually be conservatively brokered, and identities merged, across future generations.[49] The idea of cross-regional assimilation—or amalgamation—would prove far more troubling, as we shall see, in the nineteenth century, but in 1787, it was a reasonable way, it seems, to theorize the unimaginable future.

It is a testament to the incredible cultural success of federalism that even today we uncritically see reflected back from the stage of our reading a transparent playing-out of the world that was—all bell hoops and shoe buckles. If this is so, it is because *The Contrast's* guiding ethic is not the divisive work of identity politics but the federal and federalizing work of consensus across the divides of faction at any cost, and it achieves this end so successfully that even now we reproduce that consensus whenever we identify in it the canonical early national contrasts for which it is so famous. The play may seem like a window, but it is really more like a mirror—a mirror that resists the fracture of difference and reabsorbs it into bland consensus. In the end, the work done here strongly resembles the cultural work that federalism would eventually do everywhere else in the republic, from cobblers' shops to the Senate gallery.

Yet it is important to remember that when Tyler wrote the play, the outcome of federal connection was not nearly as self-evident as it seems to us in retrospect. Although local identifications based on class position would eventually become a meaningful category of national otherness—a category that was roughly coherent or equivalent across numerous geographic economies—it would achieve such coherence only with the ongoing emergence of industrial infrastructure. In 1787, however, monolithic models of lower-class people, "negers," free white men, and appropriately domestic women had not yet been pervasively worked out, any more than a national book had yet to be perfectly and ubiquitously disseminated across the vast territorial nation-space of America. In fact, it would not be until some form of mass dissemination *was* possible that coherent identities would slowly come into alignment, from east to west, north to south. It is the spread of capitalism itself (and the coincident spread of print capitalism) that created our more modern conceptions of class and which itself enacted the divisive processes that constitute our modern experience of class today. But this is a divisive kind of work we rarely assign to print culture in the early United States, precisely because we are too busy crediting it with the unionizing work of nation formation.

But class identity does not stand alone or preeminent in this respect. As that set of social identifications was emerging from the mills of Manayunk and later from the factories at Lowell, parallel languages of difference simultaneously emerged—with identity discourses like domesticity and racial superiority each in their turn imbricating themselves into the fabric of the others. These were new kinds of federal affiliation—affiliation based on one's individual position via the reference points of normative categories of subjectivity (a normativity powered by increasing cultural homogeneity across a more homogenized culture industry). One could argue that such affiliations were themselves made possible by the Constitution's initial gesture toward making individual subjects the determinative units of federal representation, a move that initiated the new discursive practice of census-taking throughout the extended republic, where other extended discursive projects soon followed. The essentialized Americanness of one's position as a republican wife, daughter, husband, and son—and the bourgeois project of elite, familial self-making such identifications imply—all unevenly emerged along the same fault lines where railroads and canals emerged: these categories of subjective identification—and communal division—were the inevitable coincidences of the rise of a vast federal marketplace for words, things, and people alike (and hence were not merely coincidental at all). The fact that those same railroads and canals diffused the emergent discourses of subjective difference or "contrast" that then interlocked with the ongoing emergence and proliferation of a recognizably American economic underclass, the gendering of American social spheres and public space, and the profound racialization of nineteenth-century American citizenship is a problem for the last third of this book. It is enough to say here that in the early national period, these were not yet the coherent or seemingly inevitable categories we postindustrial postconstitutionalists live with every day but were instead emergent fictions radically rooted in the local places that predate an effectual U.S. union. As Crèvecoeur says in *Letters from an American Farmer* (another artifact whose 1780s specificity has been largely erased by the postconstitutional we), "every thing is local."[50] Or everything *was* local—until the market revolution came to town after town after town and made a George Washington of every Manly, a Jessamy of every Jonathan, a weeping Maria of every Charlotte, an Injun Joe of every Alknomook, a Jim Crow of every black Hannah—and, I am afraid, a *Yankee Doodle* of every *Contrast.*

4. A TALE OF TWO STATUES: MATERIAL CULTURES OF REPRESENTATION

On February 17, 1787—very nearly two months to the day before *The Contrast* opened at the John Street Theater in New York City—Tyler wrote home describing his new duties as a militia officer under Benjamin Lincoln, the Revolutionary veteran in charge of putting down Shays's Rebellion in western Massachusetts. "My Good Friends," Tyler writes to his future in-laws:

> Now I wish you could look in upon me—and see your old Friend the Center the main spring of movements that he once thought would have Crazed his Brain . . . This minute Harranguing Govenour Council & House of Representatives. The next Driving 40 miles into the State of New York at the Head of a Party to apprehend Shay [—] Back again in 20 hours. Now Closing the Pases to Canada next Writing orders to the

Frontier . . . I hope to be home and Bring Shays with me if the Command of a Pocket full of money and 500 Choice men will do it [—] [If the men of] this State are not Blind to their own Interest I shall do it.[51]

Like much of Tyler's early correspondence, this letter shows a man wholly taken up with the project of inserting himself into "the Center" of a new social order. Tyler may be only half-serious here, but he clearly saw his service in Shays's Rebellion as an opportunity for advancement. Officially licensed and made exceptionally mobile through the temporary mechanism of his militia commission, Tyler was navigating not just the debris of the Revolution (in the form of border skirmishes with armed farmers) but also making his way around what was emerging before his eyes as the anti-Shaysite federal state. In such moments, Tyler displays an eager and ambitious sense of his role in putting down the rebellion and in negotiating diplomatic arrangements between Massachusetts and the states on its border—particularly Connecticut, New York, and Vermont, all of which harbored "rebels" just feet away from Massachusetts land and law. Tyler's forays into the field to "captivate Captain Shays" (as he phrased it) placed his loyalties squarely with the state of Massachusetts, but his experiences as a diplomat to other states also forced him to consider the interstate implications of such stringently state-based loyalties—and, of course, to recognize the inability of individual states to enforce such loyalty on mobile citizens like Shays or, indeed, himself.[52]

Given Tyler's service in Shays's Rebellion, it is not surprising that *The Contrast* records a world of local investments and then tries to negotiate a way to move beyond them. But places (and the ways that people both identify and are identified with them) are not the only troubling sites of contrast in this play. History too provides a lingering set of disruptive identifications that must be restructured in order for the play to achieve its intended outcome. Indeed, it is the Revolution itself—and all the ideals it had once raised about popular participation, embodied collectivity, and actual representation—that must be set aside in order for life to move forward. Jonathan is just one of many Revolutionary holdovers that *The Contrast* disciplines and reinvents over the course of five acts. In the final scene depicted by the frontispiece, Jonathan is centrally and silently absorbed into the play's constructed solution for its own (constructed) crises. But many other characters are also under federal reconstruction here, with Charlotte, Dimple, Maria, Van Rough, and even the marginal Letitia all being similarly renovated by the end of the play—all transformed into new people who must transcend their previous character traits in order to lend support to Manly and Maria's anticipated union. Even Manly, the play's putative hero, must change. Many readers have identified Manly with General Washington, but this is just one of the many misrecognitions engendered by the play's successful absorption (or repression) of the specific social crisis that created it. The real Washington was, if anything, Dimple-like in his youthful devotion not just to the letters of Lord Chesterfield (a favorite target of Tyler's satire) but to the practices of superficial self-construction that the play's New York characters have mastered to such perfect excess. Unlike Manly, furthermore (whose primary flaw is that he cannot take off his "regimental coat" and get on with a post-Revolutionary life), Washington made his fame by dramatically renouncing his military commission in front of the Continental Congress and then returning to Mount Vernon to cultivate the private life of the farmer- (rather than the soldier-) citizen (23). Tyler's Colonel Manly is not a Cincinnatus (like Washington) but an anti-Cincinnatus, a character whose whole dramatic dilemma involves his inability to give up on his Revolutionary identity and go back to his farm and reproduce. By play's end, of course, Manly has made this key adjustment: he learns to refocus his affections from his Revolutionary "family"—the "brother officers" he came to New York to represent—to his present and future family (sister Charlotte and wife Maria) (25, 61). But it is not until he trades his regimental coat for a wedding coat that the play's resolution is assured.

But it is not just the play's characters who are being asked to set aside their Revolutionary pasts. The audience too is being hailed, in Althusserian fashion, to participate in a new social order—a world marked by a new set of representational standards that are distinctively virtual and protofederal. *The Contrast* ultimately teaches its audience that everyday life is routinely fraught with dislocations that, when taken to their most absurd theoretical conclusions, look a lot like the ones that made James Otis and Daniel Dulany so suspicious of parliamentary sovereignty— and, by extension, partial representation of any kind. Tyler makes this critique a compulsory aspect of viewing the play in two ways. First, he bombards his viewers with a persistent array of unlikely asides in almost every scene, as a range of characters—from Dimple and Jessamy to Letitia, Charlotte, Van Rough, Maria, and even Jonathan—take the opportunity of being alone or isolated on the stage to reveal the "true" nature of their words or deeds. Though a theatrical commonplace, these asides were invasive enough to cause one early reviewer to make special note of Tyler's "frequent use of soliloquies," which he deemed "injudicious" and "misplaced" in an otherwise well-crafted drama.[53] That the more honest characters (like Jonathan and Manly) are just as likely to participate in these two-faced "soliloquies" as are their dissolute counterparts suggests the extent to which social behaviors in this play simply never match up in obvious ways to the individual motives that drive them, especially in the rather involved circuitry of affections mapped by the play's seduction plot. But the "misplaced" and frequent nature of the asides also shapes the playgoer's experience at another level, casting each viewer as an accomplice to the deceptions being performed not just by the characters but by their creator, forcing us, in the act of accurately processing the asides into a discernible theatrical code, to recognize and acknowledge both the theatricality of the production at hand and the routine nature—if not the outright naturalness—of that theatricality at the level of ordinary cognition.

But the banality of representation and all its attendant, everyday dislocations is pursued even more aggressively through a series of forays into what might be called cognitive slapstick, farcical moments of misrecognition that create a communal standard by inviting the audience to participate in that most coercive form of assent—a laugh. Walking around New York City, Jonathan sees a number of sights that require their viewer to distinguish reality from representation. Jonathan of course cannot make such distinctions—and that inability accounts for (though should not be reduced to) some of the funniest moments in the early national canon. In the most celebrated and cited scene of the play, for instance, Jonathan describes his experiences in the playhouse through the naïve lens of literalness that marks almost all of his visual and verbal engagements:

JENNY: Mr. Jonathan, I hear you were at the play last night.
JONATHAN: At the play! why, did you think I went to the devil's
    drawing-room! (39)

Insisting that "Oh! no, no, no! You won't catch me at a play-house," Jonathan describes in detail what theater historians tell us was not just a theater but the very theater *The Contrast* was being played in—the John Street Theater. Looking for "the hocus-pocus man," Jonathan sees "a great croud of folks going into a long entry that had lantherns over the door" and follows them in:

> JONATHAN: So I went right in, and they shewed me away clean up to the garret, just like meeting-house gallery. And so I saw a power of topping folks, all sitting round in little cabbins . . . and then there was such a squeaking with the fiddles, and such a tarnal blaze with the lights, my head was near turned. At last the people that sat near me set up such a hissing-hiss—like so many mad cats; and then they went thump, thump, thump, just like our Peleg threshing wheat, and stampt away, just like the nation. . . . Why, I vow . . . they lifted up a great green cloth, and let us look right into the next neighbor's house. Have you a good many houses in New-York made so in that 'ere way?
>
> JENNY: Not many: but did you see the family?
>
> JONATHAN: Yes, swamp it; I see'd the family.
>
> JENNY: Well, and how did you like them?
>
> JONATHAN: I vow they were pretty much like other families;—there was a poor, good natured curse of a husband, and a sad rantipole of a wife. . . .
>
> JENNY: Well, Mr. Jonathan, you were certainly at the play-house.
>
> JONATHAN: I at the play-house! Why didn't I see the play then?
>
> JENNY: Why, the people you saw were players.
>
> JONATHAN: Mercy on my soul! did I see the wicked players? . . .
>
> JESSAMY: Well, Mr. Jonathan, from your account, which I confess is very accurate, you must have been at the play-house.
>
> JONATHAN: Why, I vow I began to smell a rat. When I came away, I went to the man for my money again; you want your money, says he; yes, says I; for what, says he; why, says I, no man shall jocky me out of my money; I paid my money to see sights, and the dogs a bit of a sight have I seen, unless you call listening to people's private business a sight. Why, says he, it is the School for Scandalization.— The School for Scandalization!— Oh! ho! no wonder you New-York folks are so cute at it, when you go to school to learn it: and so I jogged off. (40 – 43)

Jonathan's peculiar and persistent inability to recognize the intimate dislocations that constitute any form of cultural life is never explained.

On the contrary, Tyler treats these repeated misrecognitions as a normal form of backcountry blockheadedness for a Yankee farm boy visiting the city for the first time, and any attempt by the reader to make realistic sense of Jonathan's perceptual troubles would involve the same myopic literal-mindedness that Tyler is lampooning in Jonathan—who is portrayed throughout the play not merely as populist and localist, but as specifically Shaysite and above all absurdly literalist. The joke, here and elsewhere, depends on the absurd oxymoron of actual representation. As Tyler knows (but Jonathan does not), no representation can ever be actual—just as a play is obviously not real. In this way, Tyler is teaching his playgoers to be good citizens (and amusing them to boot) by asking them to recognize the outrageous dislocations that make up the good humor of the play, which are then accepted as a version of social entertainment rather than real threats to the virtue of real people or, for that matter, to the virtue of the republic at large. The play thus offers a deeply rhetorical solution to the social crises it engages, for through the trope of comic misrecognition, Tyler suggests that even the most real or workaday experiences (including play going, flirting, and walking about town) are already perpetually fraught with displacements that demand obvious, even routine, perceptual adjustments on the part of those who experience them. Representation is everywhere, Tyler tells us: in playhouses, and of course, in Congress too.

This move to recuperate the everyday omnipresence of representation was necessarily entangled with ongoing attempts in the 1780s to recuperate the theater from its suspect status. Throughout the colonial period and particularly during the Revolution, theater was identified as a form of luxury and vice that could undo the people and their virtue.[54] Widely understood as antithetical to colonial political goals, theatrical entertainments were considered an essentially British (and thus Tory) activity but were also feared precisely because of their ability to corrupt the distinction between the real and the artificial. In the postwar decade, however, theater took on different meanings for different groups. Many elites, including prior patriots, supported the return of playhouses and players, along with the cultural ties to England that these entertainments necessarily implied (for the importation of British drama, British values, and British goods). For many partisans of populist reform, on the other hand, the theater remained suspect, an ongoing site for potentially false or unnatural representations epitomized by a potentially Tory but certainly

Anglophile clientele draped in the denaturalizing, imported costumes of theater-going—including "Caps, Hats, Wigs, Cardinals, and Cloaks."[55] As Heather Nathans has noted, many Pennsylvanians linked resistance to stage values with the ultimate success or failure of the radically democratic political experiments being enacted there (including the populist, unicameral legislature adopted by the new state constitution).[56] "As long as stage plays are prohibited," one 1784 observer noted, "the present constitution will stand in its vigor and simplicity, but no longer."[57] The contested relation of stage entertainments to populist political experiments may be difficult to grasp now, for in American culture today, visual entertainment is usually understood as a form of popular, and hence populist, culture. In the eighteenth century, however, theater was an *essentially* nonpopulist activity, associated not just with nondemocratic class divides (the province of the rich—and the British) but with a worldview that cast the globe in miniature, elevating parts to the status of representative or signifying wholes—the very logic of imperial virtuality that radical state constitutions like Pennsylvania's were meant to ameliorate.

In creating a character whose primary character trait is his inability to discern the real from the unreal and then sending him to a play, Tyler directly engages the populist debate about the dangers of theatrical representations while at the same time engaging more elite concerns about the fitness of the people either to assemble peacefully or even, indeed, to be in charge of themselves. While many federalists invoked "the people" as a legitimating source of authority, they nevertheless feared that those same people were not sharp enough to discern between true and false representations—that they were, in short, a nation of Jonathans in need of federal Manlys to guide their way. In the play's most slapstick moments, Tyler validates the usefulness of seeing parts as signifying wholes (something Jonathan, of course, is unable to do, but that the audience must do in order to negotiate the play's humor). In doing so, he recuperates not just theatergoing but the fact of Manly-like elites themselves, in the process reimagining the validity of a partial—as opposed to a populist—state.

Tyler's celebration of cultural representation, and the everyday dislocations it entails, is compulsively reenacted in all of Jonathan's numerous misrecognitions, each of which is coded (like his literal and absurdly moralistic response to the theater) as an outmoded vestige of Revolutionary populism. In what would have been a vivid example to Tyler's New

York audience, Jonathan rambles through the streets of Manhattan looking for "agents to Congress" but finds instead the relics of New York's
Revolutionary past eerily damaged and dismembered:

> JESSAMY: Well, have you been abroad in the city since your arrival?
>   What have you seen that is curious and entertaining?
> JONATHAN: Oh! I have seen a power of fine sights. I went to see two
>   marble-stone men and a leaden horse, that stands out in doors in all
>   weathers; and when I came where they was, one had got no head,
>   and t'other wer'n't there. They said as how the leaden man was a
>   damn'd tory, and that he took wit in his anger and rode off in the
>   time of the troubles. (28–29)

Jessamy himself, in his role as servant to the gentleman Dimple, is one
dismembered leftover of the Revolution—one who Jonathan comically
misreads as a senator in yet another in a long litany of comic misunderstandings. But the two other "sights" that Jonathan mentions here—"the
two marble-stone men and a leaden horse"—are likewise leftovers that
he similarly misrecognizes—two rare but significant examples of colonial public art that accrued meaning and history as part of New York's
struggle to define and defend its rights against imperial rule.

Jonathan, of course, is up to his old tricks here, either unwilling or
incapable of perceiving that the two "men" he describes are not men at all
but statues. They are not, furthermore, just any statues. Though hardly
recognizable today (their surviving fragments are pictured here in figures
4.4 and 4.5), these material objects would have been well known to the
play's original New York audience as local things with local histories, each
of which ironically had its literal genesis in the pamphlet debates about
actual and virtual representation with which this chapter began. The first
statue referred to—the one that "had got no head"—is William Pitt, Earl
of Chatham; the second—the one that "wer'n't there"—is King George
III. Pitt became a hero for the patriot cause when he openly championed
colonial rights on the floor of Parliament in the 1760s, declaiming that
"this kingdom has NO RIGHT to lay A TAX upon the colonies" since "the
Americans are the SONS, not the BASTARDS of England." He (like the
colonists) concluded that "the idea of a virtual representation of America
. . . is the most contemptible idea that ever entered into the head of a
man. It does not deserve a serious refutation."[58] Pitt's embrace of actual

FIGURE 4.4   Fragments of the statue of William Pitt. Joseph Wilton, sculptor. Circa 1770. Collection of The New-York Historical Society.

representation made him the darling of American colonists, who pledged to commemorate his role in the Stamp Act's repeal by commissioning not a two-dimensional portrait but a three-dimensional (and actual-sized) representation of him in the form of a statue imported from England.[59] Observing monarchical niceties, however, the legislature of New York

FIGURE 4.5   Fragment of the statue of George III (probably the horse's tail). Joseph Wilton, sculptor. Circa 1770. Collection of The New-York Historical Society.

promptly followed its order for a statue of Pitt with a second one for an even more fantastic, equestrian statue of George III.

These statues were the first erected in the state of New York and among the earliest in all the colonies. In the years leading up to the Revolution, they became popular tourist sites, but they also posed problems for the city, which was forced to play guardian to expensive pieces of the public trust at the very moment the colonial public had lost its faith in England. The records of the Common Council show that vandalism was a problem from the moment the statues were raised. On May 3, 1771, the council contracted to have an iron fence built around the king's statue at Bowling Green (replacing an earlier, ineffective wooden fence), so that the area would not become "a Recepticle of all the filth & dirt of the Neighbourhood"—a reference not just to the trash produced by certain sorts of people but to those very sorts of people themselves.[60] Less than two years later, on January 6, 1773, the legislature passed a prohibitive act "to prevent the Defacing [of] the Statues which are erected in the City of New York," instituting a weighty fine of five hundred pounds.[61]

FIGURE 4.6 *Pulling Down the Statue of George III by the 'Sons of Freedom' at Bowling Green.*
Painted by Johannes A. Oertel; engraved by John C. McRae. 1875. Library of Congress, Prints
and Photographs Division, LC-USZ62-2455.

But despite these protective measures, the statues are primarily remembered today for the way they were eventually "defaced" and destroyed. The statue of the king stood at Bowling Green for only six years.
On July 9, 1776, it was pulled down by a mob in a classic Revolutionary
crowd action after the first New York reading of the Declaration of Independence, with both soldiers and citizens participating. As one New
Yorker wrote: "The Declaration was read . . . this week; and loud Huzzas
express'd the approbation of ye Freeborn Bands. . . . The Night following, the famous gilded equestrian statue of ye British King, in this City,
was levelled with ye Dust."[62] The destruction of the king's statue did not
go unacknowledged or unreciprocated by British troops, who later mutilated the statue of Pitt in direct retaliation for the havoc wreaked on
George. By war's end, Pitt had lost not just his head but an arm. When
the British evacuated the city in 1783, they left behind only a disfigured
trunk.[63]

The story of each statue's demise sits at an ironic juncture in the history of American subject and nation formation. Viewing the story of

these crowd actions in hindsight, it is easy to view the disfigurement they performed as little more than a pantomime of violence—a theatrical version of the "real" acts of regicide enacted during the English Civil War and later the French Revolution. But the fact that this particular act of violence was displaced onto a symbolic representation rather than being performed on the literal body of the king is quintessentially American, for it was a defining feature of the rebellion in America that it was literally (geographically) displaced from the metropole and thus necessitated the circuitous use of all sorts of displaced modes of resistance that nevertheless called forth literal crowds. American resistance—to the king in particular but to Parliament as well—was thus both embodied and abstracted at the same time—enacted by real people but often abstractly mediated through symbolic acts of vandalism on signifying tavern signs, statues, and buildings.

The peculiar but powerful displacement of violence onto a mere representation of the king's person created an odd rhetorical effect in the stories about Bowling Green that circulated afterwards. Tories sought to capitalize on the symbolic parallels between the real and metaphorical act of regicide, even as they feared that literal acts of violence might eventually be turned on them since they were, ironically, among the only embodied representatives of the king to be found on the western side of the Atlantic. In London, one newspaper offered this apocryphal report: "Our readers have heard that the Provincials have melted the leaden Statue of their most gracious King, at New-York, into Bullets; but they were guilty also of a Joke, for they reserved the leaden Head, and consigned it, by the next Opportunity, to one of his Majesty's principal Ministers, who, upon Receipt of the weighty Parcel, could not easily imagine what were its Contents."[64] Another popular account sensationally claimed that the colonists had planned to display the head on a stake, like that of a criminal, but before they were able to execute the plan, British soldiers smuggled it out of the patriot camp. But neither of these stories is entirely accurate. Appalled by the beheading of the king, however symbolic, Tory New Yorkers buried the (nonleaden) pieces of the razed statue until the city was secured by British troops, at which time "the mutilated head, according to Montresor's *Journals*, was forwarded to Lord Townshend 'to convince them at home of the Infamous Disposition of the Ungrateful people of this distressed Country.'"[65] Once in London, the head became the topic of unlikely parlor conversations. As Thomas Hutchinson noted in his diary: "Lady Townshend asked me if I had a mind to see an instance of American loyalty? and going to the sopha, uncovered a large gilt head, which at once appeared to be that of the King. . . . The nose is wounded and defaced, but the gilding remains fair, and as it was well executed, it retains a striking likeness."[66]

The king's beheading became part of the lore of the Revolution for the patriot movement too. Samuel Webb simply noted without irony in his journal that the statue was "tumbled down and beheaded,"[67] but many patriots gloried in the fun, and funniness, of pulling a (lead) king off his (marble) pedestal. As William Whipple wrote to John Langdon with grim irony, "Independence was proclaimed in the army at New York last Wednesday when the leaden King in the Bowling Green was dismounted and is by this time cast into bullets for the destruction of his tools of Tyranny. May every one of them be properly commissioned."[68] Ebenezer Hazard adopted a similarly dark brand of humor, noting that the redcoats would soon have "melted majesty fired at them."[69] Isaac Bangs followed suit in his journal when he wrote, to no one in particular: "it is hoped that the Emanations of the Leaden George will make as deep impressions in the Bodies of some of his red Coated and Torie Subjects."[70] But the oddest rhetorical effect occurred in the *Pennsylvania Journal*, which reported on the incident by citing Milton, thus raising the specter of the English Civil War (and actual regicide): "the lead wherewith this monument was made, is to be run into bullets, to assimilate with the brain of our infatuated adversaries. . . . A gentlemen who was present at this ominous fall of leaden Majesty, looking back to the original's hopeful beginning pertinently exclaimed, in the language of the angel to Lucifer, 'if thou be'est he! But ah, how fallen! How chang'd!'"[71] Each of these accounts makes a knowing joke about the oddly unreal ways in which the American rebellion was being mediated through cultural representation; they all register as well, however, the visceral way in which this particular act of violence, originally displaced onto the unreal (the statue), would eventually be recirculated back into the real by way of leaden bullets shot at living soldiers.

When Jonathan wanders through the streets of New York looking at such rhetorically and historically charged "sights," Tyler is pointedly referencing the intimate histories behind them. In doing so, he openly raises not just the disfigured ghosts of the Revolution but the pervasive post-Revolutionary fear of ongoing crowd actions—the feared scene of "the people" embodied and up to no good. As the 1780s drew to a close, post-Revolutionary elites scrambled to close the Pandora's box of a rebellion powered by embodied mobilizations like the crowd action referenced by these statues. By the time Tyler took his trip to New York, the idea of the people gathered and embodied—even locally—was no longer the solution it had been during the heyday of colonial resistance (in crowd actions like the Boston Tea Party or the toppling of King George) but had turned instead into the Shaysite nightmare. By the 1780s, elites who were gathering at Annapolis and Philadelphia to rethink the structure of the Confederation were beginning to ask questions about the possibility, the necessity, and the desirability of those Enlightenment models of rational, embodied collectivity that had been championed by Paine and Jefferson—and epitomized by Rousseau's sanguine fantasy of the people gathering peacefully out of doors to see each other as they participated in celebratory festivals that would, in his ideal (small) republic, serve as the basis for communal virtue.[72]

On one hand, the ideal of embodied national collectivity proved moot once the Federal Convention committed to the idea of an extended federal sphere. As numerous delegates pointed out, it might be good Whig form to cite "the people" as the source of legitimate political authority, but the people were an abstraction that could never be literally assembled. When delegates with localist biases called for a compromise in which members of the new Congress would be elected by the direct vote of the people, it failed to pass because, as Charles Cotesworth Pinckney said, "an election of either branch by the people scattered as they are in many States . . . was totally impracticable."[73] This was the key innovation of the extended republic, as I will discuss at greater length in the next chapter: the new arrangement openly acknowledged and then exploited the fact that "We the People" could never assemble, en masse, nationally.

But the fact that the people could not physically assemble under the federal roof also posed logistical problems for future federal life. Gouvernor Morris, among others, feared that the new scheme would be an administrative nightmare, for just as the people could not be assembled, the government could not, conversely, reach out to compel the people to civic duties. When one delegate suggested individual taxation to avoid the dissent of another continental impost, Morris pointed out that "it is idle to suppose that the Genl. Govt. can stretch its hand directly into the pockets of the people scattered over so vast a Country."[74] By the time ratification was complete, the numerous logistical problems with making the extended republic a real and felt fact in the everyday life of its subjects were wearily detailed at great length by antifederalist literalists who worried every angle of the proposal. But even the problems raised by the extended republic were, in a sense, solutions—as Madison famously suggests in *Federalist* No. 10. Indeed, the fact that the government could not be embodied (as a reaching "hand") in everyday life is just the thing that made the medicine of federalism go down in the early years of constitutional reconsolidation. As Madison argued from the start, the scatteredness of different communities was a nation-building buffer: the government would not be impinged upon by embodied citizens, but neither would embodied citizens be impinged upon by the government.

David Waldstreicher has noted that the practice of virtuous assembly—the gathering of the people in their literal persons—was a key process in the formation of national subjects. But the "fetes" that Waldstreicher posits as the constituent feature of emerging American nationalism are always oddly cultural—which is to say, nonpolitical—ones. The parades, feasts, and fireworks Waldstreicher describes all involve moments in which local public space is mobilized for political purposes even as the work of official politics is being done behind closed doors in rooming houses and Senate hallways in the nation's early capitals. Throughout the 1770s and 1780s, debates emerged in the Continental Congress as to whether the proceedings of the government ought to be open or closed, and if open, whether or not a gallery (like the ones found in theaters) should be built, how big it should be, and who should be allowed to sit in it. Sam Adams, for one, favored such participation. He wrote to James Warren in 1778 complaining of "the Conduct of some our Politicians" (in Massachusetts) and asked where "the people" were as such unsavory developments unfolded: "Are the Galleries of the House open? Do the people know such a Motion was Made? A Motion so alarming to an old Whig!"[75] Noting also, however, that "your News Papers are silent upon every Subject of Importance, but the Description of a Feast," Adams's letter points to an emerging split between active political and passive cultural participation. Whether Adams knew it or not, the "old Whig" investment in popular participation was being rewritten in these years, and nowhere more so than at the national level. From the 1780s forward, the people were increasingly called on to perform federal feeling in notably nonfederal (or open but local) spaces (like "Feasts") rather than taking part in the closed but federalized space of congressional debate, where translocal human bodies were literally gathering to discuss translocal policy. And this fact attests to one of the central paradoxes of early American nationalism and one of the key theoretical insights of the extended republic—that in order for the work of nation building to proceed, it was best for the people to be both absent and unaware of just exactly what it was that their representatives were doing, in the process making representative dislocation the bond that yoked together dispersed American subjects even as it simultaneously banished the disruptive specter of populist mob activity from the (national) political imaginary.

It is no surprise, then, that debates both before and after the war focused on whether the Continental Congress, the Federal Convention, or the new Federal Congress should be open. Throughout the 1770s and the early 1780s, the answer to such questions was no. It was not until 1787 that Congress opened its first (partial) gallery, and even then only the proceedings of the House were available for public display (the Senate remained closed until 1795). Thus while galleries did eventually open the work of government to the people, they did not do so until after the constitutional coup that reorganized American representational values from ideals of embodied actuality to those of dislocated virtuality, in the process permanently refiguring the people as silent observers rather than the unruly crowds that had once demolished public property, and imperial trust, at Bowling Green.

With the reconsolidation of social and political life under the new Constitution, the threat of an assembled body politic was eventually absorbed—in part through the very mechanisms of commodity culture that Tyler's play both thematically lampoons and yet, as a stage entertainment, also participates in. The same crowds, in other words, who once wanted to tear down theaters would eventually become ticket buyers, but the movement of the people out of the center of politics and into the spectator galleries was not entirely unproblematic for elite federalists, especially after the Revolution of 1800 placed a permanently (Jeffersonian) Republican pallor on the face of the nation. The result was the emergence of, if not greater, then at least ever more visible class divides, which were mimicked in the physical space of the theater, which had been conventionally arranged in England in such a way as to foreground—and symbolically invert—economic differences among different members of the audience. In most theaters built in the post-Revolutionary United States, the cheapest seats were literally placed above the more expensive ones, leaving elite members of the audience exposed to the ridicule of the lower sorts:

Those who frequent the *Pit*, have in a particular manner been the object of . . . ill treatment [from people in the Gallery]. No sooner does a person enter it than he is summoned in a peremptory tone to *doff* his hat to these *respectable blades* in token of his *inferiority*, which if he does not immediately comply with, the vociferating lungs of a hundred *Stentors* declare he must be punished for so flagrant a violation of *their imperious commands*, and then apples and pears, sticks and stones are hurl'd at him without mercy, while scurrility and abuse are as freely poured upon him as could possibly be at *Billingsgate*; nor do they stop there, but during the whole of his sitting in the house, he becomes a marked object at whom every scoundrel aloft endeavours to vent his malice by *spitting* and emptying *beer bottles* on him, tho' very frequently the innocent suffer equally with the guilty; & they who complaisantly bowed to the insolent demands of these *Gallery despots* find their cloaths ruined and their persons bruised, as well as those who independently refuse to submit to those unreasonable and unjust demands.[76]

This 1790s passage oddly anatomizes the emerging postwar theater through both the language of the prison (the civil discourse of "the innocent" and "the guilty") and the liberal language of life, liberty, and the pursuit of happiness (the civic language of "unjust demands"). Most dramatically, this anonymous observer mobilizes a discourse about the embodied people that would find considerable currency in the reorganization of the American state from an ideal based on the virtue of the people to one based on partial representation. By positing the embodied people here as "Gallery despots" who tyrannously impose "imperious demands" undiscerningly on both "the guilty" and "the innocent," this observer takes part in a broader post-Revolutionary discourse that shifted the role of "despot" from the king and Parliament back onto the people, locally, physically, and literally imagined as a troublesome (theater) crowd.[77]

Tyler, of course, directly engages both of these wide-ranging debates—from the question (posed by elites) of whether the people could be trusted to assemble virtuously to the question (posed by the people) of whether theatrical entertainments should be accepted as part of the postwar landscape or resisted as highly suspect relics of the recent Tory past. Tyler's position on such debates—like his later politics—is profoundly federalist, but with a twist. *The Contrast* promotes the reconception of the people from political participants—Shaysite "sturgeons," as Jonathan dimly calls them (28)—to cultural consumers standing in the galleries of nation formation rather than on the floor of debate. More subtly, however, Tyler innovates the use of comic misrecognition as a trope to condition his audience to the (inevitably) partializing logic of representation, and in doing so he makes a case not only for the harmlessness of theatrical entertainments but also for the necessary dislocations of other kinds of representation—including the highly controversial version of proportional political representation that would be innovated in the months to come at the Federal Convention.

5. FROM ACTUAL TO VIRTUAL AND BACK AGAIN

Tyler's open commitment to the virtuality of the new world order—a world floated on the generative possibilities of partial representations rather than impeded by a fear of them—was a theoretically advanced one for the late 1780s. After all, while Tyler was playfully pushing the limits of perceptual misrecognitions—openly raising part-for-whole cognition as a metonymy for patriotic consent—John Trumbull was tediously traveling up and down the eastern seaboard, stuck in the marshy standard of actual representation held up for him as an ideal by both Jefferson and Adams. Trumbull was by no means looking backwards in 1787. His commitment to reproducing authentic physiognomies was, in 1787, at the cutting edge of cultural representation, taking up a standard raised (in theory) by the Revolution but that would not be attainable in graphic art for many decades to come. According to Wendy Wick, for instance, "actual" representations in physical portraiture were relatively unavailable before the 1820s.[78] While wealthy patrons might commission portraits based on real-life sittings, most people did not have access to such painters or to the portraits they produced, which tended to be hung in private houses rather than public places. Indeed, actual likenesses were almost unheard of in large historical canvasses like Trumbull's, works that depicted multiple historical actors whose names might be well known but whose faces were not. Thus a painter like Benjamin West was not held to any strict standard of actual resemblance when painting a vast historical canvas like *The Death of General Wolfe* (which is often noted for the verisimilitude not of its faces but of its contemporary costumes). For much of the eighteenth century, there was only one physical face that the geographically scattered peoples of the British Empire knew well enough to recognize as either true or untrue, a real or a fictitious likeness—and that was King George.[79] While George Washington and Benjamin Franklin would eventually join this exclusive company, the physical features of most important faces were not widely recognizable to common citizens unless they had personally met the person depicted.

There was, in short, a very low cultural expectation of absolute verisimilitude in the representation of particular human features when it came to mass disseminated engravings. Even as late as 1780, printmakers and their potential audiences were considered "geographically remote" enough from someone like George Washington that numerous "completely fictitious" yet "immensely influential" prints of Washington were issued and widely circulated on both sides of the Atlantic (see figures 4.7 and 4.8).[80] Small-scale printers, on the other hand, tended to use generic woodcuts to represent Washington and other prominent figures, merely changing the name printed beneath the woodcut on successive uses. These woodcut plates were often exchanged among different printers, with the same figure appearing in different times and places but signifying multiple identities. As Wick notes, one 1777 almanac used a primitive woodcut to depict Sam Adams, but it was, as it turns out, the same one it had used in 1773 to depict John Dryden, and it would be used as late as 1799 to depict even Washington.[81] Washington's later face recognition was the exception to this rule of interchangeability, and the widespread availability of numerous authentic Washington portraits eventually introduced a new expectation for an "actual representation," if not in every graphic portrait, then certainly in portraits of Washington. By the time Washington died in 1799, most people who had access to prints had some idea of what he looked like, just as they had once known what the king had looked like. But while most printers and engravers worked to fulfill the cultural expectation of authenticity in Washington's portraiture, other figures remained fair game. In New England, another popular almanac woodcut routinely depicted Washington alongside another figure; while Washington's identity in this pairing remained stable in the print's various appearances, the other figure's identity shifted to a new identity each time it appeared in print. In one version of the woodcut, the second figure was named Horatio Gates; in another, it was Artemus Ward.[82]

In light of Wick's account of how unusual authentic portraiture was in late-eighteenth-century America, Trumbull's commitment to authentic portraits amounts almost to a mania for recovering the real moment of independence. But as elaborate as Trumbull's labors were and as popular

GEORGE WASHINGTON, Esq.ʳ

GENERAL and COMMANDER in CHIEF of the CONTINENTAL ARMY in AMERICA.

FIGURE 4.7 *George Washington, Esqr.* Unidentified artist. London: 1775. The Emmett Collection, Miriam and Ira D. Wallach Division of Art, Prints and Photographs, The New York Public Library, Astor, Lenox, and Tilden Foundations. A totally fictitious portrait of Washington.

The true PORTRAITURE of his Excellency

George Washington Esq.r

In the Roman Dress, as Order'd by Congress for the Monument to be erected
in Philadelphia, to perpetuate to Posterity the Man who commanded the
American Forces through the late glorious Revolution.

FIGURE 4.8 Attributed to John Norman. *The True* PORTRAITURE *of His Excellency George Washington Esqr.* Circa 1783. The Yale University Art Gallery. Mabel Brady Garvan Collection. On August 7, 1783, Congress declared that an equestrian statue of Washington was to be built in honor of his service in the Revolution. This print curries an aura of authenticity by citing this legislation and declaring itself a "true portraiture" of Washington, but with the exception of Washington's head, which does not fit proportionately on this body, it is actually a copy of a portrait of Sir William de la More taken from John Guillim's seventeenth-century *Display of Heraldry*.

as the painting has proven retrospectively, *The Declaration of Independence* was not entirely successful in its own time. In the fall of 1818, Trumbull took the newly finished painting on a traveling exhibition, touring Boston, New York, Philadelphia, and Baltimore on the way to its final destination in Washington. The tour itself was "a tremendous success—the high point of Trumbull's career."[83] In a little over a month, more than six thousand New Yorkers paid 25 cents to see a painting that had taken the better part of the painter's life to create. But the tour did not translate into the wider success Trumbull had long struggled to achieve. Having worked strenuously for decades to gather the portraits and finish the federal commission, Trumbull had hoped to parlay the painting into a well-distributed engraving, diffused "not only through our own country, but the world."[84] To this end, his letters speak frequently of potential "markets," innovative methods for obtaining subscribers, and the high costs of production. But as ambitious as this fantasy of federal coverage was, Trumbull could not find buyers who wanted to own his "faithful memorial," and this weak reception became one of the greatest frustrations of his professional life. His letters from this period are saturated with complaints and pleas for "patronage" and "protection" while he is "mortified" to hear that his call for subscriptions has laid for a week under "letters and unnoticed newspapers" on a table in Congress "without one single signature" (359, 364, 362). Meanwhile, he notes with amazement that a local printer named Binns "is getting numerous subscribers for a mere verbal copy of the Declaration . . . which is already in every body's hands" (358, 360). In sharp contrast to the success of Binns's textual Declaration, only 275 patrons ever subscribed to Trumbull's visual engraving of the signing—and fewer paid for it.[85]

How could such a promising venture fail its maker? By 1818, the moment of founding that Trumbull illustrates had already passed into another kind of historical memory—one particularly suited to "mere verbal copies." Some contemporary viewers linked their disdain for the painting to the fact that Trumbull had so insistently promised to deliver the real (authentic and historical) goods on founding but had finally failed to get his facts right. Despite Trumbull's thirty-year quest for absolute verisimilitude in representing the features of individual signers, contemporary critics broadly criticized the painting for "violations of truth." One anonymous review, signed by "Detector," declared that "it may, perhaps, be a *very pretty picture*, but it is certainly no representation of the Declaration of Independence."[86] As critics like Detector were quick to point out, the painting includes several figures (most noticeably John Dickinson) who did not support independence, refused to sign the document, or had left the Continental Congress before the resolution formally came to the floor.[87] Others have noted that the painting's title cites July 4 as the scene depicted when in fact the committee of five presented the Declaration to the Congress at large not in July but in June—June 28, to be exact. When the committee did present the document, parliamentary procedure dictated that only one member bring it to the chair, and that was not likely to have been an event, as it is portrayed here, of any great magnitude. Trumbull's boasts of complete architectural authenticity aside, certain physical features were fudged as well: the two doors shown in the background of the painting were apparently never there, no military banners decorated the Philadelphia Statehouse at that early date, and the furniture is the sort Trumbull would have seen in Paris in the 1780s—not in Philadelphia in 1776.[88]

The public's rejection of Trumbull's painting reflects a number of different problems. One was that Trumbull promised to deliver something historically authentic, but his standards for authenticity had essentially become archaic by the time he finished the project. The commitment to verisimilitude in portraiture that was so novel and innovative in the late 1780s proved much less exciting to audiences in 1818. It is a paradox of this painting's production, then, that the longer Trumbull spent researching and reproducing the precise details of each founder's face, the further he journeyed into the unreal—for by 1818, the standards for what amounted to an acceptably authentic historical portrait were different, as were the standards for verisimilitude of every sort. Put simply, the facts of founding—facts about doors and flags, about individual actors and the furniture the signers sat on—were more widely available than they would have been in the 1780s or 1790s. Forty-two years after the fact, Trumbull seems to have researched himself out of a well-received masterpiece.

Still, it seems equally arguable that the engraving flopped for an entirely different reason—that Trumbull went unappreciated not because he was not literal enough (not true enough to the truth), but because he was *too much* of a literalist, attempting to cover every base, sparing "neither labor nor expense" to recover what had already been irrevocably lost in national space and historical time. Some "ideal representations" were inevitable: there were signers, for instance, who were already dead by the time he was ready to paint them, and there were many others who, by the time they were painted, had aged beyond recognition from the men they'd been in 1776.[89] But even the figures that were based on Trumbull's most painstaking life sittings are still, inevitably, representations, simulacra that when taken too seriously only serve to draw attention to the central paradox of displaced representation that the scene simultaneously illustrates and denies. In the end, the painting misses its mark not because it is unreal (every painting, novel, and play is a simulation), but because it also *seems* unreal. Trumbull's signers stand stiffly—forty-seven exquisitely accurate portraitures stuffed in the wax museum of the picture's frame. Had he been less concerned with preserving the features of each and every face, Trumbull might not have composed their bodies in such an unnatural and stiff-bodied panorama. Thus, in trying to preserve a strict ethos of precision in the portraits themselves, Trumbull sacrificed the overall *appearance* of reality, allowing the project to become defined by the very geographic and historical gaps which his Odyssean travels were meant to erase. The life-sized version of the painting installed in the Rotunda was immediately ridiculed in the Senate corridors as a "shin-piece"—a reference to the artificial quality of the bodies that stand lifeless but intricately detailed, right down to their stockings.[90] The painting may stand today as an icon, but it is an oddly flawed one: in the words of one of its most comprehensive critics, it is "static," "repetitive," and "devoid of action"—a fact that may explain why it is so often the safe choice for the bland advertising of insurance companies and investment securities.[91] But there is something else too: while the visual representation makes its owners onlookers to the moment of founding—replacing them completely by their continental representatives—the verbal text makes its owners invested speakers and participants, memorializing the unmediated act itself, as if it had somehow occurred outside of the closed circuit of representation. As a representation of the moment of founding, Trumbull's painting cannot compare to the "mere verbal copy" that had already, in 1818, become the preferred marker of America's "actual" origins.

Trumbull was not alone in trying to create a mythic representation of national founding from within a rigid set of representational ideals. Throughout the 1780s, an array of citizens—painters, authors, cartographers, statesmen, and of course playwrights and poets like Tyler—tested a series of representational strategies within which to make monolithic sense of the unfolding experience of American nationalism. But the successful mythmakers and nation-builders of this era were not literalists like Trumbull (or, as we shall see, the antifederalists). Indeed, the federalists of 1787 did not stop to worry about the apparent contradictions that peppered the local landscapes that, when taken together, made up the projected vista of the United States as a whole. Like Tyler, the federalists were willing to let the nation rest on the impenetrable paradox of a virtual nationalism, and many of their fellow citizens followed them there, adopting federalism as a "stile" of national affiliation that need not (yet) rival their state-based identities—not least because the federal hand could not yet reach onto the local stages of day-to-day life.[92]

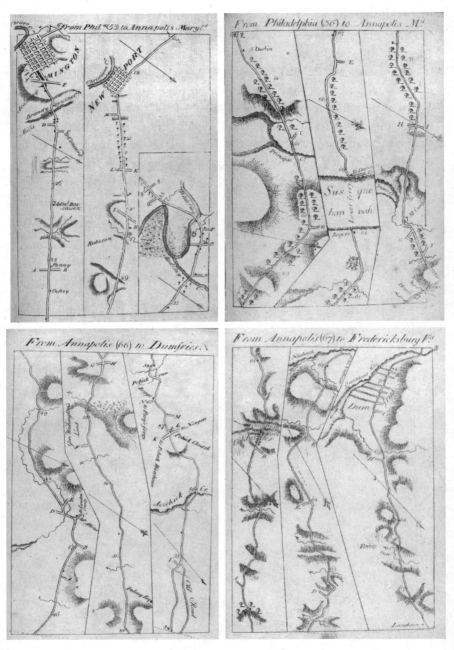

FIGURE 5.1 Christopher Colles. *A Survey of the Roads of the United States of America.* New York: s.n., 1789. Plates 53, 56, 66, and 67. Lawrence H. Slaughter Collection, The Lionel Pincus and Princess Firyal Map Division, The New York Public Library, Astor, Lenox, and Tilden Foundations.

5. METROBUILDING
THE PRODUCTION OF FEDERALIST SPACE

When he considered the amazing extent of the Country—the immense population which is to fill it, the influence which the Govt. we are to form will have, not only on the present generation of our people & their multiplied posterity, but on the whole Globe, he was lost in the magnitude of the object.

—James Madison, transcribing remarks
made by James Wilson in the Federal Convention, 25 June 1787

It is space not time that hides consequences from us.
—John Berger, *The Look of Things,* 1972

1. REVISITING THE VIRTUAL LANDSCAPE

Common Sense and *The Federalist* both worked to counter the vastness of the proposed republic through the unifying potential of a single text. But there are crucial differences in how they achieve this effect. Paine's ambitions for *Common Sense* were rooted in a popular discourse of republican diffusion, an ideology that allowed him to believe that he had authored a book that could penetrate every possible location among the numerous and still proliferating spaces of the early American republic. In this way, Paine fantasized a radically democratic model of nation building, committed to the idea that every citizen might participate, through the reading of his text, in the formation of the coming state. *The Federalist,* on the other hand, appeals to a narrow band of elite readers, many of whom were to become "federal" characters in the new national government. *The Federalist* has been elevated to the status of national masterpiece not because it was thickly disseminated in newspapers but because it was finally collected into an iconic book—a form that materially mimes the singular consensus that ratification sought to construct. *The Federalist's* success finally relies not on the fantasy of wide-scale diffusion, but on a principle of selection and collection—a decidedly non-Painite and post-Revolutionary kind of representation.

This difference poses a paradox for the cultural history of early U.S. nationalism, for it suggests competing theories of incipient national space and its relation back to the local, embodied spaces of everyday life. As I've already argued, *Common Sense* served its reader as an actual material object, held in hand and so demonstrating the groundedness of the pamphlet and its ideas as something locally produced and locally consumed. But the early national book was being imagined on another scale as well—signifying a set of relations not just at the level of the local print economies in which it was produced (where real readers bought real books) but at the more abstract level of the republic at large. *Common Sense* was made and used locally, in other words, but it was also imagined to have a life (indeed, hundreds of thousands of lives) that far exceeded these limited bounds. The material text held in hand was thus imagined to join its reader to the larger nation, one reader to the next, in one long and uninterrupted chain of textual reception—a local emblem for its own wished-for diffusion. This is the late-eighteenth-century's version of the "imagined community," but while it subtends a fantasy about the potential simultaneity of one newly national public, it is actually managing the profound spatial *seriality* of many different early national communities.

The Federalist works on a different principle, as does the government it proposes. The myth of *Common Sense* is based on a trope of diffusion, but *The Federalist* organizes itself around tropes of collection. Not only is *The Federalist* formally a collection of previously published newspaper essays but it actively posits the principle of collection as a viable model for building a national government. What did the federalists do if not construct an extended sphere of representation and then designate a geographical site (the capital) in which to collect representatives from across that imagined space? Paine sought to saturate a vast but always self-identical space through acts of reading that would have enabled a densely participatory (if still textually mediated) political culture. But *The Federalist* posits a new mechanics of government that allows the part to stand in completely for the whole. The new federal representative is intended to act without oversight or binding instructions, a substitute standing in the place of his missing constituents, just as the President's voice speaks for an absent people. Individual federalists displayed some anxiety about this procedure—as Trumbull does in his reassembly project of 1787, which attempts to insert "actual" portraits into the newly revirtualized landscape of U.S. political life. But Trumbull's painting does finally concede the necessary dislocation of the representative from those he is said to represent, placing both in separate spaces—just as federalism does by installing a "superstructure" over and somewhere beyond the microspaces of those more local, everyday cultures called states.[1]

The federalists proposed this superstructure—the "mammoth state," as Laura Rigal has called it—as a solution to the problems that had rendered the Confederation an administrative "wreck."[2] But antifederalists quickly dubbed the extended republic a "Monster" precisely because of what they diagnosed as a problem of spatial administration. No republic, they contended, could cover so much territory and still aspire to the Revolutionary ideal of actual representation:

> The idea of an uncompounded republick, on an average, one thousand miles in length, and eight hundred in breadth, and containing six millions of white inhabitants all reduced to the same standard of morals, or habits, and of laws, is in itself an absurdity, and contrary to the whole experience of mankind. The attempt made by Great-Britain to introduce such a system, struck us with horrour, and when it was proposed by some theorists that we should be represented in parliament, we uniformly declared that one legislature could not represent so many different interests for the purposes of legislation and taxation. This was the leading principle of the revolution.[3]

This writer, like many others, found the very notion of an extended republic a troubling reconstruction of the British Empire's attempt to impose virtual representation on its colonial subjects. The federal scheme of representation, he argues, does little more than readopt (or transplant) a metropolitan model of representation—revirtualizing the American populace and essentially recolonizing them from the inside out (rather than from the outside in). In constructing a new center of power, the Constitution thus undoes "the leading principle of the revolution."

But of course the irony of American nationalism is that the Revolution had to be undone in just this way in order to be remembered by the many later generations that would legitimate it as the authentic origin of "their" nation (rather than a failed experiment, like the Confederation). This chapter addresses this irony by exploring two connected problems of early U.S. nation building: first, the question of how the superstructure of federalism was spatially theorized, and second, how the material consequence of that theory, which we now call a "nation," endured historically through time to produce that mass affect we now call "nationalism." The texts to be considered include maps, essays, law, and a novel: Christopher Colles's *Survey of American Roads* (1789); Hamilton, Jay, and Madison's *The Federalist* (1787–88); the Constitution itself (1787); and William Hill Brown's *The Power of Sympathy* (1789). When read in unison against the early republic's ongoing debate about the utility of an extended social sphere, these texts make it clear that the republic-in-space and the republic-in-print were linked problems for cultural producers of every kind—from the authors, editors, and engravers who sought to represent (and reach) the emerging nation in books and pictures to the legislators and political partisans who sought to do the same through the creation of a constitutional state. These texts suggest some of the complicated ways that first-generation federalism was theorizing a new kind of space—a new set of imaginary relations between the geographic parts of the contemporary North American world that ultimately ensured a far different (because always spatially evolving) union far ahead in deep historical time. I argue here that the federalists of 1787–88 were able to install a government that then slowly called forth the material conditions of nationality, but that they did so from an original vantage point that had nothing but fiction with which to imagine such a future. This negotiation of the present and the future, of territory and perpetuity, may well be federalism's most elusive cultural innovation. Rather than making material interventions at the moment of founding, the federalists used the Constitution to restructure existing social relations in a way that allowed for new spatial conditions to emerge *later*. Nothing material changed when the ninth state ratified. Rivers were not moved; roads were not built. But a theory was installed that allowed rivers to be moved and roads to be built in the years that unfolded through each decade of the nineteenth century. The federalist project thus amounts to the successful, if unlikely, conquest of both space and time by a theory, a consolidation, on a mass scale, of both territory and history—the very matrix of what it means to be a nation.

2. The Mammoth State Mapped:
Christopher Colles's Survey of American Roads

Before there were Mapquest and Google, before the cell phone and the satellite, there was the surveyor's chain. This was how the North American continent became visible to itself—measured, mapped, split into parcels, recorded in deeds, bought, sold, and cultivated.[4] The young George Washington used the chain. He worked as a surveyor throughout Virginia's western interior in his youth; the land he eventually accumulated from this labor (and from his involvement in the Seven Years War) ensured his future fortune and at the same time determined, decades before the fact, the site at which the U.S. capital now sits. It is no coincidence that the District of Columbia lies just east of Washington's considerable western land holdings; like other Virginians, Washington hoped to make these western lands more profitable through the creation of a vast marketplace that might draw raw materials out of the interior, along the Potomac, and onto ships bound for international ports while at the same time pulling back in imported goods brought home on the same ships, distributing them to a dense web of cash-ready consumers in the Virginia interior. Like many southern planters, Washington believed the Potomac could unite eastern and western Virginia into one teeming market, but he knew that to do so, the interior had to be populated and connected to the coast. The answer to this problem of dis/connection was first the surveyor's chain and then a series of canals intended to connect those rivers into a network more far-flung than any yet known in provincial North America. The national capital, placed at the convergence point of this future network, was to be both its symbol and its beneficiary.

Washington's ambitions for an expanded trading community were, if anything, small-minded and provincial ones; they imagined the potential of such a network largely at the level of the colony and state. As the United States emerged from the Revolution as a sovereign nation-state in the 1780s, a number of Americans in different productive capacities (authors, statesman, artists, and inventors) were beginning to imagine not just integrated regions, or part-spaces, but the yet-to-be-integrated nation-space as a whole. This newly continental scale of imagined community was at the heart of Paine's fantasy of a ubiquitously consumed *Common Sense* and Mathew Carey's wish to create a nationally distributed magazine. It was also a recurring theme in the fascinating cultural career of an early industrial engineer named Christopher Colles. An Irish emigrant who witnessed the Revolution and its aftermath, Colles not only surveyed and made maps (like Washington before him) but also invented engines, built urban waterworks, designed canals, and at several points attempted to sell books across several regions simultaneously—all complex networking projects tackled before, during, and after the Revolution.

Relatively little is known about Colles's peripatetic life, compared to other early national figures. This is strange, for Colles was an immigrant to Franklin's Philadelphia in the early 1770s, a well-known citizen of New York City at the onset of the Revolution, a gunnery sergeant in New Jersey for Washington's army during most of the war, a state surveyor of western lands during and after the war, and a frequent petitioner to early national state and federal legislatures (where he sought funding and reimbursement for expenses incurred on various state projects).[5] But while Colles lived at the center of momentous events, his name is rarely mentioned in contemporary memoirs or correspondence, nor have the minor details of his life been recorded in the histories that such documents produced. He merits only a single letter, for instance, from the prolific George Washington, who warned him after the war to scale down his proposals for massive canal projects in New York State (advice offered even as Washington promoted similarly visionary canal projects in Virginia designed by a southern engineer named James Rumsey).[6] Most of the other prominent men that Colles must have known of and been known by—the Rittenhouses, Franklins, Jeffersons, and even the Paines of the American Enlightenment—never mention him at all.

Alongside this documentary void, Colles's migratory life and indigent death prevented the preservation of his own papers, either personal or scientific. To the degree that Colles's life is recorded at all, it is in a miscellany of rare print sources. He reappears, for instance, throughout early American print culture as the persistent "projector" of various scientific projects concocted to further his study and, according to several petitions, feed his large family (he fathered eleven children). He thus has a spectral presence in the minutes of the American Philosophical Society, where he repeatedly sought patronage and aid for various building projects and inventions (but was, tellingly, never asked to join). In addition to these third-person sightings, Colles stalks the archive in the first person as well, most notably in a series of printed public announcements that detail the impressive range of his study and invention. These begin with a series of newspaper advertisements inviting local Philadelphians (and later, New Yorkers) to attend lectures in his home on scientific principles. Advertised as "exhibitions," these lectures' more theoretical points were demonstrated through the use of painstakingly scaled models—machines that the American Philosophical Society (APS) found distastefully showman-like.[7] Later, Colles would publish an impressive series of brief printed pamphlets proposing various engineering projects for public subscription—every one of which eventually failed and left Colles in deeper debt than when he began them. Against this archive of exceedingly diminishing returns, only one remark remains that can be ascribed to Colles after the manner of a quotation, but it is an appropriate one: ruminating on his own propensity to imagine what seemed, to his contemporaries, to be impossible or fanciful building projects, Colles was fond of saying (and his biographers have been fond of repeating) "that had he been trained as a hatter, men would probably have come into the world without heads."[8]

Colles is nevertheless an instructive figure. While Washington was making the iconic gesture of crossing the Delaware in 1776 and Madison was taking notes at the Federal Convention of 1787, Colles was traveling the northeastern seaboard (and later the New York interior) plotting projects for which the early nation-state had, to use a variation of his own words, "no head." These increasingly ambitious projects were grounded, in part, in Colles's Painite response to the Revolution, an event that displaced him (making him, like many wartime refugees, exceptionally mobile in these years) even as it created a vast, incipiently national space onto which he could project his futuristic imagination. Colles's progression (or, in federalist parlance, his imaginative "extension") from small- to large-scale projects is evident in almost everything he did in these years. In the years just before the Revolution, for example, Colles's projects had an insistently local character. These include his cultivation of local Philadelphia and New York publics to act either as patron-collaborators for his scientific pursuits (as with the APS) or as audiences for them (as in his advertised lecture series); his numerous proposals for the construction and installation of various "mechanical contrivances" in and around the proto-industrial Delaware Valley (as in his early proposal to use a steam engine to create an inland, non-water-powered mill); and finally, his proposal, in 1774, for an early waterworks system that, had it been finished, would have provided fresh water to the entire population of New York City.[9]

Although these more localized projects continually failed for lack of interest or funding, Colles's proposals became, by the end of the war, in-

creasingly fantastical. They would eventually include a wireless telegraph
system that was to visually link the eastern seaboard in a chain of tele-
scopic signal stations; several large and small canal projects (never built),
including one that he hoped to construct aboveground (in areas where
there were no natural waterways) and another that was to have linked
New York State to the "waste lands" surrounding the Great Lakes region
(a highly nationalist objective that anticipated the Erie Canal, built four
decades later); and finally two massive cartographic printing projects that
ultimately did produce fragmentary texts, even though copies of either
are among the rarest antiquarian objects in all of early national print culture. Of all these efforts, Colles remains most famous for the first of these
two map series—his most unified and longest surviving printed text,
titled *A Survey of the Roads of the United States of America* (1789). It is because of the novelty of this text that Colles is most frequently cited today,
when he is cited at all, as the author and inventor of the first American
road map (see figure 5.1).

The road map series is one of many attempts, from the colonial period
forward, to represent an emerging federal space in its most literal territorial form, yet it attends to this problem in a number of novel ways.
Indeed, the maps that comprise the *Survey* differ strikingly from Colles's
two other extant mapping projects, which are both far more conventional cartographic efforts: first, a "plan" of the city of Limerick (the first
map Colles ever published), and second, a larger project called *The Geographical Ledger* (begun just after, and perhaps in response to, the failure
of the road map book) (see figures 5.2 and 5.3). It is unknown how large
the original map of Limerick was, but the *Ledger* maps were printed on
oversized paper and worked from a much larger scale than the Limerick map, imagining massive chunks of the northeastern coastline from
a vastly abstracted perspective and thus offering significantly less detail
than the map of Limerick, which restricts itself to a single township. In
this way, the two maps perform in miniature Colles's more general move
in these years from urban to national improvements, registering a significant shift in imaginative scale from the relatively local (a town in Ireland)
to the explicitly continental, or national (the coastline pictured in just
one of the *Ledger*'s plates, for example, includes parts of New York, Connecticut, Rhode Island, and Massachusetts).

Yet if we set aside the issue of scale, the two maps actually share many
important features, including a host of unassuming (which is to say,
highly familiar) representational strategies. Both, for example, place their

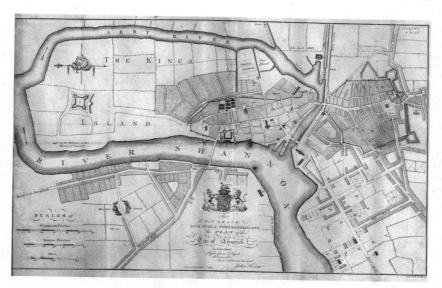

FIGURE 5.2 Christopher Colles. Map of the city of Limerick. 1769. From John Ferrar's *History of Limerick*. 1787. Photo courtesy of the Newberry Library.

viewers in the impossible, highly abstracted, and yet fairly traditional position accorded to readers of maps through the surreally ungrounded conventions of Western cartography—what Donna Haraway calls "the god-trick of seeing everywhere from nowhere."[10] Likewise, each map establishes a cartographically conventional sense of geographic orientation (a sense of north, south, east, and west) by invoking either a literal or an understood compass that organizes the space depicted on the page in such a way that north always sits at the top of the frame, east to right, west to the left, and south at the bottom. Thus while the scale and content of the two maps differ in important ways, the structure of knowledge that informs each one remains constant. One "reads" these two maps, in other words, in very much the same way.

Between these two mapping projects, however, came another one that expanded the scope of the area Colles planned to map even as it broke down that area into the most minutely scaled renderings ever produced in eighteenth-century North America (one inch and three quarters to the mile). This was the road map series of 1789, titled by Colles *A Survey of the Roads of the United States of America*. Colles's maps were based on earlier road maps he had seen in Ireland, and the form, with some important differences, dates to medieval Europe. The most impor-

FIGURE 5.3 Christopher Colles. *The Geographical Ledger and Systemized Atlas.* New York: John Buel, 1794. Collection of The New-York Historical Society. Digital ID 78724d.

tant of these differences is the way more modern map books gathered their maps within a bound book while medieval versions often unfolded horizontally on long, rolled pieces of parchment (a fact that is residually registered in some Renaissance engravings, which picture a piece of scrolled parchment on which a continuous roadmap is then graphically unfurled). The most magnificent of these modern European map books (and one that Colles probably knew) was *Britannia Depicta, or Ogilby Improv'd* (1720), which went through numerous editions in Colles's lifetime.[11] But the sensuous and tactile simulation of medieval manuscript culture (still registered in Ogilby's original *Britannia* in 1675) is a far cry from the awkward angularity of many of Colles's more primitive-looking maps. Indeed, the dense, lushly overgrown mappings and notations of *Britannia Depicta* pose a startling and instructive contrast to the starkness and sheer blankness of many of Colles's plates, which eloquently speak to the undeveloped state of early American interconnective infrastructures, even as they seek to represent and cultivate them.[12]

Colles's 1789 road maps differ radically from his other maps and, indeed, from every other extant American map from this period. Unlike Colles's city plan of Limerick, the road maps of the *Survey* are imagined in explicitly serialized form, with each roadway depicted vertically and then arranged in "strips" (like the maps that the American Automobile Association now provides its members for road trips). In fact, the *Survey*'s maps rupture our most common cartographic expectations. They abandon classical modes of spatial orientation, so that north, south, east, and west do not remain statically located from map to map. On the contrary, verticality takes precedence over convention in these maps, and every road is represented lengthwise down the page, whether it runs north to south or east to west. (See, for example, the arrows designating north and south on each strip, which shift orientation with the road and traveler.) In disavowing conventional orientation, the maps resolutely banish the familiar bird's-eye viewer (whose head is always assumed to be pointed north) and construct instead an embodied traveler who is projected into the actual landscape as if holding the map in hand and looking down at it while standing on the road in question (without knowing, as travelers often do not know, in what direction that road runs). And that is not all: the maps in Colles's *Survey* (see figure 5.4) further frustrate their viewers' more mundane expectations by never attempting to simulate the spatial unity of more conventional maps. Thus the roads are represented, within the frame of each plate, in discontinuous and spatially incongruous "com-

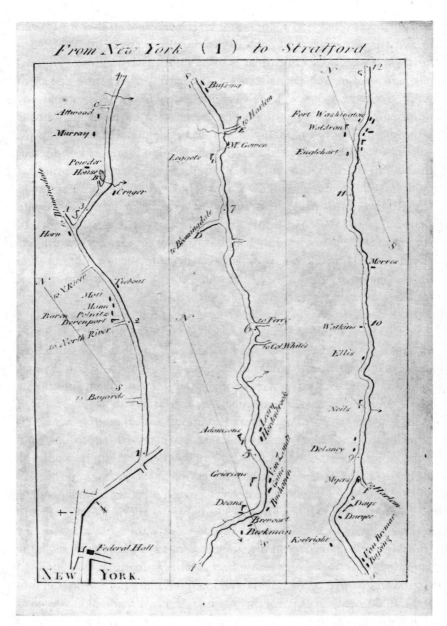

FIGURE 5.4   Christopher Colles. *A Survey of the Roads of the United States of America*. New York: s.n., 1789. Plate 1. Lawrence H. Slaughter Collection, The Lionel Pincus and Princess Firyal Map Division, The New York Public Library, Astor, Lenox, and Tilden Foundations.

partments," and the frame of each map is filled with one, two, or three distinct strips, which make no effort to actually (or mimetically) represent the space depicted. Instead, each plate is composed in such a way that the reader must do the analytical work both of deducing the relation of the (strip) parts to the whole page and of connecting these different strip-parts to the many other serialized strip maps that precede and succeed any given plate in the book as a whole. In this way, the plates implode the visual integrity one routinely expects in an Enlightenment map even as they draw attention to the artificiality of such pseudo-mimetic techniques.

These road-mapping techniques—innovative, disorienting, but (one would guess) weirdly empowering for the early national traveler—represent a crucial addition to the already complex archive of the extended republic that we have begun to assemble, an archive that is itself part of a global history of the expanding yet increasingly compressed (representable) universe scholars have come to associate with the spread of mercantile and later industrial capitalism. Colles's *Survey* is, in this sense, a captivating signpost on the roadway of American modernity. Like Trumbull's painting of the Declaration of Independence, the *Survey* appealed to a desire for literal coverage, requiring the collection and then reassembly of topographical knowledge that could be gained (like Trumbull's portraits) only through extraordinary feats of cross-country travel. Like Paine, however, Colles also fully expected that this collection of maps would eventually be reincorporated back into the local spaces it sought to represent by way of a mass diffusion of the printed road book, and to this end, Colles sought to place his subscription list with "most of the Booksellers on the continent."[13] In this way, the *Survey* might be said to (try to) broker, in its highly innovative internal arrangement, the perceptual paradox of federalism itself, powerfully countering the seeming impossibility of keeping in simultaneous view both the generalized and diffuse thing that is the nation *and* its many embodied spaces—and doing so, not coincidentally, in the form of a book.

Colles is, in other words, very much a federalist in the *Survey*. He calls forth an embodied traveler moving through a series of local spaces, pointing out countless local attractions ("a mine hole," a "red house," "Snowden's Ironworks," "Gen. Washington's Land," "Aylett's Warehouses," "Sneed's Ordinary," and so on). Yet he never relinquishes a larger—or what Hamilton would have called a "comprehensive"—conception of federal space. Indeed, the *Survey* has intensely nationalist investments that are plainly inscribed on its face from page one. Where other maps of this period routinely depict regions that are both intra- and extranational (maps of the post road, for instance, usually included both American and Canadian space), Colles's book explicitly declares itself a "Survey of the Roads of the United States of America." Though the plates themselves were not available to buyers until 1790, Colles placed the year 1789 on the title page in order to make the book's publication coincide with the ratification of the Constitution and the formation of the new government. Indeed, Colles even goes so far as to begin the book's fictional journey in Plate 1 at New York's Federal Hall, which was, in 1789, the new national capitol and the recent site of Washington's inauguration. In this way, the book makes continual literal and symbolic reference to the newly invented nation-state even as it attempts to collect and contain a map to every known space within it in the highly singular space of a book. That it does so in such a way that each represented space can also be experienced locally, by the body holding any given map on any given road, makes this an exceptional artifact in the production of federalist space.

Why would an eighteenth-century engineer, more suited finally to bridge building than engraving, want to publish a map series? Colles's *Survey* labored to master the extended spaces that continually foiled so many of his other projects but that he could never banish from view as the object of his scientific and creative desires. And in a sense, the project succeeds, at least in the way that it brings many of the wild and far-flung sites of the extended republic back, within the frame of a single book, into the realm of representational order. In many ways, however, this Colles project, like so many of the other ones, finally breaks down along the intractable axes of its own implausibility, with "the magnitude of the project" exceeding the resources available to execute it.[14] For one thing, Colles had originally planned to personally survey every road included in the *Survey*, promising his subscribers that all plates would be made "from actual mensuration, by a perambulator" of his own invention, an odometer-like device designed to allow a single person to record highly accurate mileage data (as opposed to the more common surveying chain, which required at least two people and produced a higher rate of error in the calculation of long and hilly distances).[15] But the task of gathering so much cartographic data alone, in the body of his own person, finally proved too massive an undertaking, and Colles was not able to finish what he began. The map series remains incomplete, with only eighty-three of the original one hundred plates drafted. Cartographers now speculate, furthermore, that only a small number of the completed plates were actually based on Colles's own surveys.[16]

But the problems posed by the project did not simply involve the implausibility of one man recovering, in a single text, the infinite simultaneity of national space. The project also failed because the people living along those roads had no need for a book that did such a thing, especially one with detailed maps of distant locales, where many potential readers knew they would never travel. Colles, of course, fully believed in the utility of existing networks of exchange, encouraging his prospective subscribers to imagine themselves as participants in a densely knit web of early national print culture, whereby individuals who might want to sell property or further their business enterprises could "advertise in the public newspapers that the place is marked on such a page of Colles's Survey of the roads."[17] As it turned out, however, the *Survey* was never that densely cross-referenced with local sites nor was it widely consumed enough to merit such iconic mention in the newspapers of its day. Indeed, it was only offered for sale in bookstores in two locations—New York and Philadelphia—making it unlikely that news of its existence ever reached most of its target readers in the first place.[18]

The *Survey* finally crumbled through a lack of subscriptions. While Colles had initially imagined a flexible project in which any traveler might select out only those "particular pages which are necessary for his direction,"[19] he sank deeper into debt as he was forced to sell off existing plates separately. As might be expected, local consumers bought the maps most tailored to their everyday travels (New Yorkers and Philadelphians, for example, preferring plates of the middle colonies). But only the most affluent buyers wanted a whole set, and even then, their purchase was more likely motivated out of a (federalist) desire to collect and accumulate rather than a need to own maps they might actually use. Once Colles started to sell the plates piecemeal, he was left with a motley collection of mismatched leftovers, the traces of which survive in today's most elite archives, most of which hold only partial copies of the *Survey*.[20] Colles thus failed in his attempt to collect, organize, and recirculate his map book evenly across a vast, serialized space. In his failure, however, he not only mimed those competing modes of national fantasy that preceded him (making his project simultaneously Painite and *Federalist*-like) but also finally foreshadowed—in some small, partial way—the practices of official federalism as they were soon to be practiced in the newly imagined federal state. If Colles failed, then, he failed spectacularly, and the story of his road book condenses in a single location something besides roads: it comprises a nearly seamless compendium of even the most mismatched, or seemingly opposed, of early nationalist imaginaries.

3. *The Federalist's* Spatial Fix

Like Colles (who proposed and published his *Survey* in ratification-era New York City), the federalists of 1787–88 found themselves about the business of organizing an extended field of representation that relied upon a new conception of part to whole, and, like Colles, they attempted to do so through the mediation of a printed text—that new and complicated administrative "machine" they called the Constitution. This new "frame" of government, as the Constitution was sometimes called, innovated a new and pluralized state apparatus for the emergent United States, creating a bicameral legislature, a federal judiciary, and an iconic executive that were all eventually intended to materially inhabit a single space: the capital. The Constitution—and federalism more generally—is widely understood to be a novel theory for the arrangement of these new institutions, a system of checks and balances in which the three branches of government harmoniously balance each other, just as each micro-unit is in turn balanced within itself by smaller parts (the Senate balancing the House, for instance, or the elected president balancing with the nonelected cabinet).

But federalism was more than a theory about the new government's relation to itself; in fact, it reaches beyond the construction of any single entity (even a particularly well-balanced government) to theorize instead a number of new relations at many different spatial scales. As Madison pointed out to Jefferson, the state-units were simultaneously intended to be reorganized around, and balanced with, this new thing called the federal government, while the people themselves were to be reorganized and balanced, as we shall see, with their more refined, more rational, more elite "representatives."[21] Rather than newly rearranging a single set of parts and wholes, then, the Constitution sought to rearrange parts and wholes at every scale of national life. It was thus an all-encompassing theory that reached from federal institutions through the old "medium" of the states and down to individual persons.[22] Indeed, while the Revolution sought (however imperfectly) to redistribute the social, political, and economic power of the imperial center back through the diverse sites that comprised North America's colonial periphery, federalism theorized an entirely new social mechanics that would eventually reorganize the horizontal relations of geographic space in and through the verticality of unequal social relations. As such, it marks a shift that wholly saturates the field of known spaces, both real and abstract, near and far, local and national—a novel classificatory system designed to include everyone and everything within its organizing, hierarchizing reach.

Laura Rigal has characterized federalism's drive to represent and organize the whole as an "exhibitionary complex."[23] She argues that "the arts of federalism" (in which she includes invention, authorship, painting, museum building, and ornithology, to name a few) worked together to produce the federal state as a vast spectatorial space. Such practices allowed viewers/citizens within this space to share the supposedly "elevated" view of federalism through their own local production and consumption of "a world of things," which included objects and events as diverse as magazines, parades, engravings, maps, and encyclopedias. Though Rigal does not explicitly say so, this spectatorial aspect of U.S. citizenship would eventually be managed in at least two fundamental ways—first, through the figure of the iconic president and second, through the emergence of the two-party system. Both successfully organize, simplify, and, in short, reduce the diversity of federal governance so that it can be viewed from afar. In 1789, Colles sought to create a similarly simplifying administrative master-text for members of the new nation. Colles's *Survey* is a catalogue of every major American road, joining together for the first time a series of fragmented frames that, once collected and connected, picture the impressive length and breadth of the United States. Such objects, Rigal suggests, make the American public visible to itself as members of the newly federalized republic while at the same time reframing "participation" in that republic as an act of spectatorship—or cultural consumption.[24]

But there is a difference, finally, between a will to exhibit and a successful exhibit. Colles felt this difference in the form of failure when his attempts to collect, contain, represent, and redistribute the new nation finally found no audience—or, at any rate, no mass audience that could be reached or who might, conversely, reach back with its pocketbook and pay the bill for such an object. This same fate met several of the other characters we have already met in this book, including the feckless postal inspector Hugh Finlay, whose uncompleted survey of the post road in 1773–74 led not at all to better service; the young Mathew Carey, whose plans for a national magazine had to wait several decades before they were fulfilled;

and the post-Revolutionary John Trumbull, whose arduous attempts to make the scene of founding as authentic as possible finally made his picture of it obsolete. These figures demonstrate that the vast museum-making project Rigal describes actually emerged several decades before its time: all of these first-generation Americans—from Colles to Carey to Trumbull—failed in their attempts to contain, verbally and visually, the republic's vastness in and through "the arts of federalism." Try as these authors might to represent and turn to their advantage the dislocations of the extended republic, those dislocations finally determined the very viability of their careers as cultural producers, even at a moment when "culture" was gradually emerging as a category separate from, but indispensable to, republican politics. Such projects were, in some sense, destined to fail. As the federalists knew when they reverted in 1787 to the metropolitan model of virtual representation, there simply is no representational scheme that can *literally* hold any vast space (or its human contents, their political constituents) in view. Publius makes a similar point in *Federalist* No. 35: "The idea of an actual representation of all classes by persons of each class is altogether visionary" (219). Colles's maps, of course, focus on a fledgling infrastructure (the post road), but they finally point instead to the circulatory *potential* of such connective structures. For this reason, his *Survey* was, to use Publius's words, "altogether visionary."

The recognition of the basic unrepresentability of the republic at large is a simple but crucial point, for as I have already argued, it was precisely the inability to actually see what was going on everywhere else that finally allowed each state, one by one, to ratify. The decentralization of both people and (pamphlet, essay, and newspaper) production paradoxically enabled the process of federal consolidation to proceed without widespread organized resistance, especially from those populations living in the interior who were particularly hostile to the primarily mercantile, urban (and hence coastal) interests that the Constitution most sought to protect.[25] Indeed, a system as totalizing as the U.S. Constitution would probably never have been adopted if there had been infrastructural means by which to defeat it. Fragmentation (rather than unity) and absence (rather than presence) made the difference in its adoption. Ironically enough, then, it was the very thing that made the *Survey* a failure—the inability to find or reach a consolidated American audience (a monolithic map-using, road-traveling majority)—that finally ensured ratification's success.

Key federalists clearly recognized that the unrepresentability of the republic at large was a direct consequence of its materiality—its status, that is, as a very real, large, and disconnected space. Indeed, the republic's dispersed spatial conditions form the subject matter of *The Federalist*'s most cherished contribution to American political economy: No. 10. Here Madison offers his famous exposition about the practicability and positive virtues of the extended republic, which, by dispersing known dissent, was expected to contain and control majority factions that might otherwise tyrannize the minority:

> The smaller the society . . . and the smaller the compass within which [factions] are placed, the more easily will they concert and execute their plans of oppression. Extend the sphere, and you take in a greater variety of parties and interests; you make it less probable that a majority of the whole will have a common motive to invade the rights of other citizens; or if such a common motive exists, it will be more difficult for all who feel it to discover their own strength, and to act in unison with each other. (63–64)

Madison's faith in the utility of the extended republic's dispersion is what the geographer David Harvey has called, in a different context, a "spatial fix"—a way of using geography to resolve a social problem.[26] Ratification was a crucial test case for this theory: like the other factions that Madison thought could be neutralized by extending the sphere of representation, the antifederalists simply did not have the opportunities for "communication and concert" that would have allowed them to defeat the Constitution (61). Antifederalists were thus doomed to debate the extended republic from inside the more contracted sphere of their own state cultures and the even more contracted and temporary space of local ratifying conventions, unable to "act in unison" on a national scale.

Even so, the antifederalists did recognize and theorize the problem of size, identifying it as an administrative issue that pertained not just to ratification but to the future administration of the proposed federal state. George Clinton (writing as Cato) pointed to the remoteness of the federal capital (its geographic displacement from the republic's peripheries) and insisted that the plan was impractical. Noting that the extent of many of the union's *state-units* was "almost too great for the superintendence of a republican form of government," he insisted the federal government would not be able to operate at such a remove from the object(s) of its superintendence.[27] The Federal Farmer likewise wondered how, for example, taxes could be "collected" across the vast geographic expanse projected by the proposed constitution.[28] Other antifederalists, however, sometimes argued the opposite point, painting the federal government as a monstrous hydra whose tentacles would reach into every household, impressing its will on individuals in the form of standing armies and burdensome taxes. These particular concerns were not random: the power to tax and the power to raise standing armies were, in fact, the two most dramatic powers delegated to the new government under the Constitution, and both were frequently criticized, either as the two most likely forms of force through which the new federal state might invasively enter the everyday lives of local communities or as the two most likely ways in which that state would fail to assume a lasting power. For this reason, the figures of the soldier and the tax collector recur throughout ratification debate, either as specters of the despotic abuse of state power or as figments of the federalist's "visionary," impractical scheme.

Benjamin Workman voices a mixture of these two positions when he writes, in the paranoid voice of Philadelphiensis:

> The number of inhabitants of the United States is now probably about three millions and a half . . . scattered over a continent twelve hundred miles long and eight hundred broad. Now to keep such an extensive country in subjection to one general government, a *standing army* by far too numerous for such a small number of people to maintain, must and will be garrisoned in every district through the whole.——And in case of immergency, the collecting of these scattered troops into one large body, to act against a foreign enemy, will be morally impossible. Besides they will have too much business on hand at their respective garrisons, *in awing the people,* to be spared for other purposes: There is no doubt, but to carry the arbitrary decrees of the federal judges into execution, and to protect the *tax gatherers* in collecting the revenue, will be ample employment for the military.[29]

For Workman, taxation and military occupation are intimately connected. In the circular logic of the federal state, an army will be required to ensure the hegemony of the new government; heavy taxation of individual citizens will be required for such an army to be raised; such heavy taxation will in turn require the coercive power of (that same) extensive army; and the army will thus be used primarily to protect the tax gatherer rather than the everyday citizen. Its force turned inward in this way, the military will not be able to protect the people it coerces: indeed, these armies will be so busy doing the work of tyranny that it will be "impossible" to "collect" it together in time to face the external challenges of foreign invasion. The world will thus be turned upside down: the domestic (nation) will become the site of homegrown military coercion rather than protection, and those "who do not love to work" will be paid with the taxes of those who do.

Workman's analysis is unusual in its attempt to project the spatial logic of federalism into the deep future; it is exemplary, however, in the antifederalist topoi it mobilizes. The fear of armies, the prediction of heavy taxation, the dilemma of "collection" across a vast space—all these were central features of the antifederalist critique of both the new Constitution and the extended spatial area upon which it depended. There was, however, an internal contradiction at work in the antifederalist critique of the extended republic's size. *Federalist* No. 29 points out this contradiction, lampooning the "exaggerated and improbable suggestions which have taken place respecting the power of calling for the services of the militia": "At one moment there is to be a large army to lay prostrate the liberties of the people; at another moment the militia of Virginia are to be dragged from their homes five or six hundred miles to tame the republican contumacy of Massachusetts" (186). Publius appears to be up to his old trick here of gathering together the most contrary antifederalist positions in order to make resistance to the Constitution appear confused and nonsensical. In this case, however, he does not need to manufacture a contradiction so much as to notice one. On one hand, the antifederalists fear that "a large army" will "lay prostrate the liberties of the people," with the army figured as a monstrous state apparatus that permeates the republic at large, tyrannizing its people from coast to coast. On the other hand, the antifederalists also fear the army will be stretched so thin that the militia of one state will "be dragged from their homes five or six hundred miles" in order to maintain internal peace in distant states. One of these objections poses a problem of saturation (too much of an army and not enough space to avoid it); the other poses a problem of collection (too large of a space to protect and not enough men in reach).

In moments like these, the antifederalists were struggling in part to find a way to make legible to their audiences the Constitution's novel extension of state power to the individual. Despite the word "federalism," the Constitution was not merely a compact between states (as the Articles of Confederation had been) but sought instead to extract consent from (and ultimately to exert power over) individual citizens, each alone in their body in the realm of the everyday. As Publius plainly put it, the new state will "carry its agency to the persons of the citizens," and there was little dissimulation about why this might be useful (102). As Madison knew, it is easier to compel individuals to pay their taxes than it is to get states to do so. "It was generally agreed," Madison later told Jefferson, "that the objects of the Union could not be secured by any system founded on the principle of a confederation of sovereign States. A *voluntary* observance of the federal law by all the members, could never be hoped for. A *compulsive* one could evidently never be reduced to practice. . . . Hence was embraced the alternative of a Government which instead of operating, on the States, should operate without their intervention on the individuals composing them."[30] As a bonus, the removal of the local state-unit (Georgia, Pennsylvania, New York, and so on) as an intermediary between the federal state and the individual citizen would also allow the federal state to sidestep the political corruption that men like Madison saw brewing at the state level.

Whether well intentioned or not, this extension of state power to individuals, because it depended on such an attenuated chain of representation between federal representatives and local citizens, reminded many antifederalists of the pre-Revolutionary model of virtual representation, whereby the colonies were denied meaningful mediators to speak for their interests in Parliament. In fact, the highly centralized model of power proposed by the Constitution was both a reminder of this earlier, metropolitan model and a seemingly new, terrifying experiment in what Michel Foucault calls biopower—the coercion of individual bodies by an abstract and all-encompassing power that circulates routinely and omnivorously throughout the microspaces of everyday life.[31] Many antifederalist essays and speeches thus center their fantasies about the future federal state on the figure of an individual citizen who is harassed and tortured by the absolute power of a government that has direct access to his body. An antifederalist essayist signing himself John Humble imagines the nightmare of federalism in just this way—as the spatial coincidence of state power and individual bodies. Reciting a mock pledge of allegiance to the new federal government, Humble addresses himself sarcastically to "slaves scattered through the world":

> Now we the *low born*, that is, all the people of the United States except 600 or thereabouts, *well born*, do by this our humble address, declare, and most solemnly engage, that we will allow and admit the said 600

well born, immediately to establish and confirm this most noble, most excellent and truely divine constitution: And we further declare that without any equivocation or mental reservation whatever we will support and maintain the same according to the best of our power, and after the manner and custom of all other slaves in foreign countries, namely by the sweat and toil of our body: Nor will we at any future period of time ever attempt to complain of this our *royal* government, let the consequences be what they may.—And although it appears to us that a *standing army* . . . shall be employed in collecting the *revenue* of this our king and government; yet, we again in the most solemn manner declare, that we will abide by our present determination of non-assistance and passive obedience; so that we shall not dare to molest or disturb those military gentleman in the service of our royal government. And . . . should any one of those soldiers when employed on duty in collecting the *taxes*, strike off the arms (with his sword,) of one of our *fellow slaves*, we will conceive our case remarkably fortunate if he leaves the other arm on. —And moreover because we are aware that many of our fellow slaves shall be unable to pay their *taxes* . . . [we will not] think their sentence severe unless after being hanged they are also to be both *beheaded* and *quartered.* —And finally we shall hence forth and forever, leave all *power, authority,* and *dominion* over our *persons* and *properties* in the hands of the *well born,* who were designed by Providence to *govern.* . . . We shall in future be perfectly contented if our *tongues* be left us to lick the feet of our well born masters.[32]

A veritable Declaration of Dependence, this pledge satirically reverses many of our more familiar discourses of American autonomy. As such, it negatively recalls the original scene of American independence in 1776, hailing the new government as the reincarnation of "royal government" and constructing its projected citizen as a servile slave. But why, this essayist asks, should the many submit to the unjust regime of a few? Viscerally skewering the absurdity of such submission, the speaker resists, through parody, the people's reconstitution into so many "docile bodies."[33] He does this by imagining, in the most literal terms possible, what the relation between the new federal citizen and his government might look like, gruesomely invoking that citizen as a literal body upon which the state will directly exert its force. Indeed, it is the "sweat and toil" of this individual citizen that will fund the new government; it is he who will be crippled by heavy taxation and military occupation; and it is he who will be beheaded and quartered when he fails to properly pay his debt. In the micro-imaginary space of everyday life under federalism, the body of the federal subject will in time be reduced to nothing more than a tongue—one that will be used to lick the shoes of those who run the new state rather than (in Habermasian fashion) to critique it.

In contrast to grotesque parodies like this one, *The Federalist* sought to reconstruct the new state as a positive good for the few *and* the many. Just as No. 10 argued that the extended republic would disperse faction (thus protecting the minority), other numbers argue that this dispersal will also protect the majority from the two things that local populations apparently feared most—taxation and military occupation. If the new frame of government is metropolitan (or "royal") in its scheme of representation, it will also be metropolitan in the literal distance it will maintain from its peripheries and parts. One benefit of such distance is that the federalist representative can take a more comprehensive (or federal) view of local matters from afar. More importantly, neither the representative nor the government will pose a threat to the everyday world of town and state. Instead, the mutual isolation of the national center from its own peripheries—the geographical dislocation of federal representatives from those they represent within the newly installed metropolitan government—will simultaneously protect the many from the few and the few from the many. That "reprobated" maxim, *Divide et impere*, was thus to be the answer to both anarchy *and* oligarchy, since "the people collectively from their number and from their dispersed situation, cannot be regulated in their movements by that systematic spirit of cabal and intrigue" feared by the antifederalists.[34]

Publius implies (here and elsewhere) that the people and the federal state will inhabit different (and always disarticulated) locations. The gap between these spaces is the essence of the project I call metrobuilding—a word I use to refer to the ongoing construction, under the Constitution, of a single national center where previously there had been a proliferation of centers in the form of polycentrically conceived state capitals.[35] At its most material, this project would eventually call forth a federal government consisting of a number of new, concrete institutions (the presidency, the Congress, and the Supreme Court), all territorially concentrated in a capital, a to-be-built environment that was to collect and construct actual people, buildings, and land. But long before this material set of institutions actually came into existence, the federal "superstructure" was being fantasized in the most material terms possible, repeatedly troped, both visually and verbally, as an "edifice" or a "roof" held up by the several concrete "pillars" of each ratifying state. The "grand federal edifice" was, ironically, a metaphor, but the actual (future) materiality of the projected capital-space was crucial to first-generation federalism, for it ensured a mutual buffer between those who would run the nation and those who populated it. Thus in *Federalist* No. 46, Publius emphasizes the disarticulable spaces in which citizen and representative must finally reside, evoking a concrete citizen who occupies the spaces of everyday life (or, the local) and a federal government that occupies a more distant space (in literal terms, the capital). Publius argues that as a singular entity compressed (materially) either in the form of an army or a capital, the new federal government cannot share the same space or possess the same force as the massive plurality of the states—which, when combined, constitute that ultimate source of political power ("the people"). Put simply, the everyday proves, in Publius's account of the extended republic, to be the every*where* as well, and it is the everywhereness of the United States, conceived as a totality, that finally proves impenetrable to tyranny.

To Publius, this is a question of simple math, for he essentially argues that the federal state will be no match for the sum of its parts. He repeatedly points out that the countless locations in which the people daily reside are too numerous to be successfully colonized by a fledgling government that has only limited material resources at its disposal. Though many antifederalists feared the eventual abolition of state governments, Publius insists that the federal state will always be outnumbered and overpowered in such a project: "one set of representatives would be contending against thirteen" (320). In the case of the much-feared army, he insists that the standing army imagined by the Constitution "does not exceed one hundredth part of the whole number of souls" (321). Here again, simple math dictates that the federal government will never be able to coerce the people, en masse, into anything to which they do not consent. The same logic extends to taxation. Cities, he concedes, might be "directly" taxed (due to their condensed locations), "but beyond these circles," the nation "must in a great measure escape the eye and hand of the tax-gatherer" (79). Thus to the highly localized body grotesquely evoked by John Humble, Publius counters with the equally localized body of the tax gatherer, whose "eye" and "hand" are too small to reach into the everyday spaces of local life. The federal government thus repeatedly plays "part" to the people's "whole," and just as the part must always be less threatening (because less powerful) than the whole, the federal state—as a partial representation, or projection, of "the people" and the nation at large—can never fully occupy or invade the local worlds of village, town, and state. The extended republic thus offers a spatial fix not just for faction but for tyranny as well.[36]

Though its partisans developed extensive critiques of the new Constitution, antifederalism failed, both as a coalition and a critique. Despite considerable resistance, the federalists succeeded in reconstructing a metropolitan site of power within a vastly extended field of representation, in the process resurrecting the once-imperial model of virtual representation as a newly national one. But in constructing a superstructure over and against the local worlds of town and state, the federalists did more than simply defy the Enlightenment maxim of *imperium in imperio*—however unlikely that feat alone had once seemed.[37] They succeeded precisely because they embraced the paradox inherent in such an arrangement, recognizing that federalism's two scales of competing power, when understood materially (as matters of disarticulable space), could never *actually* come into conflict. As Madison and Hamilton both knew, the newly imagined state could not have interfered, even if it had wanted to, in the local lives and affairs of American citizens; to do so, the federalists would have had to install from scratch a repressive state apparatus throughout a massive territory that had only a bare minimum of existing connective infrastructure. But in the late 1780s, no singular state institution—not even the post office—was yet capable of perpetually recirculating itself (or any material extension of its power) back through all the original sites that had constituted it—any more than Christopher Colles could make a map of every part of the post road and then distribute it back through every village and town on its path.[38]

4. MEN OF LITTLE INFORMATION: PRODUCING A FEDERALIST ELITE

One of the truisms that has followed *The Federalist Papers* into contemporary life is that it is a supremely rational text, a series of essays that coolly and deliberately reasons with its readers, addressing them as thinking rather than feeling subjects. But while *The Federalist* appears to place the question of self-government before the people (embodied in the form of the newspaper's reading audience), Publius actually deploys an astonishing number of devices that undermine the reader's capacity to discern the problem for him- or herself. In some cases, he undercuts his reader by appealing to a higher authority, as when he claims (frequently) that the justness of his arguments are self-evident and that disagreement can follow only from a flawed perception. At other moments, he calls on the superior wisdom of the Federal Convention and suggests that disagreement amounts to a vain and futile rivalry with that esteemed group. At still others, he reminds his reader of the many ways in which "the people" of the United States have been duped in the past—both by ambitious men and by newspapers, which (though sometimes cited as "expeditious messengers") usually play a large role in the problem of public misapprehension—agents of misrepresentation that "teem . . . with the most inflammatory railings," "the offspring of extreme ignorance or extreme dishonesty" (583).

Publius's tendency to deflate his reader's ability to reason is connected to the way he constructs the larger field of debate. Positioning himself as ratification's narrator, he tends to amplify, rather than minimize, the complications raised by the Constitution, and the result is a frontal assault on the reader's deliberative position. The drive to undermine and overwhelm the reader is apparent even in the opening paragraphs of No. 1:

To the People of the State of New York:

AFTER an unequivocal experience of the inefficacy of the subsisting Federal Government, you are called upon to deliberate on a new Constitution for the United States of America. The subject speaks its own importance; comprehending in its consequences, nothing less than the existence of the UNION, the safety and welfare of the parts of which it is composed, the fate of an empire, in many respects, the most interesting in the world. It has been frequently remarked, that it seems to have been reserved to the people of this country, by their conduct and example, to decide the important question, whether societies of men are really capable or not, of establishing good government from reflection and choice, or whether they are forever destined to depend, for their political constitutions, on accident and force. If there be any truth in the remark, the crisis, at which we are arrived, may with propriety be regarded as the era in which that decision is to be made; and a wrong election of the part we shall act, may, in this view, deserve to be considered as the general misfortune of mankind. (3)

This number overtly draws on Hamilton's legal background, as Publius, like a trial lawyer, asks his readers to "deliberate," like a jury, on an important question. Publius politely addresses this audience as a "you," conceding their instrumental role in the impending decision. Yet even as he places the question in front of his readers, Publius also insists that some things are beyond argument. The direness of the situation is "unequivocal," while "the subject speaks its own importance." More than that, the importance of the subject quickly exceeds the reader in his stated capacity as a citizen "of the State of New York," for the problem is not local but world-historical in importance, entailing not only "the Union" and all of its "parts," but "the fate" of both an "empire" and, indeed, the world. Slyly registering the fact that voting will be the individual's real role—indeed, his only role—under the federal constitution, Publius suggests that "the wrong election" shall not just be a vote poorly cast but will prove "the general misfortune of mankind."[39] Shifting the consequences of the debate from New York to the fate of the union, to that of an empire, and finally to that of the world, *Federalist* No. 1 outlines an overwhelming set of ever-mounting problems before the debate has even begun.

We see here, on the very first page of *The Federalist*, the same problem that confronts Christopher Colles in his *Survey of Roads*: the problem of scale, or, more specifically, the vexed relationship that we have seen emerging in the late eighteenth century between local bodies and the always-expanding universe beyond the local (the state, the nation, and the world). Representational technologies of every kind—from Colles's maps to the founders' new frame of government—sought to describe and manage this sometimes productive, sometimes troubling set of emerging translocal social relations. *The Federalist* is likewise thinking about this problem, turning it to the Constitution's advantage whenever possible. But *The Federalist* is all the more remarkable because it does not merely describe the problem of scale but also seeks, over the arduous course of eighty-five essays, to *produce* it. Like the Constitution itself, *The Federalist* installs a tiered scale of political participation, and it does this partially through the arguments it frames about human nature and partially through the rhetorical effects it generates.

Throughout the essays, Publius takes special care to construct the common citizen as one who inhabits the most local of his imagined spatial scales. This citizen is frequently invoked as a body, even as he is placed at the foot of an immense philosophical question. Toward the end of No. 1, for example, Publius again invokes a world of multiple scales, carefully locating the common citizen (congealed under the umbrella term "the vast majority") in the most limited of these scales. Indeed, he offers himself up as a point of localized identification, overtly referring to himself as a person with a body, a citizen whose motives must remain "in the depository of my own breast." In the sentences that follow, the reader is also hailed as a body (or body-part), one whose "heart" is "deeply engraved" through the violence of the Revolution with a sense of the union's utility. The identification of Publius (as a body) with the general reader's body stops there, however, as he goes on to proliferate a series of semi-discontinuous areas of debate:

> [T]he fact is, that we already hear it whispered in the private circles of those who oppose the new constitution, that the Thirteen States are of too great extent for any general system. . . . [Yet] nothing can be more evident, to those who are able to take an enlarged view of the subject, than the alternative of an adoption of the new Constitution, or a dismemberment of the Union. (7)

Against the "engraved" "hearts" of the general public, Publius posits the whispering mouths of antifederalists (who gossip "in private circles"), and against the smallness of these "private circles," he posits his own "enlarged view." In this way, the three administrative scales of the new frame of government are neatly invoked as just so many concentric circles: the people are represented as individual bodies, who (with hearts already "engraved" with a love of union) are most vulnerable to the possibility of political "dismemberment"; the state officeholders who oppose the Constitution are troped as a number of "private circles," peopled by "whisper[ing]" antifederalists driven by gossip and greed; and the emerging federal state is aligned with a more "enlarged view of the subject." The trope of scale (constructed here through the language of circles) does double work for Publius: on one hand, it organizes the disarray and potential anarchy lurking within the extended (and ever-expandable) republic; on the other hand, it turns antifederalist arguments about distance ("the great extent" of "the Thirteen States") into questions about comprehension and character—about who is and is not "able" to "see" the subject rightly.

By reframing the issue of space as a matter of scale and thus of intellectual perspective, Publius turns distance and detachment into an abstract problem rather than a material one. As I have already argued, however,

the material fact of distance was central to the federalist project of metrobuilding. Spatial discontinuity—the literal distance between such embodied spaces as the federal capital and the state capitals, or between the
federal capital and the local worlds of town and home—served the federalists as a screen in two senses. First, distance literally removed the federal
representative from the day-to-day supervision of his constituents (who,
whether intellectually "able" or not, could never "see" the government
in operation). Second, distance offered itself as the ultimate alibi for the
necessity of representative government. The people cannot be involved
in every government decision, Publius wryly declares; if they tried, "it
would leave them little time to do any thing else" (510). The implication
here is that representation is both necessary and desirable: nations require
a representative political structure so that their citizens can lead happy
and productive lives. As Royall Tyler knew (but his back-state character,
Jonathan, did not), representation is and will always be a de facto part of
everyday life. The convention's couplike work in gutting the Articles of
Confederation and replacing them with a new form of government (one
the convention was not authorized by the states to draft) is likewise explained as a necessary contraction of authority into a small body of men
who do work that the "the people" cannot (in "their dispersed situation")
do (510). "It is impossible," Publius declares, "for the people spontaneously and universally, to move in concert towards their object; and it is
therefore essential, that such changes [as we see in the Constitution] be
instituted by some *informal and unauthorized propositions,* made by some
patriotic and respectable citizen or number of citizens" (265).

Publius's reference here to "some patriotic and respectable . . . citizens" suggests the human capital that is to be invested in the federal
state's political capital. Not only does the Constitution call for a new center; it also requires a new federal elite—a small number of "patriotic and
respectable" citizens—to populate that center and govern from it. The
antifederalists balked at the production of such an elite, and they repeatedly characterized the new federal state as the pet project of an oligarchic
junto. As in other areas of debate, they focused on space as a problem in
the production of such an elite rather than seeing it, as the federalists did,
as a solution. Their critiques raised two issues in this regard. First: how
were federal representatives to be collected into a cohesive unit? (What
location would be equally available to all? How were elections to be executed? Who would pay their travel expenses?) And second, how would
this small group, once it was gathered in the singular space of the capital,

collect information about their constituents—and vice versa—in order to produce the likeness of interests, the sympathy between representative and constituent, that is required in any healthy republic?

Melancton Smith raised the latter point on the floor of the New York Ratifying Convention. "In a country, where a portion of the people live more than twelve hundred miles from the center," he argued, "one body cannot possibly legislate for the whole. . . . It is not possible to collect a set of representatives, who are acquainted with all parts of the continent. Can you find men in Georgia who are acquainted with the situation of New-Hampshire?"[40] Even if such a group could be gathered in one place, Smith argues that they would not be able to govern effectively because they would lack adequate knowledge of the objects of their governance; they would be too far removed from their constituents, literally unable to see them in their diversity and unable to physically mix with them, as Rousseau insists republican representatives must. The question here turns on two issues: sympathy (which I will discuss further on) and *information*—especially the problem of how information (or what we might call local knowledge) is to be collected and by whom. The antifederalists, today dubbed "men of little faith," imagined future federal statesmen as men of little information—just as Paine had once claimed that the king, sitting all alone at the royal center, was the most uninformed man in the British Empire.[41]

Publius's solution to this problem is to invoke once again a world of cascading but geographically distinct scales:

There is in most of the arguments which relate to distance a palpable illusion of the imagination. What are the sources of information by which the people in Montgomery county must regulate their judgment of the conduct of their representatives in the state legislature? Of personal observation they can have no benefit. This is confined to the citizens on the spot. They must therefore depend on the information of intelligent men, in whom they confide—and how must these men obtain their information? Evidently from the complection of public measures, from the public prints, from correspondences with their representatives, and with other persons who reside at the place of their deliberation. This does not apply to Montgomery County only, but to all the counties, at any considerable distance from the seat of government. (582)

Though this passage insists that its target is "distance," Publius is really constructing a theory here about how information circulates. The federalists routinely responded to arguments about "distance" by noting that the larger state units (like Massachusetts, New York, and Virginia) were already far larger than Montesquieu (the original theorist of the small-sized republic) had initially imagined.[42] Publius mobilizes this argument when he suggests that New York State is already too large for its legislature to be overseen by the likes of Montgomery County. All republican governments, he concludes, remove the government from the embodied "observation" of their constituents—even those that function on relatively smaller scales. The people of the union can expect to get their "information" about their representatives the same way the people of Montgomery County do: from "intelligent men" who have access to "public prints," "correspondences" with their representatives, and their intercourse with "persons" elsewhere. People living at every tier (county, state, and nation) are all subject, Publius suggests, to the limits of their perceptions—all constrained to information accessible "on the spot" in which their bodies circulate. Conceding the virtuality of the new state, he also insists upon the hyperactuality, or localness, of information.

But the *kind* of information each tier produces is quite different. Publius's reference to "intelligent men" echoes a model of the public sphere that we have already seen elsewhere in *The Federalist*—one in which the federal government is populated by the "most able men" who are supervised (from afar) by the less able but still "intelligent" men who run state governments. These state representatives are in turn watched over by the people at large, who inhabit the dispersed spaces of counties, towns, and villages. The virtue of this attenuated (but vertical) chain of representation is that it becomes more refined the closer to the top that it gets. In fact, Publius's faith in a world of hierarchically organized administrations is based on his belief in a hierarchy of talent and virtue. As *Federalist* No. 4 argues:

> One Government can collect and avail itself of the talents and experience of the ablest men. . . . It can move on uniform principles of policy—It can harmonize, assimilate, and protect the several parts and members, and extend the benefit of its foresight and precautions to each. . . . It can apply the resources and power of the whole to the defence of any particular part. (20–21)

This passage draws upon a commonplace of eighteenth-century political theory by arguing that a larger field of choice will yield better and more able men than a smaller area could; it will, in fact, make "the ablest men" available. But *The Federalist* does not just argue that the extended republic will make the collection of virtue easier (because more virtuous men can be had). It also suggests that this new "corps" of men will gather, embody, and manage a new kind of knowledge—a form of understanding that is not based on the part or the detail (as everyday "information" is), but that founds itself instead on the "enlarged view" of the whole. A great deal of *The Federalist* is devoted to theorizing this new kind of federal man and a new kind of federal knowledge. While conceding that the federal statesman will lack minute local knowledge (and hence will have little sympathy with his constituents), Publius turns this detachment into a virtue: "Is the man whose situation leads to extensive inquiry and information less likely to be a competent judge of [the] nature, extent and foundation [of particular locations] than one whose observation does not travel beyond the circle of his neighbours and acquaintances?" (221).[43] Ignorance and distance are rewritten in *The Federalist* as a new form of knowledge, so that the representative's removal from the country at large (in its everyday, everywhere form) finally becomes what Catherine Holland calls an "aggregating device" whereby a new "comprehensive knowledge of the whole is gathered and produced."[44] "Information" is thus trumped, in the federalist lexicon, by "comprehension," and a hierarchical relationship to knowledge is simultaneously encoded in that distinction. The federal state becomes the intellectual "head" to millions of local "members" living elsewhere.[45]

In proposing that "the ablest men" run the new government, Publius is advocating for the creation of a federal elite.[46] As the essays accrue, different models emerge for how such a group might operate and who might people it. The most repeated of these is the Federal Convention, "composed of men who possessed the confidence of the people, and many of whom had become highly distinguished by their patriotism, virtue, and wisdom, in times which tried the minds and hearts of men" (10). Cast as guardians of the Revolution, these men are nevertheless said to be more prepared in 1787 than they were in 1776 to do the difficult work of nation building: "In the mild season of peace, with minds unoccupied by other subjects, they passed many months in cool uninterrupted and daily consultations; and finally, without having been awed by power, or influenced by any passions except love for their Country, they presented and recommended to the people the plan produced by their joint and very unanimous counsels" (10–11). Patriotic, virtuous, wise, cool, careful, unawed, dispassionate, and "very unanimous," the convention is hailed by Publius as an intellectual wonder that dwarfs the capacities of both the average person and past Congresses. As a group of men who sought to put "local views" behind them for the sake of the Constitution's more "enlarged view," the convention becomes living proof that men of "comprehension" exist and can operate in concert.

But if the convention is a collective model of what the future federal state might look like, then Publius himself stands in as the exemplary individual spokesman of this new elite. *The Federalist* thus serves as an iconic and performative retort to antifederalist fears about the inevitable dispersion and unavailability of knowledge within an extended sphere. Not only is *The Federalist* finally able to "collect" itself into a monolithic artifact from the fragmentary part-essays that first circulated pell-mell in this or that newspaper, but Publius himself—as a voice, or a monolithic perspective—is a particularly effective example of such collectedness. Throughout the eighty-five essays, Publius models an encyclopedic knowledge that encompasses all of human history, criss-crossing the massive divides of space and time to draw examples from both ancient and modern history, from the Old World and the New, and from the realms of politics, law, mathematics, geography, and botany. And while the fullness and breadth of Publius's knowledge in such instances models comprehension (in its most learned sense), the essays nevertheless stoop to the level of the detail as well. In one particularly impressive display of local factoids, Publius spends an entire paper surveying the constitutions of each of the original thirteen states (though at other moments he judiciously dismisses the necessity of such a maneuver) (323–31). The essays thus demonstrate—at length—that Publius is a man of both comprehension *and* information.

What are the consequences of this performance? In offering up Publius as a model for the new federal statesman, *The Federalist* does more than simply construct *him*; it simultaneously hails its *reader* as the exemplary subject of the federalist mode of governance. Indeed, the chasm that *The Federalist* seeks to cultivate between the (dispersed) general public and a national (consolidated) elite is exactly the one that opens, in No. 1, between the pronouns "you" and "I." That chasm is marked, toward the end of that paper, with the slippery imposition of the word "we": "It may perhaps be thought superfluous to offer arguments to prove the utility of the UNION. . . . But the fact is, that we already hear it whispered in the private circles of those who oppose the new constitution, that the Thir-

teen States are of too great extent for any general system" (7). Twenty-
first-century readers might expect that this "we" connotes the union, or
identification, of the "you" and the "I" already used throughout the essay. But the "we" does not conflate Publius with his reader; instead, it
registers Publius's membership in another world entirely—the world of
the federal. Indeed, No. 1 does a great deal of work partitioning and positioning its pronouns so that by the time Publius attaches his signature
at the bottom of the page, an appreciable difference has been produced
between a "they" (the licentious antifederalist state legislators who "whisper"), a "we" (the federalists, who hear these whispers and relay them to
the reader), and a "you" (the reader, who is now being informed of these
events by the great little man himself, Publius). As a federalist, Publius
appears to have access to gossip circulating secretly "in private circles" at
the state level—information that readers, who live their lives within the
domain of the local, do not have access to. In an odd turn, Publius—and
The Federalist itself—becomes the medium that relays information to
the people at large about their own state politicians (rather than the states
serving, as they had throughout the Confederation era, as a medium between the individual citizens of each state and the Continental Congress).
And this is of course the very inversion in local-to-national relations that
the Constitution seeks to innovate in exerting its power, not through the
old medium of the states, but directly onto individuals.

Like *The Contrast* before it, then, *The Federalist* takes up a pedagogical
project, instructing its reader in the norms of the new federal citizenship.
Tyler celebrates representation for its productive potential; Publius, on
the other hand, defends it and seeks to differentiate between its constitutive elements (representative and citizen), creating a hierarchy between
the two. And if it is true that *The Federalist* finally does not simply posit
an elite speaker or a common reader but instead constructs a pedagogy
between the two, then it cannot be said to promote the production of a
thing (a government, a constitution, or ratification-as-an-outcome) so
much as it seeks to install *a relation*. Under the Constitution, this new relation is at once both material and abstract—a matter of what we might
call space and a matter of what would eventually emerge to be called
class. In the most material (and Collesean) sense, a relation must always
involve positions on a map, but in questions of politics, and especially in
questions of governance, it also involves power. The federalist project of
centralization—or metrobuilding, as I have called it here—actually exploits one set of (material) relations in order to produce this other (more

abstract) kind of power relation. Distinction—in the sense of hierarchical difference (or "class")—is thus written into the deep spatial structure of federalism. The Constitution portends a world of horizontally organized individual bodies living at a remove from and yet governed by a far more vertically organized, top-down set of power relations. This new relation of individuals (and their bodies) to some inexpressible, nonrepresentable, unviewable (because never exactly present) center of power resembles the complex that Foucault calls biopower, but it is biopower American-style. Its success, in other words, depends entirely upon its production at precisely this juncture in the history of technological development (when canals like Colles's could be imagined but not yet built) and at precisely this location (a former colonial periphery seeking to constitute itself as a new national center when no infrastructure yet subtends such a center).

Publius himself often ascribes a material and even territorial dimension to the federal power he seeks to defend—speaking of its boundaries, its shape, and its size as if it were something that might be measured, packaged, and then carried back and forth between the people and their representatives. Indeed, Publius's own relation to the reader is sometimes framed in explicitly geographic terms. In one such moment, Publius offers himself as a tour guide to a reader he feels sure is lost on the winding "road" to ratification:

> If the road, over which you will still have to pass, should in some places appear to you tedious or irksome, you will recollect, that you are in quest of information on a subject the most momentous which can engage the attention of a free people: that the field through which you have to travel is in itself spacious, and that the difficulties of the journey have been unnecessarily increased by the mazes with which sophistry has beset the way. It will be my aim to remove the obstacles to your progress in as compendious a manner, as it can be done, without sacrificing utility to dispatch. (90)

In such moments, Publius theorizes a new relationship between the common citizen and his capacity to gather and organize "information" across space. And it is hardly coincidental that the reader's confusion should be troped as a problem of long-distance (or overly "spacious") travel, for in the protoindustrial early republic, knowledge is always linked to mobility—to one's ability to be "on the spot" in this or that fortuitously eventful locale. *The Federalist*'s alienating rhetorical antics mine this larger social question about how knowledge is to be gathered and disseminated across a newly expanded national space—about who will have it, who should have it, and what varieties it will take.

We have returned, then, to the place where this section began: to the problem of what it is like to read *The Federalist*. Though Publius promises to help the reader through the difficult terrain ahead, his book only demonstrates its own version of "irksome" tediousness. This rhetorical effect was as active in 1787 as it is today. As one eighteenth-century reader noted to his son: "The Federalist unquestionably is a treatise, which displays learning and deep penetration. It is an ingenious, elaborate, and in some places, sophistical defence of the constitution." But "altho written in a correct, smooth stile it is from its prolixity, tiresome. I honestly confess, that I could not read it thro'."[47] A treatise that is at once both "tiresome" and complete (and perhaps tiresome because complete), *The Federalist* produces in its readers an intellectual version of vertigo because it moves too quickly and concentratedly across the scale of human history. Though the reader is appealed to, in No. 1, as the adjudicator of great events, he is actually irrelevant to most of these essays. Publius achieves this evisceration in large part by alienating the reader with his long-winded, arcane, overgrown, and Ciceronian prose. Rather than explaining, *The Federalist* mystifies, and rather than educating, it belabors and (too often) bores. It is a difficult book, invested in its own density and abstraction, requiring immense patience and erudition on the part of its reader. More than one reader has quit, like the one cited above, unable to "read it thro'."

My argument here relies, in part, on actual reception (the question of who has historically read this text and how they have responded to it), but it also relies on the attitude that *The Federalist* takes toward its reader. Compare *The Federalist* once again to *Common Sense*. Paine wrote a book that people could imagine was popular and of course in many places actually was. But *The Federalist* is exceedingly exclusive in the audience it imagines for itself, aggressively constructing partitions not only between itself and its alleged opposition (those antifederalist whisperers), but between itself and its inevitably less erudite and energetic reader. It is unquestionably the cornerstone, if not the doorstop, of American constitutional jurisprudence. But how many people have read *The Federalist* all the way through? While Paine worked to efface the line between elite and common readers—itself a smaller version of the line between the metropolitan center of world power and the everyday periphery—*The Federalist* emphatically reinstalls those divides.

The Constitution likewise partitions the world into several well-defined compartments, not just in the structure of the government it projects, but also in the spatial relations that emerge in the wake of its careful commitment to *imperium in imperio.* The spatial architecture of the new state calls upon each tier—the federal, the state-unit, and the local—to take its place in the machine of constitutional administration. But this new arrangement left ordinary citizens in a place far different from the one they had once occupied under the polycentrically conceived Confederation. As Sheldon Wolin writes:

> Because the Constitution proposed to establish a centered system of power, a national government, it had to create a new type of citizen, one who would accept the attenuated relationship with power implied if voting and elections were to serve as the main link between citizens and those in power. . . . [I]t needed a citizen who could identify himself with a power that was remote, abstract, and so distant that, for the most part, it would operate unseen.[48]

The Constitution, in other words, sought geographically alienated citizens as the base unit of federal representation. Like the frustrated reader who "cannot read [*The Federalist*] thro'," the new federal citizen was expected, after ratification, to voluntarily quit the scene of federal politics. The Constitution dictates this legally, since it turns the power of governance over to a small number of elected and appointed representatives who "operate unseen" in the new federal metropole (the capital), while geography does its part by making this arrangement seem just, necessary, and commonsensical. Once again, as Publius says, the people cannot make every appointment: "it would leave them little time to do any thing else" (510).

The Federalist prepares its reader to be this new citizen. It suggests, in both argument and rhetorical effect, that ratification is enough involvement for the multitude, which by its very nature is unfit to lead, not just because of its massness but by its nature as a large group primarily filled with average men. ("Had every Athenian citizen been a Socrates," Publius says, "every Athenian assembly would still have been a mob" [374].) Under the federal system, the people are meant to elect as best they can—but not to govern. Indeed, No. 1 warns that even voting might be too much involvement, since "a wrong election . . . may

... be considered as the general misfortune of mankind." A split is thus cultivated between two activities that need not really be split: consent and participation. Ratification, though it appears to put the question of self-governance before the people at large, is merely the ritual whereby this system of "superintendence" is "popularly" installed.[49] And here we see why *The Federalist* is a masterpiece—the true counterpart to the federal Constitution, as so many jurists have insisted. In cultivating his audience as a series of bodies forever constrained within the local—"members" to the metaphorical federal "head"—Publius does more than simply argue for the creation of an elite (or, for that matter, for a subordinate, or nonelite, audience); instead, the text actually produces the relation that the Constitution likewise seeks to install. *The Federalist*—whether read or unread (and indeed, all the more so if left half-read)—is an exemplary instance of culture working in tandem with power to produce the world as we know it.

5. Rogue's Island: Postmarking *The Power of Sympathy*

The strongest principle of union resides within our domestic walls. The ties of the parent exceed that of any other; as we depart from home, the next general principle of union is amongst citizens of the same state, where acquaintance, habits, and fortunes nourish affection, and attachment; enlarge the circle still further, and, as citizens of different states, though we acknowledge the same national denomination, we lose the ties of acquaintance, habits, and fortunes, and thus, by degrees, we lessen in our attachments, till, at length, we no more than acknowledge a sameness of species.
—Cato, *New-York Journal,* 25 October 1787

On June 11, 1787, as the Federal Convention sat locked in the state-house at Philadelphia, the Boston *American Herald* ran a political essay signed by someone calling himself "Harrington." In it, the author explicitly raises the question of the geographic and political expansion of the union. Addressing "the Freemen of the United States," Harrington hectors his audience about the need, politically, for more national space:

The ambition of the poor and the avarice of the rich demagogue, can never be restrained upon the narrow scale of a state government. In [a federal government on the other hand] they will check each other. . . . Should even the virtue be wanting in it, ambition will oppose ambition, and wealth will prevent danger from wealth.[50]

Larry Kramer has argued that Madison's model of the extended republic (made famous, in part, by Charles Beard's intense focus on the economic logic of *Federalist* No. 10) was in fact culturally marginal—an overintellectualized account of how the new state might operate that few of Madison's contemporaries understood or valued.[51] But like many scholars, Kramer focuses too aggressively on Madison as the author of the extended republic, when in fact the notion of an expanded sphere of federal administration was being polytheorized across a wide range of sites, by numerous authors, and in a wide variety of genres. Christopher Colles was one of these theorists, and so was Harrington, the *Herald*'s essayist. Indeed, Harrington cites the "narrow scale" of the state units as a problem a full six months before Publius uses the same phrase, calling for a balance between the states and some larger field of federal representation that very much resembles the Constitution's coming rearrangement of these spaces.

In fact, Harrington's speculations about the productive potential of geographic "extension" were hardly original. Instead, they mine a powerful body of eighteenth-century theory on the perceptual content of distance and proximity. Publius takes up this theme as well, drawing heavily (as Douglass Adair has shown) on Hume's *Treatise of Human Nature*, which devotes two chapters to the perceptual effects "of distance."[52] Publius is in agreement with both Hume and the antifederalist Cato (cited in the epigraph above) when he writes:

> It is a known fact in human nature, that its affections are commonly weak in proportion to the distance or diffusiveness of the object. Upon the same principle that a man is more attached to his family than to his neighbourhood, to his neighbourhood than to the community at large, the people of each State would be apt to feel a stronger bias towards their local governments than towards the government of the Union. . . . The operations of the national government, on the other hand, falling less immediately under the observation of the mass of the citizens, the benefits derived from it will chiefly be perceived and attended to by speculative men. Relating to more general interests, [the operations of the national government] will be less apt to come home to the feelings of the people; and in proportion, less likely to inspire a habitual sense of obligation, and an active sentiment of attachment. (107–8)

Here we see the potential downside of metrobuilding. The remoteness of the federal state shields the people from its potential tyranny while at the same time shielding the federal state from the people's daily observation. But it also presents Publius with the problem of "diffuse" (or diluted) "affections." Publius deploys this argument to appease those who fear the federal state's encroachment on states' rights, but in doing so he also makes a key concession to the antifederalist argument: he admits that there will be little feeling (or what he calls elsewhere "sympathy") between the constituent and his federal representative.[53] Following Hume, who believes that we sympathize most with that which is nearer to us in space or time, Publius concedes that distance will have affective consequences for the future state.[54]

Publius's answer to this problem is similar to the answer he finally arrives at on the problem of information. In that argument, he privileges "an enlarged view" over detailed (or local) knowledge; comprehension trumps everyday information, and the federal state becomes a "head" from which other body parts can be judiciously governed. *The Federalist*'s arguments about sympathy offer a similar concession and a similar inversion. Publius admits that the federal state will be remote and so less likely to "come home," as he puts it, "to the feelings of the people" than their current state governments. But he also uses this concession as an opportunity to further cultivate a preferred distinction between national and state administration: one, being the work of the "head," is intellectualized (it calls for men who can "harmonize" fragments into beautiful wholes); the other, stirring as it does the "affections," is the work of the more debased body. Federal representatives thus do the mental labor of national governance while state officials, who rely more on the sympathy of the people with whom they daily mingle, function on a more affective and more embodied (because always more local) level.

Like *The Federalist*, William Hill Brown's novel *The Power of Sympathy* takes up the linked problems of sympathy and space. Brown thought of himself as a federalist, and the novel can be read as straightforwardly federalist (and incipiently Federalist Party) in much of its cultural bias—including its calls for the protection of helpless women, its indictment of licentious itinerants, its nervous hand-wringing over popular (novel) reading, and its overdrawn fear of the leveling legacy of the Revolution (as when a lowly mechanic's daughter mixes promiscuously with a merchant clan). Nevertheless, its simple snobberies aside, *The Power of Sympathy* finally proves ambivalent about the very thing the federalists had created—an expanded republic, bound not by material links but by a *discourse* of union. Such a theory is, in Brown's novel, no match for the havoc that geographical and temporal dislocation might eventually wreak on innocent victims. A cautionary lesson in the consequences of such displacements, the novel records the social mayhem that follows in the wake of a slowly expanding social sphere. Indeed, the potential power of sympathy to transcend the local is by no means a good thing here, as the outcome of the novel's numerous storylines make clear. This includes a subplot in which a random traveler attracts and then abducts a country girl, causing her lover to drown himself. But it applies, as we shall see, to the main plot as well, in which Brown's protagonists, Harrington and Harriot, having been deprived of the appropriately restricted experience of a domestic home and childhood together (and who thus do not recognize one another as biological brother and sister), meet and accidentally fall in love. Only a midnight missive stops the young lover-siblings from consummating their affair in marriage (and the marriage bed). Far from ratifying the union of young lovers as a trope for the felicity of federal union, as Tyler does more generically in *The Contrast*, these lovers die for "sympathies" that disastrously transcend the local social circles in which they have lived their entire young lives.[55]

It is curious that Brown's novel should so completely reverse the central trope of Tyler's play (which, like many eighteenth-century texts, happily equates romantic union with political union). Historically, Tyler and Brown are similar figures. Both were raised in a pre-Revolutionary (but already radicalized) New England, and both were trying to establish themselves socially and financially in the chaotic 1780s. Their fates were similar as well: though socially mobile in the years before and after ratification, neither found a place at the new federal center. Tyler wound up in the boondocks of New England, a distinguished but cash-strapped state jurist in Vermont. Though he rose to be chief justice of that state's Supreme Court, he nevertheless pined for the rest of his life for more urban spaces, a sentiment expressed in letter after letter to friends and associates "Southward."[56] Brown emigrated as well, but in the other direction: he moved to North Carolina in 1792 and, except for a few obscure pieces published in local newspapers there, fell off the map of U.S. literary history before being dug up a century later as the probable author of *The Power of Sympathy*.[57] Both men are best remembered for their (dubious) structural place in the canon rather than for any particular ingenuity: Tyler as the author of the first American stage comedy; Brown as the author of the first American novel. Though they worked in different forms, both made seduction their theme and New England a crucial regional backdrop—in each case offering an extended reflection upon the relationship between local individuals and the world of the larger (and still enlarging) republic.

The likeness ends there, however, especially in the way each text handles the problem of space and its literary counterpart, setting. Tyler, as we have already seen, aggressively organizes his play around a series of geographical contrasts: Britain vs. the States, Massachusetts vs. New York, New England farmers vs. Old Dutch merchants, rural honesty vs. urban foppery. These are staid comparisons, tight dichotomies that pair up evenly with one another (city and city, state and state) to produce the promised "contrast" of the play's title. Tyler's pairings offer little room for destabilization in and of themselves; indeed, they only cause trouble to pairs *in* pairs—which is to say, when deployed in relation to one another as stable block-units. Brown, however, does something more unusual with his settings. Like Tyler, he deals throughout the novel with many different locations drawn from what we might think of as a number of different scales (city, region, nation, and empire), but unlike Tyler he does not deploy them within an organized dyadic system. Cities do not pair in Brown's novel with other cities, nor do any two settings mirror or balance each other. This is important because setting is a central metafeature of any epistolary novel—a set of stage directions that orient the reader at the top of each piece of fictional correspondence. It is the dateline of the letter, in other words, that helps the reader make sense of the world on which he or she is eavesdropping. Nothing offers more structure, more coherence, to an epistolary narrative than to have its dates and locations match one another in recognizable ways.[58]

Brown, however, is thinking differently on the eve of Washington's inauguration. He does not take up the question of space from within the fixed dialectic of local-and-national (as Tyler does) nor by positing a world of structurally homogenized spatial units (as contemporary epistolary novels like *The Coquette* do); instead, *The Power of Sympathy* explicitly theorizes the problem of proliferating and mismatching geographic scales. Brown's datelines thus range from urban settings to rural ones and include a grab-bag of cities, private estates, and states (for example: Boston, Belleview, and Rhode Island). This mixing and matching would be unremarkable if the book did not begin in its early letters by trying, like Tyler's play, to install order through commonplace geographical pairings, only to abandon them as the narrative action develops. The early letters, for example, carefully frame two key dichotomies—one moral, the other geographic. The first, a contrast between virtue and seduction, plays itself out in a series of letters between the stuffy Worthy and his more playful friend Harrington, a would-be rake. The second, a discussion of the relative pleasures of rural and urban life, plays itself out in a series of letters between Myra Harrington (the protagonist's sister and Worthy's fiancée) and her mentor, Mrs. Holmes. Myra's letters are dated at Boston; Mrs. Holmes's bear the rural postmark of her country cottage ("Belleview"). Just as the men's letters banter about virtue and seduction (with Worthy arguing for the former, Harrington for the latter), the ladies' letters banter about the relative merits of city and country. Myra chides Mrs. Holmes's seclusion in the country; Mrs. Holmes responds by remarking on the overstimulation of the city.

By deploying these pairs and playing with them, Brown's novel opens like a beautiful neoclassical couplet. It twins its own terms, balancing and counterbalancing every theme, character, and setting. Indeed, this is true not just between the two pairs of letters (and letter writers) just described, but in the relationships that emerge among all four. For instance: Worthy's and Harrington's letters are (like Myra's and Mrs. Holmes's) posted from Boston and Belleview. But rather than installing a fixed role for each setting (the city as dissipated and the country as virtuous), the novel plays the two pairings against each other, using the two sets of letters to cancel out each other's codings. Thus the male Harrington writes from the country and seeks advice from the city, while the female Harrington writes from the city and seeks advice from the country. Neither locale is privileged as more virtuous or more pleasurable, more central or more peripheral; both remain not only in play but in perfect balance; each (to borrow a word from constitutional theory) "checks" the other, producing a perfect thematic equilibrium. And then—

The novel implodes. Many critics have remarked on the plot's declension into formlessness. Cathy Davidson dubs *The Power of Sympathy* a "novel divided against itself," referring to the criss-cross of generic conventions deployed throughout the novel—from sermon to advice book to sensational seduction plot; the novel is, as she points out, both moralizing and titillating—though never on the same page.[59] The zenith of this breakdown comes in letters 11 and 12, which record a long argument among several characters who leisurely discuss (and disagree about) the vices and virtues of ladies' reading habits—especially the reading of novels like *The Power of Sympathy*. A rupture is signaled, literally, by the fact that this is not really two letters but a single letter split in two, resembling a *Federalist* essay that is continued across two numbers and suggesting for a moment a more serial (chapterlike) format than the web of semi-circular, interconnected volleys that began the novel. But the letter is not simply "divided against itself" in this way: it also shatters the most basic conventions of the letter form and opens itself up to a heteroglossia of nonepistolary narrative techniques. Rather than having Mrs. Holmes (the letter writer) directly narrate events to her correspondent, Brown introduces a series of distancing devices, including indirect narration, dialogue, and a footnote that spans several pages. In this way, he does everything he can to draw attention to the artificiality of the form in which he writes (and about which his characters, in this chapter, argue). These two letters are, in short, the most novelistic in the novel.

In this way, the novel fails to sustain the commonplace symmetries and the epistolary mode with which it began. As letters accrue, complications creep into Brown's initial pairings: an early letter from Harriot, for instance, sticks out and has no "partner." At the same time, more characters and more complex relations are introduced. Rank and wealth are added to gender as complicating factors that disquiet the surface of life at Belleview: "a mechanick's daughter," for instance, arrives at a party there, and, as Harrington remarks, "disorder and confusion immediately took place, and the amusement was put [to] an end."[60] Political affiliations are likewise added to geographic ones, when Harrington identifies himself as a democrat in contrast to Worthy's more elitist republicanism (even though Harrington at other times eschews such democratic pretensions). Most notably, subplots start and stop—sometimes at great length and in fairly rudderless fashion. It is especially unclear why the novel insistently turns to seduction-themed subplots when the main character has already disavowed seduction for the (supposedly) more virtuous option of marriage.

The novel's accruing complications are accompanied by a number of new datelines that suggest, more than anything else, a world of unlike locations—a slow accumulation of mismatched spaces that further disturbs the simple symmetries with which the novel began. By the novel's midpoint, letters have been posted not just from the city and the estate that serves as its suburban retreat (Boston and Belleview) but from a state: "RHODEISLAND." These letters provide the most perplexing postmark in the novel. As an undifferentiated state-unit, Rhode Island is offered as a third term to the city-country dichotomy, thus disturbing that initial dichotomy by proving illegible to it. The notion of "RHODEISLAND," in other words, is unassimilable to "Boston" and "Belleview" because we are never told from where in Rhode Island these letters issue relative to town and country. Though they might have been dated at "Providence" or from some private estate on its edge (thus mapping onto the novel's existing spatial imaginary), they are not. Another stitch is thus lost as the reader moves through the book, attempting to order his amusement but finding (like Harrington at his mismatched ball) only "disorder and confusion."

Brown's decision to set a central part of the novel's action in Rhode Island is significant for other reasons as well, for as we shall see, Rhode Island was one of the most overdetermined sites in North America to those living outside of it. Popularly lampooned in the newspapers of other states as "Rogues' Island," Rhode Island had persistently evaded its debts to the union throughout the Confederation period. For federalists, Rhode Island was the essence of the Shaysite nightmare: the most miniature (geographically) of the original colonies, Rhode Island was small enough to experiment with radical modes of actual representation. In the post-Revolutionary 1780s, its popularly controlled legislature passed a series of laws designed to do exactly what *Federalist* No. 10 hoped to stop, promoting the needs of the majority (in the form of debtor relief and paper money laws) against those of the minority (those property holders, merchants, and professionals huddled in Providence and Newport). Depending on how one looked at it, Rhode Island was either a haven for licentious anarchy or a democratic utopia.[61]

In its continuing commitment to actual representation, Rhode Island stands out (like the figure of Jonathan—or Manly's faded coat—in *The Contrast*) as yet another of the Confederation era's Revolutionary relics; more than any other locale in the union, Rhode Island was recognized by outsiders as the site of residual populist energies, Revolutionary leftovers that the Constitution sought to contain. Publius twice raises the example of Rhode Island in *The Federalist*, in both instances using it as a stark countertext to the federal state proposed by the Constitution. In No. 63, for example, Publius compares Rhode Island unfavorably with its happier "sister states," characterizing its population as a "misguided people" who suffer under "calamities" altogether specific to the contracted political sphere its geography engenders (423). This argument reinforces one made earlier in the essays (in No. 51), where an explicit contrast is drawn between the "narrow limits" of Rhode Island and the virtues that must ensue from the adoption of an "extended republic":

It can be little doubted that if the state of Rhode Island was separated from the confederacy and left to itself, the insecurity of rights under the

popular form of government within such narrow limits would be displayed by such reiterated oppressions of factious majorities that some
power altogether independent of the people would soon be called for
by the voice of the very factions whose misrule had proved the necessity of it. In the extended republic of the United States, and among the
great variety of interests, parties, and sects which it embraces, a coalition of a majority of the whole society could seldom take place on any
other principles than those of justice and the general good; and there
being thus less danger to a minor from the will of the major party,
there must be less pretext, also, to provide for the security of the former, by introducing into the government a will not dependent on the
latter, or, in other words, a will independent of the society itself. It is
no less certain than it is important, notwithstanding the contrary opinions which have been entertained, that the larger the society, provided
it lie within a practicable sphere, the more duly capable it will be of
self-government. And happily for the *republican cause*, the practicable
sphere may be carried to a very great extent, by a judicious modifica-
tion and mixture of the *federal principle*. (352–53)

We see here, once again, the perverse logic of the extended republic, in
which self-identity and autonomy are said to be most available under
conditions of material dispersion. In a "narrow" state, Publius suggests,
the government does not have room to govern because it literally cannot
divide itself from its people: there is too much sameness and not enough
difference. The extended republic, on the other hand, contains within it a
cacophonous "variety of interests, parties, and sects" that, paradoxically,
makes "self-government" more possible by protecting the minority from
the majority and allowing the government to differentiate itself from the
governed. In one sense Publius is simply restating a constitutional maxim
here: the idea that dispersion (of power, of people, of interests) produces
the possibility of balance. But in citing Rhode Island and specifically raising the question of size in relation to governance, Publius also suggests
that large masses of people must be governed at a physical remove—otherwise the will of the majority will overcome and obliterate the minority
(including the minority that is the government). His argument makes it
clear that federalism's metrobuilding project is not possible in a state as
geographically limited as Rhode Island.

But that is not all. As if to make the idea of a self-governing Rhode
Island that much more absurd, Publius dwarfs it further by imagining it

not just as the smallest state in the union, but as a state standing alone, divided from the union he proposes. At this moment, Publius is primarily reflecting on a potential outcome: what would happen *if* Rhode Island were separated from the union? If the idea was absurd in 1787, it seems even more so today. In 1789, however, when Brown was about to publish *The Power of Sympathy*, the possibility of a Lichtensteinian, or independent, Rhode Island had come to pass. The only state to decide the question of ratification by popular referendum (rather than via ratifying convention, as suggested by the Federal Convention), Rhode Island rejected the Constitution by a vote of 2,708 to 237.[62] Thus when Washington took office in 1789, he did not represent the people of Rhode Island because Rhode Island was not a member of the union (nor would it join until 1790). For this reason, Rhode Island was the ultimate (and closest) of American outsides in 1789.

Given Rhode Island's overdetermined status in 1789, why does *The Power of Sympathy* go there? Brown's decision to set part of the action in Rhode Island was perplexing enough to prompt one contemporary reviewer to question it: "The story of *Ophelia*, however recent and local the particulars related in it, referreth to Rhode Island for its origin."[63] The Rhode Island setting is all the more puzzling to this reviewer because Brown uses it to stage the novel's most local and fact-based storyline. Boston readers readily recognized "the story of *Ophelia*" as a thinly veiled recounting of a local scandal involving two prominent Boston families—the Mortons and the Apthorps—who were well known in local newspapers for an incestuous affair between Perez Morton and his sister-in-law, Fanny Apthorp. The affair ended in tragedy when Fanny, like many a fictional heroine, chose suicide rather than submit to a public inquiry instigated by her father. For readers who might miss the correspondence between the fictional family and the real one, Brown marks it with a meagerly concealing pseudonym: the Mortons become Martins and are banished in the novel to Rhode Island, even though they were, in real life, Brown's Boston neighbors.[64]

Traditionally there have been two explanations for this shift of scenery, both of which were immediately offered up by the novel's first two reviewers. A 1789 review signed "Civil Spy" suggests that Brown may have included Rhode Island in the novel's geographic scheme to increase sales: "Perhaps the Rhode-Islanders," he reasons, "may be so far acquainted with [the scandal], as to be profitably entertained by reading it in the author's dress" (although he adds, almost immediately, that "I am strongly inclined to believe that the story would be less familiar in Rhode-Island, than in Boston").[65] Another reviewer, signing herself "Antonia," takes up a second (and opposite) explanation when she claims that Brown shifts the action to Rhode Island to avoid spreading gossip—citing it as a virtuous attempt to dissociate the fictional storyline from its real-life counterpart.[66] Neither explanation, however, adequately addresses the mixed signals Brown sends as he packs both his central female character and his next-door neighbors off to Rhode Island. Civil Spy's half-hearted explanation—entrepreneurial ambition—carries with it its own critique: if Brown had sought to sell the book to Rhode Islanders, his mark was likely missed, because the story is "less familiar in Rhode Island, than in Boston." (Indeed, we now know the book did not sell well *anywhere*.) Antonia's explanation, on the other hand, is no more convincing, for if the setting is meant to dissociate the Ophelia story from that of the Apthorp/Mortons, why then does the novel immediately disavow that disavowal by renaming Morton as the very recognizable Martin? The question of recognition was further complicated when the printer decided to place the Apthorp/Morton scandal on the cover of the book, portraying Fanny/Ophelia's suicide as its frontispiece (figure 5.5) with the subtitle "The Story of Ophelia." As Cathy Davidson notes, "the contemporary reference is unmistakable."[67]

Though neither the initial reviewers nor later critics have been able to explain it, the Rhode Island setting is crucial because it raises a series of questions about proximity and distance—and about how our perceptions can and cannot shift between them—that are central to Brown's novel. Given the devices used to foreground it, the scandal could not, as Davidson notes, go unrecognized—no matter how far it is removed from Boston or how small its importance to the overall plot (as a subplot, the entire episode takes up only four of the novel's sixty-five letters). The novel's foregrounding devices, in fact, are no less powerful than its distancing devices; one brings the subplot front and center, the other banishes it to the background. This flip-flop irritated Civil Spy, who noted that "the frontispiece, designated from the Story of Ophelia, naturally leadeth to a conclusion, that the author considered the circumstances in that story, as greatly contributory to the promotion of the design of his undertaking." Left hanging, however, Civil Spy peevishly found that "it is not until we arrive near the end of the work, that we find anything to authorize the title."[68] But the novel's vacillations between local scandals and distant settings (or major storylines and minor subplots) are hardly

FIGURE 5.5 William Hill Brown. *The Power of Sympathy: or, The Triumph of Nature.* Boston: Isaiah Thomas, 1789. Frontispiece. Photo courtesy of the Newberry Library.

unimportant. Instead, the novel uses these devices in tandem to force its reader to shift and reshift attention from things that are near to things that are far, things that are central to the plot and things that are not. This shifting and reshifting is the perceptual work that the novel is most interested in doing: abandoning its own framing dichotomies, the novel asks its reader to move willy-nilly among a series of unlike locations—a series of shifts in scale that require the reader to take up different subject positions in relation to each part of the book. Though different from *The Federalist*, then, *The Power of Sympathy* shares something with Publius's long and arcane essays: it taxes the reader's powers of discernment, confusing us. As Davidson quips: "Boston is not Rhode Island; Martin is not Morton; truth is not fiction"[69]—nor, Civil Spy might add, is "the Story of Ophelia" (emblazoned next to the title page) the main plot of the novel.

Many readers have concluded that this much confusion amounts to very bad writing. But even those critics who have tried to make important claims for *The Power of Sympathy* have had trouble reclaiming the full field of complications that the novel raises, tending to organize it (as Davidson's remark above does) around a series of stabilizing dichotomies rather than giving full play to the numerous scales it generates or theorizing the perceptual work such shifting perspectives demand.[70] The novel's tendency to skew—and, in the process, to demand that the reader experience the disorienting limits of his or her own embodied perception— is played out even in the frontispiece. Though Davidson describes this Samuel Hill engraving as "exceptionally realistic," it is actually exceptionally *odd* in its depiction of the intensely interiorized space in which Ophelia commits suicide. If we look at the human actors involved in the "tragedy," we see a fairly accurate rendering of one of the novel's central scenes: a young woman dying, her parents attending, perceptible anguish on each and every face. And yet the larger space is less mimetically convincing because it does not observe a classical (or consistent) perspective. The problem involves Hill's attempt to relate the interior space of the drawing room to the world outside. More precisely, we can trace the image's flawed perspective to two doors: one, in the foreground, opens inward; the other, in the background, opens outward. If we map these doors geometrically within the space of the picture, their sharp lines trace themselves to two distinct vanishing points, unsettling both the scene in the center and the viewer, who must decide which of these vanishing points the eye is to inhabit. The image thus refuses to be taken in with a single glance. Indeed, it defies its viewers' attempts to integrate the scene and brings attention to the fact that our perceptions are fatally grounded in the singularity of our spatially rooted bodies. That rootedness is made plain by the fact that the viewer's eyes are finally capable of inhabiting only one (vanishing) point, or location, at a time. We cannot see both doors simultaneously but must shift between each one as we scan the scene, a disruptive visual experience that forces us to choose where and how to look—and which thus nicely approximates the novel's tendency to shift between near and far (or minor and major) narrative positions.

This raises the question of intention, for it is unlikely that the engraver and the author worked in tandem to produce this effect—any more than it is likely that the printer, Isaiah Thomas, worked in concert with Brown when he chose to foreground the Apthorp/Morton scandal in the frontispiece. Nevertheless, the frontispiece and the novel disorient us in similar ways, and this disorientation precisely replicates, in turn, that (by now) familiar feeling of being lost on the highway that Christopher Colles's road maps sought to minimize. Indeed, the four texts discussed in this chapter so far—Colles's maps, *The Federalist, The Power of Sympathy,* and Hill's engraving—all raise questions about perspective and perception. They all share, furthermore, the very thing that the federal state insists upon in its subjects—a recognition that the world consists of multiple scales and that individual observers cannot move so easily between them (either physically or perceptually)—at least not without the aid of a Publius-like guide (or, as Colles might wish, a guidebook). All four texts *enact* the difficulty of seeing parts and wholes simultaneously, but this is hardly a problem that their makers need to have knowingly theorized. Hamilton, Madison, and Colles may well have been aware of the spatial dilemma they were confronting; Brown and Hill probably were less so. All four, however, lived in a world that was coping—through newly evolving representational and technological innovations (including engravings, maps, canals, constitutions, and novels)—with the perceptual and practical problem of ongoing expansion. Knowingly or not, each text serves as a performative gloss on the relation between such an expanded world and the living bodies who must inhabit it.

This reading explains something important about Brown's novel—especially its squirrelly shifts from settings near to settings far. But it still does not account for the geographical specificity of Rhode Island per se—which was, after all, an overdetermined site in 1789, making itself an obnoxious topic of daily conversation up and down the eastern seaboard by refusing to pay its debts, control its people, or (finally) join the union. As a "sister state" who refuses to be a sister to her twelve political brethren, Rhode Island suggests a parallel to Fanny Apthorp's decision not to act as a sister (or sister-in-law) should. Other than that, the shift in setting is most remarkable for the panic it produces in the overly nervous Harrington. As he writes to his friend Worthy: "My beloved has left me for a while—she has attended Mrs. *Francis* in a journey to *Rhode-island*—and here am I—anxious—solitary—alone!" (54). Expanding on this insipid inversion of homesickness (or in kinder terms, lovesickness), Harrington sends his next letter to Harriot herself, proclaiming that "if a wish, arising from the most tender affection, could transport me to the object of my love, I persuade myself that you would not be troubled with reading this letter" (55). Unlike Thomas Paine, who exhorted his readers to "transport" themselves "to Boston" by reading *Common Sense*, Harrington insists on the inadequacy of the textual substitutions he sends in place of himself. Correspondences do not, for Harrington, correspond nearly as adequately as two bodies might; his letters are merely a representational stopgap because his desire cannot move (or "transport") him in the way he would like to be moved.

But the word "transport" connotes both travel and feeling in the eighteenth century, and it is the vexed relationship between these two meanings that finally makes sense of the novel's Rhode Island setting. This link is apparent in the four letters that Harriot sends "home" from the road. All four are addressed to Myra and describe at length the feelings that Harriot both witnesses and experiences upon being "transported" to the scene of Ophelia's suffering. The novel's first extended treatment of the theme of "sympathy," the episode produces a cascade of emotion, describing characters as "sad," "serious," "agitated," remorseful, guilty, and "anxious" (59–60). Harriot herself mimes Harrington's panicked syntax in these letters, filling them with long strings of incoherent, staccato exclamations. While Harriot does not theorize the relation between her travels and their affective consequences, she does explicitly describe why the trip, and the storyline it produces, will be useful to her reader:

> Whatever may be the other causes (if there were any besides her seduction) which drove the unhappy *Ophelia*, temerariously to end her existence, it certainly becomes us, my dear friend, to attend to them—and to draw such morals and lessons of instruction from each side of the question, as will be a mirrour by which we may regulate our conduct and amend our lives. (68)

This admonition follows another letter (also from Harriot) entirely devoted to sermonizing (if not actually eulogizing) Sarah Apthorp's dead
sister ("How frail is the heart! How dim is human foresight!") (65–67).
Both letters suggest a moral content for the Ophelia narrative, and both
take melodramatic pleasure in the tragedy they describe (as the exclama-
tion points delightfully testify, even two centuries later). The "mirrour"
here is, in a sense, the mirror of literary representation: just as Harriot
plans to make "use" of Ophelia's story for her own moral instruction, the
reader is urged, at different points in the story, to make "use" of the novel
at hand.[71] That neither Harriot nor the reader can see, in the mirror of
this story, just how closely the main plot will finally resemble this subplot
is an irony I will return to in a moment.

As it turns out, Harriot's moralistic retelling of the Ophelia story "mir-
rours" another moment of "transport" in the novel, when Harrington
experiences his own flight of feeling on a trip far from home. Twinning
Harriot's "travel" narrative with one of his own, Harrington tells Worthy
the sad story of another kind of family altogether, this one from "*Southcarolina*":

> I feel *that I have a soul*—and every man of sensibility feels it within
> himself. I will relate a circumstance I met with in my late travels
> through *Southcarolina*—I was always susceptible of *touches of nature.*
>
> I had often remarked a female slave pass by my window to a spring
> to fetch water. She had something in her air superiour to those of her
> situation—a fire that the damps of slavery had not extinguished.
>
> As I was one day walking behind her, the wind blew her tattered
> handkerchief from her neck and exposed it to my sight—I asked her
> the cause of the scar on her shoulder—She answered composedly, and
> with an earnestness that proved she was not ashamed to declare it,—
> "It is the mark of the whip," said she, and went on with the history of
> it, without my desiring her to proceed—"my boy, of about ten years
> old, was unlucky enough to break a glass tumbler—this crime was im-
> mediately inquired into—I trembled for the fate of my child, and was
> thought to be guilty. I did not deny the charge, and was tied up. My
> former good character availed nothing. Under every affliction, we may
> receive consolation; and during the smart of the whip, I rejoiced—be-
> cause I shielded with my body the lash from my child; and I rendered
> thanks to the best of beings that I was allowed to suffer for him."

"HEROICALLY spoken!" said I, "may he whom you call the best of beings continue you in the same sentiments—may thy soul be ever disposed to SYMPATHIZE with thy children, and with thy brethren and sisters in calamity—then shalt thou feel every circumstance of thy life afford thee satisfaction; and repining and melancholy shall fly from thy bosom—all thy labours will become easy—all thy burdens light, and the yoke of slavery will never gall thy neck."

I was sensibly relieved as I pronounced these words, and I felt my heart glow with feelings of exquisite delight, as I anticipated the happy time when the sighs of the slave shall no longer expire in the air of freedom. What delightful sensations are those in which the heart is interested! (103–4)

Unlike Harriot, who mixes pain in her prose's pleasure, Harrington openly "delights" in this South Carolina story. The slave mother functions perversely as an object for Harrington's own self-reflection—a metonymy for his geographically alienated position (as a northerner) toward the South at large. Here we see, as in Harriot's account of Ophelia, not just the power but the paradoxical pleasures and possibilities of sympathy: the way it makes its subject feel good—not because he is *like* the person he watches, but precisely because he is unlike that person. Harriot, for example, hopes to take instruction from Ophelia's story not because she identifies her own future with Ophelia's (ironically, she does not), but because she believes she can and will have a different future. Likewise, Harrington arrives at a feeling of common humanity ("I feel *that I have a soul*" and here is why) by overlooking the gaping breach between his experience of the slave mother's story (as a story) and her own experience of it (as an experience). Odder still, this story of human sameness (or "sympathy"), couched as it is in the starkest of human differences, allows Harrington to arrive at a more abstracted moral about sameness and difference on the vastly larger scale of national politics: "I felt my heart glow with feelings of exquisite delight, as I anticipated the happy time when the sighs of the slave shall no longer expire in the air of freedom. What delightful sensations are those in which the heart is interested!" Unlike Hector St. John de Crèvecoeur's encounter with an abused slave in *Letters from an American Farmer*, this encounter makes Harrington feel *better*, rather than worse, about the possibilities of federal union. Though the story marks a clear difference between North and

South, it also cultivates a belief that the two regions might one day be united. In this way, Harrington daydreams about the abolition of both slavery and regional difference (and thus the inevitable production of a more integrated, less split union).

In both these examples, Harrington and Harriot require distance (or a sense of differentiation) from the object they are surveying in order to experience the "sensations" of liberal sympathy. Indeed, the logic of the "mirrour" into which Harriot and Harrington gaze works much like Publius's arguments about "comprehension." According to *The Federalist*, the federal representative requires "distance" (literally) to attain an "extended" or "elevated" "view." Harrington and Harriot attain such distance, both in their travels and in their inevitably retrospective reflections on what they have seen. Harriot suggests that the outcome will be a more efficient form of self-governance ("a mirrour by which we may regulate our conduct and amend our lives") while Harrington suggests the "delightful" pleasures that might accrue from this strange mode of self-regulation.

As readers of Brown's novel, we too become subject to this maxim— albeit in slightly different form. The distance required by the reader to "harmonize" and integrate the action of the story is not spatial but narrative—which is to say, temporal. The story's meaning can only "come home" to us, in other words, after we have finished reading. The Rhode Island episode is a good example of this. Only on reflection can readers discern how the Fanny Apthorp scandal relates to the central story of Harriot and Harrington's courtship. The trip to Rhode Island, and the "incestuous connexion" it narrates, function as an exemplary case of foreshadowing, but we cannot know this until we arrive at the end of the narrative. Indeed, Brown organizes the plot in such a way that the reader learns of Harrington and Harriot's "true relation" at the same moment they do. For this reason, Harriot's ironic plan to use Ophelia's story as a "mirror" of reflection makes sense to the reader (as a moment of irony) only upon rereading. Little does Harriot (or the reader) know the first time through just how close the resemblance will finally be between Fanny's story and her own—and hence how appropriate the trope of the mirror really is.

The novel offers ample examples of such compressed ironies, moments that are illegible to the first-time reader, who has been aggressively trained from the first page to believe he is reading a novel about seduction. But unlike *Charlotte Temple* or *The Coquette*, in which seduction truly does lie at the center of the novel's climax and denouement, *The Power of Sympathy* turns instead on the unforeseen problem of incest.

Davidson has remarked on the mixed signals the narrative offers before arriving at this end: she notes, for instance, that the title page, frontispiece, and preface all foreground the theme of seduction, positioning the book as a cautionary fable for young girls.[72] The numerous subplots that wind through the body of the book likewise misdirect us into believing that we are reading a novel of seduction. On four separate occasions, Brown introduces digressive narratives within the narrative, plots only tangentially connected to the main one, and in each case the story turns on the question of seduction. Although we ultimately see that the possibility of an incestuous relation between Harrington and Harriot has been present from the outset (they are related, Elizabeth Barnes notes, right "down to the roots of their names"), we can only do so in retrospect, for the clues that might help us predict this outcome are embedded in the most miniature of details—in throwaway lines and simple puns.[73] Indeed, the "correspondences" between subplots and the main plot (embedded as they often are in double entendres) are themselves homophonic correspondences that must necessarily go unrecognized by readers who are caught up in the presentism of Brown's unfolding narrative. In this way, the novel broods (even at the cellular linguistic level of the pun) on the problem of sameness unseen.

Harriot's and Harrington's forays to *Rhodeisland* and *Southcarolina* return us once again to *The Federalist* and in particular to Publius's critique of Rhode Island as a state undivided from itself. As an undifferentiated miasma of equality, Rhode Island may well be the perfect place to plot out a story about the terrible sameness of incest. In a novel filled with inversions (where suicide becomes murder, courtship becomes incest, lovers become siblings, and death finally becomes a form of marriage), the final reversal must be in the way we read these two ultra-exteriorized extrafederal spaces. The state of Rhode Island is the ultimate outside—the perfect contrast, as *The Federalist* insists, to the diversity of the extended republic; likewise Harrington insists, in his southern sojourn, on the absolute difference between northern freedom and southern slavery. Harrington is, in fact, so invested in regional differences that the novel affords him a long soliloquy on just this theme. In a speech devoted to an explanation of his own democratic principles, Harrington produces a sketch of the cultural and climatological differences of the union's different part-spaces:

INEQUALITY among mankind is a foe to our happiness—it even affects our little parties of pleasure—Such is the fate of the human race, one order of men lords it over another; but upon what grounds its right is founded I could never yet be satisfied.

For this reason, I like a democratical better than any other kind of government; and were I a *Lycurgus* no distinction of rank should be found in my commonwealth.

In my tour through the UNITED STATES, I had an opportunity of examining and comparing the different manners and dispositions of the inhabitants of the several republicks. Those of the southern states, accustomed to a habit of domineering over their slaves, are haughtier, more tenacious of honour, and indeed possess more of an aristocratick temper than their sisters of the confederacy. As we travel to the northward, the nature of the constitution seems to operate on the minds of the people—slavery is abolished—all men are declared free and equal, and their tempers are open, generous, and communicative. It is the same in all those countries where the people enjoy independence and equal liberty. Why then should those distinctions arise which are inimical to domestick quietude? Or why should the noisy voice of those who seek distinction, so loudly reecho in the ears of peace and jollity, as to deafen the sound of the musick? For while we are disputing who shall lead off the dance, behold! the instrument gets out of tune—a string snaps—and where is our chance for dancing? (53–54)

This rather long-winded explanation of Harrington's "democratical" politics is prompted by the appearance of the "mechanick's daughter" at a Belleview ball. The specter of class difference forces from him a powerful defense of equality, just as the specter of slavery, in his previous speech, forced a meditation on sympathy. In arguing, however, that "no distinction of rank should be found in my commonwealth," Harrington actually winds up offering a survey of the quite divided commonwealth he lives in. In doing so, he ironically insists upon the union's own absolute differentiation from itself. His argument for sameness in class is, in short, predicated upon an investment in the difference between places. He only knows how to be a "democrat" because he has traveled through the "aristocratick" South.

Harrington's investment in the paradox of American sameness and difference is by no means peculiar. Difference and sameness are constitutive structural elements in both neoclassical aesthetics and neoclassical political theory. A couplet, for instance, requires sameness, but it also requires just enough difference to produce an elegant tension. Likewise,

as any federalist would tell you, the Constitution is beautiful not just because it conglomerates but because it partitions—dividing and balancing
power among its several distinct parts. As a novel, *The Power of Sympathy* meditates at length on the aesthetic and political consequences of this
conundrum, organizing itself around the trope of "sympathy"—a word
that suggests identification with another even as it requires its subject to
maintain a proper distance from that other. While Elizabeth Barnes has
argued that Brown finally seeks to seduce the reader into a bond of over-
identificatory sympathy with his characters (thus reinscribing the error
he seeks to reform), I am more doubtful of the novel's power to enfold
the reader within its world.[74] Davidson's work on the original reception
of the novel suggests that readers were not all that taken with the storyline.[75] Like readers today, many eighteenth-century readers found the
plot awkward and far-fetched. Civil Spy, in the same review that criticized Brown's choice of settings, complains loudly that the book is finally
preposterous (the reviewer had "never heard of any thing similar to it in
this part of the world").[76] This suggests that the novel seeks to produce
not an identification between the characters and its audience but a disidentification—something like the disidentification that *The Federalist*
produces in its insistent deployment of a "you" and an "I" who, it seems,
have little in common.

This is not surprising. Like many an antifederalist, *The Power of Sympathy* appears anxious about the potential obliteration of diversity under
the new compact. Many Americans feared the Constitution's consolidating nature—its power to bind the union into one thing by passing over
the states and extending itself instead to individuals—even more than
they feared geographic size. Rhode Island's undifferentiated sameness—
its inability to divide itself properly into governed and government—
thus becomes, in this case, a miniature version of what a consolidated
federal state might eventually look like, were it to dissolve the differences
of "sister" state-units and turn them all into one thing. Just as Brown
uses Rhode Island, then, to foreshadow the incestuous connection between Harrington and Harriot, he also uses Rhode Island as an early and
microcosmic example of what an expanded republic might one day look
like. Indeed, both Rhode Island *and* South Carolina are sites of radical
difference (difference from each other as well as from the union at large)
that ultimately transform into sites of sameness. The ultimate "outsides"
(or "others") to Brown's Boston, both states will, upon ratification, become "insiders"—not just sisters to the other states (as they had been

under the Confederation), but homogenous parts of some larger self-identical thing called "the union"—states like every other state in a newly consolidated, undifferentiated American nation.

Because the novel insists that difference and distance are the necessary requisites of proper self-reflection, such a homogenizing consolidation of preexisting diversities bodes poorly for the republic. As Hume notes, "contiguous objects must have an influence much superior to the distant and remote. . . . The breaking of a mirror gives us more concern when at home, than the burning of a house, when abroad, and some hundred leagues distant."[77] This is a lesson in perspective that turns, in *The Power of Sympathy*, into a lesson in proper social relations. What might happen, the novel asks, if such perspective is lost and the breaking of a mirror far from home becomes just as important as the burning of a house next door? This is in a sense what happens to Harriot over the course of her Rhode Island interlude: she thinks she is looking at something very different from her own life, something that might serve as a mirrorlike inversion of her own situation, but instead the mirror is not reversing but replicating her future. There is no difference, finally, between what happens in Rhode Island and what happens at Belleview: when paired properly, they are both tragedies about "incestuous connexion." Likewise the "mirror" of federalism may one day obliterate the world-ordering differences between here and there, you and I, North and South, small states and large states. In altering the spatial relations between the parts of the union, federalism risks altering social relations. The outcome, *The Power of Sympathy* suggests, will be a world of terrible sameness.

The Power of Sympathy's ending reinforces its own wishful insistence that there must always be an elsewhere against which the everyday can be contrasted. In the novel's last moments, Harrington decides to kill himself because he needs to be somewhere else—in a more "refined" place, a paradise where he believes that he and Harriot can finally be together because they will no longer have bodies. In his derangement, his perspective becomes skewed, and, cribbing Hamlet, he no longer observes the niceties of proper scale: "What an important little thing is man!" he tells the increasingly concerned Worthy. "His life is a day, and his space a point!" (158). The final line of both the novel and Harrington's epitaph—"*O! may we never love as these have lov'd*"—becomes just the last of the novel's many lessons, not in identification, but in emphatic and cautionary disidentification (181). Ironically, however, the line fails in fulfilling its own prescription because Harrington chooses to speak *for* the spectators who gather at his grave ("may *we* never love as these have lov'd") rather than allowing them to speak for themselves. To the very end, the boundaries between you and me, subject and object, here and there, continue to be dissolved, and they are dissolved here, as they are in the Constitution's Preamble, through the use of the pronoun "we"—that shiftiest of shifters (as Barbara Johnson says).[78] "We the People of the United States" of America (past, present, and future) could not be explained any better than this.

6. THE POWER OF SYMPATHY AND THE PROBLEM WITH PERPETUITY

Tho' distance both in space and time has a considerable effect on the imagination . . . yet the consequence of a removal in *space* are much inferior to those of a removal in *time*. . . . A *West-India* merchant will tell you, that he is not without concern about what passes in *Jamaica*; tho' few extend their views so far into futurity, as to dread very remote accidents.
—David Hume, *A Treatise of Human Nature*, 1739

Few politicians better understood federalist space (and the way bodies within it operated) than Hamilton did. Madison may get academic credit for theorizing the extended republic in his closet at Montpelier, but Hamilton was expansion's Collesean visionary: he saw the emerging federal union less as an arrangement for social fixity and stasis (as the more Jeffersonian Madison did) than as a plan that might set the groundwork for a different future. It was Hamilton, not Madison, who foresaw an inevitable Age of Manufactures displacing the yeoman republic:

An unrestrained intercourse between the States themselves will advance the trade of each, by an interchange of their respective productions, not only for the supply of reciprocal wants at home, but for exportation to foreign markets. The veins of commerce in every part will be replenished, and will acquire additional motion and vigor from a free circulation of the commodities of every part. (*FP* 71)

Writing in a largely agrarian republic that was barely viable in either political or economic terms, Hamilton was already projecting the vast commercial network of future industrial capitalism. This passage concludes a futuristic fantasy in which Hamilton imagines a truly "American" navy—one for which the South will provide wood; the middle states, iron; while the "Northern hive" provides "seamen." ("A system of Government, meant for duration," Hamilton notes, "ought to contemplate these revolutions" [276–77].) In such a future, the (now) dispersed parts of the union would eventually be tied, not by the chords of sympathy (or the proximity that might produce it) but by the bond of "common interests." These interests would, of course, be economic—matters of production and consumption. It is precisely the futurity of Hamilton's vision that makes it remarkable. His was never just a plan for a nation; it was a model of nation *building*—not a thing in and of itself but a historically contingent process begun at one point in time and then extended into a future that no federalist (not even Publius) could foresee.[79]

This is one reason why the antifederalists were never able to mount, either ideologically or materially, a successful attack on the Constitution. They could never track the elusive ways that the Constitution posited not one but two extended republics—one meant to function in the present (or near future) under conditions of immense dispersion and one that posited, in perpetuity, a far more integrated future. As I have argued throughout this book, first-generation federalism recognized and even exploited the fact that the early United States was a site of radical, serial discontinuity. But it also sought to install a continuous *history* over and against this discontinuous space, a homogenizing tradition passed down across generations that would eventually help to call forth a more integrated, continuous space. The antifederalist critique breaks down at just this juncture—at the place where the future of the nation meets its present. True to Publius's analysis, "the people" of 1787 could not assemble in one place nor could the state recirculate itself (or its agents) back through the spaces of everyday life. As my final two chapters will argue, however, the federal state did increasingly, in the antebellum period, fulfill the circulatory potential glimpsed at by Christopher Colles's networking projects, thus breaking down the buffer between the once-distant and fairly abstract sphere of the federal and the everyday spaces of local life. The result was the mass assemblage of citizen-bodies now remembered as the Civil War.

Here the differences between Madison's Publius and Hamilton's Publius become especially apparent. Madison theorized the extended republic as a technique for stabilizing contemporary social strata; in his formulation, the central feature of this arrangement was its ability to disperse the power of the majority against (the property of) the minority in order to allow existing social relations to extend themselves ad inifinitum into the future. Hamilton had other ideas; like Colles, he imagined a day when the part-spaces of the republic might finally be fully networked—a tightly bound circuit of interconnections (which we now call a "nation") that would allow the federal state to reach out to the people at large and slowly draw from them the productive potential of their local, laboring bodies, allowing the state to amass itself into an empire of Roman proportions. In his vision of the commercial republic to come, Hamilton assumes, both in *The Federalist* and his later financial programs, that this productive potential will pay dividends in the form of taxes—both direct taxes on income and indirect taxes carried on the back of a circulating "world of things" (to use Laura Rigal's phrase) that will finally allow the United States to emerge as a world power. In this way, the tiny metropolitan elite imagined in the metrobuilding fantasies of the founders links directly to the metropolitan superpower the United States has become in the world as we know it. As Michael Hardt and Antonio Negri have argued, U.S. federalism's investment in "networking" was the initial step on the way to the contemporary world condition they call "empire."[80]

Though *The Power of Sympathy* focuses its attentions on a fairly small New England circle living in the year 1789, it is also intensely concerned with the problem of the future, or perpetuity. The reproductive social logic of inheritance frames the main plot and several of the subplots, as the novel repeatedly indicts the activities of the previous (Revolutionary) generation by casting irresponsible fathers as the worst villains imaginable. Harrington and Harriot, for instance, must die in the end because their father has kept his youthful transgression a secret, refusing to allow them insight into their own origins. By focusing on the problems of parenthood, the novel asks a series of questions not just about the enlargement, or extension, of the federal "sphere" across a vast space, but about the extension of fixed social orders—including political ones—through time. Indeed, the name "Harrington"—the same name sometimes used in Boston newspapers to sign political essays—is a pointed reference to the English Civil War essayist James Harrington and thus to Boston's deep Whig inheritance.

The Constitution—itself a beneficiary of this Whig inheritance—overtly seeks to install a state in perpetuity, a stable form of government that might reproduce itself for generations. *The Federalist* recognizes this and makes the future a constitutive participant in the perfection of the federal plan: "'Tis time only," Publius declares "that can mature and perfect so compound a system, liquidate the meaning of all the parts, and adjust them to each other in a harmonious and consistent WHOLE" (553). The problem with this future state was that it would be grounded in the consent only of those living in the present moment of 1787 and 1788; although future generations were expected to fulfill the founders' plans, they would not be consulted in framing them, nor would they be given the chance to consent. In portraying two characters, then, who stumble accidentally upon their own obscure and horrible origin, *The Power of Sympathy* poses a question that many people in 1789 were asking about the nation's future self: what happens when a democracy is removed not in space but *in time* from the scene of its production? And in this sense, the book's firstness—its status as the certain point of departure for U.S. novels ever since—is crucial, for the question of origins is as central to the book's plot as it has been to the book's later life in American literary history.

What better place to explore this theme than in a seduction novel? Brown's novel must be classed as such because for much of it, that is how it behaves. And no wonder. No eighteenth-century form is more interested in the problem of social reproduction and its potential corruption. While the newspaper tries to gather up dispersed spaces, the seduction novel seeks to install clean genealogies. In a newly postmonarchical republic, such explorations of birthright can never be apolitical. The troubled relation between social and biological reproduction is in fact a deeply American theme. Pre-Revolutionary almanacs, for example, routinely charted the genealogy of the British monarchy, and Paine in turn pressed genealogy into the service of the Revolution by claiming that England was founded, in deep historical time, illegitimately (by the French "bastard," William the Conqueror). The new republic responded by vanquishing biological reproduction as the basis of its polity both politically and socially (primogeniture was abolished in the same decade that the king was sent packing). Indeed, Washington's sterility made him not a less but a more apt first president, for it ensured that no son would ever succeed him.

Brown's Boston neighbor Noah Webster (a federalist) took up the vexed issue of political perpetuity and its opposite, self-determination (or self-propagation), in a series of essays published in the *American Magazine* in 1787 and 1788. Signing himself "Giles Hickory," Webster used the essays to rehearse a number of staid federalist arguments, including one that echoes Publius's arguments about information by insisting that in a dispersed republic, the people need not know everything about what their representatives are doing (and vice versa).[81] On questions of space, Webster toed the party line. When he turned, however, to the question of "the people's" historic dispersal through time, he strayed from the federalist course:

> If . . . our posterity are bound by our constitutions, and can neither emend nor annul them, they are to all intents and purposes our slaves. . . . The very attempt to make *perpetual* constitutions, is the assumption of a right to control the opinions of future generations; and to legislate for those over whom we have as little authority as we have over a nation in Asia.[82]

Like Hume's *Treatise*, Webster thinks about distance in space and time as linked problems. Unlike either Hume or Publius, however, he refuses to see them merely as analogies for one another. Indeed, his later numbers add an unusually harsh assessment not just of perpetual constitutions but of the hubris of those who would produce them: a state conceived in "perpetuity," he declares, "implies a supposition of *perfect wisdom and probity* in the framers; which is both arrogant and impudent."[83]

Webster's essay suggests the implicit connection between Brown's incest plot and his seduction plot. Though the two appear connected by an interest in illicit and illegitimate sexual activity, Brown is far more interested in the problem of consent than he is in sex. Most American seduction narratives of the 1780s and '90s stage the consent of the seduced woman in a way that concedes her ability to make important choices for herself even as the novel calls those choices into question (whether sympathetically or not).[84] Seduction is not rape in these novels: it proceeds, instead, like a party—by way of invitation. Charlotte Temple and Eliza Wharton, for example—those famous fallen women of the 1790s—both actively participate in their own unraveling; they are given a clear choice to consent or refuse their lovers' propositions and, in choosing badly, allow the novel to explore the dangers of a free (social) will in a polity whose political base was expanding daily to include not just property owners but many traditionally marginal groups. John Adams's famous gloss on this problem—"Democracy is Lovelace, and the people are Clarissa"—nicely condenses the ideological moral of early American seduction fables.[85] As a disciplining form, such narratives function somewhat like *The Federalist*: they question the ability of some citizens to consent and the virtuousness of others to lead.

In *The Power of Sympathy*, however, the question of consent is folded into the scandal of incest. The tragedy is premised on the elder Harrington's seduction of Harriot's mother Maria and, in turn, on her consent to that seduction. These events are, however, placed squarely in the past; indeed, the novel aggressively contains them within a clearly demarcated (titled and indented) subplot. Neither Harrington nor Harriot is a party to their parents' compact. In fact, the novel is so arcanely plotted that the fate of the two characters finally rests not on the moral or immoral behavior of any one (or two) characters, but on an array of unforeseen contingencies. These include (but need not be reduced to) Harrington, Sr.'s, abandonment of his illegitimate family; the premature death of Harriot's mother; the spatial dispersal of the families in the children's younger years; the later physical proximity of the adult children; and of course the willingness of the elder characters (including Harrington, Sr., Mr. Holmes, and Mrs. Holmes) to withhold their knowledge of Myra, Harrington, and Harriot's true relation to one another.

To the degree that the parents' actions are isolated as the cause of Harrington and Harriot's tragedy, it is the father and not the mother who is held most responsible; for Brown, the problem of perpetuity is mostly a matter of paternity. Indeed, we might read the novel as yet another rehearsal of a commonplace maxim of eighteenth-century republican theory: that if future generations are to be protected, the men who produce them must be virtuous. Historiographically and culturally, the United States has long wanted to believe in just this kind of pure genealogy for itself. We speak of "founding fathers" and a "miracle at Philadelphia," binding the language of social and biological reproduction in ways that make the nation form seem desirably proximate to the more local family form. Even Centinel, that staunchest of antifederalist dissenters, took up the language of biological reproduction when he quippingly dubbed 1787's achievement "the Immaculate Convention."

But Brown's novel offers little consolation for those who might look to 1789 for a virtuous national origin. The bad father may be the novel's only villain, but he appears repeatedly in storyline after storyline. In one subplot, a young girl named Fidelia is raped because her father invites a stranger into their home; this father is a weak and elderly man who himself needs protection and so is unable to protect his daughter. In the Rhode Island interlude, Ophelia submits to the seduction of her brother-in-law, but it is her father (ironically named "Shepherd") who shames his daughter into suicide and is identified by Brown as Ophelia's "murderer." But it is the main plot that offers the worst father-failure: Harrington, Sr., a seducer whose cowardly disavowal of his illegitimate offspring brings the novel's protagonists to the brink of incest when they become secretly engaged, only to discover at the last minute their "true" relation as brother and sister.

The novel thus emphatically isolates paternity as the central object of its critique. There are no mothers in *The Power of Sympathy*, save the slave mother Harrington meets on his trip to South Carolina (and who is, tellingly, the only "good" parent in the book). This choice suggests that Brown is less interested in birth or birthrights than in the historical process of mystification that obscures human origins. The mother's body, as Hortense Spillers reminds us, is always tied to her child's material production at the moment of birth, but the father is able to leave the scene of conception as a felon leaves the scene of a crime.[86] For this reason, it makes sense that the weakness of the mother is never this novel's primary object of social critique and pedagogical reconstruction: instead, Brown explores the profoundly destabilizing ability of the father to absent himself from the consequences of his sexual conquests.

Harrington, Jr., spends most of the novel resisting his father's agency, repeatedly peppering his correspondents with clichés about self-made men that allow him to deny that his life is constrained by contingencies he cannot control. "*Independency of spirit* is my motto—I think for myself" (167). To the very end of the novel, he seeks to become the "author" of his own story (it is he, not Harriot, who feels compelled to compose a last-minute epitaph for the two of them). But Harrington is in fact *never* the author of the novel's action. His fate has been determined from the beginning by forces beyond his control—including the "power of sympathy," "the triumph of nature," and, above all, the decisions made by his father decades before he was born.

Like Harrington, the federal state's future relied upon its displacement from the scene of its production—its ability to leave behind the splintered scene of founding both materially (in its own time) and historically (for generations to come). I have argued that ratification's success initially depended on the disconnections between the nation's serialized part-spaces, but the Constitution's present-day hegemony depends just as much on our contemporary willingness to repress the memory of that dispersal. The inability of later generations to reach back in time and "see" the founding follows the same maxim about proximity and distance that I have been describing in this chapter. As Hume says,

any one may easily observe, that space or extension consists of a number of co-existent parts dispos'd in a certain order, and capable of being at once present to the sight or feeling. On the contrary, time or
succession, tho' it consists likewise of parts, never presents to us more
than one at once; nor is it possible for any two of them ever to be co-
existent. These qualities of the objects have a suitable effect on the
imagination. The parts of extension being susceptible of an union to
the senses acquire an union in fancy; and as the appearance of one part
excludes not another, the transition or passage of the thought thro' the
contiguous parts is by that means render'd more smooth and easy. On
the other hand, the incompatibility of the parts of time in their real
existence separates them in the imagination, and makes it more *difficult* for that faculty to trace any long succession or series of events. . . .
By this means any distance in time causes a greater interruption in the
thought than an equal distance in space.[87]

Hume specifically connects this semi-amnesiac condition (or "interruption") to "the order, which is always observ'd in historical narrations"—
which strive to re-create a sense of continuity rather than capturing the
jagged discontinuity of a history that must always unfold itself unknow-
ingly on the "ground" of time, bequeathing primarily unforeseen consequences to a posterity that has been largely satisfied with their inheritance
simply because they cannot see where it came from (430). My early chapters suggested the ways that a dispersed (reading) population was useful
to founding. But the Constitution's longevity suggests something equally
important: that early U.S. nation-builders finally succeeded not just because their productions were originally displaced through a process of
(assumed) dissemination across space, but because those processes (and
their effects) were also temporally dispersed across generations of (national) audiences. John Berger's claim—that "it is space not time that
hides consequences from us"[88]—is thus, in this case, only partially correct, for in the modern nation-state, it is both space *and* time that hides
consequences from us. The real men of little information are not the federalists or antifederalists of 1787–88 but us—we latter-day Americans
who, like every generation that lives under the law of the Constitution
without actually having composed or ratified it ourselves, do not consent
to the power that structures us but simply inherit it. Like Harrington,
Jr., we do not write our own destiny but are born into it, unwitting heirs

to the pseudonational but protoimperial fantasies of 1787—children of Publius, all.

7. THE FUTURE OF FEDERALIST SPACE

Where is the man who can see through the constitution to its effects?
—Denatus, *Virginia Independent Gazette*, 11 June 1788

The maps, political pamphlets, novels, and engravings described in this chapter all form an episode in the long history of what David Harvey calls "the rational ordering of space."[89] As registers of this long historical process, these objects suggest that in 1789, people were looking both backward to more local conceptions of the universe (which Harvey associates with the feudal past) *and* forward to more modern conceptions of the nation and, indeed, the planet as a totalized and finite space very much within the reach of both nationalist and capitalist networking fantasies. If this is so, it is because the extended republic was a model of social and spatial relations that sat at the generative juncture of past, present, and future. Hamilton, for one, understood the deep spatial architecture of the extended republic and its potential for expansion. But many men who supported the Constitution did not. Thus as the consensus of 1789 fractured in the 1790s along (two) party lines and the Jeffersonian Republicans emerged to displace the party of Washington and Adams, many Federalist Party federalists began to suffer the same kinds of anxiety about size and dispersion that had once plagued their opponents in the ratification debates, openly worrying about the infinite extendability of the extended republic and the feasibility of its ever more mammoth size. After Jefferson's purchase of the Louisiana Territory created a vast new federal frontier, for example, the New England Federalist Fisher Ames fretted: "The Mississippi was a boundary. . . . We were confined within some limits. Now, by adding unmeasurable worlds beyond that river we rush like a comet into infinite space."[90]

The Federalist Party was, of course, the institutional heir to the elitism first performed and projected by Publius. The federalism of 1787–89 was conceived as a hierarchical set of spatial and social relations organized around a high intellectual center (and a distant geographical one), and this model was embraced by Washington, Hamilton, Adams, and the powerful network of Federalist Party elites that formed around them in the 1790s. But Jefferson (and his party) proved less invested in the centralization of power than in the reproducibility of a series of identical, or parallel, world-units—the base of which was to be the individual homestead and the sum of which was to be the yeoman republic. Several years before the Constitution was ratified, Jefferson had already begun to imagine the material production of such an egalitarian nation-space in the Land Ordinance of 1785, which developed a template for the sale, settlement, and eventual statehood of lands in the Northwest Territories (today's Midwest). Philip Fisher notes that this plan projected a new kind of "democratic social space" onto the federal frontier by imagining a radically equalized settlement pattern across western lands.[91] In sketching out the spatial dimensions of this policy, Jefferson adopted the same tabular grid that recurs like an Enlightenment nightmare all through the *Notes on the State of Virginia* in those numerous scientific tables that seek to homogenize the "heterogeneous, incoherent, distracted mass" of data that is Virginia—and Enlightenment America.[92] Jefferson's plans for the 1785 Ordinance likewise projected onto the landscape a geometrically exact grid of endlessly replicable boxes (each box, called a township, being six miles square and subdivided into thirty-six smaller boxes). The result was a Pythagorean fantasy of pure order and equanimity laid over a materially resistant, uneven landscape—a utopian but futile effort to harmonize and equalize the everyday disequivalences inherent in nature's nation. Today, that Jeffersonian grid is inscribed like a tattoo on the American Midwest, a quaint reminder of a radically different conception of national space than our own and one that can, ironically, only be viewed aerially when we Google satellite images of Illinois or Ohio or fly in and out of the industrial transportation hubs that Jefferson would have considered "sores" on the yeoman republic's democratic body politic (*Notes* 165).

But it would be a mistake to think of the federalism I have been describing here as a countertext to Jefferson or of Jeffersonian Republicanism as its antidote. As both a party and an ideology, Jeffersonian Republicanism benefited immensely from the constitutional status quo and its spatial project. Indeed, as D. W. Meinig's research on Jeffersonian expansionism makes clear, arguments about the extended republic resurfaced in particularly unexpected ways after 1800. Federalist Party partisans, for example, ironically found themselves inhabiting the old antifederalist pole of the argument on the floor of Congress whenever they wanted to resist Jefferson's acquisitive land policies. Senator Samuel White, for example, feared that the "new immense, unbounded world" projected by Jefferson's territorial acquisitions would endanger the union by diminishing the links between the people and their chosen representatives at the center. Like some lately arrived Federal Farmer, he declares that "our citizens will be removed to the immense distance of two or three thousand miles from the capital of the Union, where they will scarcely ever feel the rays of the General Government; their affections will become alienated; [and] they will gradually begin to view us as strangers." Jeffersonian Republicans like Senator John Breckinridge, on the other hand, took up *The Federalist's* old position, channeling Publius by refuting the idea that "a Republic ought to be confined within narrow limits." Indeed, Jefferson himself embraced a classical Madisonian position on the extended republic, dusting off the maxims of *Federalist* No. 10 by pointing out how geographic extension might control (regional) factions: "who can limit the extent to which the federative principle may operate efficiently? The larger our association, the less it will be shaken by local passions."[93]

But of course early partisan politics do not map cleanly or consistently onto federalist and antifederalist positions. Rather than viewing Jefferson's rise after 1800 as a second American Revolution (displacing the federalist consensus) *or* seeing this early partisanship as a continuation of the ideological splits that formed around ratification, we would do better to see it as a subscript within a larger process, the macronarrative of which was governed by the deep federalist superstructure inscribed, first abstractly and later materially, into American territory and history by the Constitution, which was and is America's master-text.[94] The federalist paradigm was, in other words, neither reversed nor assimilated by the gradual rise of mass political parties. If anything, the tiered scales of federalism were the necessary precondition for the iconic dyad of national party politics that emerged after 1790 to display and hold conflict at the federal center. Thus while the rise of Jeffersonian Republicanism did call forth what Jeffrey Pasley describes as a national newspaper network, that network relied on a radically decentralized conception of material (print) production, held together between 1790 and 1840 by the gradual aggregation of a unified ideological apparatus at the center (the capital) in such a way that nationalism in these years came to be organized around the spectacle of (two-party) dissent, a dialogic contest that could be endlessly and identically reproduced across vast portions of relatively unintegrated space in any number of local newspapers that funneled information from the center but then redistributed it primarily through local cultures.[95]

In the end, Jefferson's mammoth spatial imaginary was (like his social imaginary) a tangle of contradictions: on one hand, it was far more
democratic than anything Publius would ever have proposed, but it was,
on the other hand, also extravagantly imperialist (and hence deeply committed to the ideals of 1787–89). Because it was made possible within an
extended *national* geography, Jefferson's homestead model was both locally democratic and yet, as Harvey has pointed out, profoundly "pulver-
izing"—a deeply fragmenting process that ultimately sliced the frontier
up into private parcels whose productive capacity was used not merely
to sustain life on a local scale but also to extend the power, prestige, and
finally the wealth of the federal state and the expanding nation at large
(255–57). Indeed, in laying out a framework for the creation of new
states, Jefferson's land policies ensured the federal state's ability not just
to sustain but to materially reproduce itself in miniature in the form of
new territory, populations, and administrative bureaucracies. Thus while
Jefferson's land policies were meant to "open the way to an egalitarian democracy," they only "ended up being a means that facilitated the proliferation of capitalist social relations"—the very relations Jefferson warns
us against in "On Manufactures" (Harvey 257). And this was possible
because the federalist nation—that awesome container of both social
power and pure violence—was the already present framework in which
such Jeffersonian imaginings took place.

Christopher Colles stood somewhere between a Federalist and a Jeffersonian spatial imaginary with his production, in 1794, of *The Geographical Ledger and Systematized Atlas*.[96] Having failed to profit from his
roadmap series, Colles turned to this grander project, abandoning in its
larger plates the locally embedded viewer imagined in the roadmap *Survey* and embracing instead the most enlarged perspective he would ever
work in cartographically. To this end, the *Ledger* (figure 5.6) assembles a
series of new plates that reassert "the god-trick of seeing everywhere from
nowhere" by once again embracing conventional orientation and the
vastly abstracted point of view required to visually image vast portions
of North American coastline.[97] The oversized maps in this series were to
be produced as a collection of unbound plates that "may be most conveniently kept and carried without damage in a port folio, and occasionally
laid together upon a clean floor or carpet and examined with satisfaction to any extent."[98] Physically assembled on a flat plane, the various
plates were intended, as an assembled "whole," to "form one uniform,
connected design"(iii), with each individual plate joining with the oth-

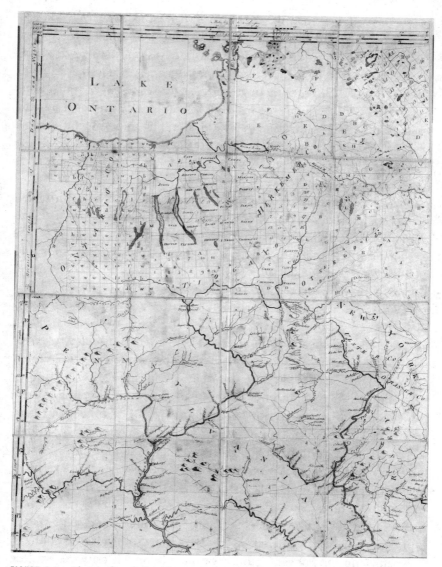

FIGURE 5.6 Christopher Colles. *The Geographical Ledger and Systemized Atlas*. New York: John Buel. 1794. Collection of The New-York Historical Society. Digital ID 78723d.

ers to form a larger map that would eventually look something like Jefferson's ever-expandable, highly reproducible, structurally self-identical grid. Instead of embedding the viewer in the landscape itself (with a miniature roadmap in hand), the *Ledger* thus imagines a map that expands "to any extent," laid out on an actual piece of real estate in front of its user, who no longer holds the map but instead stands over or inside the virtual landscape, dominating the world in miniature in much the same way that Elizabeth I does in the famous Ditchley portrait, in which the map of England lays spread out beneath her feet as an emblem of her perfect dominion over it.

But the *Ledger* does not so much repudiate as attempt to incorporate, within an even larger framework, the mixed spatial fantasies that had formerly driven the *Survey*. Indeed, the ingenuity and timeliness of *The Geographical Ledger* lie precisely in its hybrid relation to abstraction and embodiment, which Colles continued to theorize as a matter of material space to be engineered and represented through his cultural work as a scientist, mechanical genius, author, surveyor, and graphic illustrator. Though the project was never completed (only five plates are believed to have been produced), the *Ledger* was conceived as a totality of maps that would not only include every place within its geographic purview but would do so (in federalist fashion) at and in different scales, promising on its title page both the new, oversized coastal surveys that were to include multiple states *and* "an actual survey of a number of roads, specifying the true situation of every river, creek, church, mill, bridge, ford, ferry and tavern thereon, and their distances in miles." Colles thus appeared poised to enfold within this single project not just a series of new vastly abstracted map-plates but all the existing road-plates from the *Survey* as well (and many more besides). As in his other projects, furthermore, Colles not only imagined that a massive amount of dispersed local knowledge might be gathered in one place; he also believed it could be done efficiently and advantageously by one person. He criticizes existing maps of North America (and indeed, the world) as "unsatisfactory" precisely because "they are generally laid down by different authors, upon different scales, and with different modes of projection" (ii). In response to this decentralized approach, the *Ledger* introduces itself as a "united collection of topographical maps, projected by one universal principle, and laid down by one scale" (np).

But while the *Ledger* shares some crucial aspects (and even plates) with the 1789 *Survey*, it is essentially different in scope, for Colles never conceived of it as merely a national project, as the roadmap series had been. Instead, he believed the *Ledger* could be infinitely "extended to different countries as materials can be procured." Noting that "a great number of foreigners are continually arriving in this country," he imagined eventually incorporating "maps of some parts of Europe, Asia or Africa," as part of his "universal" "design" (viii). Had this project ever been completed, it would have been Colles's most fantastic and cosmopolitan representational project, an Enlightenment master-text not unlike Diderot's *Encyclopedia* in its attempt to create a "systematized" approach to the entire circumference of the known physical world, an inclusive and incorporative system not only for mapping all known spaces, but for indexing all known things within those places as well. The *Ledger*'s index is, in fact, one of its most remarkable features. In the fragment of the *Ledger* that survives, the provisional index includes hundreds of creeks, rivers, points, falls, towns, taverns, ferries, mountains, furnaces, homes, farms, public buildings, and landmarks, each one locatable on a map by virtue of two reference points (representing the horizontal and vertical planes of the grid) and then by a third letter meant to designate the location of the specific site inside the particular map-box in which it was located. The *Ledger* thus worked exactly as modern atlases do today, with each map laid out on a two-dimensional graph, so that, for example, "Minick's mill is given in the index with the letters k G m" and readers are thus instructed to "find the space G m upon the map, and the letter k [inside that space] will designate the situation of Minick's mill" (ix).

In its imperialist grandiosity, Colles's *Ledger* reveals the outer limits of federalist fantasy, which need not, in fact, be bound by national borders at all. In the end, the *Ledger* was intended to give its eighteenth-century subscribers a new mastery over an expanding universe, whether that mastery was achieved by looming over a literalized world-in-miniature laid out in boxes at their feet or by using the book's elaborately encoded index to physically locate minute features of the landscape from a vastly abstracted position of detachment. It was, Colles noted, "an entire[ly] new design . . . intended to answer the purposes of particular maps, and at the same time to form one connected map of the whole continent of America"—and perhaps, eventually, the planet.[99] In terms of its perceptual pedagogy, the *Ledger* strongly resembled two of Colles's most popular public entertainments—the microscope and the telescope, which sought to teach viewers how to smoothly rotate their attention between the near and the far, the minute and the gigantic.[100] Likewise the

Ledger sought to enable its viewers to see and phenomenologically experience both the part and the whole, the local and the global, the here and the there—all together, in jagged disunison.

In its embrace of "enlarged" views, its desire to collect the many into one (map), its attempts to master multiple scales with one text, and its desire to integrate all knowledge through a single unifying perspective, or geographic intellect, Colles's *Ledger* participates, in a particularly innovative way, in the federalist spatial imaginary emerging in the 1790s. At the same time, it does not choose sides (as newspapers all over the union were doing) in the partisan debates of those years. If anything, Colles balanced a (mercantile) Federalist Party investment in a high center with the more egalitarian (Jeffersonian Republican) investment in self-identicality, or duplication across space. The novel integration of several distinctly differentiated spatial scales ("the particular" and "the whole") was one that Colles himself knowingly connected to the elite mercantile cultures that had powered federalism's adoption as a national plan: "I have given this work the name of the *Geographical Ledger*," he notes, because "the situation of the places can be found (by means of the index and reference) as speedily as a merchant can find any particular account in his ledger" (viii). But he also clearly saw the project as an opportunity to redistribute, as it were, the informational wealth of geographical knowledge, so that every (book-owning) man might take pleasure in the aggregative work of early industrial expansion.

In the end, *The Geographical Ledger* went the way of all of Colles's projects: it failed because it lacked subscribers, because Colles did not have the resources to produce it on the terms he had proposed it, and because it was, in short, materially unfeasible for an impoverished New York tinkerer to produce a map of the world that recorded and cross-referenced every imaginable everything. In his final years, Colles would leave behind the mapping and building projects that consumed him in the 1780s and '90s and turn instead to a novel *communications* project: a semaphoric (or visual) telegraph intended to transmit intelligence across vast spaces without requiring a human body to carry it there.[101] The telegraph (which was to extend from Maine to New Orleans, connecting the Atlantic and Gulf coasts in one long chain of national conversation) never flourished. Nevertheless, it was a notable venture for Colles, for in it we can see him partially translating his conception of abstract federalist space into a peopled social space, filled not with places or things but with differentiated populations. Indeed, in the telegraph project, Colles explicitly imagines that his cultural work might unify not just American space but different kinds of people within that space—in this case, different groups divided by class. Thus in his first printed proposal for the telegraph, Colles connects the "interests of the United States of America" as a nation with the extension of "its advantages to all ranks and conditions of men, whether monied, landed, agricultural, commercial, mechanical, or manufactural"—a bounty he intends to disperse "by means of inland navigable communications," using telegraphic "intelligence boxes" that, the title page insists, can extend "to any assignable distance" and (like the nation-state itself) can be "easily kept in . . . full operation for ever." Partially constructed in the 1810s (with a line running from New York City to Sandy Hook), Colles's experimental telegraph was as close as he ever got to the collapsing nation-space that forms the subject matter of the last part of this book.

Put simply, the future of federalist space was neither Federalist Party, Jeffersonian Republican, Jacksonian, nor even ultimately Lincolnian. It was historically fated to be just one thing: relentlessly national—which is to say, domestically compressed and materially integrated to the point of collapse. In his later *Description of the Numerical Telegraph* (1813), Colles would imagine an elaborate array of preencoded messages that reveal how he expected dispersed regions to interact under the conditions of modest compression he hoped to produce with the telegraph. These include charmingly polite messages like: "What is the price of ____ with you?"; "I would be glad to know how accounts stand between us"; "It is reported ____"; "Give my compliments to____"; "Can you inform me where ___ _ lives?"; as well as abbreviations for basic commercial relationships (including words like "debtor," "creditor," and so on).[102] These blithe and even banal exchanges are a far cry from the anxious words transmitted just over thirty years later by Samuel Morse, in the first electrical telegraphic exchange. There, Morse tapped out the dilemma of his era in the iconic phrase, "What hath god wrought?"—a message that fully comprehends the problem that the national information network posed for U.S. citizens living in the midst of its historical emergence. Publius had famously declared America providentially united by virtue of geography in *Federalist* No. 2, but Morse and other early industrial engineers lived to see that geographic space providentially (and problematically) collapsed by technology—the very same technologies, in fact, that would, in time, be retroactively produced as unionizing agents (as seen, for example, in Currier and Ives's nationalist ode to industrialization in figure 1.1, which

places the telegraph alongside print culture, steam, and railroads as supremely nationalizing developments).

In the 1810s, Colles could imagine "universal communication" as a
reachable reality, an achievement "worthy of being classed with some of
the greatest improvements and most profitable speculations of the present age," aiding both merchants (by "opening a more copious field for
the extension of Commerce") and the state (who might use it in "War
and Peace").[103] But he did not foresee the perceptual and political impact of the time-space compressions those networks would eventually
produce for subjects living in their midst. Indeed, Colles seems in this
project, perhaps for the first time ever, to have been looking *backward* to
the relatively disconnected world of the high Enlightenment rather than
fully grasping the social and political consequences that greater integration would eventually produce. He thus imagined a quaint system of interregional communication that would leave a number of indispensable
buffers intact, with correspondents exchanging civil niceties, bills of sale,
and goods but never engaging in anything like the long, protracted, and
finally bloody squabble that was to arrive on America's doorstep in years
to come. Nor could he foresee that the emerging problem of class (which
he explicitly imagines his telegraph ameliorating) would be absorbed and
transformed into a more consuming national debate about several other
kinds of interconnected difference that would ensure that class would
never become a central preoccupation in (federal) America: most notably, the regional differences between white men, a translocal political
problem that would, ironically, be rewritten at the level of the local as the
social problem of racism, or ethnic difference. Colles was, like Hamilton
and Madison, a signal cultural purveyor of new conceptions of federalist
space, but even he could not imagine its true future: pure consolidation,
split into sections, followed by secession, Civil War, and, today, a nation
blasted into countless embodied identity-fragments, each nurtured in its
own consumer niche by the very market mechanisms that Colles (like
Publius) first dreamed of as early as the late 1780s.

PART THREE

THE OVEREXTENDED REPUBLIC
Slavery, Abolition, and National Space, 1790–1870

FIGURE 6.1 *Printers' Picture Gallery: Memorial of the American Anti-Slavery Society.* Broadside. New York: American Anti-Slavery Society, 1838. Library of Congress, Prints and Photographs Division, LC-USZ62-68414.

6. ABOLITIONIST NATION
THE SPACE OF ORGANIZED ABOLITION, 1790–1840

Public opinion cannot be walled in. The people of the South cannot shut it out from their borders. It knows no barriers—is not arrested by geographical boundaries—is not hemmed in by state lines or imprisoned by state legislation. It is a moral atmosphere that spreads itself noiselessly throughout the domains of intellect and intelligence. Like electricity, it mingles itself with all the elements of the moral world and imperceptibly becomes a part of the mental constitution. Neither its progress nor its power can be stayed.
> —Edward D. Barber, *Oration Delivered Before the Addison County Anti-Slavery Society*, 1836

1. ABOLITION AS MATERIAL PRACTICE

The nation-building projects of 1776 and 1787 did not require a sophisticated material infrastructure to make them work, either at the moment of founding or for many years afterwards; indeed, as I have argued so far, it was the very absence of such an infrastructure that enabled founding to proceed in the first place. But the theory of the extended republic did more for federalism than just assure its own initial success by finding a way to disperse dissent against it. It also allowed the federalists to map a new kind of state power in a space that did not yet meaningfully exist in the majority of people's everyday lives. More profoundly, it set in motion the long historical process that would eventually call forth the material conditions in which an altogether new kind of networked national space might emerge. The previous chapter suggested that *The Federalist Papers* not only defends the rearrangement of old spaces but also theorizes this new, abstract space-in-waiting, while *The Power of Sympathy* forecasts, from some strange, unconscious margin of the early national imaginary, the havoc that such an incestuously interconnected space might wreak

were it finally to meet its own self/parts face to face. This chapter extends
these arguments by addressing two new but related questions. First, what
happens when the nation emerges into conditions its framers did not predict? And second, what role did the antebellum culture industry play in
mediating the contradiction of nationality back through the body politic?

As the fourth president of the United States, it was Publius himself
(in the person of Madison) who presided over the transformations that
most permanently altered the spatial architecture of the United States.
These changes began with Jefferson's Embargo (1807–9) but stretched
out across Madison's two presidential terms (1809–17), which saw traditional trade relations with Britain disrupted by the War of 1812 and in
turn a new investment, both financially and ideologically, in a range of
internal improvements.[1] In the wake of these developments, the United
States emerged as a consolidated domestic space, a nation in its own
right, significantly less reliant on its prenational ties to Great Britain,
more able to manufacture goods for itself, and more able to distribute
those goods back through its own interior. The proliferation of internal
improvements was tied from the start to a belief in the link between technologies of communication and union. When Asa Whitney, for instance,
addressed Congress in 1845, seeking funds for the first (but not the last)
of many imagined transcontinental railroads, he mobilized a well-worn
national idiom that linked internal improvements to domestic bliss:
"Such easy and rapid communication," he argued, "would bring all our
immensely wide-spread population together as one vast city, the moral
and social effects of which must harmonize all together as one family, but
with one interest—the general good of all."[2] Whitney's enthusiasm for
national improvement persists in public discourse today, both popular
and academic. But such optimism is a central paradox in American history, for contrary to truisms that link the production of collective affect to
the existence of material institutions (from post roads to print culture),
the golden age of U.S. nation building did not in fact lead to a golden age
of U.S. nationalism but instead ushered in the era of high sectionalism
that is now marked in official U.S. history by that most divisive of adjec-
tives: "antebellum." Not only was union *not* bolstered by the antebellum
period's newfound experience of self-integration, but, as I hope to show
here, these new material conditions ultimately exposed the geographical
incoherence over which the fiction of union had originally been written.

The historical movement most devoted to exposing that fiction was
immediate abolition, a cluster of practices that emerged after 1830 to pro-

duce a distinctive critique of the national sin of slavery. This movement has often been understood as either an ideology or a discourse, sometimes even being reduced to a particular style of ("Garrisonian") argumentation. In revisiting immediate abolition as the site of both national integration and disintegration, I want to do something different here: I want to theorize it instead as an explicitly material practice. This is not to deny the discursive foundations of antislavery or to contest its status as an ideological position, but simply to insist that like anything else that happens in language, abolition is also the history of bodies and things: first of brains, tongues, hands, and ears and then of arms, legs, horses, wagons, railroads, steam engines, maps, and directories. In the United States, the project known as immediate abolition largely spread along just these railroad lines and roads, embedding its discursive self in other forms as it circulated within that continuously emerging built environment we call modernity: in newspapers, lyceums, magazines, and museums. At once a discourse and more than discourse, the historical project known as abolition knowingly embedded itself within an actual set of material structures. My argument here will be that its success would not otherwise have been possible—and that the American Anti-Slavery Society of the 1830s knew it. Like chapter 1 (which sought to lay out the circulatory spine of the American Revolution) and chapter 2 (which posed ratification as material text), this chapter lays out a materialist framework for abolition— an infrastructure in which this multifaceted, formally diverse debate took shape, circulated, and recirculated in upon itself.

As an account of abolition's institutions (including its newspapers, lecture halls, and iconic leaders), Robert Fanuzzi's *Abolition's Public Sphere* provides one of our few extended descriptions of abolition as a material practice.[3] Fanuzzi nevertheless makes an argument that I will sharply counter here: he reads immediate abolition not as a spatial but as an explicitly nonterritorial temporal critique. For him, antebellum abolition invokes a bygone, Revolutionary-era public sphere, similar to the one whose passing Habermas bemoans. Fanuzzi essentially argues that abolition represented itself "diachronically, or in relation to time, rather than synchronically, or as a community sharing the same space" (xxi). In doing so, he explicitly rejects the idea that immediate abolition was theorizing a new spatial imaginary—nor is he interested in the idea that the new spatial conditions of an emerging modernity might frame the antebellum abolitionist agenda. Instead, he argues that the immediatist movement "did not intend their campaign of mass distribution to foster the experience of simultaneity among literate subjects or produce the synchronized image of a national people" across continuous space (xxvi).

This chapter narrates the shift from Enlightenment gradualism to 1830s immediatism, and in doing so it argues the opposite point: that immediate abolition was, at base, a geographical critique—a critique both of emerging U.S. nationalism and of federalism's spatial legacy to antebellum America: the extended republic. I hope to show here that in its print campaigns of the 1830s, the AASS of 1833–40 explicitly targeted *both* the spatial and the temporal logic of early U.S. nationalism. In doing so, it accomplished something that earlier gradualist programs could neither have imagined nor materially achieved, in large part because gradualism was rooted in a world of geographic dispersal while immediatism flourished at the very moment when the United States was experiencing the time-space compressions of early industrial speedup. Amid these changes, the AASS produced an explicitly territorial critique of slavery, forcing a recognition of temporal simultaneity between distinct geographical spaces through the mechanisms available to it in the print public sphere: high-speed presses, express railroad delivery, federal postage regulations. In this way, slavery, an institution that had previously been attacked on essentially moral (or nonearthly) grounds (as a sin against either God or the universal rights of man), increasingly became entwined with the earthly narrative of U.S. territorial expansion.

My argument about the immediatism of the AASS is intentionally decentered. *Common Sense* stands today as the exemplary text of Revolutionary print culture while *The Federalist* stands as the premier artifact of constitutional ratification. If immediate abolition has such an iconic textual center, it would be William Lloyd Garrison's newspaper, *The Liberator*. And for good reason. Abolition was a splintered project between 1831 (when Garrison founded *The Liberator*) and 1863 (when Lincoln issued the Emancipation Proclamation). Garrison provides one of the few continuous figures against (and through) which to narrate that fragmentation, a man who was on the scene at almost every crucial juncture along the way. Likewise *The Liberator* offers itself as a cohesive text, even as it appears (in its format) as a diverse collection of positions and voices, an admirable cacophony that might be said to transcend Garrison's more finite editorial positions.[4] But abolition was never a one-man show. Though more difficult to narrate in this way, the antislavery movement was a cluster of practices as fragmented as the scene of antebellum culture it sought to navigate, a practice with no singular human or textual center. For this reason, the archive I have assembled here (which includes pamphlets, newspapers, administrative documents, diary entries, and memoirs) resists the reduction of the movement to one man, one text, one style, or even one principle. It is offered up instead as a set of circulating material practices that comprehended, for a time, the entire scene of antebellum cultural production, shadowing and foreshadowing the more mainstream culture industry that was developing all around it.

This is not to say, of course, that the antislavery movement did not have—or did not fancy itself to have, at least for a brief period—a geographic center. Located in New York City, the American Anti-Slavery Society of the 1830s saw itself as such a center—a high administrative peak raised above "the field" of abolition—a field it often theorizes and strategizes in its voluminous and well-documented *Reports* and its multiple periodical series. If this arrangement sounds federalist in its privileging of the center over and against the productive energies that feed it from the ground, then that is because it was. Indeed, centralization of every kind in these years follows the metrobuilding logic of a high center that oversees a vast foundation. But whereas first-generation federalism relied on the disconnection between the center and the ground, the centralized agencies of the 1830s focused on the opposite end of the project. The building of a national community in these years was a commercially motivated and industrially powered social process. It involved the growth of bigger and wider markets for things like shoes, hats, and magazines, and these projects demanded a new level of integration between the ground and its center. Under ongoing industrialization, in other words, the center became the site not just for the management or production of (nationalist) ideology (as it had been in 1787), but for the production of things— goods that must finally move across and through spaces in order to make their production meaningful (or, in capital's terms, profitable).

National voluntary associations like temperance, abolition, and evangelical reform were all part of this process; they may have been manufacturing, at their core, an ideology and a discourse, but that ideology was made material in exactly the same terms that industrial capitalism's more mundane goods were material. At one time or another, for instance, the American Anti-Slavery Society produced pamphlets, newspapers, magazines, pincushions, envelopes, scarves, and graphic broadsides (see, for example, figure 6.1 opposite the opening page of this chapter). Some of these goods were intended for local consumption in New York City, but many were dispersed into the wider field through commercial networks and the traveling lecturer system. Indeed, the AASS's traveling agents worked much the way that subscription agents worked for publishers in this period—as crucial middlemen who smoothed the transmission of goods from industrial center to the widest possible market (and who are now viewed as transitional objects in the history of national literary dissemination). It is no accident, then, that the rise of immediate abolition exactly coincides with that period in American literary history that we associate with high cultural nationalism. Abolition enfolds itself in these years within a vast culture industry, of which it must be understood to hold itself a central share.

Consider, in this regard, three documents in the history of abolitionist cultural production: Elihu Embree's Tennessee-based *Manumission Intelligencer*, Garrison's Boston-based *Liberator*, and Gamaliel Bailey's *National Era*, based in Washington, DC. Each of these texts demonstrates, in miniature, a different stage of abolitionist print culture's development as a material practice. Embree published the first U.S. periodical explicitly devoted to cultivating and connecting an abolitionist public, the Tennessee *Manumission Intelligencer* (later retitled *The Emancipator*), at Jonesborough, Tennessee, between 1819 and 1820. Underwritten by Jonesborough's local manumission society, the *Intelligencer* resembled what we might now call a newsletter, putting forth the ideals of the small group that underwrites it and articulating broad arguments against the continuance of slavery. Some years later, in 1831, William Lloyd Garrison would take on the task of printing *The Liberator* on a hand press in Boston. As one might expect, *The Liberator* was far more complexly situated than the *Intelligencer*. Indeed, Garrison was specially situated to connect the dots of the public sphere in which he circulated. He was intimately connected both to abolition's key figures in these years and, as a printer, to the wider print culture of his era. He had, for instance, already partnered with Benjamin Lundy to help co-edit, in Baltimore, the *Genius of Universal Emancipation*, and prior to that he had served as apprentice printer, master craftsman, and editor at another newspaper in New England. Even so, the first issue of *The Liberator* displays a world only slightly larger than that of the *Intelligencer*. Indeed, Garrison's relatively modest beginnings are hardly comparable to the vast marketplace that was eventually to arise around the issue of antislavery. Published at Washington City, the *National Era* of October 19, 1848, displays a far different scene.

A single page from this issue of the *National Era*, then in its second year of publication, displays advertisements from cities as diverse as Washington, DC, New York, Cincinnati, London, Edinburgh, Boston, and Louisville. Advertisements from manufacturers in these locations seek to reach a nationally dispersed audience in order to sell objects and services from the mundane to the sublime. On one page, we can find advertisements for a temperance hotel, a midwestern medical school, lard oil, cigars, "free soil" and antislavery reading rooms, as well as a crushing host of abolitionist and mainstream printed matter—including *Littell's Living Age, Godey's Lady's Book,* a Boston-based children's magazine, numerous American Anti-Slavery Society imprints, a number of British journals (the *London Quarterly Review, Edinburgh Review, Westminster Review,* and *Blackwood's*), and a prospectus for a new publication to be titled the *Louisville Examiner.*[5]

As this issue of the *National Era* demonstrates, immediate abolition lived to see and participate in a massive proliferation of its own and other print cultures—and to see them embedded, as part of an emerging culture industry, in the proliferation of other kinds of industry as well. Specialized as it may at first glance appear, then, immediate abolition offers an excellent vantage point from which to view the rise of a national culture industry and the subsequent fragmentation of that culture into a variegated field of consumption. Abolition was never simply a random witness to such changes. On the contrary, I place abolition at the center of this inquiry, rather than one of the antebellum period's many other voluntary associations (evangelical Christianity, temperance, women's rights, or working-class movements, to name a few), for a specific reason. Although each of these emerging voluntary associations (or "publics") took part in producing a more saturated, more cross-regional, more national (and thus less place-based) public sphere, only abolition devoted itself, for thirty years, to a geopolitical critique of the nation as an integrated space. Abolition is, in other words, the one nonterritorially based public in these years that organizes itself as an explicit attack on the territorially based practice of southern slaveholding. This critique was so strong that it led, in the 1840s, to a staunch disunionist position among the most radical wing of the movement. And while this disunionist position did not in itself ensure civil war (indeed, it was secession not from within the North but from outside of it that finally forced military engagement), the movement to end slavery was inextricably tied to the onset of war, its political and economic stakes, and of course its outcomes.

Like federalism, immediate abolition actively theorized the world-historical conditions that made its own material production possible. For all these reasons and more, it is abolition (rather than secession or states' rights) that ought rightfully to be viewed as federalism's most canny, if unrecognized, antebellum other.

2. THE PAST IN THE PERIPHERY: FROM EARLY GRADUALISM TO BENJAMIN LUNDY'S *LIFE* AND *GENIUS*

The macronarrative of American abolition is usually told in two temporally loaded words: gradual and immediate. Gradualism is often understood as the expectation that slavery should and would end but without the sense of urgency that marks the rise of immediate abolition after 1830. As both an organized program and a vague structure of antislavery feeling, gradual emancipation appears in retrospect to have been satisfied with predicting the slow unraveling of slavery somewhere in the deep future—even as it tended to its local wreckage in the present. To this end, gradualism was characterized by a scattered set of localist amelioration programs set alongside the annual (and later bi-annual) circulation of deferential petitions to patriarchially conceived state and federal governments. Immediate abolition, on the other hand, enacted a sharp rupture in this practice. Often associated with the founding of Garrison's Boston *Liberator* in 1831 and the New York-based American Anti-Slavery Society in 1833, "immediate abolition" was a phrase first coined in Britain by Elizabeth Heyrick, whose 1824 pamphlet *Immediate, Not Gradual Abolition* defied the (then) central tenet of Britain's national antislavery society by insisting on the immediate and total emancipation of all slaves held in the British West Indies.[6] The pamphlet then emigrated to the United States and was embraced as a defining program by radical American abolitionists in the waning days of the colonizationist movement. Taken together, side by side, after the fact, the words "gradual" and "immediate" tell an ideological tale teetering on the sharp fulcrum of righteousness. On the gradualist side, there is good will but also a sense of protraction and passivity; on the immediatist side, there is a radical utopianism unwilling to barter politically for fear of compromising a moral purpose of utter clarity. Where gradualism makes a deal with the devil and buys the word "later" in the bargain, immediatism says *now*.[7]

But if the words "gradual" and "immediate" make the temporal stakes of abolitionist history clear, they have been less useful in helping later generations see the spatial logic that underwrites each program. Viewed at the level of the local, gradual emancipation is, as immediate abolitionists would later argue, temporally vague; viewed at the level of the national or global, however—as a program for the ultimate eradication of slavery across the United States or the planet—gradualism was not temporally vague so much as geographically (and, in the U.S. case, politically) pragmatic. It describes less a moral equivocation than a sense of the profound dispersal of slavery across space. In the early United States, gradualism was just this kind of place-based doctrine, one that recognized the practical difficulty of enforcing a simultaneous (or immediate) abolition across a vast federal space—especially in the absence of connective infrastructure. Indeed, gradual abolition may best be understood, spatially, as a kind of serial abolition that sought to spread itself through and across numerous semidisconnected sceneries. Between 1788 (the year the Constitution was ratified) and 1831 (the year immediatism finds its first persistent textual trace in Garrison's *Liberator*), the former colonies—now sovereign state units—constitute just this kind of pluralized scenery.

Thomas Haskell has argued that the rise of antislavery sentiment is symptomatic of a "new cognitive style" in which previously indifferent populations become aware of the sufferings of people in remote locations and of their own moral responsibility toward such distant problems. Where such scenes would previously not have impinged on the inner life of these abolitionists-in-the-making, they slowly begin to do so in the late eighteenth century because, in Haskell's argument, the emerging market creates a new sense of connectedness between strangers, making mercantile elites more aware of their ability to affect the lives of distant populations.[8] Haskell's argument is provocative because it accounts for a number of perceptual and technological shifts that enfold themselves into the emerging history of humanitarianism in the West, but it more aptly describes metropolitan Britain's ultimate renunciation of slavery in the West Indies than the rise of abolition in the United States. In the U.S. context, Haskell's argument about "remote" consequences only becomes compelling as an account of the rise of immediate abolition in the 1830s—a sentiment that was always geographically centered in the North but ideologically focused on the (distant, if not remote) South. It is a far less compelling account of early American antislavery sentiment, which sought from the Revolution forward not to eradicate slavery from remote locations either inside or outside national borders, but to deal instead with slavery in its midst, North and South. Thus in the post-Revolutionary era, a number of state-based (usually urban-centered) societies emerged to try to end slavery and to ameliorate the condition of free blacks within their own state borders. These societies began to organize themselves nationally in the 1790s, when the Convention for Promoting the Abolition of Slavery began to meet annually (and then bi-annually) to discuss a more nationally coherent program. After the fashion of the Continental Congress before them (or the Federal Congress, which was then meeting in the same city), this group saw itself as a representative body of "the Abolition Societies, in various and distant parts of the Union."[9]

The administrative minutes of these early conventions afford an invaluable account of the material practices of early abolition in the United States. They show a group not so much unable to imagine the lives of distant populations as unable to coordinate their activities across vast distances. Even as late as the Seventh Convention in 1800, member societies were noting organizational difficulties not just at the national level but at the *state* level. New Jersey, for instance, complained in its annual report that the state had no urban center from which to do the work of spreading antislavery sentiment: "The scattered situation of this Society, occasions many embarrassments and difficulties, of which Societies that are more compact, have no experience. Those members who constitute the acting committee, are often so far apart, as to render it impracticable for them to act in concert in cases of emergency, and are obliged to content themselves with convening but three or four times a year."[10] The national society had just as much difficulty organizing itself across a vast space. Indeed, while the general convention considered its membership national (composed of societies "in various and distant parts of the Union"), the early meetings drew on a regionally compact area precisely because of the difficulties of gathering more diffuse delegates together in one spot. In 1794, for instance, representatives from nine societies participated in the first annual convention at Philadelphia, but the nine societies represented only six states; the following year, representatives from seven societies in only five states participated. In both cases, no delegates appear from anywhere either north of Connecticut or south of Maryland. In fact, the minutes for these meetings mark the conspicuous absences of societies near and far as letters arrive with apologies from member societies in New Jersey, Virginia, and Washington, PA (then considered the far west).

The first published report of the convention frankly acknowledges its gradualist program, supporting different time tracks in different states. At no time does it imagine a singular abolition of slavery. Instead it posits the project of abolition as one that will occur multiply—or serially—across several highly differentiated spaces.[11] Each society reports on its own goals and timeline, and both slavery and antislavery are thus rendered as local affairs—deeply city- and state-based practices that are discussed with absolute deference to the custom of each county and state represented. The convention never projects a unified program for these place-parts but serves instead the connective function of drawing together abolitionists from "distant" states in order to share information and strategies that may or may not translate across space. To the degree that the convention sets forth a unified (or cross-regional) program, it is one of cellular homogeneity. Individual societies are urged to take up the tools of the Enlightenment (petitions and public orations) within their local worlds in order to promote abolition and amelioration. But the content of these petitions and orations is left to individual societies, which often choose not to pursue them at all. As a Pennsylvania delegate admitted, "your advice, frequently to publish extracts . . . has not passed unnoticed; but while we admit the correctness of the reasoning . . . we have not discovered anything [in Pennsylvania] . . . which makes it necessary to act upon the recommendation."[12]

In the end, the convention's place-based program was rooted in a worldview that emphasized the geographical origins of early national identity for whites and blacks alike. Indeed, these documents articulate slavery as something geographically specific to the locations that were producing it, and its worst aftereffects were likewise minted in the coin of geography. The 1794 convention, for instance, appears most horrified by slavery as a practice that travels: "Negroes, considered merely as subjects of property, are frequently carried off, by force, from their dearest connections, and transported to places, where even the severity of their former bondage is increased; where a new climate, rigid laws, and despotic manners, render their despair complete."[13] Here, the burgeoning domestic slave trade is described as a second middle passage. For these late Enlightenment philanthropists, such forced migration—to "a new climate," with new laws and manners—is the cruelest and most inhuman of American slavery's practices. In a world in which personal identity is organized around geography—where self and place are intimately sutured to create a life—what could be worse than slavery's erasure of local origins and local roots? But the increased mobility of both slaves and slaveholding did something else as well: it exposed the (geographical) limits of the localist ameliorist programs on which gradual abolition had staked itself. Such programs could address any number of slavery's social problems in their midst as long as they remained there, but they could do nothing about them once they were exported elsewhere. At the same time, however, this early complaint points to the great fallacy on which gradualism was based: the belief that slavery would fade away after the abolition of the international trade (dictated in the Constitution) in 1808. As many historians have noted, the early gradualists believed they were subtending slavery's inevitable demise (its suffocation from replenishment from abroad). This belief was so widely subscribed to that gradualism lost its center and faded into virtual nonexistence once the benchmark of 1808 was passed. But not only did the abolition of the international trade in 1808 fail to end slavery in the United States; it actually created the internal slave trade as one of the first entirely *domestic* forms of U.S. commerce. It sealed the borders, as it were, and locked slavery in—a decision that had profound effects for the future of the United States as it slowly emerged into one nation under market capitalism.

As the *Minutes* of these early antislavery conventions make clear, gradual abolition inhabited a highly localist spatial imaginary, responding to slavery not as a coherent problem on a national scale but as something practiced across any number of disjunct, serially imagined spaces. Nowhere is this fragmented, serial, highly localized spatial imaginary more apparent than in the peripatetic career of its last real practitioner, Benjamin Lundy. Born in Sussex County, New Jersey, in 1789, Lundy was an erstwhile farmer, leather worker, printer, newspaper editor, lecturer, editorialist, pamphleteer, and committed lifelong abolitionist. More importantly for our purposes, Lundy's antislavery work was part of the larger, geographically based worldview that was being slowly displaced by the time-space compressions of early industrialization. He thus serves as a crucial transitional figure in this book's description of the emerging nation-state as well as in this chapter's discussion of abolition's emergence into a truly national project.

Lundy was a product of the waning American Enlightenment, and his life compresses in a single story all the attendant hopes and failures of the eighteenth century's most utopian representational projects. But unlike other figures I have already discussed (including Hugh Finlay, John

Trumbull, and Christopher Colles), Lundy was never merely a creature of the eighteenth century. With one foot in Paine's world and the other in Garrison's, Lundy's life exactly coincides with abolition's emergence from obscurity in the 1810s and 1820s into the national culture industry of the 1830s and early 1840s. Born on the eve of ratification, Lundy lived until 1839, witnessing from the sidelines and at times participating at the center in the rise of organized antislavery. He is most often remembered today as the editor of the *Genius of Universal Emancipation*, a sometimes monthly, sometimes weekly abolitionist newspaper, which ran semi-continuously from 1821 to 1839. Though not the first newspaper in the United States to be entirely devoted to the question of slavery, Lundy's *Genius* was the first to make a visible mark across the union, and, of the earliest abolitionist newspapers, it was by far the longest running. After Lundy died in 1839, Thomas Earle compiled his few surviving papers into a loosely organized biography titled *The Life, Travel, and Opinions of Benjamin Lundy*, which circulated widely in northern antislavery librar-ies and reading rooms in the years before the Civil War. It is from extant copies of the *Genius* and from Earle's *Life* that most of our information on Lundy derives.[14]

Lundy's early occupational history demonstrates his liminal status in the increasingly industrial relations of production that mark these tran-sitional years in the American economy. Raised on a farm in New Jersey, Lundy left home in the 1810s to train as an artisan saddler in Wheeling, Virginia (now West Virginia), but unlike skilled artisans of the previous generation, he worked only intermittently at his chosen trade throughout his life. Invited in 1818 to co-edit the *Philanthropist*, Charles Osborn's re-form newspaper based in Mount Pleasant, Ohio, Lundy sold the tools of his trade and commenced newspapering. Without serving a single day as an apprentice printer, he taught himself both the printing and the edito-rial business. At his death in 1839, the *Genius* was the longest running an-tislavery periodical in the United States, having survived eighteen years, several geographic relocations, and innumerable interruptions. Both predating and postdating the American Anti-Slavery Society's early work, Lundy's *Life* and *Genius* offer a special vantage point from which to view the emergence of abolition as a mass, national, centralized movement in the 1830s.

Yet Lundy's peculiar style of activism does not map smoothly onto ex-isting accounts of gradual-into-immediate abolition. Indeed, his career inscribes the distance between, on one hand, the serial spatial imaginary of gradual abolition and, on the other, the highly centralized and abstract space of the abolitionist nation constituted by the American Anti-Slavery Society as it demanded an immediate end to slavery. Though Lundy identified himself as an immediate abolitionist (he was, in fact, one of the first U.S. printers to set Elizabeth Heyrick's essay in type), he nevertheless paradoxically insisted that any program for immediate abolition must happen gradually. Lundy's reprinting of Heyrick's pamphlet is particularly ironic in this regard, for in introducing the notion of immediate abolition to his readers, Lundy was forced to print the pamphlet serially—in halting part-pieces—throughout the fall and winter of 1826 and 1827. Readers who wanted the full argument thus had to wait to see how it unfolded, slowly, in installments. The seriality of Lundy's reprinting of *Immediate, Not Gradual Abolition* is a perfect figure for his paradoxical career as a transitional and ambivalent immediate abolitionist, one whose antislavery practice sutures gradualism to immediatism and in doing so reveals the stakes of each.

Lundy's hybrid affiliation as a gradual immediatist found him embracing two massive life-projects that left him slightly out of step with his time: first, colonization (a waning project in the 1830s that Lundy nevertheless pursued avidly) and second, his quirkily produced newspaper, the *Genius*—a serial representational project that Lundy insisted on personally producing and disseminating, often hand-carrying it circuitously across wide spaces, in a strangely embodied attempt to take it national. I want to link these two seemingly disjointed projects here into one story by suggesting that the serial project of Lundy's life as an itinerant printer was tied to a similarly serialized spatial imaginary that found its expression in a colonizationist fantasy of far-flung communities of freed blacks relocated (voluntarily) to peripheral locales at the edges of the United States (in Haiti and Mexico). Colonization was, in fact—given Lundy's worldview—a fairly predictable solution to the pending crisis of emancipation, for Lundy's world was always a world of elsewheres, and his life was spent setting out for one after another of these other places. Indeed, as we shall see, his *Life* resembles nothing so much as one long circular journey in which every arrival merely inserted him in an absent relation to all the other elsewheres where he could not be.

The most interesting literary artifact to be produced from Lundy's activism, Earle's *Life* epitomizes the serial peregrinations and nonlinear compulsions of its biographical subject. Commissioned to write a biography by Lundy's sister, Earle strategically decided not to narrate Lundy's life in retrospect but to let Lundy's life-in-writing speak for itself. To do this, Earle collected Lundy's papers—his private correspondence, copious travel journals, and newspaper columns—and "compiled" them in rough chronological lines that continually start and re-start, like a stuck record, whenever a new set of materials is inserted. The result is a fascinating mess—a nonintegrated mass of semidisconnected materials that winds circuitously through the major events of the 1820s and 1830s, looping back and renarrating the same events in different formats (letters, editorials, journals) that refuse the unity we expect of the biography (and autobiography) form yet that often speak in the integrated voice of an "I," or first-person narrator.

These casually collated papers show a man wholly aware of his position in the midst of world-historical events. As a young apprentice working in Wheeling, Lundy found himself, quite literally, at an epic territorial conjunction, living and working on the newly opened National Road, a site that would eventually connect an increasingly free North to the still unfree South while joining both to the commercially expanding West. This geographic crossroads is exactly where, Lundy tells us, his commitments to abolition began. "Wheeling was a great thoroughfare," he recalls, "for the traffickers in human flesh. Their '*coffles*' passed through the place frequently. My heart was deeply grieved at the gross abomination; I heard the wail of a captive; I felt his pang of distress; and the iron entered my soul" (15). As his career continued, Lundy found himself on what he alternately termed the "great scene" and the "great thoroughfare" of historical debate, and he was clearly awed by the monumental scale of the problem facing him. He was at a loss to discern, for example, what an individual might do to oppose the expansion of slavery into distant (and multiple) territories: "I had lamented the sad condition of the slave, ever since I became acquainted with his wrongs and sufferings. But the question, 'What can I do?' was the continual response to the impulses of my heart" (16). His initial attempts to intervene are comically and touchingly small, given his own well-articulated conception of the scope of the problem. His first action, for instance, a few years after his departure from Wheeling, was to form a local society made up of a handful of friends and to write for them "an appeal on the subject of slavery, addressed" (grandiosely) "to the philanthropists of the United States, and circulated [in] five or six copies in manuscript" (16). Urged to have the manuscript printed, Lundy arranged for its publication under a fictitious

signature. The surviving circular—apparently handed out to local neighbors—is dated January 4, 1816—Lundy's twenty-seventh birthday.

From these modest manuscript-into-circular origins emerged one
of the most famous printer-abolitionists of the antebellum years. After
his death, Lundy was memorialized in the movement as a founder and a
pioneer. Many of these remembrances remark, for example, on Lundy's
priority as one of the first antislavery editors and lecturers. But even as
they cite the resemblance of his methods to the cause's more modern
publicity techniques, these memorials also compulsively mark his essential difference from that modernity. This difference can be summed up
in a single word: *travel*. Where others mailed antislavery tracts, Lundy
delivered them in person. Where others wrote of and to and for distant
populations, Lundy walked among them. His journals are scattered with
the records, large and small, of endless journeys: one entry notes "forty-
five miles" as "the greatest walk I have accomplished in a single day" (28);
others tally the accumulation of miles: "700 miles, on foot, and in the
winter season" (19); "eight hundred miles, one-half on foot" (20); "six
hundred miles . . . on horseback, in the winter season, and that at my
own expense" (21). On each of the numerous trips his journals record,
Lundy was, as he liked to say, "scatter[ing] the seed of antislavery" (26).
Thomas Earle notes that in the 1820s alone "Lundy had expended in the
Anti-Slavery cause, several thousand dollars of his earnings, had traveled
more than five thousand miles, on foot, and twenty thousand in other
ways, had visited nineteen states of the Union, held more than two hundred public meetings, and made two voyages to Hayti" (240). No obitu-
ary, memorial, or biographical sketch of Lundy fails to mention these
Odyssean travels. Indeed, even while he was alive, abolitionist newspapers like *Freedom's Journal* and *The Colored American* kept a running log
(when they could keep track at all) of Lundy's ongoing travels north, west,
and especially south.[15] After his death, he was rhapsodically eulogized by
Wendell Phillips Garrison as "the most unwearied of pedestrians. . . . This
little man, so slight you might think he would be blown away, traversed
a large part of the Union without a conveyance. 'Rivers and mountains,'
said an admiring disciple, 'vanish in his path; midnight finds him wend-
ing his solitary way over an unfrequented road; the sun is anticipated in
his rising.'" Thus Lundy "trudged to and fro, carrying the printed sheets
[of the *Genius*] upon his back," "preaching the gospel of freedom" with
his "his carpetbag," a "knapsack," and "his direction-book" in hand.[16]

Lundy's peculiarly embodied style of activism had consequences for the printed texts he was producing for the movement. Two modes of print production adhere within the antislavery movement in these years. The first is the classic local printer, who works in one place and produces his central antislavery texts (usually a newspaper) on a hand press. Garrison is the iconic example of this type of print production, but other well-known examples include Frederick Douglass (who published the Rochester-based *North Star*, later titled *Frederick Douglass' Newspaper*), Elijah Lovejoy (who published the Alton, Illinois-based *Observer* before being murdered by a mob in 1837), and James Birney (who published the Cincinnati-based *Philanthropist*). The second mode of print production we see in these years is the more centralized model associated with the consolidating publishing industry and pursued by the American Anti-Slavery Society from 1833 forward. Following the example of the American Tract Society, this model emphasizes the mass production and (often free) distribution of antislavery tracts and periodicals of every kind. Lundy appears, in retrospect, to epitomize the solitary figure of the Garrisonian editor-abolitionist, but in fact he fits neither model. This is because his investment in travel made it impossible for the *Genius* to be issued from a single place for any length of time. While the *Liberator* issued continuously from Boston for over thirty years, Lundy's *Genius* is a bibliographer's nightmare, issued at one time or another from (at least) six different locations, including Mount Pleasant, Ohio; Greeneville, Tennessee; Baltimore, Maryland; Washington, DC; Philadelphia, Pennsylvania; and Hennepin, Illinois. Each of these geographic imprints marks a major movement in Lundy's life. He founded the *Genius*, for example, in Mount Pleasant, where he jobbed out the presswork to a printer twenty miles away (carrying the completed sheets home on his back), and he later moved to Tennessee after inheriting the press on which Elihu Embree had been printing Jonesborough's *Manumission Intelligencer*. (Notably the press could not come to Lundy in either of these cases, so Lundy moved, by foot, in order to be near the press.) Later, upon traveling across the Alleghenies to attend the Convention of Abolitionist Societies (the first man west of the Alleghenies to do so), Lundy determined to move the paper to the east coast to be "nearer to centers of information" and away from the "isolation" of the West (85). From that time on, he slowly inched his way up the coastline, from Baltimore and Washington to Philadelphia, partly (as he tells it) because antislavery sentiment drove

him northward and partly because Washington and later Philadelphia offered a greater community on which he could rely to help him produce
and circulate the paper. In each case, his moves were spurred by a desire
to become, as he put it, "more generally acquainted with intelligent and
influential men, from every part of the Union, and thus to increase the
facilities of collecting and disseminating important information."[17]

Lundy's relation to the production and dissemination of information
was, however, always ambivalent. Indeed, the *Genius* is unique among
the print artifacts of its day because Lundy refused, as often as he could,
to split the sites of the newspaper's distribution from its production. He
did not, in other words, simply move the place of publication only to
set up shop again in one "center of information" or another. For a good
part of his life, he also took the *Genius* on the road with him as he traveled from site to site on his epic pedestrian travels. Lundy was known,
for instance, to travel with his newspaper's standing type ("his title-
letter, head lines and column-rules, leads and [other] standing matter").[18]
As Earle remarks: "It appears from a private letter which Lundy wrote
[in the 1830s] that he printed the paper at whatever place he happened
to be . . . [on whatever] printing press which he could use, and [with
whatever] funds [he could find] to defray expenses, in the course of his
journey" (245–46). Thus when the *Genius* moved its publication offices
from Washington, DC, to Philadelphia in the 1830s, the move was at best
nominal, for as Earle notes, it had "for some time before . . . been dated at
Washington, but [was] generally not printed there" (266).

Lundy sometimes made light of this unusual practice of traveling with
his type: "Thee will, no doubt, smile at the idea of an *itinerant editor!*
and, probably, laugh outright, to think of an *itinerant periodical!*"[19] But
Lundy's travels are more than just comical. At a time when production
of every kind was centralizing, Lundy remained invested in the radically
decentralized form of production afforded by his "itinerant periodical."
Thus as AASS was forming itself in the 1830s on a corporate model that
formally mimicked the reorganization of space and production under
the ongoing processes of industrial expansion, Lundy steadfastly refused
to have the *Genius* associated with any singular site of origin or with any
one group. He likewise refused, for the most part, to divide the labor of
his abolitionist undertaking, playing the parts of printer, publisher, editor, lecturer, subscription agent, fundraiser, and even collections officer.

Such practices indicate that abolition's public sphere was never a theoretical construct for Lundy. It was a material location, a field of practice

in which he felt the need to personally circulate, visiting with his body the same sites his newspaper did. As such, his travels represent a Collesean fantasy about the collection of disparate spaces, a desire to unite the travels of his text-object with his own body's movements through space. Lundy's investment in decentralized (and so polycentric) cultural production proved both useful and troublesome for him. On the positive side, his epic travels allowed him to exponentially expand his subscription list and to personally locate agents and allies on his various tours. It was Lundy, for instance, who ignited a young William Lloyd Garrison with abolitionist fervor at a time when the North was, as Lundy says, "cool" to the project of emancipation. Lundy's early traveling habits also allowed him to do something few later abolitionists could do for fear of arrest: he traveled by foot through the South, converting slaveholders to his cause and gathering firsthand information about slavery for his readers. In fact, Lundy was so successful in converting southern slaveholders to abolition that many of them began to sign their slaves over to him (always on the promise that he would settle them elsewhere)—a situation that led to the quirky (and historically doomed) colonization schemes that took up the last years of his life.

Thoreau's famous aphorism aside, Lundy's *Life* proves that the swiftest traveler is not he that goes afoot. Indeed, his life was marked by a series of losses that occurred within the gaps produced by his many long and protracted journeys. Lundy suffered a great deal, in other words, because of his tendency to circulate his body throughout the field of his antislavery work, rather than staying "at home," as we might say, within his own life. Lundy's family was the first to learn that because Lundy felt the need to be present everywhere, he wound up being always absent everywhere else. While visiting Haiti in 1825, for instance, Lundy was "detained . . . much longer than I had anticipated" and returned many months overdue to find that his wife had died in his absence: "I hastened to my dwelling, but found it deserted. All was lone and dreary within its walls. I roused some of my neighbours, but they could tell me nothing about my children. . . . On further inquiry, I found that my little ones were scattered among my friends. But 'home with all its pleasures' was gone" (24). Sacrificing a centered home life for his decentered antislavery work, Lundy placed his children "with friends in whom I could confide, and renewed my vow to devote my energies to the cause of the slave, until the nation should be effectually roused in his behalf" (24). This pattern of absence and loss persisted for the rest of Lundy's life. Traveling to Mexico in the 1830s in pursuit of yet another, more suitable colonization site, Lundy was detained so long that he found, upon his return, that he had been presumed dead and that the *Genius* (which he had left in the care of a junior partner) had been taken over by a new editor and moved to another city (177). Lundy notes that his friends were "rejoiced" to discover that "I had not lost my life." But he is not surprised, either, that they moved on without him: "This I expected would have been the case, for I was aware that they had not heard a word from me for about ten months" (177).

Lundy's shattered home life suggests what was at stake for many abolitionists in the choice of a more fixed, or centralized, location from which to produce an antislavery appeal. Immediate abolition's investment in centralized production allowed its key cultural producers to inhabit middle-class norms that were intimately tied to the production of domesticity, allowing men like Arthur and Lewis Tappan, Theodore Weld, and even Garrison to become successful husbands and fathers even as they rose in the world as successful businessmen, newspapermen, and reformers. Lundy, however, continually refused the cultural forms of domesticity—and its centered, home-based logic—in favor of a more itinerant, centerless life-story. But it was not just his children's birthdays that he missed. Lundy's pseudo-deaths (and his Lazarus-like returns) also testify to the ways that his travels forced his absence from the mainstream history of his moment. Though his letters, journals, and editorials continually suggest his understanding of the need to be at the center of debate and information, the *Life* tells another story—one in which Lundy repeatedly sought out the protracted periphery over and against the condensation of the northeastern center. Nothing makes this clearer than the way in which this printer of newspapers had trouble getting copies of other people's newspapers in the far reaches of his travels. At a time when print culture was becoming ever more rationalized and interconnectedly networked, Lundy persistently traveled to places that print had not yet penetrated—particularly the far Mexican frontier. When scouting in unsettled areas of Mexico, Lundy was forced to leave his own paper at home and rely instead on informal networks of information for news. The problem with this penchant for the periphery was that it put Lundy directly at odds, as a cultural producer, with the culture industry that was then emerging in the United States in general, and in particular within the antislavery movement. As Merton Dillon notes, Lundy returned from his sojourns to find himself an increasingly "irrelevant" "relic" to the reform movements of his time.[20] Premature rumors of Lundy's death make this marginalization painfully clear, but they also point to its cause: to disappear from the radar of recordable (American) locales is, at this moment in history, simply to disappear. To go unheard from in the American 1830s is not to exist.[21]

Lundy himself frequently remarks in his journals and letters on the "truly arduous" nature of his work in the field of antislavery (31). The ultimate effect of his need to be in his body and "on the spot" of each of his ventures was that he was almost always out in the field rather than at the center when great things happened. The American Anti-Slavery Society, for instance, formed itself in 1833, passing its constitution and then raising over the next few years a massive amount of antislavery capital that it then redistributed back into the field via lecturers and printed pamphlets. Though Lundy might have been a central figure in this process, he was instead traveling in these years on foot and by pony through Mexico, where he had only sporadic access to news of antislavery's progress. In these remarkable Mexican sojourns, Lundy absents himself from every major antislavery event of his lifetime and instead travels through a periphery as yet unintegrated into the emerging U.S. communications network, selling his personal possessions (suspenders, pants, shirts, and hats) in order to survive, sometimes being accused of being an "imposter" (a charge one can never disprove while in the middle of nowhere), and frequently being duped by confidence men who were far better at manipulating the frontier logic of Mexico's unsettled margins than Lundy was. Throughout these journeys, we see Lundy begging information from home from whatever provisional sources he can find, collecting random newspaper numbers that tell the ongoing story of U.S. antislavery reform at a vastly staggered pace from its actual unfolding in New York and Boston. At such moments, Lundy was navigating conditions that were at once both material and ideological—and absolutely unimaginable to the likes of William Lloyd Garrison, who from the outset of his career as an abolitionist rejected the spatial solution of external colonization as an answer to the problem of domestic slavery.

Lundy's travels on the Mexican frontier are the most materially and ideologically regressive (or historically backward-looking) features of his story. Traveling by foot through the wilderness, sleeping with his head on a knapsack and a gun at his side, Lundy could easily be misrecognized for some dime novel desperado—or a reactionary post-1830s colonizationist of the sort Amy Kaplan describes in *The Anarchy of Empire*.[22] But Lundy never identified his colonization projects either with the present (of the frontier) or the future (of U.S. expansion and development). Instead, he explicitly styles himself a figure of the imperial past. In a series of letters on the future of the Texas territory, for example, he signs himself "Columbus," revealing his fantasy that he might yet be a founding father. His papers in this period show him referring hopefully not to "a colony" or "the colony" that he hopes to begin in Mexico but to "my colony."[23] Sitting cross-legged in the middle of a lonely, unpopulated desert in 1835, out of reach of all newspaper coverage and personal correspondence, Lundy appears like a phantom from the early American Enlightenment, reading a fading copy of Junius by firelight rather than one of the more recognizable print objects of his day: a gift book, a reform tract, a story paper—or a copy of *The Liberator* (133).

Lundy's travels in search of an appropriate colonization site made him peripheral to the mainstream abolition movement of the 1830s, both ideologically and literally. Living at the edge of the organized (American) world, alongside both Mexican citizens and a motley array of New and Old World immigrants, Lundy fastidiously records his encounter with each random issue of a newspaper or pamphlet emanating from abolition's center. In one particularly ironic episode, he records reading a random number of a newspaper (loaned to him by a friend) that contains a now famous manifesto by James Birney, in which Birney declares his secession from the American Colonization Society and his conversion to the immediatism espoused by the AASS.[24] "It is a noble document," an enthusiastic Lundy remarks. "O, how the leaven is working!" (149). Always self-centered (in his body) rather than allowing a larger culture to organize him within the expanding structures of modernity, Lundy cannot see the fatally ironic problem that underlies his own response: the fact that Birney's conversion away from colonization actually boded poorly for Lundy's own colonization projects, which he was then in Mexico avidly pursuing. Lundy's investment in local activism led him to adopt, all through his career, just this kind of near-sightedness on issues large and small—from colonization to compensated emancipation. Lundy's journal finally concedes the epic failure of these years but rewrites the dislocations of travel as a penance of time. "After all my hardships and perils," he writes, "I am completely baffled" (128). "Conscious that I ought to be doing something else . . . I must submit . . . to *circumstansial* fate, and cherish the virtues of patience and perseverance" (146).

The word "circumstansial" points us to an important feature in Lundy's thinking, for like many gradualists, Lundy thought of slavery as an essentially place-based—or "circumstansial"—institution. In both his "itinerant" printing projects and his colonization schemes, Lundy was attempting to negotiate these place-based beliefs on the shifting ground of American expansion—which (with the advent of steam, rail, and the consumer networks that made them profitable) was less invested finally in the fixities of local geographical identity than in the possibilities of more abstracted regional and national identities. To be sure, early industrial capitalism favored mobility, but it was never the kind of quirky, itinerant, semi-evangelical mobility practiced by Lundy. Lundy saw himself as a Quaker prophet, bringing the good news of antislavery reform to communities that were themselves destined to remain fixed where they were. Antebellum culture, on the other hand, was invested not in itinerant travel but in the predictable and highly rationalized circulation of both people and things—from traveling salesmen and tourists to shoes, hats, books, and, of course, slaves. Lundy's career as a printer-peddler thus looked back to the place-based world he was born in and in doing so proved out of step with the more networked world in which he died.

Lundy's belief in the possibilities of colonization betrays his old-fashioned tendency to read race and culture in environmental (or place-based) terms—a position that owes more to Thomas Jefferson than to Andrew Jackson.[25] To this end, Lundy's many travel journals read like wry studies of regional manners that regress, at key moments, into climatological essentialism. New Englanders, for instance, are said to be as "cool" as their weather while Mexico is deemed "far better suited than Canada, for the residence of coloured emigrants" because "the frigid atmosphere of the extreme north" is assumed inappropriate to "persons . . . with a constitution inherited in some measure from the climate of Africa" (259). The belief that environment produces one's innate character was one that Jefferson, in his famous argument with Buffon, railed against (seeking to demonstrate that Native Americans—including white American colonists—were no less diminutive in stature than those of European "stock").[26] As Catherine Holland has pointed out, however, Jefferson applied his anticlimatological theories inconsistently.[27] He may have believed that the North American climate was as conducive to genius as that of Europe, but he also viewed the continent of Africa as climatologically primitive—an environmental atmosphere that had (scientifically speaking) produced a lag in civilized progress.

But Lundy was no garden-variety racist. His colonization schemes were for the most part based on a complex reading of the relationship among local geography, race, slavery, and racism. Though he sometimes essentializes identities in terms of climate, he also understands slavery to be a historically specific practice that has produced patterns of social behavior ("racism") that are deeply ingrained in the locations where they have taken hold. Lundy's reasons for preferring Haiti and Mexico as sites for colonization were not, in other words, merely motivated by climatological assumptions, nor were they ever rooted in a phobic fear of amalgamation or racial integration (as so many antebellum colonizationist programs were). Though Lundy believed Haiti and Mexico offered the best climate for African-American settlement, he also read these locations as culturally more appropriate because they were, in his view, less saturated with race-based prejudice than almost any U.S. location—including the North.[28] To this end, he persistently remarks upon the level of racial integration and acceptance he witnesses in his South American travels, frequently counterposing such examples to the current state of race relations in the United States. Speaking of Mexico's relatively low level of racism toward "coloured emigrants," he concludes: "This they cannot expect here [in the United States], for many generations to come, for the causes that produced the prejudices now existing, on the part of the white inhabitants, will have a tendency to prolong them, and to give them force and effect."[29]

Nevertheless, as complicated and unusual as Lundy's motives may have been, his colonization plans went the way of all such schemes. They failed miserably, and Lundy never fully recovered from those failures. On one hand, his Haitian settlers proved resistant to the terms of their new lives and many fled the island, preferring to return to the American North. Mexico, on the other hand, steadfastly refused to grant Lundy the land that he spent years both scouting and pleading for. Lundy finally gave up on his colony in 1836, but upon returning to antislavery's center, he promptly decided that he could not compete with the thriving culture industry that had emerged on the northeastern seaboard.[30] Finding himself in what he called "a crowd of antislavery workers," Lundy decided in 1838 to take the *Genius* west, where, one newspaper announcement suggested, "a wider field will be open for his untiring exertions."[31] "I must now look," he announced to his subscribers, "to the affairs of my own household." Lundy promised to revive the newspaper in Illinois but frankly acknowledged that "the particular place is not yet determined."[32]

Impoverished, itinerant, alone, and greatly fatigued, Lundy turned to the American Anti-Slavery Society for funding. Thus after decades of resistance, Lundy was finally interpellated into the field of more centralized cultural production projected by that organization. Before leaving for Illinois, he founded a more mainstream paper, made his first experiment in the mass production of an AASS-like pamphlet (numbering 23,000 copies), and after attending his first-ever AASS managerial workshop, was named in 1838 one of the society's managers for the state of Illinois.[33] Reinventing himself in Hennepin, Illinois, Lundy gathered his surviving (adult) children, bought a lot to build a home, and proposed marriage to a Pennsylvania woman he had met on his travels. Had he lived into the 1840s, he might well have become fully incorporated into the disembodied and yet domestically oriented techniques of the American Anti-Slavery Society—a home-owning, wife-loving, sentimentalized abolitionist, of the kind Stowe imagines in *Uncle Tom's Cabin.* Instead, Lundy died on August 22, 1839, and was instantaneously lionized by the eastern antislavery establishment as a heroic relic of a bygone era.

Archaic though Lundy's travels made him to the antislavery movement's ongoing progress, they are important to the argument of this book for several reasons. For one thing, they represent a material practice of antislavery that was inseparable from the material production of Lundy's major life-text (the *Genius*) and the antislavery program it advocated. For another, this program offers itself, for our purposes here, as an explicit countermodel to the AASS's more corporate, disembodied, mediated, and highly centralized model. Put simply, Lundy's *Life* and *Genius* reveal the stakes of antislavery's shift from a serial spatial imaginary expressed as temporal gradualism to one reorganized around immediatism and a sense of spatial simultaneity. Indeed, Lundy's career marks a crucial historical passage in U.S. cultural production. In his commitment to polycentric newspaper production, Lundy represents an attempt to inhabit, on the ground, the same kind of polycentrically conceived field of debate characteristic of the preindustrial relations of production (the political expression of which was found, once upon a time, in the Articles of Confederation). The AASS, on the other hand, must be understood as something more structurally akin to federalism itself—a vast superstructure that sought to draw its energies from people on the ground and then to control that energy by channeling it back through a fixed center. This structural similitude aside, however, federalism in the 1830s was not what it had been in 1787. Indeed, we might go so far as to say that federalism with canals, train tracks, steam presses, and telegraph wires is no longer truly "federalist" in the eighteenth-century sense of the word (in the sense, that is, of striking a balance between part and whole, local and national, state and federal). It is, instead, a theory that increasingly saturates and materially integrates the parts rather than merely balancing them at a distance. Federalism with train tracks is thus more properly called nationalism, and it is a nationalism that immediate abolition capitalized on—massively—throughout the 1830s.[34]

3. FROM PERIPHERY TO CENTER: THE RISE OF AN ABOLITIONIST CULTURE INDUSTRY, 1833–1840

If Benjamin Lundy's style of activism has a doppelganger in the history of antislavery practice, its precise geographical location would be the American Anti-Slavery Society's offices on Nassau Street in New York City, and its human content would be the young men who worked there between 1833 and 1840. These men included the likes of Lewis Tappan, Elizur Wright, R. G. Williams, Theodore Weld, Henry Stanton, Joshua Leavitt, and John Greenleaf Whittier—white, middle-class evangelical reformers who came to New York and took up the new historical position that Lundy, in his foot travels, continually refused: that of the white-collar antislavery office worker.[35] Arthur Tappan (an extraordinarily successful dry goods merchant) was the president and a chief financier of the AASS before the Panic of 1837 overturned his fortunes. But it was the Lewis Tappans, Welds, Leavitts, and Wrights who were living and theorizing, in their daily practice, the epic shift in material conditions on which immediate abolition was based.[36] The members of the AASS had, in these years, a two-pronged agenda: first, they sought to forge a new kind of (material) antislavery practice that relied upon a new conception of the relation between abolition's (semi-industrial) center and its (national) field of labor; and second, they developed a set of ideological arguments that underwrote this practice by insisting on the connections, rather than the disconnections, among the many local landscapes that slavery and antislavery inhabited. If gradualism's spatial imaginary was local and serial, in other words, then the American Anti-Slavery Society's was national and synchronic—positing the essential correspondence of every part of the union (rather than the disparateness of each part). To these AASS workers, the North, the South, and the West were one, and they proved this point, again and again, in print.

Lundy's *Genius* was only the second newspaper published in the United States devoted entirely to antislavery. It began with a mere six subscriptions, and though it grew far beyond those inauspicious origins, the long unfurling of its many volumes and issues was frequently interrupted by production lags and lapses. In the early years, these interruptions were caused by logistical obstacles that translated into low readership (Lundy's inability to collect subscription fees, problems sending papers through the mails, lack of paper). In later years, however, the *Genius* suffered not from too few antislavery consumers but from too many antislavery producers, as abolition emerged into a competitive culture industry in its own right. As early as 1833, for example, Lundy was devoting a full column in the *Genius* to a list of other antislavery newspapers then being published. While there had been none fifteen years before, he counted eighteen in 1833 in locations large and small, from urban centers like New York City, Boston, Washington, DC, and Philadelphia to the backwaters of Kentucky, North Carolina, Vermont, and Maine (*Life* 262).

The abolitionist investment in print culture was, of course, not new. The early Conventions for Promoting the Abolition of Slavery were devoted from their earliest meetings to a republican model of information diffusion, and the *Minutes* detail endless suggestions for how the antislavery message might be circulated in print. In 1794, for example, the convention met for the first time and immediately voted to take up a number of print-related projects. These included plans to disseminate printed copies of both the *Minutes* and an open circular letter to local societies; a plan to produce a series of publications based on the compilation of local materials (including an antislavery history, a compendium of laws, and a printed collection of local slavery "facts"); and statements encouraging the production of "periodical discourses" at the local level, including orations, petitions, and pamphlets—publications that will, the *Minutes* predicted, "extend" "liberality and humanity" "from the archives of your state to the practice of your citizens."[37]

The convention's faith in the power of "archives" is consistent with the Enlightenment's larger investment in the collection and diffusion of useful information. Nevertheless, in one degree or another, each of its publication measures failed. Later *Minutes* show a steady decline in the number of printed texts produced by the convention because too many copies were continually left on hand. The number of *Minutes* printed thus shrank from 1,500 in 1794 to 600 in 1800.[38] Likewise, the convention struggled with logistical problems coordinating and gathering information. The 1790s *Minutes* are packed, for example, with references to unanswered letters and unfulfilled requests. Local societies are repeatedly noted to have "not yet transmitted," "complied partially," "not yet sent," "sent no account," and "done nothing" about requests for local information. In fact, only two states in these years comply with the convention's instructions to "establish periodical discourses" (New York does so "partially," and Pennsylvania "faithfully"). One noncomplying state declares, on the other hand, that such discourses are "not deemed necessary in this state"; another claims it has "no information" on them; and eleven others "transmitted no information" at all.[39]

The most ambitious publication project proposed by the early convention was the production of an extensive history of antislavery reform, a goal that was discussed at every meeting between 1794 and 1812. Eighteen long years later, the (uncompleted) project came to an end when the historian died. The convention then did what Meredith McGill has taught us that book producers of every kind were doing in these years: it voted to import and reprint a British history of antislavery instead.[40] Having made this decision, the convention ordered copies of Thomas Clarkson's *History of the Rise, Progress, and Accomplishment of the Abolition of the African Slave-Trade* (1808) from London—a title that was destined to be the only full-length book it would ever distribute. Noting that "the want of correct information is often among the causes of the long continuance of abuses," the delegates hailed Clarkson for bringing "to light . . . a chain of enormities till then unsuspected by the mass."[41] The convention's importation of Clarkson's *History* suggests that gradual abolitionists were, in the second decade of the nineteenth century, beginning to think of slavery as a more coherent practice (explicitly described here as an interconnected "chain of enormities"). In keeping with its gradualist roots, however, the convention was always more sensitive to the temporal chain of events that constituted slavery than to its geographical circuitry—a fact registered in their ongoing interest in producing a history of slavery rather than, say, a set of maps tracking its movements.[42] This occlusion in their thinking was based on a material set of conditions that limited both the theoretical and practical horizon of their work. Indeed, their failure to collect, produce, and disseminate their own history strongly indicates that they were unable to master the basic "chain" of textual assemblage, distribution, and circulation throughout the territory their members inhabited.[43]

All these examples testify to the failure of print to link local antislavery societies in the early days of the gradualist movement, but they also raise questions about how effectively the gradualists were able to concentrate their efforts in one centralized organization or location. The gradualists were not just limited, in other words, by the absence of a network that might have connected their part-units into a more cohesive whole; they also failed to turn their meeting-space into a "center" from which their operations might emanate. They persistently thought of their activities, once again, in protracted temporal terms—occurring at regular calendrical intervals (either annually or bi-annually) rather than imagining the site of their meetings as a fixed staging ground for more nationally visible activities. Indeed, upon importing their first copy of Clarkson's *History* in 1812, the convention arranged to reprint extracts in local papers and then promptly mailed the book itself to Washington (where no delegates lived), in order to "deposit [it] in the National Library."[44] As late as 1826, they were voting to obtain tracts from London in order to disperse one copy each to the presidents of their local member societies. These activities show that the convention never thought to constitute itself as either a theoretical or a material "depository"—never, for example, founding an antislavery library (or reading room) and never keeping a fixed office. To the degree that these gradualists believed the United States had any center at all, they identified Washington, DC, and the national government as that center. Their only option, when it came to the possession of material objects (like books), was to deposit them in the National Library or to disperse them back through their member societies—the latter task proving exceedingly difficult, given that no one was centrally responsible for importing and distributing such texts.[45]

In terms of spatial theory and practice, the convention provides a stark counterpoint to the American Anti-Slavery Society of the 1830s. The convention's failure to produce itself as a geographical center goes hand in hand with the serial spatial imaginary embraced by gradualism more generally. Rather than allowing the convention site to act as a center for its member societies, each one of those societies was seen as its own center—a model based in the polycentric spatial relations of early American culture. In contrast, the AASS staged its operations from the high pinnacle of a raised center—New York City—a material location from which it sought to spread its doctrines throughout the union. New York's special geographical position vis-à-vis reform movements and mass tract distribution was evident as early as the 1820s, when the American Tract Society argued for New York's destiny as the new national "centre":

> The city of New-York, eminently distinguished by its natural and local advantages, its accumulating population and its increasing commercial prosperity and influence, seems destined, in the wisdom of Providence, to become the centre of these extended operations. . . . Merchants assemble here, and opportunities are constantly presented for sending Tracts, at a very small expense, and very frequently no expense at all, to the remotest part of the land.[46]

From this fortuitous staging ground, the AASS planned its own "extended operations" just eight years later.[47] Unlike previous "national" antislavery organizations, the AASS imagined itself from the start not as a recurring calendrical event but (like the Tract Society) a material entity with a clear and strategic location in geographical space. To this end, the AASS offices were housed on Nassau Street, where the managerial coordination between the National Society and its auxiliary member societies created a new kind of antislavery work and a new kind of antislavery worker. As Theodore Weld noted, this new work consisted largely of the clerklike labor of letter writing. Weld wrote to the Grimkés that his colleague Henry Stanton "writes perhaps forty letters a day." Such productivity thrilled Weld: "The labor he has performed this summer has been prodigiously great. He has sent off *personally* thousands of circulars and petitions and written many hundreds of letters, besides doing a world of other business. All this has been done in great haste with no leisure for details, subject to calls at every moment, and the office filled with people from morning till night."[48] Workers like Stanton and Weld pose a sharp contrast to gradualism's more relaxed pace. And quite unlike Benjamin Lundy (who spent his life circumventing and circumnavigating a fixed location from which to produce his newspaper), these new immediate abolitionists were exceptionally "fixed" (or reliable) characters—men who could be counted on, in the Executive Committee's estimation, and who were able to use the singularity of their position in New York City to direct, from afar, the circulation of antislavery doctrine and goods through various parts of the union. If Lundy went nowhere by going everywhere, New York bureaucrats like Stanton and (the later) Weld went everywhere by going nowhere.

The field of circulation thus imagined has been called, by Robert Fanuzzi, "abolition's public sphere," and the massive administrative records of the American Anti-Slavery Society prove that its activities do indeed deserve that title. The model of publicity pursued by the AASS cannot, however, rightly be termed a Habermasian public sphere, in the sense that it was never merely an ideal or theoretical set of communicative relations but was instead an organizational theory based on what we might call an "actually existing" network of exchange.[49] The AASS, in other words, imagined a circulatory project for itself—a message that it wanted to disseminate and proliferate across the nation to an increasingly reachable American public—but it achieved that end through the circulation of actual material objects and persons. These included traveling antislavery agents, personal letters, pamphlets, tracts, periodicals, and petitions. Many of these goods were, furthermore, centrally produced in New York and then disseminated back through a grassroots structure that encouraged the founding of both "local" and "state" auxiliaries. The exponential growth of these auxiliaries testifies to the success of the model: in the *Report* for its first Annual Meeting in 1834, the AASS Executive Committee noted sixty antislavery societies throughout the United States. By 1839 (a year before the AASS was to dissolve into warring factions), there were an impressive 1,650.[50]

In planning its various programs and policies, the AASS adopted a tight-handed, top-down mode of managing these local auxiliaries. Indeed, in its earliest years, the New York office sought to direct even the most local of activities in these auxiliaries, going so far as to print blank petition forms in New York on high-speed presses and then disseminating them in massive bundles to local societies, where they were then used to collect local signatures.[51] But the New York office did not just produce objects in these years. It also produced antislavery knowledge, which it circulated via traveling agents and lecturers—agents whose movements were extensively coordinated by a group called the "Agency Committee." Weld's letters make it clear that AASS agents were carefully trained by the New York office—sometimes in New York and sometimes at regional (sub-) centers, where more experienced agents traveled to offer seminars in antislavery reform to newer converts.[52] These newly trained agents, in turn, took this knowledge home with them and trained local societies on the techniques of mass resistance (particularly on the proper use of petitions and on fundraising strategies, such as cent-a-week societies). In this way, the AASS filtered its urban-generated policies down to the dispersed masses, and it did so in a way that sought to contain and control the labor of the bodies doing this work on the ground.

This last point is worth pausing over, for many scholars have noted the ways that the abolitionist movement tried to construct fugitive slave lecturers as black bodies newly arrived from the South in the 1840s.[53] But before immediate abolition turned to black lecturers like Frederick Douglass and William Wells Brown, it relied on the bodily movements of white agents like Weld, Marius Robinson, and Amos Dresser. The roles assigned to these agents were never delimited, of course, in the same ways or by the same racist logics that mark the roles later assigned to black lecturers. But the AASS did seek to exert control over the daily movements of these white agents, who were a crucial part of the society's cross-regional coordinations. Indeed, the way these agents were used was counterintuitive and novel. Rather than allowing them to move through their home constituencies (thus converting people in their own states), the main office strategized the assignments of all local agents, moving them from site to site at will and thus making them true itinerants in the service of reform. The dispersed travels of these men resemble Benjamin Lundy's, but with one crucial difference: Lundy was always the master of his own locomotion, while these traveling lecturers were exactly what the AASS called them—"agents" whose movements were directed from elsewhere. As Weld described it,

> [i]t is made the duty of the agency committee by the bye laws to assign agents to their fields of labor according to their *various adaptations*. Whatever makes it their duty to assign an agent to *any* field of labor makes it their duty to assign him to *that* field where he will do the *most* good. This committee are constantly looking over the whole field and assigning the agents different fields, as the ever varying exigencies of the cause demand, as generals dispatch bodies [of] troops to different points as the battle waxes or wanes, and *just such* troops as will do the thing *best*. Nothing is more common than to shift the *locality* of agents.[54]

Weld offers us insight here into the managerial logic that drove the AASS in these years. The division of labor he describes echoes the many divisions of labor that were permeating industrial firms throughout New York City in the 1830s (including the Tappans' multistoried dry goods firm on Pearl Street and the Harpers' expanding book factory on nearby Franklin Square). In both cases, every "working" man is assigned a task according to his abilities, while a more elite group of managers does the work of discerning who belongs where. AASS agents were thus consigned to inhabit the local in their "bodies" (they are, in Weld's analogy, like "soldiers") while the "agency committee" (the "general") takes up what *The Federalist* would call the more "comprehensive view," "looking over the whole field" from its centralized perch in the national office. In this way the AASS agents served as crucial mediators, controlled from the top, who helped to transmit knowledge and information between auxiliaries (which formed the "base" of the antislavery edifice) and New York City—which served as the singular location from which both ideology (in the form of antislavery policy) and material texts emanated.

The Federalist's "comprehensive view" is an especially apt analogy, for the AASS resembles the federal state of 1787 in several ways. The AASS was, after all, positing itself as a new center for an otherwise disorganized reform movement—just as federalism had styled itself, in 1787, as a solution to the "weak" structure of the centerless Confederation.[55] Federalism's "metrobuilding" project had two components: the creation of a material center (or capital) and the peopling of that capital with managerial "federalists"—men of "information" and "talent" who were to form the elite core of the new nation. In positing such a center, the Constitution imagined a new set of relations between parts and whole, center and periphery—just as the AASS was doing in the 1830s. *The Federalist* (among other late-eighteenth-century texts) repeatedly attempts to find a language to describe this new set of relations and its dynamic, circulatory potential. In one passage, for example, Publius asks how the United States might "turn the tide of State influence into the channels of the national government, instead of making fœderal influence flow in an opposite and adverse current" (228). In another, he picks up the same trope, arguing that "the streams of national power ought to flow immediately" from the people, who are the "original fountain of all legitimate authority" (146). It is little wonder that Publius would imagine the circulation of power as the work of natural waterways, for in 1787, rivers and streams were the primary mode of transport available to emerging national culture. The metaphor is nevertheless telling for the model of circulation it posits among the federal state, the local state, and the individual citizen. Not only does Publius describe power here as a mobile, multidirectional, and ongoing exchange that occurs between distinct sites. He also reminds us that federalism was always, in its original conception, a theory for the production of power and wealth that sought (theoretically) to link the federal state directly to "the people," living in their local capacity, and it did so by using the old unit of confederal collectivity (the local state) as the infrastructural medium through which to make this relationship work.

The AASS worked on a similar structural principle. Like federalism, the AASS was a multitiered structure, operating simultaneously on a number of different scales (local, state, and national). In Hamiltonian fashion, the New York office sought to produce itself as the center of a national field of circulatory exchange that might reach directly to individuals living in the local, and it used state auxiliaries as the "medium" through which to achieve this goal. As with federalism, furthermore, the circulatory framework imagined by the AASS was never a one-way street. The New York office circulated ideas and goods through its auxiliaries, but it also "channeled" back to itself the energy of individual members living on the ground in order to sustain itself. It did this—as Weld's uncanny metaphor of the "soldier" suggests—in terms that strongly resemble the workings of the federal state. Just as the federal government, for instance, collects taxes from individuals living within its domain, so the AASS used its network to collect dues, donations, and other monies from individuals living far and wide; at the same time, the AASS also capitalized (as any state framework does) on the labor of local populations—who, in this case, formed their own societies, wrote letters to their congressmen, and above all circulated petition after petition, submitting their pleas not just at the local level but in coordinated campaigns at the local, state, and national levels.[56] The AASS was not, of course, always successful in its attempts to "channel" the power and energy that "flowed" from its auxiliaries (indeed, as I will discuss further on, it eventually succumbed to the forces of localism at the end of the 1830s). Nevertheless, the society did emerge, for a time, through the use of these techniques, as a legible force on the national scene.[57]

The structural analogy between corporate antislavery and federalism is a useful one, but it would be a mistake to think that the AASS was merely looking back, in these years, to the past (as Benjamin Lundy so frequently did). Indeed, if anything, the organizational logic of the AASS was explicitly forward-looking, participating from an early date in the larger project of market revolution that federalism was, we might argue, installed to make possible. The ongoing process of industrialization was part of this market revolution, and as such, it brought spaces near and far into closer communication and contact in these years—a fulfillment, of sorts, of the more perfect union imagined in 1787. This process also, however, necessarily rearranged the relations between spaces in ways the founders could not have predicted. For one thing, urban areas became denser than ever before, so that cities like Boston, Baltimore, Cincinnati, and New York all emerged to play the role of new and multiple metropoles to the nation's more disparate and far-flung peripheries. This process was at once unifying and fragmenting, for the ability to enfold the nation within itself, within its ever-integrating conception of itself as a vast market of producers and consumers, created a division of labor not just on the producer side but on the consumer side as well. As industrialization centralized production, in other words, it also sought to disperse consumption—both across space and within individual households, whose members were hailed to self-differentiate in any number of ways (as juvenile, male, female, American, British, black, white, abolitionist, southern, and so on).[58]

The AASS capitalized on both these processes. Along with the American Tract Society (to whom it owed many of its publishing techniques), the AASS was one of the first truly centralized publishers of mass-market book-objects in the United States, and it marketed its books to a geographically dispersed and demographically splintered group that it explicitly differentiated along age and gender lines (promoting distinct publications for "young men," "ladies," and "children").[59] In doing so, the AASS publications office was self-consciously setting itself up as a rival to the existing culture industry—a rival whose goal, however, was to compete not in profit margin but in piety. The *Annual Report* from 1837 shows that the Executive Committee discussed the ideological shortcomings of the existing culture industry at length. The *Report* notes, for example, that the New York firm of Harper and Brothers, after receiving complaints about some "abolitionist" subject matter in one of their novels, had sent a letter to the *Charleston Mercury* "excusing themselves on the ground that they were not able to read every book they published and did not suspect anything improper." In this and similar episodes, the Harpers showed themselves willing to expurgate "true abolition stuff" (lopping off whatever offended) because it was in their "interest" to do so. The *Report* diagnoses this behavior as sheer servility:

> What trembling slave ever made greater haste to obey the tyrant in whom was vested the ownership of both his soul and body? In one short month the fiat of expurgation travels from Charleston to New-

York, the Harpers settle it with their consciences to expunge, mutilate, and falsify the work of a foreign author, and are prepared to say, that they have printed a new edition "*in which the offensive matter has been omitted.*" Here, for the sake of southern custom, is perpetrated a literary forgery, or we should rather say murder, which in a free country . . . should have brought on these publishers everlasting disgrace—yet they are "honorable men"—for they have stooped no lower than the mercantile community in which they move![60]

The Executive Committee's outrage at the crime of "literary forgery" is rather disingenuous given the AASS's own editorial policies, which were every bit as invested in the culture of editing and reprinting as the Harpers' were. The *Report*'s description, however, of how the practice of "expurgation" "travels" north goes to the heart of their understanding of how a culture circulates itself through the nation's print networks. The "mutilation" of this novel is posited, in other words, as just one of the many ways that slavery has traveled to New York and infected northern customs and manners. The example suggests that textual circulation does not always work the way we think it does, for rather than exporting northern culture (in the form of New York cultural production) into and throughout the South, the South manages in this instance to channel its customs and manners back through the conduits of exchange in which the books were originally delivered to them. This makes a "slave" of the book industry and a "tyrant" of the South. But it also prompted the AASS to turn itself into a publisher in its own right—one that might, as *The Federalist* says, "turn the tide" of southern influence back against itself in order to circulate antislavery sentiment throughout an increasingly connected union.

4. FROM SERIALITY TO SAMENESS

Like the early gradualists, the immediate abolitionists who peopled the AASS believed that slavery benefited from "the want of correct information" about its practices. The AASS was, however, far more successful in its print campaigns than the gradualists had been. Indeed, the befuddled *Minutes* of the early conventions—with their unwritten history and uncollected information—pose an instructive contrast to the AASS's hyper

print productivity in the mid-1830s. Even as late as 1829, the gradualists were producing relatively modest print runs (three thousand copies, for instance, of an annual address) and yet were unable to distribute
them anywhere but in adjacent states. Six years later, the American Anti-
Slavery Society would be publishing not just annual items but four different periodical publications as well, and they would issue them not in the
hundreds or thousands but in the hundreds of thousands. Indeed, the
earliest AASS *Annual Reports* invoke the press as "one of the most powerful engines of reform."[61] They sometimes express frustration with the difficulties that attend textual circulation, but they also offer "proof" after
"proof" that antislavery authors can produce steady sellers, citing Mrs.
Child's "Oasis" and "Appeal," Mr. Phelps' "Lecture," "compositions by
Whittier," and Jay's "Inquiry into Colonization and Antislavery."[62] Their
periodical publications were intended to take part in this trend, even if
the AASS was still mastering the art of distribution. The 1834 report, for
instance, notes that the AASS house organ—the *American Anti-Slavery
Reporter*—has been issued five times as a monthly sheet, with five thousand copies printed each time, "two to three thousand" of which were
"gratuitously distributed" while the "remainder are still on hand."[63]

Devoted from the start to the mass production of printed goods, the
AASS proselytized its members to join in the work of circulating their
tracts, pamphlets, and periodicals. As titles accumulated on the AASS
book list over the 1830s, many were emblazoned in the top right-hand
corner with the Painite mantra "Read and circulate"—a directive invari-
ably followed by the number of copies in circulation. Year after year, the
AASS actively theorized ways to gain a larger audience, urging "all to do
something" to get their imprints "into extensive circulation."[64] Even juvenile publications such *The Slave's Friend* instructed their young readers
on how to spread the printed word. A single issue, for instance, includes
a story titled "The Little Tract Distributor" (urging children to buy copies
of *The Slave's Friend* for their relatives and acquaintances), another titled
"The Collection Box" (urging children to save their pennies for new copies of the magazine), another titled "The Three Little Abolitionists" (depicting three children having a "reading party" with a "new book from
New York"), and, of course, numerous advertisements for other (New
York) imprints.[65]

In 1794, the first national antislavery convention had proclaimed the
limited circumference of its spatial imaginary by telling its members that

"liberality and humanity will extend from the archives of your state to the practice of your citizens."[66] These simple examples from *The Slave's Friend* suggest how much more expansive the AASS was in its conception of the relation between an archive and a people. Though it was not always successful, the AASS sought to "extend" its archive of printed matter into every nook of the extended republic, addressing a densely differentiated field of readers (children, ladies, gentlemen, slaveholders, and freemen) on a national scale. This extension of abolitionist print culture was intimately connected to the organization's larger nationalist message, which sought to convince readers that they were connected not just in a "great chain" of cross-regional readership, but in that "great chain of enormities" called chattel slavery.

The dense relations emerging among states are registered in AASS publications in a variety of prosaic and practical ways. The society's weekly newspaper, *The Emancipator*, used conventional newspaper layouts to emphasize a sense of connectedness between parts of the union, organizing its columns by region, including a distinct section of the paper devoted to "NEWS FROM THE SOUTH." But while similar techniques saturated every kind of periodical culture in these years (mainstream and abolitionist alike), they were never merely incidental to the AASS. On the contrary, they were knowingly annexed to an ideological agenda that emphasized national communication and connectivity as the structural apparatus through which local populations might be made to feel personally responsible for the actions of more remote ones. To this end, no meeting of the Anti-Slavery Society passed without explicitly describing the material and ideological relations connecting every part of the union. In the first Annual Meeting, for example, news was submitted about antislavery efforts in sites as diverse as Kentucky, Maine, and Georgia. Whereas in earlier years, such sites would have been viewed as disparate and disjunct entities, the AASS steadfastly presents them as unified and singular—a swath of resistance whose cries can be heard "from Louisiana to Maine." Indeed, the entire globe is posited as part of the singular chain of slavery, as one member rises to declare that

> he knew that the southern country was *not* ignorant of what was said and done in other sections of the country and in distant lands. When the subject of West India Emancipation was under discussion in Parliament, a Georgia planter was heard to say: "Let these resolutions be carried into effect in the West Indies, and in six months I shall see the

effect on my slaves." . . . Mr. Chairman! thousands of our fellow-citizens of the south will go to bed tonight with their loaded pistols under their pillows, and their muskets over the mantel piece.[67]

In such moments, the *Reports* register a new sense of spatial connection and temporal simultaneity across distant spaces. Not only are different parts of the union aware of each other (and the rest of the world); slaveholders in Georgia are also explicitly invoked as sharing the same present-tense timeframe as the abolitionists sitting in the meeting in New York ("Mr. Chairman! thousands of our fellow-citizens of the south will go to bed tonight with their loaded pistols under their pillows").

In 1835, James Birney rose in a similar meeting to make the same point in a different way, reminding everyone in the room about "the constitutional provisions which bind you to your Southern neighbors" before concluding decisively that "you are [all] participants in Southern slavery."[68] Birney called on his listeners to take responsibility for remote practices, couching his appeal in a spatial logic that emphasized the continuous linkage of regional publics across both time and space:

> But it will be said, "Slavery, to be sure, is very bad; but it is not what it used to be; liberal principles are advancing; the slaves may be happy, and so may their masters; they may go happily and lovingly through this world, and all land in heaven together." Yes: all this is said continually. Go to Kentucky, and they will tell you, "Oh slavery is not here in its severe aspect; you must go farther south to see that." Well: you go farther south; you come into Alabama; and they tell you, "It is not here that you will find the evils of slavery; you must go into Mississippi"; and in Mississippi, "You must go upon the sugar plantations," and on the sugar plantations they directed you, till lately, to the British West [Indies]! It is all a delusion. Slavery is substantially the same every where.[69]

Birney attacks the temporal and spatial logics not just of proslavery apologias but of gradualism as well. Temporally, gradualism had long deferred action by insisting that slavery "is not what it used to be" and that "liberal principles are advancing." Birney suggests that this temporal deferral was intimately linked to a sense of spatial deferral, as the buck of slavery's "evils" is passed in his speech from Kentucky to Alabama to Mississippi—all the way to the British West Indies. Against the "delusion" of geographic difference, Birney posits a simple maxim: "Slavery is substantially the same everywhere," upending the serial claims of both gradual-ism and proslavery with a simple assertion of sameness and simultaneity.[70]

Birney's argument here is part of the AASS's larger rethinking in these years of the relation of each one of the union's parts to the next. In do-ing this intellectual work, however, the AASS was also thinking about the historical relations between the existing center and periphery—in other words, the relation of the federal capital to the local worlds it represents. The serial spatial logic that underwrote gradualism was, after all, the same one that the federal union had relied upon to ensure its production at the moment of founding. As Birney noted in this meeting, however, U.S. nation-spaces were no longer as disarticulated from one another in 1835 as they had been in 1787—nor did any part of the union need to conceive of itself as hopelessly disarticulated from the federal capital:

> Look at the state of things in the District of Columbia. Are you not as much participants in the slavery existing there, as the people of Ken-tucky are in Kentucky? The people of Kentucky elect legislators who pass laws confirming slavery in that State; and you elect legislators who confirm the continuance of slavery in the District of Columbia. Where is the difference? Slavery exists by your permission; this never could have been but by the aid of Northern votes.[71]

Birney clearly recognizes the model of virtual representation upon which the District of Columbia is based. Unlike other territories in the union (which are "actually" represented by members of Congress they vote into office), the District is an entirely federalized space, recognizing no local constituency and so making the entire nation the virtual constituency of the District's "ten Miles square."[72] The idea that the District of Columbia has no local constituency of its own is, of course, a federal fiction (con-tinually resisted and resented in the contemporary District, which has produced a set of license plates emblazoned with the wry slogan, "The District of Columbia: Taxation Without Representation"). Birney, how-ever, embraces the model of a virtual, or national, constituency because it supports the case he wants to make for what we might call national consolidation—his belief, that is, that every American is "a participant" in the national crime of slavery. In this way, Birney shakes up the exist-ing balance between the federal and the local, hailing "the people" on the ground to take up their role as constituents and make their federal repre-sentatives act as they would.

Birney embraces here a more actualized brand of virtual representation than had ever been theorized before—a model based on a massive virtual constituency that nevertheless makes its presence known to the capital via modern lobbying techniques such as the mass petition drive. In doing so, he calls into question Robert Fanuzzi's central thesis: the idea that abolition's public sphere was an essentially nostalgic one, establishing "a connection with a historically absent public"—namely, the Revolutionary people of 1776—over and against a connection with the historically present American people then inhabiting the national map.[73] While such a model may aptly describe Garrison's more (geographically) circumscribed work in the *Liberator*, it does not adequately describe the scene of national antislavery as it unfolded in New York City and in AASS publications and practices. To be sure, abolitionists throughout the United States—from New England to New York and from Lundy to Lewis Tappan—were sensitive to the temporal rupture that history had produced in the ongoing project of U.S. nationalism. Slavery was often described, for example, as a sin that had been "entailed" on present generations from previous ones. But the AASS was interested in more than just representing itself "diachronically, or in relation to time"; it was also explicitly devoted to the project that Fanuzzi denies: the "synchronic" representation of the nation "as a community sharing the same space" (xxi). To execute that project, furthermore, the AASS had to embrace not the bygone models of Revolutionary (highly localist, or actual) representation, but a more virtual, or federalist, mode of representation—one that emphasized the disembodied, the abstract, the mediated, and above all, a highly centralized model of production. In producing a new culture industry at the emerging industrial center of New York City, in other words, the AASS offered itself as a new metropolitan entity—a savvy competitor, in both ideological and material production, to that which emanated from Washington, DC, which it hailed as "the slave market of America" in a series of popular prints and pamphlets, all designed to unpack the faux disintegration of national geography and federal representation.[74]

In this way, the AASS developed a new way of thinking about the relation of new (industrial) centers and the old (political) center to the nation at large. We might say that politically, the AASS wanted to collapse the distance between Washington, DC, and the local worlds it was said to represent federally. It did this, in part, by asking its local auxiliaries to perform their relation to the capital in a series of highly visible national petition campaigns that insisted on the material connectedness of the federal representative to every one of the American citizens that he virtually represented in his governance of the District. Culturally, however, the society continued to embrace the differential spatial development dividing New York from other more peripheral (or "auxiliary") locations throughout the union. The AASS managed, in this way, to insist on a more direct relation between political representatives and their constituents even as it upheld its own privilege as the virtual mediator of abolition's cultural message to the masses who consumed it. In criticizing the existing political center and replacing it with a new message and a new center, the AASS was not merely making use of an old federal model. It was actually using that old model against itself, exploiting the increasingly material relations of regional parts to national whole in order to undermine the historical ways that those relations had long been understood. In doing so, the AASS was developing a set of practices that would finally prove destructive to its own survival, for in eroding a sense of remoteness between political center and periphery, it was giving its auxiliaries the tools to resist New York as a cultural center as well.

5. A MOB OF READERS: OF SIMULTANEITY AND SECTIONALISM

In making its antislavery appeal to the American public, the AASS experimented with a variety of publicity techniques, from agents to tracts to petitions. In the mid-1830s, however, print culture emerged for a time as the preferred apparatus through which to reach distant audiences.[75] In using print in this way, the society actually performed its nationalist message, displaying, in the very circulation of its text-objects, an increasing connectedness among parts of the union. I want to end this chapter by focusing on what I take to be the two most remarkable episodes in the AASS's 1830s print campaign: the infamous mass mailing of 1835, when hundreds of thousands of periodicals were flooded through every region of the nation, and the material assemblage and publication of Theodore Weld's iconic 1839 pamphlet, *American Slavery as It Is*. The first of these is, as Richard John has noted, the most notable example of how the AASS used printed artifacts to create a disorienting and destabilizing sense of simultaneity across space; the second suggests the more localizing (or "domestic") logic the AASS was producing at its center, for readers and authors alike.[76] Both demonstrate a central thesis of this book: in short, that the more connected regions appeared to be (in print), the more regionalized (rather than nationalized) their identities became. Contrary to unionist truisms that link the spread of print culture to a more nationalist consciousness, the print campaigns of the 1830s cultivated a sense of material simultaneity across national space that, paradoxically, produced an enhanced sense of regional difference. A growing sense of simultaneity, in other words, produced not nationalism but an ever more entrenched sectionalism—an argument among white men of different regions that was, as we shall see, ironically expressed through the phobic language of racism at the most local levels.

While the 1835 campaign was funded primarily through the largesse of Arthur Tappan, it was organized through the administrative energies of his brother Lewis, who also helped run his brother's dry goods company.[77] The management skills that made Tappan good for the family business transferred seamlessly to his antislavery work. As his biographer Bertram Wyatt-Brown notes, Tappan was an arch-administrator who oversaw the AASS's publishing operations for seven years. Though he was never the attributed author or editor of anything in particular, Tappan "was intimately connected with the publication of a dozen newspapers and periodicals in the course of his life, and he contributed articles to at least three times that many both in the United States and abroad."[78] At the same time, Tappan was responsible for the mundane work of managing the AASS office, paying bills, fundraising—and masterminding the 1835 pamphlet campaign. The most managerially competent administrator the AASS ever had, Tappan had been theorizing the practice of tract dissemination from the minute he arrived in New York City in 1828. His journals frequently remark on the considerable work he did to personally spread the printed word, both as an active member of the early American Tract Society and later for the AASS. Random journal entries find Tappan personally handing out reform tracts on street corners after work, carrying bundles of papers to the docks for shipment, proofing news sheets at his printers' office at midnight, and getting articles "inserted" into local (nonabolitionist) papers whenever he could.[79] But the 1835 campaign entailed a new scale of dissemination. Its goal was less the Lundy-like spreading of actual printed texts with one's own body (on street corners and in dock yards) than the maestro-like manipulation of distant networks of exchange.

The story of the mailing is well known in American historiography. Early in 1835, Tappan presented the Executive Committee with a plan to cut back on the use of traveling agents and to invest capital instead in cheaper steam press printing and new shipping technologies.[80] The administrative *Report* for 1836 include a report from the publications office that proudly looks back on the success of the experiment, noting that the number of imprints for 1835 was "*nine* times as great as those of last year, at only about *five* times the expense."[81] But it was not just the production of these pamphlets that was technologically novel; their dissemination was unusual as well. Unlike previous mailings, the 1835 campaign directed hundreds of thousands of unsolicited antislavery periodicals to addressees all over the union—including twenty thousand prominent southerners whose names and residences were collected from a different periodical source: the city directories and trade annuals that were becoming the yellow pages of cross-regional commerce. As Richard John writes, "during the height of the mass mailing in the summer of 1835, the abolitionists sent into the slaveholding states no fewer than 175,000 separate pieces, or roughly half the total number of items that the entire New York City periodical press ordinarily sent through the mail in a comparable period of time" and one that was "roughly equivalent to the entire output of the periodical press of the South" at that time.[82]

The pamphlets arrived in multiple regions at roughly the same time and thus effected a sense of surreal simultaneity across space as mobs in multiple locations appeared to respond in unison to Tappan's antislavery appeal. Benedict Anderson has made simultaneity a fabled term in nationalism studies, but the historical varieties of simultaneity—its ragged emergence across time in this or that form—are less remarked. The 1835 mass mailing is one particularly evocative episode in this long, unfolding history (as, in the next chapter, *Uncle Tom's Cabin* and the Fugitive Slave Law will also be). Indeed, the mailing eloquently testifies to the ways that the foundational buffers of national time and space were being tested and eroded by technologies designed to network and compress the nation into a more singular, interconnected unit. It is tempting to try to contain, locate, and narrate this scene of simultaneous collapse in one or another moment or to trace it to one technology or institution. Wolfgang Schivelbusch, for example, has focused on how railways produce a sense of intimate temporal connection across space. With the rise of locomotives, he argues, "regions lose their temporal identity in an entirely concrete sense: the railroads deprive them of their local time" as the train schedule standardizes the clocks of every station stop it incorporates.[83] Richard John, on the other hand, nominates the post office as the primary agent of such transspatial imaginings, arguing that the imagined community was both made possible and then imperiled by the federal government's use of rail and water routes to speed mail delivery. But in fact, the erosion of local boundaries was a polycultural process, arriving in many forms and contexts and unfolding ceaselessly across the whole arc of nation-building time I have been describing here. The AASS mass mailing (along with railways, postal service, the expansion of telegraph lines, increased rates of tourism, and the like) was a small but important moment in this larger cultural process.

In fact, the AASS mailing resembles numerous other experiments in mass culture that were saturating the public sphere in these years. On February 26, 1836, Tappan's journal notes his participation in one such experiment: "This day," he notes, "simultaneous Temperance meetings are to be held throughout the civilized world."[84] Likewise, in 1844, the *New-York Tribune* reported (in an article reflexively titled "NEWS-PAPER REPORTING") that the *New York Sun* had stunned participants of a local banquet by printing off, before the end of their dinner, a copy of a newspaper recounting the speeches that had been made at the start of the banquet. The papers were distributed "gratuitously," chic testimonials to the *Sun's* capacity to bring up-to-the-minute news to readers.[85] Both events are signposts to the time-space compressions of these decades. They demonstrate the ways in which the world was becoming more temporally and spatially commensurate with itself, with dispersed populations feeling not just connected by a mass affect that was nevertheless grounded in a secure local identity (which is how early American nationalism worked), but a more connected world in which temporal and spatial divides were being managed and collapsed in order to engineer mass experiences with others (elsewhere). The AASS mass mailing operated on a similar principle, for it too was designed to produce a phenomenological sensation, forcing a sense of slavery as a national problem by overtly reaching out to a more national audience. And in this sense, the campaign did not seek to produce a major text so much as to engineer the mailing into a major textual *event*.

The southern response to the 1835 mailing was immediate, unified, and (given the printedness of the offending objects) strangely embodied. Towns in Louisiana and Alabama placed large cash bounties on the head of Arthur Tappan while grand juries in Alabama and Virginia indicted various officers of the society on sedition charges, actively seeking their extradition. In Charleston, a mob broke into the post office and destroyed sacks full of AASS periodicals while effigies of Tappan and Garrison burned nearby. In Nashville, a young bookseller and erstwhile antislavery lecturer named Amos Dresser was publicly whipped for having some AASS publications in his private possession. And in Washington, DC, a doctor was jailed when he went to the post office to pick up some botanical samples that were wrapped, unfortunately for him, in antislavery newspapers.[86]

The irony of the 1835 campaign is that print culture became, in its wake, the special scapegoat of the decade. As historians like Richard John, Henry Mayer, and John Nerone have documented, the mailing initiated a national debate in both abolitionist and nonabolitionist papers about the right to free speech and the free circulation of printed speech. In a letter from the Executive Committee, the AASS declared its belief that "slavery cannot stand, unless it be on the ruins of the free press."[87] As if in reverse fulfillment of this prophecy, presses throughout the union were wrecked through the rest of the decade as small-town printers were mobbed and their printing offices dismantled.[88] In October 1835, a nonabolitionist press in Utica, New York, was destroyed by a mob simply because its editor had suggested that abolitionist organizing should be protected as a form of freedom of speech.[89] In July of the following year, a Cincinnati mob entered the office of the antislavery paper *The Philanthropist*, destroyed every copy they could locate in the office, and then removed numerous parts of the press, making it unworkable. The next day, the group took out an ad in another local paper announcing that "the destruction of their Press" was only a "warning" and that if the abolitionists attempted "to re-establish their press, it will be viewed as an act of defiance to an already outraged community." When the editor ordered new parts for the dismantled press, the mob reconvened as promised, this time destroying the press completely, scattering its type in the streets, dismantling the printing office, and even searching the printer's house for paper and ink.[90] But by far the most notorious act of violence was the lynching of the Reverend Elijah Lovejoy in Alton, Illinois. Lovejoy received—and had dismantled by mobs—four different presses before he was murdered there in August 1837. As he lay dead in the street, the last of these mobs took the fourth press into the street and began destroying it the old-fashioned way—with hammer and hand. "It was done,"

one witness remembered, "in a quiet sort of way. . . . They seemed happy while engaged in breaking it in pieces."[91]

In 1836, Abraham Lincoln called such mobbings "the every-day news of the times," but in fact newspapers did not just report on mobbings; they also helped create them.[92] In the end, it was not just the AASS (or more poorly capitalized newspapers like *The Liberator*) that spread the word of abolitionist organizing: it was the highly capitalized world of the mainstream commercial penny press. Leonard Richards has shown that urban organs like the New York *Courier* and *Herald* sent correspondents to antislavery meetings in order to stoke disturbances, reporting sensationally on both urban and rural scenes of dissent, including mobbings, lynchings, and book burnings. In New York City, mainstream newspapers routinely publicized the locations of antislavery meetings and then called forth dissenters to protest at them. Thus in 1833, James Watson Webb, the editor of New York's *Courier and Enquirer*, called for local men to disrupt the first meeting of the New York City Abolition Society while at the same time handbills were disseminated calling for "Southerners" to assemble to, ironically, "manifest the *true* feelings of the State on this subject."[93]

In the South, of course, abolitionist pamphlets were always imported at a distance from their production. For this reason, it was not printers or their presses that were destroyed in southern mob actions but tracts themselves that were burned as a new states' rights argument emerged explicitly targeting the republican project of information diffusion. In a widely reprinted speech calling for the suppression of all abolitionist periodicals, Senator John Tyler of Virginia stood before his local constituency with a copy of the *Anti-Slavery Record* in his hand, denouncing abolition as a set of circulating principles that had finally come home, in the form of the abolitionist newspaper, to the South. "The unexpected evil is now upon us," he declared. "It has invaded our firesides, and under our roofs is sharpening the dagger for midnight assassination." Tyler warned his constituents that the abolitionist movement had grown from "a mere handful of obscure persons" into a national organ with

numerous presses, four of which circulated from the city of New York, with copies of three of which they had been so *extremely kind* as to favor me through the mail. These papers were circulated gratuitously among us, and at mere nominal prices to actual subscribers. He had

then in his possession one of these publications, and he would exhibit
it for the inspection of those present. (Here he drew from his pocket
the *Antislavery Record*.) . . . But I propose to show you the cheap rate
at which these papers are delivered out to actual subscribers. [He read
from the external sheet: "*Human Rights*, twenty five cents per annum;
Anti-Slavery Record, one-dollar-and-a-half *per hundred*, *Emancipator* (a paper larger than the *Whig* or *Enquirer*), fifty cents per annum;
Slave's Friend, single number, one cent."] . . . Here then, Mr. Chairman, are evidences of a powerful combination.[94]

Tyler's hysterical rhetoric of "combination" and "conspiracy" resembles
in some ways the antifederalist conspiracy theories described in chapter
3, which, at the moment of founding, vastly overstated the material capacities of the federalist coalition, misreading a theory of social relations
for actual political practice. In 1835, a similar fear of "combination" was
circulating in newspapers and speeches all over the country. One New
Hampshire man wondered how "our own New England men" could participate in such a society as the AASS. They had begun, he claimed, "the
agitation of a legal, constitutional, [and] political reform," "a systematic,
and, as far as practicable, simultaneous effort" that was making use of
"organized societies, public meetings, authorized agents, foreign emissar-
ies, [and] . . . cheap tracts [and] . . . pamphlets." Abolition had become, in
this man's words, an "organized," "regular," "systematic machinery" that
partook of the emerging machines of the age.[95] This reference to "machinery" points us to an important aspect of this episode, stamping its
fatal intersection with a specific moment in the history of U.S. industrial
expansion and finally differentiating it from the antifederalist conspiracy
theories of 1787 and 1788. Critiques like Tyler's may have hyperbolized,
in other words, but they were never nearly as exaggerated as fears of federalist conspiracy had once been, and this is because 1835 marks a far different material juncture in the history of national compression. Indeed,
if the abolitionists of 1835 had one thing in common with the federalists
of 1787, it is that they saw and exploited the material conditions under
which they made their appeal. As Garrison liked to say, abolition was the
great locomotive engine of truth, and like the railroad itself it was spreading its iron tendrils across the American landscape, disseminating with
greater rapidity and regularity than ever before the cross-regional productions—both in the form of actual newspapers and in the ideas they
expressed—of once distant and indifferent locales.

The copy of the *Anti-Slavery Record* that Tyler held up in his speech was probably the June issue for 1835. A short, twelve-page miscellany, it is perfectly representative of the materials coming out of the society's propaganda machine at the height of the mass mailing. Like other periodicals produced in New York, the *Anti-Slavery Record* was devoted to demonstrating that slavery was not a regional practice but a national one. Indeed, the first line of the pamphlet invokes the argument that the AASS most sought to dismantle: the idea that "we of the North have nothing to do with slavery"—a "standing argument" that it labels a "fallacy."[96] The back page of the pamphlet would appear to reinforce the front page's claims to nationalism by describing a list of geographically dispersed donors—local financiers who had helped send these pamphlets into the South, including individuals in New York, Connecticut, Massachusetts, Ohio, New Jersey, Pennsylvania, and Maine. The fact that this list was not national at all but sectional (with every subscriber hailing from either the North or West) tellingly demonstrates the sectional identifications that underwrote the AASS's nationalist claims, even as the circulation of the *Anti-Slavery Record* into distant (southern) locales would appear finally to fulfill them.

Tyler's phantasmatic response to this circulating piece of antebellum print culture was to pit the abstracted language of "combination," "organization," systematization, and "simultaneity" against the local language of "home" and "fireside." In invoking the feared scene of murder and mayhem within individual homes, Tyler's speech becomes just one example of how the response to the 1835 campaign was written at the impossibly local scale of home and body. Indeed, Tyler's figure of a violated domestic home-space recalls another common response to 1830s abolitionism: the fear of violated white bodies that circulated pervasively in the discourse of amalgamation. "Amalgamationist" was the most common epithet levied on organized abolition after 1835. James Watson Webb, for instance, frequently used his New York penny paper to mock Arthur Tappan and other members of the Anti-Slavery Society as "amalgamators" who threatened American life through interracial doctrines. In Cincinnati, Lyman Beecher (Stowe's father) came forward as a supporter of colonization because, like Jefferson before him, "he considered it a salutary preventive of that amalgamation, which would confound the two races and obliterate the traces of their distinction."[97] And when fellow newspaper editors in Cincinnati called him a "white traitor" who openly favored "a mixture of races," the young Gamaliel Bailey issued a public disclaimer in the *Cincinnati Daily Gazette*, proclaiming, in his opening sentence, "We are not *amalgamationists*."[98]

Leonard Richards accounts for the rise of amalgamation discourse in this decade by arguing that the AASS campaign had tapped a pervasive vein of racial animosity through every part of the country—a racism that took up the language and imagery of miscegenation to make its point.[99] But I would suggest that 1830s amalgamation discourse is a local reaction to a national (or interregional) conflict that could not otherwise be articulated at the level of the body. In making this argument, I follow scholars like David Roediger and Eric Lott, whose work suggests that racism emerges systemically in the early nineteenth century in many of its simplified and local manifestations in order to repress (in part) a larger difficulty that saturates the polity at large: the ethnic, cultural, regional, and class differences among white men. In doing so, such episodes were at the same time repressing the imperfect way those differences were being managed by the state these heterogeneous white men had created in 1787.[100] In fact, we might view federalism's historical emergence from a theory into a practice as the larger world-ordering context for understanding the discourse of amalgamation, for the antebellum fear of race-mixing strongly recalls the problem that was at the heart of antifederalist resistance to the Constitution in the late 1780s: the fear of national consolidation across regions.[101]

"Consolidation" was, of course, the antifederalist word for nationalism (as opposed to a confederation of states), and as I have already argued, it is the problem that haunts William Hill Brown's *The Power of Sympathy*. The discourse of amalgamation functions in the antebellum period much the way that incest worked in Brown's 1789 novel: both register a diffuse anxiety about national merger (or "consolidation"), but they do so, paradoxically, by imagining a problem being generated at the micro level of individual biology, through forbidden forms of sexual reproduction that produce compromised "complexions" of the sort that Hamilton, for one, hoped that federalism would ultimately eradicate.[102] In Brown's case, these conflicts are contained at the level of the imaginary and within the conventions of novelistic plot, but in the antebellum period, they enter public discourse as a widespread fear of mixed races—an anxiety that stands in for the vexed, disembodied, and nonlocal problem of intermixing regions.[103] As white men who sought to critique the behavior of other white men (across state lines), the abolitionists were, in a sense, *federal* amalgamationists—nationalists whose local voices originated from within a federal field, insistently raising into view the implications of what Garrison liked to call the unholy union between North and South. Under the pressure induced by this and other kinds of (circulating) cultural work, the polycentric cacophony of the early national period came finally to be reduced, in the 1830s, to the reductive and binarized spectacles of antebellum sectionalism and racism.

There are several ironies to the national reaction the AASS evoked in 1835. First, as this brief account suggests, the rage that the campaign prompted could never be materially directed at its proper object (the actual Tappans, Welds, and Wrights who were producing the antislavery message from afar). Amalgamation became a discursive screen for articulating this rage, and the bodies of black slaves (and, later, freemen) were continually seized on within local contexts as material targets for a racism that was generated, in part, out of sectional panic. Arguments for the suppression of printed goods operated in a similar way. The abstract ideology of cross-regional circulation became a discursive target of states' rights theorists while local printers and booksellers (from Lovejoy to Garrison to Amos Dresser) paid the price with their lynched and beaten bodies for the AASS's more disembodied, more mediated techniques. Most of these local printers were devoted to a different set of cultural values than the AASS. These small-town, small-time editors stood, as Fanuzzi has insisted, for a bygone model of local, decentralized, artisanal (or Revolutionary-era) production—the kind of hands-on labor the AASS was dismantling at its center.[104] Nevertheless, the center's physical distance from the local worlds where antislavery texts circulated allowed most AASS authors, editors, and administrators to evade the worst reactions. This is, of course, precisely why the federalist model of management was so attractive in the first place, for (as Hamilton and Madison argued in *The Federalist*), no matter how integrated a nation's spaces become, its center is never instantly reachable (in any embodied sense) by all the populations that inhabit it. Though the AASS's auxiliaries would eventually pull it apart from the outside in, no national mob of multiregional readers could materially converge and assemble, en masse (in totality), in New York City and direct its massive rage at the actual persons responsible for publishing the local story of slavery in nationally disseminated newspapers. Local publics thus had no choice but to symbolically burn effigies of the Tappans from afar, even as they lynched, mobbed, shot, tarred, feathered, and whipped whatever enslaved and antislavery bodies they could find within their midst.[105]

The final irony here is that these antebellum mobs were never really mobs of readers—at least not readers of the items they destroyed. Lovejoy was shot and his mutilated body displayed on the streets of Alton simply because he planned to print a modest newspaper on that spot. The *Alton Observer* did not have a mass circulation, and the mob that killed him clearly did not plan to subscribe to it (although they could have seen imprints of it). In the South more generally, it is almost certain that the mobs that convened to loot post offices and menace book agents were not actually reading the printed materials they destroyed. But if antebellum mobs were not the readers of abolitionist texts, many of them were readers of other kinds of texts—including newspapers, magazines, penny papers, story papers, and gift books. Though the South would continue to lag notably behind the North in literacy, reading was becoming "a necessity of life" not just, as William Gilmore tells us, in New England but everywhere a train or steamboat traveled.[106] This became more true as the South emerged in the 1840s and 1850s into a cotton kingdom with strong ties to the textile mills of Lowell, factories which in turn shipped their coats and cravats both south and west, out along the Erie Canal, down the Mississippi, and into homes all over America.[107] The febrile networks of exchange that the Tappans saw emerging in stacks of silk scarves and predictably circulated newspapers in the 1830s were nothing like the conduits of exchange that would make *Uncle Tom's Cabin* a widely circulated "national" bestseller in the 1850s. But of course by then, the reality of interregional commerce and communication had in many ways caught up with the hysterical and conspiratorial rhetoric of circulation (and the fear of merger) that made the 1830s the beginning of the end for the old federalist model and the start of a new, nationally induced sense of regionalism.

6. FACTS FROM HOME: THEODORE WELD'S *AMERICAN SLAVERY AS IT IS*

As the AASS's most effective antislavery lecturer in the 1830s, Theodore Weld temporarily lived in Lundy-land, occupying the ground of the vast superstructure of national abolition for several years before eventually leaving the field to take a job in New York.[108] Upon settling into that job, Weld did what many a white-collar worker has done ever since: he moved to New Jersey and commenced a daily commute between his home in Fort Lee and his desk in Manhattan, a series of looping pilgrimages between his workplace's urban center and his home-space's suburban fringe that, as we shall see, mimics the circular movement of his printed appeals on behalf of the slave as they moved from his desk out onto the desks of fellow antislavery workers in auxiliaries throughout the nation. It was from his office on Nassau Street, in the still-emerging publishing capital of the nation, that Weld coordinated the production of *Slavery as It Is* in late 1838 and early 1839. If there is a single AASS text that approaches the status of the iconic, it would be Weld's material history of slavery, a gruesomely gothic documentary account of what exactly happens to a human body when subjected to the practice of chattel slavery. But this material history of slavery has a fascinating material history in its own right, as a text. Indeed, the book's production history exemplifies the New York Society's increasing reliance on networks of exchange not just to disseminate but to assemble their antislavery message even as it demonstrates how those networks enabled a new kind of middle-class antislavery worker to remain fixed, at home, while he gathered his material.

As a material practice of collection, selection, and assemblage, *American Slavery as It Is* operated on an inverse logic from the one that powered the 1835 pamphlet campaign, even if it made similar use of the emerging built environment of American modernity (the same market networks, railroads and business directories). Weld initiated his search for materials by drafting a personalized circular letter calling for "witnesses" to "testify" to their first-hand observations of slave culture. This letter was reproduced lithographically (rather than printed) and then disseminated in the mails to AASS auxiliaries and to known antislavery leaders in each state. The decision to send the circular in lithographic form was just the first of many hybrid material practices that ultimately produced the book. Still a relatively new art technology in the 1830s, lithography relies on a simple principle, with text handwritten on a specially prepared limestone and then—when one seeks to mass produce—run through a mechanical printing press. The process is thus peculiarly mixed, joining handwork and presswork, a visual technology with a textual one, the uniqueness of human penmanship with the repetitions of mechanical reproduction. Forestalling the impersonality of the mass circular, Weld used this format in an attempt to cultivate a more intimate connection between himself and his correspondents, rather like the personal appeals he had been making for some years oratorically as he traveled in person as an AASS lecturer.

But while Weld expected personal replies in the thousands, responses were limited, and he was ultimately forced to devise a different technique for collecting his material. Weld's solution to this problem shows us both the limits and the potential of the antislavery network, for he finally found his source material in the highly impersonal form of the antebellum newspaper—or, more precisely, the many southern-based papers that circulated through the offices of New York City's merchant community. Having seen southern papers on display in the New York Commercial Reading Room (a repository for papers from all over the country), Weld learned that the papers were sold for waste when their newsworthiness expired. Seizing upon this opportunity, Weld purchased these "waste" papers in bulk, poring over their advertisements and articles, from which he culled his evidence for *American Slavery as It Is.* Though Weld subtitled the book "Testimony of a Thousand Witnesses," his use of these newspapers never involved the active participation of most of the southern voices it cited; if anything, *Slavery as It Is* did little more than eavesdrop (from a peculiar distance) on a faraway region. In some ways, this technique recalls Publius's 1787 promise to deliver the lowdown on antifederalist "whispering" to his scattered readers. But while *The Federalist's* readers needed Publius to serve as a human medium between themselves and those being eavesdropped upon, Weld found he could go to the "source" of southern slavery indirectly—skipping the human informant and relying instead on the mediation of newspapers that were not even originally addressed to him.

But if the content of *Slavery as It Is* depended on public networks, its actual assemblage relied upon the very thing such networks were creating locally: a private group of friends and family. While the newspapers themselves, in other words, came from outside the abolitionist nation (in the form of mainstream newspapers discarded by New York merchants who were themselves financially invested in the protection of the slave economy), the labor of assembling them into a coherent treatise fell within the domain of Weld's inner domestic circle. This work was divided between Weld, his wife Angelina Grimké, and her sister Sarah Grimké, with Weld carrying stacks of papers home on his daily commute while the Grimkés performed "their daily researches" at the kitchen table in Fort Lee. As Weld later recalled, he provided the Grimkés with "the raw material for the manufacture of 'Slavery As It Is,'" while "those dear souls spent six months, averaging more than six hours a day, in searching through thousands upon thousands of Southern newspapers" and then "marking and cutting out facts of slave-holding disclosures."[109] The labor involved was hardly menial. As Weld notes, "after the work was finished we were curious to know how many newspapers had been examined. So we went up to our attic and took an inventory of bundles, as they were packed heap upon heap. When our count had reached *twenty thousand* newspapers, we said: 'There, let that suffice.'"[110]

The book was the only real bestseller the AASS ever produced. Upon publication, the pamphlet sold for 37 1/2 cents (or $25 for a hundred copies). According to AASS records, 22,000 copies sold in four months, and more than 100,000 sold within a year. The book was stereotyped and went through multiple printings, becoming even more popular than the AASS's most stalwart, mainstream sellers, including the popular *Anti-Slavery Almanac,* which was routinely hawked on the streets of New York by newsboys.[111] Weld's method of clipping materials from the southern papers and labeling it "testimony" was never questioned by northern readers and went largely unremarked by southern ones, since the book was primarily disseminated in the North. Indeed, the method was picked up and elaborated on in ensuing years in numerous other AASS publications, which increasingly relied on the journalistic practice of "clipping" not just from southern papers but from Weld's particular selection of southern items in *Slavery as It Is.* Dickens would later use Weld's book as the source for his account of U.S. slavery in the *American Notes,* and Stowe would famously make Weld her most recurrent source for *Uncle Tom's Cabin.*[112] Extant reviews hailed *Slavery as It Is* as a truthful and powerful addition to the cause. The Boston *Zion's Herald* called it "a mass of solid facts," assembled by "a master-workman."[113] An anonymous correspondent to the *Emancipator* (the AASS news organ) suggested that readers use the book as a "stumper" in potential arguments with slaveholders, urging them to do as he did and pull it from their pockets in order to "give the names, places, and dates from Southern papers" if an interlocutor should accuse them of lying or exaggerating. This practice, the correspondent noted (without irony), will silence the slaveholder and cause him to "change color" on the spot.[114]

Weld's use of newspaper clippings mirrors the literary model of dissemination that was prevalent in this period; indeed, the technique is paradigmatic of an 1830s print culture that was, as Meredith McGill has shown, structured to its core around the project of republican diffusion, open access to information, and reprinting. Here we see the larger stakes of these choices, for *Slavery as It Is* was a quintessentially hybrid project, in which Weld sought to gather his materials and then redistribute them back through a print market that was still materially organized to resist centralized production. The production of the individual testimonies and the individual newspaper items were, in other words, all products of local worlds—both manuscript (in the case of testimonies) and print (in the case of news clippings). These scattered local worlds were brought together through the force of the national market (which was daily driving information to centralized sites like New York City and its mercantile reading rooms) and through abolition's integrative project—which found a way to turn these waste papers into something that might be collected (between book covers) and redistributed back through the nation-parts from which the original "testimony" had been gathered. Weld's use of southern clippings thus displays the decentralized nature of local print cultures of the 1830s and points to the greater centralization that was to come in the later 1840s and 1850s.

The story of the book's initial compilation proves that *Slavery as It Is* was (like abolition more generally) a collective project—even if we remember it today as a book written "by" Theodore Weld. The monolithic way that we commemorate Weld as the singular and central author of this text reiterates the book's own singularizing belief in its ability to deliver an unambiguous (or self-identical) account of a practice that originates at a geographical remove from the site of the text's home-production (in Fort Lee and New York). This project was, of course, deeply self-contradictory. On one hand, the book was invested in and fed a fantasy of unmediated description—offering "a mass of incontrovertible facts" intended to transparently "exhibit" "slavery as it is."[115] On the other hand, it chose to do so in highly partial and partializing ways. For example, Weld relied almost exclusively on white testimony (he used no slave "witnesses" in the book), just as he sought to divide the book's cultural labor across sections, pitting the cultural productions of the South (in the form of its newspapers) against the cultural consumption of the North, where the AASS hyped *Slavery as It Is* as a "thrilling" encyclopedia of horror. In a similarly differentiating move, Weld printed the names and residences of the southerners who had unwittingly provided "testimony" via newspapers, but he sometimes omitted this information in entries provided by those who had willingly provided responses to the original lithographed circular.

American Slavery as It Is thus arrays before us a number of emerging antebellum splits that Weld simultaneously relies upon and denies. The division of labor performed by the family Weld was, it turns out, well suited to such a denial. Stephen Browne has called *Slavery as It Is* "a stylistic token for managing the complex demands of ideology and duty," arguing that Weld resorts to a "sentimental" style that allows readers of the text to feel the pain of slavery from their home-side hearths without ever actually acting. I would add that the book's production was also, materially speaking, a domestic project that was enabled in the first place by a set of uneven geographical developments not just between North and South but between industrial center and periphery.[116] Sarah would later insist that it was neither Weld nor even the New York Commercial Reading Room that had provided the necessary newspapers but God himself who "in his providence has put into our hands these weapons prepared by the South."[117] Grimké's faith in divine providence willfully elides the material arrangements I have described here (from Weld's circular daily commute to the larger networks of information slowly being erected across the nation). In fact, Sarah only half-grudgingly acknowledges the earthly origin of the newspapers themselves when she calls the news items "weapons prepared by the South." In doing so, she gives credit to the South for the production of the facts but assigns all circulatory agency to the Lord—without reference to the railway, the ferry, the business firm, the bookstore, the reading room, or, indeed, her brother-in-law's white-collar desk job in Manhattan. It is not surprising, however, that Weld's middle-class commute between his office and his home (and the division of labor those two sites entailed) should be occluded, nor that its absence in Grimké's narrative should further fudge the workings of the larger and more worldly market in which abolition was embedded. This is exactly how high sentimental culture of the 1850s would eventually manage the impersonality of capitalism's spread—by ideologically anchoring itself in localized images of middle-class home and family, the modern world's ever narrowing conception of both a "here" and "us."

Coda: On the Future of the Culture Industry

Though the AASS arrived early on the scene of national consolidation, it did not survive it. Just as the nationalist consensus of 1787 was replaced, in the 1790s, by a two-party system that both managed and displayed conflict at the center and in the field, so immediate abolition erupted into factions that were finally contained by the well-known schism of 1840, in which radical Garrisonians took over the New York-based national society and eventually removed its operations to New England while the more socially conservative Tappanites seceded to create a new society, named the American and Foreign Anti-Slavery Society. Historiographically, this moment in abolitionist history is usually narrated as a spectacular dyadic split between moderate New York evangelicals like the Tappans and Bostonian hotheads like Garrison.[118] But in fact, the AASS had tremendous difficulty with *all* its auxiliaries—not just with Garrison's New England chapter. The theory on which AASS was organized—a federal model in which ideology and objects were produced in New York, distributed back through the body politic (in the form of auxiliaries), and then rerouted to the political center in the form of petitions—failed to hold at the center. In 1839, the *Annual Report* took note of these emerging tensions, and the Executive Committee passed a resolution diluting its own authority and promising "not [to] interfere directly or indirectly, by sending or employing agents or otherwise, in the conduct of the cause, in any State within which a State Society exists, without the assent of such Society."[119] Nevertheless, the AASS could not withstand the tensions that were accumulating within the abolitionist nation, a world whose energies were still more centrifugal than centralized in these years, and in 1840 the national society collapsed.

Even so, the AASS had profoundly reshaped the way abolition was materially organized on the ground, bequeathing to its reformist heirs a model of cross-regional organization, a new kind of culture industry, and a geopolitical critique of slavery as a national institution.[120] This critique was successful enough to no longer be novel in the 1850s—in large part because it had been cannily situated, all along, on the fault lines of a modernity that never stopped marching onward: articulated, literally, in factories, on the decks of steamboats, in newspaper columns, and in railroad cars. We might say that the federal union's shifting passage into a more integrated nationalism no longer *needed* the AASS to keep exposing it in the 1840s and 1850s, as it was instead picked up and described in cultural productions of every kind. Indeed, that national literary flowering that we call the American Renaissance is a locomotive whose tracks run directly though Lewis Tappan's office, and vice versa. The abolitionist culture industry is thus an excellent vantage point from which to view the workings of American culture writ large in these years. In the 1830s and 1840s, in other words, the expanding republic had finally been introduced to itself for the very first time, and that meeting sets the stage for the great socio-literary problems of the 1850s that form the subject matter of the last chapter of this book.

FIGURE 7.1 *Citizens of Boston!* Broadside. Boston: circa 1850s. Courtesy of the Division of Rare and Manuscript Collections, Cornell University Library.

7. SLAVERY ON THE MOVE
FROM FUGITIVE SLAVE TO VIRTUAL CITIZEN

Slavery is here. It is not a stationary matter.
—Charles Francis Adams, "What Makes Slavery a Question of National Concern?" 1855

1. THE COLOR LINE AND THE STATE LINE

No one needs to write the material history of *Uncle Tom's Cabin*. Enough chapters, articles, biographies, and book-histories have already been composed on Stowe's relationship with her editors and publishers, on the fabled circulation of her book, and on its reproduction across countless forms, genres, and artifacts. *Uncle Tom's Cabin* arrived at bookstores at a moment of American history that remains well preserved in libraries all over the United States. Magazines, newspapers, and private letters all survive to tell the story of Stowe's success, as do the financial papers of many of the companies who printed, published, and distributed Stowe's bestseller across the United States. Scholars in search of *Uncle Tom*'s material history can plumb an archive that includes correspondence, receipts, book orders, memoirs, and even canceled checks; they can follow the book's circulation in advertisements, magazines, and its many serialized and excerpted reprintings. *Uncle Tom* is not the mystified object for book historians that *Common Sense* is. The sale of hundreds of thousands of novels in 1852 is far more plausible, and its history more recoverable, than the sale of hundreds of thousands of pamphlets in 1776. This is because 1852 was, nationally speaking, what 1776 could not have been: a moment of profound economic and geographic integration rather than a moment of disintegrated origin.[1]

Uncle Tom's Cabin is alluded to in thousands of printed artifacts of the 1850s. In one widely circulated newspaper announcement, Stowe's publisher, John P. Jewett, helped trumpet the book's fabled reception in terms we are likely to find familiar:

> *Uncle Tom's Cabin.*—We are informed by Messrs. Jewett & Company, the publishers of the above thrilling work, that they are now printing the Fiftieth thousand copies, making One Hundred thousand volumes issued in eight weeks! This is without a precedent in the history of book publishing in this country. The demand continues without abatement. Our readers can judge of the labor of producing so great a number of books in so short a time when informed that it has taken 3000 reams of medium paper, weighing 30 lbs. to the ream—90,000 lbs. of paper; and that three or four of Adams's power presses have been kept running at the most rapid rate, day and night, stopping only on the Sabbath; and that from 125 to 200 bookbinders have been constantly at work in binding. Weight of books when bound about 110,000 lbs. or 55 tons. These have been principally transported in small boxes or packages by Messrs. Kinleys & Co. and Thompson & Co.'s Expresses. What could have been done towards transporting so large a number of packages in so short a time, only a few years since?[2]

This blurb strongly resembles popular accounts of *Common Sense*: it cites massive circulation numbers, notes a compressed time frame for such consumption, and generally objectifies the text's circulation as a cultural phenomenon "without precedent in the history of book publishing in this country!" (a claim comparable to Paine's description of *Common Sense* as "the greatest sale that any performance ever had since the use of letters" [2:1163]). In fact, there is no doubt that Stowe's publisher achieved in this advertising campaign something very similar to what Paine originally did for *Common Sense*: he helped generate a wider reception by *representing* a wide reception to a reading public eager to be involved in the novelties and news of the day.

But there are important differences. For one thing, Jewett's numbers are verifiable, as Paine's were not. For another, an actual material process is made visible here, rather than being obscured as it often is in accounts of *Common Sense*'s magical diffusion. The announcement does distinguish between a more abstracted audience (implied by the agentless statement, "demand continues without abatement") and the more micro audience of the newspaper (concretely named "our readers"). But it never abstracts the labor power involved in producing this bestseller. Instead it clearly describes the production and distribution process, which is peopled by actual workers: "Messrs. Jewett & Company, the publishers" "are now printing" the book on "Adams's power presses," with "125 to 200 bookbinders" "constantly at work in binding" copies that are then "transported . . . by Messrs. Kinleys & Co. and Thompson & Co.'s Expresses." Rather than mystifying the book's material production, the announcement details it, and it does so precisely because it wants to mark *Uncle Tom's Cabin* as a memorable moment in the unfolding history of national development—hence the closing question: "What could have been done towards transporting so large a number of packages in so short a time, only a few years since?"

More than any artifact of the nineteenth century, *Uncle Tom's Cabin* stands for both a circulating thing and a set of circulating ideas. It does not simply *figure* a densely intertwined cross-regional public (as *Common Sense* historically has). Instead, *Uncle Tom's Cabin* actually engaged one, not just because it was itself so widely distributed and consumed but because it entered a cultural marketplace that, like a hall of mirrors, absorbed and reproduced Stowe's central characters and storylines ad infinitum across a vast space that was becoming more visible to itself as an entity because of an interconnected system of cultural representation (or culture industry) that variously hailed, attacked, expurgated, pirated, misquoted, rewrote, and simply reprinted *Uncle Tom's Cabin* in any number of local and translocal venues, including newspapers, magazines, theaters, advertisements, magazines, speeches, stores, and museum displays. There were no "Common Sense" dolls or tobacco tins in 1776, but as numerous cultural historians have noted, Topsy dolls and Uncle Tom textiles were widely produced and widely consumed after 1852, as were, of course, actual copies of *Uncle Tom's Cabin*.[3] The irony of this "national" scene of reception is that having reached this massive, geographically dispersed audience, Stowe's novel did not unite it. *Uncle Tom* is at every turn what Paine's pamphlet was not: a bestseller that speaks to a large, nationally dispersed reading constituency from a centralized location but one that manages, in reaching that constituency, to divide rather than to unite it politically.[4]

Instead of adding to the material history of *Uncle Tom's Cabin*, this chapter assumes the circulatory utility of the 1850s domestic book market and turns instead to the collapsed nation-space that the book figured for its readers both in its phenomenal circulation and in its picaresque storylines. *Uncle Tom's Cabin* did not literally circulate everywhere, but it did circulate at a crucial moment in the history of national compression and thus stands as an iconic index of the collapse between different parts of the extended republic as they consolidated into one tautological, self-same, and (as it turns out) intolerable thing: a nation. As D.W. Meinig notes: "by the late 1850s the entire national population—excepting only the Far West and Texas—was within six days' travel of New York City or Philadelphia, a remarkable compression of the operational distance-scale of the nation."[5] This compression was the ongoing work of a growing infrastructure that ensured that local sites everywhere "were no longer spatially individual" (as Wolfgang Schivelbusch notes) but interlinked by material structures that were systemically conceived as "one vast national market."[6]

Stowe's novel was not alone in registering this ongoing shift in the relations between parts of the union. The crisis posed by national consolidation is reflected in any number of texts of the 1850s, visual and verbal—from almanacs, novels, maps, and posters to cartoons, political speeches, and "nationalist" local color paintings (like Richard Caton Woodville's *War News from Mexico*, discussed in chapter 3). To take just one visual example: in 1856, Horace Greeley's *Tribune* published a political pamphlet that included a recently revised national map (figure 7.2). This map represents an early version of the now familiar U.S. nation-logo, a territorial hieroglyph that fulfills Manifest Destiny by designating all horizontal space between the Atlantic and Pacific oceans as rightfully belonging to the United States. Nevertheless, the map fails to present the unified continent as united in any simple way. Instead, it articulates a well-known paradox of antebellum territorial expansion, indexing the stark sectional splits emerging among regions (North, South, and West) even as it evokes a feared scene of national merger (expressed here as regional encroachment). The map imagines the ongoing dissolution of sectional boundaries in typically racist terms, constructing a visual fantasy that collapses region and race into a wordless narrative about federal amalgamation. Thus the nightmare of national consolidation is encoded in the ink that produces the map, with the "black" slave states menacing a shrinking body of free "white" states and bleeding their darkness west,

FREEDOM AND SLAVERY, AND THE COVETED TERRITORIES

FIGURE 7.2 *The Border Ruffian Code in Kansas.* New York: Tribune Office, 1856. GLC 08471. The Gilder Lehrman Collection, courtesy of the Gilder Lehrman Institute of American History, New York. Not to be reproduced without written permission.

into the preponderantly gray states beyond the Mississippi, where only California is guaranteed to be free (and hence white). The map visually figures slavery as a spreading geographic stain poised to cover the continent, even as its textual apparatus speaks to the "mixed" condition of antebellum American political life under the federal Constitution. Thus the right-hand side of the map describes the numerical consequences of the Federal Convention's three-fifths compromise, pointing out that southern members of Congress stand at the center of a mixed field of (federal) representation that is already both black and white (in this map's terms, that is, both northern and southern) and hence already consolidated in precisely the color-coded terms the map otherwise represents as a crisis. The bottom left-hand side of the map, on the other hand, emphasizes a different kind of merger, counting "the number of slaves in the United States" (3,204,313), the far smaller "number of slave holders" (347,525), and finally balancing between them the uncounted "number of white slaves of the North who are owned by this small but iron willed oligarchy" of slave owners, hailing white northerners as already one with their black southern slave neighbors in a way that once again merges black and white interests and makes that merger precisely the point of the pamphlet's phobic critique.

Greeley's map is a popular representation of a territorial critique that was no longer, by 1854, merely abolitionist at base. Indeed, for people all over the United States, the drama of national consolidation was being acted out in the 1850s in a number of highly visible juridical texts that all contributed to a dissolving sense of difference across national space even as they took up the often more local question of free versus slave, white versus black. This body of new law begins with the expansion of national boundaries in the U.S.–Mexican War and the consequent passage of the Compromise of 1850 (with its infamous Fugitive Slave Law), an omnibus bill designed to manage the integration of that new territory even as it sought to appease all existing sections. It then extends deep into the decade with the Kansas-Nebraska Act of 1854, which erased the Mason-Dixon line as the legal boundary between free and slave states, thus letting slavery loose, as it were, from its previous containment in the South. And it ends with the Dred Scott case of 1857, in which the rights of southern slaveholders to move their human property in and out of free states— or across the free/slave divide—were determined to be constitutionally guaranteed. Dred Scott was, in fact, a particularly devastating revision of intersectional relations: like Kansas-Nebraska, Dred Scott breached slavery's fixed location within the so-called slave states, but it did so not just at the more abstracted scale of section (by erasing, for instance, a single imaginary line between North and South), but at the more local and plural scale of individual states. Thus after 1857, no free state could actually guarantee its soil as free because of the Taney Court's extension of an early version of due process to southern slaveholders. All of these developments were, in turn, widely debated in the presidential election of 1860, which itself finally led to the literal redistribution of bodies-across-borders entailed by any war: the massive deployment of northern troops into the South in 1861–65 (and beyond) and the consequent displacement of large refugee populations.[7]

This chapter uses the Fugitive Slave Law of 1850 and its diverse archive to think about the intersection of books, bodies, and nation from within that scene of cultural panic we now call antebellum sectionalism. If the color line was (as Du Bois suggests) the central problem of the twentieth century, then the state line was surely the central problem of the mid-nineteenth century. Yet the cultural history of the 1850s suggests that these two lines were never disconnected problems, as different in kind as they might be. As we shall see, each represents a different kind of American identity— one geographic, or place-based (and hence backward looking), and the other racial, or body-based (and hence forward looking). This chapter interrogates this shift, asking how people came to identify with and be identified as mobile individuals rather than geographically fixed citizens of the collective bargaining units called states, regions, and sections. At the moment of founding, location in space—or "place"—had provided the surest route to a fixed personal identity. The Constitution acknowledges the ongoing importance of place by allowing local states to retain their role as administrative substructures within the grander scheme of federalism. Even Publius concedes that citizens must necessarily identify most powerfully with their local states and state representatives because proximity breeds sympathy. Under the compressing pressures of national consolidation, however, place became a bygone mode of political and affective affiliation, as individual actors and the federal state itself became more invested in locating identity not in places but in persons. In the 1850s, we can thus see the very ground of American identity shifting alongside emerging networks of exchange.

I elaborate this unfolding history through readings of three literary texts: Stowe's *Uncle Tom's Cabin* (1851–52), Solomon Northup's *Twelve Years a Slave* (1853), and William Wells Brown's *Clotel* (1853). Stowe's novel, because it sutures the nation to itself in the very process of being circulated as a book-object, is one of our most enduring literary signs for the long historical process of reimagining the relation among the local, the regional, and the national. But as I argue here, *Uncle Tom's Cabin* actually relies upon a nostalgic theory of national space over and against a radical critique of ongoing and irreversible national history, leading Stowe to try to realign the color line and the state line through a colonizationist fantasy that would appear to make race and nation perfectly coincident. Solomon Northup, on the other hand, contests Stowe's account of national space on empirical grounds, emphasizing the geographical gaps between North and South (and insisting on the inability of distinct locations to be fused into one thing), especially via the circulation of written texts. In doing so, however, he too invests in an old, geographic (or place-based) understanding of American identity that looks back to the early days of the Confederation, refusing to acknowledge the ongoing integration of the tiered scales of federalism.

William Wells Brown's *Clotel* is, in a sense, the 1850s' most innovative response to these two ways of reading national space and identity (one based on race, the other on geography). Fleeing the hand of a newly localized and embodied federal state, Brown returns to London, the place

where the eighteenth-century idea of virtual representation was first theorized, and it is from that geographically displaced location and within
the open form of the novel that Brown crafts his solution to the now
century-old question of actual (or embodied) versus virtual (or displaced) identity. It is here, in the first African-American novel, that we
get from Brown what neither Stowe nor Northup can give us: a full account of the problem of U.S. nation building, of slavery's role in it, and of
history's role in both. *Clotel* details, in other words, the very thing I have
been describing throughout this book: the consequences of nationalism's
long, cross-generational, cross-regional emergence for the particular
bodies living in its midst.

2. THE FUGITIVE-IN-SPACE
AND THE FUGITIVE-IN-PRINT, 1787–1850

On May 24, 1854, slavery came (back) to Massachusetts in the person of
Anthony Burns. A fugitive slave who had escaped from Virginia in March
1854, Burns had been living in Boston for two months when he was arrested one evening on his way home from work and claimed, under the
auspices of the Fugitive Slave Law of 1850, as the property of Charles Suttle. For the next week, the city, the state, and the nation focused on the
spectacle of Burns's trial and Boston's response to it (see figure 7.1). The
episode was especially memorable for the impressive machinery the federal government set in motion to help Suttle collect Burns from the Boston jail. After a failed rescue attempt (in which one federal marshal was
killed) and under the ongoing threat of riot, the U.S. president Franklin
Pierce ordered marines and artillery to assist in Burns's rendition back
to Virginia. Chains and padlocks were placed on the courthouse, and
upon being legally deemed Suttle's property, Burns was taken into custody aboard a federal frigate, which lay waiting in the harbor to transport
him back to Virginia at the federal government's expense. Pierce was kept
updated about the case via telegraph and ultimately allocated over 2,000
troops and $50,000 to retrieving Burns—an embarrassingly large number,
given that his freedom was purchased for $1,300 just a few months later.[8]

Charles Emery Stevens notes that Burns's rendition was "the first time
that the armed power of the United States had ever been arrayed against
the people of Massachusetts" (143), and the response throughout Boston was reminiscent of pre-Revolutionary resistance to the armed power

of the British Crown. The people came out, en masse, in their bodies, to watch the federal government declare that place had no bearing on Anthony Burns's identity: he was a slave in Virginia and a slave in Massachusetts. Contemporary accounts describe as many as 50,000 people turning out to witness Burns's march from the courthouse to the ship. One Bostonian later recalled "the mustering of thousands of Abolitionists, who quit their business, their farms, their shops, their offices, to be the sad *spectators*, if, indeed, they could not be the *rescuers* of Burns."[9] In a Boston tradition dating back to the 1760s, windows were dressed in black, gates were hung with funereal bunting, and an empty coffin marked "Liberty" moved through the streets, creating, for a day, a surreal continuum between the old days of the Stamp Act and the new ones under the Fugitive Slave Act.

Burns's case generated a number of well-known literary artifacts, among them Walt Whitman's "A Boston Ballad."[10] In an ironic revision of "Yankee Doodle," the poem's speaker visits Boston to watch the Burns rendition, a scene which resembles a Fourth of July parade, complete with drums, fifes, flag, and cannon: "I rose this morning early to get betimes in Boston town, / . . . I love to look on the stars and stripes . . . I hope the fifes will play Yankee Doodle." In a gothic twist, however, the speaker is joined in his spectatorship by a group of dead Revolutionary soldiers "called . . . out of the earth" on mouldering crutches, "woodenlegged . . . bandaged and bloodless," to watch their grandsons watch Burns return to slavery. The result is a grotesque scene of national collectivity across time that captures all the con/fusions of 1850s nationalism. In the space between the courthouse and the ship, the North comes face to face with the South, the past comes face to face with the present, but more importantly the two different *scales* first constituted by the Constitution in 1787—the federal and the state—finally stand on one geographic ground. To this end, the intense localism of the people watching "the show"–the "Jonathans," the "Yankee phantoms," and the "gentlemen of Boston"—is placed in direct tension with the "federal" scene that unfolds before them—"the President's marshal," "the government cannon," "the federal foot and dragoons," "the stars and stripes."

In keeping with the poem's Revolutionary backdrop, Whitman links the arrival of federal troops in 1854 to the old imperial arrangements under colonial rule, identifying the return of the fugitive slave with the return of the pre-Revolutionary king. Having watched Burns be reenslaved through federal force, the speaker urges "the gentlemen of Boston" to send "a committee to England," where "they shall get a grant from the Parliament, and go with a cart to the royal vault," "dig out King George's coffin," and "box up his bones for a journey." Shipped home to "Boston bay" in "a swift Yankee clipper," the king's skeleton (the "regal ribs," "the skull . . . and crown") will serve as the "centrepiece" for a new kind of nationalist celebration, complete with "the President's marshal," "the government cannon," "the roarers from Congress," armed soldiers, and, finally, "orderly citizens" who "look" instead of act. The poem ends with a direct address both to the king and his Yankee subject: "You have got your revenge, old buster! . . . The crown is come to its own, and more than its own. // Stick your hands in your pockets, Jonathan . . . you are a made man from this day, / You are mighty cute . . . and here is one of your bargains."

Whitman's references to the British monarchy suggest that by 1854, the problem of the virtual had returned with a vengeance in the form of the Fugitive Slave Law, with the king reincarnated in the form of the increasingly centralized yet encroaching federal state. The poem thus uncannily stages a new relation between citizen and state that is at the same time an old relation—one that was framed, Whitman suggests, by the "mighty cute" "bargain" of 1787 (the three-fifths compromise) but not fulfilled until Webster and Clay's second bargain (the Compromise of 1850) authorized southern slaveholders to travel north and seize slaves in northern cities. The Revolutionary dead look on in dismay as their able-bodied descendents do nothing to stop Burns's seizure: "What is all this chattering of bare gums?" asks the speaker: "For shame, old maniacs! . . . / Here gape your smart grandsons . . . their wives gaze at them from the windows, / See how well-dressed . . . see how orderly they conduct themselves." But in fact, these third- and fourth-generation Americans are exactly what the old maniacs' Constitution had made them: well-dressed consumers of federal spectacle rather than political participants.

It is appropriate that the Boston public should be rendered by Whitman as just so many bodies—beings synecdochically reduced to gaping mouths, chattering gums, skeletal frames, and watchful eyes. As I have pointed out in previous chapters, federalism's subject was imagined from the start as an individual, a body whose local labor might be networked and funneled upward (in the form of taxes and military power) in order to produce the awesome power of a potentially imperial centralized state. I have described this process as metrobuilding but also suggested the material limits placed on that project at the moment of its emergence. Burns's case suggests that over the course of many decades, the relation between the federal state and the individual citizen changed. The federal state that had once had difficulty collecting a simple impost used, on this occasion, fifty thousand tax dollars to enforce the customs of Virginia on the people of Massachusetts—and it did so through the force of an army marched from one end of the continent to the other aboard a federal frigate and under the direct command of the president of the United States (that spectral residue of British monarchy).[11]

The irony of Whitman's poem is that it stages these conflicts with no apparent memory of how the debate about centralized power had originally been framed—which is to say, between federalists and antifederalists. Whether Whitman knows it or not, at least some of the "old maniacs" he describes here would have been "antis" who had feared all along the extension of federal power into every day life. Publius had, in *The Federalist*, mocked the idea that "the militia of Virginia [would] be dragged from their homes five or six hundred miles" to Massachusetts (186). His prediction that such arrangements were impractical was accurate—for several decades. By 1850, however, the antifederalist nightmare that the local states might someday be abolished began, in a sense, to come true, as some of the most meaningful differences between states, regions, and sections were erased under federal law. Whitman's poem illustrates this process nicely, showing how locations that had once been meaningfully disjunct were becoming newly linked in these years and how the tiered scales of federalism, which were once materially disarticulate, could now come face to face with one another in the form of soldier-bodies and citizen-bodies. Whitman's poem describes this moment and sees its circular origin in the American founding—that Janus-faced moment in American history that both looked back and rejected empire and yet looked forward as well, and embraced it.

Anthony Burns returns us to the theoretical problem at the heart of this book: the relationship, inscribed under the federal Constitution, between the national and the local, relations that were revisited and revised after the Civil War with the addition of the three constitutional amendments that end slavery, extend the franchise to newly emancipated slaves, and establish due process. As Lauren Berlant has pointed out, "modern American citizenship is derived primarily not from Enlightenment Constitutional dicta but rather from the enfranchisement of African Americans" in the Fourteenth Amendment. Berlant identifies this and other amendments to the Constitution as "a record of the nation's gradual recognition that it needs officially to theorize an ideal relation between its abstract 'citizen' and the person who lives, embodied, an everyday life."[12] I would characterize it somewhat differently, in light of the history unfolded here. The Fourteenth Amendment may retheorize the relationship between two kinds of citizens-in-one (an abstract and a real one), but it also does important historical work, restructuring the relation of individual citizens (in or out of their bodies) to a federal state that had once been entirely removed (and so abstract), but that had finally come home to specific locations in the 1850s and '60s in human form. Put simply, the problem of abstraction has a history that produces different versions of the same problem at various temporal intervals, and the intervals that interest me most in this chapter are the ones between 1787 and 1860. I will argue that in the decades leading up to secession, civil war, emancipation, and the recodification of U.S. citizenship under the Thirteenth, Fourteenth, and Fifteenth Amendments, the federal state did something new: it developed the material capacity to circulate itself back through the part-spaces that had once comprised it via structures of (seemingly) pure representation. These structures (among them a dispersed and disconnected print culture) had once assured the nation's separation from itself (via a kind of practical disaggregation that maintained a distinct boundary between state and state *and* between the federal government and the states en masse). But like everything else, representation has a material history that develops over time, and by the 1850s, the staid structures of early federal representation no longer worked as they once had. My object in this chapter is to describe some of the consequences of this shift, not (as in the last chapter) for regions or sections, but for the local bodies of individual subjects living inside those regions and sections.

The Fugitive Slave Law was part of this transformation. A provision of the Compromise of 1850, the law was designed to pacify the South and thus gain concessions on those articles that sought in turn to pacify the North. But a federal code for fugitive slave recovery was not new. Instead, the 1850 law renovated the original but unenforced fugitive slave clause embedded within the U.S. Constitution. In the blandest language imaginable, the Convention of 1787 had constructed, along with the three-fifths clause, the following concession to slaveholding interests: "No Person held to Service or Labour in one State, under the Laws thereof, escaping into another, shall, in Consequence of any Law or Regulation therein, be discharged from such Service or Labour, but shall be delivered up on Claim of the Party to whom such Service or Labour may be due."[13] While this original clause was composed of a single sentence (and its legislative follow-up, the Fugitive Slave Law of 1793, a mere page), Congress's 1850 revisions innovated at length on the original law's language in an effort to override the elaborate local machinery of personal liberty laws in the North. The 1850 law comprises thousands of words, embedded in dense legalese. In the massive archive of printed response that followed the law's passage, it is not unusual to see the law quoted in full and then comprehensively critiqued in broadsides, essays, sermons, speeches, almanacs, novels, and of course newspapers (figures 7.3 and 7.4). The 1850 law was so controversial and debate upon it so common that one is tempted to say that the fugitive slave was the central public figure of the decade. If this is not strictly true, it is at least safe to say that fugitives slaves were key figures in federalism's ongoing transformation from a theory into a more material national practice.

The text of the 1850 law seeks to clarify and materialize the relations between the local and the national in four particular ways. First, it explicitly embodies the agents of the federal government, who populate the law's various articles in the physical persons of "commissioners," "marshals," "deputy marshals," and "clerks." Second, it works to locate and contain both the fugitive and his slave-catcher (deemed either "an attorney" or "an agent") by marking out the jurisdictions where each begins and ends his journey (from slave state to free state and back again, accompanied by mediating texts, called "certificates," that authenticate the transition from one site to the next). Third, it racializes its fugitive subject, who in the Constitution had been left racially unmarked in order to include escaped indentured servants of any race. And finally, it compels all citizen-spectators to participate in the scene of retrieval, empowering federal marshals and commissioners "to summon and call to their aid . . . bystanders," noting that "all good citizens are hereby commanded to aid and assist in the prompt and efficient execution of this law, whenever their services may be required" (section 5). In this way, the 1850 law seeks to localize and contain the mobility not just of the fugitive slave but of white men of "other" sections (southern slave owners and slave catchers) and of the federal state itself.

And no wonder. The boundary-crossing travels of southern fugitives called into crisis the common understanding of federalism's internal arrangements. Prior to the networks produced by the market revolution (and exploited by both fugitive slaves and the culture industry), different scales of national life were insistently troped as materially distinct and yet structurally homologous to one another—from the level of the national

THE FUGITIVE SLAVE LAW.

A bill to amend the act entitled "An act respecting fugitives from justice, and persons escaping from the service of their masters."

Be it enacted by the Senate and House of Representatives of the United States of America in Congress assembled, That the persons who have been, or may hereafter be, appointed commissioners, in virtue of any act of Congress, by the circuit courts of the United States, and who, in consequence of such appointment, are authorised to exercise the powers that any justice of the peace or other magistrate of any of the United States may exercise in respect to offenders for any crime or offence against the United States, by arresting, imprisoning, or bailing the same under and by virtue of the thirty-third section of the act of the twenty-fourth of September, seventeen hundred and eighty-nine, entitled "An act to establish the judicial courts of the United States," shall be, and are hereby authorized and required to exercise and discharge all the powers and duties conferred by this act.

Sec. 2. *And be it further enacted,* That the superior court of each organized territory of the United States shall have the same power to appoint commissioners to take acknowledgments of bail and affidavit, and to take depositions of witnesses in civil causes, which is now possessed by the circuit courts of the United States; and all commissioners who shall hereafter be appointed for such purposes by the superior court of any organized territory of the United States shall possess all the powers and exercise all the duties conferred by law upon the commissioners appointed by the circuit courts of the United States for similar purposes, and shall moreover exercise and discharge all the powers and duties conferred by this act.

Sec. 3. *And be it further enacted,* That the circuit courts of the United States, and the superior courts of each organized territory of the United States, shall from time to time enlarge the number of commissioners, with a view to afford reasonable facilities to reclaim fugitives from labor, and to the prompt discharge of the duties imposed by this act.

Sec 4. *And be it further enacted,* That the commissioners above named shall have concurrent jurisdiction with the judges of the circuit and district courts of the United States, in their respective circuits and districts within the several States, and the judges of the superior courts of the Territories, severally and collectively, in term time and vacation; and shall grant certificates to such claimants, upon satisfactory proof being made, with authority to take and remove such fugitives from service or labor, under the restrictions herein contained, to the State or Territory from which such persons may have escaped or fled.

Sec. 5. *And be it further enacted,* That it shall be the duty of all marshals and deputy marshals to obey and execute all warrants and precepts issued under the provisions of this act, when to them directed, and should any marshal or deputy marshal refuse to receive such warrant or other process, when tendered, or to use all proper means diligently to execute the same, he shall, on conviction thereof, be fined in the sum of one thousand dollars to the use of such claimant, on the motion of such claimant, by the circuit or district court for the district of such marshal; and after arrest of such fugitive by such marshal or his deputy, or whilst at any time in his custody, under the provisions of this act, should such fugitive escape, whether with or without the assent of such marshal or his deputy, such marshal shall be liable, on his official bond, to be prosecuted, for the benefit of such claimant, for the full value of the service or labor of said fugitive in the State, Territory or district whence he escaped; and the better to enable the said commissioners, when thus appointed, to execute their duties faithfully and efficiently, in conformity with the requirements of the constitution of the United States and of this act, they are hereby authorized and empowered, within their counties respectively, to appoint in writing under their hands, any one or more suitable persons, from time to time, to execute all such warrants and other process as may be issued by them in the lawful performance of their respective duties; with an authority to such commissioners, or the persons to be appointed by them, to execute process as aforesaid, to summon and call to their aid the bystanders, or *posse comitatus* of the proper county, when necessary to insure a faithful observance of the clause of the constitution referred to, in conformity with the provisions of this act; and all good citizens are hereby commanded to aid and assist in the prompt and efficient execution of this law, whenever their services may be required, as aforesaid, for that purpose; and said warrants shall run and be executed by said officers anywhere in the State within which they are issued.

Sec. 6. *And be it further enacted,* That when a person held to service or labor in any State or Territory of the United States has heretofore or shall hereafter escape into another State or Territory of the United States, the person or persons to whom such service or labor may be due, or his, her or their agent or attorney, duly authorised, by power of attorney, in writing, acknowledged and certified under the seal of some legal office or court of the State or Territory in which the same may be executed, may pursue and reclaim such fugitive person, either by procuring a warrant from some one of the courts, judges, or commissioners aforesaid, of the proper circuit, district or county, for the apprehension of such fugitive from service or labor, or by seizing and arresting such fugitive, where the same can be done without process, and by taking or causing such person to be taken, forthwith before such court, judge or commissioner, whose duty it shall be to hear and determine the case of such claimant in a summary manner; and upon satisfactory proof being made, by deposition or affidavit, in writing, to be taken and certified by such court, judge, or commissioner, or by other satisfactory testimony, duly taken and certified by some court, magistrate, justice of the peace, or other legal officer authorized to administer an oath and take depositions under the laws of the State or Territory from which such person owing service or labor may have escaped, with a certificate of such magistracy or other authority, as aforesaid, with the seal of the proper court or officer thereto attached, which seal shall be sufficient to establish the competency of the proof, and with proof, also by affidavit, of the identity of the person whose service or labor is claimed to be due as aforesaid, that the person so arrested does in fact owe service or labor to the person or persons claiming him or her, in the State or Territory from which such fugitive may have escaped as aforesaid, and that said person escaped, to make out and deliver to such claimant, his or her agent or attorney, a certificate setting forth the substantial facts as to the service or labor due from such fugitive to the claimant, and of his or her escape from the State or Territory in which such service or labor was due to the State or Territory in which he or she was arrested, with authority to such claimant, or his or her agent or attorney, to use such reasonable force and restraint as may be necessary under the circumstances of the case, to take and remove such fugitive person back to the State or Territory from whence he or she may have escaped as aforesaid. In no trial or hearing under this act shall the testimony of such alleged fugitive be admitted in evidence; and the certificates in this and the first section mentioned shall be conclusive of the right of the person or persons in whose favor granted to remove such fugitive to the State or Territory from which he escaped, and shall prevent all molestation of said person or persons by any process issued by any court, judge, magistrate, or other person whomsoever.

Sec. 7. *And be it further enacted,* That any person who shall knowingly and willingly obstruct, hinder, or prevent such claimant, his agent or attorney, or any person or persons lawfully assisting him, her, or them, from arresting such a fugitive from service or labor, either with or [illegible]ss as aforesaid; or shall res[illegible]pt to rescue, such fugitive [illegible] or labor, or from the custody of [illegible]mant, his or her agent or attorney or other persons or persons lawfully assisting as aforesaid, when so arrested, pursuant to the authority herein given and declared; or shall aid, abet, or assist such person, so owing service or labor as aforesaid, directly or indirectly, to escape from such claimant, his agent or attorney, or other person or persons legally authorized as aforesaid; or shall harbor or conceal such fugitive, so as to prevent the discovery and arrest of such person, after notice or knowledge of the fact that such person was a fugitive from service or labor as aforesaid, shall, for either of said offences, be subject to a fine not exceeding one thousand dollars, and imprisonment not exceeding six months, by indictment and conviction before the District Court of the United States for the district in which such offence may have been committed, or before the proper court of criminal jurisdiction, if committed within any one of the organized Territories of the United States; and shall moreover forfeit and pay, by way of civil damages to the party injured by such illegal conduct, the sum of one thousand dollars for each fugitive so lost as aforesaid, to be recovered by action of debt in any of the District or Territorial Courts aforesaid, within whose jurisdiction the said offence may have been committed.

Sec. 8. *And be it further enacted,* That the marshals, their deputies, and the clerks of the said district and territorial courts, shall be paid for their services the like fees as may be allowed to them for similar services in other cases; and where such services are rendered exclusively in the arrest, custody, and delivery of the fugitive to the claimant, his or her agent or attorney, or where such supposed fugitive may be discharged out of the custody from the want of sufficient proof as aforesaid, then such fees are to be paid in the whole by such complainant, his agent or attorney; and in all cases where the proceedings are before a commissioner, he shall be entitled to a fee of ten dollars in full for his services in each case, upon the delivery of the said certificate to the claimant, his or her agent or attorney; or a fee of five dollars in cases where proof shall not, in the opinion of such commissioner, warrant such certificate and delivery, inclusive of all services incident to such arrest and examination, to be paid, in either case, by the claimant, his or her agent or attorney. The person or persons authorized to execute the process to be issued by such commissioners for the arrest and detention of fugitives from service or labor as aforesaid shall also be entitled to a fee of five dollars each for each person he or they may arrest and take before any such commissioner as aforesaid, at the instance and request of such claimant, with such other fees as may be deemed reasonable by such commissioner for such other additional services as may be necessarily performed by him or them: such as attending to the examination, keeping the fugitive in custody, and providing him with food and lodging during his detention, and until the final determination of such commissioner; and in general for performing such other duties as may be required by such claimant, his or her attorney or agent, or commissioner in the premises; such fees to be made up in conformity with the fees usually charged by the officers of the courts of justice within the proper district or county, as near as may be practicable, and paid by such claimants, their agents or attorneys, whether such supposed fugitive from service or labor be ordered to be delivered to such claimants by the final determination of such commissioners or not.

Sec. 9. *And be it further enacted,* That upon affidavit made by the claimant of such fugitive, his agent or attorney, after such certificate has been issued, that he has reason to apprehend that such fugitive will be rescued by force from his or their possession before he can be taken beyond the limits of the State in which the arrest is made, it shall be the duty of the officer making the arrest to retain such fugitive in his custody, and to remove him to the State whence he fled, and there to deliver him to said claimant, his agent or attorney. And to this end the officer aforesaid is hereby authorized and required to employ so many persons as he may deem necessary, to overcome such force, and to retain them in his service so long as circumstances may require; the said officer and his assistants, while so employed, to receive the same compensation, and to be allowed the same expenses as are now allowed by law for the transportation of criminals, to be certified by the judge of the district within which the arrest is made, and paid out of the treasury of the United States.

Sec. 10. *And be it further enacted,* That when any person held to service or labor in any State or Territory, or in the District of Columbia, shall escape therefrom, the party to whom such service or labor shall be due, his, her, or their agent or attorney, may apply to any court of record therein, or judge thereof in vacation, and make such satisfactory proof to such court, or judge, in vacation, of the escape aforesaid, and that the person escaping owed service or labor to such party.— Whereupon the court shall cause a record to be made of the matters so proved, and also a general description of the person so escaping, with such convenient certainty as may be; and a transcript of such record authenticated by the attestation of the clerk, and of the seal of the said court, being produced in any other State, Territory, or District in which the person so escaping may be found, and being exhibited to any judge, commissioner, or other officer, authorized by the law of the United States to cause persons escaping from service or labor to be delivered up, shall be held and taken to be full and conclusive evidence of the fact of escape, and that the service or labor of the person escaping is due to the party in such record mentioned. And upon the production by the said party of other and further evidence, if necessary, either oral or by affidavit, in addition to what is contained in the said record of the identity of the person escaping, he or she shall be delivered up to the claimant. And the said court, commissioner, judge or other person authorized by this act to grant certificates to claimants of fugitives, shall, upon the production of the record and other evidences aforesaid, grant to such claimant a certificate of his right to take any such person identified and proved to be owing service or labor as aforesaid, which certificate shall authorize such claimant to seize or arrest and transport such person to the State or Territory from which he escaped: *Provided,* That nothing herein contained shall be construed as requiring the production of a transcript of such record as evidence as aforesaid; but in its absence, the claim shall be heard and determined upon other satisfactory proofs competent in law.

SYNOPSIS OF THE LAW.

1. It clothes any ruffian who may be commissioned to act in this new and infamous office of *Slave-Catcher,* with magisterial and judicial authority. 2. It commands and requires good citizens to aid in this heartless and brutal business, imposing the work of bloodhounds upon them. 3. It authorizes such kidnappers and rascals as may choose to do so, to arrest or seize persons without "due process of law." 4. It jeopardizes the liberty of every colored person, by requiring merely a *"general description,"* and by casting out the evidence of the person arrested. 5. It seeks to annul the writ of Habens Corpus, which tends to secure justice and liberty by delivering a person from false imprisonment, or by removing a case from one court to another. 6. It imposes excessive fines. 7. It denies the citizen a Jury Trial, where his liberty, and perhaps his life, is at stake.

Objections.—It violates the spirit and letter of the Constitution, in the form and manner of seizures or arrests; in its requirements upon good citizens, in imposing excessive fines, in crushing the Habeas Corpus, and in depriving the person arrested of a trial by a jury of his peers. 2. It contravenes the Law of Nature, which is the foundation of all human laws, and which, being dictated by the Almighty himself, is of course superior in obligation to any other. Therefore this enactment of Congress is both unjust and unreasonable, consequently becomes of no binding force—is null and void.

Let it be placed among the abominations!

S. M. Africanus, Hartford, Ct.

I.

Shame on the costly mockery of piling stone on stone
To those who won *our* liberties, the Heroes dead and gone,
While we look coldly on and see law-shielded ruffians slay
The men who fain would win *their own,* the Heroes of *to-day!*

II.

Are we pledged to craven silence? O fling it to the wind,
The parchment wall that bars us from the least of human kind—
That makes us cringe and temporise, and dumbly stand at rest,
While Pity's burning flood of words upheaves within the breast.

III.

Though we break our fathers' promise, we have nobler duties first,
The traitor to humanity is the traitor most accursed:—
Man is more than Constitutions; better rot beneath the sod,
Than be true to Church and State, while we're doubly false to God.

FIGURE 7.4 *The Fugitive Slave Law.* Broadside. Hartford, CT: circa 1850. Library of Congress, Prints and Photographs Division, rbpe 33700200.

to that of the state and then down the scale to the local levels of county, township, and home. The base unit of all such homologies was always the individual person, a trope that dates back to the cosmological phantasmagoria of medieval iconography, which posits man at the center of an escalating universe—or in the middle of the great chain of being. This paradigm persists into the modern period, where we can find it repeatedly deployed throughout foundational U.S. texts whenever a Paine or a Publius seeks to describe the logic of the nation or the federal state. "Until an independence is declared," Paine writes in *Common Sense*, "the continent will feel itself like a man who continues putting off some unpleasant business" (1:39). Publius likewise frequently compares the "passions" of a nation to the "passions" of a man, as he does in No. 6, where the behavior of one person (Pericles) stands in as an analogy for the behavior of an entire kingdom (28–29).[14] As I have already argued, the units in each of these cascading homologies function at the moment of founding as self-contained organisms—structurally similar nesting dolls that rest one inside the other, with little material connection between each other. Thus in the great chain of federalism, the "superstructure" of the nation always exists elsewhere, looming over and beyond individual citizens in the form of various bureaucracies which are administered at several geographical removes from one another: the town, the state, and the federal. The material emergence, however, of what Michael Hardt and Antonio Negri call "network culture" disrupts this fragile nesting arrangement, so that the logic of imperium in imperio finally encounters the limits of its own abstraction inside the proliferating built environment of nineteenth-century America.[15]

Like other traveling figures described in this book (from Hugh Finlay to Christopher Colles), the fugitive slave makes clear the connections between the parts of the union at the level of these once disarticulated spaces and scales. For one thing, the fugitive slave is always the resident of two states: the slave state he or she has left (and which continues to claim the fugitive as its own) and the free state he or she has arrived in (and which likewise claims the fugitive as its own in the name of its state sovereignty). In the act of moving between these two spaces and becoming the object of their competing claims, the fugitive becomes a special and spectacular kind of federal subject, one whose case, because it crosses and confuses local jurisdictions, must finally be determined by a national (and nationally visible) arbiter: the federal government. But if the fugitive slave resembles other figures I have already discussed, there is a crucial difference. Unlike a Christopher Colles or a Hugh Finlay, these fugitives from slavery were never isolated "projectors" of the future potential of U.S. network power. They were instead contemporary fixtures within an *existing* network—everyday icons of interstate relations that arrived, in the 1850s, on many different American doorsteps (including judicial ones) and were then repackaged in print for a nation of reader-citizens who consumed their stories in newspaper articles, slave narratives, novels, poems, stories, and tracts. In this way, the figure of the fugitive slave criss-crosses the national network, making its stakes and contradictions visible to those living within those no longer self-contained administrative units called states, counties, towns, and villages. Their stories (and the popularity of those stories) suggest that the overextended republic was shrinking in these years, both materially (through the time-space compression of technological and industrial development) and imaginatively. Lauren Berlant is correct, then, in noting that modern American citizenship is structured (or, in the Fourteenth Amendment, is restructured) around the seemingly anomalous experience of African-American slavery. I would simply add that it is not the emancipated slave who first forces the need for this new structure; it is, instead, the fugitive slave who, in occupying the contradictory local spaces of two states (and two sections) as well as two statuses at once (free and slave, human and thing), exposes the discontinuities upon which national consensus rests even as he predicts their ultimate integration within the national spaces of print, law, and finally war.

As icons of interstate commerce and community, fugitives in this period escaped by any and every (federal) means possible, making their way not only via the phantom "Underground Railroad" but, as Lisa Brawley notes, through an array of developing technologies that involved real rails and real roads.[16] Like Benjamin Lundy, many fugitives moved on foot. But most capitalized, as the American Anti-Slavery Society of the 1830s did, on the emerging relations of industrial production in its most material forms. William and Ellen Craft and Frederick Douglass traveled north by steamboat and rail. In the most famous manipulation of emerging U.S. infrastructure, Henry Box Brown packaged himself in a crate and mailed himself, express, from Richmond to Philadelphia in a relatively speedy twenty-six hours. Even Harriet Jacobs, who for seven years escaped her would-be rapist/master by standing still—locked, nearly to the point of paralysis, in the crawlspace above her grandmother's house—made use of this emerging infrastructure by directing a fraudulent letter campaign, using the mails and then newspaper ads to decoy her whereabouts, thus virtually inhabiting the cities in which her mail was postmarked (New York and Boston) while her body stayed home in Edenton, North Carolina. Thus in 1835, as the AASS was sending its pamphlets south, Jacobs's letters were crossing into the North, receiving postmarks in northern cities and then returning south by way of Hugh Finlay's distant descendant: the federal postman.[17] But these are only the best known of such travelers. As William Still's mammoth 1872 memoir of the Underground Railroad makes clear, countless fugitives traveled in every direction and by every means possible in these years.[18]

I have already argued that the freestanding political pamphlet was, during the American Revolution, one of few speaking commodities in the emerging market zone Benedict Anderson characterizes as the nation. Fugitive slaves would eventually prove a second such speaking commodity for northern book-buying publics. In their bondage and their freedom, fugitive slaves were doubly (if differently) commodified: once sold as slaves, they were later sold as stories—among the most popular literary subjects in antebellum print culture.[19] Lydia Maria Child made the connection between slave narrators and their books explicit when she described one fugitive slave as a tale "bound in black," enfolding the slave's circulating body within the circulating logic of print capitalism.[20] Many critics have peripherally engaged the more constraining aspect of this analogy (compressed here in the word "bound") by describing the "bondage" produced by conventional print forms in the abolitionist public sphere, which are rightly noted to have been expressively restrictive. I want to do something different, however, by thinking more literally about how the circulating bodies of fugitive slaves took up the nation-building work once performed by circulating texts—though, as we shall see, to very different ends. If the serial publication of a text like *The Federalist* figures consensus at the moment of founding (and yet reveals in retrospect the early republic's fragmented discontinuity from site to site), then fugitive slaves did the opposite: mobile slaves were spectacular indexes of the later republic's ongoing integration even as they helped expose a highly divisive contest between sections that finally led to civil war.

This difference is a historical effect, for the literature of fugitive slavery makes vividly clear that the material world of the 1830s, '40s, and '50s was significantly different from the one in which the Constitution had originally been ratified. In the same postal correspondences in which Madison sent copies of *The Federalist* home to Virginia friends in the late

1780s, he also engaged his family in an ongoing discussion about a particular fugitive slave named Anthony. In the very letters in which Madison tries to convince local doubters that this new-fangled contraption called the extended republic is desirable and practicable, he also makes a number of frustrated remarks about the fact that this man Anthony has escaped and eluded capture. Though Madison suspected that Anthony had gone to Philadelphia, he tells his family that he cannot get definitive information from his sources about the fugitive's whereabouts and ironically concludes that he will have to go there personally, for only a first-hand investigation will give him the local, on-the-spot information he requires. Though he made several trips, however, Madison never found what he was looking for. Anthony successfully eluded capture, and his success is important to the argument of this book in two ways. First, it demonstrates the precarious and partial ways that information and people circulated in the early republic—a vast space fraught with potential loopholes, lapses, opportunities for duplicity, and, in short, places to hide. Second, it shows us a case in which this was a problem for Madison, the federalist, but a solution for Anthony, his slave. In the 1780s, in other words, Anthony was able to slip through the interstices of the early national information network and make a new life for himself somewhere far away from Madison and his many local (Philadelphia) contacts.[21]

Sixty years later, fugitive slaves did not always fare quite so well escaping the federal information net, especially those who chose to run north (instead of west or south).[22] The Fugitive Slave Law of 1850 was responsible for helping to locate and return to slavery that other, more famous Anthony: Anthony Burns. The stories of these two Anthonies set side by side argue powerfully against the unities of time and space that the federal Constitution had initially tried to install. The world had changed significantly between 1787 and 1854, and it did so in ways that seriously challenged the delicate balance of spatial power that the framers had originally envisioned. The federalists of 1787 had relied upon certain indispensable kinds of disconnection from one community to the next—as did Madison's Anthony—and that is one reason why they were fearless in their projection of an extended republic made up of so many disjunct communities. This faith in geographic difference, and dispersion's power to manage it, is the essence of federalism's spatial fix. The extended republic was expected to isolate potential factions (like antifederalists—and abolitionists), who, with fewer opportunities for "communication and concert" would pose no serious threat to the federal center

(*FP* 61). As I argued in the first two sections of this book, the disconnections among different parts of the union finally allowed the framers to
ignore differences (and in some cases, samenesses) that would eventually
become more visible and more troublesome. These included a number of
regionally specific cultural practices—slavery being, of course, the most
notable among them. But such differences would, just two generations
later, finally begin to saturate an increasingly connected, more nationalized public sphere in such a way that, as Thoreau claimed, slavery finally
seemed to come to Massachusetts.

In marking the shift in material conditions between 1787 and 1854,
I do not mean to suggest that the Fugitive Slave Law of 1850 was *actually* able to locate and return every fugitive slave within its jurisdiction.
No law—either in print or execution—can penetrate every space it seeks
to structure, and for this reason, the process of national consolidation
begun in 1787 continues to this day, without end. There was, however,
after 1850 a discernible shift away from local (state-based) tactics in the
pursuit of fugitives like Madison's Anthony and toward a more centralized model involving the mobilization of a massive federal apparatus. Indeed, the very topos of fugitive slave recovery circulated as a conversation
within a more densely integrated network of representation that relied
on a series of connections that were, at base, material (involving roads,
rails, and steamboats). The federal government made this shift visible
and newly meaningful by deploying one of its own material incarnations
(the army) into local sites like Boston in order to seize and return fugitive
slaves. But antebellum print culture—that infinitely expanding tangle of
newspapers, magazines, handbills, advertisements, posters, novels, and
the like—played the more important role by representing and circulating news, opinion, and narratives about the Fugitive Slave Law in artifacts that were far less locally bound than the newspapers and pamphlets
of the early republic had once been. While some of these artifacts were
produced locally and others imported from some other, more metropolitan elsewhere (whether New York or Washington, DC), most overlapped with one another at a much denser rate than the printed texts of
1787 once had. In Publius's day, newspapers circulated up and down the
post road (either whole or in pieces), exchanged primarily among a community of printers who each printed some (but not all) pieces of these
exchanged items in a locally produced newspaper for local consumption.
In the antebellum era, the scene of textual exchange was less contained
than this, and the 1850s in particular produced fragmented but spectacu-

MRS. STOWE'S
FIRST GEOGRAPHY.

LESSON I.
MEASUREMENT.

DEAR CHILDREN: I have taught a little flock of children of my own; and this has led me to think a great deal about young folks like you. And when I have seen how much pleasure can be made for children by my way of teaching geography, I have wished that you, too, could share it. And so I have made this little book for you.

(7)

---

16   FIRST GEOGRAPHY.

Always, in bounding, begin north, then east, then south, and then west. This is the right order.

Now, you may make a map of the school-house yard. First draw a two-inch square; then turn your faces *north*, and put down crosses and dots, to show where the school house and other large and small things are placed, according to the points of the compass. Then *bound* the map you have drawn, by mentioning in the right order the things that are north, east, south, and west of the school-house yard. Thus: It is bounded north by Mr. Smith's lot, east by the street, south by Mr. Brown's lot, and west by Mr. Jones's lot.

Next you may draw such a figure as this on your slate; only make it a good deal larger. Then turn your faces to the north.

In the middle square write the name of the town where you live. Then write in the square above it the name of the town north of you; in the east square write the name of the place east of you; in the south square the place south of you; and in the west square the town west of you. If there are places north-east or south-east, north-west or south-west, write them in the corner squares.

FIGURE 7.5   Harriet Beecher Stowe. *First Geography for Children*. Boston: Phillips, Sampson & Co. 1855. Photo courtesy of the Newberry Library.

lar evidence of a rapidly compressing national network—with the Fugitive Slave Law working, as we shall see, as one particularly powerful index of such compression and *Uncle Tom's Cabin* working as another.

3. STOWE'S SPATIAL FIX: THE GEOGRAPHY OF *UNCLE TOM'S CABIN*

Uncle Tom's Cabin ends with the decision to "send George Harris to Liberia."[23] In lines Stowe would live to regret, George (an ex-slave) embraces a colonizationist project that can only be called ethnic nationalism:

The desire and yearning of my soul is for an African *nationality*. I want a people that shall have a tangible, separate existence of its own; and where am I to look for it? . . . On the shores of Africa I see a republic,—a republic formed of picked men, who, by energy and self-educating force, have, in many cases, individually, raised themselves above a condition of slavery. Having gone through a preparatory stage of feebleness, this republic has, at last, become an acknowledged nation on the face of the earth,—acknowledged by both France and England. There it is my wish to go, and find myself a people.[24]

For most northern abolitionists in 1852, colonization was an all but defunct solution to the problems of slavery and impending emancipation. Indeed, Garrison began his career as a New England abolitionist in the 1830s with an absolute renunciation of colonization.[25] It is no surprise, then, that the *Liberator*'s review of *Uncle Tom's Cabin* begins with a litany of compliments but ends bluntly on the problem of Liberia: "The work, towards its conclusion, contains some objectionable sentiments respecting African colonization, which we regret to see."[26] Immediate abolition had always insisted that the solution to slavery must be located within the nation rather than outside of it. *Uncle Tom's Cabin* likewise targets the American interior, albeit on a more local scale—portraying American kitchens and living rooms, as well as that more tender interior sanctuary of sentimentalism, the hearts and minds of the middle class. But it also arrives, finally, at a long-outmoded colonizationist solution that, on an ethnic model, relinks race and nation, biological essence and geographical place.

The novel's investment in geographic identity is not entirely surprising, given that Stowe spent her life as an author constructing well-conceived spatial imaginaries, from her antislavery fiction (critical of the South) to her many local color pieces (based on a nostalgic identification with New England). Her first foray into the field of national geography came in 1833, when she authored the *Primary Geography for Children* for Catherine Beecher's textbook series (a text that was reissued, at the height of Stowe's popularity, in 1855).[27] The *Geography* offers a taxonomy of nineteenth-century spaces—both national (the Western, Middle, Eastern, and the "Southern or Slave States") and global. Its imaginary is also insistently place-based, with the world's five "races" catalogued in explicitly territorial terms that recall George Harris's enthusiastic embrace of ethnic nationalism ("the European, the Asiatic, the African, the American, and the Malayan"). As a spatial primer, however, the *Geography*'s primary objective is the rather Collesean task of teaching its young readers how to read and draw maps of local, regional, national, and finally global space. As Stowe notes, "the first thing to be learned in geography is, *what a map is, and how to make one*" (8).

In this pedagogical project, Stowe takes a high federalist approach. "*General views*" are privileged (after the fashion of a Publius) over "*disconnected details*" (4, 3). Indeed, the *Geography* stakes itself on a "generalized and systematized" pedagogy that places a premium on the ability to imagine an expanded and expanding world: "The child is made to commence at home, and gradually to enlarge his ideas of extension, till town, country, continent, and finally the whole world, are presented on maps" (3, 4). This picture of the extended republic is, however, always rooted in the local act of reading and writing/drawing, as Stowe engages her readers in a series of exercises designed to help them understand both the empirical and representational relation between the local and the nonlocal. These lessons (which aim to teach the principles of both scale and orientation) begin with the production of an abstract grid that closely resembles the Jeffersonian grid once used as a template for the Land Ordinance of 1785. The central box of Stowe's grid is designated as the place in which the student is sitting (so that in the initial exercise, the center box represents the schoolroom and the boxes around it represent the houses that surround the schoolhouse); successive installments of the exercise then encourage the apprentice mapmaker to escalate his vision into ever more abstracted mappings—including depictions of town, state, and nation (again, in each case, with the mapmaker's own location placed at the center of the grid). The end result is, Stowe suggests, a "complete picture" (5), but it is also an early example of two key principles that would emerge in Stowe's later writings: first, a sense of relational orientation (North, South, East, and West) that nevertheless places New England at the center (since Stowe assumes here—as she often does later as well—a primarily New England audience); and second, the desire to make a "map" of the world that places her reader's body and home at the center. Scale, Stowe seems to suggest, is a trick of perception that must be mastered by the young and old alike: within the representational domain of the map, a large country can be the same size as a small city, depending on scale—a problem that can best be managed by keeping track of one's own embeddedness within the abstract structure of representation called, here, "geography."

Uncle Tom's Cabin is likewise a geography—a spatial primer in the increasingly nationalized geography of the early 1850s, but one that poses a crisis for any reader seeking to locate himself within an extended yet differentiated field of (federal) representation. The novel's events are staged across a shifting series of terrains, each one a temporary backdrop to a body in transit. To draw a map of the novel's action is to draw a map of North America. The story begins in the heart of the continent (on a farm in Kentucky) and then tracks its characters' forced migrations across national space, the literal navigation of which is minutely narrated, with roads, rivers, steamboats, horses, and carriages described at length at each point of transit: from Kentucky to Ohio to Canada (in one plotline) and from Kentucky to New Orleans to the Red River (in the other). But if *Uncle Tom's Cabin* takes the nation at large as its setting (rather than focusing on any one site), then the nation is looking small, parochial, stagey, and, as many readers have pointed out, hypersectionalized. There is no "West" to speak of here. Instead, Stowe orchestrates an epic conflict between a reified North and South, each embedded in the other's daily practices through the workings of an ever more integrated marketplace (as in the famous auction depicted in "The Slave Warehouse" chapter, which begins in New Orleans and ends, via telegraph wire, in New York City).[28] There are not parts to the nation or part-spaces beyond this dyadic split but just the stark, unsatisfactory binary of North versus South sectionalism. Indeed, the novel is a tale not just of two sections but of two everythings: two slaves sold down the river and two options for each of them (resistance or submission), which in stark geo- and cosmographic terms translates into freedom in Canada or death on the Red River, redemption on Earth (in Liberia) for the Harrises or resurrection (in Heaven) for Tom.

Amy Kaplan has recently revisited the spatial politics of the domestic novel of the 1850s, arguing that George Harris's embrace of colonization is not just a "racist failure of Stowe's political imagination" but instead "underwrites the racial politics of the domestic imagination" more generally.[29] For Kaplan, the domestic novel "turns an imperial nation into a home by producing and colonizing specters of the foreign that lurk inside and outside its ever shifting borders."[30] Kaplan points out that while these novels dismantle the separate (gendered) spheres of home and state, female and male, they also frequently introduce a new set of separate (racial) spheres organized around a global program of apartheid that would return American blacks to Africa as missionaries and nation-builders in their own right. This colonizationist project effects two ends: it extends the global power of the United States abroad by having emancipated

"American" slaves take the lead in Christianizing Africa, and it leaves the new imperial center, the United States, white at its center.

Though Kaplan does not say so, her argument centers on the problem of scale. She describes a juncture in U.S. history when home and nation are starting to work in tandem to think about a larger imperial project in noncontiguous U.S. spaces. This shift outward is exactly how other nineteenth-century thinkers were theorizing that imperialism might resolve the interior contradictions of nationalism, providing an external location about which internally divided populations might be able to unite—a screen for the projection and production of national harmony.[31] So it is in Kaplan's argument, which shows how nineteenth-century domestic novels unite the once divided interests of men and women through the unifying project of global empire building. But while Kaplan does not remark on it, such work unites not just different genders but different scales (the micro scale of home and the macro scale of nation), each acting in concert with each other while playing that unity off against an African outside, or elsewhere, shrinking the differences between home and nation through the more macro project of global conquest.

This kind of multitiered spatial fix would have been unimaginable in an earlier period, when the tiered scales of home, state, nation, and continent were not understood to work in concert but were instead frequently seen as pragmatically disconnected—disarticulable to one another in space and (travel) time. When de Tocqueville, for instance, describes "the dwelling" of the frontier home as "a little world, an ark of civilization amid an ocean of foliage," he is articulating a fantasy that organizes itself around the integrity of each little locality within a larger microcosmic chain of attenuated geographic coordinates. In this model, local sites function insularly unto themselves and retain an integrity based on the uniqueness of their own material location in space; like Noah's "ark," they serve as microcosms of a larger world that works in a structurally similar way but does so at a safe physical remove (across a distant "ocean of foliage").[32] My argument here is that the logic of such microcosms is historically disrupted in the nineteenth century by the production of networks that reorder the world—networks of communication and commerce that reveal that the points and dots that make up these insular worlds, these self-sufficient "arks of civilization," are not permanently dispersed, each occupying a safe distance from the next, but are instead intimately connected by a tangled skein of mass transit—a transit both enacted and figured by the winding pathways of steam travel, railroad tracks, and of course the proliferating web of self-representation known as print culture.

Stowe's novel describes just such an emerging skein of criss-crossing dots. Indeed, it is abundantly clear that Stowe has fully absorbed the national simultaneity argument first put forward by the AASS, which in the 1830s had insisted that slavery was not local but national and that all citizens everywhere were responsible for it. Unlike her earlier *Geography* textbook, which sought to empower its readers to see themselves as distinguished parts in a massive but still highly self-differentiated whole, *Uncle Tom's Cabin* displays a world that is, as John Berger has said of modern life more generally, "indivisible."[33] The novel is devoted to demonstrating that once-distinct spatial scales (and hence, regional differences) have collapsed under the circulating regimes of the domestic slave market. There is no clear partition, Stowe insists, between northern and southern interests in regard to slavery: to be a northerner is to be an American in *Uncle Tom's Cabin*; to be an American is to be half-southern and thus to be a slaveholder—whether one resides in New Orleans or Nantucket. (Simon Legree is the exemplum of this principle: born in Vermont, he is the most ruthless southerner in the novel.) To the idea of sectional merger, however, Stowe attaches mergers and confusions of many other kinds—with women acting like men, men acting like women, slaves behaving virtuously, and masters behaving servilely. The once-meaningful differences of gender, status, and region are thus all shown to be in a crisis of correspondence—of claustrophobic, tautological sameness, or self-suture—a problem plainly provoked by slavery and the domestic national market that sustains it.

The novel makes clear, however, that the overintegration of once-distinct sections is not merely a matter of economic interest between northern merchants and southern slaveholders. Stowe also explores the political encroachment of Washington, DC, into particular homes, making the state and the market two sides of an incursion into the local. In one well-known chapter, a senator who has supported the Fugitive Slave Law arrives home (in Ohio) to find his wife feeding Eliza and Harry in their kitchen. The senator tries to stem his wife's sentimental understanding of her duty by deploying the logic of federal union and national consensus:

> But, Mary, just listen to me. Your feelings are all quite right, dear, and interesting, and I love you for them; but, then, dear, we mustn't suffer our feelings to run away with our judgment; you must consider it's

not a matter of private feeling,—there are great public interests involved,—there is such a state of public agitation rising, that we must
put aside our private feelings. (84)

Senator Bird makes an argument here that can never fly in a sentimental novel: he implores Mrs. Bird to forgo the sanctity of the local nest,
insisting that "private feelings" can no longer be entertained in the face
of "public" imperatives and that local customs must be adapted to federal law. His argument implies, as Webster's compromise does on a larger
scale, that the local world of "private feeling" is now saturated with "public interests" that were once distant. The North is no longer a place elsewhere, or outside, of slave culture but increasingly must understand itself
as part of a great bundle of interconnected national "interests." The idea
that local attachments might be erased in this way horrifies Mrs. Bird
(who wins the argument), but it also captivates many northern citizens
in these years, as almost any newspaper after 1854 will show.

Stowe's polarization of "sympathy" and "interest" recalls Publius's
disquisitions on these two modes of attachment in 1787. *Federalist* No.
6, for example, argues that "commercial republics, like ours, will never
be disposed to waste themselves in ruinous contentions with each other.
They will be governed by mutual interest, and will cultivate a spirit of
mutual amity" (31). *Federalist* No. 56, on the other hand, describes sympathy as something that arises from "local objects" and will most likely
bind the citizen to his local state rather than the federal state (384–90).
In the early federalist imaginary, "sympathy" is always aligned with the
local while "interest" is aligned with the national. But this, of course, was
before moving bodies like Eliza and Harry's begin to place pressure on
these two once disarticulated scales of national (versus local) life.

Stowe's novel is, in fact, famous precisely for the ways that it diffuses,
on a national scale, the once local affect we call "sentiment." But *Uncle
Tom's Cabin* is not really as nationalist a text as it may at first seem, even
if we grant that its primary theme is the problem of spatial compression I
have been describing here. Stowe is, in fact, very much an old-fashioned
federalist, in that she would appear to be lamenting the ongoing collapse
between the scales of national life as destructive rather than productive.
To this end, she seeks both to describe America's fall into nationalism *and*
to reinstall the equipoise of an older, more disintegrated model in which
the (different) parts of the nation balance the whole at a distance. We can
see this high federalist strain in the way that her work both federalizes

(in the sense of making "accurate" information about a regional practice more nationally available) and yet simultaneously reregionalizes (in the sense of representing the differences that, ideally, separate different ways of life and so reinforcing the different moral economies of North and South). Like many immediate abolitionists, Stowe describes a material collapse of meaningful boundaries even as she seeks the respite of local (ideological) difference.

This contradictory move is the key to understanding the novel's attempt to achieve closure through colonization. *Uncle Tom's Cabin* clearly participates in a wider, more sectionally based form of cultural panic— the fear of fused identities and collapsed national scales (with nation, region, home, and self all emerging as one disturbingly coagulated site of "interest"). This is the fear that underwrites Stowe's colonizationist ending, but it is less an attempt to forestall racial amalgamation than to evade the ongoing emergence of nationalism itself: the consolidation of a single, nonregionalized identity among whites of different locales. Stowe can find no other solution to the self-sameness of the1850s nation (and the seemingly closed circuit of its increasingly compressed national network) than to exteriorize (or colonize) its unwanted parts at the level of individual bodies, deporting her freedmen beyond state borders—to Canada, to Liberia, and to heaven. In a very real sense, then, Stowe seeks to reinstall the line between states by appealing to a color line that is itself made coincident with the nation-state as a whole (with America ultimately remaining white as black freedmen return to Africa). By ending the novel on the project of colonization, Stowe fantasizes a solution to the problem of sameness that ultimately requires her to reinstall the foundational splits upon which local identities (North and South, male and female) depend. The novel suggests that when Tom goes to heaven and George, Eliza, and Topsy leave for Liberia—when the figure of the slave in transit is finally removed from the national frame—then men will be men again, New England will be northern again, and America will be white again.

Though Stowe later claimed that if she had to do it again, she would rewrite the ending, colonization is the novel's most predictable spatial solution, given its many con/fusions and its self-saturated national setting. Not only does this choice create an outside that appears otherwise lost under the integrating regimes of domestic market capitalism. But in removing its characters' futures to another continent, the novel also reestablishes a geographic identification of race with nation, of bodies with

places, over and against a definition of race that casts it as portable biological essence (and hence autonomous and mobile at the level of the individual and transferable at the level of region—a model that would have
allowed regions to be racially integrated, or heterogeneously filled with
many different kinds of bodies at once). By stepping back and rescaling
the problems she faces—differences that organize themselves around
the axes of gender, race, and location—Stowe seeks an old solution to
an old problem. But we should not read her recurrence to colonization
as wholly residual. The spatial fix of colonization, though not politically
progressive, is actually the most forward-looking feature of Stowe's novel,
forecasting, from empire's threshold, the colonizing projects to come, not
just in the late-nineteenth-century United States but across the world.

4. Inside and Outside the Loop: Solomon Northup's *Twelve Years a Slave*

For many readers, *Uncle Tom's Cabin* dissolved into an issue of fact or
fiction. Unable to stem its circulation (and thus divide the novel from
its own material manifestations in rail cars, steamers, stages, and drawing rooms), *Uncle Tom's* critics sought to split the novel from itself on
the grounds of faulty knowledge, interrupting its successful circulation
by appealing to a discrepancy between a northern set of signifiers and a
southern signified. Stowe's response was, famously, *A Key to Uncle Tom's
Cabin*—an elaborate defense of the novel's characters and events based,
like Weld's *Slavery as It Is*, on documentary sources.[34] The commotion
over the facticity of *Uncle Tom's Cabin* indicates that for American audiences, the word *actual* never went away. The status of corrupt representation was every bit as important in the reception of Stowe's novel as it had
been in the early days of republic. And while few northern abolitionists
knew the South from first-hand experience, they persistently and paradoxically invoked the Revolutionary inheritance of actual representation
every time they cited the language of inalienable rights and self-evident
truths. In upholding these fictions, immediate abolition mapped a two-
part agenda: first, it sought the fusion of all that had been alienated from
itself under slavery (God and man, word and thing, the nation then and
the nation now, North and South, black and white). At the same time,
however, such commitments confusedly bound abolition (like other
Protestant reform movements of the period) to a vision of the factual,

the empirical, or what I have called throughout this book the *actual* over and against the virtualities of the nation or other regions.[35]

Strictly speaking, these two agendas were mutually contradictory. How could abolitionists living out their lives in New York and New England fuse their northern selves with a southern self they had never seen firsthand? It's little wonder that southern testimony became a key component in abolitionist discourse, which compulsively amassed the conversion narratives of reformed slaveholders (like James Birney and the Grimkés); indigenous southern "archives"—usually newspaper ads and articles; and finally, the testimony of fugitive slaves ("native informants," as Lisa Brawley calls them), who described their experiences in lectures and slave narratives sponsored by both national and regional antislavery societies. Weld, in *Slavery as It Is*, focused on the first two of these categories, assembling a large archive of white testimony. Stowe, in composing the *Key*, relied on all three, as well drawing on the accruing archive of abolition itself (with Weld serving as a primary source).

Frederick Douglass's resistance to being paraded in front of northern audiences as "a brand new fact" is well known; so is Harriet Jacobs's refusal to be appropriated *after* the fact by Stowe.[36] We might add to this more famous pairing the autobiographical "slave" narrative of Solomon Northup, whose remarkable story is cited, with a thousand others, in Stowe's *Key*. Born a free African-American citizen of New York State, Northup was tricked in 1841 into leaving his home in Saratoga Springs by kidnappers who engaged him to play his fiddle for a traveling circus in Washington, DC. Once in the capital city, Northup was drugged, placed in a slave pen, and severely whipped until he stopped claiming his freedom.[37] Transported by slave ship to New Orleans, he was eventually sold onto a cotton plantation on the Red River in Louisiana—the same place where Simon Legree lives (and Tom dies) in *Uncle Tom's Cabin*. Upon returning to the North after twelve years in slavery, Northup gave an interview about his experience that was reprinted in numerous northern newspapers (Stowe found her copy, for instance, in the *New York Times*). Upon resettling in New York, Northup commenced authoring in his own right, publishing an extended memoir titled *Twelve Years a Slave* that went through several large printings.[38]

Stowe gives Northup four full columns (or about two pages) in the *Key*, categorizing his story under the subheading "kidnapping." Northup returns the favor of this acknowledgment by dedicating *Twelve Years a Slave* to Stowe ("whose name, throughout the world, is identified with the great reform") and by citing his narrative as "another *Key to Uncle Tom's Cabin*." But Northup's references to Stowe within the text are less salutary. Appearing at regular intervals, these allusions are most often asides that emphasize the profound difference between fictional accounts of slavery and its factual experience:

> Men may write fictions portraying lowly life as it is, or as it is not— may expatiate with owlish gravity upon the bliss of ignorance—discourse flippantly from arm chairs of the pleasures of slave life; but let them toil with him in the field—sleep with him in the cabin—feed with him on husks; let them behold him scourged, hunted, trampled on, and they will come back with another story in their mouths. (158)

Northup obliquely references Stowe here (her subtitle to *Uncle Tom's Cabin* had been "Life Among the Lowly") at the same moment he is remarking on the truthfulness of his own account over and against "fictions portraying lowly life as it is, or as it is not." In doing so, he ironically deploys a critique that was usually associated with the proslavery, or southern, side of the debate. Indeed, the phrase "lowly life as it is" simultaneously refers to Stowe's novel and to Mary Eastman's popular proslavery response to it, *Aunt Phillis's Cabin, or Southern Life as It Is* (1852) (itself a pointed allusion to Weld's *Slavery as It Is*). By collapsing Stowe's title with Eastman's, Northup manages to obfuscate the target of his critique even as he suggests that the two might not be as different as they seem.

But many of Northup's references to *Uncle Tom's Cabin* are more direct. On several occasions, he draws an explicit analogy between himself and Tom in ways that suggest that Stowe has produced a crisis for him— a need to explain why he survived the Red River when Tom did not. In one such example, Northup is named the driver on his plantation and pointedly remarks: "I dared not show any lenity, not having the Christian fortitude of a certain well-known Uncle Tom. . . . In that way, only, I escaped the immediate martyrdom he suffered, and, withal, saved my companions much suffering" (172). Here and elsewhere, Northup insists on his difference from Tom and defends it, mildly reproaching Stowe for not recognizing that there might be better ways to help one's fellow slaves (since Northup ultimately "saved [his] companions much suffering," as Tom could not). Northup's vexed relation to *Uncle Tom* recurs later in the narrative, where he makes his most pointed criticism of Stowe, not so much targeting her portrait of southern life "as it is, or is not" as taking issue with her representation of *him*, as a brand new fact, in the supposedly factual *Key*:

> The allusion to myself in the work recently issued, entitled "A Key to Uncle Tom's Cabin," contains the first part of this letter [a document about Northup], omitting the postscript. Neither are the full names of the gentlemen to whom it is directed correctly stated, there being a slight discrepancy, probably a typographical error. To the postscript more than to the body of the communication am I indebted for my liberation, as will presently be seen. (213)

We might view this as an elaborate way for Northup to try to convince readers that they need to read both *A Key* and *Twelve Years*, except that the remark is placed near the end of the narrative and so has little selling power. Instead, this passage once again calls Stowe's facticity into question, insisting on Northup's more authentic brand of knowledge, even at the level of documentary evidence. Stowe's novel may have circulated more widely than Northup's narrative, but Northup's body had circulated more widely than Stowe's.

Here and elsewhere, Northup shows a remarkable faith in the evidence of texts, but his conception of textuality is at direct odds with Stowe's representation of it in *Uncle Tom's Cabin*. While Stowe famously declares that "mail for [Tom] had no existence," Northup can think of nothing else while in slavery. Indeed, much of *Twelve Years a Slave* documents Northup's attempt to gain control over a basic circulating representation of his situation: a letter to friends who might help locate him. Indeed, the book could well be called "Twelve Years to Post a Letter," for Northup's experience of slavery exactly coincides with his lack of access to the federal post office and to the basic materials (pen, ink, and paper) whereby any literate free American might insert himself into the disembodied circuits of national life:

> My great object always was to invent means of getting a letter secretly into the post-office, directed to some of my friends or family at the North. The difficulty of such an achievement cannot be comprehended by one unacquainted with the severe restrictions imposed upon me. In the first place, I was deprived of pen, ink, and paper. In the second place, a slave cannot leave his plantation without a pass, nor will a post-master mail a letter for one without written instructions from his

owner. I was in slavery nine years, and always watchful and on the alert, before I met with the good fortune of obtaining a sheet of paper. (175)

In this way, the narrative recounts Northup's twelve-year odyssey to locate a piece of paper and a pen—items not readily available to him in either a New Orleans slave pen or a Red River cotton field. Northup eventually "appropriates" a single sheet of foolscap, "concealing it . . . under the board on which I slept." The letter that gains him his freedom is produced with this pilfered foolscap, ink made from the bark of a white maple tree, and a pen "manufactured" from the wing feathers of a duck (175). As an account of Northup's travel across sectional boundaries (first as a body and later, in ink, as signature on a letter), *Twelve Years a Slave* serves as a rejoinder to the geography of *Uncle Tom's Cabin*—both to its theory of national space and to its understanding of how bodies and information circulate in that space. Indeed, as an extended account of Northup's textual deprivation—his inability, that is, to circulate himself as a representation through a virtual network of national information—*Twelve Years a Slave* is a rebuke not just to *Uncle Tom's Cabin's* representation of "slavery as it is, or is not," but to that novel's status as an always self-identical, because omnicirculating, object within the print network to which Northup was, as a slave, continually denied access.

Northup goes to great lengths, for example, to show the edges of the circuit in which Stowe's novel can be said to travel, the impenetrable locations in (and from) which certain kinds of information have yet to be integrated. Sometimes these edges appear material (or geographical), while at other times they appear ideological. He speaks, for instance, of "the remoter depths of Slavery" (63)—which he reached when living on the Red River's Bayou Boeuf, lying, as it does, beyond "the termination of the railroad tracks" (64). In such moments, Northup registers slavery's reach as both a vertical location in an abstract chain of power (the "depths" of slavery) and as the horizontal edge of an empirical map ("the termination of the railroad tracks"). Though Stowe claims to present a trustworthy representation of the Red River region, Northup goes out of his way to emphasize the ways in which his geographic experiences elude representation—or are distorted by it. Indeed, his ultimate deliverance is nearly foiled by the illegibility of his geographical position on a map that his liberators have trouble reading: the town of Marksville, from which Northup's appeal is postmarked, "although occupying a prominent position, and standing out in impressive italics on the map of Louisiana, is, in fact, but a small and insignificant hamlet" (228–29), while Bayou Boeuf (at which the letter was written and by-lined) "was twenty-three miles distant [from Marksville], and was the name applied to the section of country extending between fifty and a hundred miles, on both sides of that stream" (229). Though seemingly legible as representations on a map (and in Stowe's novel), these Red River locales prove difficult to locate on foot or in person. Northup's ultimate release finally reads like an unlikely Cinderella story, as agents from the North arrive, only to find that the only way to locate him is to "repair to the Bayou, and traveling up one side and down the other its whole length [i.e., 150 miles], inquire at each plantation" for someone matching Northup's description (229).

But while Northup's predicament is a material one (in that he finds himself beyond the reach of pen, paper, and postage for over a decade), his narrative also emphasizes the ideological structure of emerging material infrastructures—especially the uneven access afforded to different persons inscribed within the supposedly transparent and increasingly totalizing reach of antebellum postal routes, rail lines, and telegraph wires. Northup's fellow slaves have only a vague sense of national space, not as a real-world network of places but as an imagined space of freedom. To one such slave (named Patsey), slavery "was one long dream of liberty. Far away, to her fancy an immeasurable distance, she knew there was a land of freedom. A thousand times she had heard that somewhere in the distant North there were no slaves—no masters. In her imagination it was an enchanted region, the Paradise of the earth" (200). But unlike either Uncle Tom or Patsey, Northup carries with him geographic knowledge about the place he lives in and all the other elsewheres where he once was and might one day be. He has an acute awareness of his "real situation" and "the hopelessness of any effort to escape through the wide forests" that surround the Red River region (67). But while this predicament disturbs him, he nevertheless has enough prior knowledge of the world to imagine other locations in a way that his fellow slaves do not (as when he remarks, in the same passage, that "my heart was at home in Saratoga" [67]). Indeed, Northup's deliverance is premised on his knowledge of faraway places: it is in speaking with a Canadian itinerant named Bass (the friend who ultimately helps him post his letter north) that Northup finally reveals himself as something no slave on the Red River can be: a traveler who has moved as freely through the North as Bass himself has. Northup shocks Bass with his extensive geographical knowledge:

"Oh, I know where Canada is," said I, "I have been there myself."

"Yes, I expect you are well acquainted all through that country," [Bass] remarked, laughing incredulously.

"As sure as I live, Master Bass," I replied, "I have been there. I have been in Montreal and Kingston, and Queenston, and a great many places in Canada, and I have been in York State, too—in Buffalo, and Rochester, and Albany, and can tell you the names of the villages on the Erie canal and the Champlain canal."

Bass turned round and gazed at me a long time without uttering a syllable. (208–9)

This scene points out a crucial fact of Northup's captivity: his ability to access the national network (and the freedom such circulation promises) is in some ways a material, or geographical, matter and in other ways an ideological issue shaped by the contingencies of place. It is never, however, what his master Epps thinks it is: a matter of innate biological aptitude reducible to his race (a fact I will return to in a moment).

Just as Northup is denied free circulation in his body, he is denied entrance into the circuit of national print culture while he remains in the South. His access to the world of print does not depend on his knowledge or skill but on where he happens to be at any given moment in time. He can enter the circuit of representation and experience its freedoms, in other words, only from certain distinct locations on the national map. "Beyond the reach of [Epps's] inhuman thong, and standing on the soil of the free State where I was born, thanks be to Heaven, I can raise my head once more among men. I can speak of the wrongs I have suffered, and of those who inflicted them, with upraised eyes" (138). It is place, in the end, rather than race that makes Northup free and unfree, an author or a slave, part of the circuit of representation or an outcast from it. Thus on his return North, Northup not only circulates his body and his story through the representational structures of the national book market but does so with extraordinary success, as the book's high circulation numbers and his general celebrity attest.

Frederick Douglass' Paper (among others) took special note of the discrepancy between Northup's enslavement in "the obscurest section of the Red River region" and his later celebrity as the author of "a most interesting narrative" "read by hundreds of thousands of his fellow citizens."[39] Indeed, Douglass emphasized Northup's success by reprinting at steady intervals extensive puffs from Northup's publishers trumpeting its successful circulation across a wide geographic space. After the fashion of a Stowe advertisement, the earliest ads declare that "17,000 copies have sold in 4 months" while later ones proudly announce that the "FOUR-TEENTH THOUSAND" copy is "NOW READY," reprinting favorable cita-tions from twelve different reviews located in cities as diverse as Buffalo, New York, Detroit, Rochester, Cincinnati, Syracuse, Cayuga (Ohio), and Pittsburgh.[40] But this only proves Northup's investment in the North as a self-making site: the book illustrates (as a plot and as an object circulat-ing through stores in Syracuse and Pittsburgh) that Northup could be (simultaneously, it seems) a slave in the South and a celebrated author in other regions. The successful sale of the narrative across the scattered Northeast and West thus fulfills the place-based logic of his twelve-year ordeal, set as it is against the scene of textual deprivation he experiences at Bayou Boeuf.

Both in its plotline and in its circulatory afterlife as a celebrated book-object in its own right, Northup's story reveals loopholes in the model of mass circulation we associate with *Uncle Tom's Cabin*. While *Twelve Years a Slave* was frequently yoked to *Uncle Tom* in newspaper and maga-zine reviews, Northup actually points out one of the biggest problems in Stowe's conception of national space, for Northup's story denies the saturation (or self-sameness) of space that Stowe's novel describes, and in some sense, performs.[41] In doing so, it exposes *Uncle Tom's Cabin* as just another partial (printed) representation of slavery "as it is, or is not." To the degree that Northup fails to enter the circuit of such circulating representations (and he does fail—for twelve years), it is not because he does not know how to enter it or because it cannot reach him. It is be-cause it is a circuit that only *seems* to saturate the world of known spaces but that is nevertheless closed to certain readers and writers (like himself) through structures of power that are hyperlocal (and thus more vertical than horizontal). In this way, Northup's narrative portrays a new kind of virtual nation: one that exists for some subjects and not for others—no matter how extensive its material structures come to be.

Northup's story is important to the argument of this book, then, for several reasons. It suggests that the nation's networks were more evenly developed in the 1850s than they had once been, but it also shows that even at the height of its self-understanding as a fused series of parts (a na-tion rather than a series of well-bounded sections or disaggregated state-parts), the United States was never a fully self-saturated space, even in print. Print may have emerged more evenly and produced more connections between the parts of the union after 1850, but Northup's struggles to escape (back) into freedom prove that the privileges of print culture were never evenly distributed. The more actual the nation became and the more connected its parts were in 1850, 1860, and beyond, the more virtual (or hyper-) the space of national belonging became. In this way, Northup's narrative rebukes Stowe's claustrophobic fantasy of a nation so self-sutured at the ground that it needs to extract and colonize its own dark difference.

5. THE FULTON OF INDIAN CREEK: RACE AND PLACE IN *TWELVE YEARS A SLAVE*

Throughout his narrative, Northup is invested in a place-based reading of social difference, which he explicitly opposes to a more biological reading (of the sort Stowe finally embraces)—a conflict aggressively staged in a conversation between his owner (Epps) and his "liberator"/friend (Bass). Here, Epps mouths a proslavery truism by insisting that slavery is premised on an absolute difference between the white and black races (one that he compares to the species difference "between a white man and a baboon") (206). The more sympathetic Bass, on the other hand, argues instead that the conditions of enslavement are made possible by the uneven circulation of information:

"There are monkeys among white people as well as black, when you come to that," coolly remarked Bass. "I know some white men that use arguments no sensible monkey would. But let that pass. These niggers are human beings. If they don't know as much as their masters, whose fault is it? They are not *allowed* to know anything. You have books and papers, and can go where you please, and gather intelligence in a thousand ways. But your slaves have no privileges. You'd whip one of them if caught reading a book. They are held in bondage, generation after generation, deprived of mental improvement, and who can expect them to possess much knowledge?"

. . .

"If you lived up among the Yankees in New-England," said Epps, "I expect you'd be one of them cursed fanatics that know more than the constitution, and go about peddling clocks and coaxing niggers to run away."

"If I was in New-England," returned Bass, "I would be just what I am here." (206–7)

In keeping with his general character, Epps lays out different rules for black and white men, suggesting they differ by virtue of race while white men differ (even from themselves) by virtue of the geographical locale (or place) that they happen to inhabit. Epps argues, in other words, that Bass's identity is likely to change based on his location, his placement in space: if Bass "lived up among the Yankees in New-England," Epps suggests, he would be an abolitionist. Bass, of course, denies this premise, insisting that he is autonomous, consistent, and self-identical no matter where he is: "If I was in New-England," he says, "I would be just what I am here." At the same time, however, he recognizes that his self-identicality is premised on his intellectual, social, and geographic mobility. As he tells Epps: "you have books and papers, and can go where you please, and gather intelligence in a thousand ways. But your slaves have no privileges. You'd whip one of them if caught reading a book."

In thinking through the question of where identity ultimately resides (in a racially marked body or in a geographic place), Northup agrees, in a sense, with Bass, suggesting that self-identicality (or consistency of character) across space is a privilege afforded largely to white men. But where Bass emphasizes the circulation of information and knowledge in the production of southern slave identities, Northup tends to emphasize the literal geographic consequences of one's placement in space. Where geography means nothing to a man like Bass (who remains the same person in New England that he is on the Red River), it means everything to Northup—who finds himself free in one state and unfree in another, even though he is every bit as learned and well traveled as either Bass or Epps. As we shall see, this recognition of his own differential identity in space ultimately leads Northup to reinvest in the very spatial construct Stowe diagnoses as lost: the sectional line dividing North from South. His reification of these regions is based, however, on a consistent understanding of how American identity is meaningfully constructed on the ground.

This may explain why an explicitly *northern* freedom becomes Northup's fetish. The lived experience of freedom is such a fundamental condition of identity for Northup that he is only able to identify and bond with those who have known it firsthand. Early in the narrative, for instance, Northup meets two falsely enslaved freemen, with whom he develops a special affective bond. One, "a man of intelligence and information," has much in common with Northup:

> His name was Robert. Like myself, he had been born free, and had a wife and two children in Cincinnati. He said he had come south with two men, who had hired him in the city of his residence. Without free papers, he had been seized at Fredericksburgh, placed in confinement, and beaten until he had learned, as I had, the necessity and the policy of silence. He had been in Goodin's pen about three weeks. To this man I became much attached. We could sympathize with, and understand each other. (38)

Northup's and Robert's fates temporarily coincide when they are literally connected by an iron chain and placed on a New Orleans-bound ship. While on this middle passage, they meet a third freeman named Arthur, who, in contrast to "the policy of silence" adopted by Northup and Robert, arrives "protest[ing], in a loud voice, against the treatment he was receiving, and demand[ing] to be released" (41). In the larger narrative, Robert and Arthur represent two potential outcomes—and affects—for Northup. Robert is "melancholy" while Arthur is angry; perhaps for this reason, Robert dies quickly while Arthur lives to be rescued upon arrival in New Orleans. While on board, however, the differences between the three are collapsed in their common memory and common desire for northern freedom, which expresses itself in a plan, first formulated by Northup, to seize the ship:

> There was not another slave we dared to trust. Brought up in fear and ignorance as they are, it can scarcely be conceived how servilely they will cringe before a white man's look. It was not safe to deposit so bold a secret with any of them, and finally we three resolved to take upon ourselves alone the fearful responsibility of the attempt. (44–45)

Like Frederick Douglass, who, in his 1845 autobiography, describes the slave songs of his peers from a position of cultivated detachment and difference, Northup marks his difference from "real" slaves, whom he frequently describes as servile and cringing beings so damaged by their environment that they cannot be trusted. While Northup, Robert, and Arthur are men of "intelligence and information," the slaves they travel with are constructed as ignorant and untrustworthy. In this way, Northup cultivates a bond, not just with other freemen within the narrative, but with every free man who reads it.

Importantly, however, these characterizations are never elaborated in racial terms but are understood instead as the effects of slavery, which is in turn characterized in geographic terms as an explicitly southern institution. Northup thus rejects racial essentialisms but embraces what we might call geographic essentialisms—the idea of essences produced by location. To this end, Northup valorizes freedom—and his own status as a northern freeman—over and against the debasing and geographically based effects of southern slavery. Indeed, the terms "northern" and "freedom" are interchangeable for Northup, and he draws, throughout his years in slavery, on a base of knowledge produced by his experiences of freedom, importing northern know-how into his everyday work-life on the Red River. At one point, he produces what he characterizes as a "Northern" axe-handle, replacing the southern fashion of using "a round, straight stick" with the "crooked one . . . to which I had been accustomed at the North." His master responds "with astonishment, unable to determine" what it is, and Northup betrays no small amount of pride in noting that his master was "forcibly struck with the novelty of the idea" and "kept it in the house a long time, and when his friends called, was wont to exhibit it as a curiosity" (133).

"Novelty," ingenuity, efficiency, skill—not to mention the desire to produce and display "curiosities"—are all ideological productions of the northern wage economy—just as the axe-handle is a material one. Northup further reveals his investment in that economy and its values when he innovates a makeshift canal to transport his master's lumber up the Red River, an efficient alternative to moving it overland. "I ascertained the distance from the mills to the point on the latter bayou, where our lumber was to be delivered, was but a few miles less by land than by water. Provided the creek could be made navigable for rafts, it occurred to me that the expense of transportation would be materially diminished" (70). Northup's project is successful, but given his inability to circulate freely through the national network, his construction of this miniature canal might be the most ironic moment of his enslavement, expressing his faith in the very structures of commercial mobility that had both whisked him to slavery (he was moved south by both rail and boat) and that nevertheless denied him, for twelve long years, transit home. In Northup's narrative, the canal episode is meant to prove, once again, his essential difference from the southerners who surround him:

> At this business I think I was quite skillful, not having forgotten my experience years before on the Champlain canal. I labored hard, being extremely anxious to succeed, both from a desire to please my master, and to show Adam Taydem [the foreman] that my scheme was not such a visionary one as he incessantly pronounced it. (70–71)

Northup notes that the arrival of the first raft through the canal "created a sensation": "on all sides I heard Ford's Platt [Northup's slave name] pronounced the 'smartest nigger in the Pine Woods'—in fact I was the Fulton of Indian Creek" (70). Poignantly, Northup must hear himself "pronounced" worthy by a name other than his own, and he appears to respond to this enforced alienation by taking up, in turn, his own new name, dubbing himself "the Fulton of Indian Creek." Though never fully recognized for who he is, Northup revels in his ability to excel and astonish the men who surround him. But as this episode shows, the ignorance Northup describes at such moments is never racialized. Northup's white overseers and masters are as ignorant of the innovations he brings to his labor as any of their slaves are—and vice versa. Like many a northerner after 1850, Northup genuinely seems to believe in the benefits that accrue to free men through free labor—including the skill, efficiency, pride, and exceptional drive "to succeed" that he displays in building his canal. Northup learns these principles in New York but carries them with him into the South, where they serve as imports of a very local kind of knowledge and selfhood. To the degree that Northup becomes "the Fulton of Indian Creek"—the ingenious inventor who can participate fully in the densely connected circuit that is national culture (rather than remaining a slave forever excluded from that circuit)—it is because he has so fully imbibed the mores of the northern wage economy that made him what he is.

Northup's geographic essentialism is characteristic of the sectionalist identifications that mark U.S. culture in these years, and it holds within it the same paradox that would eventually undo those sectionalisms. On one hand, he takes pride in his origin as a northerner, from whence his status as a freeman derives; on the other hand, he deplores the fact that this condition is not mobile (that he cannot, in other words, be as

self-identical across state lines—or sections—as Bass is). One of these
positions is place-based (valorizing region of origin as the key producer
of character); the other seeks to detach identity from place and make it
more mobile. This contradiction suggests that there are two conflicting
ways of reading identity in this period: one based on geographically conceived identity politics, and the other based on a far more mobile and
highly individualized kind of identity politics in which the only border
that matters is the biological border of each individual body. Of the two,
geo-identity (as we might call it) would appear to be the more regressive
model, rooted in the climatological theories of the Enlightenment and
the social structures of a less mobile, more agrarian society. Bio-identity,
on the other hand (based in the individual body), is far more suited to
capitalism's mobile networks. While it is tempting, however, to link the
first with the (underdeveloped) South and the second with the (developing) North, it is clear that the shift from geographic notions of identity to
more biological ones actually occurred on a massive scale that, ironically,
knew no geographical boundaries. The conflict between the two was, in
fact, the epic cultural dilemma of Northup's era.

6. IMPRINTED IDENTITIES AND IDENTITIES IN PRINT: FICTIONAL FUGITIVES IN *CLOTEL*

Northup's book was a freak of 1850s literary culture: his was not the tale
of a fugitive slave gone north but of a freeman gone south, and to the
degree that *Twelve Years a Slave* is a slave narrative, it only enters those
precincts by proxy, for, as Northup reminds us repeatedly, he never "really" was a slave. While *Twelve Years a Slave* is an artifact of the 1850s,
then, it was never a direct response to the Fugitive Slave Law in the same
way that Stowe's novel was or, as we shall see, that William Wells Brown's
Clotel was. One might go so far as to say that the Fugitive Slave Law had
no negative consequences at all for Northup and that he was a safer man
within its logic than without it, since his rescue depended finally on the
continuity of his (free) identity across space, a continuity-of-status-
across-space similar to that guaranteed by the Fugitive Slave Law. But
the logic of the slave law was less utilitarian for other national travelers
after 1850, especially for the fugitives it targeted as slaves for life, regardless of their state of residence. William Wells Brown was such a traveler,
finding himself newly vulnerable to southern repatriation after 1850 even

though he had lived in the North for sixteen years. In *Clotel*, published in England in 1853, Brown responds to the law by refusing the fiction of differential space (North/South) and differential identity (free/slave) on which Northup's restoration depends, pointing out that under the Fugitive Slave Law "liberty in the so-called Free States was more a name than a reality."[42] More than that, Brown vexes the logic of that law (in which identity is posited as continuous across a unified field of fugitive exchange) by destabilizing the idea of *any* continuous individual identity (male or female, black or white, free or unfree) or any kind of regional integrity (within states or across sections). In doing so, he takes a third road (untaken by either Stowe or Northup), delinking individual identity both from the body (as either raced or gendered) and from location in space. The irony of this choice is that it takes Brown to the most unexpected of places: first (geographically) to England (where he avoided capture until his freedom was secured in 1854) and then, in *Clotel*, to the scene of American origins, written in explicitly Revolutionary terms as a Jeffersonian genealogy. From these two displaced points, Brown unfolds his narrative of American life up to and inside of the American 1850s.

Clotel is comprised of two distinct texts: a prefatory narrative of Brown's life told in the third person and the novel proper. The autobiographical narrative tells one man's story while the novel describes slavery's shattering geographical and temporal effects on an entire family. Chapter 1 of the novel proper (titled "The Negro Sale") stages the family's breakup as Clotel (the daughter of Thomas Jefferson) is purchased by her white lover Horatio Green, while her mother (Currer, Jefferson's lover) and sister Althesa are purchased by a trader for the out-of-state market. Currer and Althesa subsequently experience another separation when purchased in New Orleans by different owners. This structure of splitting and resplitting is then reenacted at several temporal intervals and across generations, recurring for both Althesa's and Clotel's children (Althesa, for instance, has two girls who will be sold separately upon her death; Clotel is likewise forcibly separated from her daughter). Brown thus elaborates on slavery's elongated family tree—representing the rhizomatic proliferation of several generations of families living always at some remove from their scene (and family) of origin. In this way, the novel records American slavery's double diaspora, tracking both temporal/intergenerational dislocations and the more familiar problem (staged by Stowe) of geographical dislocation from one's husband, wife, mother, brother—and so on.

Critics have tended to focus on one of two issues in the novel. First, the problem of genre: while *Clotel* is usually cited as the first African-American novel, Brown adopts an experimental format that makes this designation nettlesome. A pastiche of materials published elsewhere and of Brown's own invention, *Clotel* does not look like any other novel of the 1850s—no matter who wrote it. Unlike someone like Phillis Wheatley (who took up, in her neoclassical lyrics, the most conventional and recognizable version of the form in which she chose to write), Brown refuses to let *Clotel* look like a novel. This problem alone has raised a rich vein of critical rumination on the relative ficticity and facticity of *Clotel's* novel-pieces and their relation to prior forms available to African-American authors—notably, the slave narrative, with its twin burdens of absolute truthfulness and authenticity. Alongside this formal approach to the novel, a second critical tradition has emerged more recently around questions of identity—especially Brown's understanding of the constructedness of social categories like gender and race. I want to suggest here that these two questions—one of form, one of identity—are actually already connected in Brown's novel. In fact, if we look carefully at how black identity was being constructed both before and after the adoption of the Fugitive Slave Law, we can see that the novel's experimental technique is in large part a critique of the identity-driven politics of the 1850s and of the evidentiary biases that authorized them. These biases saturated both the public sphere (finding their way into newspapers, narratives, and novels) as well as the state apparatus that structured such productions (notably, the Fugitive Slave Law itself). Brown, in writing *Clotel*, is thinking about both.[43]

While many critics have pointed out that *Clotel* marks a shift in the strategies of representation embraced by African-American authors (from autobiographical, fact-based narratives to fiction), none has remarked on the possibility that this strategy might have been a direct response to the material conditions fugitives faced in these years—a response, in particular, to a law that was itself remarkable for a coincidental shift in its strategies of *identification*.[44] But the Fugitive Slave Law did more than institute new techniques for identifying fugitives. As Brown knew, these techniques reflexively affected how such fugitives self-identified within the representational architecture of antebellum American culture. For over twenty years, fugitives had been migrating north via the underground railroad under an intense burden of proof. As Lara Cohen has shown in her work on antebellum fraud, slaves who arrived in northern cities seeking help from either white abolitionists or black communities were met with pervasive skepticism about their potential identities as imposters and confidence men.[45] Stories about fugitive slaves who used disguises to escape captivity circulated widely in these years—not just in slave narratives but in routine newspaper accounts. The *Liberator*, for example, reported admiringly in 1837 on a "runaway slave from Georgia" who "passed himself off . . . as an Indian, and one of the Chiefs of the Cherokee nation, calling himself 'Falling Water.'"[46]

But disguise was never a one-way enterprise. Just as real fugitives adopted new personas to escape slavery, so too was the persona of the fugitive slave used as a disguise to hoodwink unsuspecting abolitionists. Garrison's *Liberator*, among others, printed many items in these years tracking the movements of such imposters, and some of their exploits rival the brilliance and artifice of a Stephen Burroughs (a well-known Enlightenment confidence man, whose cons possessed a Franklinian elegance). Garrison reports on one occasion, for example, on a "colored man" transparently calling himself "Charles Traveller," who "lectured on a system of emigration, and was raising money to purchase a printing press. Several persons in Erie, who had given him testimonials, have publicly signified their conviction that they have been imposed upon."[47] *The North Star* for March 1, 1850, likewise reprints a cautionary tale from the New York *Tribune* about the differences between "the true fugitive" and "a pretended one." It warns that a "colored man calling his name William Johnson, is on a tour of speculation among the friends of the colored race in the Northern and Eastern States." Johnson had apparently claimed "that he had escaped from Slavery three or four years since and was now in search of his wife residing somewhere in the north." Though "his address is good and statements very plausible" (allowing him to obtain "a few letters of introduction to gentlemen prominent for their benevolence"), Johnson was in fact an imposter who, the paper reported, had "deserted his wife and left her entirely unprovided for."[48]

As these examples suggest, newspapers played a crucial role in tracking the movements of such confidence men. *Frederick Douglass' Paper* for September 30, 1853, reports on a fugitive slave imposter "calling himself Thomas Clarkson" and asks "Papers in Western New York, and in Ohio" to reprint the report. Douglass's paper printed a similar appeal on December 7, 1855, running an exposé of a man named "O. C. Gilbert" under the title "AN IMPOSTER AGAIN IMPOSED." Though Gilbert (a man of "plausible address") "has been reasoned with, and condemned, and exposed," the *Paper* reports that he continues to pass himself off as a fugitive to new people in new places. In an effort to end the adventures of this serial imposter, the article concludes with a physical description of Gilbert that reads very much like a fugitive slave advertisement: "a large robust man, about five feet nine or ten inches in height, dark brown, or black complexion, partially bald, and quite bow-legged." Warning that his exploits will "yet lead him to the State Prison," the editor asks "all the papers [to] pass him around"—circulating his story across the region through which he is moving.[49]

In response to such fraudulent fugitives, the abolitionist community developed techniques to help verify the accounts of fugitives arriving from distant locations. John White Browne, an agent for the Committee of Vigilance in Boston, kept a detailed log of his interviews with newly arrived slaves and maintained an elaborate network of correspondents in other aid societies in order to do background checks on unknown characters. Samuel May likewise noted that whenever a fugitive contacted him, he was always careful to check the story of the slave's travels against his "Atlas."[50] John Bailey, writing an open letter to the *Liberator* in 1846, claimed that fake fugitives appeared regularly: "They are strangers, and we take them in. In so doing, we are sometimes taken in ourselves. . . . We spare no pains in endeavoring to ascertain the truth of their stories, but do not always succeed, and after being at considerable expense on their account, find them to be imposters. Three or four weeks since, a colored man came here, saying he was from the South, but [in fact he came] last from Boston." To protect against frauds like these, Bailey proposed a system of "certificates" designed to authenticate the fugitive's movement—a fairly ironic solution, given the Fugitive Slave Law's use of the same technique just four years later. Bailey reasoned that such certificates, if issued as closely as possible to the slave's point of origin (for instance, at the "border states"), would prevent frauds from being perpetuated by imposters who capitalized on geographic distance to tell tall tales. The certificate system was meant to ensure that "one could not come from the north, pretending to be from the south."[51]

Establishing authentic identities was important to organized abolition for several reasons. For one thing, as Bailey noted, "whatever is gained by the imposter, lessens the chance of the real fugitive." There were only so many "resources" to pass around. But a fixed notion of the difference between the "pretended" and the "real" was also the very basis upon which antislavery made its critique—at a vast distance—of slavery and its practices. For (white) abolition's account of slavery to appear authentic to other white populations, it required that fugitives from slavery be likewise authentic. The fugitive slave had to be, as Dwight McBride has said, a "fulfillment of the prophecy of abolitionist discourse . . . the 'real' evidence . . . of what ha[d] been told before."[52] The stakes of this problem exploded visibly into national (and nonabolitionist) print culture in the vexed *Narrative of James Williams* (1838), the first fugitive slave narrative funded by the AASS as part of its popular pamphlet series. Williams was a rare find for the AASS: a fugitive not just of slavery but of its harshest conditions in the cotton districts of the deep South. On arrival in New York, Williams was subjected to intense scrutiny, undergoing comprehensive interviews "again and again" with various members of the AASS Executive Committee, who tried to finds holes in his story.[53] Satisfied with his "testimony," the committee authorized John Greenleaf Whittier to take down Williams's story and sell it as a pamphlet—yet another of the AASS's attempts, in these years, to tell the story of southern slavery as it was. The *Narrative* was widely advertised throughout the North as an "authentic" tale of life in the deep South; as one article suggested with pride, the AASS had found, in Williams, "the real Archy Moore."[54]

In the months following the publication of Williams's *Narrative*, however, questions emerged about the truthfulness of its claims. Local information emerged from Alabama (appearing first in newspapers and then circulating northward), refuting Williams's account of his life there.[55] Though the narrative was internally consistent, Williams had used false names, opening a space for his southern readers to cast him as a liar and to reject his narrative as inauthentic. Williams's absence from the scene of this debate (he was sent to England to ensure his safety) only exacerbated matters, making it appear that he had duped the AASS and then fled. Though modern scholars continue to debate whether Williams's *Narrative* was actually a hoax, the historical effects of the episode were profound for abolitionist print culture. Not only did AASS pull the *Narrative* from its list and libraries, but it issued a long statement (in print) apologizing for its lack of authenticity—effectively siding with Williams's detractors.[56] The Williams affair affected Theodore Weld's decision, the following year, to write a material history of slavery (*Slavery as It Is*) without what he viewed as the potentially compromised testimony of former slaves. The lingering memory of Williams's troubles likewise undoubtedly played a role in Douglass's decision to cite real names and real locations in his 1845 *Narrative*, even though it endangered his freedom by making him a more visible target for retrieval.[57]

Even as brief a history as this reveals a dialectic between the problem of identification (faced by local communities, whose philanthropy was challenged by imposters) and the problem of self-representation (faced by fugitives, who frequently had to find ways to establish their histories as authentic at a vast distance from their origins and without anyone to corroborate their claims). I would suggest that this dialectic underwent a transformation—a reversal even—after 1850. Before the passage of the Fugitive Slave Law, newly arrived fugitives were primarily seeking ways to establish local credibility in ways that might foster roots in the community and help establish new geographic identities as free New Yorkers, Philadelphians, Bostonians, and so on. Under such an imperative, the truth-telling form of the slave narrative made sense as a strategy of representation. After the passage of the Fugitive Slave Law, however, the route to a secure and free identity grew trickier, for the more established one's identity after 1850, the more easily one might be retrieved under the auspices of the law. To tell the truth by providing the details of one's history, one's origin, or (as we shall see) one's race was to provide evidence of self-identity that might be used to reenslave rather than ensure passage into freedom.

The problem of how to read the signs of race and enslavement in individual bodies removed from some prior geographical context proliferated throughout the South in the decades preceding the Civil War. Walter Johnson and Ariela Gross have each described a number of racial determination cases in antebellum southern courts—cases in which a person's race had to be judicially established, either because a slave defendant was suing for freedom (on the grounds that he was white) or because a slave-owning claimant was trying to retrieve a person as a slave and attempting to prove that the person in question was black and a former slave, rather than free and white.[58] These court cases indicate that race was a vexed category of identity in these years—especially when placed under the pressure of evidentiary law, which was usually forced to rely either on textual evidence (in the form of affidavits) or on "eyewitness" testimony in order to establish the slave (and sometimes the racial) status of runaways who claimed they were free (and sometimes white). As numerous judges and juries came to recognize, slavery was an institution that shattered a clear sense of origins in ways that made a person's race and even his life history increasingly difficult to establish beyond a reasonable doubt.

Under the auspices of the Fugitive Slave Law, the same set of legal problems came North in 1850. The body of the fugitive slave became, under this law, an object of federal scrutiny and subjection, even as the federal government itself became more embodied in local contexts (in the form of the "marshals," "judges," and "commissioners" who were expected to execute the law on the ground). The Fugitive Slave Law thus intersects with the larger history of American identity, which was increasingly being located in these years in mobile bodies rather than in or at sites of origin. We might say that the problem of personal identity was being *rescaled* at this moment and under this law, as identities that had once been rooted in particular geographical locations were increasingly attached to nothing more than a body moving through space. Such mobility made the space that makes an identity meaningful vaster than ever before, encompassing not just the location of one's birth or residence but the entire circumference of one's potential travels.

The trick under the Fugitive Slave Law was, of course, how to establish a method of identification for these moving bodies. How could the law establish the identity of the slave at a distance from his or her point of origin? The evidentiary machinery for producing "satisfactory proof" of "the identity of the person" in question was notoriously flimsy. The alleged slaves themselves were, following legal conventions across many states, not allowed to testify on their own behalf. "Proof" of their identity as fugitive slaves was sometimes produced though eyewitnesses with actual knowledge of their identities and origins (usually former owners who traveled north to reclaim them), but more often, the identification was established through the mediation of the owner's "agent" (a lawyer or hired slave catcher) who produced (or asked the court to produce) an "affidavit" or "certificate" establishing the owner's claim.[59]

Here we see the primary dilemma at the heart of the law's execution: the problem of how to establish proof of identity after the fact of a body's circulation away from its (putative) starting point. To this end, the word "proof" recurs eight times in the language of the Fugitive Slave Law (usually paired with the word "satisfactory" or "sufficient"), while the word "identity" appears twice in these moments. Section 4, for example, states that "certificates" should be granted to slaveholders by their local courts "upon satisfactory proof being made" that their slave has escaped. Section 6 dictates that once this certificate is presented in any northern state, "the case of such claimant" must be attended to "in a summary manner; and upon satisfactory proof [of the slave's identity] being made, by deposition or affidavit, in writing," another certificate is granted and the alleged slave is to be transferred to the claimant's custody. Section 6 dictates that once a certificate is issued authorizing the slaveholder to repossess his fugitive slave, the judicial seal on that certificate "shall be sufficient to establish the competency of the proof, and with proof, also by affidavit, of the identity of the person whose service or labor is claimed to be due." Section 8 outlines the process that must be followed when "satisfactory proof" is not established (dictating that the "supposed fugitive may be discharged out of custody for the want of sufficient proof"), but the law never actually details the threshold of "satisfact[ion]."

As many northerners pointed out, the law's procedures opened a palpable space for misidentification. As George Stroud asked in 1856:

> Can a person in Alabama, or anywhere else, so describe the *personal appearance* of another that, by reading the description, a third person can certainly know to whom it applies? Will it be said he may be described by *scars* from *casualties* or from ARTIFICIAL *marks? A brand of a letter or letters of the alphabet* approximates most nearly to reliable evidence of this kind. But even this would give no certainty; and, at all events, unless the description *in all other particulars* could be made in the same affidavit, a single correspondence in artificial marks would prove nothing.[60]

Stroud betrays a devastating skepticism here about the ability of texts to communicate transparently the facts of identity across distance. Not only was proof of identity being established in these cases through the mediation of a series of self-interested, unreliable, and thus compromised texts (the "certificates" and "affidavits" compiled at the slave-holding site of origin), but a number of impersonal mechanisms were likewise implanted within the language of the law to ensure a high rate of retrieval. Section 8, for example, provides a financial incentive for federal commissioners to find for the claimant (rather than the "fugitive") by allocating a five-dollar fee in all cases where a claim is denied but a ten-dollar fee in cases where the claim is upheld and the fugitive returned to slavery. Commissioners deemed remiss in their execution of the law, furthermore, were vulnerable to a thousand-dollar fine, while federal marshals were held fiscally responsible for the "value" of the fugitive in case of escape (section 5).[61]

Daniel Webster was frequently forced to defend not just the accommodationist logic of the Compromise of 1850, but the new slave law's potential for misidentification and fraud. In a speech before Congress delivered on July 17, 1850, Webster insisted that there was "an exaggerated sense of the actual evil of the reclamation of fugitive slaves, felt by Massachusetts and the other New England States." He argued that

> there has not been a case within the knowledge of this generation, in which a man has been taken back from Massachusetts into slavery by process of law—not one. . . . Not only has there been no case, so far as I can learn, of the reclamation of a slave by his master, which ended in taking him back to slavery, in this generation, but I will add that, as far as I have been able to go back in my researches, as far as I have been able to hear and learn, in all that region, there has been no one case of false claim.[62]

Webster was wrong of course, for, as Samuel May pointed out (at great length), there were historical cases of each kind of problem. It is in fact especially ironic that Webster hedges his claims so dramatically ("as far as I have been able to go back in my researches, as far as I have been able to hear and learn"), for the tendency of hearsay "researches" to be incomplete is precisely what opens the space for fraud and misidentification.

With its commitment to the fictional form of the novel and its persistent troubling of the notion of fixed, easily readable, or essentialized personal identities, *Clotel* not only intersects the debate over the Fugitive Slave Law but actively engages it as an object of critique, interrogating at length the techniques of identification whereby the law sought to effect its ends. The effects of this law were very much on Brown's mind as he wrote the novel in England in the early 1850s. In fact, *Clotel* explicitly opens and closes with long discussions of the Fugitive Slave Law. In his preface, Brown makes a point of telling his British audience that "the entire white population of the United States, North and South, are bound by their oath to the constitution, and their adhesion to the Fugitive Slave Law, to hunt down the runaway slave and return him to his claimant" (iii–iv). The *Narrative* likewise ends by describing the effects the 1850 law has had on Brown's movements, noting that "it was Mr. Brown's intention to have returned to the United States to his family ere this. But the passage of the infamous 'Fugitive Slave Law' prevented his returning" (51).

In a canny display of what his life was like before and after the passage of the law, Brown also reproduces in the *Narrative* two letters from his former owner, Enoch Price. The first, dated at "St. Louis, Jan. 10th, 1848," represents Price's relation to Brown (the fugitive) as one of hopeless geographic distance and difference, muted but not overcome by a series of textual mediations. In this letter, Price notes that he has recently "received a pamphlet, or a narrative, so called on the title page, of the Life of William W. Brown," and he identifies the author as "a slave belonging to me" (36–37). In an attempt to establish his claim to Brown, Price goes on to offer his own counter-"narrative" of the financial transactions that led to his ownership of Brown and asks his northern correspondent to go "see him, and see if what I say is not the truth" (37). He then offers to sell Brown to the "Anti-Slavery Society of Boston, or Massachusetts" by way of his "agent in Boston" for "just half what I paid for him" (37). At no point in the letter does Price threaten to travel to Boston to retrieve Brown, nor does he assume (as the later Fugitive Slave Law does) that Brown's identity can be established merely through the intercession of mediating texts or agents. On the contrary, he suggests that his correspondent physically visit Brown in order to get *him* to corroborate Price's account as "the truth"—asking Brown, in other words, to identify himself *as* himself for the purposes of sealing the transaction. The second letter, dated at "St. Louis, Feb. 16th, 1852," takes a new relation to the question of Brown's retrieval. Here, Price asserts that he is no longer willing, as he was in 1848, to sell Brown at "half price" because "since that time the laws of the United States are materially changed" (51). The material change is put quite bluntly: "the Fugitive Slave Bill has passed since then. I can now take him anywhere in the United States, and I have everything arranged for his arrest if he lands at any port in the United States" (51–52).

Brown was in England when Price wrote the second letter, and he responds to its threats by declaring himself beyond Price's reach, as long as he remains abroad. Brown remarks at length, for example, on the "change that is brought about by a trip of nine days in an Atlantic steamer": "My old master may make his appearance here, with the constitution of the United States in his pocket, the fugitive slave law in one hand and the chains in the other, and claim me as his property; but all will avail him nothing" (41). In an odd throwback to the grammar of 1776, Brown goes on to declare himself "free" and "equal" to Price while on British soil while indicting his former master with the monarchical title of "tyrant" (41). That he should do so from the center of the former empire is ironic indeed—especially in a text as invested in America's Jeffersonian origins as this one is. Like Whitman, then, Brown connects the master-text of 1787 with its heir in 1850 (explicitly linking the Constitution and the Fugitive Slave Law as two texts that overlap within a material field of historical circulation), but rather than citing England as the metropolitan source of America's present day corruption, he ironically hails it (and its geographical displacement from the United States) as a site of freedom. Here and elsewhere, Brown would appear both to know where America came from and to realize its historical passage into a new set of spatial relations.[63]

Brown explicitly references the Fugitive Slave Law in numerous places throughout *Clotel*. There are also, however, many more implicit ways that the novel responds to the world-altering logic of the law, for Brown repeatedly both references and refuses the kinds of identification upon which the 1850 law is premised—forms of identification that the novel links to the long history of factitious authentication that marks African-American literary representation within the abolitionist movement. To this end, *Clotel* does not simply refuse the form of the slave narrative and replace it with an 1850s-style fiction (after the fashion of a Hildreth or a Hawthorne). Instead, Brown explicitly invokes the nonfictional form of the slave narrative by offering his own autobiographical *Narrative* as a preface to the novel. In a paradoxical move, however, he refuses to divide the labor of knowledge and authority between a knowing slave narrator and a trusted white authenticator, serving instead as his own amanuensis. Where most fugitive slave authors, in other words, were writing autobiographies and prefacing them with an authenticating essay or letter written by a white abolitionist, Brown writes a *novel* and prefaces it with an autobiography of his own. The prefatory *Narrative* does, however, split Brown's narrated self from his narrating self, adopting the third-person pronoun where, in his original 1847 narrative, there had been only an "I"—an "I" that is for the most part banished in the 1853 preface to *Clotel* but that nevertheless slips into the text at disconcerting intervals in ways that draw attention to Brown's use of the alienating and alienated pronoun "he." Brown's third-person objectification of his own life history has produced a tradition of reading the prefatory *Narrative* as an authenticating document (intended to fend off the taint of deception and dishonor that might accrue to the novel form). But I would point instead to the ways that the third-person narrator opens a palpable wedge between signifier and signified, rather than closing down that gap as more conventional (first person) autobiographical narrators tend to do. Why speak, in other words, from the displaced position of a "he" when one can speak with the self-identicality of an "I"?

More than 150 years later, critics still do not agree on the answer to this question. Some insist that the prefatory narrative and its experimentation with point of view is meant, as Robert Stepto suggests, to "authenticate" Brown's references to slavery throughout the novel; others argue (as I would) the opposite, noting the ways that Brown keeps "the question [of authenticity] open by vexing any attempt to delineate the boundary between fact and fiction."[64] But the answer to this question is perhaps less interesting than the confusion it continues to generate. Indeed, the same willful opacity doggedly follows *Clotel*'s readers into the novel itself, where Brown continually blurs (via his remarkable use of documentary sources) the lines that are usually so compulsively and meticulously maintained within abolitionist print culture: the line between history and fiction, truth and fantasy, the real and the unreal. Drawing (as he tells us in the novel's "Conclusion") on numerous sources—including the testimony of fugitive slaves, a short story by Lydia Maria Child, and the ephemera of several "American Abolitionist journals"—Brown insists upon the truth-value of the novel's various plotlines. As many readers have noted, however, Brown's avowals and disavowals of his source material are never consistent. Some of his sources are openly cited (as with Child's 1842 story, "The Quadroons"), but others are left uncited (as in the wholesale reproduction of several passages from John Beard's 1853 *Life of Toussaint L'Ouverture*). In similar fashion, some events are explicitly noted as historical (or "true") when they are in fact fictional, while others are cited as fictional when they are in fact well known to be historical. To the degree that history is mobilized at all, it is inserted into the narrative in ways that skew rather than anchor. Indeed, the novel's most recurrent trope may well be the numerous anachronisms that flauntingly undo its most basic claims to historicism even as they tangle up Brown's central plotlines with unexpected twists and turns.[65]

Clotel is, in short, a novel of mixed messages, from the first page to the last. Even once the preface is behind us and we embark on reading the novel proper, the fictive action is delayed by several paragraphs of essayistic exposition. When the "story" does begin, it begins in peculiar (because nonfictional) fashion—with the citation of a "documentary" newspaper:

> At the close of the year—the following advertisement appeared in a newspaper published in Richmond, the capital of the state of Virginia:—"Notice: Thirty-eight negroes will be offered for sale on Mon-

day, November 10th, at twelve o'clock, being the entire stock of the late John Graves, Esq. The negroes are in good condition, some of them very prime; among them are several mechanics, able-bodied field hands, plough-boys, and women with children at the breast, and some of them very prolific in their generating qualities, affording a rare opportunity to any one who wishes to raise a strong and healthy lot of servants for their own use. Also several mulatto girls of rare personal qualities: two of them very superior. Any gentleman or lady wishing to purchase, can take any of the above slaves on trial for a week, for which no charge will be made." Amongst the above slaves to be sold were Currer and her two daughters, Clotel and Althesa. (59–60)

The advertisement cited here is not just from a real newspaper but from one cited by Weld in *Slavery as It Is*.[66] Thus at the moment the novel's "imagined" action begins ("At the close of the year—"), we are diverted by the insertion of a historical document whose previous intent was to verify the "truth" of slavery "as it is." In this way, Brown declares at this most crucial juncture of African-American literature—the start of a new genre (the first African-American *novel*)—his intention to mix fact and fiction, and he does it in a way that explicitly references the long and vexed history that facts have played in abolitionist representation. Carla Peterson notes that Brown was considered "the most faithful of black Garrisonians" and argues that his use of fiction in *Clotel* is "an indirect protest" against the abolitionist movement's desire to fix and use black identities.[67] Brown's assault, however, on the truth-telling capacities of northern abolitionist print culture could not be more direct. The novel draws attention from the beginning to the idea that "facts" are themselves mediated through structures of representation that must always register a loss or a displacement from some prior moment within the real that cannot be recovered. Brown thus demonstrates immediately his understanding that no representation can ever be actual.[68]

Alongside this aestheticized deconstruction of the line between the real and the unreal, Brown plays out in chapter 1 an extended disquisition on a different kind of unstable line—the racial distinction between black and white, which, he argues, is increasingly threatened by the ubiquity of the American mulatto. Brown declares: "in all the cities and towns of the slave states, the real negro, or clear black, does not amount to more than one in every four of the slave population. This fact is, of itself, the best evidence of the degraded and immoral condition of the relation of master and slave in the United States of America" (55). In this moment, slavery's amalgamating sexual practice meets the zenith of a new social logic, and the result is a sentence that tests the boundaries of logic, as something that is disappearing—"the real negro"—is cited as "the best evidence" that slavery has produced about its true being. In these sentences, Brown places acute pressure on our common (legal) understanding of the words "real" and "evidence." While the evidence cited is still based on something "real," the diminishing nature of that reality suggests that an epistemological crisis—a soon-to-be-absence—is brewing.

This early focus on "the real negro" is in keeping with the book's larger concerns. As many readers have noticed, *Clotel* takes up the question of "the real" at great length, persistently questioning the relationship between "reality" and "evidence."[69] We might say that Brown takes Jefferson's glib claim about self-evident truths as his ironic epigram and then pursues the problem of non-self-evidence as his central theme. He does so in two registers: formally (by mixing and matching documentary and nondocumentary sources) and biologically (by dissolving the fixities of personal identity markers within individual bodies). Nothing could be more appropriate in a novel centered on the founding fathers' progeny, for this is the very dialectic upon which American federalism depends—premised, as it is, on achieving a perfect balance between the form of government and the bodies of its citizens, between representation and that which is represented. Brown thus resurrects the very thing that Jefferson's Declaration sought to banish: the vitality of virtual representation (a model that insists that representation's gaps are productive ones), rather than trying to manufacture some more authentic relation to the real. The century-old notion of an "actual" "representation" is once again refused in favor of a redefined (imagined) "real."

Clotel places the fugitive slave at the epicenter of this problem. Brown's most concerted attempts to dissolve individual identity categories come, for example, at the novel's most mobile (or "fugitive") juncture: in the chapter called "Escape of Clotel." This is the longest and perhaps most critical chapter in *Clotel*. Not coincidentally, it is also the one in which bodies are most frequently described as being in motion across the lines of state and region. Brown begins, for example, with the "inside" stories of several other fugitive slaves, describing the strategies of misrepresentation by which they make their unlikely escapes. In one case, the fugitive travels in open daylight with a pig, under the pretense that he is moving it to market for his master—driving the animal all the way to Ohio, where it is exchanged for money and a new suit of clothes. In another, two slaves execute an escape technique that Brown knowingly calls the "ride and tie":

> [O]ne was on horseback, the other was walking before him with his arms tightly bound, and a long rope leading from the man on foot to the one on horseback. "Oh, ho, that's a runaway rascal, I suppose," said a farmer, who met them on the road. "Yes, sir, he bin runaway, and I got him fast. Marser will tan his jacket for him nicely when he gets him." "You are a trustworthy fellow, I imagine," continued the farmer. "Oh yes, sir; marser puts a heap of confidence in dis nigger." And the slaves traveled on. When the one on foot was fatigued they would change positions, the other being tied and driven on foot. (165)

Neither of these examples is exceptional in the history of the Underground Railroad or African-American literature more generally, which frequently describes such trickery as a means of survival.[70] Nevertheless, the second episode is made more interesting by what happens to one of the fugitives once he reaches the North. Captured and "compelled" (under torture) "to reveal the name of his owner and his place of residence," the slave is taken into custody by mercenary slave catchers who, on their return home, drink themselves numb and allow their captive to escape a second time:

> The chains were soon off, and the negro stealthily making his way to the window: he stopped and said to himself, "These men are villains, they are enemies to all who like me are trying to be free. Then why not I teach them a lesson?" He then undressed himself, took the clothes of one of the men, dressed himself in them, and escaped through the window, and, a moment more, he was on the high road to Canada. (165–66)

Here the "ride and tie" strategy is redeployed—but with a twist: instead of swapping identities with his slave companion, the fugitive assumes the identity of his pursuers by dressing himself in their clothes. The episode demonstrates, in a particularly apt and ironic way, that the willing and artful exchange of identities is the most direct route to freedom. And as numerous such examples suggest, it is not so much the content of any one kind of identity that ensures survival as the willingness to circulate freely through and across many different kinds of identities.

The "ride and tie" is just one of many such episodes scattered throughout the antebellum archive. As Cindy Weinstein has noted, "the plots of slave narratives often hinge on the necessity of unrecognizability," and unrecognizability as an effect is often produced through an exchange not just of clothes but of other bodily markers of identity—including those that speak to race and gender, which are taken on and put off like so many hats and scarves in numerous antebellum slave narratives.[71] Brown's discussion of the "ride and tie" frames a chapter that pursues this trope, appropriately enough, in a range of guises. In this chapter alone, Brown narrates an extraordinarily high number of scenes of what we might simply call misidentification (in some cases self-initiated and in others unintentional)—scenes of cross-dressing, racial passing, and random misrecognitions of the everyday kind. These include not just slaves dressed up as slave catchers, but a mulatto woman passing as a white man; two white men misrecognized as black men; a man being treated like a box of freight (on a Jim Crow car); and Brown himself masquerading in literary garments first provided by (among others) William and Ellen Craft.

In one of the novel's more well-known twists, for example, Clotel finds herself crossing the lines of both race and gender, passing as a white man while her friend William remains fixed in his role of slave by playing the part of her body servant:

> [A]ll persons taking negroes with them have to give bail that such negroes are not runaway slaves. The law upon this point is very stringent: all steamboats and other public conveyances are liable to a fine for every slave that escapes by them, besides paying the full value for the slave. After a delay of four hours, Mr. Johnson and servant took passage on the steamer Rodolph, for Pittsburgh. It is usual, before the departure of the boats, for an officer to examine every part of the vessel to see that no slave secretes himself on board, "Where are you going?" asked the officer of William, as he was doing his duty on this occasion. "I am going with marser," was the quick reply. "Who is your master?" "Mr. Johnson, sir, a gentleman in the cabin." "You must take him to the office and satisfy that captain that all is right, or you can't go on this boat." William informed his master what the officer had said. The boat was on the eve of going, and no time could be lost, yet they knew not

what to do. At last they went to the office, and Mr. Johnson, addressing
the captain, said, "I am informed that my boy can't go with me unless I
give security that he belongs to me." "Yes," replied the captain, "that is
the law." "A very strange law indeed," rejoined Mr. Johnson, "that one
can't take his property with him." (169–70)

This scene stages a moment of testimony quite similar to the testimony
that claimants must offer under the Fugitive Slave Law—if, of course,
such testimony were offered in reverse. Instead of a white man trying to
claim another man as a runaway in order to transport him south, this
scene finds Clotel, a black woman, trying to claim that a man is *not* a runaway in order to transport him north. In doing so, Clotel performs one of
the novel's most peculiar moments of passing—not because she is passing as white man (a literary commonplace by 1853), but because she ven-
triloquizes the argument for federal mobility that underlies the Fugitive
Slave Law ("'A very strange law indeed,' rejoined Mr. Johnson, 'that one
can't take his property with him'"). Here we see the real stakes of these
scenes of passing and misrecognition for Brown, for the scene suggests
that the logic of the Fugitive Slave Law might, given the right strategies
of misrepresentation, work *in favor* of the fugitive it seeks to confine. Enhanced mobility, in other words, if coupled with enhanced confusion—
dislocation joined, as it were, to misidentification—provides the perfect
point of resistance to the law's attempts to ensure mobility through more
stringent modes of identification.

Brown's refusal to uphold the legible outlines of the genres he works
in—and even the stories he "steals"—goes hand in hand with his refusal
of conventional identity categories. In the chapter just cited, Brown takes
the well-known story of Ellen and William Craft and bends it to his own
use, making several notable changes.[72] As many readers have noted, these
revisions introduce yet another kind of instability into the narrative as
Brown once again intentionally crosses history with fiction, tangling old
plotlines with new ones so often that it becomes difficult to locate the
original from within Brown's redeployment of other people's stories and
settings. Robert Levine aptly dubs such moments "kidnappings" (following the etymology of "plagiary," which means, literally, "to kidnap")—a
perfect characterization in light of my discussion here of the slave law,
which was often derided, throughout the North, as a legal form of kidnapping. In such moments, Levine notes, Brown "steals the texts of a
culture that steals black bodies."[73] I would merely add that Brown is not

just taking back texts in *Clotel*; he is crafting a strategy for taking back the bodies too, openly embracing misrepresentation as the safest passage to freedom over and against the old truth-telling way embraced by the Crafts, not in their escape but in their narrative. In 1846, John Bailey argued that "whatever is gained by the imposter, lessens the chance of the real fugitive."[74] After 1850, however, the Craft-like strategies of misrepresentation mobilized to escape the South were increasingly necessary to sustain life *in the North*. Indeed, the "real fugitive" after 1850 becomes as rare as "the real Negro," as fugitives (including Brown and the Crafts) left the States for non-U.S. territories.

Brown takes up the genre of the novel, then, not just because he wants to try on a new form or needs to defy his colleagues in organized antislavery (two common explanations for his shift to fiction in these years), but because he recognizes fiction as a practice perfectly suited to the new conditions that attend the relation of free men to the state that seeks to reenslave them. Like many African-American authors after 1850, Brown turns away from the old standard of actual and authentic representation and embraces the slippery possibilities of the (seemingly) unreal and inauthentic. The characters of *Clotel* thus emerge, across a tangled skein of new and old plotlines, as patently virtual projections—emphatically fictional person(a)s whose identities remain fluid throughout, much as the narrative's components (or part-pieces) remain impossible to locate. Unlike either Stowe or Northup, Brown refuses the binaries that increasingly constituted a fixed individual identity in these years—binaries such as free/unfree, black/white, male/female, North/South, and, of course, real/unreal or true/false. Nor does he characterize the instability of such dissolving binarisms as a crisis to be resolved (as Stowe does—all the way to Liberia). Instead, he casts them as solutions that his characters productively ride across the arc of the book and down through the decades of American history that the book depicts.[75]

Regional identity (of the sort Northup values) is given special attention in this regard, as Brown makes a point of showing that even the most fixed regional identities are already mediated through structures of representation that are, in turn, tied to structures of mobility. Thus in the chapter titled "A Ride in a Stage Coach," a cross-dressing Clotel witnesses a political, cultural, and sectional debate between two of this period's most recognizable regional stereotypes: the New England Yankee and the southern planter. Not only does Brown stage this argument inside a moving stagecoach (with both parties in transit between identifiable places), but he knowingly pokes fun at how the sectional identities in question are textually mediated and manufactured from afar, even when the people who espouse them sit face-to-face in a contracted space. Thus the southerner insists that "I know you Connecticut people *like a book*" (198, my emphasis) while the Yankee, in the spirit of Theodore Weld, takes a New Orleans newspaper from his pocket in order to proffer irrefutable evidence (in the form of advertisements) for his belief that "you people of the Slave States have no regard for the Sabbath" (199).

I argued in an earlier chapter that "the first American contrasts" were not organized around race, class, or even gender so much as around the place-based affiliations of state and region. *Clotel* reveals, however, that even amid the intense sectionalism of the 1850s, the stakes of American identity were already less rooted in geography than in the mobile bodies of individual persons. These bickering sectionalists are parodic specters of an outgoing order in a nation where identity has already become detached from specific sectional locations through the agency of mobile bodies. Indeed, to the notion of mixed races, Brown develops and joins the notion of *mixed regions,* peopling his South with characters that cannot be categorized as either northern or southern. One such site is the Peck plantation, where we meet a stock northern traveler named Mr. Carlton. In generic plantation fiction, such travelers serve as anthropologically minded tourists surveying the indigenous culture of an alien South; here, however, Carlton arrives in Natchez, Mississippi, only to meet a number of other travelers, all in various states of removal from their own sites of origin. This is true of the slaves (many of whom have been imported from the "slave producing states" of the Southeast to the "slave consuming states" of the Southwest). But it is also true of the white people—all of whom have likewise arrived from elsewhere. The Reverend John Peck, for example, is a transplanted "native of the state of Connecticut" (87); his daughter Georgiana, though "a native of the South," is "by education and sympathy" "a Northerner" (91); Ned Huckelby, the slave driver, is "from Maryland" (104); Mr. Snyder, the jaded preacher-apologist, was "brought up in the Mohawk Valley, in the state of New York" (93); while their neighbor, Mr. J. C. Hobbs, is "a Tennessean" (105).

Peck's plantation figures a South that is profoundly non-self-identical. Not only is no one a local "native," but almost no one acts as he thinks or thinks as she acts. The "Reverend" Peck is a cruel master while his daughter Georgiana is elevated to the masculinized role of "liberator" (an explicit counterpart to Stowe's George Shelby). In the sermon chapters, we witness Mr. Snyder, a displaced New Yorker, giving a sermon, and then in succeeding scenes we witness both his audience's false reception of it and his own account of his false delivery. The split revealed—repeatedly, in everyone, everywhere—is an externalized version of the split within the ambivalent Carlton himself (between belief and unbelief), but it is also a version of the split developed more concretely within the Peck household between an antislavery daughter and her proslavery father. The incoherence of the white characters on the Peck plantation thus echoes and reaffirms the incoherence of the black characters—and vice versa. Both, in turn, foreshadow the identity-shifting episodes that are to come later in the novel, as black women like Clotel take up the garb of white men and white men like Daniel Webster are received publicly as black men.

Brown's disavowal of conventional identity markers may account for the novel's 1853 ending—with its only two surviving characters joined in a marriage that is both deracinated and deterritorialized. George Green arrives (like Brown) in London, only to leave his past and his race behind him in America. He "never once mentioned the fact of his being a slave" (231) and he becomes, in effect, a wealthy Englishman. Similarly, Clotel's daughter Mary escapes from slavery through marriage and becomes "Mrs. Devenant"—a French heiress whose new name makes her temporarily unrecognizable to both the reader and her former lover. Both George and Mary thus occupy a cosmopolitan world at the end of the novel, a world filled with unraced, decidedly non-American cultural objects—from the biography of Leo X that George reads in a graveyard (like some lately arrived Werther, lounging on a tomb) to the lush Italian and German paintings and the "rich Turkey carpet" (235) that decorate Mary's Paris parlor. *Clotel's* displaced but happy ending is in fact produced by one of these cosmopolitan cultural objects: George's copy of *The Life of Leo X* (which has his name written on the flyleaf) is the plot device that finally reunites George and Mary.[76] As on so many other occasions, a printed text is the answer as Brown rewrites African Americans not just into American national history but into European literary history as well. But even here Brown insists on a new kind of identity and identification bound neither to location nor to (racial) biology but situated instead on the shifting ground of culture. In this way, his characters trade in the fixities of authenticity for the security of more mediated (because historically malleable and geographically displaced) identities. No longer fugitives of American slavery, George and Mary are virtual citizens of the

world, just as they were always already self-made characters in *Clotel*'s
virtual world.

7. Federalism's Subject:
The Strange History of White Slaves

A crowd began to collect about us. When they heard that I was seized as a fugitive slave,
some of them appeared not a little outraged at the idea that a white man should be subject
to such an indignity. They seemed to think that it was only the black whom it was lawful to
kidnap in this way.
— Richard Hildreth, *The White Slave*, 1852

Suppose . . . the slaves should suddenly become white?
— William Lloyd Garrison, Park Street Address, 4 July 1829

I have suggested that the Fugitive Slave Law registers an important shift
in the material reorganization of relations under the Constitution. In the
case of Anthony Burns, that new relation was made visible when federal
troops came to Boston to retrieve Burns in the shadow of Faneuil Hall,
a federal frigate lying in Boston Harbor just as British men-of-war once
did. Although fugitive slave cases like Burns's initially look like a conflict
between the laws of two states (in Burns's case, Massachusetts and Virginia), they actually also involve a larger conflict between the federal and
the local state, a problem Whitman foregrounds in "A Boston Ballad"
by casting centralized government as the royalist skeleton in America's
closet. Burns's subjection into slavery demonstrated, in short, the federal
government's ability to reach into a local world and compel an individual
body to do its bidding. I would like to complete my work here by asking,
as *Clotel* does, what the stakes of such a federalist spectacle might be for
other kinds of (nonfugitive) bodies living under its operation.

The 1850 Fugitive Slave Law did something the 1793 fugitive law had
not done: it explicitly identified its subject as a fugitive from race-based
chattel slavery—a change that would seem to make the nation safer than
ever before for white mobility.[77] In sending federal troops into Boston,
however, President Pierce revealed that the state could do more than just
compel a black man into slavery: it could also compel the white men of
Massachusetts to help it. Though Daniel Webster repeatedly denied that
the law would compel northerners to act against their will, the language
of the law did in fact "command" "all good citizens" "to aid and assist

in the prompt and efficient execution of this law, whenever their services may be required" (section 5). As Henry Clay declared on the floor of the Senate (in one of his many defenses of the compromise he had brokered), the law implicates not just "every State in the Union" but "extends to every man in the Union, and devolves upon him the obligation to assist in the recovery of a fugitive slave from labor. . . . Every man present, whether an officer or agent of the State governments, or private individual, is bound to assist in the execution of the laws of their country."[78] In this way, northerners became increasingly aware of how the federal "bargain" extended to them, and renditions like Burns's demonstrated their own subjection to the logic and power of the federal state, even as that power was being actively focused on the body of a black fugitive. Thus while the new slave law targeted a narrowly defined (racialized) fugitive, it nevertheless had broader implications for citizens of every kind. Indeed, in characterizing the fugitive slave as an individual with a mobile body that could nevertheless be retrieved at a distance from his journey's region of origin, the new law hailed not just the slave but all of federalism's mobile subjects, each in his or her own moveable body.[79]

The new law's extension to individual citizens had profound racial consequences—though not, perhaps, the ones we might expect. Like the anti-abolitionist hysteria described in chapter 6 (which began as a regional reaction against northern encroachment but ultimately expressed itself as a phobic reaction to mixed-race, or amalgamated, bodies), the Fugitive Slave Law of 1850 triggered a regional panic that was expressed, in part, as biological panic. The law induced a sense of regional encroachment—of borders crossed and boundaries blurred—that developed, initially, on the broad scale of state and nation. Samuel May opined that "nothing was left undone to introduce the tactics, discipline, and customs of the Southern plantation into our Northern cities and towns, in order to enforce the Fugitive law."[80] But the law also had consequences for the individuals who found themselves living within these compromised regions, individuals who felt themselves newly visible to the integrating gaze of the federal state. Indeed, the regional reaction we call sectionalism was being dramatically rewritten in these years at the scale of the body as the biological reaction called racism—a racism specifically couched as a fear of falling not from northernness into southernness (or Bostonianness into Americanness) but from whiteness into blackness, from freedom into slavery, from autonomy into (federal) subjection.

Though the 1850 law targeted a racialized fugitive, Americans were notoriously difficult to identify racially. We have already seen that the law tried to establish, at a distance from their origin, the identities of formerly enslaved individuals living in the North. Race could not, however, serve as the only index of slave status in such situations; indeed, "color" was doubly unreliable in this context, because of the widespread presence in the North both of mulattoes (understood in this case as persons who looked white but who might potentially be escaped slaves) and freemen (persons who looked, or were, black but who were, like Solomon Northup, free). The very fungibility of identity-across-space celebrated by Brown in *Clotel* proved rather more troublesome for white populations, many of whom fantasized themselves potentially vulnerable to seizure under the law's loose rules of identification and evidence. As Brown knew, a devastating problem emerges for a white supremacist culture when whiteness can neither be assumed nor proven. If the "real negro" is slowly disappearing (as Brown claims), then where is the real white? And if we cannot tell the difference between the two, then how do we know who is and is not being "lawfully" kidnapped?

We find one answer to this question in the phantasmatic figure of the antebellum white slave. The phrase "white slavery" appears frequently in the antebellum archive but develops enormous slippage in these years, as the categories of both whiteness and slavery came under intense critical scrutiny.[81] As David Roediger has pointed out, the phrase "white slavery" was increasingly embraced in the 1830s and '40s by nascent working-class movements to describe the degraded conditions of white workers, whose misery was described as virtual slavery. Thus Warren Burton, in 1839, published a screed titled *White Slavery: A New Emancipation Cause*, arguing that the working "people of America" had increasingly been "reduc[ed]" "more or less to the condition of *slaves*" when it was, he hoped to show, "their legislative and executive officers" who should be treated as their "*hired men.*" As Roediger notes, the very notion of "white slavery" worked as an oxymoron—a perverse pairing of two words that should never be joined. Burton thus deploys the terms in the hopes of creating a chiasmic backlash, inverting the condition of white working citizens to their legislators.[82] A later pamphlet titled "Abolition Philanthropy!" (1862) frames the problem more polemically, warning that even though the Fugitive Slave Law was resisted when applied to "Southern Negroes," it is considered "Good Enough for Free Citizens of Foreign

Birth!" In this way the pamphlet attempts to link abolition and nativism as a joint conspiracy against European immigrants. To this end, it compares the "cargoes of poor Germans and Irishmen" pouring into North America to the African slave trade and argues that "Negro Equality and the Degradation of the White Foreigner go Hand in Hand." "The same hand which is stretched out to elevate the Negro is lifted to strike down the white citizen in the land of his adoption." Predicting "HANDCUFFS FOR WHITE MEN!" and "SHOULDER STRAPS FOR NEGROES!" the pamphlet rallies white immigrant workers by suggesting that the Pennsylvania Legislature is about to "APPLY THE FUGITIVE-SLAVE LAW TO WHITE MEN" (incorrectly calling this "THE FIRST ATTEMPT OF THE KIND EVER MADE ON THIS CONTINENT").[83] Though speaking to different problems, both Burton's pamphlet and "Abolition Philanthropy!" deploy the same rhetorical technique. Rather than creating a point of contact, or unity, between workers and slaves, the notion of white slavery reifies both terms in that phrase and polarizes them—insisting on the rightful freedom of whites by comparing their condition to the presumed unfreedom of blacks. It is a formula, here and elsewhere, not for multiracial identification but for intraracial jockeying—a measure not of the essential sameness of white and black men but of the wrongful differences that have emerged between white men of different social classes.

The perversity of the phrase "white slavery" was not lost on abolitionists, who took it up to far different purposes. Rather than metaphorizing the idea of slavery, abolitionists worked instead to make it more real even as they destabilized the word "white." Thus Richard Hildreth, on reissuing his 1836 abolitionist novel *The Slave; or, the Memoirs of Archy Moore*, retitled it, in 1852, *The White Slave* (the title usually used today).[84] In both editions, Hildreth includes a scene in which the mulatto Archy Moore is "seized as a fugitive slave," in the middle of a white northern crowd. "Some of them appeared not a little outraged," he wryly notes, "at the idea that a white man should be subject to such an indignity."[85] As elsewhere in the abolitionist archive, the phrase "white slave" refers here to mulattoes who, like Archy Moore, are "decidedly whiter" than other slaves.[86] The same point is made—at length—in a popular AASS pamphlet titled *White Slavery in the United States* (1855), which details the vagaries of racial determination from state to state by listing advertisement after advertisement (à la Theodore Weld) for escaped slaves who are all described with the word "white," thus eroding the fixity of racial categories in ways that are meant to produce an uncomfortable identification of the (white) northern reader with the "white slaves" being described.[87]

Both these uses of the phrase "white slave" are part-metaphors in which one term slips and unmoors the other. A worker who is a white slave is not "really" a slave, just as a mulatto who is a white slave is not, by antebellum understandings of race, "really" white. Indeed, before the 1850s, the phrase "white slave" was most likely to be used literally, with no slippage in either term, only if the usage in question was historically removed from the present day. In 1847, for example, Charles Sumner delivered a retrospective lecture titled *White Slavery in the Barbary States*, which recounted a distant episode from the days of the early republic. The 1850s saw numerous such publications—tales of white American sailors sent into slavery in distant lands and distant times.[88] These accounts demonstrate an ongoing interest in the potential for white unfreedom, but they also mark that potential as part of a past associated with the nation's earliest history. As members of a new nation—without stable foreign relations or a navy to defend itself—early Americans were more available for such seizures; to be a second or third generation removed from the founding, however, was to be doubly free of such dangers. As one antebellum ship's captain wrote in his *Memoir*: "Nobody in this country will admit, for a moment, that there can be any such thing as property in a white man. The institution of slavery could not last for a day, if the slaves were all white."[89]

After 1850, however, something peculiar happens in the history of white slaves: both terms take a turn for the literal as accounts of free white persons held in slavery begin to circulate more widely.[90] We see the fear of such a possibility in "Abolition Philanthropy!" (which argues that the Fugitive Slave Law will soon be applied to white indentured laborers and immigrants), a not so oblique extension of the logic of Horace Greeley's black-and-white map of "Freedom and Slavery" (discussed at the beginning of this chapter), which hails northern citizens as "white slaves" to southern political agendas. But far more literal accounts circulated in these years describing white people being turned into actual chattel slaves. In 1852, for example, William Goodell devoted a section of his mammoth history of the slave trade to this kind of white slavery, contending that "it is known that . . . white persons have been kidnapped who had no African blood in their veins."[91] Stowe likewise includes a chapter on white slavery in *A Key to Uncle Tom's Cabin* (1853), citing two factual cases before concluding:

> That kidnappers may steal and sell white children at the South now, is evident. . . . When the mind once becomes familiarized with the process of slavery,—of enslaving first black, then Indian, then mulatto, then quadroon, and when blue eyes and golden hair are advertised as properties of *negroes*,—what protection will there be for poor white people, especially as under the present fugitive slave law they can be openly carried away without a jury trial?[92]

Samuel May agreed, arguing in 1856 that the Fugitive Slave Law is "fast threatening to include white citizens also"; by 1861, he was declaring that "the number of ACTUALLY FREE persons, STOLEN, KIDNAPPED, from the Northern States and, in utter defiance of law and justice alike, HURRIED into slavery, is to be reckoned by hundreds."[93]

The possibility of white chattel slavery had obvious propagandistic potential for abolitionists like Goodell, Stowe, and May. But the figure of the white slave recurs compulsively in print culture after 1850, from novels to newspaper stories to political debate. In an exchange on the Senate floor on August 19, 1850, for example, several U.S. senators debated the likelihood of such kidnappings and misidentifications as they tried to hammer out the details of the Fugitive Slave Law while it was still under revision.[94] This exchange is ironic, given that all through this debate, Solomon Northup sat enslaved on the Red River. But these senators were less concerned with the kidnapping of free black people than free white people. One senator asks another, for example, "whether he ever knew of any instance in which a man claimed as a slave by a claimant from a slave State was found to be a free man and not a slave." His colleague answers:

> MR. WALKER: I remember a case, which happened a few years since, in Pennsylvania. The person claimed was a female, and was pursued from the State of Maryland. She was taken, and was not discharged until there was a tedious investigation in the courts of Pennsylvania, in which it was ascertained that she was the child of poor Irish parents, who had been but a short time in the country, and that her mother had died in the hospital at Baltimore.
>
> MR. BUTLER: Was she white?
>
> MR. WALKER: She was.

Having detailed this and another case of explicitly racial misidentification, the senator declares: "we see the danger that persons who are free are in of falling into the category of slaves." The senators then discuss how best to minimize the possibility of misidentifying, and enslaving, white persons. A southern senator named Underwood suggests a textual, or documentary, solution: "To prevent the possibility of such frauds, I would suggest . . . that the record [of a missing slave] should be made up in the county whence the slave fled" so that the federal commissioner (on the northern end) should have "nothing but to decide the question of identity." This solution resembles, in some ways, a passport—the system of documentary identification that states have long used to fix (or, gain a monopoly on) what John Torpey calls "the legitimate means of movement" by their citizens.[95] But Senator Underwood never worked out the wrinkles in his plan, undisturbed by the fact that these identity papers would be drawn up in the absence of the person being described and by interested rather than impartial parties. His description of how these "records" will be used to establish a contested identity is, in fact, almost comically simple-minded. He imagines the slaveholder arriving in a northern city and saying, "Here is the record—the description giving the character of the slave, whether male or female, his or her age, and appearance, and color, and all necessary particulars. Then your commissioner or magistrate—call him what you please—has nothing to do but to decide the question of identity. And why do you want a jury for that purpose?"[96]

Senator Underwood's faith in the reliability of description and documentary "records" ironically echoes the faith in long-distance representation that had long underwritten the abolitionist project. In texts like *Slavery as It Is* and *A Key to Uncle Tom's Cabin* (not to mention *Twelve Years a Slave*), antislavery wed itself not just to the truth but to an accumulating antebellum print archive as the earthly location of that truth. As I have already suggested, Brown uses *Clotel* to directly engage and explode the fantasy of transparent description and identification that drives both abolitionist print culture and the slave law. In the process, he widens the imagined scope of the law from targets like himself to those once unthinkable (but increasingly visible) subjects: white slaves.[97]

Clotel knowingly participates in contemporary discourses on white slavery in several ways. For one thing, Brown deploys the common working-class analogy between wage labor and slave labor, unpacking its logic and discarding it: "The English labourer may be oppressed," he notes, "he may be cheated, defrauded, swindled, and even starved; but it is not slavery under which he groans" (145). For another, he continually focuses, throughout the book, on the shifting color line implied by the word "mulatto." Clotel, for example, is a "white slave" of the same kind that Hildreth's Archy Moore is (she both looks white and is descended from a prominent white father). Likewise George Green is "as white as most white persons" and is "often taken for a free white person by those who . . . know him" (222). Finally, Clotel's daughter Mary is not only described as "white" but, like the white children in Stowe's *Key*, is tanned by her mistress so she will look more black (153–54).[98]

But alongside these more familiar white slaves, Brown also explores the possibility of the third kind of white slave—the kind that is neither metaphorical nor racially mixed. He takes both terms literally, for example, in his discussion of Salome Miller, a falsely enslaved German immigrant who is both "really" white and "really" a slave. Indeed, in an ironic turn that is consistent with Brown's wider penchant for reversing identities, the one character who tries to intercede on Miller's behalf is Clotel's sister Althesa—who is "really" black and "really" a slave but who is nevertheless living freely as the wife of a white man in New Orleans. In describing Miller's case (which is based on the historical case of Salome Müller), Brown connects her inability to escape servitude to the evidentiary machinery of southern law. He describes in great detail, for example, how difficult it is to make a positive identification of Miller, in relation both to her race and to her status as either free or unfree:

> In Louisiana as well as many others of the slave states, great obstacles are thrown in the way of persons who have been wrongfully reduced to slavery regaining their freedom. A person claiming to be free must prove his right to his liberty. This, it will be seen, throws the burden of proof upon the slave, who, in all probability, finds it out of his power to procure such evidence. And if any free person shall attempt to aid a freeman in regaining his freedom, he is compelled to enter into security in the sum of one thousand dollars, and if the person claiming to be free shall fail to establish such fact, the thousand dollars are forfeited to the state. This cruel and oppressive law has kept many a freeman from espousing the cause of persons unjustly held as slaves. (141)

The "burden of proof" described here is remarkably similar to the burden of proof placed on fugitives under the 1850 Fugitive Slave Law (as are the incentives and disincentives enacted through fines and fees). Because of this burden of proof, Miller remains a slave until a living link to her free white past is found to testify to her German origin. Her story suggests that the only way identity can be authoritatively established is through the testimony of someone who knows the alleged slave's history personally, a form of "evidence" which, Brown notes, an average person "finds it out of his power to procure"—especially once geographically dislocated from his or her free past (as Solomon Northup was) and confined, without resources, within the "remote regions" of slavery.

Remarkably, the Miller episode is the only moment in *Clotel* in which misidentification has dire consequences. For the most part, *Clotel* embraces fungibility as a solution to the essentializing fixities of antebellum identity categories (organized, as they are, around a series of binaries that the novel repeatedly exposes as unstable: black/white, man/woman, free/unfree, North/South). By including this chapter about "A Free Woman Reduced to Slavery," however, Brown introduces a question that troubles the foundation of antebellum American culture: in a world increasingly organized around long-distance mobility and pasted together through structures of representation, how can one provide "satisfactory" or "sufficient" "proof" that he or she is "actually" white?

Clotel proves that any moving body is vulnerable to misidentification. Kidnappers in white slave narratives usually target immigrants (like Salome Müller or the "child of Irish parents" cited in congressional debate). But Brown suggests that even the most privileged white men might be vulnerable to the same kinds of racial misrecognition. In the same chapter in which Clotel escapes, for example, Brown introduces an extraordinary image: two prominent American white men who are misrecognized as black men. The first of these, Thomas Corwin, is a senator from Ohio, whom Brown dubs "one of the blackest white men in the United States." The second is the more famous (and for our purposes, more interesting) Daniel Webster, the northern legislator most identified with the successful passage of the Fugitive Slave Law:

On the 6th inst., the Hon. Daniel Webster and family entered Edgartown, on a visit for health and recreation. Arriving at the hotel, without alighting from the coach, the landlord was sent for to see if suitable accommodation could be had. That dignitary appearing, and surveying Mr. Webster, while the hon. senator addressed him, seemed woefully to mistake the dark features of the traveller as he sat back in the corner of the carriage, and to suppose him a *coloured man,* particularly as there were two coloured servants of Mr. W. outside. So he promptly declared that there was no room for him and his family, and he could not be accommodated there—at the same time suggesting that he might perhaps find accommodation at some of the huts "up back," to which he pointed. So deeply did the prejudice of looks possess him, that he appeared not to notice that the stranger introduced himself to him as Daniel Webster, or to be so ignorant as not to have heard of such a personage; and turning away, he expressed to the driver his astonishment that he should bring *black* people there for *him* to take in. It was not till he had been repeatedly assured and made to understand that the said Daniel Webster was a real live senator of the United States, that he perceived his awkward mistake and the distinguished honour which he and his house were so near missing. (174–75)

In momentarily turning Webster black, Brown is making at least two jokes at once. On one hand, a black Daniel Webster figures Webster the political turncoat, who sometimes reversed himself to make political deals. On the other hand, it also figures Webster the consolidationist (or compromiser)—the northerner who went to bed with the South to seal a "mixed" nationalist deal (instead of embracing states rights, as his Massachusetts constituents wanted him to). In any case, the scene serves as a reminder that concerns about national consolidation were frequently routed in this period through the figure of the mulatto and the dread of amalgamation. Sectional anxieties about political encroachment (staged nationally as a series of political contests between white men of different regions) are once again rewritten at the micro scale of the body as a fantasy about blood-mixing, or racial miscegenation. In *Clotel,* we get a twist on this trope, as the United States senator most associated with the Compromise of 1850 is presented as a white supremacist culture's most paradoxical production: a black white man.

Notably, like many of the identity-shifting episodes in *Clotel,* this scene is not about the relative whiteness, blackness, or mixed race of Daniel Webster, or even about his own artful performance of such identities, so much as it is about a confused act of reading on the part of the innkeeper.[99] Paul Gilmore has argued that the identity-shifting episodes throughout *Clotel* constitute Brown's open avowal of a performative rather than an essentialist model of raced and gendered identities. To this end, Brown plays different kinds of conventionally essentialized identities off one another at their most explosive points of intersection. Race is thus "a mask" that depends upon the "simultaneous construction of ideas about gender," and Gilmore offers this as an answer to why Brown turns to the novel at this point in his career.[100] "Brown turns to fiction *not* to escape the problematic of stereotyped black representability, but to negotiate the objectification and commodification of the black image by revealing its instability" (39). In this way, *Clotel* "foregrounds the performative nature of race and gender in both abolitionism" and the wider culture industry (particularly minstrelsy) (43). Brown thus exposes race as "an illusion" (44) that is performed, with the best example being Brown's famous blacking up episode—in which he describes the custom among slave traders of altering the looks of their slave-goods through the use of black polish (a doubly ironic use of blackface) that is intended to make the slaves look blacker, younger, and healthier.

Clotel does, of course, undermine "the idea of one authentic representation of black manhood" (46), but as my earlier discussion indicates, it also undermines the idea of *any* fixed representation. As Carla Peterson argues, *Clotel* devotes itself to undoing "essentialist notions of identity" at multiple levels and in multiple registers (as do several other African-American fictions of the 1850s).[101] All markers of identity are up for grabs in *Clotel*: race, gender, class, region, and (finally) nationality are each exposed as provisional sites of selfhood as Brown's characters (black and white, male and female, Vermonters and Tennesseans) are routinely and repeatedly misrecognized by people they do and do not know—sometimes to further the plot but more often for no narrative reason at all. The emphasis in many such moments is not on the *performance* of race (or any other identity) but on the reader's role in producing it. Daniel Webster, for example, is performing neither whiteness nor blackness when he enters the inn, but he is nevertheless misrecognized in raced, and racist, terms. The innkeeper just happens to be a very bad reader of the signs of both race and status. Likewise, many of the slaves throughout *Clotel* are coached to behave (or "perform") in specific ways, but in most of these cases, they fail to fulfill their performative charges. Nevertheless, they continue to be constructed, read, and misread by the characters around them.

Consider two of *Clotel*'s more obvious examples of performance gone bad. In the first, several slaves are coached on how to answer religious questions in order to assure a Yankee traveler of their master's piety. In a comic twist, the faux catechism does not take: "Of course you know who made you?" asks the Yankee, and the slave responds: "De overseer told us last night who made us, but indeed I forgot the gentman's name" (134). In a similar episode, several slaves are prepared for market and coached on how to "sell" themselves to prospective buyers by lying about their ages. Come market time, however, the slaves are tripped up by a series of mathematical questions that reveal inconsistencies in their stories (84–85). In both examples, the slaves comically "fail" to perform their offices. Gilmore rightly notes that such moments draw on the racist assumptions of the minstrel stage in order to produce intellectual slapstick. As in many such instances, however, it is never made clear to *Clotel*'s reader whether the slaves are (as their interlocutors assume) "actually" ignorant or—as in other episodes—intentionally missignifying. Brown provides his readers no interpretive cover in these moments, no narrative security against which we might anchor our reading. These episodes are, in fact, most remarkable for the ways they expose the reader's own potential to be duped—persistently hailing us to take up the innkeeper's position (as misreader) by refusing to point us in the proper direction.

In this way, *Clotel* undermines the reading strategies its readers are most likely to bring to it. How, then, is a reader to answer the question of who is and is not white—or black, male, female, free, enslaved, wily, dull, worthy, or licentious? This question begins as a game in *Clotel* and ends as an epistemological crisis that empties out the evidentiary grounds on which American slavery is enforced across space. These questions cannot finally be answered in a novel that willfully cultivates the idea that the truth is unknowable and that personal identity is fungible, not just in ways that we control (or "perform"), but in ways that construct us from the outside in (as in those acts of social reading and unintentional misrecognition that produce, among other things, a black Daniel Webster). *Clotel* works against the idea that there is an epistemologically verifiable difference between black and white Americans—an argument that is eloquently embodied, as we shall see, in the figure of Jefferson's daughter, the slave.[102]

In destabilizing the presumably fixed privileges of both whiteness and freedom, Brown stakes out a site where a white person might discover not just his own complicity in the Fugitive Slave Law but his vulnerability to it. *Clotel*'s color-crossings thus serve triple duty: they entertain; they critique; but, practically speaking, they also place a new demand on Brown's white audience. Rather than hailing white readers to identify affectively

with heroic mulattoes and tragic mulattas through the mechanism of sentimental sympathy, Brown resurrects that old federalist chestnut—self-
interest—and weaves it into the fabric of his narrative. Ventriloquizing
the voice of the average white citizen in yet another of the novel's endless
role-playing reversals, Brown asks: "Who questions the right of mankind
to be free? / Yet, what are the rights of the *negro* to me? / I'm well fed
and clothed, I have plenty of pelf— / I'll care for the blacks when I turn
black myself" (181). By placing pressure on perceived categories of identity and proving them easily confused, Brown suggests to his readers that
under the right circumstances, anyone could "turn black" (or, indeed,
white). In the postcompromise era, such color-crossings were not likely,
but the figure of the white slave proves they had become thinkable—a
telling sign of a larger transformation.[103] Under the ongoing pressures of
federalist integration—nationalism, circa 1850—the gap between the
words "white" and "slave" would, in fact, only further compress.

8. The Material History of Nation-States

Clotel's interest in obfuscated origins goes beyond Salome Miller. In fact,
the novel uses the everyday dislocations of slavery to think about the similarly dislocated nature of nationalism's imagined community—which,
like slavery, is premised on a series of temporal and geographic displacements of its subjects from their origins. Slave law states that "slavery is hereditary and perpetual."[104] After 1861, Lincoln would instruct
the secessionist South that the condition of political subjects under the
Constitution was likewise "hereditary and perpetual"—a binding social compact that no state could choose to dissolve. To this end, Lincoln
ominously announced in his first inaugural that "the Union is perpetual"
and warned that "it *will* constitutionally defend and maintain itself."[105]
Though there are, of course, many meaningful differences between slavery and nationalism, one of the more significant structural differences,
in terms of inheritance, is that under slavery, one follows the condition
of the mother while under nationalism, one follows the condition of the
(founding) fathers. The brilliance of *Clotel* is that Brown finds, in "the
president's daughter," a figure that joins both these heirs in a single body.
In doing so, Brown identifies nationalism's subjects with slavery's subjects—white citizens with black slaves—and he does so not by recurring

to an affective (or "sentimental") identification but by tracing, historically, the *material* production of both of these kinds of subjectivity across
time and space.[106]

Chattel slavery initially erased the origins of slaves in the forced migration from Africa (which dissolved a sense of geographical origins)
and in the forced separation of slave families (which dissolved a sense
of biological origins across generations). The first was initially a product of the external slave trade, abolished by Congress in 1808; the second
was repeated endlessly in the proliferating internal trade, a thriving commerce inadvertently but disastrously intensified by that 1808 abolition
and finally leading, of course, to more scenes of forced geographic dislocation inside the domestic market. *Clotel* places the problem of such
dislocations at its center. The prefatory *Narrative* deploys six scenes of
separation in rapid succession, spanning nine concerted pages, with most
routed through the perspective of the lost child (rather than the more
conventional figure of the mourning mother). These separations form
the backbone of Brown's *Narrative* and constitute its most consistent and
recurrent theme: "Nothing was more grievous to the sensitive feelings of
William," Brown tells us, "than seeing the separation of families" (9).

The novel proper tells the same story at the micro level of one family.
As a narrative architecture, *Clotel* is specifically designed to rejoin Clotel's
disarticulated family unit. Brown resists doing this, however, in the way
that conventional abolitionist narratives do—through fantastic reunions
at the level of plot. Stowe is again exemplary in this regard, using the final
pages of *Uncle Tom's Cabin* to reunite not just George, Eliza, and Harry
into an appropriately nuclearized family but to restore the solitary Cassy
to her blood relatives as well. *Clotel* emphatically refuses this tidy strategy. Clotel's sister Althesa tries, for example, to purchase her mother's
freedom but fails because the owner refuses to sell; later in the novel, the
slaves on that plantation are emancipated en masse, but by then both Althesa and her mother are dead. It is not, then, through narrative content
but through narrative *structure* that Brown reconnects Clotel's scattered
family of origin. That word Benedict Anderson has taught us to be so
sensitive to—the word *meanwhile*—enables Brown to phantasmatically
rearticulate Clotel's family unit within the reading-space of the novel
without forcing him to resolve the problem diegetically—as a matter
of plot. Thus the first two chapters stage three destinations for Clotel's
family (Natchez, New Orleans, and Richmond), and for the rest of the

novel, Brown shifts without remark among all three (and the new set-tings they generate through subsequent offspring and subsequent slave sales). In this way, the novel works to resuture the separated family even as it insists, at the level of plot, upon their irreversible loss (of each other) within the diaspora of the national slave trade.

Here again we see Brown's striking difference from Stowe. For Stowe (as for many antebellum Americans), the nation is imagined as a wholly spatial problem—a series of distinct places whose relations have become overly entwined and whose boundaries have collapsed. *Uncle Tom's Cabin* imagines this problem within a very specific moment in U.S. history—and hence plucked out of a larger ongoing national narrative, making it anomalous and, at the end of the novel, reversible. Stowe manages in this way to produce an iconic account both of slavery's wrongs and of its po-tential resolutions, but she does so by evading the problem of space-in-history—the unfolding process of territorial conquest and identification we call nation building. *Uncle Tom's Cabin* heartily rebukes the living con-tent of the nation, reconnecting its distant dots (much as a fugitive slave narrative does), but it never disavows the nation's inherently problematic structure as a cross-generational spatial form. The result is Stowe's wish-ful fantasy that history's relations might be erased and rearranged under a new set of spatial relations (African colonization)—without any sense that even these new spatial relations will eventually undergo historical displacements from themselves and cause new problems.

Clotel is thus more than just a novel about a family of slaves whose connections to one another are disrupted by travel and by history. It is also, by virtue of its ensemble cast of highly mobile characters, its subtitle ("The President's Daughter"), and its plot, a genealogy of the nation and of its human content (its people) as they exist not phantasmatically—as an ideological projection of nationalist sentiment—but in their bodies, as material facts of life. I have been describing throughout this book the many ways in which the nation as a form relies upon the dislocations of its subjects from the scene of their origins—both in space and in time.[107] Brown is interested in precisely this problem, and he renders it in vividly materialist fashion, for *Clotel* describes a nation populated by its found-ers' progeny—literalized and made material in the children and grand-children of Thomas Jefferson. To Stowe's critique of the nation as a spa-tially flawed form that can no longer operate at an appropriate remove from itself, Brown adds a deep, historical, and yet uncannily materialist critique. *Clotel*'s nation is not just a space but a history that produces three things across generations: a new territory, an accumulating archive (of stories, facts, and figures), and a dispersed people (portrayed here in the presidentially produced figures of Clotel, Althesa, Jane, Ellen, and Mary). It is what this book has claimed a nation must always be: a material history of space, things, and people.

CONCLUSION
THE DUE PROCESS OF NATIONALISM

All persons born or naturalized in the United States, and subject to the jurisdiction thereof, are citizens of the United States and of the state wherein they reside. No state shall make or enforce any law which shall abridge the privileges or immunities of citizens of the United States; nor shall any state deprive any person of life, liberty, or property, without due process of law; nor deny to any person within its jurisdiction the equal protection of the laws.
———United States Constitution, Fourteenth Amendment, Section 1

"If you lived up among the Yankees in New-England," said Epps, "I expect you'd be one of them cursed fanatics that know more than the constitution, and go about peddling clocks and coaxing niggers to run away."

"If I was in New-England," returned Bass, "I would be just what I am here."
———Solomon Northup, *Twelve Years a Slave*, 1853

In American historiography, the Fugitive Slave Law is often narrated as part of the larger failure of the 1850 Compromise. But in many ways, the law points not to the exhausted past but to a future that extends well beyond emancipation. One might argue in fact that the logic of the Fugitive Slave Law is perfectly if paradoxically consistent with that of those postwar amendments that might seem to undo it. The war produced three major amendments to the Constitution: one abolished slavery; the next one established due process and equal protection; and the last one guaranteed the right to vote regardless of race. Like the 1850 law, all these amendments rely upon a new relation between the individual citizen and the federal state, whereby the citizen is for the first time constitutionally "seen" by that state as an embodied individual, a raced and a reachable subject. It is remarkable enough that an individual body would be racially marked within the language of the Constitution (as in the Fifteenth Amendment) and that a special protection is articulated there precisely on that basis. But it is more remarkable that the Constitution became capable, after 1870, of thinking of individuals at the local scale of their biological being——in short, that the federal citizen is understood to be raced at all (regardless of who or what color he is). Seen in this way, the achievement, though spectacular, becomes politically dubious, for we see the liberal myth of equal access guaranteed in terms of race at this moment precisely because the state bears a new, potentially oppressive relation to individuals living within the once inaccessible world of the local.

The original Constitution is not, of course, interested in individuals in quite this way. Though Publius (among others) knew that the Constitution imagines federalism's subject as an individual (rather than a geopolitical entity like a state or region), the Constitution seeks to effect that monumental shift (in the relation between national and local, near and far, here and there) by erecting an abstract structure to manage such relations, both in its own time and deep into the unforeseen future. There are few "characters" in the Constitution, in the literary sense of the word. Indeed, the "persons" most often mentioned in articles 1 through 5 are the nameless and interchangeable bureaucrats who will manage the theoretical structure installed by the Constitution—the president, the senator, the representative, the judge. Virtual characters all, they are likewise placed in the virtual space of a guaranteed but as yet unchosen (and so not quite real) location: the "ten Miles square" capital that would become Washington, DC—itself one of the greatest of American contradictions: a site of taxation, without representation. While it is true that "the People" are present, as putative speakers, in the Preamble's opening declaration, they disappear immediately inside of that circuitous locution, and if we are to look for them after the Preamble (as actual persons, inhabiting their local capacity as individuals who live at some remove from their government), we must skip over the Constitution itself and look instead to its (first) sequel: the Bill of Rights. This is, as it were, the constitutional location of the local, for here, "persons" are openly articulated as federalism's true subject, individual beings with rights (to free speech, to jury trials, to gun ownership) that either must be protected *from* an encroaching federal state or can, alternatively, be protected *by* that state.[1]

This new, more material relation between state and citizen is evident in the three amendments that emerge from the Civil War. Unlike the Bill of Rights, these amendments are not afterthoughts to the original arrangement framed at the moment of ratification but are instead the after-*effects* of an ongoing historical process. They mark the permanent rejection of place (and place collectivity—such as statehood and sectionalism) as the keys to American identity, which is rewritten instead in the form of the more mobile, individualized identities we see being legislated (unsuccessfully, it turns out) in the Fugitive Slave Law. The rejection of place is evident not just in the abolition of the territorially based institution of slavery, but in the Fourteenth Amendment's aggressive outline of punishment for southern Confederates (obliquely referred to in the second, third, and fourth articles as "participan[nts]" in "insurrection or rebellion" against the United States). The crime of these Confederate insurrectionists was in maintaining a loyalty to their local states and regions over and against a loyalty to the nation at large. The Fourteenth Amendment thoroughly vanquishes this kind of regional and state-based loyalty, denying rebels both the right to vote and compensation for their losses even as it erects a series of new protections for those whose identities shall hereafter inhere not in geography (making them part of a regional community), but within their own individual bodies, as subjects of a consolidated megastate—a nation. Though race is the obvious (or explicit) mode of personal identity upheld and protected under these three amendments, all three work together to usher in a new era of that regime Foucault calls biopower by codifying a new kind of bio-identity. That regime was begun in 1787 with the theoretical extension of federal power to individuals (bypassing the states) and finishes here, in 1868, with the promised "equal protection" of such individuals regardless of their location in space or the (ostensible) racial content of their unique biologies. But these three amendments are less interested in insisting on a particular race for the federal subject they imagine than in insisting that this new federal subject has an individual body with a race necessarily attached to it—a person with a biological history that is visible and meaningful to the state that is said to protect it, even if only because it is not supposed to mean anything in particular.

Christopher Gadsden famously declared at the onset of the Revolution that "there ought to be no New England men, no New Yorker, &c., known on the Continent, but all of us Americans."[2] That pretty sentiment was not constitutionally codified until passage of the Fourteenth Amendment ensured equal (federal) protection and due process to all, regardless of regional origin or biological/racial genealogy. In extending this bounty to the individual citizen (protected in his explicitly raced—and implicitly gendered—body), the United States finally did away constitutionally with the last remnants of the Confederation and of the local, regional, and state-based identities for which the Revolution had been fought. The United States thus emerged as an actual nation, fulfilling the consolidationist fantasies of its original framers by reaching out, through densely mediated structures of representation that no Publius could have dreamed of, to every individual citizen—virtually equal, all.

ABBREVIATIONS FOR WORKS FREQUENTLY CITED

AASS: The American Anti-Slavery Society.

CAF: Herbert J. Storing, ed., *The Complete Anti-Federalist*, 7 vols. (Chicago: University of Chicago Press, 1981).

DHRC: Merrill Jensen, John P. Kaminski, and Gaspare J. Saladino, eds., *The Documentary History of the Ratification of the Constitution*, 19 vols. (Madison: State Historical Society of Wisconsin, 1976–<2003>).

LDC: Paul H. Smith et al., eds., *Letters of Delegates to Congress, 1774–1789*, 26 vols. (Washington: Library of Congress: U.S. Govt. Printing Office, 1976–2000).

LMCC: Edmund C. Burnett, ed., *Letters of Members of the Continental Congress*, 8 vols. (Washington: The Carnegie Institution, 1921–36).

LWGG: Gilbert H. Barnes and Dwight L. Dumond, eds., *Letters of Theodore Dwight Weld, Angelina Grimké and Sarah Grimké, 1822–1844*, 2 vols. (Gloucester, MA: P. Smith, 1965).

PAH: Harold C. Syrett, ed., *Papers of Alexander Hamilton*, 27 vols. (New York: Columbia University Press, 1961–87).

PJM: William T. Hutchinson and William M. E. Rachal et al., eds., *Papers of James Madison*, 17 vols. (Chicago and Charlottesville: University of Chicago Press and University of Virginia Press, 1962–91).

RFC: Max Farrand, ed., *Records of the Federal Convention of 1787*, 4 vols. (New Haven: Yale University Press, 1966).

WMQ: *William and Mary Quarterly*.

NOTES

Introduction. A View from the Capitol

1. John Torpey, *The Invention of the Passport: Surveillance, Citizenship, and the State* (New York: Cambridge University Press, 2000), 12–13. As Rogers Brubaker says: "We should not ask, 'what is a nation' but rather: 'how is nationhood as a political and cultural form institutionalized within and among states?'" Rogers Brubaker, *Nationalism Reframed: Nationhood and the National Question in the New Europe* (1982; New York: Cambridge University Press, 1996), 19. For theoretical approaches that emphasize the materiality of nationalism, see John Breuilly, *Nationalism and the State*, 2d ed. (Chicago: University of Chicago Press, 1994); Karl Deutsch, *Nationalism and Social Communication*, 2d ed. (Cambridge: MIT Press, 1966); Anthony Giddens, *The Nation-State and Violence* (Berkeley: University of California Press, 1985); Michael Mann, "The Nation-State in Europe and Other Continents: Diversifying, Developing, Not Dying," in *Mapping the Nation*, ed. Gopal Balakrishnan (New York: Verso, 1996), 281–94. For materialist historiographic approaches, see Richard D. Brown, *Knowledge Is Power: The Diffusion of Information in Early America, 1700–1865* (New York: Oxford University Press, 1989); Richard R. John, *Spreading the News: The American Postal System from Franklin to Morse* (Cambridge: Harvard University Press, 1995); and Eugen Weber, *Peasants into Frenchmen: The Modernization of Rural France,*

1870–1914 (Stanford: Stanford University Press, 1976). On the distinction between nationalism as an idea and as a practice, see David Waldstreicher, *In the
Midst of Perpetual Fetes: The Making of American Nationalism, 1776–1820* (Chapel Hill: Published for the Omohundro Institute of Early American History and
Culture by the University of North Carolina Press, 1997), 17–52.

CHAPTER 1. U.S. PRINT CULTURE

1. Brown, *Knowledge Is Power*, 269.

2. Benedict Anderson, *Imagined Communities: Reflections on the Origin and
Spread of Nationalism* (1983; New York: Verso, 1991), 11.

3. John L. Brooke, "To be 'Read by the Whole People': Press, Party, and Public
Sphere in the United States, 1790–1840," *Proceedings of the American Antiquarian
Society* 110, no. 1 (2000): 41–118; and Alexander Saxton, *The Rise and Fall of the
White Republic: Class Politics and Mass Culture in Nineteenth-Century America*
(New York: Verso, 1990).

4. Anderson explicitly frames *Imagined Communities* as a response to the more
skeptical accounts of nationalism that preceded him, including Ernest Gellner's
"modernization thesis" in *Nations and Nationalism* (Ithaca: Cornell University
Press, 1983).

5. Finlay and John Foxcroft replaced Benjamin Franklin, who was dismissed
from his position as postmaster general in 1774 for (as he liked to say) "being
too much of an American." Cited in Frank H. Norton, ed., *Journal Kept by Hugh
Finlay* (Brooklyn: F.H. Norton, 1867), xxi.

6. *Pennsylvania Gazette*, 3 and 10 January 1776.

7. Cited in Catherine A. Holland, *The Body Politic: Foundings, Citizenship, and
Difference in the American Political Imagination* (New York: Routledge, 2001),
62.

8. The modular aspect of Anderson's approach (his desire to create an argument that will fit any nation anywhere) has left him vulnerable to comparative
critiques organized around more local evidence. See Partha Chatterjee, *The Nation and Its Fragments: Colonial and Postcolonial Histories* (Princeton: Princeton
University Press, 1993); and Ed White, "Early American Nations as Imagined
Communities," *American Quarterly* 56 (2000): 49–81.

9. Richard D. Brown, *The Strength of a People: The Idea of an Informed Citi-
zenry in America, 1650–1870* (Chapel Hill: University of North Carolina Press,
1996).

10. *American Museum* (January 1787): xvii, 10.

11. The most successful corporate book projects of this era were encyclopedias
financed by European capital. Similarly ambitious ventures by American printers

ers often met with disaster. See Laura Rigal, *The American Manufactory: Art, Labor, and the World of Things in the Early Republic* (Princeton: Princeton University Press, 1998), 151–53; and James Green, "The Middle Colonies, 1720–1790: Part 1, English Books and Printing in the Age of Franklin," in Hugh Amory and David D. Hall, eds., *The Colonial Book in the Atlantic World* (Cambridge: Cambridge University Press, 2000), 248–98.

12. Mathew Carey, *Autobiography* (Brooklyn: E. L. Schwaab, 1942), 22. As Green notes, Carey wanted something "that would give him wider scope than a local newspaper." But while "it was the most ambitious magazine yet published in America," the *Columbian Magazine* failed because "Carey could not get his partners to promote it as widely as he wanted and so the profits were too small, when divided by six, to be worth his while." James N. Green, *Mathew Carey: Publisher and Patriot* (Philadelphia: The Library Company, 1985), 6.

13. Cross-regional printing and publishing ventures were rare but not unheard of in the late 1780s, since urban printers maintained loose business contacts with colleagues in other regions. Benjamin Franklin was famously linked to other colonies through a network of family, friends, and past apprentices. Franklin often placed former apprentices in business, however, to get them out of Philadelphia, and his contact with many of them was limited, even when goods were exchanged and accounts kept. This was the case for Robert Aitken, a Philadelphia bookseller who sent William Young, a small Charleston printer, fifty-five volumes on exchange in 1784, only to have all but five returned eleven years later. The books exchanged in such trades were usually not American imprints but the castoff refuse of the European book trade—unlikely and random volumes that often had little or no value. See Rosalind Remer, *Printers and Men of Capital: Philadelphia Book Publishers in the New Republic* (Philadelphia: University of Pennsylvania Press, 1996), 84.

14. Carey did eventually become the pioneer of organized, cross-regional distribution, but his path was not a simple one. He is best remembered for *Charlotte Temple*'s success in the 1790s and for his erstwhile partnership with Mason Locke Weems, the itinerant book peddler who traveled alone through Maryland and Virginia hawking Carey's wares. But throughout the 1790s, Carey's fascination with the chimera of national distribution continually disabled his more successful local, if increasingly regionalized, trade. As James Green notes, "Weems sold immense quantities of books, but the expense of distributing them over so wide an area and of maintaining stock in so many branch stores was so great that Carey's profits were wiped out." By the end of the decade, he was so badly in debt that he took out a desperate ad in the *Pennsylvania Gazette*: "Books Selling Very Cheap. Mathew Carey, Proposing to quit the Book Selling business, offers his large and valuable collection of Books for sale." But his proposition prompted no responses. Green, *Mathew Carey*, 12.

15. Benjamin Franklin, *The Autobiography of Benjamin Franklin: A Genetic Text*, ed. J. A. Leo LeMay and Paul M. Zall (Knoxville: University of Tennessee Press, 1981), 68.

16. Joseph Dennie wrote to Tyler in New Hampshire noting how difficult it was "for the Bostonians to supply themselves with a book that slumbers in a stall at Walpole." Cited in Cathy N. Davidson, *Revolution and the Word: The Rise of the Novel in America* (New York: Oxford University Press, 1986), 21; and in William Charvat, *Literary Publishing in America, 1790–1850* (1959; Amherst: University of Massachusetts Press, 1993), 25–26. For case studies of local print cultures, see Amory and Hall, eds., *The Colonial Book in the Atlantic World*; David D. Hall and John B. Hench, eds., *Needs and Opportunities in the History of the Book: America, 1639–1876* (Worcester, MA: American Antiquarian Society, 1987); and David D. Hall, *Cultures of Print: Essays in the History of the Book* (Amherst: University of Massachusetts Press, 1996).

17. Hugh Henry Brackenridge, *Modern Chivalry*, ed. Claude M. Newlin (New York: American Book Company, 1937), 250.

18. Brown, *Knowledge Is Power*, 247, 254–55.

19. Ibid., 271. There are important exceptions. Massachusetts, for instance, was densely literate and more connected from town to town than other colonies just before and after the Revolution. But even in Massachusetts, Brown cites notable levels of insularity well into the nineteenth century. See also William J. Gilmore, *Reading Becomes a Necessity of Life: Material and Cultural Life in Rural New England, 1780–1835* (Knoxville: University of Tennessee Press, 1989).

20. See Davidson, *Revolution and the Word*; Cathy N. Davidson, ed., *Reading in America: Literature and Social History* (Baltimore: Johns Hopkins University Press, 1989); Michael Warner, *Letters of the Republic: Publication and the Public Sphere in Eighteenth-Century America* (Cambridge: Harvard University Press, 1990); and Larzer Ziff, *Writing in the New Nation: Prose, Print, and Politics in the Early United States* (New Haven: Yale University Press, 1991).

21. For an account that challenges abstract print paradigms by thinking about material conditions, see Robert A. Gross, "Print and the Public Sphere in Early America," in *The State of U.S. History*, ed. Melvyn Stokes (New York: Berg Press, 2002).

22. On the emergence of a more integrated national market, see Charles Grier Sellers, *The Market Revolution: Jacksonian America, 1815–1846* (New York: Oxford University Press, 1991).

23. Cass R. Sunstein, *Legal Reasoning and Political Conflict* (New York: Oxford University Press, 1996), 35–61.

24. On the limited ability of American newspapers to link different communities together via domestic news networks in these years, see Richard L. Merritt, *Symbols of American Community, 1735–1775* (New Haven: Yale University Press, 1966); Frank Luther Mott, *American Journalism: A History of Newspapers*

in the United States through 260 years, 1690–1950 (New York: Macmillan, 1950); and Allan R. Pred, *Urban Growth and the Circulation of Information: The United States System of Cities, 1790–1840* (Cambridge: Harvard University Press, 1973), 20–77.

25. See, for example, Jay Grossman, *Reconstituting the American Renaissance: Emerson, Whitman, and the Politics of Representation* (Durham: Duke University Press, 2003); and Warner, *Letters of the Republic*, 97–117.

26. On the importance of representation in American political economy, see Grossman, *Reconstituting the American Renaissance*, 28–74; and Thomas Gustafson, *Representative Words: Politics, Literature, and the American Language, 1776–1865* (New York: Cambridge University Press, 1992), 19–36. On the difference between actual and virtual representation, see Bernard Bailyn, *Ideological Origins of the American Revolution* (Cambridge: Belknap, 1967), 160–75; and Gordon S. Wood, *The Creation of the American Republic, 1776–1787* (New York: W. W. Norton, 1969), 173–88, 363–72.

27. Christopher Looby, *Voicing America: Language, Literary Form, and the Origins of the United States* (Chicago: University of Chicago Press, 1996), 1.

28. On the post office and the U.S. "imagined community," see John, *Spreading the News*, 112–68, 257–80.

29. On *The Federalist*'s distribution, see Elaine F. Crane, "Publius in the Provinces: Where Was *The Federalist* Reprinted Outside of New York City?," *WMQ*, 3d ser., 21, no. 4 (1964): 589–92; and Albert Furtwangler, *The Authority of Publius: A Reading of the Federalist Papers* (Ithaca: Cornell University Press, 1984).

30. Henry Carey, *The Slave Trade, Domestic and Foreign* (1853; Philadelphia: Henry Carey Baird, 1867), 375. Lisa Brawley has suggested that the fear of regionally specific practices that "travel" north is most often emblematized in the figure of the fugitive slave and the form of the slave narrative. Lisa Brawley, "Frederick Douglass's *My Bondage and My Freedom* and the Fugitive Tourist Industry," *Novel* 30 (1996): 98–128.

31. Eric Foner, *Free Soil, Free Labor, Free Men: The Ideology of the Republican Party before the Civil War* (1970; New York: Oxford University Press, 1995).

Chapter 2. Disseminating *Common Sense*

1. Warner, *Letters of the Republic*, esp. 73–96.

2. For a standard treatment, see Jack Fruchtman Jr.'s "*Common Sense*," in *A Companion to the American Revolution*, ed. Jack P. Greene and J. R. Pole (Malden, MA: Blackwell, 2000), 254–57, which cites large circulation numbers but never describes the pamphlet's physical production and circulation. The only comprehensive account of *Common Sense*'s actual publication history is Richard Gimbel's introduction to *Thomas Paine: A Bibliographical Checklist of Common*

Sense (New Haven: Yale University Press, 1956), 15–57. See also Scott Liell, *46 Pages: Thomas Paine, Common Sense, and the Turning Point to American Independence* (New York: Running Press, 2004), 83–120.

3. Philip S. Foner, ed., *The Complete Writings of Thomas Paine*, 2 vols. (New York: Citadel, 1945), 2:1163.

4. Howard Zinn, "Pamphleteering in America," in *Artists in Times of War* (New York: Seven Stories Press, 2003), 93–94.

5. Michel-Rolph Trouillot, *Silencing the Past: Power and the Production of History* (Boston: Beacon Press, 1995), 29. Meredith McGill has recently argued that the "culture of reprinting" in the 1830s has been obscured by our tendency, in literary studies, to isolate authors as the meaning-making focus of our study. I argue here that the fragmentary, chaotic culture of Revolutionary reprinting has been not just obscured but repressed inside a historical narrative that reproduces power from above by attributing it to the world below—and that this materiality has been forgotten in favor not just of a Great Author and a Great Text but of a Great People and a Great Nation. Meredith L. McGill, *American Literature and the Culture of Reprinting, 1834–1853* (Philadelphia: University of Pennsylvania Press, 2003).

6. Grant Thorburn, "Anecdote of Thomas Paine," in the Colonel Richard Gimbel Collection of Thomas Paine Papers, American Philosophical Society.

7. The phrase "common sense" presents a case study in the development of colonial vernaculars. Between 1740 and 1783, the *Pennsylvania Gazette* used this phrase 120 times, but only 10 date from before 1766—a year marked by resistance to the Stamp Act. The greatest cluster of uses emerges in two moments— the 1760s and then 1776, when *Common Sense* was frequently referred to editorially and in advertisements.

8. Sir Herbert Butterfield defines "the Whig interpretation of history" as "the tendency in many historians . . . to praise revolutions provided they have been successful, to emphasize certain principles of progress in the past and to produce a story which is the ratification if not the glorification of the present." *The Whig Interpretation of History* (1931; New York: W. W. Norton, 1965), v. I use the phrase similarly, to refer to popular accounts of 1776 as a progressive and populist revolution.

9. Henry Cabot Lodge, *The Story of the Revolution*, 2 vols. (New York: Charles Scribner's Sons, 1898), 1:154.

10. Thomas R. Adams, *American Independence: The Growth of an Idea* (Austin, TX: Jenkins and Reese, 1980), xi.

11. In addition to the twenty-five known American editions, there is one 1776 imprint with no printer's colophon, reading only "Printed for the Thirteen Colonies." This could have been printed domestically or imported, although it seems likely, given the phrasing, that it was produced abroad. Gimbel, *Thomas Paine*, 91.

12. Adams, *American Independence*, xi–xii. The eighteenth-century British book trade was centralized in London and served a more massive market than anything American publishing could coordinate until the rise of the railroad in the nineteenth century reorganized the American book industry. As Rosalind Remer notes, "London remained the undisputed center of the British book trade," while "there was no one city in America that controlled or monopolized the national trade." *Printers and Men of Capital*, 40. *Common Sense* is a case in point: London editions outnumber all American editions combined. London produced thirty-five editions between 1776 and 1800 as opposed to North America's twenty-eight.

13. Moncure Daniel Conway, ed., *The Writings of Thomas Paine*, 4 vols. (New York: G. P. Putnam's Sons, 1894–96), 1:67; Foner, ed., *Complete Writings*, 1:xiv.

14. John Fiske, *The American Revolution*, 2 vols. (New York: Houghton Mifflin, 1891), 1:175.

15. W. E. Woodward, *George Washington: The Image and the Man* (New York: Liveright, 1926), 282.

16. Lynn Montross, *The Reluctant Rebels* (New York: Harper and Brothers, 1950), 112.

17. Greene and Pole, eds., *Companion to the American Revolution*, 193, 212, 254.

18. Zinn, "Pamphleteering in America," 93–94. More generalist sources like history textbooks also routinely cite circulation numbers. One notes that "*Common Sense* exploded on the American scene like a bombshell. Within three months of publication, it sold 120,000 copies." Mary Beth Norton et al., *A People and a Nation: A History of the United States*, 2 vols., 6th ed. (New York: Houghton Mifflin, 2001), 1:153. Another is more wary, concluding that *Common Sense* "reached hundreds of thousands of homes." James A. Henretta et al., *America: A Concise History*, 2 vols. (Boston: Bedford/St. Martin's, 1999), 1:147.

19. Eric Foner finds 150,000 to be the most common figure, noting that "Paine later claimed *Common Sense* had sold at least 150,000 copies, and most historians have accepted this figure as accurate." *Tom Paine and Revolutionary America* (New York: Oxford University Press, 1976), 79.

20. There are no extant letters between Paine and printers of *Common Sense*, although later correspondence sometimes shows Paine trying to control his work's publication. The American Philosophical Society holds several later pieces of correspondence between Paine and American newspaper editors as well as an early letter to the Honorable Supreme Executive Council of Pennsylvania outlining a plan to import a large quantity of paper and oversee production of a two-volume edition of "my several pieces, beginning with Common Sense." Though he sought "the loan of fifteen hundred pounds" to execute this project, his request was not seriously considered and the edition did not appear. Letter of The Honorable Supreme Executive, 11 October 1779, in the Colonel Richard Gimbel

Collection of Thomas Paine Papers, American Philosophical Society. Such letters indicate ambition but display limited business savvy. As Benjamin Franklin Bache recalled, Paine often urged techniques that furthered dissemination but generated no profits. Remer, *Printers and Men of Capital*, 30.

21. Robert Middlekauff, *The Glorious Cause: The American Revolution, 1763–1789* (New York: Oxford University Press, 1982), 320.

22. The colonial printer "tended to produce material of local interest and sponsorship for local markets. While commodities such as molasses, tobacco, and humans linked colonial regions, printed matter was not considered a particularly valuable commodity for trade." Remer, *Printers and Men of Capital*, 4.

23. James Gilreath, "American Book Distribution," in *Needs and Opportunities in the History of the Book*, ed. Hall and Hench, 111.

24. Ibid., 128.

25. Remer, *Printers and Men of Capital*, 17. David D. Hall similarly prioritizes "local items" when he says that "farmers, artisans, and merchants . . . bought little more than almanacs and Bibles—if that." He also usefully notes regional disparities: "the leading Virginia printer-bookseller was issuing 6,000 almanacs a year" while "a *single* northern almanac had annual sales of 50,000 copies." David D. Hall, "Books and Reading in Eighteenth-Century America," in *Of Consuming Interests: The Style of Life in the Eighteenth Century*, ed. Cary Carson et al. (Charlottesville: University Press of Virginia, 1994), 363–64.

26. For an example of a first-generation historian who does cite Paine, see Edmund Randolph, *History of Virginia* (Charlottesville: University Press of Virginia, 1970), 233–34, who claims that *Common Sense* reached both "the learned" and "the unlearned." It's unclear, however, whether this passing remark refers to Paine's influence in Virginia or more nationally.

27. Arthur H. Shaffer, *The Politics of History: Writing the History of the American Revolution, 1783–1815* (Chicago: Precedent Publishing, 1975), 32–35, 174–75.

28. Gordon S. Wood, "Rhetoric and Reality in the American Revolution," *WMQ*, 3d ser., 23, no. 1 (1966): 3–32.

29. Michael Zuckerman, "Rhetoric, Reality, and the Revolution: The Genteel Radicalism of Gordon Wood," *WMQ*, 3d ser., 51, no. 4 (1994): 697.

30. William Duane, ed., *Extracts from the Diary of Christopher Marshall* (Albany: J. Munsell Publishers, 1877), 57.

31. A. Owen Aldridge, *Thomas Paine's American Ideology* (Newark: University of Delaware Press, 1984), 41; Robert A. Ferguson, "Writing the Revolution," in *The Cambridge History of American Literature*, 8 vols., ed. Sacvan Bercovitch (New York: Cambridge University Press, 1994–99), 1:456.

32. Paine cites these numbers and reflects on his dispute with Bell in a letter to Henry Laurens that details the business side of the early Philadelphia printings,

including the rate charged per pamphlet and his own "out-of-pocket" expenses, which in 1779 amounted to nearly forty pounds (2:1163–64).

33. See Carl Van Doren, *Benjamin Franklin* (New York: Viking Press, 1938), 548; and Gimbel, *Thomas Paine*, 17. The source for Aitken's numbers is his wastebook, one of few extant records of actual orders for *Common Sense*. Aitken was a friend of Franklin's and a respected Philadelphia Whig. His popular bookstore probably provided many members of the Continental Congress with their first copies of the pamphlet.

34. Bradford's edition contains Paine's appendix on the Quakers, included to deny Bell an authoritative edition to reprint. Bell responded by issuing a "complete edition" that pirated this appendix and also added six new items by other authors. Bell describes these as "Large Additions to *Common Sense*," but all except one were unrelated. Bell offered this enlarged edition free to anyone who had purchased his original edition. These expanded editions undoubtedly reached large numbers of new readers in Philadelphia and outlying areas. It is also likely, however, that they earned each printer repeat buyers who sought the new material (some receiving it free from Bell, others buying new copies from either printer). To distinguish their products, the Bradfords placed a note on their title page that read "N.B. The New Addition here given increases the Work upwards of a third," while Bell prominently listed each new item on his title page. The four editions differed significantly: the appended Bell edition expanded from 79 pages to 147; the Bradfords', from 50 pages to 99.

35. *Pennsylvania Evening Post*, 27 January, 30 January, 1 February, and 22 February 1776.

36. The colonial population for 1776 is estimated at around three million (one-fifth of them black slaves), with most living in rural areas. Estimates for specific cities and towns are harder to find and often noncomparable (in terms of who is and is not counted). Conventional estimates range from 25,000 to 40,000 for Philadelphia and from 12,000 to 15,000 for Boston.

37. William Bell Clark, ed., *Naval Documents of the American Revolution*, 10 vols. (Washington, DC: United States Government Printing Office, 1964), 4:213.

38. On Paine's Philadelphia, see Foner, *Tom Paine*, 19–70, 73.

39. On early American book distribution, see Gilreath, "American Book Distribution." On local print cultures, see Amory and Hall, eds., *The Colonial Book in the Atlantic World*.

40. Gimbel, *Thomas Paine*, 78–91. Parts of Canada, Maine, and Vermont were important Revolutionary locales—both literally (as battlegrounds) and figuratively (as objects of debate)—but there is no evidence that Paine's pamphlet reached these sites in any notable way. Though presses operated throughout the Revolution in Quebec, Montreal, and Nova Scotia, *Common Sense* was not reprinted there. Maine and Vermont, on the other hand, continued to figure

in the post-1776 war and were eventually declared independent from Great Britain because of it. While both had burgeoning populations in 1776, there was no press to service them (except more southern New England presses) until Vermont was declared independent and hired a government printer in 1778. The furthest western press, meanwhile, was established at New Orleans in 1768, printing mostly French and Spanish titles. While copies of *Common Sense* did eventually reach the West Indies and Europe, there is no mention of its availability in the Spanish-ruled regions of Louisiana—or anywhere west of Lancaster, Pennsylvania. The secondary literature on local print cultures is vast. See James S. Leamon, *Revolution Downeast: The War for American Independence in Maine* (Amherst: University of Massachusetts Press, 1993); Douglas C. McMurtrie, *The Royalist Printers at Shelburne, Nova Scotia* (Chicago: np, 1933); Marie Tremaine, ed., *Canadian Book of Printing: How Printing Came to Canada* (Toronto: Toronto Public Libraries, 1940); Marcus A. McCorison, ed., *Vermont Imprints, 1778–1820* (Worcester: American Antiquarian Society, 1963); R. Webb Noyes, *A Bibliography of Maine Imprints to 1820* (Stonington, ME: np, 1930); Douglas C. McMurtrie, *Louisiana Imprints, 1768–1810* (Hattiesburg, MI: The Book Farm, 1942) and *Early Printing in New Orleans, 1764–1810* (New Orleans: Searcy & Pfaff, 1929). On *Common Sense*'s quiet reception in the West Indies, see Andrew Jackson O'Shaughnessy, *An Empire Divided: The American Revolution and the British Caribbean* (Philadelphia: University of Pennsylvania Press, 2000), 143.

41. Postal service was routinely disrupted in 1775 and 1776. William Goddard ran a private courier service (named the Constitutional Post) between Philadelphia and New York but never successfully extended it to New England or the deep South. Jerrilyn Greene Marston claims that "the failure to fully implement Goddard's plan in 1774 . . . added to the chaos of 1776." Postal service was overseen provisionally and unevenly by local committees of correspondence until Congress was able to regularize service in the spring of 1776 (halfway through the window of reception for Paine's *Common Sense*). Jerrilyn Marston, *King and Congress: The Transfer of Political Legitimacy, 1774–1776* (Princeton: Princeton University Press, 1987), 228–29.

42. Working presses that might have but did not reprint *Common Sense* include those at Burlington, Wilmington, Annapolis, Baltimore, Newbern, and Williamsburg. For a comprehensive listing of 1776 printers and their imprints, see Charles Evans, *American Bibliography*, 14 vols. (New York: Peter Smith, 1941–59), 5:216–301. Although newspapers in New Jersey and Delaware never advertised the pamphlet (as other colonies routinely did), readers in these areas undoubtedly had access to the Bell and Bradford editions. Maryland newspapers do not appear to have advertised the pamphlet but did reprint the anti–*Common Sense* editorialist Cato, which may or may not indicate wide interest in Paine's pamphlet there. The more southern colonies, which put out only one edition

of their own, almost certainly received fewer Philadelphia imprints than nearby New Jersey and Delaware and show far fewer traces of its presence in their newspapers.

43. *Boston Gazette*, 4 March 1776. Seven Boston-area papers were consulted, including the *Gazette*. No *Common Sense* advertisements were found for 1776 in the *Boston News-Letter, Continental Journal, Independent Chronicle*, or *Massachusetts Spy*. The [Cambridge] *New-England Chronicle* printed one ad, in its 28 March–4 April issue, for Ezekial Russell's "2d Salem Edition"; the [Boston] *New-England Chronicle* likewise printed one ad, on 6 June, noting "a few" copies "may be had."

44. *Boston Gazette*, 8 April 1776.

45. This advertisement refers to one of two imprints available in New Hampshire: one bears the line "NEWBURY PORT, Reprinted, / for SAMUEL PHILLIPS, jun. Of Andover," while the other reads "NEWBURY PORT, Reprinted, / By JOHN MYCALL, and to be Sold at the *Printing Office*." Though these are counted in *Common Sense* lore as two different editions, Gimbel notes that they are identical except for the title-page and would appear to represent a joint venture struck from the same typeset. Gimbel, *Thomas Paine*, 78, 88. See also advertisements in the Newburyport *Essex Journal*, which advertises Phillips's edition of *Common Sense* as being "Now in the Press, and will be published in about a fortnight" on 19 and 26 April and "Just Published" on 18 May.

46. Albany, for example, maintained the only New York State press outside of New York City, but in 1775 its owners buried it and moved on, first to Norwich and then to New York City, leaving upstate New York dependent on imprints that circulated northward from New York City and south from smaller New England towns. McMurtrie, *Royalist Printers*, 4.

47. See, for example, the provincial government's announcement in the *Essex Journal and New Hampshire Packet*, 23 February 1776, calling on committees of correspondence to organize citizens to collect rags for local paper-mills "to promote the public good."

48. *Connecticut Courant*, 19 February 1776. Watson did eventually publish the essay in pamphlet form, but it did not appear until April. See *Connecticut Courant*, 8 April 1776. Philip Foner claims that *Common Sense*'s "more trenchant paragraphs were reprinted in newspapers all over the country" (*Complete Writings*, 1:xiv), and many popular histories also assume this to be the case. But newspaper serializations (or extracts) like Watson's were rare, although the pamphlet was routinely advertised as a pamphlet in northeastern newspapers.

49. Gimbel, *Thomas Paine*, 89–90. See *Newport Mercury*, 8 April 1776, for this edition's only advertisement. Southwick's paper and cash troubles continued through 1776: on 20 May 1776, he urged his subscribers to settle their accounts or else the newspaper "cannot publish even a half-sheet longer." Later that year,

he buried his press rather than allow the British to seize it but continued to work itinerantly, teaming with printers in Watertown, Attleborough, and Providence before returning to Newport to reestablish the *Mercury* in late 1779.

50. Thomas Paine, *Common Sense* (Salem: Ezekial Russell, 1776), 28.

51. On the problems faced by Boston-area printers throughout the Revolution, including the troubled partnership of Edes & Gill (printers of *Common Sense*), see Benjamin Franklin V, ed., *Boston Printers, Publishers, and Booksellers: 1640–1800* (Boston: G. K. Hall & Company, 1980). Although Edes & Gill were "by far the most active political printers in Boston," they struggled to stay in business throughout 1775 and 1776 (124). Edes fled Boston for Watertown in April 1775, where he faced a scarcity of ink, paper, and types (as Franklin notes, "the most frequent advertisement in [Edes's Watertown] *Gazette* was Edes's own plea for 'clean Cotton and Linenn *RAGS*'" [131]). Gill remained in Boston but stopped publishing, spending part of 1776 in jail (128). Though the Edes & Gill edition of *Common Sense* was produced with their joint Queens Street (Boston) imprint, it appeared after the partnership split and was probably produced at Edes's Watertown shop.

52. Gimbel, *Thomas Paine*, 49.

53. Liell, *46 Pages*, 101, 105; *Connecticut Gazette*, 22 March 1776; Gary B. Nash, *The Unknown American Revolution: The Unruly Birth of Democracy and the Struggle to Create America* (New York: Viking Press, 2005), 189–90; and Norton et al., *People and a Nation*, 1:153.

54. On the uneven transition from older models of social relations to more market-driven ones in three American port cities (all of which reprinted *Common Sense*), see Gary B. Nash, *The Urban Crucible: The Northern Seaports and the Origins of the American Revolution* (Cambridge: Harvard University Press, 1986). While Paine believed the pamphlet was a monumental financial success, he himself lost money on it, never having received any dividends from his first printer and dying in debt to the second one for the costs of creating the appended edition.

55. On Paine's Philadelphia patrons, see Aldridge, *Thomas Paine's American Ideology*, 36–37.

56. Pauline Maier, *American Scripture: Making the Declaration of Independence* (New York: Vintage, 1997), 34.

57. *LDC*, 3:88.

58. In this case, the delegate (Samuel Ward) suggests that the local printer "print the Appendix separately to compleat the work." *LDC*, 3:330.

59. In Savannah, for example, the *Georgia Gazette* was suspended after 7 February and did not resume that year, while in Norfolk, the local press was seized in January and taken aboard a British frigate, where it was used to run off anti-American propaganda that read "Printed on board the ship William off Norfolk, 1776."

60. *Pennsylvania Evening Post*, 25 January 1776.

61. *LDC*, 3:558; Washington to Joseph Reed, 1 April 1776, in *The Papers of George Washington, Revolutionary War Series*, ed. Philander D. Chase, 15 vols. (Charlottesville: University Press of Virginia, 1985–2006), 4:11.

62. Thomas Jefferson, *Notes on the State of Virginia*, ed. William Peden (1954; Chapel Hill: University of North Carolina Press, 1995), 122.

63. Holton suggests the pamphlet was popular with Virginia smallholders despite elite resistance, but he doesn't discuss the pamphlet's physical production there. Even so, *Common Sense* forms only a modest part of his larger thesis: that Virginia elites were "forced" into embracing independence by more common Virginians. Woody Holton, *Forced Founders: Indians, Debtors, Slaves, and the Making of the American Revolution in Virginia* (Chapel Hill: University of North Carolina Press, 1999), 196–97.

64. Joseph Hewes sent one copy to Samuel Johnston as a "Curiosity," deferentially noting that he did not know "how you might relish independency." One week later, however, Hewes sent forward multiple copies at the urging of his Philadelphia colleague John Penn. *LDC*, 3:247.

65. *LDC*, 3:194.

66. William J. Van Schreeven, comp., and Robert L. Scribner, ed., *Revolutionary Virginia: The Road to Independence*, 7 vols. (Charlottesville: University Press of Virginia, 1973–83), 6:284.

67. Brief extracts appear 2 February and 5 April. The *Gazette* later published, throughout April and May, a miscellaneous number of anti–*Common Sense* Cato letters but none of Paine's Forester responses. The paper also ran the first number of the anti–*Common Sense* Cassandra on 25 May. Other pertinent items include a 9 March advertisement for hundreds of books that does not include *Common Sense*; a 27 April note (datelined at Cambridge, 4 April) that reports "A favourite Toast in the best companies is, 'May the INDEPENDENT principles of COMMON SENSE be confirmed throughout the United Colonies'"; a 27 September note (datelined at New London on 30 August) that relays information received from the *London Evening Post* (dated in London, 21 May), noting that the pamphlet "they say" "has been ascribed to Mr. Adams, one of the Delegates of the Continental Congress," is in press in London.

68. Jerome J. Nadelhaft, *The Disorders of War: The Revolution in South Carolina* (Orono: University of Maine at Orono Press, 1981), 9–10.

69. *LDC*, 3:289–90.

70. Congress did not overtly control the dissemination of printed texts out of Philadelphia in this period, but its members did influence the transmission of information and sometimes sought to do more. In one notable example, Congress attempted to extend the patriot network into Canada (the so-called fourteenth colony), sending a number of soldiers, diplomats, and a printer to Montreal just prior to declaring independence. The military and diplomatic delegations

quickly withdrew under British pressure, but the printer stayed. Though he eventually established a press and newspaper, he never reprinted *Common Sense* or any other patriot material. Tremaine, *Canadian Book of Printing*, 32.

71. It is possible that Philadelphia and congressional elites powered the pamphlet's initial emergence out of Philadelphia, promoting it as a populist signpost of the coming Revolution in the North in ways that were successful enough to actually produce a populist outpouring of support for independence in more southern colonies like Virginia, where local elites were (according to Woody Holton) still resisting the idea of independence as late as April and May. But this is exactly the kind of differential (cross- and inter-regional vs. national) model of reception that has not yet been theorized for *Common Sense*. Holton, *Forced Founders*, 196–97.

72. *Common Sense* is not cited as often as one might expect in Revolutionary diaries. Of thirty-six diaries consulted from various regions dating from January to July 1776, only five mention *Common Sense*—one by Philadelphia Whig Christopher Marshall; one by South Carolina Provincial Congressmen John Drayton (who was present when Christopher Gadsden tried to read Paine's essay in the Provincial Congress there); one by Nicholas Cresswell, a Tory living in Alexandria, Virginia; one by Ambrose Serle, an urban New Yorker; and one by Landon Carter, a conservative Virginia planter. See Duane, ed., *Extracts from the Diary of Christopher Marshall*, 57; John Drayton, *Memoirs of the American Revolution as Relating to the State of South Carolina* (New York: New York Times, 1969); Nicholas Cresswell, *The Journal of Nicholas Cresswell, 1774–1777* (Port Washington, NY: Kennikat Press, 1968), 136; Ambrose Serle, *The American Journal of Ambrose Serle* (New York: New York Times, 1969), 39; Jack P. Greene, ed., *The Diary of Colonel Landon Carter of Sabine Hall, 1752–1778*, 2 vols. (Charlottesville: Published for the Virginia Historical Society [by] the University Press of Virginia, 1965), 2:1016.

73. It is possible there were 1776 imprints on hand after the war. Bell advertised *Common Sense* as late as 1783, an indication that he had either imported British copies or still had his own on hand. Robert Bell, *Just published . . . A catalogue of a large collection of new and old books* (Philadelphia: Robert Bell, 1783), 22.

74. Lodge, *Story of the Revolution*, 1:154.

75. Foner, ed., *Complete Writings*, 1:xiv.

76. The OED locates the origins of the word "bestseller" in the late-nineteenth-century United States.

77. Trouillot, *Silencing the Past*, 29.

78. T. H. Breen, *The Marketplace of Revolution: How Consumer Politics Shaped American Independence* (New York: Oxford University Press, 2004).

79. See, for example, Laurel Thatcher Ulrich, *The Age of Homespun: Objects and Stories in the Creation of an American Myth* (New York: Alfred A. Knopf, 2001).

80. This episode resembles the time-space compressions of a more industrialized modernity, even if it was in this case accidental and many months in the making. On time-space compression in the Enlightenment, see David Harvey, *The Condition of Postmodernity: An Enquiry into the Origins of Cultural Change* (Cambridge: Blackwell, 1989), 240–59.

81. On imperial deferral, see Christopher Looby, "Franklin's Purloined Letters," *Arizona Quarterly* 46, no. 2 (1990): 1–12.

82. *Pennsylvania Evening Post*, 3 February 1776. Paine first explains the strategy of publishing *Common Sense* as a pamphlet (rather than serially inserting it in newspapers) during his dispute with the printer Bell. Notably, Paine did not pursue this stand-alone strategy with *The Crisis*. Its numbers were composed piecemeal and then produced variously as freestanding broadsides and serial newspaper installments (many of them widely reprinted in the Northeast), which were only later collected as a pamphlet. Even in *The Crisis*, however, Paine was working on the same intellectual and political problems posed in *Common Sense*, trying to turn dispersed objects (essays and colonies) into continental wholes. For example, though bibliographers today usually number *The Crisis* in twelve parts (with two supernumerary pieces), Paine thought of the series as consisting of thirteen numbers, thus making it commensurate with the number of original colonies.

83. Paine himself believed *Common Sense* had precipitated the Declaration of Independence and hence the nation: "I think the importance of the pamphlet was such that if it had not appeared, and that at the exact time it did, the Congress would not now have been sitting where they are. . . . Independence followed in six months after it, although before it was published it was a dangerous doctrine to speak of, and that because it was not understood" (2:1163).

84. Jacques Derrida, "Declarations of Independence," *New Political Science* 15 (1986): 7–15.

85. Tories like Ambrose Serle assigned all agency for independence to Congress, believing it "to have been their Object from the Beginning." Serle, *The American Journal*, ed. Edward H. Tatum, Jr. (San Marino, CA: The Huntington Library, 1940), 30–31.

86. Charles Francis Adams, ed., *Works of John Adams*, 10 vols. (Boston: Little, Brown, 1850–56), 10:172; Lodge, *Story of the Revolution*, 1:154.

87. Max Horkheimer and Theodor W. Adorno, *Dialectic of Enlightenment*, trans. John Cumming (New York: Continuum, 1972), 3–5.

88. F. W. Maitland, *The Constitutional History of England* (1908; Cambridge: Cambridge University Press, 1913), 445.

89. Robert A. Ferguson, "The Commonalities of *Common Sense*," *WMQ*, 3d ser., 57, no. 3 (2000): 465–504.

90. See, for example, Bernard Bailyn, "Common Sense," in *Fundamental Testaments of the American Revolution* (Washington, DC: Library of Congress,

1973), 7–24; and Samuel H. Beer, *To Make a Nation: The Rediscovery of American Federalism* (Cambridge: Belknap Press, 1993), 206–7.

91. George W. Corner, ed., *The Autobiography of Benjamin Rush* (1948; Westport, CT: Greenwood Press, 1970), 113–14.

92. Thomas Adams notes that most American political pamphlets during the Revolution were printed at the author's expense and circulated only as far as their authors could carry them, with many disseminated in manuscript. While such pamphlets were routinely addressed to large populations, their circulation was usually local. *American Independence*, xi.

93. Jonathan Boucher, *Reminiscences of an American Loyalist, 1738–1789* (Boston: Houghton Mifflin, 1925), 132–34.

94. *LMCC*, 1:420–21.

95. R. W. Gibbes, ed., *Documentary History of the American Revolution* (New York: Appleton, 1853–57), 8.

96. *LDC*, 1:28.

97. David M. Potter and Thomas G. Manning, eds., *Nationalism and Sectionalism in America* (New York: Holt, 1949), 40.

98. Merritt, *Symbols of American Community*, 5.

99. Josiah Tucker, *Cui Bono?* (Glocester: Printed by R. Raikes, for T. Cadell, 1781), 117–19.

100. *Pennsylvania Journal*, 22 November and 6 December 1775. On Paine's authorship, see Aldridge, *Thomas Paine's American Ideology*, 33, 35.

101. Boston was a strategic choice: anti-Massachusetts sentiment was common in the 1770s. Southern delegates to the Continental Congress, for example, frequently criticized their Massachusetts colleagues for their "purely democratical" leanings, "low cunning," and "levelling principles." *LMCC*, 3:517–18.

102. *LMCC*, 3:50.

103. For critiques and revisions of the public sphere model that place special pressure on its nonuniversal subject and its historiographic timeline, see diverse contributions in Craig J. Calhoun, ed., *Habermas and the Public Sphere* (Cambridge: MIT Press, 1992); Oskar Negt and Alexander Kluge, *Public Sphere and Experience: Toward an Analysis of the Bourgeois and Proletarian Public Sphere*, trans. Peter Labanyi et al. (Minneapolis: University of Minnesota Press, 1993); James Van Horn Melton, *The Rise of the Public in Enlightenment Europe* (New York: Cambridge University Press, 2001); David Zaret, *Origins of Democratic Culture: Printing, Petitions, and the Public Sphere in Early-Modern England* (Princeton: Princeton University Press, 2000); and "Alternative Histories of the Public Sphere," Special Issue of *WMQ*, 3d ser., 62, no. 1 (2005). For overviews of these debates, see John L. Brooke, "Consent, Civil Society, and the Public Sphere in the Age of Revolution and the Early American Republic," in *Beyond the Founders: New Approaches to the Political History of the Early American Republic*, ed. Jeffrey L. Pasley, Andrew W. Robertson, and David Waldstreicher (Chapel Hill:

University of North Carolina Press, 2004), 207–50; Gross, "Print and the Public Sphere in Early America," 245–64; and Harold Mah, "Phantasies of the Public Sphere: Rethinking the Habermas of Historians," *Journal of Modern History* 72, no. 1 (2000): 153–82.

104. Jürgen Habermas, *The Structural Transformation of the Public Sphere: An Inquiry Into a Category of Bourgeois Society*, trans. Thomas Burger (Cambridge: MIT Press, 1989), 36; and Gordon S. Wood, *The Radicalism of the American Revolution* (New York: Vintage, 1993), 233. Compare the standard account of *Common Sense*'s circulation ("every American able to read, had read 'Common Sense'") to Habermas's comment on Richardson: "of Richardson's *Pamela*, it can be said that it was read by the entire public, that is, by 'everybody' who could read at all" (174). Habermas's "public," though putatively including "everybody," is also pragmatically (if paradoxically) delimited, with "the entire public" explicitly understood as bourgeois and urban. But Lodge's protonational public is more populist than that—intending to *really* include "everyone" (no scare quotes in sight). In this way, the myth of *Common Sense* diminishes the difference between that which is bourgeois and that which is populist (in print)—much as Whig history seeks to do more generally. Lodge, *Story of the Revolution*, 154.

105. L. H. Butterfield, ed., *The Diary and Autobiography of John Adams* (Cambridge: Harvard University Press, 1961), 3:334.

106. On Paine's early experiences in Lewes and London, see Foner, *Tom Paine*, 1–17; Jack Fruchtman, Jr., *Thomas Paine: Apostle of Freedom* (New York: Four Walls Eight Windows, 1994), 30–36; and David Freeman Hawke, *Paine* (New York: Harper and Row, 1974), 7–21.

107. Scholars sometimes echo Paine's understanding of the *Excise* pamphlet as an act of nonauthorship, distinguishing it as having been "printed for the House of Commons" rather than "published" for readers. See Jack P. Greene, "Paine, America, and the 'Modernization' of Political Consciousness," *Political Science Quarterly* 93, no. 1 (1978): 74–75.

108. *Pennsylvania Evening Post*, 1 February 1776.

109. Ibid., 25 January 1776.

110. For Paine's initial remarks and his several rejoinders to Bell, see ibid., 25 January, 27 January, 30 January, 3 February, and 20 February 1776.

111. For Bell's many advertisements and attacks, see ibid., 25 January, 27 January, 30 January, 1 February, 3 February, and 22 February 1776. Bell's accusations here echo John Adams's later claim that Paine had plumbed commonplace arguments that had been circulating in Philadelphia for a year. Butterfield, ed., *Diary and Autobiography of John Adams*, 3:333–34.

112. Ibid., 3:333. Paine inhabited a novel position in this regard, for as Foner notes, most colonial pamphleteers came from "the upper social strata of lawyers, merchants, planters, and ministers." *Tom Paine*, 85.

113. *Pennsylvania Evening Post*, 30 January 1776.

114. Ibid. Paine wanted all profits to go to patriot soldiers fighting in Quebec, imagining Canada to be part of *Common Sense*'s "continental" political imaginary. But even while Paine was writing, Quebec had already decisively fallen to the British—news that did not reach Philadelphia until many months later.

115. *Pennsylvania Evening Post*, 1 February 1776.

116. On early American tavern culture, see Peter Thompson, *Rum Punch and Revolution: Taverngoing & Public Life in Eighteenth Century Philadelphia* (Philadelphia: University of Pennsylvania Press, 1999); and David W. Conroy, *In Public Houses: Drink and the Revolution of Authority in Colonial Massachusetts* (Chapel Hill: University of North Carolina Press, 1995).

117. On Paine's place in partisan city politics, see Foner, *Tom Paine*, 107–82.

118. *Pennsylvania Evening Post*, 6 February 1776.

119. On Philadelphia's tiered social structure, see Foner, *Tom Paine;* Nash, *Urban Crucible*, esp. 194–99, 240–46; Steven Rosswurm, *Arms, Country, and Class: The Philadelphia Militia and the "Lower Sort" during the American Revolution, 1775–1783* (New Brunswick: Rutgers University Press, 1987); Richard Alan Ryerson, *"The Revolution Is Now Begun": The Radical Committees of Philadelphia, 1765–1776* (Philadelphia: University of Pennsylvania Press, 1978); and Billy G. Smith, *The "Lower Sort": Philadelphia's Laboring People, 1750–1800* (Ithaca: Cornell University Press, 1990).

120. Francis Jordan, Jr., *The Life of William Henry of Lancaster, Pa 1729–1786* (Lancaster, PA: The New Era Printing Company, 1910), 85–86.

121. Michael Warner, "The Mass Public and the Mass Subject," in *Habermas and the Public Sphere*, ed. Calhoun, 382–83.

122. *Pennsylvania Evening Post*, 3 February 1776.

123. Ibid., 22 February 1776.

124. Moncure Daniel Conway, *Life of Thomas Paine* (London: Watts, 1909), 205.

125. *Pennsylvania Gazette*, 20 August 1783.

126. There was a Revolutionary captain named Edward Paine (1746–1841) whose grave in Painesville, Ohio, is memorialized with a statue. But Watson's print references *The Crisis* and *Common Sense* and so clearly intends to depict Thomas Paine.

127. Foner, *Tom Paine*, 107, 161. Foner is quoting Robert Bell.

128. France and England maintain numerous public monuments to the author of *The Rights of Man*, but Philadelphia (where the U.S. Park Service maintains Franklin's print shop, the Liberty Bell, and Independence Hall) has dedicated no monument to Paine other than a small plaque commemorating *Common Sense* and a service alley in Old City named "Thomas Paine Way."

129. Benjamin Rush, *The Drunkard's Emblem: Or, an Enquiry into the Effects of Ardent Spirits on the Human Body and Mind* (Newmarket, VA: Ambrose Henkel and Co., 1814), 4–5. Cited in Thompson, *Rum Punch and Revolution*, 182–83.

130. Grant Thorburn, "Anecdote of Thomas Paine," in the Colonel Richard Gimbel Collection of Thomas Paine Papers, American Philosophical Society. Thorburn "received this anecdote" from Aaron Burr, "Burr being second in command at that Feast of Reason."

131. The notable exception is Foner's *Tom Paine*, which nevertheless notes "the exclusion of Paine from the roster of revolutionary leaders canonized in nineteenth century popular culture" (xiii).

132. The word "upheaval" belongs to Gordon Wood, who argues that the Revolution was "one of the greatest revolutions the world has known, a momentous upheaval . . . as radical and social as any revolution in history." *Radicalism of the American Revolution*, 5.

CHAPTER 3. THE REPUBLIC IN PRINT

1. Anderson, *Imagined Communities*, 19. Neither image of course has a more authentic claim to representing the actual material conditions of the 1780s or 1840s. The book cover cribs a scene of community life first imagined in 1848, but Woodville himself was probably nostalgically evoking an outmoded scene that was satisfying to audiences in 1848 precisely because they had less and less access to such experiences in their daily life.

2. Bryan Wolf, "All the World's a Code: Art and Ideology in Nineteenth Century American Painting," *Art Journal* 44, no. 4 (1984): 332.

3. Gerald J. Baldasty, *The Commercialization of News in the Nineteenth Century* (Madison: University of Wisconsin Press, 1992); Mott, *American Journalism*; David Paul Nord, *Communities of Journalism: A History of American Newspapers and Their Readers* (Urbana: University of Illinois Press, 2001); Dan Schiller, *Objectivity and the News: The Public and the Rise of Commercial Journalism* (Philadelphia: University of Pennsylvania Press, 1981); Michael Schudson, *Discovering the News: A Social History of American Newspapers* (New York: Basic Books, 1978); and Paul Starr, *The Creation of the Media: Political Origins of Modern Communication* (New York: Basic Books, 2004).

4. On early American print production, see Lawrence C. Wroth, *The Colonial Printer* (1931; New York: Dover, 1995).

5. Pred, *Urban Growth*, 22. On early national newspaper circulation more generally, see also Mott, *American Journalism*; and Merritt, *Symbols of American Community*.

6. On the circulation of newspapers during ratification, see John K. Alexander, *The Selling of the Constitutional Convention: A History of News Coverage* (Madison: Madison House, 1990), esp. 2–54. As Alexander notes, there were 76 newspapers in 1787: 58 weekly, 2 biweekly, 11 semiweekly, and 5 daily (as well as 2 magazines) (4). On their circulation, he follows Mott's estimate for the year

1800: 700 copies per newspaper (though each paper would have had multiple readers). The circulation numbers for newspapers in 1787, however, would have been considerably lower because ratification preceded the rise of the two-party system, which produced an explosion of newsprint in the 1790s. For accounts of newspaper production and circulation in the early republic more generally (especially postratification), see Brooke, "To Be 'Read by the Whole People'"; and Jeffrey L. Pasley, *"The Tyranny of Printers": Newspaper Politics in the Early American Republic* (Charlottesville: University Press of Virginia, 2001).

7. Pred, *Urban Growth*, 32–34.

8. *Report to the President and Directors of the Literary Fund of the University of Virginia* (1825). See Furtwangler, *The Authority of Publius*, 37.

9. Clinton Rossiter, ed., *The Federalist Papers* (New York: New American Library, 1961), vii.

10. James G. Wilson, "The Sacred Text: The Supreme Court's Use of *The Federalist Papers*," *Brigham Young University Law Review* 65 (1985). Different generations do, however, use *The Federalist* in different ways. See Jack N. Rakove, "Early Uses of *The Federalist*," in *Saving the Revolution: The Federalist Papers and the American Founding*, ed. Charles R. Kesler (New York: Free Press, 1987), 234–49.

11. Jay Fliegelman, *Declaring Independence: Jefferson, Natural Language and the Culture of Performance* (Stanford: Stanford University Press, 1993); Christopher Grasso, *A Speaking Aristocracy: Transforming Public Discourse in Eighteenth-Century Connecticut* (Chapel Hill: Published for the Omohundro Institute of Early American History and Culture by the University of North Carolina Press, 1999); Sandra M. Gustafson, *Eloquence Is Power: Oratory and Performance in Early America* (Chapel Hill: Published for the Omohundro Institute of Early American History and Culture by the University of North Carolina Press, 2000); Looby, *Voicing America*; and David S. Shields, *Civil Tongues & Polite Letters in British America* (Chapel Hill: Published for the Omohundro Institute of Early American History and Culture by the University of North Carolina Press, 1997).

12. Hamilton's identity as the author of the Caesar papers has been contested, but given his position in New York State politics and his well-documented love of all things imperial, I find his authorship likely.

13. Crane, "Publius in the Provinces," 589–92.

14. Elizabeth Fleet, "Madison's 'Detatched Memoranda,'" *WMQ*, 3d ser., 3, no. 4 (1946): 564.

15. See *PAH*, 4:332 and 5:201; and *PJM*, 10:254, 283, 290, 295, 375.

16. *New-York Journal*, 1 January 1788.

17. For reprintings in and outside of New York, see Jacob E. Cooke, ed., *The Federalist* (Middletown, CT: Wesleyan University Press, 1961), and Crane, "Publius in the Provinces."

18. "Politically, ratification was complex and convoluted. . . . Much of the

time, information was sketchy, and because the mails were slow and travel was hard, coordination between states and regions was difficult if not impossible." Michael Allen Gillespie and Michael Lienesch, eds., Introduction to *Ratifying the Constitution* (Lawrence: University Press of Kansas, 1989), 5–6. See also David J. Siemers, *Ratifying the Republic: Antifederalists and Federalists in Constitutional Time* (Stanford: Stanford University Press, 2002), esp. 1, 19, 24, 133; and Sheldon Wolin, *The Presence of the Past: Essays on the State and the Constitution* (Baltimore: Johns Hopkins University Press, 1989), 88.

19. *Independent Journal*, 17 November 1787. See Cooke, *The Federalist*, xiii.

20. Hamilton kept a working relationship with every printer in the city, parsing out small government printing jobs to each one throughout the ratification debates. For traces of these relationships, see his cash book, reprinted in *PAH*, 3:9, 29–32. On the competition between New York printers to print *The Federalist*, see printer Samuel Loudon's letter to Hamilton, 22 May 1789, *PAH*, 5:341–42.

21. *Daily Advertiser*, 3 January 1788.

22. *The Federalist*, 2 vols. (New York: J. and A. McLean, 1788), l:iii–iv.

23. Fleet, "Madison's 'Detached Memoranda,'" 565.

24. Madison to Edmund Randolph, 2 December 1787, *PJM*, 10:290.

25. Ironically, Hamilton mounts this critique in a paper that was published out of sequence, making his attack on antifederalist incoherence appear momentarily incoherent itself. Initially published as No. 35, this essay was renumbered 29 in the collected *Federalist* of 1788.

26. The antifederalists have long been viewed as ideologically fragmented. Cecilia Kenyon, for example, notes their failure to produce a single thesis in her classic anthology of antifederalist writings, *The Antifederalists* (Indianapolis: Bobbs-Merrill, 1966), xxxviii.

27. Jonathan Elliot, *The Debates in the Several State Conventions*, 5 vols. (Philadelphia: J. B. Lippincott, 1836–59), 2:394.

28. Wolin, *The Presence of the Past*, 136. For an impressive synthesis of antifederalist thought that nevertheless allows for a complicated array of variety, see Saul Cornell, *The Other Founders: Anti-Federalism and the Dissenting Tradition in America, 1788–1828* (Chapel Hill: University of North Carolina Press, 1999).

29. The words "slave" and "slavery" do not enter the Constitution until the Thirteenth and Fourteenth Amendments. Slaves are, however, elusively referred to in three places in the original Constitution: (1) Article I, Section 2, details the three-fifths compromise, whereby "Representatives and Taxes" are apportioned by population, "which shall be determined by adding to the whole Number of free Persons, including those bound to Service for a Term of Years, and excluding Indians not taxed, three fifths of all other Persons"; (2) Article I, Section 9, protects "the migration and importation of such persons as any of the States now existing shall think proper to admit" (i.e., the slave trade) until 1808; and (3) Ar-

ticle IV, Section 2, puts forward the federal government's first fugitive slave law, deeming that "no person held to Service or labor in one State" shall be allowed to escape their condition by fleeing to another state. In each case, slaves are semantically disguised as "persons" and are twice explicitly linked with two other peripheral populations: indentured laborers (in the fugitive slave clause) and emigrants (in the slave trade clause). Madison (himself a slave owner) believed that slavery should not be mentioned in the Constitution, directly or indirectly: he found the slave trade clause "more dishonorable to the National character than to say nothing about it in the Constitution" and "thought it wrong to admit in the Constitution the idea that there could be property in men." *PJM*, 10:157.

30. "No Union with Slaveholders" is a Garrisonian slogan dating to the 1840s, but slavery was at the center of the Federal Convention's compromises. Madison noted in later years that "the States were divided into different interests . . . principally from their having or not having slaves." Delegates from the three southernmost states insisted that slavery be protected: Charles Cotesworth Pinckney flatly declared that "S. Carolina & Georgia cannot do without slaves." See Gillespie and Lienesch, *Ratifying the Constitution*, 208–9. As David Ramsay later wrote to the New Englander Benjamin Lincoln: "Your delegates never did a more political thing than in standing by those of South Carolina about Negroes." Bernard Bailyn, ed., *The Debate on the Constitution*, 2 vols. (New York: Library of America, 1993), 2:117.

31. Ralph Ketcham, ed., *The Anti-Federalist Papers and the Constitutional Convention Debates* (New York: New American Library, 1986).

32. *New-York Journal*, 16 May 1788.

33. See Furtwangler, *The Authority of Publius*, 30–33; and Cooke, ed., *The Federalist*, xix–xxx.

34. Washington to Hamilton, 28 August 1788, *PAH*, 5:207.

35. *CAF*, 2:186.

36. William Maclay, *Journal of William Maclay* (New York: A & C Boni, 1927), 73–74.

37. Madison to Jefferson, 8 February 1825, in *The Writings of James Madison*, 9 vols. (New York: G.P. Putnam's Sons, 1900–10), 9:218.

38. Roland Barthes, "The Death of the Author," in *Image-Music-Text*, trans. Stephen Heath (London: Fontana, 1977), 142.

39. On the limits of impersonality in the early republic, see Gross, "Print and the Public Sphere in America," 252–54.

40. *CAF*, 2:183.

41. *CAF*, 2:154.

42. For an excellent account of this debate, see *DHRC*, 13:312–23.

43. *DHRC*, 13:316.

44. [Boston] *Independent Chronicle*, 4 October 1787. See *DHRC*, 13:315.

45. [Boston] *American Herald*, 22 October 1787. See *DHRC*, 13:313.

46. Ibid.

47. This fact reflects the conditions of preindustrial newspaper production: with local printers playing the part, in many cases, of publisher, editor, and author, it is no surprise that items directly engaging the politics and patronage systems of the printing trade would be among the most reprinted from city to city.

48. [Philadelphia] *Independent Gazetteer*, 29 October 1787. See *DHRC*, 13:319.

49. [Philadelphia] *Freeman's Journal*, 31 October 1787. See *DHRC*, 13:320.

50. The dread of local recognition had its counterpart in the desire to be visible when visibility would pay dividends. When Bryan, for instance, sought to distinguish himself in a private letter to New York's Governor Clinton, he named himself as the author of the essays. Burton Alva Konkle, *George Bryan and the Constitution of Pennsylvania* (Philadelphia: William J. Campbell, 1922), 309. Despite this self-avowal, the attribution of the Centinel essays remains in question. Most scholars believe Samuel Bryan wrote the papers, but some believe his father (George Bryan) may have co-authored them (as *The Federalist* was co-authored). Both cases suggest that co-authorship was a good way to keep readers guessing about who was writing what.

51. *Massachusetts Gazette*, 16 October 1787. See *DHRC*, 13:317.

52. Smith noted in a private letter that "Hamilton is the champion [—] he speaks frequently, very long and very vehemently [and] has, like Publius, much to say not very applicable to the subject." Smith to Nathan Dane, 28 June 1788, in Bailyn, ed., *Debate on the Constitution*, 2:823. To a political ally, Governor George Clinton similarly wrote: "I steal this Moment while . . . the little Great Man [is] employed in repeating over Parts of Publius to us, to drop you a line." Clinton to John Lamb, [27?] June 1788. Quoted in Furtwangler, *Authority of Publius*, 23.

53. [Philadelphia] *Freeman's Journal*, 5 March 1788.

54. Hamilton and Madison did sometimes attempt to screen their involvement, even from allies. Several letters between Madison and the Philadelphia federalist Tench Coxe show Coxe asking for confirmation of rumors that attribute authorship of *The Federalist* partly to Madison. He was apparently admonished for his curiosity, however, because later letters show him deferentially apologizing: "I would not by any means wish a request of the circle of gentlemen, who wrote the papers under the Signature of Publius, which I think with you would be disagreeable and improper. I am to ask your pardon for the trouble I have given you on that Subject, but was led to it from hearing that Mr. Jay had written the two first Numbers. I therefore presumed that there might be no impropriety in a confidential communication concerning the remainder. However I confess I think the secrecy both political & delicate, and am now only anxious that you should excuse the trouble I gave you." Tench Coxe to Madison, 10 and 26 September 1788, *PJM*, 11:248, 268. On one remarkable occasion, Hamilton feigned

ignorance of Publius's identity in a letter to Madison that he clearly feared might be intercepted. Hamilton to Madison, 3 April 1788, *PJM*, 11:7. Madison likewise feared interception at certain moments: his admission of his authorship to Jefferson was encrypted in cipher. Madison to Jefferson, 10 August 1788, *PJM*, 11:227.

55. Paul Downes, *Democracy, Revolution, and Monarchism in Early American Literature* (New York: Cambridge University Press, 2002), 16.

56. [Philadelphia] *Independent Gazetteer*, 5 January 1788.

57. Wood, *Creation of the American Republic*, 471–518.

58. *RFC*, 1:48.

59. *PJM*, 10:329.

60. *PJM*, 10:330.

61. *PJM*, 11:5–6.

62. Washington to Madison, 7 December 1787, *PJM*, 10:297; and Madison to Washington, 20 December 1787, *PJM*, 10:334. For the original news item, see the [Philadelphia] *Independent Gazetteer*, 24 November 1787 (later reprinted in the [Baltimore] *Maryland Journal*, 30 November 1787). For Jay's response, see the *Pennsylvania Packet*, 7 December 1787.

63. As Jay Fliegelman notes, the early republic was "a society obsessed with misrepresentations." *Prodigals and Pilgrims: The American Revolution against Patriarchal Authority, 1750–1800* (New York: Cambridge University Press, 1982), 247. On the widespread anxiety over misrepresentation in the 1780s, see Robert A. Gross, "The Confidence Man and the Preacher: The Cultural Politics of Shays's Rebellion," in *In Debt to Shays*, ed. Robert A. Gross (Charlottesville: University Press of Virginia, 1993).

64. *CAF*, 5:211.

65. *CAF*, 2:32.

66. *RFC*, 1:8.

67. *RFC*, 1:9, 15.

68. James Madison, *Notes of the Debates in the Federal Convention* (New York: W. W. Norton, 1987), 654.

69. Ibid., 658–59.

70. Ibid., 659. When the initial motion to maintain secrecy passed 10–1 (New York and Rhode Island absent, Maryland dissenting), Washington was characteristically uncomfortable and wanted detailed instructions as to who should and should not be given access to the documents. The convention determined that the records should be sealed until after ratification was complete, at which time the new federal Congress would instruct Washington on what to do. After the convention, Washington maintained possession of the documents, keeping them throughout most of his administration as president. In 1796, almost as an afterthought, he deposited them in the Department of State where, according to Farrand, they remained untouched until Congress ordered them printed in

1818. John Quincy Adams, who was given the job of overseeing their publication, found them woefully incomplete and incoherent—"no better than the daily minutes from which the regular Journal ought to have been, but never was, made out." *RFC*, 1:xi–xii.

71. For arguments for and against original intent, see Edwin Meese III, "Interpreting the Constitution," and William J. Brennan, Jr., "The Constitution of the United States: Contemporary Ratification," in *Interpreting the Constitution: The Debate over Original Intent*, ed. Jack N. Rakove (Boston: Northeastern University Press, 1990), 13–22, 23–34. On the documentary record, see *RFC*, 1: xi–xxv; and James H. Hutson, "The Creation of the Constitution: The Integrity of the Documentary Record," in *Interpreting the Constitution*, 151–78.

72. *RFC*, 1:xi.

73. For a complete list of extant notes made by delegates, see *RFC*, 1:xi–xxv.

74. Many antifederalists bemoaned the "rush" of ratification, complaining that they were not given time to assemble their critique or coordinate with antifederalists in other states. See Gillespie and Lienesch, *Ratifying the Constitution*, 5–6.

75. *DHRC*, 17:395–98.

76. The phrase is originally Centinel's. See *CAF*, 2:198. For a critique of the convention's secrecy, see also Luther Martin's *Genuine Information* in *CAF*, 2:19–82.

77. Rosemarie Zagarri, *The Politics of Size: Representation in the United States 1776–1850* (Ithaca: Cornell University Press, 1987).

78. Washington to Madison, 10 October 1787, *PJM*, 10:189.

79. *DHRC*, 14:228.

80. *DHRC*, 15:133–35.

81. *DHRC*, 17:69–73.

82. See, for instance, Washington to Madison, 7 December 1787, *PJM*, 10:297, discussed above.

83. [Providence, RI] *United States Chronicle*, 17 July 1788.

84. *CAF*, 2:17.

85. Washington to Joseph Jones, 22 July 1780.

86. Washington to Madison, 5 February 1788, *PJM*, 10:469.

87. Washington to the Marquis de La Fayette, 7 February 1788, in *The Papers of George Washington, Confederation Series*, ed. W. W. Abbot and Dorothy Twohig, 6 vols. (Charlottesville: University Press of Virginia, 1992–97), 6:95–98.

88. *Daily Advertiser*, 4 July 1788. See also *PAH*, 5:135.

89. The court stenographer, Francis Childs, explained his excision of this argument from the official record thus: "As this dispute was of a delicate nature, and as a statement of the circumstances, however cautiously formed, may wear a complexion not perfectly satisfactory to the parties; the Editor presumes, that

the public will excuse an entire omission of the subject." Francis Childs, *Debates and Proceedings of the Constitutional Convention of the State of New-York* (Poughkeepsie: Vassar Brothers Institute, 1905), 123.

90. *PAH*, 5:57–58.

91. Madison uses the same language when describing the emerging split between himself and Hamilton, even as early as 1787–88. While the two Publiuses initially shared their ideas before sending individual numbers of *The Federalist* to press, they finally agreed to forgo such communications, it being "found most agreeable to each, not to give a positive sanction to all the doctrines and sentiments of the other; there being a known difference in the general complexion of their political theories." Fleet, "Madison's 'Detatched Memoranda,'" 565.

92. *CAF*, 3:118. As George Bryan later recalled: "The evidence of a preconcerted system, in those who are called the Federalists, appears rather from the effort than from any certain knowledge beforehand. The thing, however, must have been easy to them from their situation in the great towns and many of them being wealthy men and merchants, who have continual correspondence with each other. . . . Letters were frequently intercepted, and some of them selected and published by the Federalists. Private conversation was listened to by eavesdroppers. Pamphlets and newspapers were stopped and destroyed. This was the more easily done as most of the towns, even down to the smallest villages, were in possession of the Federalists. I can say nothing about the post office." Bryan's memory of the antifederalist campaign is quite different: "Those in opposition seem to have had no pre-concert, nor any suspicion of what was coming forward. The same objections were made in different parts of the Continent, almost at the same time, merely as they were obviously dictated by their subject. Local ideas seem to have entered very little into the subject." See Konkle, *George Bryan*, 306.

93. *CAF*, 2:188.

94. *CAF*, 2:181.

95. *CAF*, 2:190.

96. *CAF*, 2:183.

97. *CAF*, 3:113.

98. Ibid.

99. Ibid.

100. *CAF*, 3:118.

101. *CAF*, 3:117–18.

102. Gordon S. Wood, "Conspiracy and the Paranoid Style: Causality and Deceit in the Eighteenth Century," *WMQ*, 3d ser., 39, no. 3 (1982): 401–41.

103. Ed White, "The Value of Conspiracy Theory," *American Literary History* 14, no. 1 (2002): 10–14.

104. *American Museum* (August 1788): 142–46.

105. Richard Hofstadter, *The Paranoid Style in American Politics and Other Essays* (New York: Knopf, 1965), 36.

106. *CAF*, 2:187.

107. Hamilton twice urged Madison to send timely news of ratification's outcome in Virginia: "I believe you meet nearly at the time we do. It will be of vast importance that an exact communication should be kept up between us at that period; and the moment any decisive question is taken, if favourable, I request you to dispatch an express to me with pointed orders to make all possible diligence, by changing horses &c. All expenses shall be thankfully and liberally repaid." Hamilton to Madison, 19 May 1788, *PJM*, 11:54. See also Hamilton to Madison, 8 June 1788, *PJM*, 11:100. Madison was less invested in getting news quickly, but his letters between the Federal Convention and ratification of the ninth state persistently seek out "news," "information," and intelligences from each state and every section.

108. Washington to Madison, 7 December 1787, *PJM*, 10:296–97.

Chapter 4. Virtual Nation

1. Charles Inglis, *The True Interest of America* (Philadelphia: James Humphreys, 1776), 48, 53.

2. John Adams to Abigail Adams, 19 March 1776, in *Adams Family Correspondence*, ed. L. H. Butterfield, 7 vols. (1963; Cambridge: Belknap, 1973), 1:363.

3. If anything, the problem of geographic dispersion was more daunting in the United States because the states were faced with the problem of how to connect the parts of a contiguous land mass—with all the problems of land travel and few of the conveniences of water travel, except where waterways connected important seaports to each other on the eastern seaboard. Given this dilemma, it's no wonder that critics attacked *Common Sense* on the basis of its strangely utilitarian arguments about the unmanageable size of the empire. Loyalists easily reversed this argument, putting it into more recognizable terms as a choice between concentrated, centralized monarchy and diffuse republicanism. As Charles Inglis argued, "America is too extensive" for republican government: "that form may do well enough for a single city, or small territory; but would be utterly improper for such a continent as this. America is too unwieldy for the feeble, dilatory administration of democracy." *True Interest*, 53.

4. The classic British position is Thomas Whately, *The Regulations Lately Made Concerning the Colonies and the Taxes Imposed Upon Them, Considered* (London, 1765). Important American responses include James Otis, *Considerations on Behalf of the Colonies* (London, 1765); and Daniel Dulany, *Considerations on*

the Propriety of Imposing Taxes in the British Colonies (Annapolis, 1765). All are reprinted in Bernard Bailyn, ed., *Pamphlets of the American Revolution, 1750–1776* (Cambridge: Belknap, 1965). Whately argued that "none are actually, all are virtually represented in Parliament; for every member of Parliament sits in the House not as a representative of his own constituents but as one of that august assembly by which all the commons of Great Britain are represented" (602). Otis retorted that "you could 'as well prove that the British House of Commons in fact represent all the people of the globe as those in America'" (95). But it was Dulany who offered the most convincing counterargument, insisting that different citizens had different needs and that no "identity of interests" existed between metropolitan and colonial citizens (604). Dulany's *Considerations* went through five colonial editions and two London editions within a year, as well as being read aloud in Parliament, where Pitt called it "a textbook of American rights" (599). Dulany refused representative logic so completely that he eventually opposed not just Parliament's sovereignty over colonial interests but the Continental Congress's as well, which he found equally arbitrary—a position that left him at the margins of further Revolutionary activity (603, 606).

5. Thomas Jefferson, *Writings* (New York: Library of America, 1984), 20.

6. On the history of these relations, see Jack P. Greene, *Peripheries and Center: Constitutional Development in the Extended Polities of the British Empire and the United States, 1607–1788* (Athens: University of Georgia Press, 1986).

7. The moment of independence is rhetorically performed through a present-tense declaration: "We . . . do . . . publish and declare, That these United Colonies are, and of Right ought to be Free and Independent States; that they are Absolved of all Allegiance to the British Crown, and that all political connection between them and the State of Great Britain, is and ought to be totally dissolved."

8. On the Declaration's performativity, see Fliegelman, *Declaring Independence.*

9. John Trumbull, *Autobiography, Reminiscences, and Letters of John Trumbull from 1756 to 1841* (New York: Wiley and Putnam, 1841), 416–18.

10. John Trumbull, *Proposals . . . for publishing by subscription, two prints* (New York: J. Fenno, 1790), 2.

11. For a scholarly version of this narrative, see Bernard Bailyn's appended introduction to *Ideological Origins of the American Revolution* (1967; Cambridge: Belknap, 1992), in which he argues for the Constitution not as a rupture of revolutionary ideology but as its "fulfillment." Many historians have, of course, challenged this idea.

12. See, among others, Waldstreicher, *In the Midst of Perpetual Fetes*, 53–107.

13. See, for example, Roberta Borkat, "Lord Chesterfield and Yankee Doodle: Royall Tyler's *The Contrast*," *Midwest Quarterly* 17 (1976): 436–39; John Lauber, "*The Contrast*: A Study in the Concept of Innocence," *English Language Notes* 1

(1963): 33–37; Lucy Rinehart, "A Nation's 'Noble Spectacle,'" *American Drama* 3, no. 2 (1994): 29–52; Donald Siebert, "Royall Tyler's 'Bold Example': *The Contrast* and the English Comedy of Manners," *Early American Literature* 13, no.1 (1978): 3–11; and Roger B. Stein, "Royall Tyler and the Question of Our Speech," *New England Quarterly* 38, no. 4 (1965): 454–74.

14. Richard S. Pressman, "Class Positioning and Shays' Rebellion: Resolving the Contradictions of The Contrast," *Early American Literature* 21, no. 2 (1986): 87–102; and Davidson, *Revolution and the Word*, 212–19. See also John Evelev, "The Contrast: The Problem of Theatricality and Political and Social Crisis in Post-Revolutionary America," *Early American Literature* 31, no. 1 (1996): 74–97; and Gross, "The Confidence Man and the Preacher."

15. Davidson, *Revolution and the Word*, 83–109.

16. Elizabeth Carter Wills, comp., and James Gilreath, ed., *Federal Copyright Records, 1790–1800* (Washington, DC: Library of Congress, 1987), 1.

17. The fact that Tyler gave copyright to Wignell at all is significant. Later in life, Tyler consistently refused to cede copyright even to his publishers. But by that time, it was more meaningful because more regulated. See G. Thomas Tanselle, "Author and Publisher in 1800: Letters of Royall Tyler and Joseph Nancrede," *The Harvard Library Bulletin* 15, no. 12 (1967): 129–39.

18. Wignell's letter of presentation was faithfully logged by Washington's secretary Tobias Lear, but no other letters between Wignell and Washington ever changed hands. Though Washington never saw *The Contrast* performed, he did see Wignell act on two occasions—once in Philadelphia in 1787 (during the Federal Convention) and once in New York in 1789 (just after his inauguration). *The Papers of George Washington, Presidential Series*, ed. Dorothy Twohig, 12 vols. (Charlottesville: University Press of Virginia, 1987–2005), 5:416–17.

19. On *The Contrast*'s performance history, see George O. Seilhamer, *A History of the American Theatre* (1888; New York: B. Blom, 1968), 2:232 (also 215, 222, 246); and Helen Tyler Brown, "Introduction" to *The Contrast* (Boston: Houghton Mifflin, 1920), xix–xxxii. According to Brown, post-1790s performances consisted of two in Philadelphia (in July 1790), one in Williamsburg (in 1791), and two in Boston (in October 1792 and May 1795). A broadside survives, however, advertising at least one performance "by Mr. McGRATH's COMPANY OF COMEDIANS" in Frederick-Town, Maryland, in 1791. The same broadside claims the play has been "*Performed with* Universal Applause *at the Theatres [in], Philadelphia, New-York, Baltimore, Alexandria & George-Town*," but there is no archival evidence to suggest that it actually did play in all of these locations. *Theatre, Frederick-Town* (Frederick-Town: John Winter, 1791).

20. New York and Maryland were the only two states not to pass post-Revolutionary antitheater laws. Kenneth Silverman, *A Cultural History of the American Revolution: Painting, Music, Literature, and the Theatre . . . 1763–1789* (New York: T.Y. Crowell, 1976), 549–57.

21. The standard seating capacity of a theater in the 1780s was about a thousand. This means that if each theater was filled to capacity every time the play was shown prior to early 1790 (and if no one saw it twice), then seven thousand (at most) saw it performed, not counting the Philadelphia reading. "In regard to the reading," Seilhamer notes, "the Philadelphia newspapers are silent." Seilhamer, *History of American Theatre*, 2:236.

22. For a history of theater closures from the Revolution through the 1790s, see Silverman, *Cultural History*, 539–57; David R. Brigham, *Public Culture in the Early Republic* (Washington, DC: Smithsonian Press, 1995), 8–22; and Heather S. Nathans, *Early American Theatre from the Revolution to Thomas Jefferson: Into the Hands of the People* (New York: Cambridge University Press, 2003).

23. Silverman, *Cultural History*, 557; Weldon B. Durham, ed., *American Theatre Companies, 1749–1887* (New York: Greenwood Press, 1986), 15.

24. Jean-Christophe Agnew, *Worlds Apart: The Market and the Theater in Anglo-American Thought, 1550–1750* (New York: Cambridge University Press, 1986), 150.

25. Siebert is the exception: he notes that no character is European but remains mired in the classic contrast of America versus Europe. "Royall Tyler's 'Bold Example,'" 4, 10.

26. When Europeans are mentioned, they are cast not as competitors to American virtue but as models for it. See Manly's kind words for "that brave Gallic hero, the Marquis de Lafayette" and for the "true Castilian frankness" of his "old brother officer," the Spanish ambassador. Royall Tyler, *The Contrast* (Philadelphia: Prichard & Hall, 1790), 25, 76.

27. Regional antagonism was a problem throughout the war. Even Washington initially considered Massachusetts Bay men "the most indifferent kind of People," "an exceeding dirty & nasty people." By 1777, however, Washington insisted that "I do not believe that any of the states produce better men." *The Writings of George Washington*, ed. Worthington Chauncey Ford, 19 vols. (New York: Putnams, 1889–1893), 4:313, 5:189. On variants of *Yankee Doodle*, see S. Foster Damon, *Yankee Doodle* (Providence, RI: s.n., 1959), which notes that *The Contrast*'s Marblehead verse appears nowhere else in print. On the tune's use in Anglo-American theater, see Silverman, *Cultural History*, 272–77; and J. A. Leo Lemay, "The American Origins of 'Yankee Doodle,'" *WMQ*, 3d ser., 33, no. 3 (1976): 435–64.

28. Marius B. Péladeau, ed., *The Verse of Royall Tyler* (Charlottesville: University Press of Virginia, 1968), 7–8.

29. The only ongoing argument about "The Prologue" is who wrote it. See Seilhamer, *History of American Theater*, 2:227; and Péladeau, ed., *Verse of Royall Tyler*, 7.

30. Lauren Berlant notes that "by 1789, it was clear that state membership was primary, and the only route of federal citizenship. But the purchase of the North-

west Territory (1787) also made it possible to think national identity without a state affiliation (this possibility was codified by statute in 1795)." Although she does not say so, the Constitution's "great compromise" engineers a similar solution to the problem of how "to think national identity without"—or, at any rate, alongside—"a state affiliation." *The Anatomy of National Fantasy: Hawthorne, Utopia, and Everyday Life* (Chicago: University of Chicago Press, 1991), 15.

31. Wood, *Creation of the American Republic*, 537.

32. See Jack N. Rakove, "The Great Compromise: Ideas, Interests, and the Politics of Constitution Making," *WMQ*, 3d ser., 44, no. 3 (1987): 442.

33. On the importance of state-based identity under the Articles of Confederation, see Peter S. Onuf, *Origins of the Federal Republic: Jurisdictional Controversies in the United States, 1775–1787* (Philadelphia: University of Pennsylvania Press, 1983).

34. Inglis, *True Interest*, 53.

35. Richard Leffler, "The Constitution of the United States: The End of the Revolution," in *The Reluctant Pillar: New York and the Adoption of the Federal Constitution*, ed. Stephen L. Schechter (Troy, NY: Russell Sage College, 1989), 37.

36. *LDC*, 21:381. According to Kenneth Bowling, postwar New York was a vortex of ostentatious display and consumption, a social scene heightened by the arrival of congressional tourists: "sumptuous dinners, crowds of invitations, and a frenzy of visits kept the members entertained during the early weeks of 1785. By the end of the year, elegant private parties, fortnightly concerts, and theater three nights a week provided entertainment. So many members married New York women that one wit dubbed the place, 'Calypso's Island.' Accustomed to criticizing Philadelphia and the towns in which Congress had previously resided, congressmen embraced New York and complained only about the higher cost of living." "New York City: The First Federal Capital," in *Well Begun: Chronicles of the Early National Period*, ed. Stephen L. Schechter and Richard B. Bernstein (Albany: New York State Commission on the Bicentennial of the U.S. Constitution, 1989). But not every member of Congress embraced New York. For a critical account of life in New York City, see David Howell to William Greene, 24 December 1783, *LDC*, 21:228.

37. Madison, *Notes*, 7; Anderson, *Imagined Communities*, 57.

38. Madison, *Notes*, 14.

39. On the impost, see Worthington Chauncey Ford, ed., *Journals of the Continental Congress*, 34 vols. (Washington, DC: U.S. Government Printing Office, 1904–37), 30:7–10. New Jersey was so frustrated when it learned that New York had refused to pass the Impost that it reneged on its own ratification of the bill. Leffler, "The Constitution of the United States," 37.

40. One convention delegate morosely predicted that New York was too "attached" to its trade to join the union. See Madison, *Notes*, 350. New York's

reputation as a haven of self-interested luxury wasn't helped when its legislature shelved consideration of the Continental Impost while spending most of its in-session hours debating the reopening of theaters. See Nathan Dane to Edward Pulling, 8 January 1786, *LDC*, 23:85–86.

41. See, for example, *The Contrast*, 1, 5, 26, 29–30, 37, 49, 72. Most of Tyler's later works (*May-Day, The Algerine Captive*, and *The Yankey in London*) are likewise variations on the travel narrative.

42. Grayson to Madison, 24 May 1787, *LDC*, 20:287.

43. The play had four New York performances, but advertisements after the first one announced significant "alterations." This might have been intended to draw repeat visitors but wasn't standard. Wignell probably did improvise on Tyler's text. On editorial "alterations" in Wignell's surviving stage promptbooks, see Ruth Harsha McKenzie, "Organization, Production, and Management at the Chestnut Street Theater, Philadelphia, from 1791 to 1820" (Ph.D. diss., Stanford University, 1952), 301–4.

44. *Daily Advertiser*, 18 April 1787.

45. John M. Murrin, "A Roof without Walls: The Dilemma of American National Identity," in *Beyond Confederation: Origins of the Constitution and American National Identity*, ed. Richard R. Beeman, Stephen Botein, and Edward C. Carter (Chapel Hill: Published for the Institute of Early American History and Culture by the University of North Carolina Press, 1987), 343.

46. Green (citing Peter Onuf), *Peripheries and Center*, 196–97. This is, in Stephen Patterson's words, "the Federalist frame of reference"—something Tyler inhabits completely. Stephen E. Patterson, "The Federalist Reaction to Shays's Rebellion," in *In Debt to Shays*, ed. Gross, 101.

47. Notably, the play had not yet been performed and had few subscribers north of New York.

48. Region was the most pervasive site of cultural difference in this period, but diverse communities eventually found ways to stand affectively united on the basis of the very factions that, in local life, threatened to rend them (like the class conflicts we see across regions throughout the 1780s). Many local communities experienced structurally similar sorts of interior differences, and the reproducibility of these differences from one local community to the next is what the *national* community could hold forth as a consensus of resemblances (or, to use Dulany's phrase, an identity of interests). At the national level, local difference thus became sameness—if not too closely scrutinized. In fact, the genius of the extended republic was that it was to be disconnected enough—literally—that rigorous scrutiny of one region by another was not to be expected.

49. David Waldstreicher similarly argues that women were ideal screens for national unity precisely because they were marked as apolitical entities. *In the Midst of Perpetual Fetes*, 82–84, 166–72, 234–41.

50. J. Hector St. John de Crèvecoeur, *Letters from an American Farmer* (London: Thomas Davies and Lockyer Davis, 1782), 21.

51. Royall Tyler to the Palmers, 17 February 1787. Royall Tyler Collection, Gift of Helen Tyler Brown, Vermont Historical Society.

52. Tyler reported in March that Connecticut had not yet issued a "proclamation" "for the apprehension of the Rebel Ringleaders," but he concluded such a proclamation would be futile because "the Rebels . . . are Confessedly Out of their Reach." Royall Tyler to Governor Bowdoin, 12 March 1787. Royall Tyler Collection, Gift of Helen Tyler Brown, Vermont Historical Society. In a report written to the Massachusetts legislature later that year, Tyler was bleak about the prospects of interstate cooperation, detailing numerous evasions of Massachusetts' request that Vermont not harbor known Shaysites. Vermont's governor initially refused to cooperate "upon the Pretext that he did not know how it would operate in the opinions of the People at large." Later, he "openly opposed the Report . . . upon principles of Policy," arguing that he could not "impede" emigration into Vermont. Next he refused "upon Principles of Prudence—That People were violently opposed to the measure," "that men were then in arms," and "that he Feared an Insurrection." And so on. Tyler concluded that "there being no prospect left of your memorialist . . . he took his leave of Gov. Chittington. . . . Your memorialist upon the Foregoing Facts . . . is led to conclude that the bulk of the People in Vermont are for affording protection to the Rebels and that no immediate bid . . . will be granted or if Granted will be effectual." Memorial from Royall Tyler to the Legislature of Massachusetts, 1787. Royall Tyler Collection, Gift of Helen Tyler Brown, Vermont Historical Society.

53. *Daily Advertiser*, 18 April 1787.

54. On 12 October 1778, the Continental Congress issued an order "earnestly" recommending "the several states, to take the most effectual measures . . . for the suppressing of theatrical entertainments, horse racing, gaming, and such other diversions as are productive of idleness, dissipation, and a general depravity of principals and manners." Congress amended this on 16 October to include not just civilians and foot soldiers but army officers (including Washington) who were then enjoying nightly camp shows—a staple of eighteenth-century military life: "Whereas frequenting play houses and theatrical entertainments has a fatal tendency to divert the minds of the people from a due attention to the means necessary for the defence of their country, and the preservation of their liberties: // *Resolved*, That any person holding an office under the United States, who shall act, promote, encourage, or attend such plays, shall be deemed unworthy to hold such office, and shall be accordingly dismissed." Ford, ed., *Journals of the Continental Congress*, 12:1001–02, 1018–20. After the Revolution, several states passed vagrancy laws that "classified actors with beggars, peddlers, and fortune-tellers, effectually ending theater." Silverman, *Cultural History*, 557.

55. In 1766, a New York theater that had been closed because of the Stamp Act was reopened with "disastrous results." Mark Fearnow, "American Colonial Disturbances as Political Theatre," *Theatre Survey* 33 (1991): 55. As Paul Gilje writes: "On opening night a mob arrived, huzzahed, shouted 'Liberty, Liberty,' and drove the theater patrons helter-skelter into the street, often with the loss of 'their Caps, Hats, Wigs, Cardinals, and Cloaks'. . . The building was 'Torn to Pieces' and the debris dragged to the Common, where it was burned in a public spectacle." *The Road to Mobocracy: Popular Disorder in New York City, 1763–1834* (Chapel Hill: University of North Carolina Press, 1987), 51. See also *Weyman's Gazette*, 12 May 1766; and *Gazette Post-Boy*, 8 May 1766.

56. Nathans, *Early American Theater*, 51.

57. *Independent Gazetteer*, 21 February 1784. In Massachusetts an elite observer of the Shays conflict made the converse argument, connecting the rebellion to "the want of theaters, dances, shows and other public amusements" in the backcountry. Silverman, *Cultural History*, 553.

58. Pitt's remarks were extracted in the *Pennsylvania Gazette*, 24 December 1767. His argument that "the Americans are the SONS, not the BASTARDS of England" recalls Benedict Anderson's insight that "the fatality of trans-Atlantic birth" had turned American colonists into British aliens. *Imagined Communities*, 57.

59. Formally dedicated on 7 September 1770, the statue of Pitt stood at a prominent intersection on Wall Street. See *New-York Journal*, 13 September 1770.

60. Isaac Newton Phelps Stokes, *The Iconography of Manhattan Island, 1489–1909*, 6 vols. (New York: Robert H. Dodd, 1915–28), 3:819.

61. Ibid., 3:833.

62. Solomon Drowne to William Drowne, 13 July 1776, in Abraham Tomlinson and Henry B. Dawson, eds., *New York City during the American Revolution* (New York: Mercantile Library Association, 1861), 80.

63. Stokes, *Iconography*, 3:814.

64. *St. James's Chronicle*, 7–10 March 1778. See also Stokes, *Iconography*, 4:1063.

65. Stokes, *Iconography* 1:356.

66. Thomas Hutchinson, *The Diary and Letters of His Excellency Thomas Hutchinson*, 2 vols. (London: S. Low, Marston, Searle & Rivington, 1883), 2:167–68.

67. Samuel Blachley Webb, *Correspondence and Journals*, ed. Worthington Chauncey Ford, 3 vols. (New York and Lancaster, PA: Wickersham Press, 1893), 1:153.

68. William Whipple to John Langdon, 16 July 1776, *LDC*, 4:477.

69. *Proceedings of the New York Historical Association*, 7 vols. (New York: Press of the Historical Society, 1844–49), 4:992.

70. Isaac Bangs, *Journal* (Cambridge: John Wilson and Son, 1890), 57.

71. *Pennsylvania Journal*, 17 July 1776.

72. On the "republican entertainments" most conducive to virtue in small republics, see Jean-Jacques Rousseau, *Politics and the Arts: Letter to M. D'Alembert on the Theatre*, trans. Allan Bloom (Ithaca: Cornell University Press, 1960). Rousseau's model of virtuous embodied collectivity was elaborated precisely as an argument against theatrical entertainments, where, according to Laura Rigal, "citizens were not brought together but deprived of one another by a confining idleness and false display." "'Raising the Roof': Authors, Spectators, and Artisans in the Grand Federal Procession of 1788," *Theatre Journal* 48, no. 3 (1996): 259.

73. Madison, *Notes*, 78.

74. Ibid., 412.

75. Samuel Adams to James Warren, 17 October 1778, *LDC*, 25:66.

76. [Philadelphia] *General Advertiser*, 25 October 1794. See also Brigham, *Public Culture*, 28.

77. The irony is that under the British monarchy, "the people" were made marginal and virtual by virtue of their dislocation from the metropole and yet were often embraced by colonial elites as virtuous, reasonable, worthy, nondespotic—and not really dangerous. The people of the emerging republic, however, seem to have become nonvirtual and self-identical by virtue of their geographical proximity to their own political center(s) and were consequently deemed nonvirtuous, irrational, unworthy, despotic—and, as bodies, dangerous. It is, among other things, the work of federalism to remarginalize, or revirtualize, the people's relation to the state, as it had once been virtualized under British rule.

78. Wendy C. Wick, *George Washington, An American Icon: The Eighteenth-Century Graphic Portraits* (Washington, DC: Smithsonian Institution, 1982), 4.

79. Harold Holzer, *Washington and Lincoln Portrayed: National Icons in Popular Prints* (Jefferson: McFarland, 1993), xx.

80. Holzer, *Washington and Lincoln*, 12; Wick, *George Washington*, 18.

81. Wick, *George Washington*, 4.

82. Ibid., 8–9, 20. In Europe, where production standards and consumer expectations were higher, spurious claims to a portrait's authenticity were sometimes engraved and even forged onto them, but in the United States, this level of pretense was unnecessary. Ibid., 9, 20.

83. Helen A. Cooper, *John Trumbull: The Hand and Spirit of a Painter* (New Haven: Yale University Press, 1982), 78.

84. Trumbull, *Autobiography*, 365.

85. Cooper, *John Trumbull*, 78.

86. Ibid.

87. Trumbull claimed he took the advice of Jefferson and Adams on the issue of who to include in the painting. "They concurred in the advice, that with regard to the characters to be introduced, the signatures of the original act, (which

is still preserved in the office of state,) ought to be the general guide." In several instances, however, the painting does add figures other than "the signatures of the original act." *Autobiography*, 417.

88. On the painting's inaccuracies, see Albert Furtwangler, *American Silhouettes: Rhetorical Identities of the Founders* (New Haven: Yale University Press, 1987), 6; and Cooper, *John Trumbull*, 76–80.

89. When the original signer was dead, Trumbull scrupulously met with the family and approximated a likeness from relatives or other portraits (another in a long series of displacements from the original). One portrait was painted from the verbal descriptions of friends and family, and another was done from memory.

90. Cooper, *John Trumbull*, 80.

91. Ibid., 78.

92. In Charles Brockden Brown's *Alcuin*, for example, a female feminist character claims that she is willing, for the sake of the union, "to be stiled a federalist" even though she knows that the federalists, as a party, are against women's rights. Federalism is proposed as a "stile" of affiliation that does not impose on one's local convictions or embodied reality. The federal state thus imagined is pre-Orwellian precisely because it is not yet industrial: it does not and cannot, at this point, inhabit the same temporal or spatial realities as the citizen's literal body. *Alcuin* (Kent, OH: Kent State University Press, 1987), 22.

Chapter 5. Metrobuilding

1. *Massachusetts Centinel*, 30 January 1788; *The Federalist*, 233.

2. Rigal, *American Manufactory*, 91–113. The word "wreck" comes from *The Federalist*, 44.

3. *Massachusetts Gazette*, 3 December 1787.

4. On the material production of national space, see Wilbur Zelinsky, *Nation into State: The Shifting Symbolic Foundations of American Nationalism* (Chapel Hill: University of North Carolina Press, 1988).

5. Cartographers remain interested in Colles's maps, but Colles is also sometimes remembered as the first man to build a functioning steam engine in North America. See Greville Bathe, *An Engineer's Miscellany* (Philadelphia: Patterson and White, 1938), 117–30.

6. In discouraging Colles's plan, Washington cited "insuperable difficulties," including "the present juvenile state of the Country, the abundance of land, the scarcity of laborers, and the want of resources." Washington to Colles, 25 January 1783, *The Writings of George Washington*, ed. John C. Fitzpatrick, 39 vols. (Washington, DC: U.S. Government Printing Office, 1931–44), 26:64–65.

7. *Early Proceedings of the American Philosophical Society* (Philadelphia: Mc-

Calla and Stavely, 1884), 82–83. For early lecture advertisements, see *Pennsylvania Packet*, 13 January, 27 January, 17 February, and 23 March 1772; and Christopher Colles, *Syllabus of a Course of Lectures in Natural Experimental Philosophy* (Philadelphia: John Dunlap, 1773). Despite the APS's disdain for Colles's "exhibitions," his career emulates the model of public science that was then flourishing in London. See Larry Stewart, *The Rise of Public Science: Rhetoric, Technology, and Natural Philosophy in Newtonian Britain, 1660–1750* (New York: Cambridge University Press, 1992); and Jan Golinski, *Science as Public Culture: Chemistry and Enlightenment in Britain, 1760–1820* (New York: Cambridge University Press, 1992).

8. Walter W. Ristow, "Introduction," in Christopher Colles, *A Survey of the Roads of the Unites States of America* (1789; Cambridge: Belknap, 1961), 3.

9. Several advertisements for "various mechanical contrivances particularly adapted" "to moderate the price of labor" appear in the *Pennsylvania Packet*, 26 August 1771; 22 September 1773; and 29 September 1773. On the waterworks project, see Christopher Colles, *Copy of a Proposal of Christopher Colles for furnishing the City of New-York with a Constant Supply of FRESH WATER* (New York: Hugh Gaine, 1774).

10. Donna Haraway, "Situated Knowledges: The Science Question in Feminism and the Privilege of Partial Perspective," *Feminist Studies* 14, no. 3 (1988): 581.

11. Colles cites several British precursors, noting that the *Survey* would be done "in the manner of Ogilvie's roads of England; and of Taylor and Skinner's roads of Ireland." *New-York Packet*, 1 April 1790.

12. As David Harvey notes in *The Condition of Postmodernity*, "the tradition of medieval mapping typically emphasizes the sensuous rather than the rational and objective qualities of spatial order" that would emerge later in the Renaissance and then dominate the Enlightenment (243; see also 242–49).

13. Christopher Colles, *Proposals for Publishing a Survey of the Roads of the United States of America* (New York: s.n., 1789).

14. For Colles's unsuccessful petition to Congress and the postmaster general, see *New-York Packet*, 1 April 1790.

15. Colles, *Proposals for Publishing a Survey*.

16. Measurements were probably borrowed from Washington's war department, with which Colles was connected during the Revolution. Ristow, "Introduction," 73–81.

17. Colles, *Proposals for Publishing a Survey*.

18. Ristow, "Introduction," 77.

19. Colles, *Proposals for Publishing a Survey*.

20. The *Survey* is listed, for example, in an 1823 inventory of Thomas Jefferson's Library, but there is no reason to believe Jefferson used all (or, indeed, any) of its plates. The gap between mere ownership and actual use gestures toward a

more fundamental gap, in Colles's cultural work, between potentiality and utility. For this and similar maps, guidebooks, atlases, geographies, and travel narratives owned by Jefferson, see *Thomas Jefferson's Library: A Catalog with the Entries in His Own Order*, ed. James Gilreath and Douglas L. Wilson (Washington, DC: Library of Congress, 1989), 98–107.

21. Madison to Jefferson, 24 October 1787, *PJM*, 10:207.

22. On the "medium" of the states and state legislatures, see *Federalist* Nos. 27 and 28.

23. This phrase is Tony Bennett's. See "The Exhibitionary Complex," *New Formations* 4 (1988): 73–102.

24. Rigal, *American Manufactory*, 21–54, 179–203.

25. When Madison describes the need to protect the minority from the majority, he is talking about the minority of property owners over and against an often rural majority whose interests included, most troublingly to the federalists, debtor relief and paper money laws.

26. David Harvey, "The Spatial Fix: Hegel, Von Thünen and Marx," in *Spaces of Capital: Towards a Critical Geography* (New York: Routledge, 2001), 284–311.

27. *New-York Journal*, 25 October 1787.

28. *CAF*, 2:239–43.

29. *CAF*, 3:114.

30. Madison to Jefferson, 24 October 1787, *PJM*, 10:207.

31. Michel Foucault, *The History of Sexuality, Volume I: An Introduction*, trans. Robert Hurley (New York: Vintage, 1980), 135–45. Foucault describes biopower as "an indispensable element in the development of capitalism" (140–41)—"a power to *foster* life or *disallow* it to the point of death" that he contrasts with earlier forms of sovereign power (characterized as "the ancient right to *take* life or *let* live") (138). Devoted to the simultaneous "disciplines of the body and the regulations of the population" (139), biopower "has to qualify, measure, appraise, and hierarchize, rather than display itself in its murderous splendor; it does not have to draw the line that separates the enemies of the sovereign from his obedient subjects; it effects distributions around the norm" (144). As such, it resembles not just the bureaucratic federalist state imagined in 1787 but the many cultural technologies that emerge to tend and subtend that state—what Rigal in *The American Manufactory* calls "the arts of federalism."

32. *CAF*, 3:89–90.

33. Michel Foucault, *Discipline and Punish: The Birth of the Prison*, trans. Alan Sheridan (New York: Vintage, 1979), 135–69. Of course for Foucault, the soldier's body is docile as well—a fact that John Humble cannot acknowledge.

34. Madison to Jefferson, 24 October 1787, *PJM*, 10:214; *The Federalist*, 510.

35. The debate over where the new capital was to be physically located was the first order of business when the First Federal Congress convened in 1789. See Kenneth R. Bowling, *Creating the Federal City, 1774–1800: Potomac Fever*

(Washington, DC: American Institute of Architects Press, 1988), and *Creation of Washington, DC: The Idea and Location of the American Capital* (Fairfax, VA: George Mason University Press, 1991).

36. No wonder, then, that *The Federalist* was one of the most cited texts on the floor of southern secession conventions in 1861. In his attempt to appease state legislators, Publius constructs a powerful defense of states' rights, the consequences of which he cannot foresee. See Jack N. Rakove, "Early Uses of *The Federalist,*" in *Saving the Revolution: The Federalist Papers and the American Founding,* ed. Charles R. Kesler (New York: Free Press, 1987), 234–49.

37. Many believed this problem would kill the plan: "the Imperium in imperio will be the fruitful Source of a thousand jarring Principles, wch. will make the new Machine, notwithstanding all the Oil you can give it, to go heavily along." Reverend James Madison to James Madison, Jr., 9 February 1788, *PJM,* 10:488.

38. Federalism's spatial fix was not without internal contradictions. While No. 10 poses a dispersed population as an antidote to the dangers of faction, later numbers suggest that the federal state will be subject to the surveillance of its parts—especially its state-parts. Should tyranny emerge at the center (or if, as many antifederalists feared, the central government should try to abolish the state governments), Publius argues that the peripheries will rise up and resist. But this fantasy marks a point of subtle contradiction within his larger argument. Such a revolt would suggest, contrary to No. 10, that the parts of the union will be able to unite and organize in unison when they find it necessary.

39. Hamilton held a famously dim opinion of the common voter. In a speech before the New York Assembly several months before the Federal Convention, Hamilton noted the "unlettered" state of New York's voters, estimating that one-third to one-half of the electorate in New York State were illiterate. *PAH,* 4:31. Albert Furtwangler argues that Hamilton's numbers were off: he estimates New York State literacy in 1787 at 70 percent. *Authority of Publius,* 20. That number does not account, however, for the differential density of such literacy in cities as opposed to other areas. Hamilton's disdain for common audiences—or rather, his persistent sense that there were two audiences to whom he was addressing himself (one elite, one common)—is reflected in his frequent choice of arcane pseudonyms that would have meant one thing to his more "classically educated audience" and quite another to the less educated. See "A Note on Certain of Hamilton's Pseudonyms," *WMQ,* 3d ser., 12, no. 2 (1955): 282–97, which suggests that many of Hamilton's pseudonyms refer to little-known aristocrats from the Roman Empire, all of whom "share . . . a profound contempt for the people whom they rule and serve so devotedly" (286). Even Publius is described, in Plutarch, as one who tricks the people into submission—so successfully that they ironically bestow upon him the name "Poplicola, or people lover" (283–84, n4).

40. *CAF,* 6:171.

41. Cecelia M. Kenyon, "Men of Little Faith: The Anti-Federalists on the Na-

ture of Representative Government," *WMQ*, 3d ser., 12, no. 1 (1955): 3–43. Paine writes: "There is something exceedingly ridiculous in the composition of monarchy; it first excludes a man from the means of information, yet empowers him to act in cases where the highest judgment is required. The state of a king shuts him from the world, yet the business of a king requires him to know it thoroughly; wherefore the different parts, by unnaturally opposing and destroying each other, prove the whole character to be absurd and useless"(1:8).

42. On the small republic, see Montesquieu, *Spirit of the Laws* (1748): "It is natural for a republic to have only a small territory; otherwise it cannot long subsist. . . . In an extensive republic the public good is sacrificed to a thousand private views; it is subordinate to exceptions, and depends on accidents. In a small one, the interest of the public is more obvious, better understood, and more within the reach of every citizen." Philip B. Kurland and Ralph Lerner, eds., *The Founders' Constitution*, 5 vols. (Chicago: University of Chicago Press, 1987), 1:246.

43. *The Federalist* suggests there is a limit to national intelligence: a federal statesman "should be acquainted with the general genius, habits, and modes of thinking of the people at large, and with the resources of the country. And this is all that can reasonably be meant by a knowledge of the interests and feelings of the people" (222).

44. Holland, *Body Politic*, 91.

45. This metaphor appears four times in *The Federalist* to describe the relation of federal states to their parts. See Nos. 25, 31, 44, 45.

46. The different parts of Publius, in the persons of Madison and Hamilton, had different visions of who this elite might be. Madison sought someone above local prejudice while Hamilton favored merchants ("speculative men"), a predilection undoubtedly tied to his experience as a merchant apprentice in the West Indies.

47. *DHRC*, 15:517, 521–22.

48. Wolin, *Presence of the Past*, 189.

49. Ibid., 82–89. Wolin borrows the word "superintendance" from *The Federalist*, 136.

50. [Boston] *American Herald*, 11 June 1787.

51. Larry D. Kramer, "Madison's Audience," *Harvard Law Review* 112 (1999): 611–79.

52. David Hume, *A Treatise of Human Nature*, ed. L. A. Selby-Bigge (Oxford: Clarendon Press, 1978), 426–38. Douglass Adair, "That Politics May Be Reduced to a 'Science': David Hume, James Madison, and the Tenth *Federalist*," *Huntington Library Quarterly* 20 (1957): 350.

53. Publius argues this detachment will be most acute in the case of the judiciary and the president, neither of whom are expected to circulate back through home constituencies. The legislature alone becomes a "depository" for the feelings of the people—the House more so than the Senate because the eighteenth-

century Senate was appointed and the appointments were less frequent than the House's elections.

54. Even federalists who supported the Constitution's recentralization of power were concerned about how distance might hamper the quality of representation. James Wilson thought it necessary to have representation "because it is impossible for the people to act collectively," but he also warned that the legislature must know "the mind or sense of the people." Madison likewise warned that the people must not "be lost sight of altogether"; there must be "a necessary sympathy" between representative and constituent. Madison, *Notes*, 73–74, 40.

55. On the politics of early national sympathy, see Elizabeth Barnes, *States of Sympathy: Seduction and Democracy in the American Novel* (New York: Columbia University Press, 1997); and Julia A. Stern, *The Plight of Feeling: Sympathy and Dissent in the Early American Novel* (Chicago: University of Chicago Press, 1997).

56. Royall Tyler Collection, Gift of Helen Tyler Brown, Vermont Historical Society.

57. Davidson, *Revolution and the Word*, 85–86. Brown's career was shorter, since he died only a few years after arriving in North Carolina. See Richard Walser, "North Carolina Sojourn of the First American Novelist," *North Carolina Historical Review* 28 (1951): 138–55.

58. For instance, in Hannah Foster's *The Coquette* (1797) (also an epistolary novel), letters are almost always dated from structurally similar spatial units: towns (Hartford, Hampshire, New-Haven, and Boston). In this way, the town becomes the social unit of collectivity that the novel explores.

59. Davidson, *Revolution and the Word*, 98–101.

60. William Hill Brown, *The Power of Sympathy*, ed. William S. Kable (Columbus: Ohio State University Press, 1970), 52–53.

61. Alexander, *Selling of the Constitutional Convention*, 23.

62. The vote was badly skewed because the federalists boycotted the referendum in order to undermine its authority and call its outcome into question. That they were willing to do so indicates that they knew they were going to lose. Irwin H. Polishook, "An Independence Day Celebration in Rhode Island, 1788," *Huntington Library Quarterly* 30, no. 1 (1966): 85–93.

63. *Massachusetts Centinel*, 7 February 1789.

64. Davidson, *Revolution and the Word*, 90.

65. *Massachusetts Centinel*, 7 February 1789.

66. *Herald of Freedom*, 10 February 1789.

67. Davidson, *Revolution and the Word*, 90.

68. *Massachusetts Centinel*, 7 and 14 February 1789.

69. Davidson, *Revolution and the Word*, 96.

70. Few critics, for example, forgo the structuring dichotomy of "national" versus "local." Isaiah Thomas was the first to situate the novel in this way, mar-

keting the book as the first American novel but at the same time using the Boston subplot as his frontispiece, thus capitalizing on the local scandal with local readers. As a marketing technique, these choices make sense: Thomas knew the novel would circulate primarily through his established consumer base in and around Boston. But his national pitch makes sense too, for this is how nationalism worked in the early republic: locally produced objects circulated locally yet were inflected with knowledge of and gestures to the nonlocal.

71. On the novel's pedagogical project, see Brown's dedication and preface.

72. Davidson, *Revolution and the Word*, 91.

73. Barnes, *States of Sympathy*, 34.

74. Ibid., 39.

75. Davidson reconstructs these responses from handwritten marginalia in extant first editions. *Revolution and the Word*, 95.

76. *Massachusetts Centinel*, 7 February 1789.

77. Hume, *Treatise of Human Nature*, 428–29.

78. "The pronoun 'we' has historically proven to be the most empowering and shiftiest shifter of them all. It is through the 'we' that discourses of false universality are created." Barbara E. Johnson, "Response" [to Henry Louis Gates], in *Afro-American Literary Study in the 1990s*, ed. Houston A. Baker and Patricia Redmond (Chicago: University of Chicago Press, 1989), 43.

79. On this mercantile "projection," see Stanley M. Elkins and Eric L. McKitrick, *The Age of Federalism* (New York: Oxford University Press, 1993), 92–131.

80. Michael Hardt and Antonio Negri, *Empire* (Cambridge: Harvard University Press, 2000), 160–82. On Enlightenment networking more generally, see Armand Mattelart, *The Invention of Communication*, trans. Susan Emanuel (Minneapolis: University of Minnesota Press, 1996).

81. *American Magazine* (December 1787): 9–10. In later numbers, Webster argues against the use of binding instructions because the people at large can never know "the general good." "A law which is, in its operation, *general*, must be founded on the best general information." *American Magazine* (March 1788): 205.

82. *American Magazine* (December 1787): 14. Webster's position was a Revolutionary staple. It echoes a central argument of Paine's *The Rights of Man* as well as Jefferson's theory of generational sovereignty (in which he favored a revolution every nineteen years).

83. *American Magazine* (February 1788): 139.

84. On the figure of the coquette as a test case in consent, see Carroll Smith-Rosenberg, "Domesticating 'Virtue': Coquettes and Revolutionaries in Young America," in *Literature and the Body: Essays on Populations and Persons*, ed. Elaine Scarry (Baltimore: Johns Hopkins University Press, 1988), 160–83; and Gillian Brown, *The Consent of the Governed: The Lockean Legacy in Early American Culture* (Cambridge: Harvard University Press, 2001), 123–47.

85. *Correspondence between the Hon. John Adams . . . and the late Wm. Cunningham, Esq.* (Boston: E. M. Cunningham, 1823), 19. See also Fliegelman, *Prodigals and Pilgrims*, 237.

86. Hortense J. Spillers, "Mama's Baby, Papa's Maybe: An American Grammar Book," *Diacritics* 17, no. 2 (1987): 64–81. The analogy to crime is Brown's: he explicitly frames the "seducer" in each subplot as a criminal.

87. Hume, *Treatise of Human Nature*, 429–30.

88. John Berger, *The Look of Things* (New York: Viking, 1974), 40.

89. Harvey, *Condition of Postmodernity*, 246.

90. Cited in Potter and Manning, eds., *Nationalism and Sectionalism*, 69.

91. Philip Fisher, "Democratic Social Space: Whitman, Melville, and the Promise of American Transparency," in *Representations* 24 (1988): 60–101. The 1785 Ordinance laid the basis for the Northwest Ordinance of 1787, which served as official U.S. land policy until the passage of the Homestead Act in 1862.

92. Jefferson, *Notes*, 85.

93. For these and other partisan arguments over Jefferson's "extension" of the extended republic, see D. W. Meinig, *The Shaping of America: A Geographical Perspective on 500 Years of History*, 4 vols. (New Haven: Yale University Press, 1986–2000), 2:11–14. White's fear of dispersion is particularly ironic, given his orthodox federalist position on social hierarchies: "What we have most to fear to our government and our liberties must come . . . from the licentiousness of democracy." *The Debates and Proceedings in the Congress of the United States, 1803–1805* (Boston: Gales and Seaton, 1852), 151.

94. See Elkins and McKitrick's magisterial account of both federalism writ large and the two-party system operating inside of it in *Age of Federalism*, esp. 257–302.

95. Pasley's comprehensive account emphasizes the regionalized nature of this network, which had radically different production and distribution capacities in North and South. '*Tyranny of Printers*,' 158–59, 259–64. See also Brooke, "To Be 'Read By the Whole People,'" which theorizes the decentralization of the partisan network and its consequent failure to produce a densely unified field of open, widely accessible (or "national") debate before 1840.

96. For an indication of how Colles thought western space might be settled in grids of "150 acres each" that nevertheless assume the presence of both "sober, honest, industrious farmers" and more urbanized "workmen," see Christopher Colles, *Proposals for the Speedy Settlement of the Waste and Unappropriated Lands on the Western Frontiers* (New York: Samuel Loudon, 1785), 4. Like most of Colles's proposals, this one imagines a networked commercial republic, where residents in the interior might, through the use of inland (aboveground) canals, "be enabled to send their produce to market, from whence they may have returns in money or foreign commodities" (5).

97. Haraway, "Situated Knowledges," 581.

98. Christopher Colles, *The Geographical Ledger and Systematized Atlas* (New York: John Buel, 1794), iv.

99. *Daily Advertiser*, 11 October 1794.

100. On the telescope and microscope, see *Daily Advertiser*, 31 July 1789; and Christopher Colles, *An Account of the Astonishing Beauties and Operations of Nature . . . Displayed by the Solar Microscope* (New York: Samuel Wood, 1815).

101. Christopher Colles, *Proposal of a Design for the Promotion of the Interests of the United States of America . . . By Means of Inland Navigable Communications* (New York: Samuel Wood, 1808).

102. Christopher Colles, *Description of the Numerical Telegraph* (Brooklyn: Alden Spooner, 1813), 8–9.

103. *The Statesman*, 20 October 1812.

6. ABOLITIONIST NATION

1. On this transition, see Drew R. McCoy, *The Elusive Republic: Political Economy in Jeffersonian America* (1980; New York: Norton, 1982); Meinig, *Shaping of America*, 2:334–52; and Sellers, *Market Revolution*.

2. Cited in David Rumsey and Edith M. Punt, eds., *Cartographica Extraordinaire: The Historical Map Transformed* (Redlands, CA: ESRI Press, 2004), 100.

3. Robert Fanuzzi, *Abolition's Public Sphere* (Minneapolis: University of Minnesota Press, 2003). See also Henry Mayer, *All on Fire: William Lloyd Garrison and the Abolition of Slavery* (New York: St. Martins Press, 1998).

4. See Fanuzzi, *Abolition's Public Sphere*, 43–82.

5. *National Era* 2, 19 October 1848.

6. Elizabeth Heyrick, *Immediate, Not Gradual Abolition* (London: Hatchard and Son, 1824).

7. On the shift from gradual to immediate abolition, see Richard S. Newman, *The Transformation of American Abolitionism: Fighting Slavery in the Early Republic* (Chapel Hill: University of North Carolina Press, 2002). Immediatism was initially attacked as temporally and spatially impractical, but as one correspondent to *The Liberator* noted: "I know that many objections have been raised to the doctrine of immediate emancipation on the ground that whatever requires action, requires time and therefore cannot be done *instantaneously*. . . . But let me ask.—Because a man cannot accomplish the whole of an enterprise at one blow, is it any less important that he *begins* his work *immediately*?" *The Liberator*, 19 April 1834.

8. Thomas L. Haskell, "Capitalism and the Origins of the Humanitarian Sensibility," in *The Antislavery Debate: Capitalism and Abolitionism as a Problem in*

Historical Interpretation, ed. Thomas Bender (Berkeley: University of California Press, 1992), 107–60.

9. *Minutes of the Proceedings of a Convention of Delegates from the Abolition Societies Established in Different Parts of the United States, Assembled at Philadelphia*, Session One (Philadelphia: Zachariah Poulson, Jr., 1794), 11. Future references to the convention's *Minutes* will be cited by session number, publication year, and page, except when new bibliographic information is available.

10. *Minutes*, Session Seven (1801), 8. This was consistent with antislavery practice before the Revolution. As Winthrop Jordan notes, most pre-Revolutionary "antislavery societies were ostensibly state-wide, but in fact their memberships and activities centered in the larger cities, where organization was most feasible." Winthrop Jordan, *White over Black: American Attitudes toward the Negro, 1550–1812* (Chapel Hill: Published for the Institute of Early American History and Culture by the University of North Carolina Press, 1968), 343.

11. *Minutes*, Session One (1794), 19.

12. *Minutes*, Session Twelve (1809), 14.

13. *Minutes*, Session One (1794), 14.

14. Thomas Earle, *The Life, Travels, and Opinions of Benjamin Lundy* (Philadelphia: W. D. Parrish, 1847). While Earle is usually cited as the author of Lundy's *Life*, the book is more aptly described as a compilation of Lundy's extant papers. Thus when I cite Earle, it is usually one of three Lundy sources being cited: his journals, letters, or editorials from the *Genius*.

15. See, for instance, the [New York] *Freedom's Journal* for 21 March 1828.

16. Wendell Phillips Garrison, "In Lundy's Land," *The Pennsylvania Magazine of History and Biography* 19, no. 3 (1895), 343.

17. *Genius of Universal Emancipation* (October 1830).

18. Garrison, "In Lundy's Land," 343.

19. Lundy to Elizabeth Chandler, 2 April 1831. Cited in Merton L. Dillon, *Benjamin Lundy and the Struggle for Negro Freedom* (Urbana: University of Illinois Press, 1966), 170.

20. Ibid., 208.

21. Lundy was sensitive to the gaps his travel produced, which he usually registers in the discourse of geography. For example, he often describes new places in his travel journals through comparative similes to some other location from which he is absent. In several entries written in Mexico, he writes that "every thing was as still as a Sabbath in Boston, or as any other day of the week in Burlington, N.J." (Earle 156–57); that "the weather [is] as warm as that of June in New Jersey" (164); and that "yesterday was as warm here as a hot June day north of the Potomac" (165). These place-based similes construct the areas in which he travels as an essentially differential and differentiated landscape rather than one cohesive territory sharing the same clock.

22. Kaplan describes antebellum colonization programs as imperialist projects in which freed blacks would be removed from the domestic sphere to Africa, where they would, through their leadership on that continent, enhance the American presence abroad. Amy Kaplan, *The Anarchy of Empire in the Making of U.S. Culture* (Cambridge: Harvard University Press, 2002), 23–50.

23. Lundy's "Columbus" essays appeared serially in the Philadelphia *National Gazette* throughout 1836, and Lundy personally disseminated them in the mail to friends and politicians, including John Quincy Adams (then congressman from Massachusetts). See Dillon, *Benjamin Lundy*, 227–31. Jefferson and Washington were other founding fathers Lundy admired. He favored Jefferson as a source for epigrams on the masthead of the *Genius* and once attempted (unsuccessfully) to curry favor with the Mexican leader Santa Anna by presenting him with a portrait of Washington he carried with him in his travels.

24. James G. Birney, *Letter on Colonization* (New York: Office of the Anti-Slavery Reporter, 1834).

25. We can see Lundy's tendency to look for old solutions in yet another aspect of his colonization scheme: his willingness to use indenture as a temporary solution to the problem of emancipation. Indenture was already a bygone practice in the 1820s and '30s, decades that witnessed the accelerated reorganization of labor around industrial wage models. In his Haiti ventures, Lundy sought to defray the expense of settlement by having his emancipated slaves indentured to Haitian planters—an arrangement that many fled, leaving Lundy to deal with an irate Haitian government. On Lundy's Haitian projects, see Dillon, *Benjamin Lundy*, 88–95, 98–102, 142–43.

26. Jefferson, *Notes*, 26–72.

27. Holland, *Body Politic*, 19–56.

28. On Lundy's climatological bias, see Dillon, *Benjamin Lundy*, 88–89.

29. *Genius of Universal Emancipation* (October 1824).

30. Upon returning from Mexico the first time, Lundy was sent to debtor's prison for debts related to the *Genius*. The debts were cleared before he left for his second Mexican tour, but when he returned, the paper was again insolvent. Dillon, *Benjamin Lundy*, 212–13.

31. [New York] *Colored American*, 4 August 1838.

32. [Philadelphia] *National Enquirer*, 22 February and 8 March 1838.

33. Dillon, *Benjamin Lundy*, 237, 252.

34. *The Federalist* explains this distinction nicely: "The difference between a federal and national government as it relates to the *operation of the Government* is supposed to consist in this, that in the former, the powers operate on the political bodies composing the confederacy, in their political capacities: In the latter, on the individual citizens, composing the nation, in their individual capacities." A confederation, in other words, is a union of states, or geographic units, that enter the compact of union as collective bargaining units. A nation, on the other hand,

bypasses the state-unit as a mediator and extends its membership and power directly to "individuals" (255).

35. On the office atmosphere at the AASS, see *LWGG*, 1:436, 463–64. Weld describes the office as an energized rush of activity, "with Wright, Stanton, and Leavitt jabbering all the time . . . hum, hum, buzz, buzz, all the time" (1:436). Melville's depiction of office doldrums in "Bartleby" aside, Weld thrived on the life of an office worker, finding his days filled with "questions and discussions and a tap on the shoulder at least as often as once in a minute or two" (1:463).

36. Unsurprisingly, each later took up relatively modern bureaucratic occupations. Lewis Tappan founded the first American credit reporting agency; Weld became a political lobbyist (of sorts) in Washington, DC; Leavitt crusaded for "cheap postage" reform; and Wright became an actuary and life insurance executive.

37. *Minutes*, Session One (1794), 29, 17.

38. *Minutes*, Session Seven (1801), 34.

39. *Minutes*, Session Four (1797), 42–43.

40. *Minutes*, Session Thirteen (1812), 23.

41. "To this deficiency of information was ascribed, in part, the chilling indifference" of the general public. *Minutes*, Session Sixteen (1819), 21–22.

42. Compare this to the many AASS publications that emphasized geography—including numerous maps, graphic prints, and almanacs.

43. The *Minutes* show how little writing and publishing on slavery was being done even as late as 1818: "We deem it a matter for regret, that while the talents of our writers and public speakers are put in requisition to rouse the attention of the nation, to subjects of comparatively small importance . . . *this* subject, so important to the happiness of millions in its actual state,—so portentous in its aspect to millions yet unborn,—and involving questions of the first magnitude to an enlightened people, should engage so small a share of public feeling, or public exertion" (23). "To effect this desirable union of talents and energy, more general and correct information of the real state of things among us appears to be a pre-requisite. . . . We would therefore respectfully suggest to the Convention the taking of measures for collecting and circulating such facts as may tend to elucidate this dark subject; and awaken throughout the Union, a more lively interest on behalf of the wretched African, and of our national character." *Minutes*, Session Sixteen (1819), 24.

44. *Minutes*, Session Thirteen (1812), 23.

45. *Minutes*, Session Twenty (1827), 28. To the degree that the early conventions considered geography at all, it emerged as a point of contention between delegates, who (like the Federal Congress before them) squabbled endlessly among themselves about where to meet because some members felt they had to travel too far to attend the meetings. For most of its existence, the convention met in Philadelphia. Toward the end of the 1820s, however, many members

began to lobby for a more centrally located meeting site—favoring Washington, DC. The delegates ultimately compromised, voting to meet biannually in rotating locations (Philadelphia and Washington, DC). *Minutes, Session Twenty* (1827), 16; and *Minutes, Session Twenty-One* (1829), 14. As Zagarri notes in *The Politics of Size*, rotating between two sites was common for post-Revolutionary state capitals, 8–27.

46. "If the signs of the times call for a National Institution, where might we look for the seat of its operations, unless where there are greater facilities of ingress and egress, and more extended, constant, and direct intercommunications with foreign ports, and every part of our interior, than are to be found in any other locality in the nation? When the canals which are now in progress shall be completed, there will be a direct inland water communication between this port and every village of note in the extended country West of the Allegheny Mountains. Already one-third part of all the foreign goods brought into the United States are entered at this port, and here put up for merchants in every part of the Union." *The Address of the Executive Committee of the American Tract Society to the Christian Public* (New York: American Tract Society, 1825), 10.

47. The AASS has obvious links—both in terms of abstract ideology and concrete personnel—to the two other benevolent organizations devoted to mass publishing projects in these years: the American Tract Society (ATS) and the American Bible Society (ABS), which were financed at different times from the same sources of (Congregationalist, New York-based, merchant) wealth that would ultimately fund the AASS. The Tract Society was devoted to the mass production of cheap, ephemeral pamphlets, and the mantra "read and circulate" (later adopted by the AASS) came directly from them. The ABS, on the other hand, was invested in the far more specialized project of placing a Bible in the hands of every American family. The Tract Society thus innovated most compellingly in terms of (mass) production, but the ABS, while it had to produce a large number of Bibles (and did so by building in its headquarters one of the first mass printing facilities in New York City), also focused on totalized dissemination. Indeed, the ABS seems to be the first organization in the age of mass production to fantasize the complete and total saturation of the U.S. with a single text, expressing a desire to reach everyone (white) in America. The AASS emerged in the historical wake of these other institutions and then did its work alongside them as they, like it, grew into well-capitalized affairs in the heart of Manhattan—the same location, not coincidentally, from which publishing concerns like the Harper Brothers built their antebellum empires. See David Paul Nord, *Faith in Reading: Religious Publishing and the Birth of Mass Media in America* (New York: Oxford University Press, 2004); and Peter J. Wosh, *Spreading the Word: The Bible Business in Nineteenth-Century America* (Ithaca: Cornell University Press, 1994).

48. *LWGG*, 1:463–64.

49. I borrow this phrase (and part of my argument) from Nancy Fraser. See "Rethinking the Public Sphere: A Contribution to the Critique of Actually Existing Democracy" in *Habermas and the Public Sphere*, ed. Calhoun, 109–42. Christopher Castiglia makes a similar point about the amaterialism of public sphere theory in "Abolition's Racial Interiors and the Making of White Civic Depth," *American Literary History* 14, no. 1 (2002): 32–59.

50. AASS, *Sixth Annual Report* (New York: AASS, 1839), 51.

51. Barnes and Dumond, "Introduction," *LWGG*, 1:xii. This process was not unilinear, however. According to Barnes and Dumond, the AASS believed in the "'*neighborhood influence*'" "'for which nothing can be made a substitute . . . as information is thus carried where our editors and lecturers are utterly unable to penetrate.' As the number of volunteer workers increased [at the local level], agents were [eventually] withdrawn; and by 1840 the thousands of petition volunteers possessed the field. . . . Once the volunteers had rightly learned how to circulate petitions and send them in, central command of their labors was no longer necessary" (xiii). Thus after 1838, state and national societies ceded control of petitions to local groups. "Thereafter petitions were printed in blank on village presses, circulated in the neighborhoods, and transmitted directly to" congressmen (xiii).

52. Weld was often pressed to train field agents but by the late 1830s he declined to do so. Unlike others in the AASS, Weld believed agents could be picked and prepared via "correspondence" rather than on-the-spot seminars. *LWGG*, 2:773.

53. See, for example, Fanuzzi, *Abolition's Public Sphere*, 83–128.

54. *LWGG*, 1:460. See also 1:459–63.

55. As the *First Annual Report* notes, there had been "no concentration of effort, no kindling up of general sympathy" before the New England Anti-Slavery Society opened its doors in 1833. In establishing itself in New York, the AASS hoped to extend the New England example further through the union. AASS, *First Annual Report* (1834), 39.

56. The cent-a-week society is one example of how the AASS channeled money upward from grass-roots locations after the Panic of 1837 dried up large philanthropic donations. As one instructional manual notes, "Lecturers who speak in [God's] behalf must live, and books and tracts cost money. The past irregular contributions have been insufficient, and we have pressing calls for *enlarged* operations." Nathaniel Southard, *Why Work for the Slave? Addressed to the Treasurers and Collectors in the Anti-Slavery Cent-a-Week Societies* (New York: AASS, 1838), front flyleaf.

57. The funds generated and spent (mostly on printing) by the AASS are astounding. In their first year, they spent just over $1,048, but just three years later, they reported expenditures of $38,304. These funds were raised by collecting local donations, dunning auxiliaries, and targeting wealthy philanthropists—a

project managed by the society's "financial officer," one of many administrative posts that proliferated in the New York office between 1833 and 1840. For a minute accounting of the AASS's financial status, see the *Annual Reports* for 1833–40.

58. Ronald Zboray makes a similar point: as a national literature emerged, he argues, so did "many different 'publics.' . . . Economic development had fragmented the reading public by age, gender, ethnicity, region, occupation, and class." See Ronald J. Zboray, *A Fictive People: Antebellum Economic Development and the American Reading Public* (New York: Oxford University Press, 1993), 192.

59. For a discussion of these demographic groups, see the *Second Annual Report* (1835), 48–53.

60. AASS, *Fourth Annual Report* (1837), 58–59. On the distinctive regional strategies pursued later in this period by the Harpers, see Zboray, *A Fictive People*, 62–65.

61. AASS, *First Annual Report* (1834), 41. The Constitution and the Declaration of Sentiments adopted in 1833 famously describes the material practice that came to be associated with immediate abolition: "We shall organize Anti-Slavery Societies, if possible, in every city, town and village, in our land. We shall send forth agents to lift up the voice of remonstrance, of warning, of entreaty, and in rebuke. We shall circulate, unsparingly and extensively, anti-slavery tracts and periodicals. We shall enlist the pulpit and the press in the cause of the suffering and the dumb. . . . We shall spare no exertions nor means to bring the whole nation to speedy repentance." *The Constitution of the American Anti-Slavery Society* (New York: AASS, 1838), 8–9.

62. AASS, *Second Annual Report* (1835), 53.

63. AASS, *First Annual Report* (1834), 41.

64. AASS, *Second Annual Report* (1835), 48.

65. AASS, *The Slave's Friend*, vol. 1 (1836).

66. *Minutes*, First Session (1794), 17.

67. AASS, *First Annual Report* (1834), 22.

68. AASS, *Second Annual Report* (1835), 6. Birney's comments echo and affirm the AASS's generalized message in these years. For a similar argument, see the AASS *Third Annual Report* (1836), where Gerrit Smith speaks on "the often-repeated declaration, that the Northern States have nothing to do with slavery" (11). "Do none of those, who object to our suffering our compassions to stray so far as into the Southern States, aid in the Foreign Missionary enterprise? Are none of them enlisted in the blessed work of lifting up the wretched Hindoo and Burman, and Sandwich Islander out of their deep degradation; and of turning them from their idols to serve the living God. But, how much more remote are these objects of their charity than are the Southern slaves! The great distance of the slaves from us cannot be the real objection to our interesting our hearts in

their condition: for such an objection is never raised to our sympathizing with those who are far more remote from us" (12).

69. AASS, *Second Annual Report* (1835), 7.

70. Birney's attack on the logic of "elsewhere" is also a handy critique of colonization, which posits a foreign outside as a solution to the domestic, or "inside," problem of emancipation. The AASS consistently removed the line between insides and outsides, heres and theres, in order to argue (as Birney does here) that every place is the same as every other place. Birney was a particularly compelling figure to make this argument, for he was himself a southerner (having lived in Kentucky and Alabama) and thus spoke with the authority of personal experience. Once a devoted colonizationist, Birney was the most nationally visible of the AASS's converts to immediatism. For similar "nationalist" arguments on the interconnectedness of North and South, see Charles C. Burleigh, *Slavery and the North* (New York: AASS, 1855); and Susan C. Cabot, *What Have We, as Individuals, to Do with Slavery?* (New York: AASS, 1855).

71. AASS, *Second Annual Report* (1835), 7.

72. United States Constitution (art. 1, sec. 8).

73. Fanuzzi, *Abolition's Public Sphere*, xxi. Fanuzzi's primary sources are *The Liberator* and the work of the New England Anti-Slavery Society of the 1830s, '40s, and '50s—not the American Anti-Slavery Society of the 1830s. Nevertheless, since he frames his argument in relation to a generalized abolitionist "public sphere," his work merits attention here.

74. The capital's response was to refuse the inversion: Congress issued a gag order on the issue of slavery that stayed in effect from 1836 to 1844; during this period, petitions were accumulated but "laid on the table" and ignored. The gag was formally repealed in 1844, but Washington's brief refusal to engage its politically active periphery created fodder for the abolitionist side of the argument: "As to those petitions, now piled up in monumental security . . . we have heard of the great library in Egypt, of seven hundred thousand volumes; but here is a library of seven hundred thousand authors, and all on one subject, all for humanity, and there is not a trifling thought or an insignificant word in all that vast collection." AASS, *Fifth Annual Report* (1838), 41. See William Lee Miller, *Arguing about Slavery: The Great Battle in the United States Congress* (New York: Knopf, 1996).

75. The AASS's investment in print peaked in 1835. Resistance to mass mail campaigns helped revive interest in the use of lecturers, leading to the indoctrination of "The Seventy" (a newly trained corps of antislavery agents). The Seventy were, however, imbricated in the already existing apparatus of the society, a large part of which involved printed appeals.

76. John uses this episode to describe the limits of "imagined community." *Spreading the News*, 257–80.

77. Lewis Tappan was by no means a conventional author, even though he

did write and publish frequently. Indeed, if his life has a distinct literary location, it must be in his handwritten manuscripts, a series of elaborate and meticulously kept letter books and diaries that left a comprehensive record of his work as a reader, editor, publisher, and consumer of antebellum culture of many different kinds (including picture galleries, theaters, and factory tours). But he was an especially avid reader, and his journals describe in detail the delight Tappan took in reading new titles as they came off the press, from Franklin's *Life*, to the first edition of a "pamphlet" called *The Sketch-Book*, to Cooper's *The Spy*—many of which he read out loud to his family in the evenings. In the pleasure he takes in his literacy and in his steadfast desire to become a coherent and virtuous middle-class self through the practice of keeping a diary, Tappan resembles the clerks described by Thomas Augst in *The Clerk's Tale: Young Men and Moral Life in Nineteenth-Century America* (Chicago: University of Chicago Press, 2003). On Tappan's administrative skills, see Lawrence J. Friedman, "Confidence and Pertinacity in Evangelical Abolitionism: Lewis Tappan's Circle," *American Quarterly* 31, no. 1 (1979): 81–106.

78. Bertram Wyatt-Brown, *Lewis Tappan and the Evangelical War against Slavery* (1969; Baton Rouge: Louisiana State University Press, 1997), 143–44.

79. *The Papers of Lewis Tappan* [microform] (Washington, DC: Library of Congress, 1975). Tappan's journals date from 1814 to 1869, but my discussion here refers to those that cover the years 1828–40.

80. Wyatt-Brown notes that in 1835 "monthly costs rose to nearly one thousand dollars for printing alone, four times the sum expended on the lecture tours of salaried agents. Twenty-five to fifty thousand copies of each publication rolled off the presses each week. . . . By mid-July . . . great bundles of papers, numbering 175,000 separate items, piled up in the New York City post office, awaiting delivery to hundreds of communities over the nation." AASS printed over a million impressions of antislavery literature in 1835, and in this way, antislavery became "a subject no American could ignore." *Lewis Tappan*, 144–45. Henry Mayer likewise notes that the AASS made a strategic decision to "spend far more on printing than on lecture agents, but the pamphlets would, with the help of new railroads and improved postal service, carry the word faster and prepare the ground for the organizers. Use of the mails, moreover, would enable the AASS to get its message to ministers, legislators, and editors in the South, where—all agreed—it would be too risky to assign field agents." The decision to outsource AASS's printing jobs to a steam press may have been influenced by the fact that the society had recently moved into new quarters right across the street from the legendary four-story Harper and Brothers establishment, which used multiple steam presses and employed masses of workers. *All on Fire*, 195. New steam technology was an effective use of antislavery capital. The *First Annual Report* states that in 1833 the society printed an estimated 25,000 copies of the *Anti-Slavery Reporter* but only managed to distribute half of these (41). By 1835, it produced

and distributed hundreds of thousands of similar periodicals, primarily via U.S. mail, which used rail and steam routes in much of its delivery. In July alone, the society printed 175,000 pieces, well more than had been printed in the entire year before. Some 20,000 of these were targeted for the South via directories. For precise accountings of how much money was invested in print campaigns in these years, see economic disclosures in AASS, *First, Second,* and *Third Annual Reports* (1834, 1835, and 1836).

81. AASS, *Third Annual Report* (1836), 35.

82. Aware that federal law required postal officers to deliver every newspaper that had "been issued in the proper format," the AASS took special care "to issue two of their four major publications, the *Emancipator* and the *Anti-Slavery Record,* in a newspaper format, and to issue their two other principal publications . . . in a magazine format that was indistinguishable . . . from [the] many magazines that postal officers routinely admitted into the mail" under the newspaper regulation. John, *Spreading the News,* 261, 262.

83. Wolfgang Schivelbusch, *The Railway Journey: Trains and Travel in the 19th Century,* trans. Anselm Hollo (New York: Urizen, 1979), 48; and John, *Spreading the News,* 257–80.

84. 1836 Journal, in *The Papers of Lewis Tappan* [microform].

85. *New-York Tribune,* 26 April 1844.

86. Leonard L. Richards, *Gentlemen of Property and Standing: Anti-Abolition Mobs in Jacksonian America* (New York: Oxford University Press, 1970), 17; Mayer, *All on Fire,* 196–99; John, *Spreading the Word,* 257–80; *The Narrative of Amos Dresser* (New York: AASS, 1836).

87. "Letter of the Executive Committee of the American Anti-Slavery Society to the Executive Committee of the Ohio Anti-Slavery Society," reprinted in *A Collection of Valuable Documents* (Boston: Isaac Knapp, 1836), 70.

88. John C. Nerone cites 134 cases of antiabolitionist violence, many directed against printers, presses, editors, lecturers, and newspapers. *Violence Against the Press: Policing the Public Sphere in U.S. History* (New York: Oxford University Press, 1994), 93.

89. Richards, *Gentlemen of Property and Standing,* 91–92.

90. Cited and described in ibid., 95–100.

91. *Alton Trials* (New York: J. F. Trow, 1838), 95–96. Lovejoy's family further linked abolition with freedom of the press and the free circulation of ideas by titling his posthumous autobiography *The Memoir of the Rev. Elijah P. Lovejoy, Who Was Murdered in Defence of the Liberty of the Press at Alton, Illinois, Nov. 7, 1837,* ed. Joseph C. and Owen Lovejoy (New York: John S. Taylor, 1838).

92. "Address to the Young Men's Lyceum of Springfield, Illinois," in *Speeches and Writings of Abraham Lincoln,* ed. Don E. Fehrenbacher, 2 vols. (New York: Library of America, 1989), 1:29.

93. Richards, *Gentlemen of Property and Standing,* 27–28.

94. *Richmond Whig*, 23 August 1835. The speech was delivered on 22 August at the Gloucester Courthouse in Virginia and is quoted at greater length in Richards, *Gentlemen of Property and Standing*, 56–57.

95. Richards, *Gentlemen of Property and Standing*, 59.

96. Describing the execution of the Fugitive Slave clause of the Constitution, the article insists: "the very fact that innocent men are imprisoned among us, in the name of LAW and the CONSTITUTION, *to support slavery*, is proof superlative that we *have* something to do with slavery." *Anti-Slavery Record* 1, no. 6 (June 1835): 61.

97. Richards, *Gentlemen of Property and Standing*, 32, 42.

98. Ibid., 43. *Cincinnati Daily Gazette*, 17 September 1841. Of one disrupted abolitionist meeting, Richards notes that the abolitionists dispersed and reconvened elsewhere, but the antislavery mob found a black janitor on the premises and forced him to play the part of Arthur Tappan in a mock meeting. In this way, the mob inserted a free black man in the place of a white one, performing the feared outcome of abolitionist meddling even as they passed a series of mock resolutions against "immediate amalgamation" (29–30).

99. The term "miscegenation" was coined in the 1860s and replaced the popular antebellum variant, "amalgamation." See Richards, *Gentlemen of Property and Standing*, 30–32, 40–46, 94–95, 114–15, 122, 166; and Linda K. Kerber, "Abolitionists and Amalgamators: The New York City Race Riots of 1834," *New York History* 48 (1967): 28–39. Kerber points out that these riots staged a class conflict between white men in urban areas; I would add that they also stage a regional conflict between white men of different locations.

100. On the ways that race relations manage conflicts between white men, see David R. Roediger, *The Wages of Whiteness: Race and the Making of the American Working Class* (New York: Verso, 1991); and Eric Lott, *Love and Theft: Blackface Minstrelsy and the American Working Class* (New York: Oxford University Press, 1993).

101. Eva Saks makes a similar point, arguing that miscegenation was a site for working out (legally) the competing claims of federalism. "Representing Miscegenation Law," *Raritan* 8, no. 2 (1988): 39–69. On the phantasmatic relation of mixed racial bodies to the political project of the union, see also Shirley Samuels, "Miscegenated America: The Civil War," *American Literary History* 9, no. 3 (1997): 482–501.

102. As Hamilton noted, "under the regular and gentle influence of general laws, these varying interests will be constantly assimilating, till they embrace each other, and assume the same complexion." *PAH*, 5:57–58.

103. Saks makes this point nicely in "Representing Miscegenation Law," noting that "the human body often stands for the national body" and concluding that in the Reconstruction period, "the jurisprudence of miscegenation was the site for working out political issues of federalism and race, and the human body

the fractured medium of this struggle" (42). My work here suggests the ways that states' rights and white supremacy were linked even at a much earlier date.

104. As Fanuzzi points out, Garrison was the epitome of this model of production. Four years earlier, when southerners heard that Garrison had begun publishing *The Liberator* in Boston, they sent a letter to Boston's mayor requesting that the paper be shut down. When Otis looked into the charge, all he found was a one room office in which Garrison and his partner both lived and worked, serving a subscription list of less than 300. The single hand-cranked printing press on which *The Liberator* was produced required both men to do their own presswork, folding, bundling, and mailing—a process that took up hundreds of hours in the production of a single number. Otis later recalled that in 1831 "no member of the city government, nor any person of my acquaintance, had ever heard of the publication." Mayer, *All on Fire*, 114. On the restricted scope of *The Liberator*'s circulation, see also Augusta Rohrbach, *Truth Stranger than Fiction: Race, Realism, and the US Literary Marketplace* (New York: Palgrave, 2002), 3–4.

105. New York antislavery workers treated these distant and dispersed threats as if they were immediate and local. Both Tappans sent their families out of the city, Arthur Tappan's neighborhood was patrolled by special police units, and Elizur Wright used "bars and planks an inch thick" to block the doors into the society's office, which he also evacuated of all printed materials, for fear that it would be looted and the capital invested in it lost. Mayer, *All on Fire*, 196–97; and John, *Spreading the Word*, 257–80.

106. Gilmore, *Reading Becomes a Necessity of Life*; Isabelle Lehuu, *Carnival on the Page: Popular Print Media in Antebellum America* (Chapel Hill: University of North Carolina Press, 2000); Starr, *Creation of the Media*; and Zboray, *A Fictive People*. Zboray notes that even as late as 1850 the illiteracy rate in the Old South was 1 in every 16 white adults (compared to 1 in every 156 elsewhere), 196.

107. As Mayer writes, "ninety thousand bales of Southern cotton were unloaded in Boston in 1835, double the amount of five years earlier. Arrayed in bulky stacks that stood higher than houses, the crop symbolized a commercial alliance with slavery that turned the staple crop into factory milled textiles for the inland market, with the Boston Lowells and Lawrences profiting not only from the work of the mill towns that bore their names but the railroads that carried the products across the region. Rail lines to Worcester, Lowell, and Providence all began operations from Boston in 1835 that would soon give the city a western rail connection to Albany and Buffalo and put the market of the Great Lakes basin within its reach." *All on Fire*, 192–93.

108. Weld's early letters to his antislavery peers catalogue the trauma these early travels inscribed on his body. In one case, he survived a life threatening carriage accident. He also suffered many bouts of illness and fatigue before his voice finally gave out in 1836. In later years, the Agency Committee would repeatedly attempt to reenlist Weld's voice and body in the cause, asking him to travel across

the country locating and training new agents. Weld refused these requests after his marriage, however, preferring the fixities of the center to the mobility of the field. See *LWGG*, 2:773.

109. Catherine H. Birney, *The Grimké Sisters: Sarah and Angelina Grimké, the First American Women Advocates of Abolition and Woman's Rights* (New York: C.T. Dillingham, 1885), 258.

110. Ibid.

111. *LWGG*, 2:835. See also Benjamin Platt Thomas, *Theodore Weld, Crusader for Freedom* (New Brunswick: Rutgers University Press, 1950), 174.

112. On Dickens's use of Weld, see Louise H. Johnson, "The Source of the Chapter on Slavery in Dickens's *American Notes*," *American Literature* 14, no. 4 (1943): 427–30; and McGill, *American Literature and the Culture of Reprinting*, 127–29.

113. Reprinted in *The Emancipator*, 13 June 1839.

114. Thomas, *Theodore Weld*, 171–72.

115. Sarah Grimké to Elizabeth Pease, 10 April 1839, in Larry Ceplair, ed., *The Public Years of Sarah and Angelina Grimké: Selected Writings, 1835–1839* (New York: Columbia University Press, 1989), 331–32. In 1838, Lydia Maria Child "confided" to Weld her desire to touch and see the workings of slavery up close: "I have often wished you could collect a variety of the instruments of torture used, and deposit them at the A.S. Office. I believe such a collection would do a vast deal of good." *Slavery as It Is* was, in a sense, the fulfillment of this museumizing fantasy, a wish to gather material objects that was transformed, in Weld's hands, into a collection of material facts. See Stephen H. Browne, "'Like Gory Spectres': Representing Evil in Theodore Weld's *American Slavery as It Is*," *Quarterly Journal of Speech* 80 (1994): 283.

116. Browne, "'Like Gory Spectres,'" 279. See also Castiglia, "Abolition's Racial Interiors." While I focus on the literal production of home spaces and far-off spaces, Castiglia describes the more affective center of abolitionist subjectivity and interiority—self-production as opposed to home-production.

117. Sarah Grimké to Jane Smith, 24 January 1838. Cited in Thomas, *Theodore Weld*, 168–69. See also Sarah Grimké to Elizabeth Pease, 10 April 1839, in Ceplair, ed., *Public Years of Sarah and Angelina Grimké*, 331–32.

118. See, for instance, Wyatt-Brown, *Lewis Tappan*, 185–204.

119. AASS, *Sixth Annual Report* (1839), 36.

120. The 1839 *Annual Report* notes that the most "correct index" of antislavery sentiment throughout the country "is the patronage of the Anti-Slavery press, and the yielding of the ordinary newspaper press to become the channel of Anti-Slavery discussion. There now exist not less than 9 weekly, 1 semi-monthly, and 4 monthly papers, mainly, if not exclusively, devoted to abolition." The circulation of these papers was estimated then at 25,000 copies, with subscriptions each year amounting to $40,000. AASS, *Sixth Annual Report* (1839), 51.

Chapter 7. Slavery on the Move

1. On the material history of *Uncle Tom's Cabin*, see Susan Geary, "The Domestic Novel as a Commercial Commodity: Making a Best Seller in the 1850s," *The Papers of the Bibliographical Society of America* 70, no. 3 (1976): 365–93; Thomas F. Gossett, *Uncle Tom's Cabin and American Culture* (Dallas: Southern Methodist University Press, 1985), 185–211; E. Bruce Kirkham, *The Building of Uncle Tom's Cabin* (Knoxville: University of Tennessee Press, 1977); Susan Belasco Smith, "Serialization and the Nature of *Uncle Tom's Cabin*," in *Periodical Literature in Nineteenth-Century America*, ed. Kenneth M. Price and Susan Belasco Smith (Charlottesville: University Press of Virginia, 1995), 69–89; and Michael Winship, "'The Greatest Book of Its Kind': A Publishing History of *Uncle Tom's Cabin*" (Worcester, MA: American Antiquarian Society, 1999). The novel saturated the North and West in cheap and ornate editions, popular ephemera, and stage adaptations, and while evidence of southern circulation is "sketchy," it clearly did circulate in the South, with notably large orders documented in Mississippi, New Orleans, and Georgia. Cindy Weinstein, "*Uncle Tom's Cabin* and the South" in *Cambridge Companion to Harriet Beecher Stowe*, ed. Cindy Weinstein (New York: Cambridge University Press, 2004), 39–57. Frederick Law Olmsted recalled seeing it sold on southern steamboats: "Among the peddlers there were two of 'cheap literature,' and among their yellow covers, each had two or three copies of the cheap edition (pamphlet) of Uncle Tom's Cabin. They did not cry it out as they did the other books they had, but held it forth among others, so its title could be seen. One of them told me he carried it because gentlemen often inquired for it, and he sold a good many: at least three copies were sold to passengers on the boat." *A Journey in the Seaboard Slave States* (New York: Dix and Edwards, 1856), 606.

2. *Independent*, 13 May 1852.

3. On the culture industry generated by *Uncle Tom's Cabin* in the nineteenth century, see Lott, *Love and Theft*, 211–33; Gossett, *Uncle Tom's Cabin and American Culture*, 164–84; and Ronald J. Zboray and Mary Saracino Zboray, "Books, Reading, and the World of Goods in Antebellum New England," *American Quarterly* 48, no. 4 (1996): 587–622.

4. For a description of cross-regional book distribution in the 1850s, see Zboray, *A Fictive People*, 55–68.

5. Meinig, *Shaping of America*, 2:346.

6. Schivelbusch, *Railway Journey*, 197; Meinig, *Shaping of America*, 2:347.

7. On these developments, see Don E. Fehrenbacher, *The Dred Scott Case: Its Significance in American Law and Politics* (New York: Oxford University Press, 1978).

8. Anthony Burns was the last fugitive to be removed from Massachusetts under the Fugitive Slave Law. For a contemporary account, see Charles Emery

Stevens's 1856 *Anthony Burns: A History* (New York: Negro Universities Press, 1969). See also Albert J. Von Frank, *The Trials of Anthony Burns: Freedom and Slavery in Emerson's Boston* (Cambridge: Harvard University Press, 1998); Stanley W. Campbell, *The Slave Catchers: Enforcement of the Fugitive Slave Law, 1850–1860* (Chapel Hill: University of North Carolina Press, 1970), 124–32; Jane H. Pease and William H. Pease, *The Fugitive Slave Law and Anthony Burns: A Problem in Law Enforcement* (Philadelphia: J. B. Lippincott, 1975). According to Campbell, "the cost to the government for the rendition of Burns has been a matter of considerable speculation" (130). In citing the cost at $50,000, I follow the Peases' estimate (52).

9. Austin Bearse, *Reminiscences of Fugitive-Slave Law Days in Boston* (Boston: Printed by W. Richardson, 1880), 15.

10. Walt Whitman, *Leaves of Grass* (Brooklyn: s.n., 1855), 89–90.

11. Stevens, *Anthony Burns*, 273–74; Campbell, *Slave Catchers*, 127; Von Frank, *Trials of Anthony Burns*, 72.

12. Berlant, *Anatomy of National Fantasy*, 13.

13. U.S. Constitution, art. 4, sec. 2, clause 3 (1787). This clause remained in effect until the adoption of the Thirteenth Amendment, but Congress passed a Fugitive Slave Bill in 1793 elaborating on the constitutional provisions.

14. On the human body as the base unit of analogy for larger political systems, see Mary Douglas, *Natural Symbols: Explorations in Cosmology* (1970; New York: Routledge, 1996).

15. Hardt and Negri, *Empire*, 160–82.

16. Lisa C. Brawley, "Fugitive Nation: Slavery, Travel and Technologies of American Identity, 1830–1860" (Ph.D. diss., University of Chicago, 1995). See also Fergus M. Bordewich, *Bound For Canaan: The Underground Railroad and the War for the Soul of America* (New York: Amistad, 2005); John Hope Franklin and Loren Schweninger, *Runaway Slaves: Rebels on the Plantation* (New York: Oxford University Press, 1999); David Waldstreicher, *Runaway America: Benjamin Franklin, Slavery, and the American Revolution* (New York: Hill and Wang, 2004).

17. Brawley, "Fugitive Nation," 258–60.

18. William Still, *The Underground Rail Road* (Philadelphia: Porter and Coates, 1872).

19. "The shelves of booksellers groan under the weight of Sambo's woes, done up in covers!" "Black Letters; Or Uncle Tom-Foolery in Literature," *Grahams Magazine* 42 (February 1853): 209.

20. Lydia Maria Child, *Letters of Lydia Maria Child* (Boston: Houghton, Mifflin, and Company, 1883), 58.

21. On Anthony, see *PJM*, 9:153–55, 10:118–19, and 11:208, 235–36, 247–48. On conditions attending escape and recovery in 1780s Virginia, see Lathan Algerna Windley, "A Profile of Runaway Slaves in Virginia and South Carolina from 1730 through 1787" (Ph.D. diss., University of Iowa, 1974).

22. Franklin and Schweninger, *Runaway Slaves*, 109–23.

23. *The Thirteenth Annual Report of the American & Foreign Anti-Slavery Society* (New York: Lewis J. Bates, 1853), 193.

24. Harriet Beecher Stowe, *Uncle Tom's Cabin; or, Life Among the Lowly* (Cambridge: Belknap, 1962), 444.

25. William Lloyd Garrison, *Thoughts on African Colonization* (Boston: Garrison and Knapp, 1832).

26. *Liberator*, 26 March 1852. On the reception of Stowe's ending, see Robert S. Levine, "*Uncle Tom's Cabin* in *Frederick Douglass' Paper*: An Analysis of Reception," *American Literature* 64, no. 1 (1992): 71–93.

27. Harriet Beecher Stowe, *First Geography for Children* (Boston: Phillips, Sampson, and Company, 1855).

28. Wendell Phillips describes a similar scene of national collapse in 1857, the very wording of which echoes Stowe's slave auction chapter: "The New York pulpit is today one end of a magnetic telegraph, of which the New Orleans cotton market is the other. The New York stock market is one end of the magnetic telegraph, and the Charleston *Mercury* is the other." Wendell Phillips, *Speech . . . at the Worcester Disunion Convention, January 15, 1857* (Boston: AASS, 1857).

29. Amy Kaplan, "Manifest Domesticity," *American Literature* 70, no. 3 (1998): 602. See also Kaplan, *Anarchy of Empire*, 23–50.

30. Kaplan, "Manifest Domesticity," 602.

31. Harvey, "The Spatial Fix," 284–311.

32. Cited in Kaplan, "Manifest Domesticity," 590.

33. Berger, *The Look of Things*, 40.

34. Cindy Weinstein notes that the reception of *Uncle Tom's Cabin* raised questions "about the very nature of evidence itself" (85). *Family, Kinship, and Sympathy in Nineteenth-Century American Literature* (New York: Cambridge University Press, 2004).

35. On the documentary burden placed on African-American narrative by organized abolition, see William L. Andrews, "The Novelization of Voice in Early African American Narrative," *PMLA* 105, no. 1 (1990): 23–34 (esp. 23–24); Barbara Foley, "History, Fiction, and the Ground Between: The Uses of the Documentary Mode in Black Literature," *PMLA* 95, no. 3 (1980): 389–403 (esp. 392); and Robert B. Stepto, *From Behind the Veil: A Study of Afro-American Narrative* (1979; Urbana: University of Illinois Press, 1991), 3–31.

36. Douglass wryly refers to himself as "a brand new fact" when he is "introduced to the Abolitionists" in *My Bondage and My Freedom* (New York: Miller, Orton, and Mulligan, 1855), 361. On Jacobs's resistance to Stowe, see Jean Fagan Yellin, introduction to *Incidents in the Life of a Slave Girl Written by Herself* (Cambridge: Harvard University Press, 1987), xviii–xix.

37. Kidnapping was common from the eighteenth century to the 1850s. See,

for example, Daniel E. Meaders, comp., *Kidnappers in Philadelphia: Isaac Hopper's Tales of Oppression, 1780–1843* (New York: Garland, 1994).

38. Solomon Northup, *Twelve Years a Slave: Narrative of Solomon Northup* (Baton Rouge: Louisiana State University Press, 1968).

39. *Frederick Douglass' Paper*, 4 August 1854.

40. Ibid., 26 August and 9 September 1853. The book was successful enough to be cited in a magazine article about how ordinary people might become writers. Northup's circulation numbers (cited at 20,000) are listed alongside those of other antebellum bestsellers, including Fanny Fern's *Fern Leaves* (45,000) and Ik Marvel's *Reveries of a Bachelor* (70,000). The same article details how Stowe spent her writing profits. William T. Coggeshall, "Labor and Luck of Authors," *The Ladies' Repository: A Monthly Periodical, Devoted to Literature, Arts, and Religion* 19, no. 1 (1859): 20–24.

41. Journalists were especially intrigued by potential links between Northup and Uncle Tom. The *New York Daily Times* for 20 January 1853 remarks that "the condition of this colored man [while living on the Red River] was of a character nearly approaching that described by Mrs. Stowe, as the condition of 'Uncle Tom,' while in that region."

42. William Wells Brown, *Clotel; or, The President's Daughter: A Narrative of Slave Life in the United States* (London: Partridge and Oakey, 1853), 176.

43. On the problem of fact versus fiction in *Clotel*, see Andrews, "The Novelization of Voice," 23–34; Peter A. Dorsey, "De-Authorizing Slavery: Realism in Stowe's *Uncle Tom's Cabin* and Brown's *Clotel*," *ESQ: A Journal of the American Renaissance* 41, no. 4 (1995): 256–88; Ann duCille, *The Coupling Convention: Sex, Text and Tradition in Black Women's Fiction* (New York: Oxford University Press, 1993), 17–29; Foley, "History, Fiction, and the Ground Between," 389–403; Robert S. Levine, introduction to *Clotel; or The President's Daughter* by William Wells Brown (New York: Bedford/St. Martin's, 2000), 3–27; Carla L. Peterson, "Capitalism, Black (Under)Development, and the Production of the African-American Novel in the 1850s," *American Literary History* 4, no. 4 (1992): 559–83; Lee Schweninger, "*Clotel* and the Historicity of the Anecdote," *MELUS* 24, no. 1 (1999): 21–36; Stepto, *From Behind the Veil*, 3–31. On identity, see Paul Gilmore, *The Genuine Article: Race, Mass Culture, and American Literary Manhood* (Durham: Duke University Press, 2001), 37–66; Levine, introduction to *Clotel*, 3–27; Robert Reid-Pharr, *Conjugal Union: The Body, the House, and the Black American* (New York: Oxford University Press, 1999), 37–64; and Peterson, "Capitalism."

44. On the African-American shift to fiction after 1850, see Peterson, "Capitalism," 559–83; Andrews, "The Novelization of Voice," 23–34; and Richard Yarborough, "The First-Person in Afro-American Fiction," in *Afro-American Literary Study in the 1990s*, ed. Houston A. Baker, Jr. and Patricia Redmond (Chicago: University of Chicago Press, 1989), 105–21.

45. Lara Langer Cohen, "Counterfeit Presentments: Fraud and the Production of Nineteenth-Century American Literature" (Ph.D. diss., Yale University, 2006), 138–92.

46. *Liberator*, 8 September 1837.

47. *Liberator*, 24 April 1857.

48. *North Star*, 1 March 1850.

49. For other 1850s slave imposters, see *Anti-Slavery Standard*, 31 October 1850; *Frederick Douglass' Paper*, 10 February 1854; [Toronto] *Provincial Freeman*, 17 June 1854; *Frederick Douglass' Paper*, 17 August 1855; and *Provincial Freeman*, 29 September 1855 and 29 March 1856. Lara Cohen cites two other notable sources in "Counterfeit Presentments": "An Impudent Imposter," *Liberator*, 25 December 1857; and *New-York Tribune*, 25 January 1858. In most cases, other newspapers and their reports are prominently cited in attempts to cross-reference and contain not fugitive mobility per se but the plasticity of fugitive slave representation and the economic activities of "swindlers."

50. Samuel J. May, *Some Recollections of Our Antislavery Conflict* (Boston: Fields, Osgood, and Co., 1869), 279. W. C. Nell to William Lloyd Garrison, 24 March 1842, cited in Irving H. Bartlett, "Abolitionists, Fugitives, and Imposters in Boston, 1846–1847," *New England Quarterly* 55, no. 1 (1982): 108. Bartlett reproduces John Browne's entire 1847 diary—an invaluable document, since Browne's Agent's Record is "probably the only collection of detailed narratives written at the time by an abolitionist who was actually receiving fugitives and attempting to settle them in free society" (98). Browne provided fugitives a range of help, and the more extravagant the need, the more carefully he scrutinized the fugitive's tale, verifying it through a series of authenticating letters exchanged with anyone elsewhere who might know the fugitive's "character" and "story." Imposters' files were marked "Letter on file" for future reference (106–7). But even seasoned philanthropists were sometimes duped. Browne's Record details the exploits of "one William Brown" who received money and clothing in Boston but later traveled through New York State raising money under the aliases "Dr. Brown" and "Professor Brown." Feeling himself tricked by Brown, Samuel May placed an article in *The Liberator* identifying him as a fraud, but Brown was no common imposter: he responded by suing May and "the Fugitive Aid Society" for the libel of publicly "denouncing him as an imposter and a dishonest man." Bartlett, "Abolitionists, Fugitives, and Imposters," 109. The *Liberator* for 10 February 1860 later reported that the case was resolved in nobody's favor.

51. *Liberator*, 20 March 1846. Harriet Wilson depicts a similar scenario in *Our Nig* (1859). Here, Frado marries an abolitionist lecturer, a "fine, straight negro" who represents himself as a fugitive slave but who soon after abandons her "with the disclosure that he had never seen the South, and that his illiterate harangues were humbugs for hungry abolitionists." Harriet E. Wilson, *Our Nig; or, Sketches from the Life of a Free Black* (Boston: G. C. Rand and Avery, 1859), 127–28.

52. Dwight A. McBride, *Impossible Witnesses: Truth, Abolitionism, and Slave Testimony* (New York: New York University Press, 2001), 5.

53. Letter to the editors of the *New York Commercial Advertiser*, reprinted in *Pennsylvania Freeman*, 11 October 1838.

54. *Emancipator*, 12 April 1838. On the reception of Williams's *Narrative*, see Cohen, "Counterfeit Presentments," 138–92; and Ann Fabian, *The Unvarnished Truth: Personal Narratives in Nineteenth-Century America* (Berkeley: University of California Press, 2000), 79–86.

55. On 19 April 1838, the *Emancipator* printed a notice from the *Alabama Beacon* dated 22 March, attacking "the lying Abolition pamphlet entitled the 'Narrative of James Williams'" as "a foul fester of falsehood." The *Emancipator* responded tentatively: "We hope the editor of the Beacon will make a thorough investigation. . . . The story of James Williams made a strong impression of truthfulness on the minds of all, in this city, who heard it from his lips. If it is a 'foul fester of falsehood,' we shall be glad to be undeceived."

56. On 25 October 1838, the *Emancipator* announced that some "statements in the narrative . . . are wholly false" and discontinued future sales. Nevertheless, the *Narrative* was reinstated the following year and advertised and discussed in such papers as the [Cincinnati] *Philanthropist* (7 and 21 May 1839) and the *African Repository and Colonial Journal* (June 1839). It continued to be sold by the AASS alongside an array of other volumes, both fictional and nonfictional, throughout the 1840s and 1850s.

57. Douglass is the gold standard of authenticity, but even his *Narrative* was attacked as a "catalogue of lies." See Albert E. Stone, "Identity and Art in Frederick Douglass's *Narrative*," in *Critical Essays on Frederick Douglass*, ed. William L. Andrews (Boston: G. K. Hall, 1991), 66–67.

58. Walter Johnson, "The Slave Trader, the White Slave, and the Politics of Racial Determination in the 1850s," *Journal of American History* 87, no. 1 (2000): 13–38; and Ariela J. Gross, "Litigating Whiteness: Trials of Racial Determination in the Nineteenth-Century South," *Yale Law Journal* 108, no. 1 (1998): 109–88. These cases were followed in the North in both the abolitionist and mainstream press. See *Liberator*, 15 December 1837, which reprints an article from the *New York Sun* describing a racial determination suit in Kentucky in which the judge "excluded all evidence founded on reputation, and placed the verdict of the jury on the presence or absence of any of the characteristics of the African," after which the woman was "set free."

59. Fugitive Slave Act of 1850, ch. 60, 9 Stat. 462 (repealed 1864) (amending the Fugitive Slave Act of 1793).

60. George M. Stroud, *A Sketch of the Laws Relating to Slavery in the Several States of the United States of America*, 2d ed. (Philadelphia: Henry Longstreth, 1856), 276–77. Stroud goes on to describe a case of mistaken identity, in which the wrong man was sent into slavery.

61. On these and other problems, see Lysander Spooner, *A Defence for Fugitive Slaves* (Boston: B. Marsh, 1850). Spooner derides the law for "shutting the mouth of an accused person, and compelling him to rely on such stray evidence as may chance to fall in his way" (23). On the law's vague references to "satisfactory proof" "made by '*affidavit*' alone," see esp. 18–19, 23. On the likelihood of mistaking "*the identity* of the person arrested with the person escaped," see 19. For a comprehensive record of cases executed under the Fugitive Slave Law, including numerous examples of intentional misidentification ("kidnapping") and unintentional misidentification, see Samuel May, *The Fugitive Slave Law and Its Victims* (New York: AASS, 1856).

62. Samuel May reprints and rebuts Webster's remarks in *Fugitive Slave Law and Its Victims* (1856), 8.

63. England compared favorably to the United States in these years, not just because of its distance and legal protections, but because of its less racist social reception of American fugitives, including Brown. See "Return of William Wells Brown," *Provincial Freeman*, 21 October 1854.

64. Stepto, *From Behind the Veil*, 30; Andrews, "The Novelization of Voice," 33.

65. On *Clotel's* anachronisms and inconsistencies, see William E. Farrison, *William Wells Brown: Author & Reformer* (Chicago: University of Chicago Press, 1969), 215–31, esp. 218–26.

66. Notably, Brown tampers with the Weld advertisement, lifting only key phrases. See Levine, introduction to *Clotel*, 85 n8, 269–70.

67. Peterson, "Capitalism," 569.

68. On the fantasy of unmediated experience, see Joan W. Scott, "The Evidence of Experience," in *The Lesbian and Gay Studies Reader*, ed. Henry Abelove, Michèle Aina Barale, and David M. Halperin (New York: Routledge, 1993), 397–415. Like Brown, Scott contests the idea that "the facts of history speak for themselves" (400).

69. See, for example, Andrews, "The Novelization of Voice," 23–34; Dorsey, "De-Authorizing Slavery," 256–88; duCille, *The Coupling Convention*, 17–29; Levine, introduction to *Clotel*, 3–27; and Schweninger, "*Clotel* and the Historicity of the Anecdote," 21–36.

70. See, for example, *Narrative of the Life of Frederick Douglass, an American Slave. Written by Himself* (Boston: Anti-Slavery Office, 1845), 15–20; and Henry Louis Gates, Jr., *The Signifying Monkey: A Theory of Afro-American Literary Criticism* (New York: Oxford University Press, 1988), 3–88.

71. Weinstein, *Family, Kinship, and Sympathy*, 216. On identity exchange on the Underground Railroad, see Bearse, *Reminiscences of Fugitive-Slave Law Days*. Bearse moved many fugitives through Boston and into Canada after passage of the Fugitive Slave Act, and every escape involves not just a change of clothes but an exchange of identities with some local personality (usually effected through an exchange of clothes).

72. Brown was well acquainted with the Crafts' story. He was the first writer to describe their escape in northern newspaper stories and frequently lectured with them. Barbara McCaskill, "'Yours Very Truly': Ellen Craft—The Fugitive as Text and Artifact," *African American Review* 28, no. 4 (1994): 509–29.

73. Levine, introduction to *Clotel*, 6.

74. *Liberator*, 28 August 1846.

75. Brown embraces fictional fugitives within the novel form, but he also sometimes admired real-life imposters. In an 1855 letter, Brown described an encounter with a small-time confidence man who infiltrated an antislavery meeting in Portland, Maine: "Did you ever see an empty-headed, slim, thin faced, gaunt looking, well dressed coloured man who calls himself John Randolph, son of the original old Virginia[n]? I remember to have seen him in the office, previous to my going to England. On Sunday night last, while Newell Foster was looking after the '*Spirits*,' this scamp looked after the contribution box, or rather hat, helped himself, and went home." Randolph "spirited away" "some ten or twelve dollars, in silver" in plain view of Brown, who nevertheless found the episode humorous. "I had to laugh," he concludes, "at the fellow's boldness." William Wells Brown to Samuel May, 18 July 1855. Cited in W. Edward Farrison, "Phylon Profile, XVI: William Wells Brown," *Phylon* 9, no.1 (1948): 21.

76. This is the same book that Brown himself is reading at the end of his prefatory *Narrative*—the last in a series of playful crossovers between real people and novelistic characters. Like George and Mary, Brown too is approaching the shifting ground of a more open cultural world at the end of *Clotel*. The "Conclusion" is the first chapter to leave behind the American archive: rather than citing an abolitionist truism or poem as an epigraph (as every other chapter does), Brown ends with an inscription from Byron.

77. The 1793 law targeted slave fugitives, indentured servants, and criminals of any race. For newspaper advertisements for "white" fugitives under the original Law, see Daniel Meaders, comp., *Eighteenth-Century White Slaves: Fugitive Notices* (Westport, CT: Greenwood Press, 1993); and Daniel Meaders, comp., *Dead or Alive: Fugitive Slaves and White Indentured Servants Before 1830* (New York: Garland, 1993).

78. Extracts from Clay's speech were reprinted in the *Liberator*, 22 February 1850.

79. For a critique of the 1850 law's attempt to bind individuals, see Spooner, *Defence for Fugitive Slaves*, 27–30. A freethinker, lawyer, anarchist, abolitionist, and (apparently) strict constructionist, Spooner argued that "the constitution contemplates no such submission on the part of the people. . . . The right and the physical power of the people to resist injustice, are really the only securities that any people ever can have for their liberties" (27, 30).

80. May, *Fugitive Slave Law and Its Victims*, 7. Emerson extended this logic into a defense of civil disobedience. Helping fugitives escape "is not meddling

with other people's affairs: this is hindering other people from meddling with us." Ralph Waldo Emerson, "The Fugitive Slave Law," in *The Complete Works of Ralph Waldo Emerson*, 12 vols. (Boston: Houghton Mifflin, 1883–93), 11:187.

81. On whiteness as a socially and historically constructed "property," see Theodore W. Allen, *The Invention of the White Race: The Origin of Racial Oppression in Anglo-America* (New York: Verso, 1997); Noel Ignatiev, *How the Irish Became White* (New York: Routledge, 1995); Cheryl I. Harris, "Whiteness as Property," *Harvard Law Review* 106, no. 8 (1993): 1709–91; and Roediger, *Wages of Whiteness*.

82. Warren Burton, *White Slavery* (Worcester, MA: M. D. Phillips, 1839), 20, 23; Roediger, *Wages of Whiteness*, 65–87.

83. The bill would have reinstituted indenture and resurrected the protections provided by the original fugitive slave laws of 1789 and 1793, which enabled the recovery of "criminal fugitives, [indentured] servants, or slaves." This clause of the later bill invokes the Constitution but otherwise reads very much like the 1850 act: "In case of an emigrant or emigrants imported by this company leaving this State before the sums due this company shall have been fully paid, it shall be competent for any of the officers of this company to claim said emigrants as persons escaping from service or labor, due under the third section, article fourth, of the Constitution of the United States, and bring them back to State, and the costs of such recovery shall be added to the amount to be repaid to said company by said emigrant or emigrants." *Abolition Philanthropy!* (Philadelphia: Printed at the Age Office, 1862).

84. Richard Hildreth, *The Slave; or, Memoirs of Archy Moore*, 2 vols. (Boston: John H. Eastburn, 1836); Richard Hildreth, *The White Slave; or, Memoirs of a Fugitive* (Boston: Tappan and Whittemore, 1852).

85. Hildreth, *White Slave* (1852), 223.

86. On the mulatto white slave, see Nancy Bentley, "White Slaves: The Mulatto Hero in Antebellum Fiction," *American Literature* 65, no. 3 (1993): 501–22. See also Christine MacDonald, "Judging Jurisdictions: Geography and Race in Slave Law and Literature of the 1830s," *American Literature* 71, no. 4 (1999): 625–55.

87. The phrase "almost white" recurs hundreds of times in newspapers in the 1830s, '40s, and '50s. For *Liberator* stories about "white slaves" that seek to establish an identification with white readers, see 18 March and 22 July 1842; and 6 November 1846.

88. Charles Sumner, *White Slavery in the Barbary States* (Boston: W. D. Ticknor, 1847). On Barbary slave narratives, see Paul Baepler, ed., *White Slaves, African Masters: An Anthology of American Barbary Captivity Narratives* (Chicago: University of Chicago Press, 1999).

89. Daniel Drayton, *Personal Memoir* (Boston: B. Marsh, 1855), 121. Drayton was an illiterate ship's captain who in 1847 went to prison for trying to help several Washington, DC, slaves escape aboard his boat. His claim that "the institu-

tion of slavery could not last for a day, if the slaves were all white" sounds like the racist truism described by Nancy Bentley (the idea that only those with "white" blood are heroic enough to resist their enslavement). Drayton goes on to argue however that "I do not see that because their complexions are different they are any the less men on that account" (121).

90. Although interest in white slavery was remarkably high after 1850, there were of course earlier narratives about white slaves. Karen Sánchez-Eppler, for example, discusses Lydia Maria Child's interest in the potential of white slavery, which dates to the early 1830s, noting that Child's early *Anti-Slavery Catechism* "asserts the difficulty of distinguishing the bodies of slaves from the bodies of free people" (15). In Child's account of Mary French, a free white girl is stolen, painted black, washed cleaned by her own tears, and then freed (30). *Touching Liberty: Abolition, Feminism, and the Politics of the Body* (Berkeley: University of California Press, 1993), 30–31. See also *Emancipator*, 25 January 1838.

91. William Goodell, *Slavery and Anti-Slavery: A History of the Great Struggle in Both Hemispheres* (New York: W. Harned, 1852), 142.

92. Harriet Beecher Stowe, *A Key to Uncle Tom's Cabin* (Boston: John P. Jewett, 1853), 184.

93. May, *Fugitive Slave Law and Its Victims* (1856), 29; May, *Fugitive Slave Law and Its Victims* (1861), 161.

94. *Congressional Globe*, 19 August 1850, 31st Congress, 1st session, appendix, 1586.

95. Torpey, *Invention of the Passport*, 8. Torpey describes the ways that states "develop the capacity to 'embrace' their own citizens in order to extract from them the resources they need to reproduce themselves over time" (2). He notes that the use of passports and other identity papers "followed the shift of orientations from the local to the 'national' level" of administration (8). The Fugitive Slave Law is, of course, part of this shift.

96. *Congressional Globe*, 19 August 1850, 31st Congress, 1st session, appendix, 1586. See also May, *Fugitive Slave Law and Its Victims* (1856), which insists that the Fugitive Slave Law is "fast threatening to include white citizens also" and offers two examples (29, 33). May also describes a free woman who was seized under the law; although "over sixty witnesses, from Pennsylvania, attended to testify to her being free-born, and that she was not the person she was claimed to be," she nevertheless "in great bodily terror" "confessed herself [to be] the alleged slave" (15). Brown ironically revises this scene of self-misidentification in *Clotel* when he tells the tale of a white man named Buddington, who, in order to marry a wealthy free black heiress in New Orleans, "was obliged to swear that he had negro blood in his veins" (182).

97. Whites who were not in danger of being enslaved were nevertheless increasingly subject to the technologies of identification that underwrote the law. Lisa Brawley notes that Lewis Tappan invented one such technology in the 1840s:

the modern credit report. Mobilizing the "well-organized abolitionist network" he had cultivated in the 1830s, Tappan created a nationwide system of "regionally dispersed correspondents" who "gathered information on potential customers" which was then sold to merchants in urban centers. These reports extended from bill-paying behavior and reputed financial worth to minute physical descriptions that strongly resemble fugitive slave advertisements. "Fugitive Nation," 2–5.

98. Brown was compiling and exhibiting in these years a visual historical panorama that contained a panel depicting the "tanning of a white boy": "it is not an uncommon occurrence for a white boy of poor parents to be reduced to a state of chattel slavery, in a Slave State. The writer was personally acquainted with a white boy in St Louis, Missouri, who was taken to New Orleans and sold into slavery." William Wells Brown, *A Description of William Wells Brown's Original Panoramic Views of the Scenes in the Life of an American Slave* (London: Charles Gilpin, 1849), 22. The same story appears in the *Narrative of William W. Brown, a Fugitive Slave* (Boston: Published at the Anti-Slavery Office, 1847), 26. See also Reid-Pharr, *Conjugal Union*, 46.

99. On the reading techniques that help construct passing subjects, see Amy Robinson, "It Takes One to Know One: Passing and Communities of Common Interest," *Critical Inquiry* 20, no. 4 (1994): 715–36. Rather than approaching the problem of passing from the point of view of production (or "performance"), Robinson emphasizes the centrality of reception, arguing that identity politics must be understood as a form of reading.

100. Gilmore, *The Genuine Article*, 39.

101. Peterson, "Capitalism," 564.

102. Robert Reid-Pharr makes a similar point in *Conjugal Union*, noting that Clotel's "body specifically refuses the logic of infinitely expanding binarisms that would have allowed for the production of knowable 'blackness.' Clotel's mixed-race body is understood by Brown as the very site at which the splits (racial, sexual, psychological, and ideological) that plague America can be healed—domesticated, if you will—thus producing in one not so dark body that which is properly and inevitably American" (45).

103. On the unthinkability of certain ideas in Western slave cultures, see Trouillet's account of the Haitian Revolution in *Silencing the Past*, 70–107.

104. George M. Stroud, *A Sketch of the Laws Relating to Slavery* (New York: AASS, 1843), 39.

105. Lincoln's first inaugural describes this perpetuity as a "legal" fact "confirmed by the history of the Union itself." *Speeches and Writings*, 2:217–18.

106. Paine made this connection in 1791 in addressing the question of cross-generational political structures: "Man has no property in man; neither has any generation a property in the generations which are to follow" (1:251). There are of course many examples in Enlightenment thinking of free white men metaphorically comparing their own political condition to chattel slavery. The differ-

ence here is that Paine is describing not an existing set of relations (colonialism under the British crown) but a future inherited set of conditions (nationalism). On Brown's nationalist genealogy, see Russ Castronovo, *Fathering the Nation: American Genealogies of Slavery and Freedom* (Berkeley: University of California Press, 1995), 157–89; and William Edward Farrison, "Clotel, Thomas Jefferson, and Sally Hemings," *CLA Journal* 17 (1973): 147–74.

107. Hortense Spillers implicitly marks this similarity, noting slavery's tendency to produce what we now think of as "imagined communities" over and against the more local kinds that are disrupted by the trade: "The point remains that captive persons were *forced* into patterns of *dispersal,* beginning with the Trade itself, into the *horizontal* relatedness of language groups, discourse formations, bloodlines, names, and properties by the legal arrangements of enslavement." For this reason, "the captive person developed, time and again, certain ethical and sentimental features that tied her and him, *across* the landscape to others, often sold from hand to hand, of the same and different blood in a common fabric of memory and inspiration." "Mama's Baby, Papa's Maybe," 75.

Conclusion. The Due Process of Nationalism

1. Herbert J. Storing, *What the Anti-Federalists Were For* (Chicago: University of Chicago Press, 1981), 64–70; and Akhil Reed Amar, *The Bill of Rights: Creation and Reconstruction* (New Haven: Yale University Press, 1998).

2. Gibbes, ed., *Documentary History of the American Revolution,* 8.

INDEX

"Ablest men" model, 254–55
abolition: as anti-federalist rebuke, 27; centralization of abolition movements, 328–38; constitutional amendments, 441; critique of colonization in *Uncle Tom's Cabin*, 384; dissemination of print transcending local vernacular culture, 27–28; gradualism versus immediatism, 310–44; Lundy as anachronism, 321–24; Lundy's role in the growth of antislavery movements, 315–21; Weld's *American Slavery as It Is*, 354–59. *See also* American Anti-Slavery Society; colonization projects; gradual abolition; immediate abolition
"Abolition Philanthropy!" (pamphlet), 427–28, 429
Abolition's Public Sphere (Fanuzzi), 305–6
actual representation: authenticity in portraiture, 214–15; definition, 25, 163; federalism's rejection of, 225, 240; immediate abolition's attempts to actually represent slavery, 391–92; imperial dispersion and, 163–69, 473–74*n*4; impossibility of, 168; Pitt embracing, 204–5; Rhode Island's

commitment to, 268; Trumbull's commitment to, 165–66, 214, 219–20; Tyler's satirization of in *The Contrast*, 200–203
Adams, John: authenticity of Trumbull's painting, 166; *Common Sense*'s reception, 53; criticism of *Common Sense*, 161–62; federal elites, 291–92; on Paine's authorship, 81; on Paine's social status, 86; on seduction fables, 287
Adams, John Quincy: correspondence with Lundy, 492*n*23; on Federal Convention's commitment to secrecy, 470–71*n*70
Adams, Samuel: *Common Sense*, 51; fictitious likenesses of, 215; open versus closed government proceedings, 211; Trumbull painting, 166
advertisements: *Clotel*, 416–17; *Common Sense*, 456*n*42, 457*n*43; diversity of in *National Era*, 309; *Twelve Years a Slave*, 398; *Uncle Tom's Cabin*, 364; Weld's use of in *American Slavery as It Is*, 356
African-American literature. *See* Clotel
Age of Manufacturing, 283
Age of Reason, The (Paine), 101